THE SIEGE OF JERUSALEM

EARLY ENGLISH TEXT SOCIETY

No. 320

2003

Bodleian Library, MS Laud misc. 656, fol. 7ᵛ.

THE SIEGE OF JERUSALEM

EDITED BY

RALPH HANNA
AND
DAVID LAWTON

Published for
THE EARLY ENGLISH TEXT SOCIETY
by the
OXFORD UNIVERSITY PRESS
2003

OXFORD
UNIVERSITY PRESS

Great Clarendon Street, Oxford OX2 6DP

Oxford University Press is a department of the University of Oxford.
It furthers the University's objective of excellence in research, scholarship,
and education by publishing worldwide in

Oxford New York

Auckland Bangkok Buenos Aires Cape Town Chennai
Dar es Salaam Delhi Hong Kong Istanbul Karachi Kolkata
Kuala Lumpur Madrid Melbourne Mexico City Mumbai Nairobi
São Paulo Shanghai Singapore Taipei Tokyo Toronto

Oxford is a registered trade mark of Oxford University Press
in the UK and in certain other countries

Published in the United States
by Oxford University Press Inc., New York

© Early English Text Society, 2003

The moral rights of the author have been asserted
Database right Oxford University Press (maker)

First published 2003

British Library Cataloguing in Publication Data

Data available

Library of Congress Cataloging in Publication Data

Data applied for

ISBN 0-19-722323-0

1 3 5 7 9 10 8 6 4 2

Typeset by Joshua Associates Ltd., Oxford
Printed in Great Britain
on acid-free paper by
Print Wright Ltd., Ipswich

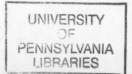

ACKNOWLEDGEMENTS

Given that this book has had a famously virtual existence for a very long time (although not quite so long as that period between Eugen Kölbing's proof-sheets and Mabel Day's completion of his edition, our predecessor), we have benefited from the counsel and aid of many. Dom Lawton was an infant when we began and when we did most of the work; we measure how long we have let publication slide by the fact that he is now a young man.

As editors, our primary debts have been to the custodians of the books we have used, libraries and their staffs. We are grateful to the British Library, Lambeth Palace Library, the Firestone Library at Princeton (and especially Jean Preston), and Cambridge University Library (and particularly Godfrey Waller, perpetually bright and welcoming and a great finder of things lost). Two libraries deserve special notice; they have been persistently central to our work and have extended us unusual kindnesses: the Henry E. Huntington Library, San Marino, and Duke Humfrey's Library in the Bodleian. We would especially single out the exceptional aid we have received over the years from Mary L. Robertson, Mary Wright, and Fred Perez at the Huntington; and from William Hodges, Russell Edwards, Jean-Pierre Maillon, and Alan Carter in Duke Humfrey.

Nearly as important as the libraries was another institution, the English Department of the University of California, Riverside. Largely through the good offices of our former colleagues, particularly John Ganim, Stephen G. Axelrod, and William O. Harris, the two of us were able to share a position for the year 1990–91 and thus get most of our editorial work behind us. The Humanities Research Institute, the University of California, Irvine also provided funds that underwrote David's stay in California; we are grateful to the HRI staff for many courtesies, as well as to Stephen A. Barney for putting together this arrangement (and for directing us to the wealth of material in Whiting's *Proverbs*).

John Alford deserves particular thanks, in the main for his forbearance. His Colleagues Press was originally to have published this volume, and John suffered through many years of frustration at our failure to conclude. We remain particularly grateful to have retained his friendship through our delays.

Our immediate scholarly cadre has been equally patient with us during our protracted bouts with the edition. Hoyt N. Duggan has remained immensely helpful and interested over the years (and will tell us immediately how many bad b-verses we have chosen to print). Thorlac Turville-Petre, master of all things alliterative, has been generous with good counsel on a wide variety of matters. Mary Hamel has taken an exceptional interest in our work, and John Thompson has been a fount of information about Robert Thornton. As the period between our inception of the project and its achievement lengthened, a new generation of scholars with an interest in the poem appeared—Elisa Van Court, Christine Chism, and particularly Bonnie Millar; we are grateful to them for trying to revive our enthusiasm for *The Siege of Jerusalem* and for allowing us to see (and sometimes appropriate bits from) their work in variously unpublished forms. We have also benefited, over many years, from the sage counsel of two palaeographers intimately aware of the problems posed by the books with which we here deal. A. I. Doyle, in particular, has goaded us and fed us information about the scribe of Lambeth Palace 491 and his connections with John Carpenter; Malcolm B. Parkes has offered us extensive advice on many questions we had not thought to ask and has been particularly helpful in confirming (he, of course, already knew this) that we were looking at John Frampton's hand in a book not normally noted as his work.

The honour of publication in this series has entailed other indebtednesses. Derek Pearsall showed his customary generosity and humanity in his reading of our typescript for the Early English Text Society; we hope he will not be disappointed in what we have made of his suggestions for improvement. And for a firm editorial hand and magnificent help with the printers, we, like all EETS contributors, are much in the debt of Helen L. Spencer, the Editorial Secretary.

In a book so intimately concerned with the detection of the errors of others, we must sorrowfully acknowledge that other errors will exist, and will be completely of our own manufacture.

CONTENTS

ILLUSTRATIONS

ABBREVIATIONS

A   British Library, MS Additional 31042

AA   *The Awntyrs off Arthure at the Terne Wathelyn*, ed. Ralph Hanna (Manchester, 1974).

BF   *La Vengeance de Nostre-Seigneur: The Old and Middle French Prose Versions: The Cura Sanitatis Tiberii (The Mission of Volusian)* . . ., ed. Alvin E. Ford, Studies and Texts 115 (Toronto, 1993), pp. 74–138.

C   British Library, MS Cotton Caligula A.ii

Cln   *Cleanness*, ed. J. J. Anderson (Manchester, 1977).

D   Lambeth Palace Library, MS 491

DPR   *On the Properties of Things: John Trevisa's Translation of Bartholomaeus Anglicus De Proprietatibus Rerum: A Critical Text*, ed. M. C. Seymour et al., 2 vols. (Oxford, 1975).

DT   *The Geste Hystoriale of the Destruction of Troy*, ed. George A. Panton and David Donaldson, EETS os 39, 56 (1869–74).

E   Huntington Library, MS HM 128

EETS   Early English Text Society; os Original Series (only noted through vol. 125); es Extra Series, ss Supplementary Series

Erk   'St. Erkenwald', ed. Turville-Petre, pp. 101–19.

Ex   Exeter, Devon Record Office, MS 2507

GGK   *Sir Gawain and the Green Knight*, ed. J. R. R. Tolkien and E. V. Gordon, rev. Norman Davis, 2nd edn. (Oxford, 1968).

IMEV   Brown, Carleton, and Rossell Hope Robbins, *The Index of Middle English Verse* (New York, 1943), with Robbins and John L. Cutler, *Supplement to IMEV* (Lexington KY, 1965).

IPMEP   Lewis, R. E., N. F. Blake, and A. S. G. Edwards, *Index of Printed Middle English Prose* (New York, 1985).

Jos   Flavius Josephus, 'De Bello Iudaico libri septem', *Opera ad multorum codicum latinorum, eorundemque*

	vetustissimorum fidem recognita et castigata, ed. Desiderius Erasmus (Cologne, 1524), fols. 227^r–326^r, with citations of the Greek text from *Josephus*, vols. 2–3, ed. H. St. J. Thackeray, Loeb Library (Cambridge MA, 1956–57).
Ker	N. R. Ker, *Medieval Libraries of Great Britain: A List of Surviving Books*, Royal Historical Society Guides and Handbooks 3, 2nd edn. (London, 1964).
Kölbing-Day	*The Siege of Jerusalem*, ed. E. Kölbing and Mabel Day EETS 188 (1932).
L	Bodleian Library, MS. Laud misc. 656
LA	Jacobus de Voragine, *Legenda aurea, vulgo historia lombardica dicta*, ed. Th. Graesse, 3rd edn. (1890; Osnabruck, 1969).
LALME	Angus McIntosh, M. L. Samuels, and Michael Benskin, *A Linguistic Atlas of Late Mediaeval English*, 4 vols. (Aberdeen, 1986).
Lewis-McIntosh	Lewis, Robert E., and Angus McIntosh, *A Descriptive Guide to the Manuscripts of* The Prick of Conscience, Medium Ævum Monographs n.s. 12 (Oxford, 1982).
MA	*Morte Arthure*, ed. Mary Hamel (New York, 1984).
MED	*Middle English Dictionary*, numerous fascicles (Ann Arbor, 1954–2001).
Mum	*Mum and the Sothsegger*, ed. Mabel Day and Robert Steele, EETS 199 (1936), pp. 27–78.
Nicodemus	*The Gospel of Nicodemus*, ed. H. C. Kim, Toronto Medieval Latin Texts 2 (Toronto, 1973).
OCist	the Cistercian order
OED	*The Oxford English Dictionary*, 13 vols. (Oxford, 1933).
OSB	the Benedictine order
P	Princeton University Library, MS Taylor Medieval 11
Pat	*Patience*, ed. J. J. Anderson (Manchester, 1969).
Pearl	*Pearl*, ed. E. V. Gordon (Oxford, 1953).
Poly	Ranulph Higden, *Polychronicon*, customarily cited, for portions parallel to *The Siege*, by line from our edition in Appendix B; citations from other portions from *Polychronicon Ranulphi Higden Monachi Cestrensis*, ed. Churchill Babington and Joseph R. Lumby, Rolls Series 41, 9 vols. (London, 1865–86).

PPA	*Piers Plowman: The A Version*, ed. George Kane (London, 1960).
PPB	*Piers Plowman: The B Version*, ed. George Kane and E. Talbot Donaldson (London, 1975).
PPC	*Piers Plowman: The C Version*, ed. George Russell and George Kane (London, 1997).
PRO	Public Record Office
PTA	'The Parlement of the Thre Ages', ed. Turville-Petre, pp. 67–100.
RR	'Richard the Redeles', ed. Mabel Day and Robert Steele, EETS 199 (1936), pp. 1–26.
STC	*A Short-Title Catalogue of Books Printed . . . 1475–1640*, ed. by A. W. Pollard et al., 2nd edn., 3 vols. (London, 1976–91).
Sus	'A Pistel of Susan', ed. Turville-Petre, pp. 120–39.
Turville-Petre	Thorlac Turville-Petre, *Alliterative Poetry of the Later Middle Ages: An Anthology* (London, 1989), and esp. the edition of *The Siege of Jerusalem* (lines 525–728 only), pp. 158–69.
U	Cambridge University Library, MS Mm.v.14
V	British Library, MS Cotton Vespasian E.xvi
VS	'Vindicta salvatoris', customarily cited, for portions parallel to *The Siege*, by line from our edition in Appendix A; the verse divisions are derived from the standard, but very different, text, *Evangelia apocrypha*, ed. Constantin von Tischendorf, 2nd edn. (Leipzig, 1876), pp. 471–86.
WA	*The Wars of Alexander*, ed. Hoyt N. Duggan and Thorlac Turville-Petre, EETS ss 10 (1989).
Whiting	Bartlett J. Whiting, *Proverbs, Sentences, and Proverbial Phrases from English Writings Mainly Before 1500* (Cambridge MA, 1968).
WP	*William of Palerne: An alliterative romance*, ed. G. H. V. Bunt (Groningen, 1985).
WW	'Wynnere and Wastoure', ed. Turville-Petre, pp. 38–66.

GRAMMATICAL ABBREVIATIONS

acc.	accusative
adj.	adjective
adv.	adverb
card.	cardinal (number)
conj.	conjunction
dat.	dative
def.	definite
dem.	demonstrative
imp.	imperative mood of a verb
interj.	interjection
ME	Middle English
n.	noun
nom.	nominative
num.	number
OE	Old English
OF	Old French
ON	Old Norse (the normal forms of Old Icelandic)
ord.	ordinal (number)
p.	participle (in combinations, e.g. pr. p. present participle; pp. past participle)
pl.	plural
poss.	possessive
prep.	preposition
pr.	present tense of verbs
pron.	pronoun
pt.	preterite/past tense of verbs
rel.	relative
sg.	singular
subj.	subjunctive mood of a verb
3 sg.	third person singular (and analogous forms)
v.	verb/infinitive

INTRODUCTION

THE MANUSCRIPTS

There are nine known copies of the Middle English alliterative poem *The Siege of Jerusalem*. Of these, six are more or less full copies (two lack single leaves with consequent textual lacunae), two quite substantial fragments, and one a piece of a single leaf.

L Bodleian Library, MS Laud Misc. 656   s. xiv ex.

Contents: I. Fols. ii, 1–116 a booklet containing:

1. Fols. 1^v–19^r *THE SIEGE OF JERUSALEM* (IMEV 1583); fol. 1 blank.

2. Fols. 19^v–114^r *Piers Plowman C* (IMEV 1459); fols. 114^v, $115a^{rv}$, the subsequent $115b^{rv}$, and 116^{rv} are blank.

II. Fols. 117–31 a booklet containing:

1. Fols. 117^r–18^r an unpublished exposition of the Creed, inc. 'Genesis 15°. capitulo Abraham bileued in god and hit was reckened'.

2. Fols. 118^r–24^v an unpublished exposition of the Decalogue, elsewhere in Westminster School, MS 3 and Cambridge, Trinity College, MS B.14.54, inc. 'Euery man and woman scholde bisily desire and couete to lerne'.

3. Fols. 124^v–25^v unpublished biblical excerpts, primarily from the wisdom books, inc. 'Hit is writen in þe boke of Machabeus the viij. capitulo þe wraþ of god'; the remainder blank, save for later pentrials.

Vellum. 133 fols. (fol. ii is part of quire 1; two fols. 115a and 115b), 206 mm. × 145 mm. (writing area for prose portions 175–183 mm. × 115–120 mm.), in 34–44 long lines. Collation: 1^{14} 2–8^{12} 9–10^{10} (fol. 116, the end of booklet I) 11^8 12^{10} (-3, -8. -9) (comprising booklet II). Brown ink. Written in anglicana, one scribe responsible for *The Siege*, perhaps a second for the remainder.

Brown bounding lines on left, upper, and lower margins; no rules or prickings. A single catchword, at fol. 13^v, no signatures. Three-line unflourished red lombardic capitals in *The Siege*, unfilled blanks with guide letters elsewhere. The text of *The Siege* is divided into four parts by multiline capitals at lines 445, 897, and 1113.

Copied by northwest Oxfordshire scribes; see Samuels, p. 239 (we refer to many secondary materials by author only; full particulars appear in the Bibliography at the end of the Introduction); the signature of John Cempe of Ticehurst, Kent (s. xv ex.); thereafter untraceable until owned by Archbishop William Laud (his *ex libris* 1633). Binding: original reddish brown leather over wooden boards.

Previous descriptions: Gisela Guddat-Figge, *Catalogue of Manuscripts Containing Middle English Romances* (Munich, 1976), pp. 287–88; Ralph Hanna, 'The Origins and Production of Westminster School MS 3', *Studies in Bibliography* 41 (1988), 197–218 (211). Doyle (pp. 93–96 and nn.) discusses briefly all the manuscripts, save the recently discovered Ex; T. Turville-Petre (1977, pp. 34, 44) comments on all save P and Ex.

P Princeton Univ. Library, MS Taylor Medieval 11   s. xiv ex.

Contents: 1. Fols. 1ra–96vb the unpublished *Speculum vitae* (IMEV 245).

2. Fols. 97ra–104va the unpublished mid fourteenth-century prose translation of ps.-Bonaventura *Meditaciones passionis Cristi*, inc. 'The tyme neghand and comand of þe rutes and mercyes of the lorde'; see Elizabeth Zeeman (Salter), 'Continuity and Change in Middle English Versions of the *Meditationes Vitae Christi*', *Medium Ævum* 26 (1957), 25–31.

3. Fols. 104vb–110vb THE SIEGE OF JERUSALEM (IMEV 1583), ending fragmentarily at line 1143, with most of the last page illegible, even under ultra-violet light.

Vellum (rather worn throughout, with substantial water damage at front and rear). 112 fols. (35, 59 [twice] repeated, 95 omitted in the foliation), 350 mm. × 270 mm. (writing area 275–80 mm. × 190 mm. in double columns), usually in 42 lines. Collation: 1–2^{12} 3^{10} 4^{12} 5^{14} 6^{10} 7^{12} 8^8 9^{12} 10^{10} (the final folio used as a pastedown in an earlier binding). Brownish ink. Written in a squarish anglicana formata.

Bounded and ruled, usually in pencil, occasionally red ink; some prickings remain. Catchwords at quire ends, no signatures. Elaborate running titles by the scribe in item 1, to indicate the septenary subjects; headings in red by the scribe. Blue lombards with red flourishing at textual divisions (four-line at initia, two-line for medial

THE MANUSCRIPTS xv

divisions), red-slashed capitals at line heads; in the prose elongated ascenders with decorative loops normal on top line. The (incomplete) text of *The Siege* is divided into six parts by multiline capitals and marginal notations ('ij[-vj] passus') at lines 305, 445, 637, 897, and 1113.

Fol. 1 bears the *ex libris* 'liber beate Marie de Bolton in C⟨ ⟩'; the remainder has become progressively illegible, but was clearer when Ker could read 'C⟨rauen⟩' and thus associated the book (p. 11) with the house of Augustinian canons at Bolton in Craven. A. I. Doyle cautions us, however, by pointing out that Ker's initial reading was 'in T⟨ower⟩', and thus that the book may have belonged to an unidentified private chapel (although not that of Castle Bolton, North Yorks., with a different dedication). LALME (3, 651–52, LP 598, grid 366 492) places the scribal dialect considerably to the north and west, in the extreme tip of West Yorks. (near Sedbergh, Westmorland). Sold by the Petre family at Sotheby, London, 10 March 1952, lot 143; to Quaritch, catalogue 704, item 350; to Laurence Witten; to Robert Taylor, passing to Princeton University on his death in 1985. Binding: turn of the century white vellum over bookboard.

Previous descriptions: The Sotheby catalogue.

A British Library, MS Additional 31042   s. xv med.

For a very full, although not uncontroversial, description, see John J. Thompson, *Robert Thornton and the London Thornton Manuscript: British Library MS Additional 31042*, Manuscript Studies 2 (Cambridge, 1987). Thompson provides (10–18) a full list of contents: thirty-one items, all verse: these include the alliterative poems *THE SIEGE OF JERUSALEM* (IMEV 1583, fols. 50ʳ–66ʳ: lacking lines 293–369 through loss of a leaf), 'The Quatrefoil of Love' (IMEV 1453, fols. 98ʳ–101ᵛ), *The Parlement of the Thre Ages* (IMEV 1556, fols. 169ʳ–76ᵛ), and *Wynnere and Wastoure* (IMEV 3137, fols. 176ᵛ–81ᵛ).

Paper. There are ten different stocks: the most narrowly datable of these fall within the period 1437–50. Thompson lists (pp. 71–72) the stocks; a substantial part of his discussion (pp. 22–34) seeks to establish a collation for the volume on the basis of the sequences of watermarks. 179 fols. (fols. 1, 2, 182, and 183 are flyleaves), 270 mm. × 200 mm. (writing area varies, in *The Siege* 222 mm. × 120–25 mm.), in varying line formats, *The Siege* in 37–40 long lines. Collation: one can make only tentative identifications, based on watermark sequences, since the leaves are now mounted individually. Following Ralph Hanna, 'The London Thornton Manuscript: A Corrected Collation', *Studies in Bibliography* 37 (1984), 122–30, largely in agreement with Thompson: $1^{?}$ (six leaves, fols. 3–8) 2^{24} (fol. 32, end of booklet I) 3^{22} (-22) 4^{20} 5^{26} (-5, -8, -26) $6^{?}$ (six leaves, fols. 97–102, the end of booklet II) $7^{18?}$ (-1, -10, -11) $8^{?}$ (seven leaves, fols. 118–24, the end of booklet III) 9^{22} (-20, -21, -22) 10^{26} (-26) (fol. 168, the end of booklet IV) $11^{18?}$ (if so, -14, -15, -16, -17, -18; fols. 169–81, comprising booklet V). Black to grayish ink. Written in a sprawling and ill-formed anglicana, the hand of Robert Thornton, gentleman of East Newton, North Yorks.; for biographical information, see George R. Keiser, 'Lincoln Cathedral Library MS 91: Life and Milieu of the Scribe', *Studies in Bibliography* 32 (1979), 158–79; and 'More Light on the Life and Milieu of Robert Thornton', *Studies in Bibliography* 36 (1983), 111–19. Thornton also copied, in part simultaneously with this manuscript, Lincoln Cathedral 91 (including the alliterative poems *Morte Arthure*, *The Awntyrs off Arthure at þe Terne Wathelyn*, and 'St John the Evangelist'); see further Ralph Hanna, 'The Growth of Robert Thornton's Books', *Studies in Bibliography* 40 (1987), 51–61.

Bounded in brownish ink, no rules or prickings. Very occasional catchwords (for example, fols. 8^{v} and 32^{v}), no signatures. Headings generally in text ink, as are many initia (often with penwork decoration, especially heads and sprays); textual divisions typically three-line red lombards. The text of *The Siege* is divided into five parts by the intracolumnar heading 'Passus' and multiline capitals at lines 445, 637, 897, and 1113; additional decorated capitals appear at lines 25, 53, and 268a.

Ownership after Thornton uncertain; the manuscript contains signatures of William Frost (s. xv) and John Nettleton (s. xvi ex.), presumably the later of the book-collectors of that name from Hutton Cranswick, East Yorks. Thereafter, the manuscript cannot be traced until it was sent from America to a London bookseller in 1879, whence it was purchased by the British Museum. Binding: the British Library's standard twentieth-century half-morocco over bookboard.

Previous descriptions: Karl Brunner, 'HS. Brit. Mus. Additional 31042', *Archiv für das Studium der neueren Sprachen und Literaturen* 132 (1914), 316–27; Karen Stern, 'The London "Thornton" Miscellany', *Scriptorium*, 30 (1976) 26–37, 201–18; Guddat-Figge, pp. 159–63; Thompson.

V British Library, MS Cotton Vespasian E.xvi   s. xv med.

Contents: Fols. 1–37 comprise two groups of leaves from manuscripts unrelated to that containing *The Siege*.

I. Fols. 38–69 the head of a booklet containing:

1. Fols. 38^r–69^v the prose *Three Kings of Cologne* (IPMEP 290), ending fragmentarily at p. 152/23 of the edition, ed. C. Horstmann, EETS os 85 (1886).

II. Fols. 70–77 a quire, probably, given the signatures (see below), not a booklet but an extension of the previous production, containing:

1. Fols. 70^r–75^v THE SIEGE OF JERUSALEM (IMEV 1583), beginning imperfectly at line 966.

2. Fols. 76^r–77^v a Latin calendar tract, verses with prose commentary, ending imperfectly, inc. 'Cum in vnaquaque sciencia est vnum generale in quod resoluuntur omnia'.

III. Fols. 78–85 a booklet containing:

1. Fols. 78^r–82^v a Latin tract on the pulse, acephalous, inc. 'brachium et ideo pulsus sinistro brachio contulimus'.

2. Fols. 83^r–85^r an unpublished discussion of physiognomy, inc. 'Among all þinges who þat woll knowe the mervelous science'. Fol. 85^v is blank.

Vellum. 48 fols., 215 mm. × 155 mm. (writing area in *Siege* 160 mm. × 105 mm.), in 29–36 long lines. Collation: 1–4^8 (fol. 69, end of part I) 5^8 (fol. 77, end of booklet I) 6^8 (comprising booklet II). Brownish black ink. Written by four different scribes, each section a different hand and the two items of the second booklet different hands; the first scribe writes anglicana with some secretary forms, the other scribes secretary (that of the scribe who copied *The Siege* might be of s. xv$^{3/4}$).

In *The Siege* pages bounded in pencil, and a few leaves show signs of similar rulings; no prickings. No catchwords; signatures, none in the same ink as the scribal hand, on the opening leaves of quires in the first two sections (fols. 38–69 = *a-d* and *x-xiij*; fols. 70–77 = *xvj*, implying the loss of two intermediate quires after fol. 69). In the first two sections, three-line blue lombards with red flourishing at textual divisions, no headings or running titles. The (fragmentary) text of

The Siege is divided into two parts by a marginal notation 'Septimus passus' and a multiline capital at line 1113; an additional decorated capital appears at line 1025.

LALME (3, 422–23, LP 553, grid 494 309) analyzes the language of *Three Kings* and places its scribe near Oakham, Rutland. LALME alleges that this scribe copied, *inter alia*, all English portions of V: such a view does not sort either with our inspection of the hands or with the forms used in *The Siege*, which do not correspond with those reported as LP 553. Thus, to take a few examples, *The Siege* shows routine þey (þei once, 1168), þeire (her at 1067, 1096, 1168, 1339), hem (þem once, 1168), not LP 553's þey, þeire, þam (þem) ((hem)); regular present participles in -ande (-aunde 990 and 1223, -aunt 1289, -yng 1339), not LP 553's -yng(e); verb present plurals in -yn -in -en, not LP 553's invariable -e-forms and alternations of -n with -s/-z and -th; and self/selve(n) but also frequent silve(n) (970, 990, 1201, 1298), not LP 553's regular self(e). A large number of these forms—unlike the present participle above—seem unlikely relicts from an antecedent *Siege* manuscript. Either the *Siege* scribe reflects mixed training—a number of his forms can be paralleled in Leicester, the Soke, or south Lincs., although all of them in no single recorded LP—his many agreements with LP 553 (for example, hit, moche, yette, þough, þrough, ben 'are', no(u)ght 'not') being the forms of the Oakham area; or LALME's LP 553 may show some interference from the *Three Kings* exemplar. Further signs pointing to such an east Midland provenance include fols. 2–11, which contain a 'liber cartarum ecclesie beate Marie Lincolniensis', that is, Lincoln Cathedral. Binding: the library's modern half morocco.

Previous descriptions: Guddat-Figge, pp. 178–79.

Ex Exeter, Devon Record Office, MS 2507 s. xv²

Contents: *THE SIEGE OF JERUSALEM*, the openings of lines 985–1017 (original ra) and conclusions of lines 1106–23, 1196, 1125–38 (original vb).

Paper (since the original was almost certainly folded in folio, no watermarks appear in this fragment, from the gutter of its leaf). A strip, currently c. 280 mm. × 55–60 mm. (current vertical writing area c. 260–270 mm., originally at least 325 mm. × 275? mm. in double columns); 33 lines survive on each side, but the original leaf was probably in 40 and 41 lines (seven or eight lines lost+985–1017 =

surviving ra, 1018–58 = lost rb, 1059–98 = lost va, lost 1099–
1105+1106–23, 1196, 1125–38 = surviving vb). Written in a careful
anglicana.

Bounded and occasionally ruled, no prickings. One paraph, at the
head of line 985.

The fragment is far too brief for any definitive linguistic analysis,
although it generally appears to be in a central north Midland dialect
(Notts.? Derbys.?). The copyist has -es in the present third person
singular but -en in the plural, o for OE ā, *shall*, *them*. One unusual
form, 1006 *thurw* "through" (although at the edge of the fragment
and conceivably the remains of *thurwe* or *thurwh* or *thurwʒ*) is
recorded in LALME (3, 591–92, grid 472 456) as the majority
form of but a single scribe, LP 228, from the upper Derwent valley
just northeast of York City (perhaps Kirkham OSA ?). The fragment
forms part of the binding of the late sixteenth-century memorandum
book of Furse of Morshead, a family from Kingsbridge, south Devon.

Previous descriptions: Michael Swanton, 'A Further Manuscript
of *The Siege of Jerusalem*', *Scriptorium* 44 (1990), 103–4, with citation
of 'diagnostic variants'.

U Cambridge University Library, MS Mm.v.14   s. xv$^{1/4}$

Contents: I. Fols. 2–139 a booklet containing:

1. Fols. 2^r–139^v Guido delle Colonne's *Historia destructionis Troie*.

II. Fols. 140–86 a booklet containing:

1. Fols. 140^r–85^r the prose *Historia de preliis Alexandri Magni*; fols.
185^v–86^v are ruled but blank.

III. Fols. 187–207 a booklet containing:

1. Fols. 187^r–206^v THE SIEGE OF JERUSALEM (IMEV 1583).
Fol. 207 is blank.

Vellum. 206 fols. (fol. 1 is a flyleaf), 250 mm. × 175 mm. (writing
area 162 mm. × 110 mm., about 100–105 mm. in the verse), in 32
long lines. Collation: 1–17^8 9^4 (-3, -4, both visible stubs) (fol. 139, the
end of booklet I) 20–24^8 25^8 (-8) (fol. 186, the end of booklet II) 26–
27^8 28$^?$ (perhaps a single followed by two bifolia?) (comprising booklet
III). Black ink. Written in anglicana formata, the hand of the London
scribe Richard Frampton (*fl. c.*1412), who also copied PRO D.L. 42,
1 and 2 (Duchy of Lancaster coucher books); Glasgow University
Library, MS Hunterian T.4.1 (the same two Latin historical texts
reproduced here, the Latin ps.-Turpin Chronicle, and Latin oriental

materials—Marco Polo, Odoric, and Mandeville); Huntington Library, MS HM 19920 (*Statuta* to 1408); British Library, MS Cotton Claudius D.ii, fols. 44, 139–268 (*Statuta antiqua*); and a two-volume breviary for Henry IV (now lost). For Frampton, see A. I. Doyle and Malcolm B. Parkes, 'The Production of Copies of the Canterbury Tales and the Confessio Amantis in the Early Fifteenth Century', *Medieval Scribes, Manuscripts and Libraries: Essays Presented to N. R. Ker*, ed. by Parkes and Andrew G. Watson (London, 1978), pp. 163–210 (192) and Doyle, p. 144 n19.

Bounded and ruled in black and reddish-brown ink, no prickings. Catchwords in decorative boxes, often cut away; no signatures. At initia and major divisions of the prose four-line champes, blue or violet on gold leaf, with full marginal extenders in the same to form buds and knots; two-line blue lombards on red flourishing at passus divisions of *The Siege*; alternating blue on red and red on blue paraphs to mark eight-line divisions in *The Siege* (from fol. 204^r, although Frampton left directions for them, the decoration not provided; paraphs in different colours and some capitals slashed in ochre in prose texts). No running titles. The text of *The Siege* is divided into eight parts by the intracolumnar heading 'Primus[-Septimus] Passus' (implying that lines 1–188 form a prologue) and the two-line capitals at lines 189, 305, 445, 637, 738, 897, and 1113.

Although Frampton's copying career as we know it is associated with London (and very strongly with the Duchy of Lancaster), the text includes a substantial veneer of northern and north Midland spellings, probably reproduced from Frampton's archetype. The manuscript contains a variety of notes and signatures: 'Sumpsimus domine dei genitricis (?)', Edwardus Savage capellanus, Johannes Redmayn, Richard Broyes (?) (all s. xv or xv/xvi), Johannes Kyngston of Endberi sends greeting to Henry VIII (s. xvi), Arthur Maynwaring (1569), Sir Robert Cotton. Binding: modern half-morocco (with leather corners) and marbled paper.

Previous descriptions: Guddat-Figge, pp. 108–9.

D Lambeth Palace Library, MS 491, part 1   s. xv^{1/4}

Contents: I. Fols. 1–216 a booklet containing:

1. Fols. 1^r–205^v the prose *Brut* (IPMEP 374), beginning fragmentarily at p. 19/29 of the edition, ed. Friedrich W. D. Brie, EETS 131, 136 (1906–8) and extending through the reign of Edward III.

2. Fols. 206^r–16^v *THE SIEGE OF JERUSALEM*, lines 1–636 (IMEV 1583); for an explanation of the copying procedures, whereby the text was split between two different codicological units through a rough casting-off at the head of passus 4 (line 637) see Ralph Hanna, 'Booklets in Medieval Manuscripts: Further Considerations', *Studies in Bibliography* 39 (1986), 100–11 (105–6) and the discussion of the poem's passus divisions, pp. lxxi–iv below.

II. Fols. 217–74 a booklet containing:

   1. Fols. 217^r–27^v *THE SIEGE OF JERUSALEM* concluded.

   2. Fols. 228^r–74^v the prose *Three Kings of Cologne* (cf. IPMEP 290); this distinct version ed. Frank Schaer, *The Three Kings of Cologne edited from London, Lambeth Palace MS 491*, Middle English Texts 31 (Heidelberg, 2000).

III. Fols. 275–90 a booklet containing:

   1. Fols. 275^r–86^v *The Awntyrs off Arthure at þe Terne Wathelyn* (IMEV 1566); ed. Hanna.

   2. Fols. 287^r–90^v *The Book of Hunting* (IMEV 4064), ending fragmentarily at line 349; ed. Arne Zettersten, 'The Lambeth Manuscript of the *Boke of Huntyng*', *Neuphilologische Mitteilungen* 70 (1969), 106–21; and Rachel Hands, *English Hawking and Hunting in The Boke of St. Albans* (London, 1975), pp. 168–86.

Vellum and paper, each quire formed by wrapping a single vellum sheet around a series of paper leaves. There are three different paper stocks, in independent blocks covering a succession of quires: (1) in quires 2–13, Monts like Briquet 11685 (Trevise 1405, with variants to 1414), and cf. 11687 (Padua 1408–15) and 11689 (Florence 1411–21); (2) in quires 14–16, Lettre N not in Briquet, most closely resembling 8431, a type common 1414–20, but here on the chainline and apparently lacking cross; (3) in quires 17–21, Ciseaux like Briquet 3656 (Perpignan 1397, with north Italian variants to 1413), perhaps cf. 3656 (Aix-en-Provence 1426). 291 fols. (150 repeated in the foliation), 222 mm. × 141 mm. (writing area 175 mm. × 80–85 mm.), in 26–31 long lines. Collation: [1 lost] 2^{16} (-7, -10) 3–5^{16} 6^{16} (-5, -7, -10, -12) 7^{16} (-2, -15) 8^{16} (-4, -5, -6, -10, -11, -12, -13) 9^{16} (-7, -10) 10^{16} (-7, -10, -14) 11^{16} 12^{16} (-7) 13^{16} (-9) 14–16^{16} (fol. 216, the end of booklet I) 17^{16} 18^{16} (-2, -15) 19^{16} 20^{16} (-3, -14, -15, -16) (fol. 274, the end of booklet II) 21^{16} (comprising booklet III). Brownish ink. Written in a rather splayed anglicana; the scribe, a London professional, also copied Huntington Library, MS HM 114 (including a conflation of all three versions of

Piers Plowman, *Mandeville's Travels*, the alliterative poem *Susannah* [IMEV 3553], and Chaucer's *Troilus*) and the core of British Library, Harley 3943 (another *Troilus*, from the same archetype as the preceding but left a fragment and completed by later scribes). A. I. Doyle generously informs us that the hand also appears in City of London Record Office, Letter Book I, fols. 223^r (15 Jan. × 7 August 7 Hen. V), 224^v, 226^v–27^r, 228^r, 229^r–31^v; and several stints in the London *Liber Albus* (Cust. 12), previously noted as a single hand H. T. Riley, *Munimenta Gildhallae Londoniensis: Liber Albus . . .*, Rolls Series 12, i (London, 1859), p. xxii n2. This volume was prepared in 1419 under the direction of John Carpenter, Secretary of the City; see William Kellaway, 'John Carpenter's Liber Albus', *Guildhall Studies* 3 (1978), 67–84.

Bounded in lead, usually only marking off corners of the writing area, no rules or prickings. Catchwords at quire ends, usually framed. Two sets of leaf signatures: in the first halves of quires 2–20, rectos signed at the page foot with letter plus arabic numeral, although most cropped (fols. 1–274 = b–v); each recto fols. 1–205 signed in upper right corner with quire and leaf number, both in arabic (running 2.1–16.5). Regular running titles and headings by the scribe in red (again, none in the 'unfinished' quire 21, which also lacks titles). Two-line high red or blue lombards at textual divisions; in prose, occasional paraphs and slashed capitals in red and blue. The text of *The Siege* has no major divisions but about forty-five scattered paraphs; codicological information (see above) seems to indicate that the exemplar had at least a passus division at line 637.

After four leaves of modern paper (fols. 291–94), a separate codex (fols. 295–329) follows, described Lewis-McIntosh, pp. 80–81.

LALME (3, 115, LP 6030, grid 578 190) places the scribe's dialect near Rayleigh, Essex. The manuscript contains a variety of names scribbled in (s. xv²), including Thomas Patsall, John Patsall, Thomas Sharp, and John Pysant. Perhaps most revelatory is Thomas Patsall's inscription on fol. 22^v 'in the tone of barakyng', that is, Barking, Essex; see further Julia Boffey and Carol Meale, 'Selecting the Text: Rawlinson C.86 and some other books for London readers', *Regionalism in Late Medieval Manuscripts and Texts*, ed. Felicity Riddy (Cambridge, 1991), pp. 143–69 (161–62 and n. 63). The book belonged to Archbishop Richard Bancroft (d. 1610) and has been part of the Archbishops' collections since. Binding: the library's standard modern red half-morocco.

Previous descriptions: Karl D. Bülbring, 'Über die Handschrift Nr. 491 der Lambeth-Bibliothek', *Archiv für das Studium der neueren Sprachen und Literaturen* 86 (1891), 383–92; A. G. Hopper, 'The Lambeth Palace Manuscript of *The Awntyrs off Arthure*', *Leeds Studies in English* 3 (1934), 37–43; Guddat-Figge, pp. 226–28.

E Huntington Library, MS HM 128   s. xv in.

Contents: I. Fols. 1–96 a booklet containing:

1. Fols. 1^r–94^r *The Prick of Conscience*, southern recension (IMEV 3429); fol. 94^v blank.

2. Fols. 95^r–96^r *Piers Plowman* B 2.208–3.73 (IMEV 1459), the two leaves now bound in reversed order; fol. 95^v blank.

II. Fols. 97–112 a booklet containing:

1. Fols. 97^r–112^v a Latin 'Expositio sequentiarum' for Sarum use, apparently related to that printed by de Worde (STC 16110).

III. Fols. 113–219 a booklet containing:

1. Fols. 113^r–205^r *Piers Plowman* B (IMEV 1459).

2. Fols. 205^r–16^r *THE SIEGE OF JERUSALEM* (IMEV 1583).

3. Fols. 216^v–19^r 'How the Good Wife Taught her Daughter' (IMEV 1673); fol. 219^v blank.

Vellum. 219 fols., 240 mm. × 168 mm. (writing area varies, within *Siege* 205 mm. × 140 mm.), in varying line formats, *Siege* in 55–65 long lines. Collation: 1–12^8 (fol. 96, the end of booklet I) 13–14^8 (fol. 112, the end of booklet II) 15–27^8 $28^?$ (fol. 217–19, three leaves; these materials comprising booklet III). Quires 3 and 4 are bound in reverse order; for an explanation of the odd bit of *Piers* on fols. 95^r–96^r, see R. B. Haselden, 'The Fragment of *Piers Plowman* in Ashburnham No. CXXX', *Modern Philology* 29 (1932), 391–94. *The Siege* in a brownish ink. Written in various types of anglicana with some secretary letter-forms by six scribes, the fifth of whom copied only *The Siege* and whose hand, like that of scribe 6 (who copied only 'Good Wife'), looks somewhat later than the others, perhaps s. $xv^{2/4}$. Arguably, the *Siege* scribe began adding a text to a partially filled last quire, and he and scribe 6 extended the manuscript as necessary.

Bounded and ruled in pencil; no prickings. No catchwords or signatures. In *The Siege*, decoration is restricted to an opening heading by the same hand which provided headings in the Latin and the *Piers* (not that of any of the text scribes), three- and four-line red lombards at textual divisions, and red paraphs at the head of each quatrain. The continuity of decorative features indicates that the manuscript, however ad lib the provision of texts at the end, was a corporate product and remained in situ. The text of *The Siege* is divided into nine parts by multiline capitals at lines 189, 445, 637, 738, 897, 953, 1113, and 1177.

LALME (3, 530, LP 6910, grid 423 238) places this scribe in extreme southern Warwickshire. The editors also (3, 534–35, LP 8040, grid 421 248) identify the language of scribe 1 (*Prick* and the opening of *Piers*) with that of an adjacent area in southwestern Warwickshire. These neighbouring sets of spellings would suggest that, if the manuscript comes from a communal environment, the manuscript might be identified with such a neighbourhood religious house as Alcester (OSB) or Evesham (Worcs., OSB). Signatures of Betoun Brygges (s. xv), Alleksander London (s. xv/xvi), Richard Rychard (s. xvi), and John Sarum, that is, John Jewel, bishop 1559–71 ?; on the front pastedown, John Bale's note on the authorship of *Piers*; see George Kane, *Piers Plowman: The Evidence for Authorship* (London, 1965), pp. 37–42 and plate 3. The preceding note, 'Robert or william langland made pers plough⟨ma⟩n', is in the hand of Ralph Coppinger, who also owned Bodleian Library, MS Laud misc. 581, with *Piers* B; like Nicholas Brigham, who appears to have been the main source of Bale's ascription, Coppinger was a Customs collector in the 1540s. See further James Alsop, 'Nicholas Brigham (d. 1558), scholar, antiquary, and crown servant', *Sixteenth Century Journal* 12, i (1981), 49–67. The manuscript is untraceable until the nineteenth century, when it belonged successively to Adam Clarke (his sale 1836, lot 352), Thorpe the bookseller, C. W. Loscombe (his sale 1854, lot 1167), and Lord Ashburnham (Ashburnham App. 130; his sale 1899, lot 78); then Quaritch cat. 193, item 54; and Ross C. Winans; acquired by the Huntington in 1918. Binding: early sixteenth-century blindstamped leather (Oldham's rolls HM. a (17–23)), with pastedowns from a manuscript of John of Salisbury's *Epistolae*, s. xiv/xv.

Previous descriptions: Seymour de Ricci, *A Census of Medieval and Renaissance Manuscripts in the United States and Canada*, 2 vols. (1935; rep. New York, 1961), 1, 54; PPB (Kane-Donaldson), pp. 9–10; Guddat-Figge, pp. 303–4; Lewis-McIntosh, pp. 146–47; Consuelo Dutschke, *Guide to Medieval and Renaissance Manuscripts in the Huntington Library*, 2 vols. (San Marino, 1989), 1, 161–63.

C British Library, MS Cotton Caligula A.ii, part 1 s. xv$^{3/4}$

Contents: Guddat-Figge, pp. 170–71, gives a full and accurate listing—forty-one items, all verse, save for John of Burgundy's plague tract (IPMEP 659, fols. 65^v–66^v), a form of confession (Jolliffe C.18, fols. 69^v–70^r), and a brief Latin chronicle (fols. 109^r–10^v); among the contents are the alliterative poems *Susannah* (IMEV 3553, fols. 3^r–5^r), *THE SIEGE OF JERUSALEM* (IMEV 1583, fols. 111^r–25^r; lacking lines 167–248 through loss of a leaf), and *Chevalere Assigne* (IMEV 272, fols. 125^v–29^v).

Paper. There are four different stocks, appearing successively: (1) in quire 1, Raisin very like Briquet 12999 (Sion 1451), perhaps more narrowly identifiable with Piccard XIV, 1, 578 (Nürnberg 1452, although a common type *c*.1425–60); (2) in quires 2–3, Roue very like Heawood 4029 and Briquet 13247 (Berne, Thoune, Chateauroux 1445–48) and cf. 13246 (Switzerland and France *c*.1432–60); (3) in quires 3 (one sheet; the quire also includes at least one sheet with no watermark) and 4, Lettre B most like Briquet 7980 (Bergamo 1423) and 7984 (Castroleone 1453, Castronovo 1459, Pavia 1447); (4) in quires 5–7, Tête de boeuf, resembling Briquet 14180–81, but more narrowly identifiable with Piccard II, 7, 123–28, 132, 134, 142 (various locales in western Germany 1453–76). 137 fols. (an older foliation is correct: 1 and 2 are modern paper flyleaves, 140 and 141 are binding leaves associated with the juncture with part II of the volume), 210 mm. × 145 mm. (writing area and format vary, within *The Siege* 180 mm. × 120 mm.), *The Siege* in 37–39 long lines. Collation: one can make only tentative identifications, based on watermark sequences, since the leaves are now mounted individually. On this basis 1^{12} (-1) (= fols. 3–13, a separate booklet) 2^{20} (= fols. 14–33) 3$^{16+6?}$ (fols. 44–49 an unwatermarked group, inserted off-centre after original folding? = fols. 34–55) 4$^?$ (no coherent sequence of watermarks emerges in fols. 56–81) 5^{20} (= fols. 82–101) 6^{20} (-8, -13) (= fols. 102–19) 7^{20} (= fols. 120–39). Brownish ink. Written in secretary.

Bounded in brown ink, no rules or pricks. No catchwords or signatures. Scribal running titles in text ink, red- and ochre- slashed capitals at line heads. Paraphs in the text hand. The text of *The Siege* is divided into six parts by marginal notations 'passus' (the last four numbered 'iiij-vij') opposite lines 445, 639 (the head of fol. 117^v), 737, 896, and 1113.

Part II of the manuscript, which has a signature (s. xvi) of Thomas

Cooke de Mylton, that is, Milton, Cambs., contains constitutions of the Carthusian order, 1411–1504. But the juxtaposition of the two codices postdates their acquisition by Robert Cotton: part I was originally Vespasian D.viii, part II Vespasian D.xxi (although they already appear as the single Caligula A.ii in the 1696 catalogue of the library).

IMEV 2411, which appears at fols. 57^v–58^r, memorializes Ralph, Lord Cromwell of Tattershall, Lincs., who died 1454/5. Frances McSparran, *Octovian Imperator*, Middle English Texts 11 (Heidelberg, 1979), pp. 24–25, reports M. L. Samuels's view that C's language is very mixed but shows strongest evidence of Kentish provenance. However, our experience with the forms of *The Siege* would suggest that Samuels has in fact identified a substrate peculiar to the transmission of *Octavian*, perhaps a London-Essex text: within *The Siege* scarcely any form occurs that one would associate with Kent. Here rather, the scribe seems to have assimilated, probably from relicts in his archetype, a melange of various East Anglian forms, focussed in no single area. Various aspects of the scribe's language show passing affinities with forms peculiar to (1) the western juncture of Norfolk and Suffolk with Ely and Cambs., (2) to King's Lynn and immediately adjacent Lincs. (congruent with Tattershall provenance); (3) to East Suffolk; and (4) to south central Norfolk. These may provide nothing more than evidence of protracted copying history in this area. Binding: the Library's modern half-morocco.

Previous descriptions: Guddat-Figge, pp. 169–72.

In addition to these survivors, other copies must have existed—at least the six (O, O′, and four archetypes) we below demonstrate (see p. lxvii) one must postulate to explain the descent of the text. Hamel (1990, esp. pp. 354–58) has noted records of at least two such lost copies. One appears as item no. 7 in the primarily English book-list of the Welles family (British Library, MS Royal 15 D.ii, fol. 211^v, s. xv ex.): 'A boke cald ye sheys of jherusalem'. The Welles's came from near Louth (Lincs.), a locale suggestive of connections with copies like the surviving V, C, and perhaps Ex. Hamel cites, on the basis of a reference at Joel T. Rosenthal, 'Aristocratic Cultural Patronage and Book Bequests', *Bulletin of the John Rylands University Library* 64 (1982), 522–48 (545), a second lost copy from the will of a Lady Basset. Joanna of Brittany, second wife and widow of Ralph, Lord Basset of Drayton Bassett (Staffs.), in 1402 left her domestic chaplain

John Spynk 'vnum librum anglicum vocatur le Sege de ierusalem' (register of archbishop Thomas Arundel, 1, fol. 195^v; cf. GEC, 2, 3–6). And T. Turville-Petre (1977, p. 118) provides, in passing, evidence for a lost copy of Scottish provenance: the opening line of the sixteenth-century burlesque *Gyre Carling* echoes *The Siege* line 1.

Our descriptions should reveal that our one-volume presentation of *The Siege* differs decidedly from any medieval experience of the work. No surviving manuscript presents *The Siege* as an isolated 'literary text', as an EETS volume does: in every case, the poem has been contextualized through its juxtaposition with other works. Such collocations might well query modern generic categories such as 'romance' (although by and large, the context in C supports such a reading) or 'alliterative history'. And certainly, they reveal *The Siege* as capable of polyvocal recuperations during its textual life. Thus, L, P, D, and probably V present *The Siege* in a context where it should read as a quasi-Scriptural narrative, a pendant to the Passion; such a reading accords well with one source of the poem, the apocryphal *Vindicta salvatoris*. Our copy A combines such an interest with one in specifically crusading poetry, since Robert Thornton's second booklet places *The Siege* in proximity to the Charlemagne poems *The Siege of Milan* and *Roland and Otuel*. And Frampton's copy, U, construes the poem as learned classical history, a tale of Roman conquest, a reading in accord with other sources of the poem, Ranulph Higden's *Polychronicon* and Josephus's *Bellum Iudaicum*.

AUTHORSHIP AND RECEPTION

DIALECT AND DATE

In seeking to determine the authorial dialect of *The Siege*, we follow the useful model provided by M. L. Samuels's demonstration, 'Langland's Dialect'. We attempt, from that minimal information available in poems composed in alliterative long-lines, to isolate in the edited text of *The Siege* features simultaneously authorial and subject to differential dialect analysis. However, in undertaking this task, we initially accept the proviso that some well-attested textual features quite clearly represent no one's Middle English dialect. For example, in order to facilitate alliteration, the author assumes that a range of what we will show to be his own 'northern' forms in /g/ are automatically translatable into /j/ forms of other Middle English dialects. Thus, he alliterates on expected 'northern' *geuen* 'given' in line 278 but the more southerly past tense *ȝaf* in 1087; on *agayn* in 952 but *aȝen* in 650. (Compare WA xxxvi–vii.) That such readings represent a convenience driven purely by demands of initial rhyme may be demonstrated, however, by the form *ȝete* 369, which is archetypal (in both L and P), if not confirmed by alliteration: this represents, not an OE -ȝīetan (assumed, rather than ON geta, in lines 979, 1173; but alliteration on /g/ in 925, 1180), but rather ON gǽta 'heed'—to our knowledge, after the mid fourteenth century, predominantly a northernism and never subject to /g/-/j/ dialectical variation.[1] (In 'northern' dialects, the word 'gate' has /j/ forms derived from Old Northumbrian,[2] and its universal alliteration on /j/—line 1219 is ambiguous—is not remarkable.)

Nonetheless, some features required either by alliterative initial rhyme or by b-verse metrical constraints do seem potentially pointers toward the author's dialect—although many of these might be borrowed, as is the author's use of *ȝaf*, across local dialectical lines from other linguistic communities. Such features include five confirmed by alliterative requirements:

1. OE *hw* crossrhymes with /kw/ from OE *cw* and OF *qu* at lines 11, 507, 626, a rhyme elsewhere in the corpus limited to WA, DT, MA, PTA, and AA. For the expected cross-rhymes of /hw/ and *w*, for example, line 201, and of /kw/ and *k*, for example, line 181, see the discussion at WA xxxvii.

2. The third person plural pronoun objective case never rhymes on /θ/ but always on vowel or /h/; see lines 115, 120, 980, 995, 1068, 1314.[3]

3. On a few, admittedly ambiguous, occasions when it may bear rhyme, the modal 'shall' must have a form in /s/, viz. *sall*; see lines 383, 990, 1220. In these lines, alliteration on this low-stress word seems to us potentially likely in a context where (a) a-verses with three staves are quite frequent (only exceeded quantitatively by usage in the Cotton Nero canon); and (b) rhymes frequently depend upon relatively low-stress words. Moreover, /s/-/ʃ/ crossrhyme is vir-

---

[1] See MED geten v.2 and note the preponderance of uses there cited, from such texts as *Cursor Mundi*, DT, and AA (but also WP 2407).

[2] See A. Campbell, *Old English Grammar* (Oxford, 1959), pp. 69–70; and cf. AA 179.

[3] The nature of the initial phoneme is immaterial, so long as it is /h/ or vowel. Although most often lines have uniform vocalic or /h/ alliteration, clear crossrhymes occur, and many more lines have potential crossrhymes, depending on one's interpretation of the number of words which alliterate.

tually unrecorded in *The Siege*, even in the scribal manuscript versions (see our note to line 319).

4. The word 'church' alliterates on both /tʃ/ (see line 143) and /k/ (see line 240).

5. In addition to the normal Middle English technique whereby /s/ and its clusters /sp/, /st/, /ʃ/, and /sk/ alliterate apart from one another (the last does not occur in *The Siege*), the poem invariably rhymes /sw/ only with itself; see lines 321, 540, 1149, 1176. (/s/-/sw/ crossrhymes occur in WA, DT, and MA.) As a result, a number of lines in which the word *so* alliterates or may alliterate (subject to those same caveats already noted under 3 above; see 565, 764, 976, 1042, 1159), would confirm a form in /s/, not /sw/.

Three further features are confirmed by metrical requirements of the b-verse, as well as relict spellings in a variety of manuscripts:

6. Most normally (see lines 128, 590, 1167, 1187, but contrast line 1078), the word *each* must be disyllabic. Given the certain absence of *-e* from the author's dialect and the widely dispersed relict forms of the MSS., the authorial form seems to have been of the type *ilka*, *ilk a*, or *ilkan*.

7. On the one occasion when judgement is possible (see line 897),[4] the word *much* must be disyllabic, probably a *mikel*-type.

8. In lines 978 and 1027, although the lines would be metrical with either mono- or disyllabic forms, they would read more tautly with the monosyllabic pp. *tan(e)* 'taken', a form widely dispersed in the MSS. as an archetypal relict. (But contrast required *taken* in 1233, as we print it.) Moreover, however the scribal alternation in 586 is interpreted—*made* alternates with *ma/mo* 'more'—the variation suggests that the archetype had the form *ma* 'make'. Our decision for the word 'more' here assumes hypercorrection on the part of a scribe conscientiously translating original *ma* (and inferentially *ta*) forms into those of his own dialect.

We find that, on the basis of materials gathered in LALME, all these eight features could represent a geographically specific authorial dialect—a small area in the West Riding of Yorkshire, a neighbourhood centred around Barnoldswick and Earby. This linguistic

---

[4] Line 149 might provide a second example. Rather than tinker with copy-text on purely dialectical grounds, we print L *myche yloued*, which would require a monosyllable, but other manuscripts suggest an original *mykel loued* (the disyllable required in AD to render the versions reported by the scribes metrical).

community most closely resembles the forms provided by six of LALME's linguistic profiles:

LP 5 British Library, MS Egerton 927, inferentially from Salley (OCist) (but not listed at Ker, p. 177), since it contains the adaptation of Grosseteste's *Château d'Amour* ascribed to a Salley monk, printed in *The Minor Poems of the Vernon Manuscript, Part I*, ed. C. Horstmann, EETS os 98 (1892), pp. 407–42.

LP 18 British Library, MS Cotton Vespasian A.iii, containing *Cursor Mundi*, ed. Richard Morris, EETS os 57 et seq. (1874–93).

LP 191 British Library, MS Harley 1770, containing an unprinted copy of 'The Surtees Psalter' (IMEV 3103); the book belonged to the Augustinian canons of Kirkham, 12 miles northeast of York (Ker, p. 106). Compare the description of our manuscript Ex above.

LP 364 British Library, MS Cotton Vespasian D.vii, also containing a copy of 'The Surtees Psalter', printed *Yorkshire Writers*, ed. K. Horstmann, 2 vols. (London, 1895–96), 2, 130–273.

LP 601 Bodleian Library, MS Bodley 425, another copy of this verse psalter, unpublished.

LP 603 British Library, MS Egerton 614, another copy of this psalter, psalms 1–9 printed *Yorkshire Writers*, 2, 130–43 and collated throughout.

In addition, two copies of *The Prick of Conscience*, placed by LALME in immediately adjacent areas of northeast Lancs. (near Colne), show similar but partially distinguishable forms (for discussions, see Lewis-McIntosh, pp. 53–54 and 76–77, respectively):

LP 154 Trinity College, Dublin, MS 158, part 1

LP 365 British Library, MS Additional 32578

The latter of these manuscripts, according to its colophon (fol. 103^r), partly in a later correcting hand, was copied in 1405 'secundum manum Iohannes Farnelay capellani manentis in Bolton" (but not listed at Ker, p. 11). Although this inscription may not refer to Bolton in Craven (there are at least three other Yorkshire Boltons—by Bowland, on Swale, and Percy), compare the description of our manuscript P and the discussion of the Fairfax 24 *Bible en françois* under 'Sources' below.

We predicate our limitation of authorial dialect to the Barnoldswick-Earby area upon our ability to construct from LALME materials three local isoglosses in the 'northwest Midlands' (broadly Lancs., Cheshire, north Derbys., and adjacent areas of the

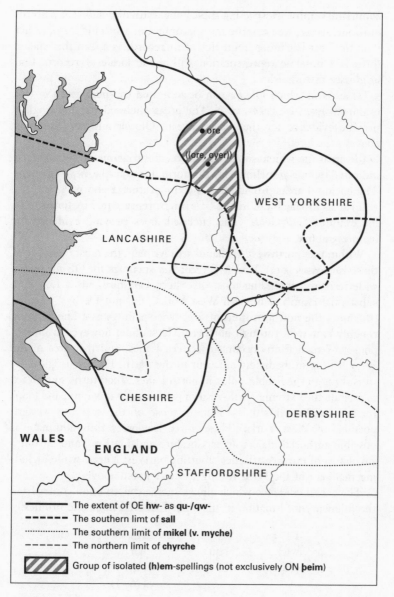

Figure 1. Placement of the authorial dialect of *The Siege of Jerusalem*.

West Riding). In constructing these lines separating different patterns of formal usage, we construe the appearance of a specific form, rather than the overwhelming frequency of its record, as a sign that such a form is a possible representation within the locale of record. Our isoglosses distinguish:

(a) areas in which OE *hw* can be indicated by spellings in *q*- (for example, *qu*-, *qw*-, *qwh*-, *qh*-). The areas enclosed by this isogloss provide evidence for the coalescence of OE *hw* and *cw* (feature 1 above).

(b) areas in which some derivative of OE *heom* is retained, as indicated by non-*þ* spellings for this form, for example, *hem*, *ham*, *am*. The enclosed areas provide evidence for feature 2 above.

(c) areas in which OE *sceal*, *scolde* can be represented by forms in *s*-, for example, *sall*, *sulde*. The enclosed areas provide evidence for feature 3 above.

Within the 'northwest Midland' area we map, the most inclusive of these isoglosses is (a). LALME records *q*-spellings for OE *hw* over a wide territory, including most of eastern Cheshire, all of Lancs., a substantial chunk of western West Yorks., but not Derbys. Isogloss (b) shows the northern limit of *hem*-type spellings as a line running roughly east-west through northern Merseyside; however, a limited pocket of such forms occurs in eastern Lancs. and that area of the West Riding immediately adjacent to the north. Finally, isogloss (c) runs through the Ribble valley in north Lancs., then turns southward to include the extreme north-eastern portion of that county, and loops further southward still to include most of the extreme western portions of West Yorks. These three isoglosses thus eliminate as possible authorial dialect areas Cheshire and Derbys., and all but a small area of northeast Lancs. abutting on West Yorks. while including that area of the West Riding we have noted above.

The actual evidence which allows such a construction comes from the following information in the eight LALME linguistic profiles:

	LP 5	18	191	364
'wh-'	wh[5]	qu	wh	wh
	((qw))	(w)	(w)	(w)
			((qw))	

---

[5] One might note the limitations of LALME in this particular profile; the editors' form of categorizing the evidence here forces them to ignore the telling backspelling at 'Castle' 668 *whoke* ('quaked').

'them'	thaim	yam (yaim) ((ham))	yam (am)	yam (am)
'shall'	sal	sal	sal	sal

	601	603	154	365
'wh-'	wh (qw) ((qwh, w))	wh ((qw, w, qh))	wh, w	wh
'them'	yame, yam, am ((hem))	yam ((yaim, am))	ham ((yam, yaim))	yaime +V[6]
'shall'	sal	sal	sall	sall ((shalle))

Identification of this area of the West Riding with the dialect of the *Siege* poet receives further confirmation from our other five putatively authorial forms. All those forms required for metrical/alliterative purposes are widely attested in the linguistic profiles:

	LP 5	18	191	364
'church'	kirk	kyrc	kirk ((kirke))	kirke
'so'[7]	so	sua, sa ((so))	swa (sa)	swa ((sa, swo))
'each'	ilka, ilk	ilk ((ilka, ilkan))	ilka (ilkan)	ilka (ilkan)
'much'	mekel +V	mikil	mikel	mikel
'make/ take'[8]	mas, ta, tan(e)	ta, tan	mas, tas, tan	mas, tas

	601	603	154	365
'church'	kirke	kirk	kyrk +V	kirke
'so'	so, so *rh* (swo)	swa (so *rh*) ((swo))		so

[6] We use '+V' to indicate a further variety of forms, the variation not germane to our specific linguistic argument.

[7] This word is unaccountably unsurveyed in LALME. The forms cited here are the result of our quick scans of the MSS and printed editions. We have not checked LP 154 for this form.

[8] Simply those forms recorded in LALME, since the MS may not provide the full paradigm.

'each'	ilka	ilke,	ilk	ilke, ilk
	(ilk,	ilka,		
	ilkon)	ilkon		
'much'	mikel	mikel	mekyll,	mykill
			mykyll	((mych))
'make/ take'		mas, tas		

The first of the forms requires comment: the LALME map 'church' shows a large bulge of *ch*-forms far up into eastern Lancs. If Langland could accession the quite distant form *kirk* when he required /k/ alliteration (as in PPB 5.1), the confirmed *ch*-lines in *The Siege* amount to reliance on forms very nearly local. And to return to the opening of our discussion, the eight linguistic profiles above show universal /g/, not /j/, for all forms of the verb *give*; and, for example, LP 5 has routine *ȝate* 'gate' (see 'Castle', lines 457, 698, 787).

Moreover, evidence confirming this authorial dialect occurs in a few further features of fairly widespread distribution, including the area we identify as that of composition. For example, line 1219 requires the trisyllabic *agaynes/aȝaynes* 'against,' recorded (with *g*-spelling) in all our linguistic profiles except LP 5 (*agayn*) and LP 18 (*agains*). Line 292 requires trisyllabic *abouten*, not recorded in LALME from any of these linguistic profiles, but certainly available by analogy from *o-*, *a-bouen* in LP 18, 364, and 365. And line 820 requires a disyllabic form of type *oþer* for 'or;' in the area we survey, this is by and large a Merseyside/Cheshire feature.[9] Although Duggan (1986, pp. 579–80) argues for the disyllabic form as an option universally open to alliterative poets, such a form appears potentially part of the authorial dialect repertoire (compare LP 364 ore (or), LP 601 or but oyer + oyer 'either + or', LP 603 or ((ore, oyer))). And a wealth of forms routine in the linguistic profiles we here survey appear as widespread relics in the various manuscripts of *The Siege*, for example, er/ar 'are', wald(e) 'would', fra/fro 'from', þof 'though' (usually yof, of in the LPs, to the confusion of many *Siege* scribes; see our note to line 7), als 'as', sin/sen 'since' conj., thurgh 'through', -and(e) pr. p. , -es pr. 3 sg. (most LPs alternate -es and -en in the plural, LP 601 -en only), ded(e) 'death', nouther/ nowther/ nauther 'neither', withouten, ar/or 'ere' conj., noght 'not' (and in U routine -th spellings for -ght, as in LP 191 (noth) and LP

---

[9] See LALME dot map 493 (1, 428).

603 ((noth))—and compare mouth 'might'), strenght/strengh 'strength', and til 'to' (esp. preceding vowels and h-).

Internal evidence for the probable date at which *The Siege* was composed is sparse. One can suggest only rough *termini a quo* and *ad quem*. The first is provided by the author's use of Ranulph Higden's *Polychronicon*, demonstrated by Kölbing and Day. This universal history was composed relatively nearby, at St Werburgh's, Chester (OSB), and it routinely circulated along various monastic grapevines; see John Taylor, *The Universal Chronicle of Ranulf Higden* (Oxford, 1966), pp. 105–9, 152–59. It could have been available almost immediately upon 'publication', *c.*1340. The date of the earliest *Siege* manuscript provides a *terminus ad quem*: this is probably in the 1390s, given the likely copying of L in the fourteenth century (and compare P, at the latest *c.*1400). On the whole, given the loss of at least one, and more probably two, generation(s) of copies between the original and the surviving manuscripts (minimally a corrupt archetype of all surviving copies; see 'The Relations of the Manuscripts' below), composition during the 1370s or 1380s would seem an appropriate and conservative inference.

In the past, considerations of dating *The Siege* have turned upon the relationship of the poem to DT. Kölbing and Day (pp. xxvi–ix) were the first to insist upon the derivative nature of *The Siege*. This they found especially evident in a few protracted passages nearly identical in the two poems, most strikingly *Siege* 57–75 and parts of DT 1983–96; *Siege* 617–21 and DT 10462–64; *Siege* 729–33 and DT 7348–53.

The last of these passages typifies the usual argument for the derivative nature of *The Siege*. John Clerk in DT here follows and expands a hint in his sources: Guido delle Colonne's *Historia* 18 opens with a rhetorical description of falling night (although only DT 7349, unparalleled in *The Siege*, really approximates direct translation). Since, Kölbing and Day claim, the passage occurred in DT's source, but the *Siege* poet was only elaborating his, DT must be the prior poem.[10] In such a view, Kölbing and Day have been followed by the poem's few recent commentators. Their arguments plainly underwrite Pearsall's efforts (1977, p. 169) at seeing *Siege* as 'decadent', perhaps especially in its 'imitative style'; both Spearing's

---

[10] Yet even here, Kölbing and Day ignore the fact that *Siege* 731, with its difficult verb *rysten* (see our text note), in fact would more easily explain the form of DT 7351 than the reverse hypothesis. The line has no parallel in Guido.

(pp. 171 and 257 n35) and Lawton's (1982, p. 4) accounts also reproduce their logic.

However, our study of the dialect and date of *The Siege*, when coupled with other recent studies, may cast a different light on these problems. If we are correct in placing *The Siege* poet in the area of Barnoldswick, West Yorks., the relationship between DT and *The Siege* may admit of an interpretation other than strict literary borrowing. For T. Turville-Petre (1988) demonstrates that the initia of DT's books spell out 'M. I[O]HANNES CLERK DE WHALELE', that is, Master John Clerk of Whalley. The poem, on that basis, would have been written in Whalley (Lancs.), perhaps only a dozen miles to the west of Barnoldswick. In fact, in the present state of our knowledge, the poets responsible for the two poems lived in closer geographical proximity to one another than the authors of any other pair of poems, save those of the Cotton Nero group. Thus, the poets' similarities in diction may simply demonstrate their reliance upon a specific local tradition of alliterative verse, a common word-hoard and poetic grammar more closely related than simply a general 'alliterative tradition' (compare T. Turville-Petre 1988, p. 267).

But the alternative of direct borrowing may not be so easily dismissed, and, if one poem has been derived from the other, it is considerably more likely that DT has pillaged *The Siege* than the reverse. First of all, charges of *The Siege*'s lateness and, thus, decadence (like those lodged by Pearsall), are exceedingly ill-taken: with the exception of WP, PP, and perhaps the Gawain-poet, no other alliterative poem shows so early a visible circulation. And from such a perspective, DT must be seen as a very belated work indeed; the single surviving copy, Glasgow University Library, MS Hunterian V.2.8, was copied by Sir Thomas Chetham of Nuthurst, Lancs., c.1540.[11] Moreover, Edward Wilson (1990) has recently argued that the poem was composed nearly contemporaneously with Chetham's copying. Wilson's view, dependent upon the identification of a specific John Clerk of Whalley (who died 1539) with the author, we do not find thoroughly compelling: as Turville-Petre (1988, p. 268) points out, the name is common enough to imagine association with other John Clerks, including some who may simply have failed to leave a trace in surviving records. But Wilson's general insistence on DT's belatedness seems to us provocative. One can easily imagine

[11] First noted by C. A. Luttrell, 'Three North-West Midland Manuscripts', *Neophilologus* 42 (1958), 38–50 (46–48).

this poem as the work of a fifteenth-century alliterative afficionado; such a dating might well explain the poet's wooden handling of the alliterative long-line and (in sharp contrast to the grammatical intricacies of *The Siege*) his tendency to think in blocks of full lines arranged as repetitive appositives.

Moreover, even if both poems are products of the fourteenth century, in the light of our discussion above, it is more probable that *The Siege* is the earlier. As has been pointed out since early in this century (Kölbing and Day, p. xxix, cite Sir Israel Gollancz for this view), DT 8053–54 contain a direct reference to Chaucer's *Troilus*:

> Whoso wilnes to wit   of þaire wo fir,
> Turne hym to Troilus,   and talke þere ynoghe.

Most modern opinion would, of course, date the completion of Chaucer's poem *c*.1385–86.[12] Placing DT, the longest of all the poems in the alliterative corpus, after this date yet early enough to allow its dissemination, the collection of sources for and the composition of *The Siege*, and the dissemination of both the visible *Siege* manuscripts and their archetypes before the 1390s, for us stretches probability considerably. However, imagining *Siege* as a poem which probably predates Chaucer's *Troilus* obviates such an unlikely scenario (and probably places DT, at the earliest, toward 1400). But in any event, if overt literary borrowings are at issue, we believe that John Clerk is more apt to be *The Siege* poet's debtor than the reverse.[13]

THE SOURCES

In literary-historical terms, *The Siege* has always been closely associated with the central tradition of Middle English alliterative poetry in long-lines. And whatever the merit of past views that the poem depends upon DT, connections with that poem highlight the poet's interests in those historical concerns integral to the alliterative movement. Not just John Clerk, but the authors of Alexander A, WA,

---

[12] See also C. David Benson, 'A Chaucerian Allusion and the Date of the Alliterative "Destruction of Troy"', *Notes and Queries* 219 (1974), 206–7.

[13] Compare Turville-Petre, *Alliterative Poetry*, p. 170, and McKay Sundwall, 'The *Destruction of Troy*, Chaucer's *Troilus and Criseyde*, and Lydgate's *Troy Book*', *Review of English Studies* 26 (1975), 313–17, who argues that DT postdates Lydgate's Troy Book, completed 1420.

and MA, rely upon chronicle histories for their subjects and thematic conceptions.[14] And, as has been evident since Kölbing and Day first discussed the sources of *The Siege* (pp. xv–xxvi), this poem, to some extent, shares their interests in learned accounts of past heroic deeds.

But as Kölbing and Day alertly, yet only partially, realized, *The Siege* poet proves considerably more venturesome than his historian colleagues. They, with only passing exceptions (for example, reliance upon the Alexander legend in MA), reproduce at length single historical texts on which they implicitly confer an utter veracity and authority. In contrast, the poet responsible for *The Siege* might be described as the encyclopedist of the movement. Like those *compilatores* who strove to produce exhaustive records of human knowledge, *The Siege* poet assiduously gathered accounts of his chosen topic, Titus's destruction of Jerusalem in 70 C.E.; these narratives, diverse in their emphases, he attempted, with general success (although see, for example, our notes to lines 209, 216–17) to integrate into a single account, more extensive than that offered by any source in isolation.[15]

In his researches, the poet uncovered five texts which offered information of (to him) varying relevance about the first-century wars of the Romans and the Jews. Of three of these, Kölbing and Day were well aware. They noted the poet's reliance, in the first two hundred lines of his account, on the apocryphal *Vindicta salvatoris*, a work perhaps of the early eighth century (hereafter VS). This describes the healing of Titus (but not of Vespasian) through news of Jesus's miracles and of the Vernicle and describes his subsequent destruction of Jerusalem. And Kölbing and Day saw that vast sections of the poem after about line 789 had been derived from a fourteenth-century chronicle source, Ranulph Higden's *Polychronicon* (interestingly, a compilation, in this case composed, like the poem itself, of citations; hereafter Poly). The poet of *The Siege* reproduced primarily Higden's Book 4, chapters 9–10; the latter includes a description of the Roman civil wars of 68–69 C.E. and Higden's cento from Josephus's *De bello Iudaico*. A third source Kölbing and Day identified offers only dispersed information about the destruction of Jerusalem, much of which the poet absorbed into his own account; from Jacobus de

---

[14] Although, in the case of MA, never with quite the specific detail of, say, the passing use of Geoffrey of Monmouth at Erk 205–16. Cf. Pearsall 1977, pp. 162–9, where the poems are grouped; and see Ralph Hanna, 'Alliterative Poetry' in *The Cambridge History of Medieval English Literature*, ed. David Wallace (Cambridge, 1999), pp. 488–512 passim.

[15] For an extensive and detailed account of the sources (and much else), see Millar.

Voragine's *Legenda aurea* (hereafter LA), he derived the story of
Titus's illness and his healing by the learned Jew Josephus (lines
1027–66), as well as several isolated details (for example, Vespasian's
illness in lines 33–36, Nero's death in lines 903–20 passim, the
supposed length of the actual siege in line 1173). In Appendixes A
and B, we offer, as did Kölbing and Day before us; see pp. 83–9)
texts of relevant portions of VS and Poly, with marginal notation of
parallel passages in *The Siege*. These amply demonstrate the
derivative nature of substantial portions of the narrative, and,
perhaps more importantly, often have motivated the decisions
between English variants which have produced our text. Given
the poet's fragmentary use of LA, we simply cite relevant readings
in the appropriate textual notes.

Kölbing and Day's study, of course, involved one major failure:
they did not adequately account for the narrative of nearly six
hundred lines of *The Siege* (roughly lines 200–788). Thus, the
weakest part of their discussion was their fitful effort to assimilate
materials in this portion of the poem to details from various versions
of the *Vindicta* or of extensive French materials concerning *La
Vengeance de Nostre Seigneur* (for the latter of which, see most
helpfully Ford's volumes).[16] Phyllis Moe remedied this deficiency:
in the course of her researches on the Middle English biblical and
apocryphal narratives of Cleveland Public Library, MS W q091.92-
C468, fols. 77^r–99^v (s. xv$^{3/4}$), she discovered that these tales (edited as
Middle English Prose) formed a translation from a French work. This,
the *Bible en françois* (hereafter BF, for its quite diverse contents, see
Middle English Prose, pp. 8–9), was probably composed in the 1260s
(p. 31); in the colophon of one of the seventeen manuscripts Moe
knew, its author is identified as 'magister Rogerus dictus de
Argentolio, clericus scolarius Parisius' (Bibliothèque nationale, MS
fr. 1850, fol. 51^r). This Roger of Argenteuil has resisted any further
identification.[17] And Moe demonstrated, in large measure from its
retention of many narrative features distinctive to BF (see pp. 24–28),

---

[16] Some derivative of the French *Vengeance* lies behind the two other Middle English
accounts of the destruction of Jerusalem, *Titus and Vespasian* (IMEV 1881) and its
offspring, *The Siege in Prose* (IPMEP 51). For the sources of these texts, both later than
and unconnected with *The Siege*, see, most recently, *The Siege in Prose*, pp. 17–18.

[17] He appears, for example, in neither of Glorieux's *Repertoire* of Paris masters; see
Middle English Prose, pp. 17 n17, 19 n19. Contrary to Moe's view that this might be a
scribal signature, we take 'Explicit diuina scriptura `ab´reuiata quam magister Rogerus . . .
fecit' to be a clear statement of authorship.

that the same French text provided *The Siege* poet's sole source for lines 205–80 and 321–728. To Moe's account we would only add that a few sporadic details near the end of the poem may also rely upon Roger's work. A third Appendix, with relevant portions of this narrative and marginal notation of parallels in *The Siege*, is rendered unnecessary by Ford's edition (BF), and we simply refer to it. (Considerably fuller detail about the transmission of Roger's work is available in BF, pp. 74–127.)

The *Siege* poet's fifth source, which has never been seriously investigated, differs markedly in kind both from the legendary anti-Semitic emphases of VS, LA, or BF,[18] and from Higden's chronicle. We believe that the poet, on a number of occasions, especially in the second half of his poem, utilized a learned classical history, one written in frank imitation of Thucydides, Josephus's *De bello Iudaico*. Making a case for the poet's access to Josephus involves immediate difficulties: ultimately, in some respect, *The Jewish Wars* conveys that information which is simultaneously the source of all other accounts. Thus, only exact verbal and narrative correspondences without parallel in other sources can convince one of any relationship between *The Siege* and *De bello*. So far as we are aware, such a demonstration has been undertaken only once in the past, in T. Kopka's 1887 Breslau dissertation, which is unavailable to us (but see *Titus*, pp. 31–38). Kopka unfortunately relied upon 'Hegisippus', the free late fourth-century Latin translation of Josephus often attributed to Ambrose. He could find there only three points of contact with *The Siege*. These Kölbing and Day demolished in short order (p. xxi). Rather more promising is the literal translation of Josephus's *Jewish Wars*, usually attributed to Rufinus of Aquileia (*fl.* *c.*385–410) and standard in the Middle Ages. It includes close verbal and narrative parallels to substantial portions of *The Siege*—including both passages unparalleled in any of the conventionally designated sources and embellishments of passages which the poet also demonstrably derived from his other sources.

Scholars still differ about the mode by which Josephus's two great Greek works, *The Antiquities* and *The Jewish War*, were produced. And similar mysteries surround the early translations of the second text, the ultimate source for all later accounts of the siege. As Blatt

[18] These have, of course, in an era of race, class, and gender studies, proved instrumental in the few critical discussions; see Hamel 1992, Hanna 1992, Van Court, Price, Lawton 1997, and Chism. Exceptionally, Hebron analyses the siege descriptions.

noted (pp. 12, 17) in his edition of the first five books of *The Antiquities*, that text was translated at Vivarium as part of Cassiodorus's huge bibliographical project.[19] But Cassiodorus, who calls Josephus 'paene secundus Livius' (p. 55/16), knew at least some preexisting translation of *The Jewish War*, although his reference renders it impossible to decide which: 'alios septem libros *Captivitatis Iudaicae* mirabili nitore conscripsit, quam translationem alii Hieronymo, alii Ambrosio, alii deputant Rufino' (p. 55/22–24).[20]

As Cassiodorus's applause for Josephus would almost have guaranteed, the Rufinian translation had an immense European circulation. Something over two hundred manuscripts of the Latin *De bello Iudaico* survive, in virtually all cases as a pendant, often at the end of the second volume of a multivolume collection, to the more extensive *Antiquities*. And the work was certainly well known in England: at least fifteen copies produced there survive, in the main volumes in the late twelfth-century double-column folio format usually reserved for the presentation of patristic authors. These we know through Blatt's extensive researches, probably complete for England (since he checked his list with, and received notice of additional copies from, N. R. Ker). And we have spotchecked lists of significant passages against about half of these manuscripts (those starred below). The relevant copies, virtually all members of Blatt's 'Norman manuscript family' of *The Antiquities* (see pp. 87–94, manuscripts nos 154–71), ordered by the sigla we have tentatively assigned, and with indications of medieval provenances, include:

*A London, British Library, MS Arundel 94 (s. xii ex.), fols. 83^v–205^r, the sample discussed below at 188vb–89ra

*B London, British Library, MS Burney 325 (s. xiii in.), fols. 1^r–160^r (in the Middle Ages, at the Hereford Franciscan convent; see Ker, p. 100), sample at 139vb–40ra

*C Oxford, Bodleian Library, MS Lat. th. c.6 (s. xii^2), fols. 2^r–130^v (perhaps continental), sample at 112^{vab}

D Durham Cathedral, MS B.II.1 (s. xii med.), fols. 189va–268ra (a Durham Cathedral book in the Middle Ages; see Ker, p. 66)

*E Oxford, Bodleian Library, MS Auct. E inf. 3 (s. xiii^2), fols. 203^r–97^r, sample at 282va

[19] As our subsequent discussion will indicate, we remain immensely in Blatt's debt for a vast amount of information. So far as we can tell, only this single volume, a fragment of Blatt's project, has ever been published.

[20] We cite Cassiodorus, *Institutiones* from R. A. B. Mynors's edition (Oxford, 1937).

G Glasgow, University Library, MS Hunterian S.1.4 (s. xii), fols. 205^r–92^v (perhaps at the Hertford Benedictine priory in the Middle Ages; see Ker, p. 101)

*H London, British Library, MS Harley 5116 (s. xiii), fols. 208^r–97^r (from the Coventry Franciscans; see Ker, p. 55), sample at 284rb

*J Cambridge, St. John's College, MS A.8 (s. xii ex.), fols. 102^r–245^r (from Christ Church, Canterbury OSB; see Ker, p. 31), sample at 275va

L Lincoln Cathedral, MS 145 (C.1.6) (s. xii med.), fols. 143^v–204^r (a Lincoln Cathedral book; see Ker, p. 117)

M^1 Oxford, Merton College, MS 316 (s. xii), fols. 1^r–162^r (a Merton College book; see F. M. Powicke, *The Medieval Books of Merton College* [Oxford, 1931], p. 219)

M^2 Oxford, Merton College, MS 317 (s. xii/xiii), fols. 72^v–95^r, 111^v–39^v (again, from Merton College; see Powicke, p. 122)

*R^1 London, British Library, MS Royal 13 D.vii (s. xii ex.), fols. 83^v–211^r (a St. Albans book; see Ker, p. 167), sample at 192vb–93ra

*R^2 London, British Library, MS Royal 13 E.viii (s. xiii/xiv), fols. 186^r–266^r, sample at 254^{vab}

V Valencia, Biblioteca de la Catedral, MS 29 (s. xii), fols. 179^v–244^r

W Worcester Cathedral, MS F.9 (s. xiii ex.), fols. 229^r–324^v (not certainly a medieval book of Worcester Cathedral Priory; see Ker, p. 210)

All other copies in British libraries were produced outside England. In addition to these MSS, we have routinely consulted and cite (largely for ease of reference) the 1524 Cologne print, so far as we know, the last published version of the Latin *Jewish Wars*.

Our belief in the poet's access to Josephus might be illustrated from any number of points in *The Siege*. But one of the poem's most affecting passages provides a compact, and to us telling, demonstration. This is lines 1081–1100, the horrifying scene in which Mary eats her baby. As Van Court and Millar have noted, the poet has suppressed substantial emphases of the sources, whatever they are construed to be, here: Mary loses a particularly challenging speech, and the scene is no longer the ultimate example of Jewish perfidy; that those who break in upon Mary are 'sediciosi', John and Simon's brigands, and that her contempt for them partially motivates her act, are details here elided. But the account the poet does reproduce

shows, as is usual in his combination of discrete sources, a rather
dextrous interweaving between Higden's exact language and less
verbally exact materials not in *Polychronicon* but directly from
Josephus. Although any single one of these might be taken as
merely accidental agreement in a common dramatic embellishment,
the number of such coincidences in short compass militates against
such a conclusion.

We cite the two passages extensively. For Higden's account, we
simply reproduce lines 130–50 from the full text provided in
Appendix B. The text of Josephus follows the forms of the 1524
print (our sigil p). We have emended the text to correspond with a
putative copy available in fourteenth-century England on the basis of
the eight manuscripts starred and with sample folios noted in the list
above.[21] In each text, we print in bold-face and provide parenthetical
(half-)line references for those portions the poet reproduces from that
version directly. Higden's report, derived from Josephus, states:

Egesippus, libro quinto, et Iosephus septimo. Tunc contingit illud factum tam
horrendum quam famosum Marie alienigene, que **fame tabescens** (1081b
or 1093b) **paruulum quem genuerat** (1082a, compare 1096a) alloquitur in
hunc modum, 'Fili mi, seua omnia te **circumstant** (1084), bellum, fames,
incendia, latrones; **redde uel semel matri quod ab ea sumpsisti** (1087a).
Redi (1087b) **in id secretum a quo existi** (1088a). Feci quandoque quod
pietatis erat, faciamus modo quod fames persuadet'. Hec dicens filium **igne
torruit** (1082b); partem comedit, partem reseruauit; sed nidor **incense
carnis** (1089a) sediciosos allexit, quos obiurgans mulier sic affatur, 'Silete;
non fui auara, partem **uobis** (1095a) seruando', et ad portionem reseruatam
sic loquitur, 'Gratus es mihi, fili mi, vite mee dilatator, percussorum
repressor; qui venerunt necaturi iam facti sunt conuiue. Gustate ergo
quod matrem nouistis gustasse, aut certe totum reliquum incoporabo. Ne
pudeat uos mulierem imitari quam sic epulari fecistis'. Repleuit ilico urbem
tanti sceleris nefas, et Titum in tantum commouit ut manus eleuans sic
effaretur, 'Ad bellum hominum venimus; sed, ut video, contra beluas
dimicamus. Quin etiam fere rapaces a propria spetie abstinent, etiam in
summa necessitate suos fetus fouent; sed isti proprios deuorant. Ipsos ergo
deleamus, quorum feda sunt omnia'.

[21] In the capitulation of the print, which we follow universally, this is Book 7, Chapter
8 (the manuscripts have book and chapter divisions, but unnumbered and unrubricated),
fol. 312[r]. This corresponds to 6.205–12 in the Greek text, to which parallel references are
always provided. For these purposes, we always cite the Loeb Library (for this passage,
3:435–37). Our emendations of the print stand as a measure of its proximity to the poem:
generally speaking, it is accurate enough, but frequent minor lections will not have
corresponded exactly to the poet's copy.

Josephus's fuller account of the outrage runs:

Plus uero quam fames iracundia succendebat. Igitur [impet]u animi ac necessitate impulsa, rebus aduersis contra naturam excitatur; raptoque filio, quem la[c]tentem habebat, 'Miserum te', ait, 'infans in bello et fame et seditione cui [r]eseruauero? Apud Romanos [quidem] etiam, si uixeris, seruiturus es; fames autem praeuenit seruitutem; his uero seditiosi saeuiores 5 sunt. Esto igitur mihi cibus, et seditiosis furia, et humane uitae fabula quae sola deest calamitatibus Iudaeorum'. Et hoc simul dicens, occidit filium coctumque medium comedit, adopertum autem reliquum [re]seruauit. Ecce [autem] **aderant** (1091a)[22] seditiosi, et contaminatissimi nidoris odore capti, **mortem** (1091b) ei statim (nisi **quod parasset** [1092a] **ostenderet**[23] 10 [1092b]) **minabantur** (1091b). Illa uero bonam partem se reseruasse respondens, **aperit** (1095b) filii reliquias. Illos autem confestim **horror cepit atque dementia** (1096b), uisuque ipso diriguerunt. At mulier: 'Et hic [meus]', inquit, 'est uere filius et facinus meum: comedite, nam et ego comedi. Nolo + sitis aut foemina molliores aut matre misericordiores. Quod 15 si uos pietatem colitis et mea sacrificia repudiatis, ego quidem comedi, reliquum [autem] eius me manebit'. Post hoc **illi quidem trementes exierunt** (1097), ad hoc solum timidi uixque h[un]c cib[um] matri cesser[unt]. Mox autem repleta est eo scelere tota ciuitas, et unusquisque ante oculos sibi cladem illam proponens tanquam hoc ipse admisisset 20 horrebat.[24]

In addition to the Josephan materials we print in bold-face here, at least three other details of the passage are potentially from this source. Line 1081a designates Mary 'a *myld* wyf', which echoes the description of Nero's slain wife in 901: given that context, the word may here mean 'gracious, well-mannered, noble' (compare MED milde a.,

---

[22] Cf. *Oxford Latin Dictionary*, s.v. adsum, sense 15 'to be upon someone'; and Josephus's description of the brigands' usual actions, 6.11,f. 304[v] (5.432, 3:335): 'Nam sic ubi clausam domum uidissent, eos qui intus erant, cibum capere hoc suspicabantur indicio, statimque ruptis foribus irruebant' (cf. the paraphrase, *Polychronicon* 124–25). *Legenda aurea* ch. 67 (p. 302), which here quotes Eusebius's quotation of Josephus, may absolve one of the need to evoke the original at this point: 'in domum irruant et, nisi carnem prodat, mortem minantur'. But the appearance of this single passage in the *Legenda* is outweighed by the numerous examples we will shortly cite; the *Legenda* cannot be the source of any of these.

[23] We assume the poet's 'layned' has been generated as the antonym of Josephus's 'ostenderet'.

[24] A full collation of the nine witnesses: 1 impetu] ui p. 2 aduersis contra] aduersus BE. 3 lactentem] latentem pC. 4 reseruauero] te seruauero p (*fere recte*); ser/uabo C. quidem etiam] etiam pC; quidem J. 6 igitur] *om.* E. 8 reseruauit] seruauit p. 9 autem] *om.* p. 10 quod] que C. 11 se] se illis EJR¹R². 14 meus] *om.* p; omnes E. 15 sitis] ut sitis p. 16 pietatem] pietate BE. 17 autem eius] eius p; autem H. hoc] hec CEHJR¹R². 18 hunc cibum] hoc cibi pE; hoc cibo BC. 19 cesserunt] cessere p.

sense 6b, and compare sense 2). That would correspond to an earlier
bit of Josephus's account, 'genere ac diuitiis nobilis' (in the Greek,
6.201, 3:435); but this sentence also appears in *Legenda aurea* ch. 67
(p. 302). Although 1082a quite adequately represents *Polychronicon*'s
'paruulum quem genuerat' and there are no English variants, this line
might display intenser 'wit' were one to read 'barn þat 30 bre[d]'. In
such a reading, *bred* might represent MED breden v.3, sense 3b
'fostered', a fairly exact reflection of Josephus's 'lactentem'. And
finally, lines 1085–86 reduce material the poet could have found in
either *Polychronicon* or Josephus. But where Higden simply gives an
ungraded list of four items, 'bellum, fames, incendia, latrones',
truncating Josephus's three-member sentence to two members
(another suppression of the 'seditiosos') would readily produce the
bellum-fames distinction (although not its exact terms) of these lines.
But compare *Polychronicon* 107, a paraphrase of this Josephan
sentence: 'foris captiuitas, intus fames, utrobique formido'.

This demonstration from a single passage seems to us compelling.
The poet supplied details, often not especially exact in their verbal
form, from consultation or memory of a Latin Josephus. In the
context of use we have demonstrated from the twenty lines which
describe Mary, other examples require much less extensive treatment.
But the sheer number of instances, perhaps thirty in all, cumulatively
extends the force of our argument. These further examples include:

49, 85 *Sensteus of Surye*: Although as we indicate in the note to line
49, the reference at Poly 63 to 'Cestius preses' may sufficiently
account for his presence in the poem, it occurs in a radically different
context and lacks any provincial identification. But Cestius is a major
actor in early stages of Josephus's narrative; compare the first
reference to him, 2.13, fol. 259ᵛ (2.280, 2:433): 'Donec autem in
Syria Cestius Gallus prouinciam regebat . . .'. Eventually, as unrest
grew in Judea, he invaded the province; at the moment when he
might have quashed the revolt by sacking Jerusalem (November 66
C.E.), he unaccountably withdrew and was eventually routed during
his retreat. See Josephus 2.22–24, fols. 266ʳ–67ᵛ (2.499–555, 2:517–
37). Cestius's failures required the appointment of a new commander,
Vespasian; compare 265–68 below.

52 *his tribute . . . þat þey withtake wolde*: In VS, Nathan brings
tribute; in BF, tribute does not represent a major reason for the war
and is eventually collected and passed to Rome; insofar as the issue is
mentioned in Poly, it only occurs in MSS variants. The question of

tribute arises, briefly yet pregnantly, in Agrippa's long speech seeking to dissuade the Jews from rebellion (late spring 66 C.E.). Josephus 2.16, fol. 263^r (2.403–4, 2:481) reports: 'Sed opera uestra, inquit, talia sunt, qualia aduersum Romanos pugnantium. Neque enim Caesari uectigal dedistis . . .'.

265–68 This transition, as well as the account of Vespasian's appointment which follows, both 'medievalized' and written to accord with the interests of VS, depends upon Josephus 3.1, fol. 270^v (3.1–4, 2:575): following Cestius's failures, 'Neronem autem, ubi res apud Iudaeam non prospere gestas accepit, latens quidem quod necesse fuit cum timore stupor inuadit; aperte autem superbiam simulans . . . Veruntamen curis angebatur mentis eius perturbatio, cum deliberaret cuinam commotum crederet orientem, qui una et Iudaeos rebellantes ulcisceretur, proximasque his nationes simili modo correptas ante caperet. Inuenit igitur Vespasianum his necessitatibus parem, et qui tanti belli magnitudinem suscipere posset'.

305–12, 321–24 This passage depends in a general way upon Josephus's description of the Galilean campaign with which Vespasian began his efforts to reduce Palestine. BF 200–3 certainly includes relevant general information of a sort which could have generated the entire account (and the second independent clause there quite adequately accounts for 321–24): 'et touz les juis que il trouvoit metoit a l'espee et a ocision'. But BF 201–2 does place the action 'd'entor Jherusalem', whereas the poet explicitly identifies the campaign with the Roman province, Syria (305; compare 49 and 85), which, as Josephus notes, included both Galilee and Judea. And, only in 323–24, after this carnage, do the Romans approach Jerusalem. Moreover, the emphatic insistence on fire (306–8) resembles much more closely Josephus 3.3, fol. 272^r (3.62–63, 2:595): 'bellum accendit Romanis, indigne ferentibus insidias. Et propterea nec die nec nocte ab agrorum depopulatione cessantibus, sed passim deripientibus quicquid rerum in his reperissent. Qui tamen cum mortem pugnacibus semper inferrent, imbelles seruitium capiebant. *Ignis uero et sanguis Galilaeam totam repleuerat*, nec quisquam expers eius acerbitatis aut cladis erat'. And compare further 3.6, fol. 276^v (3.134, 2:617), the description of the sack of Gabara and subsequent harrying: 'Incendit autem non solum ciuitatem, sed etiam omnes circum uicos et municipia; quaedam penitus desolata, nonnulla uero quorum habitantes ipse cepisset'.

438 *Sire Sabyn of Surrie*: Kölbing and Day (p. xxiii and n4) quite

plausibly suggest that the unassuming Syrian (see Poly 150–57) who makes the first ascent of the walls of Jerusalem has been transformed into a Roman general. And certainly his nationality has been carried over into this figure, if only for alliterative convenience. But one should note that the poet's elevation of the mercenary into a prominent Roman leader may echo Josephus's applause for a tribune of the fifteenth legion, prominent both in the taking of Jotapata and in the first entry into Jerusalem. See 3.13, fol. 277^r (3.324, 2:667): 'Hora igitur quae fuerat indicata, otiose ibat ad muros, primusque incedebat Titus cum uno ex chiliarchis Domitio Sabino'; and 6.10, fol. 302^v (5.340, 3:307), where Titus protects a retreat: 'Missilibus hostes [Titus] abigebat, et cum eo Domitius Sabinus, uir bonus etiam in illo praelio comprobatus'.

505–20 Although portions of the passage certainly reflect the analogous speech in BF 367–77, Titus's oration to his troops before the sack of Tarichaeae, at Josephus 3.17, fol. 280^{rv} (3.472–84, 2:709–13), may have contributed to the emphases of lines 512, 517–18, and 520a.

666b–68 The lines have no clear parallel at BF 450 (which answers *Siege* 665–66a). But the references to high banks may reflect the emergency efforts undertaken by Josephus as Jewish commander, a crash building programme to heighten the walls of Jotapata, when faced by the Roman ramps; compare Josephus 3.7, fol. 274^r (3.171 and 174, 2:627–29): 'Erecto autem propemodum aggere pauloque minus aequato propugnaculis, indignum esse ratus Iosephus nihil contra moliri quod oppido saluti foret, conuocat fabros murumque altius iubet extolli. . . . Hisque [leather shields] ante fabros oppositis, illi murum die noctuque operando, ad uiginti cubitorum altitudinem erexerunt, crebris etiam turribus in eo constructis, minisque ualidissimus aptatis'.

789–96 Although 795b certainly reflects Poly 74–75, 791b corresponds more closely to Josephus 3.8, fol. 274^v (3.186–88, 2:631) 'demersa undis' than to Poly 71 'aquis infusas'. Similarly 793a reproduces Josephus 'omnes repente aqua perfluerent', and the poet reserves Poly 72 'paulatim vaporantibus aquis' for 794a.

801–4 This passage probably reflects portions of Josephus 3.9, fol. 275^r (3.219–20, 2:639–41), which intrude between the anecdotes of the wet skins and the chaff-sacks. Rather than concentrating on the ram itself (see our note to line 802), the poet reproduces portions of the account which describe the covering fire necessary to protect those who wield the machine: 'Itaque Romani quidem ballistis, caeterisque missilium machinis, ut facilius ferirentur, qui de muris obstare tentassent, proprius adhibitis utebantur. Neque sagittarii aut fundibulatores longius aberrant. Cum uero ea causa muros nemo auderet ascendere, ipsi arietem applicabant'.

816b Perhaps a Josephan detail: Poly 79–80 stipulates no weapon, but compare Josephus 3.9, fol. 275^v (3.236, 2:645): 'Vespasiani plantam *sagitta* percussam leuiter uulnerat, quia uis *teli* spatio defecisset'. But the following distich is, as typically when wounds are at issue, the poet's elaboration, and this detail may be as well.

826–32 *cloue* 826b answers Josephus 3.9, fol. 275^v (3.246, 2:647) 'auulsum', not paralleled at Poly 81–82. Following *brayn* in this halfline, 827a probably also reflects Josephus, who distinguishes the victim's 'caput' from the projectile 'caluaria'; Poly 81 has but a single reference to 'occipicium', the back of the head, not the brain-pan. And 832a coalesces a Josephan detail from this description with that of the unfortunate mother and child: the *burne*'s brain-pan flies off 'ueluti funda excussa', as if (a stone) fired from a sling.

857–84 Poly includes no parallel episode, but the entire council scene answers Vespasian's elaborated logic for withdrawing his troops from hostilities at the siege of Jotapota; see Josephus 3.8, fol. 274^v (3.178–80, 2:629). In the siege of Jerusalem proper, Titus halts the battle once, but for only five days; see 6.11, fol. 303^r (5.348, 3:309).

897ff. The articulation of this Roman history with the Jewish War, objected to by Spearing (p. 166) as unnecessary and irrelevant elaboration, is foreign to Poly. There, the history simply follows the regnal order of the emperors Nero through Vespasian (in 4.9 and Appendix B, lines 22–46), with the end of the chapter (Appendix B, lines 47ff.) devoted to the war. But Josephus carefully switches back and forth between contemporary events in Palestine and in Rome. Such alternations of subject are integral to Josephus's account: they 'prove' his prophetic powers and his claim to be a valuable royal servant. At Jotapata after his capture, he saved himself by predicting to Vespasian that he would be named emperor.[25]

939–40 This passage simply reproduces Poly 36. But the poet, on the basis of three later references (994, 1129, 1186) to Vespasian's younger son (and later emperor) Domitian, probably knew this passage (or other, later ones where Domitian appears) from Josephus;

[25] For an argument that the lines are equally integral to *The Siege*, see Hanna 1992, pp. 110–11.

see 5.13, fol. 295ʳ (4.645–49; 3:191–93), where Domitian joins his uncle Sabinus's rising but manages to escape. Neither Poly 4.10 nor 4.12 includes any notice—which would be nonhistorical—of Domitian's participation in the wars.

957–1012 This passage has no parallel in Poly and apparently is the poet's rendition of Jos 5.10, fols. 293ᵛ–94ʳ (4.592–604, 3:173–79). There Vespasian's men, cognizant that lesser generals contend for the crown, elect their leader emperor. Compare the preparation for this moment at the climax of the poet's original arming of the hero passage, lines 767–68.

1075 Although the poet might have derived this detail from LA (see the note to line 1075), his persistent recourse to Jos 7.7, fol. 312ʳ (see 1079 and 1143–44 below) suggests that the information may come from that locus (here 6.197, 3:433, where it immediately precedes the sentence we cite in our discussion of 1143–44 below): 'Denique nec cingulis nec calciamentis abstinuere, coriaque scutis detracta mandebant'.

1079 The wolf-simile has a series of near parallels in Josephus. Compare 6.14, fol. 306ᵛ (5.526, 3:363): 'Nec enim uel animas affectio mansueta uel corpora dolor tangebat, qui etiam mortuam plebem quasi canes lacerabant'; 7.7, fol. 312ʳ (6.196, 3:433): 'Ipsos autem spes egestate uictus hiantes, ueluti canes rabidos'.

1080 The line is broadly equivalent to Josephus 6.11, fol. 304ᵛ (5. 429, 3:335): 'Cum potentiores quidem plus haberent, infirmiores autem iniuriam deplorarent'.

1109–12 The discussion of Jewish mining efforts probably reflects Josephus 6.12, fol. 305ᵛ (5.469, 3:347): 'Iam uero admotis aggeribus, Iohannes suffossa intus terra usque ad aggeres Antoniam uersus, depositis per cuniculum sudibus, opera suspendit, illataque sylua pice ac bitumine illita, ignem immittit. Succensis autem fulcimentis, fossa repente subsedit, cumque magno sonitu in ea aggeres decidere'.

1115 *kaue*: In Josephus, the attack simply comes from a gate of the city. *kaue*, however, refers to the mining activities of preceding lines—the ME word can mean 'tunnel or pit', as well as 'cave'. But the use of subterranean passages forms a standard motif of Jewish warfare in Josephus; compare the author/hero 'in quendam profundum puteum' at 3.14, fol. 277ᵛ (3.341, 2:673); or the references to 'cloacis' and 'subterraneis' at 7.14, fol. 315ᵛ (6.370 and 372, 3:483, 485). BF 573 refers to Jews, after the fall of Jerusalem, hiding 'es caves et es boves de la cité', but this passage is more relevant to one of the parallels to line 1246 which we discuss below.

1121–32 Although no battle occurs during the ambush proper (see 1109–13n, 1121n), the poet may here elaborate upon the immediately subsequent Jewish surprise attack on the tenth legion, at 6.3, fol. 297^{rv} (5.75–97, 3:223–29). There Titus comes with reinforcements to drive off the Jewish sally and then, virtually singlehandedly, repels a second attack.

1135–40 Although Poly 96–98 provide an adequate source, the poet's exact terms may reflect Josephus 6.12, fol. 305^{rv} (5.455–59, 3:343–45): Titus 'ad Iohannem et Simonem intromisit [maimed prisoners] ut . . . saltem nunc desinerent, admonens nec uere compellerent ad excidium ciuitatis, sed lucrarentur in extremis mutata uoluntate et proprias animas et patriam tantam et templum, cuius participem non habebant. . . . Ad haec in muris stantes, et ipsi Caesari et patri eius maledicebant, mortemque se contemnere clamabant, eamque seruituti recte preferre'.

1143–44 Probably suggested by two comments in Josephus (and, of course, echoed in the 'poor escheat' of line 1309); compare 6.16, fol. 307^{v} (5.571, 3:377), where Jewish defectors report 'frumenti quidem modium uendisse [p ueniisse] talento'; and 7.7, fol. 312^{r} (6.198, 3:433): 'Quinetiam foeni ueteris laceramenta uictui habebantur, cuius nonnulli exiguum pondus quatuor Atticis uenundabant'.

1155b Not from Poly 110–11 but Josephus 6.14, fol. 306^{v} (5.519, 3:361): Titus 'ingemuit, et extentis manibus deum testabatur'. Similar detail appears in LA ch. 67 (p. 302).

1159–62 Although the passage has adequate parallels at Poly 111–15 and 117–21 (but see our next example), the transition in fact directly answers Josephus 6.11, fol. 304^{v} (5.420–21, 3:333): 'Haec Iosepho uociferante cum lachrymis, seditiosi quidem neque animos flexerunt, neque tutam sibi mutationem fore iudicauerunt. Populus uero ad profugiendum commotus est'.

1168–69 The first line reflects Josephus 6.11, fol. 304^{v} (5.421, 3:333), not Poly. Compare Josephus 'ne latrones eos deprehenderent' and 'solidos' (Poly 114–15 'ne insidiatores aliquid palam reperirent' and 113 'bunones aureos'). And although 1169a probably derives from Poly 115–16 'ab vno in omnes opinio manavit' (Josephus 'fama percrebuit'), the *bourd* later in the line corresponds to Josephus 6.15, fol. 307^{r} (5.551, 3:371) 'arte'.

1188–96, 1209–12 The materials surrounding Sabin's climb on the

wall are derived from Josephus's proximate description at 7.1, fol.
308ᵛ (6.23–28, 3:385), of the first assault on Antonia: 'Iudaeis autem
inde digressis, Romani machinas admouere quamuis ab Antonia saxis
atque igni ferroque peterentur, et quodcunque hostibus telum
necessitas attulisset. . . . [Romani] quidem crebris in se missilibus
iactis, cum nullis periculis desuper uenientibus lassarentur, arietum
opus urgebant. Cum uero inferiores essent, ac lapidibus frangerentur,
alii scutis super corpore concameratis, fundamenta manibus et
uectibus suffodiebant, itaque saxis quattuor [p quatitur] obstinato
labore concussis. Quietem utrisque nox attulit, et in ea murus
arietibus labefactatus, ex qua parte prioribus Iohannes aggeribus
insiniando, murum suffoderat, subsidente cuniculo repente labitur'.
But the fall of this wall in Josephus only reveals a second behind it,
much to the Romans' consternation: it is that structure which Sabin
climbs (historically c.22 July 70 C.E.).

   1197 For *Sabyn of Surrye*, see 438 above.

   1223b Although the poet may merely respond to demands of
rhyme (and the following line clearly comes from Poly), this verse
corresponds to Josephus 7.12, fol. 314ʳ (6.289, 3:461) 'supra ciuitatem', not Poly 164 'supra templum'.

   1234b The 'last word' reflects Josephus 7.12, fol. 314ᵛ (6.309,
3:467): 'Cum autem ad extremum addidisset'.

   1246 Perhaps inspired by, or another passage from, Josephus;
compare 7.12, fol. 315ʳ (6.355, 3:479): 'nec minus ciuitatis mortuis
plenae uici ardebant domusque sumo consumptae'; 7.14, fol. 315ᵛ
(6.369; 3:483): 'nullusque in ciuitate locus uacuus erat, sed cuncta
mortuos habebant, quos fames aut latrones confecerant; et cadauer-
ibus eorum plena erant omnia, qui alimentorum penuria uel seditione
perierant'; or the description of the Romans digging in caverns to find
the last fugitives at 7.17, fol. 317ʳ (6.431, 3:501): 'Saevus autem
corporum odor introeuntibus occurrebat, adeo ut statim multi
recederent'. This last passage continues in a vein relevant to Titus's
subsequent despoliation: 'Alii plura habendi cupiditate, congesta
cadauera calcantes, se immergerent. Multae nanque opes in cuniculis
inueniebantur nefasque omnem uiam lucri faciebat'. But the detail
may be considered obvious and certainly occurs in other sources; VS
16, for example, mentions the 'fetor magnus' in the city.

   Identification of certain passages in *The Siege* as Josephan in
inspiration does not simply correct a past judgement about the
poet's sources. It serves to re-emphasize the poem's links with the

alliterative historical tradition: just like John Clerk and the author of
WA, the *Siege* poet drew upon learned historical source texts, not
simply the excerpted compilation which he found in Poly. Such texts
obviously imply access to a considerable library, and at the fourteenth-century date we hypothesize for the poem pretty certainly a
monastic one. (Manuscript U of *The Siege* and its twin Glasgow
manuscript are probably the earliest examples of the Latin *originalia*
in the lay booktrade, and the oldest reference to a lay-owned Higden
is contemporary with them.)[26] These facts imply that the poem was
likely composed in the situation that Pearsall (1981; 1982, pp. 45–46)
has laid out as the classic metier of alliterative poetry—in a monastic
context as 'edifying entertainment' for a secular patron.

Given our placement of the author's dialect in the area of
Barnoldswick, West Yorks., and always assuming that he actually
practised his craft in his home country, one can speculate further
about likely sites of composition. Three monasteries ringed the dialect
area in which we place *The Siege* poet: Whalley (Lancs., OCist), Salley
(or Sawley, on the West Yorks.-Lancs. border, also OCist), and
Bolton in Craven (West Yorks., OSA).[27] Moreover, in spite of
minimal library survivals—very few volumes and no medieval catalogue from any of the three houses—evidence exists that copies of
some source texts were available here. Whalley's copy of Poly survives
as British Library, MS Harley 3600 (see Ker, p. 197); although this
book was copied too late (s. xv) to be the author's actual source, as a
proximate copy we utilize its readings in Appendix B.

Most interestingly, the only known copy of Roger's *Bible en
françois* produced in England[28] (unknown to Moe) survives and is a
Bolton book. This is Bodleian Library, MS Fairfax 24, which lacks
any medieval *ex libris* (hence the query at Ker, p. 11) but bears
Charles Fairfax's notation 'Ex prioratu beate Marie de Bolton in

---

[26] Adam of Usk, civil and canon lawyer, owned a *Polychronicon*, now British Library,
MS Additional 10104, s. xv$^{1/4}$ (Taylor, pp. 129–30). And a copy now lost belonged to
Henry IV; see Jeremy Griffiths and Derek Pearsall, eds., *Book Production and Publishing in
Britain 1375–1475* (Cambridge, 1989), p. 203.

[27] If, as will shortly be argued, the poem was composed at Bolton, the demographic
evidence about known canons would lend credence to a Barnoldswick man among their
number. Sixty-one of the eighty canons in the period 1267–1381 are traceable: only two
came from outside Yorkshire, and fifty-one from either the abbey neighbourhood, its
estates, or the West Riding (Kershaw, p. 12).

[28] Although not the only copy for which there is evidence of English use: the
translation of *Middle English Prose* required a manuscript of the French, in this case of
the textual family Moe calls y (see pp. 14–19).

Craven, com. Ebor.', together with the information that the book came to him as a gift from 'Geo. Clapham, armige[r] de Beamsley' (fol. 1^r), a place less than two miles from the abbey ruins. Moreover, Fairfax and his friend Roger Dodsworth were responsible seventeenth-century antiquarians, conversant with other Bolton materials now lost (compare Bodleian Library, MS Dodsworth 144, fols. 1^r–77^r, his 1634 transcript of the only Bolton cartulary now known, then the property of the Ingilbys of Ripley Castle).

Fairfax 24 is a composite volume, comprised of segments from three originally separate manuscripts. The first of these (fols. 1^r–20^r, s. xiv in.) is primarily devoted to Peter Langtoft's Anglo-Norman chronicle of Edward I; it conceivably might be identified with the chronicle whose purchase is entered in the Bolton accounts of 1305–14 (A. H. Thompson, p. 98). The current fols. 62^r–63^r contain Anglo-Norman of s. xiv med.; they in fact represent the flyleaf and pastedown from an earlier binding. BF, in a hand of s. xiv$^{2/4}$, occupies the remainder of the manuscript (fols. 21^r–61^r): fol. 21^r has been rubbed to illegibility, a sign that this section of the composite book probably existed unbound for a protracted period. BF, incomplete at the end, consumes four quires, all with catchwords but no signatures: 1^{12} 2^{12} (-10, an unnumbered small fragment of the leaf is intact) 3^{12} (-4, -5, -6, -7, -8, -9) 4^{12}: the internal losses, quite unfortunately, all fall within those portions of BF used by the *Siege* poet, and thus BF, lines 34–83 and 334-end are lacking. But within these limits, this text, on the basis of its divisions a representative of Moe's textual family x (*Middle English Prose*, pp. 14–19), provides overall that version most proximate to *The Siege* of the four copies of BF (Moe's C, P, and a) we have examined. Although Fairfax 24 includes a handful of local readings which less directly correspond to *The Siege* than those of other copies, these remain relatively minor and, in most cases, the poet could well have intuited the readings he provides even from the erroneous manuscript.[29]

[29] Such readings include: *Siege* 234 (BF 144-45) O *om.* du pueple, but perhaps an obvious supply in a line rhyming /p/; *Siege* 247 (BF 162) O *om.* a plorer; *Siege* 330 (BF 264) O *om.* sus, but a second example appears in the same clause; *Siege* 393 (BF 300) O trozietes C dreciez, but in a line where /d/ alliteration seems inevitable, the poet could well have translated O's reading 'dressed' in any case; *Siege* 402 (BF 302) O asignifioit C acegnoit; *Siege* 442 (BF 297) O *om.* pour le hernois garder, but 442 seems an inevitable way to fill out the four-line unit; *Siege* 683 (BF 498–500; see the text note) the sentence appears in no surviving x manuscript of *Bible* (see *Middle English Prose* p. 101, 86/1–4n), but as an easily repeatable omission through homoarchy, may not represent an error of the archetype x.

Indeed, of all three area monastic houses, Bolton would seem the most likely site for composition. Although only four volumes survive from the medieval library, these show a sustained interest in vernacular texts.[30] In addition to the French of Fairfax 24, these include the medieval 'orientalist's' bible, *Mandeville's Travels* (the French copy in British Library, MS Harley 212) and manuscript P of *The Siege*. And this account does not include another vernacular book with possible local connections, the *Prick of Conscience* manuscript British Library, MS Additional 32578, which we have used in our dialect study above (and not because of Bolton connections). And to move away from the library behind the poem, Van Court, on the basis of what she sees as a distinctively Augustinian cast in the poet's attitude toward the Jews, would also favour Bolton as the site of composition.

If the text was composed at Bolton, it was presumably prepared for the house's secular patrons. These were the Clifford family, earls (and castelans) of nearby Skipton. The abbey functioned as the Clifford pantheon, the normal site of family burials. But the fourteenth-century state of affairs at Bolton turns out to be particularly unhelpful in pursuing narrower historical identifications: no records survive between the recovery from the Scottish raids of the 1310s and the late fifteenth century (Thompson, p. 99). But at least the middle quarters of the fourteenth century seem to have been a particularly vital period at Bolton, on the basis of architectural evidence alone (Thompson, p. 94 and passim; Kershaw, pp. 173–78). And the house may have expanded its membership by as much as 70 per cent between the dispersal of 1318–19 and the 1379 poll tax.[31] One can gain some idea of the house's eagerness to exploit its patronal connections through early fourteenth-century account entries that record substantial expenses to entertain the Cliffords (and Thomas, earl of Lancaster) (Thompson, pp. 95–96; Kershaw, pp. 132–42). In any event, if the text is a product of Bolton and prepared for a usual patron of the abbey, one should probably associate it with the fifth lord Clifford, Roger, titular head of the family 1345–89 (he came to majority only in 1354); he married a Warwick Beauchamp, was sheriff of Cumberland

---

[30] Although the survivals are very likely skewed: among the 1305–14 book purchases Thompson mentions are Peter Lombard's *Sentences*, a *Veritates theologiae* (presumably ps.-Aquinas, in fact Hugh Ripelin of Strassburg), and the constitutions of the Augustinian order.

[31] Thompson (pp. 90–92) notes fourteen canons removed on the first occasion; Kershaw (p. 11) cites nineteen canons and five lay brothers from the poll tax.

and Westmorland, served in Scotland and France, and testified in the Scrope-Grosvenor affair. In our dating, the initial addressee of the poem might also have been his son Thomas, the sixth lord (1363–91); he was a knight of the King's Chamber under Richard II (GEC, 3, 292).

THE DISSEMINATION OF THE POEM:
THE RELATIONSHIP OF THE MANUSCRIPTS

Three scholars, two of them contemporaneously and in ignorance of one another's work, have discussed the relationship of *Siege* manuscripts. In 1931, Hulbert, who did not know our manuscript P, found that the manuscripts represent three main groups—in our sigla, L, AV, and UDEC; although certain that the transmission of L had been independent of all other copies, Hulbert professed himself unable to decide whether the other six codices had descended from a common archetype or independently from the source (p. 605). And he noted (p. 609) that after line 900, C had been subjected to conflation from a copy like AV. In the introduction to the EETS edition of 1932 (pp. ix–xi), Mabel Day, again in ignorance of P, and on the basis of a highly selective group of 'gross errors', arrived at essentially similar conclusions, although she was considerably less clear than Hulbert about the status of C (compare 'There also seems to have been some cross-connection between C and AV', p. xi).[32] Finally, T. Turville-Petre (p. 159), on the basis of his edition of lines 525–728, found that P and L are related and that UDEC form a group, 'of which D is the best representative'. We here attempt to test these various theses.

Our presentation of the evidence for manuscript affiliation resembles in most respects that of Kane and Donaldson in PPB. Like them, we have found that our confidence in our ability to recognize errors—including, on the open evidence of the text we print as opposed to that provided by our predecessors, errors not 'palpable' to all students—has enabled us at most points to establish a provisional text of the poem. We routinely signal our considerations of the variants in a range of contested lemmata in the Textual Notes. The provisional text we constructed through such judgements automatically, through noninclusion, identifies certain readings as erroneous,

---

[32] The stemma as Day constructs it (p. x) implies that the text can be constructed exclusively from agreements of L(P)AV and that textual degeneration occurs universally elsewhere.

and thus susceptible to examination for possible information they may provide about the transmission history of *The Siege*.

Yet we must equally acknowledge a substantial number of hesitations among readings. These we have sought to formalize. Although the information we present below is, like Kane and Donaldson's stemma for PPB, the result of our printed, final readings, it is not the first stemma we constructed (although equivalent to it, with adjustments of detail). Like Kane and Donaldson, we believe that the only effective demonstration of manuscript relations is a final act—a representation of shared deviation from an edited text. But at a mediate stage in editing, a point at which a residue of insolubilia—variations clearly not indifferent yet not clearly susceptible to *our* open resolution—remained, attestation became for us a relevant consideration: the ability to identify some manuscript agreements as potentially only testimony to a common archetype during some stage in transmission was helpful in resolving such difficulties. We thus used, at a mediate, yet relatively advanced, point in our procedures our developing sense of those relations to be embodied in a stemma as an inductive tool to aid us in difficult cases.

We thus present the results of our editorial considerations as materials toward a transmission history, not as that tool which at most places has enabled us to edit the text. In doing so, we adopt, not simply Kane and Donaldson's insistence upon the totality of the evidence,[33] but also what they identify as the three 'assumptions of convenience' necessary to any stemmatic study. First, we assume that persistent agreements in error, agreements widely attested, must result from a shared archetype, rather than convergence or conflation. Second, we assume that genetically-created agreements persist, that they are displayed at least relatively strongly throughout the entire work. Finally, we assume that groups which emerge in a survey of shared variation must, to demonstrate true genetic descent, be congruent: that is, identifying on the basis of our first two assumptions that, say, manuscripts AB share one archetype and manuscripts CD another, must indicate that necessarily more fragmentarily attested agreements such as BC and AD are in fact nongenetic. As

---

[33] Although we are confident that errors and inconsistencies occur in our report, we have intended to report here all agreements in substantive error (including grammatical variants), including a few forms which may be dialectical variants. Our only conscious exclusions have been the variants from/fro, to/tille, eche/ilk/ilka (except when metrically significant and thus substantive; similarly a few examples of hem/them variation where *h*- provides alliteration), o/a(n)/one, ne/nor, ʒede/wente.

will become evident from our summary of the evidence below, the variants of *The Siege* involve at different moments and in different ways severe tests of the second and third of these assumptions. In these instances, the effort to present a stemmatic history of transmission is severely challenged: to explain the generation of the nine surviving witnesses we must introduce hypotheses of relationship essentially non- or anti-stemmatic. These considerations, at least in some measure codicological, rather than editorial, indicate ways in which our presentation quite properly outlines, not a diagrammatic editorial tool (to which, in any event, we had recourse in only a small minority of instances) but a textual history, an outline of the stages by which *The Siege* became (and subsisted as) a living Middle English literary work.

Our evidence in the main confirms, yet renders substantially more precise, the opinions of Hulbert and Day. To begin with, all surviving copies of *The Siege of Jerusalem* derive from a single archetype O'. This lost manuscript was not identical to authorial holograph (O), although it was, for lines it included, a reasonably accurate facsimile at nearly all points. The most convincing evidence for the existence of O' comes from lines missing in all copies of the poem. A number of such instances, for example, lines 27–28, 43–44, 1335–36, may be identified by failure of lines to organize into those four-line units we will shortly identify as integral parts of the poem. Other such losses are more frankly putative, predicated upon our sense as editors of narrative discontinuity. Such a loss may occur, as Kölbing and Day also thought, after line 216 (see their note); we think, in part on the basis of the poet's allusion to source details not included in the transmitted text, in part because of signs of eyeskip, that such losses mark the Vitellius narrative, perhaps at lines 938, 940, and 942.

A small number of local readings also may testify to failures in O'. Examples would include 264 *a* and a series of readings which confuse speech and narration in lines 720ff. And such readings occur especially frequently where forms necessary for metrical b-verses have disappeared from all surviving copies, inferentially because of O''s faulty rendition, for example, 710 *topsailes*, 793 *dryeden*. Frequently some difficulty arises in ascertaining whether observed manuscript variation in fact responds to an already corrupt reading of O' or simply represents divergent renditions of an O reading which O' had communicated. Compare *aireþ* 259: did O' read *kaireþ*, or have all manuscripts responded independently to transmitted O *aireþ*? Or, at line 637, we are reasonably certain that O' erroneously read *Sone* or *Als sone*; D, an adept scribe extremely attentive to the formal requirements of alliterative poetry, here exercizes the prerogatives of an editor, and his effort at repairing the nonalliterating line of his exemplar strikes us as an apt reconstruction. Such a demonstration that all manuscripts descend from a copy already scribally corrupt, albeit in a very limited minority of instances, means, of course, that, even were one to edit by stemmatic recension, one could construct only a scribal copy, not an authorial work.

Having indicated the existence of O', 'the archetype of all surviving manuscripts', we pass to the next task in constructing a transmission history. This requires that we present the evidence of all erroneous agreements among surviving copies. Such a display seeks to answer two basic questions: (1) Do consistent pairs or trios of manuscripts appear in such persistent erroneous agreement that we may believe they are copies made from the same immediate exemplar? (2) Do larger groups of manuscripts appear in such persistent agreement that we may believe that they descend from intermediate hyparchetypes, whatever the relations of smaller groups?

Certain logistical problems, the results of accidents in the survival of the witnesses, complicate these procedures. Two of our codices are substantial fragments—P complete for the first 1000+ lines, V providing only about 350 lines from the end of the text. In addition, as Hulbert and Day noted, C, especially in later portions of the poem, appears to have constructed its text through peculiar means. To accommodate these vicissitudes of the witnesses, we choose to divide the poem into three sections and to present our evidence separately for each of them. We thus begin with a survey of what we hope represents a 'clear' portion of the text—all those lines preceding *Siege* 621 in which the seven fullest manuscripts LPAUDEC are present (C lacks lines 167–248, A lacks lines 293–369), 461 lines total. As it turns out, the relations of the manuscripts in this portion of the poem are reasonably clear; and these relations are confirmed, *mutatis mutandis*, by parallel findings in those portions where either C or A is absent. Such a grouping of the copies provides a framework for consideration of any later deviant behavior of the C scribe, as well as for any later shuffling of relations. And, given our discovery of the fixity of these groups, the more fragmentary manuscripts V and Ex, extant only late in the poem, may simply be associated with already identified forms of the text.

We first examine shared agreement in error for lines 1–166 (at which point C lacks a folio), 249–92 (at which point A lacks a folio), 370–620. In this portion of the poem, the ten most frequently attested erroneous agreements, in terms of persistence of attestation, are: UDEC 203×, UDC 116×, PA 84×, DE 68×, UC 62×, AUDEC 56×, PAUDEC 51×, UD 37×, EC 32×, and PUDEC 28×. (We provide the full array of agreements in error in Appendix C below.)

These materials largely confirm Hulbert's view of the text, with some further clarifications. Simply on the overwhelming weight of the agreement in variation, each of the groups UDEC and PA descends from a separate archetype; moreover, evidence for PAUDEC is surprisingly strong (although for the most part recorded in trivial readings). Such variants attested in these six manuscripts are concentrated in two areas. PAUDEC tend toward logical and regularized verb tenses, rather than L's more fluid movement between past and present tenses. And they frequently agree in supplementing b-verses of the structure / × × . . / (×) by adding an unstressed syllable at the head, often a logical connective with the a-verse. In addition, L fails to show any strong agreements with any other text (LPA 10×, LP 8×, LA 7×, LE 6×): this showing implies that this single manuscript has a separate line of descent, its own archetype. The very strongly attested group UDC probably in many cases adds to the already overwhelming evidence for a common archetype behind UDEC. E is the single most deviant of all the manuscripts, and the only one which with some consistency cannot readily be collated against the others: were the quality of its scribal rewritings more compelling, it might deserve parallel text presentation. But on many of those occasions when UDC agree, their agreement is, in part, constructed by E's having created its own unique reading. (A similar argument should probably be invoked in the case of more sporadic PAUDC variation: these agreements might be construed as further evidence for the strong group PAUDEC.)

Two further points can be made. First, the strongest evidence is that UDEC have, for this portion of the poem, two subarchetypes, one for DE and one for UC (130 examples). However, this view is complicated by a considerable amount of agreement in variation across these putative archetypal lines (UD, EC, UE, and DC agree 117×). On such a showing, it is unclear whether such subarchetypes indeed existed, in which case the manuscripts simply show random agreement in convergent readings available within this limited portion of the tradition.

Second, the evidence suggests—a point at which Hulbert finally threw up his hands—that the archetypes behind PA and UDEC are themselves only second-generation descendants of an archetype which lies behind all six manuscripts. Not only do all six manuscripts agree in error together on a substantial number of occasions, but among prominent variant groups are AUDEC and PUDEC (re-enforced generally by infrequent PAUEC, PADEC, PAUDE, and, given the nature of E, by somewhat less prominent groups AUDC and PUDC). Such readings are susceptible of two possible interpreta-tions: (a) there is a group PAUDEC, whose readings may be determined by such majority agreements as AUDEC and PUDEC, and the odd manuscript of which (usually P, occasionally A) either varies independently or has conflated in the reading of L; (b) there are only the two groups PA and UDEC, each from a separate archetype, with spot contamination (the readings are a bit too prevalent to be taken as simply accidental) of the UDEC archetype into the indi-vidual manuscripts P and A. Generally speaking, we incline to a version of the first of these views. For us, the most persuasive reading of the evidence is that the archetype behind UDEC was of the same derivation as that behind PA and, on occasion, in fact retained the archetypal reading, lost in the archetype available to PA. We would thus schematize the descent of the manuscripts in this portion of *The Siege*: L { [PA] [UDEC] }, while allowing the possibility that UDEC may represent two subfamilies [UC][DE].

At a later stage in our argument, we will insert V and Ex, which contain only late portions of the poem, into this schema. For the present, we would only note that our definition of the poem's descent in this portion explains the overwhelming weight of the evidence. Such a stemma accounts for 386 variants attesting to UDEC (UDEC + UDC), 84 attesting to PA, 51 clear examples of PAUDEC (and 142 further more attenuated examples of the types PAUDC, AUDEC, and AUDC); and assuming variation among UDEC to be 'free', rather than among subfamilies, it explains 247 agreements involving two and 67 involving three of these manu-scripts. The only variants in 'frequently-occurring groups' cited above not explained are 114 examples of either P or A with some of UDEC; to these one may add the modestly attested groupings merely listed, another 171 variants. The stemma we would draw thus accounts for about 77 per cent of the variants in this portion of the poem (977 of 1262). Given that 50 per cent agreement of all variants should identify a putative stemma (although it would be quite hazardous, even if one wished to, to edit with it), this seems to us a very high level of consistency in agreement.

Further, this evidence is consistent, *mutatis mutandis*, with that available from the 180 lines preceding line 620 heretofore undiscussed, where one of the manuscripts is completely absent. Thus, in *Siege* 293–369, where A is absent (and consequently P must stand alone as representative of the PA archetype), one finds the same hierarchy of variants: UDEC occurs 54×, UDC 26× (PA cannot, of course, occur at all), DE 19×, PUDEC 15× (here including both that variant and PAUDEC agreements), UC 14×. PUDC occurs only 5× (probably examples of PAUDC and of PUDEC, with E on its frequent random walk), and the remaining variants, including some groups more prominent than the last mentioned, comprise two- and three-text agreements among UDEC.

In *Siege* 167–248, where C is absent, the results are necessarily (and thus predictably) murkier: a substantial number of widely attested variant groups includes C. But with some disruptions, the hierarchy of variants is again recognizable: 41 examples of UDE (here representing primarily UDEC, given the infrequency of UDE in portions with all MSS present), 17 of DE, 16 of UD (here both that agreement and examples of UDC, surprisingly weakly attested), 15 of PA, 13 of PAUDE (again, primarily representing PAUDEC), 10 of EU, 9 of AUDE. The other widely attested variants here comprise scattering variation, inferentially examples of accidental convergence, which we have used above as querying our stemma, agreements of P and A with one or more of UDC (AE, for example 11×).

We have limited this survey to variants recorded before line 621 for one particularly good reason. As both Hulbert and Day saw, at some point C affiliations with UDE seem to become attenuated, and the manuscript offers readings which resemble those of P and A. We believe that this apparent change of affiliation, about which neither past student of the poem was especially specific, in fact reflects an alteration in the procedures of copying C: at a point shortly after line 620, the supply of manuscript available to the C scribe changed in two discernible ways. First, the copyist obtained a second exemplar, unrelated to that from which he had been copying and most like the surviving A (contrast the minimal number of AC variants, only twelve, in those textual portions we have surveyed above); from this, he chose readings eclectically, first a bit sporadically, then gaining intensity after about line 900 or so. But, in addition to this act of conflation, the evidence suggests that the scribe's UDEC source, to which he continued to refer, also changed in character. Before this point, so far as we can tell, C's source most closely resembled U (up to line 620, UC occurs 62× v. EC 32×, DC 23×); hereafter, the variants suggest that this textual source was much more like E (although a great many of these might be construed as accidental convergence, there are some striking agreements in unpredictable readings).

We thus examine separately the common erroneous variants from line 620 to line 965 (the fragmentary text of V begins at line 966). In this portion of the poem, the ten most commonly attested agreements in variation include: AC 79×, UDE 71×, UDEC 69×, UD 59×, PA 49×, EC 46×, UDC 41×, DE 37×, DC 33×, and AUDEC 30×.

This evidence confirms in general a stemma like that outlined above, with the proviso that C has become a conflate. That is, one would wish to redraw the diagram of manuscript relationships as: L { [PA] > C < [UDE] }. L again shows no close agreements with any other manuscript: although its strongest associations are with P (LP 7×), this figure is overwhelmed in the context of 49 PA agreements. A common archetype for PAUDEC is attested in some 85 variants—the 21 examples of all six MSS. agreeing in error, 30 examples of AUDEC and 16 of PUDEC, 8 of PAUDC (where E rewrites in isolation), 10 of PUDE (where conflated C follows A). In addition, AUDE occurs only 5× but may also be construed as support for the archetype: since the A-like manuscript used by C for its conflation was not A, PC variation may in fact speak to representation of the PA archetype in C's source manuscript.

The lower archetypes for the groups PA and UDE, with C wavering between them, depending on local readings selected, are also well attested. Evidence for the PA archetype comes from 67 variants, agreements of PA and PAC. 181 variants testify to the UDEC archetype: 71 examples of UDE, 69 of UDEC, and 41 of UDC (where E again varies in isolation). Of course, 110 of these readings show C still deriving portions of its text from an archetype of the same type with which the scribe began his copying (as do also such agreements as EC, DC, and UC, 105 in all). Similarly, 98 variants offer evidence of conflation into C from the PA archetype, for, beyond the 79 AC agreements, the most strongly attested shared variation in the sample, the nineteen readings shared by PC are, again, inferentially evidence for a PA source most closely resembling A but not identical with A in all detail.

Once again, we cannot argue with conviction for further divisions within the group UDEC. There appears to be strong evidence for rearrangement of manuscript relations vis-à-vis what we have described in earlier portions of the poem. There substantial, but barely majority, evidence suggested common archetypes available to DE and to UC. However, in this portion of the poem, the strongest record of variational groups suggests a reformation of relationships. The previously strong agreements in error appear here considerably attenuated (DE 37×, UC 26×), and the most widely attested would suggest that now UD share an archetype against EC (105 total variants). However, over the whole sample, at least 122 variants speak against this split.

Analysis of smaller textual portions reveals, however, that such a reformulation of relationships among UDEC occurs here and that it is genetic in nature. That is, the onset of conflation from a copy like A into C occurs very soon after line 620, and it certainly has a disruptive force on other relationships. (Contrast, for example, the strength of UDEC agreements against UDE agreements in this portion of the poem with that portion previously analyzed.) But, although through-out lines 621–965, UD/EC variation is stronger than the previous UC/DE variation, it becomes particularly so in the last hundred lines of the sample. There DE appear in shared error 5× and UC 4×, but UD 23× and EC 15×; in fact, 38 variants speak for subgroupings UD/EC, and only 18 oppose them (DC 4×, UE 5× in this section). Thus, it appears likely that C not only engaged in conflation with an A-related manuscript during this textual portion but that, quite independently of such motivated conflation, C's original UDEC-type exemplar itself included a minor shift of textual affiliation, probably somewhere toward line 850 or 860. (This evidence would be consonant with the exemplar having been produced from loose quires; if these were in ten-leaf units with twenty-odd lines to the side, at the end of the second such, the scribe of the archetype behind C may well have intruded a quire copied from a text with slightly different antecedents.)

Explicit C conflation implies that one should trust the stemma for editorial purposes only at peril. In fact, given that C's act of conflation

is isolable and definable in the aggregate, in this portion of the poem,
two stemmata operate simultaneously on a lemma by lemma basis: at
those points where C conflates, the stemma is L { [PAC] [UDE] }, at
others the L { [PA] [UDEC] } familiar from earlier textual portions.
Of course, the points at which one stemma rather than the other is
applicable remain thoroughly unpredictable, being based upon the
discretion and taste of the C scribe.

Nevertheless, the relationships we have outlined above again
explain the great preponderance of the evidence. Of the 964
agreements in error, we have drawn upon 684 in our examples
above. The percentage of variant readings our variable stemmata
explain (71 per cent) thus turns out to be surprisingly comparable to
our previous results.

At line 966, V begins; about ninety lines later (1056), P ceases to be
universally legible, and the text breaks off after a further eighty lines.
In this portion of the poem, the ten most frequently observed
agreements in variation are: UDE 91×, EC 71×, AV 64×, UD
65×, UDEC 57×, DE 50×, AVC 45×, UE 36×, AVUDEC 35×,
UC 34×.

These data more or less confirm those genetic relationships already
examined, that is, these extend straight to the end of the poem. Once
again, ample evidence suggests that L descends from an archetype
distinct from that available to other copyists. L shows no close
relationships with any other manuscripts: its most commonly attested
agreements in error, 7× with C, 5× with A, 4× with P, are
minuscule. And substantial numbers of erroneous readings testify
to an archetype common to (P)AVUDEC. Best evidence comes from
54 readings where all these texts agree in error (PAVUDEC,
AVUDEC, PAUDEC); secondary support emerges in 73 other
readings of the types AUDEC (30×), (P)AVUDC (12×), and
AUDE or AUDC (20× and 11×, respectively), where one member
of PAV has a secondary reading also conflated into C or where E
varies in isolation).

Similarly, the same middle-level archetypes receive strong confirmation from the recorded variants. A single archetype behind
UDE, and at times C, is evidenced by 175 agreements of UDE,
UDEC, and UDC (the last, in cases where E constructs his
personalized text). And V clearly derives from the archetype earlier
shared by PA: there are eight examples of PAV agreement (given the
damage to P, these come from about one-quarter of the text, and thus

the showing is nearly as strong as support for UDC). In addition, AV occurs 64×, PA 16×, PV 8×, a total of 88 variants testifying to a family PAV.

Evidence for the C conflation persists. Fully 118 variants represent the PAV contribution to this textual state (AVC 45×, AC 32×, VC 34×, PAVC 7×); in addition, there are two examples of PC and one of PVC during the brief space when P is present. The contribution from PAV is clear, but as the relative frequency of agreements noted above would suggest, C's source manuscript can only be stipulated as a descendant of this archetype and not linked with any specific survivor (although it resembled P less than it did A or V). And in addition to 84 variants testifying to C's continuing reliance upon a text of the UD(E) type (UDEC, UDC), there are 109 further occasions when C agrees in error with one of these manuscripts (EC, UC, DC) and nineteen when it agrees with two (DEC, UEC). All in all, the procedures by which C has been constructed seem generally consistent from line 621 to the end of the poem.

In this portion of the text, subarchetypal groupings continue to be as murky as they have been before. The pair AV appears extremely frequently; the copies agree in error 64×. But, in a much briefer portion of the text, sixteen examples of PA and eight of PV occur. Such variants qualify the value of any evidence for a narrower placement of V, for example, will not support a putative rendering of this group as [P (AV)]. In the group UDEC, the shifted relations of the codices which begin after line 621 persist and become stronger: 136 variants testify to the grouping [(UD) (EC)]. This split into two groupings explains a majority, if a rather bare one (52 per cent), of the evidence for the entire section; it is countered by 124 agreements of DE, UE, UC, and DC. However, as noted above, EC and UD seem certainly genetic for about one hundred lines of the text (roughly 865–965). That genetic grouping appears to continue for the first hundred odd lines of this textual portion, although not thereafter: in lines 965–1064, it explains forty-one variants but not thirty-two others (about 56 per cent of the evidence). The evidence again is consonant with an isolated textual source foreign to the usual UDEC archetype.

Thus, for this portion of the poem, the relevant schema would seem: L { [PAV] > C < [UDE] }. Above we cite 800 raw variants in support such a reading of the evidence, while 311 remain undiscussed and thus contradict this construction. The stemma thus would explain about 72 per cent of the total evidence, a figure comparable to that in earlier portions of the poem. If one were to attempt to account for P's absence by weighting its variants, quadrupling them, in order to give some sense of their force, were P to exist intact for the full text, the figure would probably approach comparability with the results for portions of the text preceding line 621.

Finally, we consider an isolable problem, the relations of the tiny fragment Ex. This narrow paper strip provides portions of sixty-six lines (985–1017, 1106–23, 1125–38, 1196). Within this section, in addition to a handful of unique errors, Ex shows twenty-two erroneous agreements:

AVUDCEx 1005 wol, 1007 heste, 1013 þe[1] (3)
VCEx 991 fers, 1002 hym (2)
UEx 1109 þey, 1125 an (2)
AVCEx 1121 yþrelled, 1136 stoken (2)
CEx 1014 kysseþ, 1111 bygonne (2)

The following agreements occur one time each: LEx, AVEx, ACEx, PAVEx, UDCEx, AVECEx, PAVCEx, LADCEx, PAVUDCEx, AVUDECEx, PAUDECEx.

From this evidence, we believe that Ex should be associated with the group comprised of P (here frequently absent), AV, and C (where it conflates readings from this group). The raw number of observed variants offers only a passing indication of such affiliations; but in a scan of the twenty-two total variants, Ex agrees with C on 17 occasions, with A on 14, and with V on 13. And it concurs with these manuscripts in several highly distinctive localized variants: 1136 cited above as evidence for AVCEx; 1133 *hym sone*; 991 *fers* (compare Ex *Ferre* with VC *ferfurthe*) and the exchange of lines 1124 and 1196 (agrees with PAVC). Further, Ex agrees in isolation with UDE(C) errors only on three occasions (1014 *kysseþ* with UDC and the two examples of UEx variation cited above) and frequently has a correct PAV(C) reading where these copies err (for example, 1125 Ex *herter*, a unique reading resembling PAV). Given the strength of associations with C, the best likelihood is that this fragment represents a manuscript derived from a descendant of the PAV archetype like that available to C for its PAV conflation.

Thus, nearly three-quarters of the erroneous agreements of the manuscripts support a single transmission history. *The Siege*, as we know it, descends in this way:

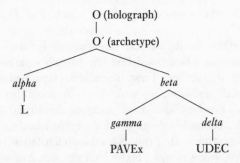

But at points after line 621, these lines of descent alternate with a second set: our copy C, on an essentially free-choice basis, accesses both its *delta*-derived exemplar and a second, unrelated one, a *gamma* manuscript not apparently identical with any surviving copy. Thus, for a substantial number of later lemmata, relevant portions of the descent of copies have the form:

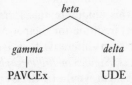

Such descent easily translates into an historical narrative of textual dissemination. For, perhaps unsurprisingly, the apparent genetic disposition of the copies parallels their geographical distribution;[34] at least as a hypothesis, *The Siege* text appears to have developed in various nonauthentic ways as a result of geographical dispersion. In this process, L, the oldest of the manuscripts, stands apart and remains nearly completely inexplicable: in provenance, Oxfordshire, it is relatively isolated from all other copies (most proximate is the clearly unrelated and much later E), and we have no way of explaining those processes of transmission by which *alpha*, the hyparchetype bearing the most accurate representation of the archetype O′,

---

[34] 'Perhaps unsurprisingly', since demonstrations of this sort do not typify most efforts at discussing textual transmissions. Such alignments of provenance and archetypal origin need considerably more investigation in a wide range of texts. Hanna has argued that both textual contexts and locale of production may in individual instances precisely underlie genetic relations; see 'The Middle English *Vitae Patrum* Collection', *Mediaeval Studies* 49 (1987), 411–42 (418–23); and 'Studies in the Manuscripts of *Piers Plowman*', *Yearbook of Langland Studies* 7 (1993), 1–25 (20–21).

travelled from the Yorkshire locale in which *The Siege* was composed.[35]

On the other hand, we can be reasonably certain that the hyparchetype *beta* was a 'local text' circulating in areas reasonably proximate to the author. First, the oldest representatives of the *gamma* textual tradition, P and A, both have firm Yorkshire provenances. Further, the most accurate rendition of the *delta* archetype, U, contains a large residue of northern/north Midland spellings consonant with prior Yorkshire circulation. These facts imply that not only was *beta* a text which circulated in what was very likely the *Siege* poet's home territories but that both *beta* derivatives, *gamma* and *delta*, were originally prepared there.

The descendants of *gamma* are not, however, limited simply to Yorkshire circulation. By the mid fifteenth century, copies from this textual tradition appear to have leached southward into the eastern central Midlands, Lincolnshire and adjacent counties. Thus, from the 1450s and 1460s, we have evidence from three copies of more southerly dispersal of this unique textual form: V, Ex, and C could all rely upon the *gamma* tradition for their work. This history can be paralleled for other northern alliterative texts (see Hanna, 'The Scribe of Huntington HM 114', *Studies in Bibliography* 42 [1989], 120–33); perhaps especially congruent would be the transmission of the south Yorkshire poem Sus, available contemporary with *The Siege* in south Lincs. to the scribe of Morgan Library M818 (who also copied a second Yorkshire text, Rolle's *Form of Living*) and to our manuscript C.

The group *delta* reflects the most southerly dispersal of *The Siege*. Both our copies U and D represent London work of the period *c*.1410–25, and testify to a relatively early movement out of the poet's home locale, in which *beta* had circulated. Here we may be dealing with some variety of patronal distribution, in which the fruits of a provincial culture have been marketed by that patron within the ambit of a developing national capital-based culture (compare Hanna, 'Sir Thomas Berkeley and His Patronage', *Speculum* 64 [1989], 878–916 [909–13]).

At least two possible mechanisms for such distribution suggest themselves. On the one hand, if one imagines *The Siege* as having

[35] Although given our discussion of authorial dialect and possible locales of composition above, one might suggest some transmission through the networks associated with monastic orders. There were three Cistercian and five Augustinian houses in Oxfordshire.

been composed at Bolton Abbey, the poem might have been distributed by the abbey's patrons, the Clifford earls of Skipton. Thomas, the sixth lord, a knight of the King's Chamber under Richard II, could well have been the medium by which the text came south to the capital. On the other hand, Richard Frampton, the scribe of U, did most of his identifiable copying for the Duchy of Lancaster; the text could have been available to him through Duchy sources, and might have come south with other materials from Duchy headquarters in Pontefract (West Yorks.).

And another alternative is worth mentioning. Although U generally appears closer to *delta* than D, that does not mean that it is the temporally prior manuscript. And in spite of his London workplace, the scribe of D was a prolific alliterative copyist. It is perfectly possible that the appearance of a *delta* exemplar in the capital resulted from the activities of those who patronized his other copyings, people capable of providing him with exemplars for Sus and AA.

If *delta* or a derivative archetype was available in London *c*.1410–25, other copies from this source probably reflect dispersal from this second centre, rather than from Yorkshire. Thus, the Warwickshire scribal team responsible for the developing manuscript E and the scribe of C are both apt to have accessed archetypes from the central booktrade for provincial use. Marks of such procedures appear elsewhere in the production of these books; the C scribe, for example, copied several romances always identified as 'southern' or 'south-eastern' in origin, and E derived its PPB from an archetype traceable in London for a century and a half.[36] In the case of C, recognition of the rather spotty quality of the available *delta* archetype—it was the least satisfactory, by and large, of the four textual versions stemmatics would require us to hypothesize—may have stimulated a search for a second text to use in correction. This scribe, uniquely in the surviving evidence, appears to have worked in a place where more than a single textual source might be available.

Textual divisions

This transmission history of *The Siege* allows us to speak to further matters of literary history. For we can do more than simply map the

---

[36] From the time it was used in Cambridge, Trinity College, MS B.15.17 until Robert Crowley drew on it for copy-text for his 1550 prints.

travels of the text; our assessment of the manuscript relations allows some comment on larger features of the text possibly authorial. These concern matters of more than a single lection or even line, the grouping of the single verses into larger poetic units.

Fitfully, for slightly more than a century, students of the form have argued the question broached by Max Kaluza, whether poems in alliterative long-lines involve the use of larger structural units (see Duggan 1977, pp. 224–26, for a summary of the discussion). Most recent opinion has ratified Kaluza's view that some poems, at least, fall into four-line units, often marked in manuscripts by paraphs at the head of each; thus, most scholars would see such line-groups as integral units of composition in WA, Pat, Cln, Erk, in addition to *The Siege* (compare T. Turville-Petre 1977, pp. 60–62). Moreover, a wide range of recently discovered alliterative fragments reinforces one's sense of the general accessibility of the technique (see Day 1939, Brewer, Wilson 1979—both these poems clearly in quatrains, with abab rhyme—, and perhaps the text printed by Kennedy).

Our text, as we present it, follows this recent consensus, which includes Kölbing and Day (see p. ix), and is divided into four-line units. Transmissional evidence for the feature in tenuous, only provided in *delta*. UEC have regular paraphs to divide the text into four- (EC) or eight-line (U) units, in the main automatically supplied, regardless of context. But the text we construct routinely falls into such units, and our assessment of manuscript variation indicates that they are authorial, whether explicitly marked in the extant manuscripts or not. Moreover, in only a very few places might four-line units in the *textus receptus* have resulted from simple accidents of transmission (although compare lines 937–44, where apparent quatrain divisions may now reflect non-authorial behaviour subsequent to the loss of lines).

Further, very few serious challenges to composition in four-line units occur in the manuscripts. At lines 25–28, four-line units fail, but the sentence there lacks any verb, and lines have presumably dropped out. Again, at lines 41–44, another failure to divide into four-line units, the corruption in 42 convinces us that a pair of nonadjacent lines have been fused. And at lines 1333–36, where only L provides evidence, that copy has arguably lost a distich. Elsewhere, failures of lines to group into fours (and frequently the supply of scribal lines to remedy the deficiency) are limited to only portions of the manuscript tradition correctible by comparison with other copies (for example, lines 1233–36a, 1309–12).

But however well they are attested, the purpose of such units has remained unclear. Duggan (1977, p. 226) comments: 'We can, I think, reject out of hand the suggestion that printing these poems in quatrains might somehow change the texture of the poetry'. But one might profitably consider whether such multiline units change, not a reader's perception, but a poet's compositional habits. And in the case of *The Siege* at least, we believe it does. The poet perceived his mode of composition in a way perhaps fundamentally different from other alliterative poets; in addition to his adherence to traditional forms of composition by the formulaic phrase, he quite persistently shaped his developing narrative within syntactic patterns conceived as joining at least distichs, 'half-stanzas' or 'hemistichs', if not the full four-line unit (compare Duggan 1977, p. 236).

Kaluza's contention that alliterative composition frequently proceeded by strophes has proved far more controversial than his insistence upon four-line units. Kaluza argued that in *The Siege* 'the quatrains are grouped into twelve-line stanzas, which are again combined in groups of three to form a 36-line stanza, and that the poem itself is divided into three parts, each containing twelve great stanzas' (Kölbing-Day, p. ixn). This theory Day (1931–32) destroyed by reference to the textual divisions of five manuscripts. But in the light of the most recent work on WA (Duggan 1977 and the Duggan-Turville-Petre edition), which has demonstrated that that poem is constructed in quatrains joined into twenty-four line units, with such strophes grouped into probably twenty-eight original passus, some reexamination of evidence from *The Siege* is in order.

The individual manuscripts divide the poem in a variety of different ways. We eliminate from consideration those multiline capitals attested by but a single manuscript (A 25, 53, 268a; E 953, 1177; V 1025). Our manuscript D includes no largescale divisions of the text, only a scattered series of paraphs (all these are noted in our collation). The divisions of the remaining texts may be displayed in a table: here we use 'x' to indicate simply a multiline capital, 'p' to indicate some notation of a new passus, and Roman numerals to indicate an actual passus numeration (those of VU we bracket, because the scribes always spell out the Latin in full).

	L	P	A	V	U	E	C
189				–	[i]	x	
305		ij		–	[ii]		
445	x	iij	p	–	[iii]	x	p
637		iiij	p	–	[iv]	x	iiij (639)
738				–	[v]	x	v
897	x	v	p	–	[vi]	x	vj
1113	x	vj	p	[vii]	[vii]	x	vij

We would only note before passing on to further analysis that codicological detail implies that D's archetype included passus divisions as well. The initial 636 lines of *The Siege* appear in the scribe's quire 16, where the writing splays out, the number of lines per page decreases, and finally the scribe leaves most of a leaf blank with an instruction to consult the next one (at the head of quire 17). For whatever reason, we believe that the scribe copied lines 637–1340 of *The Siege* first, into a blank quire: but rather than using a studied procedure, like compositors' casting off in producing print-books, he seems simply to have guessed that materials down to line 636 would fill the vacant end of his quire 16, which proved in fact untrue. But the point at which the scribe divided the text is one of its most widely attested passus divisions, and that textual break would seem the only real motivation for the erratic way in which he split his text.

Our table demonstrates that we cannot prove that passus divisions are in fact authorial, or certainly that they existed in O'. They did occur in a clearly reconstructible form in *delta* and also occurred, although less clearly reconstructible, in *gamma*. Inferentially, they descend from at least as far up the stemma as the hyparchetype *beta*, and the few agreements with L's otherwise unparalleled four large capitals suggest some divisions may have appeared in O'. However, the most widely attested divisions occur after lines certainly authorial and certainly marking some variety of textual breaks (these corre-spond to L's only divisions):

> 444 And baners beden hem forþ— now blesse vs our Lorde
> 896 þis lyf þey ledde longe: oure Lord ȝyue vs ioye
> 1112 Grobben faste on þe grounde, and God gyue vs ioye

Whether the author intended formal divisions or the scribes responded to what can be construed as such we cannot determine; in no case does the poem rely on such utterly clear markers as WW

216–17 and 366–67; WA 740, 2971, 3331, 3593–95, 4147, 4841, 5200, 5752; DT 96, 662, 2724, 4028, 8420, 8970 (and compare 524, 1004, 1579, 1843, 4699). But the same b-verses in *Siege* 896 and 1112 and DT 6064 and 9399 indicate that lines of this type probably constitute an authorial concluding formula.

The various divisions of the manuscripts also leave some doubt as to how many units the poem might be construed to have. Manuscripts descending from *delta* show eight divisions of the poem, a prologue and seven passus. One of these, the division at line 738, is surely wrong: it occurs at mid-quatrain and simply imitates the evening/morning passus division at 636/637. And two others, at 189 and 305, are ill-attested, but the second probably confirmed as at least the reading of *beta* by U's agreement with P. Of manuscripts descending from *gamma*, P, with six divisions, the first beginning at the head of the poem, appears closest to the archetype, but the 'Septimus passus' at V 1113 implies that P may be a division short.[37] In this reading of the evidence, which we adopt with some trepidation in our edition (we should perhaps simply follow P), the lost portions of V presumably agreed with UE in having a prologue and an early passus division—in those manuscripts extant, at line 189. Although the division occurs in mid-speech, it distinguishes Titus's healing proper and his determination to make war from his sacramentally Christian actualization of such a decision.

But however we divide the poem, we remain confident that Day was correct in her criticism of Kaluza's theory that the poem was written in strophes. Whether we indicate a passus break at line 189 or not, none of the resulting units includes numbers of lines which reveal any common modules—indeed, several involve multiples of reasonably large prime numbers (1–$188 = 47 \times 4$; 189–$304 = 29 \times 4$; 1113–$1340 = 19 \times 12$). And only one of the units involves a multiple of twenty-four lines, the usual strophe in WA: 445–$636 = 192$ lines $= 24 \times 8$. Obviously, the supply of lines now lost, some of which we postulate, would render textual units more like those of WA. But such suppositions cannot be of much argumentative weight, and we conclude that, although composed in four-line units, *The Siege*, like

---

[37] C's 'vij' at this juncture is not parallel: although the scribe only begins numbering passus after he has begun conflating from a *gamma* copy, his agreement with U in beginning 'Passus 5' at 738 suggests that his divisions (and their numeration) come from his *delta* copy, perhaps the specifically E-tinged version of that archetype we have discussed above.

such poems as Pat, Cln, and Erk, simply joins an arbitrary number of such units in each of its passus.

STYLE

Metre and Formula

Metrically, *The Siege of Jerusalem* is anything but 'the very model of a decadent poetic' (Pearsall 1977, p. 169). It is as close as one can find to being perfectly representative of later Middle English alliterative poetry: highly competent, lacking in mannerism, and conforming to the most recent metrical descriptions of Duggan and J. Turville-Petre. *The Siege of Jerusalem* is therefore an alliterative poem in which the only patterns of alliteration within the line are aa(a)/ax and permissible variants; in which stress and alliteration coincide (though we note and have accepted a handful of lines of the '*Piers Plowman* type', in which a normally unstressed syllable is raised to metrical prominence (see Lawton 1993, pp. 157–60); and in which the b-verse is structured according to a series of syllabic, metrical, and rhythmical constraints.

Acceptance of the last point entails more than a metrical principle. *The Siege of Jerusalem*, like other Middle English alliterative poems, is the product of a system that is 'grammetrical' (Lawrence), in which lexical and grammatical features are combined in the rhythmical patterning of the line. The most significant contribution to understanding such a system in Middle English alliterative poetry remains Ronald Waldron's (based on his pioneering and extensive 1953 M.A. thesis). Waldron significantly revises earlier conceptions of 'the alliterative phrase' (for example, the tabulations of Oakden, 2, 263–363). Rather than a fixed lexical collocation, Waldron argues that the phrase should be seen as 'a complete formula with a certain rhythmical value . . . fulfilling a rhythmical need as well as an alliterative one' (p. 794). Waldron demonstrates several sorts of pattern, some of which involve lexical collocations or one constant stressed word and some of which do not, some of which are variable in syntactic or rhythmical pattern or both. The essay offers many examples of formulaic patterns which consist of 'a framework of unstressed words and a constant rhythmical and syntactic pattern' (p. 793).

Such extensive evidence of different but interlinked patterns of verbal, syntactic, and rhythmical relation is extremely valuable in forming an understanding of what alliterative poetry involves. Questions of metre in alliterative poetry give rise to considerations of lexis, grammar, and rhythm. While initially, Waldron's critics were inclined to suggest that he isolated only the commonplaces of grammatical structure, in fact his work demonstrates beyond doubt patterns of selection and statistically significant recurrence. There seems to us little potential for an explanation markedly different from Waldron's own of what Waldron found. His conclusions are based on the oral-formulaic theory of Parry and Lord and on adaptations of that theory to literate contexts—especially Old English poetry—in spite of Parry's insistence that such formulaic composition was incompatible with literacy (see Borroff, pp. 61–64). All who have maintained Waldron's position have echoed a version of his belief in continuity from Old English to Middle English: 'It seems beyond doubt that there was some sort of continuity in the use of alliterative meter between the eleventh and the fourteenth century, although there are virtually no written records' (p. 792).

This position has been powerfully restated by Duggan against a generation that has been more inclined to look at 'written records' (although see Hanna 1995). His view appears inseparable from an insistence on the formulaic quality of alliterative verse, given the intensely phonological nature of formulas. Yet Waldron's final articulation is careful and acute:

What we shall expect to find is, at most, the *remains* of an oral technique embedded in written literature. But even this will give us grounds for seeing the alliterative style, as it is found in the later Middle Ages, as still essentially an oral style. . . . It would be rash to go on to say that this poetry must therefore be of oral origins. The most we can say is that it was written by poets who were familiar with a body of formulas which probably originated in a tradition of oral composition and for readers who still retained a taste for the conventions of an oral style. (p. 793)

Issues of this kind have always been controversial. We restate their relevance. Not only do they arise out of considerations of metre, but they also draw attention to one of the most extraordinary tensions in Middle English alliterative poetry, especially so in *The Siege of Jerusalem*, between 'an oral style' and 'written literature'. This is a tension to be found at several levels of composition: for example, in the passus endings, where conventions of oral presentation may coincide with a chapter division of the source; or in the syntax of the poem, which combines frequent parataxis and asyndeton in the transition from line to line or from verse to verse with a developed hypotaxis over all that competes with, and often overdoes, its sources. It is a creative tension inherent in the verse form itself, which requires complex metrical description yet is also justly epitomized as 'a sort of talking style' (Paull F. Baum, quoted by Lawton 1988, p. 228). In attempting to comprehend the opposites of bookishness and orality, not to deny them, one will understand *The Siege of Jerusalem*. This combination of apparent opposites is quite over-determined; it is the mark of rhetoric, with its public interest in justice and good government.

Syntax

Formulas and 'moulds' of the kinds proposed by Waldron are powerful resources for syntactic formalization. They are an alliterative system that enables and interacts with literal translation by resolving word-order in terms of rhythm. Another important syntactic resource, in our view (see Lawton 1980) is the quatrain.

The technique, as practiced in *The Siege*, involves a difficult oscillation. Not only must the poet play out the traditional phrasal grammar of the single long-line, but he is simultaneously involved in thinking out two- to five-line sense units as well. A single quatrain from early in the poem neatly enacts a transition between the linearity of traditional alliterative collocations and more elaborately structured syntactic units:

> þe wolcon wanned anon   and þe water skeweþ;
> Cloudes clateren on lofte   as þey cleue wolde;
> þe racke myd a rede wynde   roof on þe myddel
> And sone sette on þe se   out of þe souþ syde. (57–60)

The first three half-lines offer broadly repetitive paratactic patterns typical (or, perhaps, most typical) of even the least inspired alliterative verse. Each is comprised of a subject-verb unit, in the heavier a-verses pointed by alliteration (including the emphatic hyperalliterative /kl/ of line 58a) and varying with the off-verse 57b both in this initial rhyme linking subject and verb (vs. the non-alliterating off-verse verb) and in the inclusion of brief nonalliterating adverbial elements.

But such linearity is dissipated by the off-verse 58b and, most definitively, by the intricate sentence of the second distich—both of

which rely on careful subordination which partly qualifies the forward
movement, the action emphasis of the passage. The *cleaving*, the
breaking apart of the clouds, threatened in the first two lines, is
actualized in the second pair; but the description of this process of
actualization emphasizes, not simply action but the agent of action.
And that agent, a violent south wind, enters the poem through
subordinated prepositional phrases, separated by a full line of poetry
yet necessarily linked in sense. Thus, while 'roof' answers 'cleue' and is
extended into 'sette' (but without phonological parallel, as in the initial
lines); and while the adverb 'sone', now bearing alliteration, fulfils the
promise of earlier 'anon', equally prominent are the 'rede wynde', 'þe
souþ syde', and the echo of 'myd' in 'myddel', all features which
interrupt the ongoing motion and change of the passage—if only
ironically. 'Sette', as subsequent lines will indicate, does not point
toward cessation but to a renewal of yet more intense activity.

Thus, in this technique, the traditional phrasal grammar of the
single long-line quite regularly plays against more elaborately structured multiline sentences. The poet exhibits here that love for and
delight in the baroquely ornamental always associated with the
alliterative movement. And he creates far more intricate grammatical
patterns than are customarily the case in such poetry (flat units like
lines 273–80 are distinctly uncommon here), the sort of stylistic
performance Spearing (pp. 139–41; compare pp. 168–69, 171–72) has
analysed and applauded. Unravelling such syntax, which frequently
requires consultation of the sources (compare our note to line 474 for
a very minor, yet telling, example) will occupy a substantial number
of the Textual Notes. Simultaneously, we would note the cost to the
poet in terms of conventional features of alliterative technique widely
applauded: some of the intraquatrain repetitiveness (for example,
665–68) and much of the avoidance of traditional alliterative synonyms, with concomitant rhetorical emphasis on words considered
'low-stress' or 'prosaic' elsewhere in the tradition, may be attributed
to the pressure exerted by the poet's ornate syntactic emphases.

The quatrains of *The Siege of Jerusalem* are therefore syntactic
devices like the rhyme royal stanza of *Troilus and Criseyde* and consist
mainly of one or two self-contained syntactic units. There is also
evidence of artful verbal interlacing between quatrains (see lines 988–
89). In some cases where this is not so, one quatrain forms part of a
larger pattern itself modelled out of and marked by the boundaries of
quatrains (for example, lines 661–80, 697–708). That leaves only a

few exceptions, in which quatrain boundaries are transgressed syntactically, and here the enjambment across quatrains seems artful and dramatic. The fall of the 'burnes in þe bretages', for example, that begins in line 577 amid the chaos of war, so that they 'starke-blynde wexen', is sustained until the first line of the following quatrain: 'And vnder dromedaries diȝeden sone' (581).

Within the quatrain, enjambment from line to line is far more frequent in *The Siege of Jerusalem* than may long have appeared to readers of Kölbing and Day. Mabel Day inherited from Kölbing an initial set of punctuations that she judged to be both unsatisfactory and misleading (see, for example, p. 91, 1–8 n); but she was not able to repair all the damage, coming from an editorial apprenticeship with Gollancz and (wrongly) convinced with him that Middle English alliterative poetry is predominantly end-stopped. Editorial punctuation is a major intervention in all medieval texts, not least alliterative ones (Lawton 1980). We have sought here to punctuate in a way that points the larger syntactic patterns of the poem, and draws attention to the particular skill with which they are composed. Outstanding here is the poet's capacity to produce relatively short but stirring speeches using the formulaic and collocational resources of the alliterative movement, which so suited self-conscious verbal rhetoric (see, for example, Sir Sabin's speech at lines 985–1000). The variation between hypotaxis in these and local parataxis in the battle sequences is demonstrably artful, a matter of rhetorical technique, as are the frequent transitions between direct and indirect speech, with the more troublesome of which we deal in the Notes.

One extraordinary, if unobtrusive, area of achievement is the strength of the b-verse in this poem compared with others of the alliterative tradition. In the case of DT, for example, it is possible to assess the action of long narrative sequences by scanning the a-verse alone (Lawton 1980a). In *The Siege*, by contrast, the b-verses contribute forcefully, both to the action and to achieving an ironic and sometimes sardonic tone. This testifies to the sparing use in *The Siege of Jerusalem* of the ready-made filler tag and of temporizing and invariable set phrases, an impression that perhaps serves another, that the ornate syntax is not matched by the poem's lexis.

Lexis

The lexis of *The Siege of Jerusalem* does not lend itself to easy characterization, and is in this respect typical of the style of the whole

poem. We often have occasion to note echoes of other alliterative
poems and whole sequences that seem to be derived not from any one
source but from the alliterative movement itself, and which bring
with them specialized alliterative vocabulary.

But there is not the density of such vocabulary in *The Siege of
Jerusalem* that distinguishes MA or the poems of Cotton Nero A.x. It
is not that the poem is devoid of the lexis Oakden called 'chiefly
alliterative' (see 2, 175–95, esp. p. 181), but rather that such
specifically alliterative vocabulary coexists and competes with a
language less specifically ornate. For example, the poet is well
aware of alliterating synonyms for 'man' and uses them frequently—*athel* adj. 1×, *burne* 30×, *freke* 15×, *gome* 10×, *kempe* 1×,
lede 12×, *renke* 5×, *schalke* 1×, *segge* 21×, *wye* 18×. But he is as or
more apt to use *man*, whether alliterating or modified by an
alliterating adjective (38×), or a commonplace term designating
rank—*baron* 5×, *duke* 11×, *king* 39×, *knight* 22×, *lord(ing)* 14×,
prince 20×. Similarly, although he knows and uses on a handful of
occasions such verbs of motion as *ayre*, *chese*, *ferk*, *kayre*, *strike*, and
tee, their appearances in the poem are overwhelmed by reliance on
such commonplace terms as *come*, *go*, *turn*, and *wende* (some ninety
uses in total). Thus, among formal alliterative poems *The Siege* stands
closest to the *Piers Plowman* group in its sparing use of vocabulary that
is mainly restricted to the alliterative tradition, such as synonyms for
'man,' verbs of motion, idealizing adjectives and so on (see Borroff).
But this is, in the main, a relative statement: the *Siege*-poet scarcely
shares Langland's resolute avoidance of such vocabulary.

Yet it would be far from true to describe the lexis of the poem as
plain or uninventive: the sheer size of the Glossary is surprising. That
glossary demonstrates at least a competent response to the technical
demands of alliterative poetry (for the key words of each line), as well
as the *Siege*-poet's response to the range of his material. In its 1340
lines, *The Siege of Jerusalem* has a vast amount of plot covering the
fields of political, military, and salvation history. The poetic handling
of the divergent source materials extends from freehand amplification
to compression and narrative summary: a predictable range, but one
that speaks to the assurance with which the poet combines eclectic
materials and which argues for literary judgement and a sense of
purpose. The lexis follows that range, which is a range of semantic
fields: alliterative *topoi* such as battles and seastorms; highly detailed
military, mechanical, and engineering lexis, used with technical

precision; political, diplomatic, and legal language; the theological and the affective, including invective.

The tendency to avoid alliterative cliché is echoed across the wider context in the avoidance of unnecessary lexical repetition, and the inventiveness with which alliterative sets are compiled to allow the maximum narrative development in each line. For example, Vespasian's 'bees' would dictate the alliteration of the line in which they occur, and would necessitate a subsequent additional line to describe the fact that they clustered in his nose, were it not for poet's resource in using the ON derivative *bikere* 34. There is little of the lexical stretching associated with alliterative poetry; on the contrary, the poet seems concerned with accuracy in denotation and limitation of lexical meaning. The mixture of precision and lexical inventiveness in his work extends to a preparedness to plunder sources:

> A tabernacle in þe tour   atyred was riche,
> Piȝt as a paueloun   on pileres of seluere.

> A which of white seluere   walwed þerynne
> On foure goions of gold   þat hit fram grounde bare,
> A chosen chayre þerby   an chaundelers twelfe
> Betyn al with bournde gold   with brennande sergis. (467–72)

Compare: Li tabernacles estoit fez en guise de paveillon et i auoit doze pilers d'argent qui les soustenoient, et avoit el mileu une huche a feste ausi con une chaise toute d'argent asise sus quatre lions d'or. Et tout entor avoit doze chandeliers d'argent et en chascun chandelier avoit ung cierge de cire virge tout ardant. (BF 353–57)

In these lines no fewer than seven key nouns are pulled directly from the source: *tabernacle*, *paueloun*, *pileres*, *which* (although see our textual note), *chayre*, *chaundelers*, and even *sergis*, not to mention that *goions of gold* may reflect some form of the source reading 'lions d'or' (see our note). Such use of the sources is not uncommon, and is resourceful in alliterative terms: the source's 'quarriaus' becomes *quarels* 657, and 'quarniaus' becomes *kernels* 660. It is sometimes disconcerting, on perusing the sources, to see how close the borrowing has been, including such ordinary words as *toures* 659 or *Vnarmen* 634.

What the sources do not contribute to the lexis, for the most part, is the unusual number of compounds and similes in the poem. Although the poet moderates alliterative lexis, he is often capable of startling feats of word-combination, for example, *again-turn*, *bale-fire*, *bale-tree*, *feather-hame*, *gleed-fire*, *God-riche*, *steel-ware*, perhaps *whale-stream*. And his similes run the full gamut: many are nearly commonplace, proverbial comparisons; others approach epic similes (see for example, lines 564, 676, 785: those of 533–36, unusually, are suggested by the *Bible en françois*). Such usages are the lexical equivalents of the rhetorically developed speeches mentioned in our discussion of the poet's syntax: they are his most literary reshaping of his sources, and an index of the unobtrusively high style he cultivates as his mode of translation.

Techniques of Translation

The poet's versatility, rather than any uniformity of style or approach, is his most evident characteristic. This is as true in the case of sustained translation from any one source, as in Passus iii (from the *Bible en françois*), as it is in the case of Passus iv, where the translation from at least two different sources is punctuated by freehand amplification not directly based on any known source.

Passus iii (lines 445–636) corresponds to a chapter in the *Bible en françois*, except for a minor change at the end (discussed below pp. lxxxiii–iv), that is probably motivated. The first twenty lines are freehand amplification of the *topos* of coming out for battle, before the very close translation of lines 467–72, quoted above. There follows another type of passage, closely based on two sentences of the source but reshaped and amplified in a minor way to exploit the full alliterative potential of the catalogue of biblical stories (compare PTA 422–61, more distantly 599–602):

> Lered men of þe lawe   þat loude couþe synge
> With sawters seten hym by   and þe psalmys tolde
> Of douȝty Dauid þe kyng   and oþer dere storijs
> Of Iosue þe noble Iewe   and Iudas þe knyȝt.
>
> Cayphas of þe kyst   kyppid a rolle
> And radde how þe folke ran   þroȝ þe rede water
> Whan Pharao and his ferde   were in þe floode drouned,
> And myche of Moyses lawe   he mynned þat tyme. (477–84)

Compare: Et tenoit en sa main le livre Moÿses, et lisoit les estoires de Joseph et de Pharaon. Et dedenz cil chastel estoient li mestre de la loi qui chantoient les loanges Dauid le roi. (BF 362–64)

The passage has been redesigned, transposing the order of Caiaphas and the other clerks: the poet's confidence that Caiaphas is a climactic and focal point is reproduced in the inversion of lines 581–84, where Caiaphas's name is withheld until the end of the quatrain. What in the source seems a fairly routine business is turned into a set piece, in which a sometimes ironic use of alliterative collocations (as in line 477a) becomes a tonal resource for sarcasm or worse, where the source is flatly descriptive. Thus in the next line (485), 'When þis faiþles folke to þe feld comen', the source has the subject neutrally as 'li juif' (BF 365); the potential of an alliterative collocation sets up a sharp phrase that is repeated in line 513.

Thus the passage opens with three different modes of reproducing its source: freehand amplification, close translation, and translation by minor amplification and the substitution of alliterative collocations for individual words of the source. This sets the pattern for the rest of the passus, with the more common types being freehand amplification and collocational substitution. Vespasian's speech is introduced by a fine example of the latter:

> Vaspasian dyuyseþ þe vale alle aboute
> þat was with baneres ouerbrad to þe borwe ȝatis.
> To barouns and bolde men þat hym aboute were
> Seiþ, 'lordynges a londe, lestenyþ my speche'. (489–92)

Compare: Lors dist Vaspasiens a ses barons, 'Biau seignor . . . . (BF 367)

It then proceeds by freehand amplification (lines 493–508), with its significant and scholarly addition referring back to Nero and questions of unpaid tribute from another source (505–8), and the thematically relevant reminder of Christ's crucifixion, with its overt source tag ('As preueþ his passioun, whoso þe paas redeþ', line 504), which alludes, however, to the Bible itself, not the immediate source. Then the speech returns to collocational substitution on the alliterative themes of lordship and mastery. Line 509 translates 'souviegne'; lines 511 and 512 are developments of 'seignorie':

> Bot more þing in our mode myneþ today,
> þat by resoun to Rome þe realte fallyþ,
> Boþe þe myȝt and þe mayn, maistre and oþer,
> And lordschip of eche londe þat liþe vnder heuen. (509–12)

Compare: Et pour Dieu souviegne vos de qui le pueple des Romains doit
avoir seignorie et fierté seür touz autres pueples. (BF 374–76)

The peroration likewise follows the sense of the French, which
aspires to the rhetorical, too. But the English poet outdoes it in the
strength of his alliterative vocabulary and the sense of moral rightness
that it is used to convey:

> For þei ben feynt at þe fiȝt,   fals of byleue,
> And wel wenen at a wap   alle þe world quelle,
> Noþer grounded on God   ne on no grace tristen
> Bot alle in sternes of stoure   and in strengþ one.
>
> And we ben diȝt today   Driȝten to serue—
> Hey Heuen-kyng,   hede to þyn owne! (517–22)

Compare: Quar ce sont genz sanz foi et sanz cuer; et bien i pert qu'il ne s'i
fient qu'en lor forterreces. (BF 373–74)

Again, the order of the French has been reshuffled to shape the
climax. Battle is commenced within two lines, with the English poet
now drastically abbreviating the extensive response of the lords in
the French (BF 377–83) to one uncompromising line, 'Today þat
fleþe any fote   þe fende haue his soule!' (line 524), and the manner
in which it is uttered changed from 'moult doucement' (BF 378) to
aloude (523; compare the energetic movements of lines 617–20, only
partly justified by the source, BF 429–34). This is a rare example of
condensation; on the whole, the English poet is content to match
his French source, amplifying it in minor ways by collocational
translation, and considerably dilating battle material and speech, but
being careful to convey details of the campaign (for example, lines
581–88) as well as the stage effects of war (for example, lines 557–
64)—and apparently adding one highly specific, observant and
practical detail, the need for one hundred rubbish removers,
rydders, to bury the dead (571–72). The battle sequences end
with further collocational substitution (601–8, 613–20) and close
translation (621–26) framing significant freehand amplification: the
poet's insistence that the Romans were entirely without injury, as if
they had just arrived from Rome (609–12, 631–32). The invention
of this detail justifies the apparent shift from the next chapter of the
French of one quatrain of close translation followed by a closing
editorial comment:

Princes to her pauelouns   passen on swyþe,
Vnarmen hem as-tyt   and alle þe ny3t resten
With wacche vmbe þe walles   to many wyes sorowe.
þey wolle no3t þe heþen here   þus harmeles be lafte. (633–36)

Compare: Tantost Vaspasien et son ost se ralierent ensemble et vindrent a
lor tres et a leur paveillons et se desarmerent. Puis se reposerent . . . . (BF
437–38)

This simply and logically finishes the day's business, leaving the next
day to a new passus.

Passus iii, then, shows three or four different stylistic modes of
proceeding in translation from one source, which are varied with art,
intelligence and a demonstrable capability to give the material a
literary shape. The continuity of these modes in Passus iv negotiates
the shift from one source, the *Bible en françois*, to another, the
Polychronicon, through long passages of seemingly independent
amplification that may well show the influence not only of Josephus
(870ff.; see p. xlvii above) but in key set sequences, of Guido's
Historia destructionis Troie. The popularity and influence of this major
Latin example of fashionable *amplificatio* have been canvassed by
Jacobs, who argues that poets of the alliterative movement are
influenced directly by the Latin—thus accounting for at least some
of the resemblances claimed between *The Siege* and DT, for others of
which we have suggested a different explanation (see 'Dialect and
Date' above, pp. xxxvi–vii).

Such an argument may extend to the otherwise apparently
unprecedented passage from lines 729 to 788: night falls (729–37);
Vespasian is sleepless and 'walwyþ and wyndiþ and waltreþ aboute'
(739); at first light he 'bounys of bedde, busked hym fayre' (745) in an
extended arming sequence (746–68); then approaches the city walls to
deliver an impromptu morning boast in the enemy's direction (771–
88). There is in this a literary development of Vespasian as hero that
is absent from all the sources, but serves both alliterative bravura and
the work's narrative logic, the elevation of Vespasian to Emperor.
Even when the poet turns to the *Polychronicon* (and *De bello Iudaico*)
for Josephus's ruse of the wet laundry (789–96), Vespasian is given a
chance to respond with laughter at the contrivance (797–800). It is
totally in keeping with this epic advancement of Vespasian, and the
frequent supply of direct speech for him, that the poet should have
provided him with a further speech to crown the expanded account of

the killing of Caiaphas and his clerks (718–24; see our note). There remains throughout an eye for military and strategic details. When a source is consulted for these, it is consulted carefully and the significance spelt out—as, above all, with the use of the noxious vapour of carrion, 'þe stynk of þe stewe' (687), to spread disease in Jerusalem, and the blocking of all external sources of running water for the city (685–92).

The first really sustained close translation of Passus iv does not occur, however, until lines 801–32 and once more concerns Josephus and his clever tactics:

> þerof was Iosophus war   þat myche of werre couþe
> And sette on þe walle side   sakkes myd chaf
> Aȝens þe streyngþe of þe stroke   þer þe stones hytte
> þat alle dered noȝt a dyȝ   bot grete dyt made.
>
> þe Romayns runne to anon   and on roddes knytte
> Siþes for þe sackes   þat selly were kene,
> Raȝten to þe ropis,   rent hem in sondere
> þat all dasschande doun   into þe diche flatten. (805–12)

Compare: Inde Uespasianus ictu arietis murum conturbat, sed Iosephus saccos paleis repletos ictibus opponens, plagam delusam emollit, nam solida melius per molliora deluduntur; sed e contra Romani falces contis ligantes funes saccorum succiderunt. (Poly 74–78)

This is close translation, all the way to the acceptance of *sakkes* from the Latin 'saccos', but the change of text and language do not lead to a marked difference in technique from those used in Passus iii. From there on to the end of Passus iv is more independent amplification, developed from Josephus, in which Titus counsels a siege and the uses of hunger. As the population of Jerusalem starves, the Romans will take rest and recreation in the hunt:

> 'For we wol hunten at þe hart   þis heþes aboute
> And hure raches renne   amonge þis rowe bonkes;
> Ride to þe reuer   and rere vp þe foules,
> Se faucouns fle,   fele of þe beste—
>
> Ech segge to þe solas   þat hymself lykeþ.' (889–93)

This is the sequence Spearing praises most highly in his perceptive and persuasive account of *The Siege of Jerusalem*. Here he finds, at the

least, a sustained high level of poetic craft. Spearing writes of its use
of clashing and incongruous modes, its 'contrast of horror and
beauty', 'its combination of serene beauty and unbearable horror,
both perfectly under the poet's control and brought together, so far as
one can tell, with deliberate intention' (p. 172). Everything that we
have observed of the poem's style leads us to second Spearing's praise
(qualified as it is; for him, the poem is 'a brilliant and repellent work
of art') and to echo his confidence in the translator's 'deliberate
intention'. There is indeed an air of purpose in the structure and
dispositio of this text.

THE TEXT

As did our two predecessors, Kölbing-Day and Turville-Petre, we
utilize manuscript L as the base-text for our presentation of *The
Siege*. This decision, born of equal parts necessity and convenience,
involves certain irritations. Past scholars have followed L from
necessity because it is the manuscript most complete (P, A, V, and
C, for example, have major losses which remove them from consideration) and because, given its independent derivation from O',
which we have demonstrated above, the manuscript requires considerably less editorial intervention to create a putative text, whether
archetypal or authorial, than would U, D, or E.

At the same time, following L's forms regularly, as we do, proves
less than an optimal situation. The manuscript cannot function as a
conventional 'copy-text',[38] in the sense that it does not approximate
authorial forms, either in spelling or morphology. (We should have
most preferred to use the Bolton copy, P, secondarily Thornton's
Yorkshire A.) After considering the prospect for some time, we have
resisted any normalization and simply follow the manuscript. Thus,
the reader will have to endure L's dialectical peculiarities, forms
considerably removed from the poet's West Yorkshirisms and, in the
main, foreign to those of any published alliterative poem outside the
PP tradition. Among such grotesqueries, all of which we print
following our base-text, we would signal: eche (a) (for ilk, ilka, or

---

[38] For the term, see Walter W. Greg, 'The Rationale of Copy-Text', *Studies in
Bibliography* 3 (1950), 19–36; and for its relevance, D. C. Greetham, 'The Place of
Fredson Bowers in Mediaeval Editing', *Papers of the Bibliographical Society of America* 82
(1988), 53–69.

ilkan), myd (for wiþ), þei and þou '(al)though' (for þof), -yþ
terminations in verb presents (for -es), sschip 71, hy 140 (for þey),
-sulf 155, Garde 262 (for gert), ibretaged 413, Iosophus, rich 307 and
794 (for rike or reke 'smoke, vapour'), kay3t 948, hey3t 977, sille 1311,
worschup 986, propfred 1156. In addition, L contains a number of
phonological oddments, in the main reflexes of a West Saxon dialect;
these we comment upon in our textual notes.

    L involves few difficulties of transcription, and we have followed
the forms of the manuscript while imposing modern accidentals.
Thus, word-division, capitalization, and punctuation are our own.
(With regard to the second, in L, many forms are indistinguisable, for
example, a/A, w/W; lines frequently begin with non-capital forms,
for example, b and l nearly universally; and the scribe's usage, for
example, occasional forms like 13 Mannes, titus universally, is simply
inconvenient.) We have expanded all abbreviations silently, on the
whole a transparent procedure, since these most frequently involve
only the usual reduced set, derived from Latin scripts, customary in
vernacular English texts. We do, however, note the following minor
difficulties:

    1. The scribe almost invariably uses the tironian sign for 'and', and
full forms appear only five times in the whole text: And 36, 364, 734;
an 452, 1138 (?). But this sign must on at least two occasions (172,
454) mean An. The form an also appears as an infrequent spelling for
the prep. 'on' (55, 351, 452, 547), and on at least one occasion (471),
the scribe has written on, instead of an intended an.[39] He presumably
has both forms of the word, but we have chosen to universalize the
more commonly attested (and more familiar) one—and have treated
172 and 454 as if emendations.

    2. We have universally expanded -r' (with a distinct loop) as -re.
Several forms in L demand such a treatment (for example, nonbr' 458,
togedr' 561), and in many other uses where it might seem optional, its
effect appears to us beneficial, for example, wer' and werr' passim.
There are sporadic indications that abbreviation in this form reflects
an earlier, grammatical system, for example, a siker man 438 versus
xij. siker' kny3tes 346; but equally signs that the forms have become

---

[39] More attenuated evidence for the form comes from similar errors: in 417 L
equivocates, covers all possibilities, and provides dittographic & on for correct On
(perhaps An in L's archetype; cf. the other MSS at 1138); in 936, he reads þan for
correct An/And. A further confusion is implied by two instances in which L writes & for
as (202, 665).

strictly graphemic representations, for example, *vnder'* (3, 5, but also *vnder*), *her'* for both OE *hēr* and *heora*.

3. There are a few other eccentricities, for example, 138 *dempt'* (dempte, the full form attested elsewhere), 571 *maist'* (maistre 'mastery'). On those two occasions (857, 908) when it certainly represents the pp. 'done', we have ignored the common mark of abbreviation in *don'*, which we otherwise would expand *doun*.

4. Abbreviation in L is extensive (for example, affecting virtually all examples of *r* + vowel or vowel + *r*), and a few abbreviations unusual, although scarcely unparalleled, in English texts occur, for example, s'^e (secunde 114), *-m't-* (-ment- 100), *c͞oes* (comunes 318), *dd* (Dauid 479), *l͞res* (lettres 960). The scribe, we suspect, may have been an accomplished Latin copyist and brought some of his habits over into English.

We universally indicate interlineations (both in our transcription of the base-text and in the *corpus lectionum*) by including the relevant reading between forward and reverse primes ' ` ´ '. Particularly in our report of P readings in the collations, we enclose illegible sequences of letters in angle brackets '⟨ ⟩'.

All our corrections of L, based upon our interpretation of the full variant corpus, are marked in the text. We indicate all materials we have added, all our 'positive emendations' (for example, *man > berne*), and all rearrangements of word order by the customary square brackets. Given L's status as 'base-text', we put all emendations, including lines supplied from other manuscripts, into its forms. In contrast to much current practice, we also signal materials we have deleted; we place a '+' at all points in the text from which letters or words have been removed.

Beneath the text, we provide a full *corpus lectionum*, in the main an account of all rejected readings. We cite these competing variants in the fixed order (L)PAVUDECEx, which, with the exception of Ex, is both genetic and preferential. The form of the variant is that of the first manuscript cited and implies nothing about the exact forms in the manuscripts indicated by subsequent sigla. This apparatus includes all substantive variants (we take the presence of separate entries in OED and/or MED as our standard for such a judgement), all grammatical variants, all variants which might be substantive (for example, P *strange* 17, almost certainly 'strong', but perhaps 'strange'), and all syllabic variants in b-verses. (Relatively few of

these in fact challenge the metrical constraints identified in Duggan
1986 and 1988; but they may provide indications of predictable
scribal handlings of various b-verse frames, information without
parallel elsewhere in this verse tradition.) We attempt no record of
-e, which was almost certainly silent for our poet. The only variants
we deliberately exclude are *atte* : *at þe* (but *atte:at* we record as
indicating the omission of *-te = þe*); *on* + sb.:*a-* + sb.; *þe toþer* : *þat
oþer*.

Dialectical forms in the various witnesses provide some minor
problems. We universally interpret E's peculiar *wol*, *fook*, and *feyʒtles*
as 'full', 'folk', and 'faithless', respectively. And, with the exception of
the form *tan(e)* for *tak(en)*, we take no note of such dialecticisms as
C's occasional East Anglianisms, for example, common examples of *d*
for *þ* (unless they create forms possibly substantive variants). Where
P or A or both are the source of emendations, their position without
citation after a lemma indicates that they have the same word and
form we print, although the manuscript(s) may in fact present
nonidentical northern morphology. Thus, at 82 hem] ADC, A
actually reads *þam*. However, when alliterative rhyme is at issue
(for example, 66 *hem*), we provide the dialect variants (just as we do
when we correct L's southern ʒ-forms to rhyming forms in *g-*).

We italicize all non-manuscript material in the record of the variant
corpus. This includes our frequent reliance upon obvious abbreviations, designed to reduce the repetition of manuscript readings: we
use not simply the conventional *om.* (the word or phrase is omitted in
the following copies), *int.* (interlined), and *marg.* (added marginally),
but also: *trs.* (the two words are transposed; *trs. phrs.* indicates two
adjacent phrases have been transposed), *canc.* (the word is cancelled),
prec. (preceding), *precs.* (precedes), *fols.* (follows), *corr.* or *corr. to*
(corrected). Italics also identify the readings of our predecessors,
which always follow our citation of the manuscript evidence.

We exclude two types of readings from the variant corpus. We
usually ignore scribal selfcorrections (expunction, cancellation, etc.),
in favour of presenting the 'final scribal text'; we do include examples
we deem significant for any reason. And we adopt a 'double standard'
for potential metrical variants, variations of syllabic representation of
a single lexical item (for example, *suþ*:*siþen*:*siþenes*). These we record,
and then universally, only in b-verses: they may there determine
metricality.

Our collation differs from many others in our effort at recording features associated with manuscript presentation, *ordinatio*. One such set of features we indicate universally is clearly substantive, namely the notation of the midline caesura, regular in LVUEC. Where, in these copies, its placement varies from the text we print or where it is absent, we indicate that fact and use the solidus '/' to indicate the caesura. In individual variants, citation typically has the form 'lemma] / variant PAUDEC' (alternately 'lemma] variant / PAUDEC'), which means 'the caesura precedes (follows) the variant reading in all those manuscripts cited which mark the caesura'; we record caesurae omitted in those copies at the end of all variant readings for the single line.

We also record all manuscript divisions. UEC present regular paraphs, generally to set off eight- (U) and four-line (EC) units; these are, for the most part, automatic, mechanical, and thus unhelpful (given lost lines). However, we have recorded the same, but more widely dispersed, punctuation of D, potentially of import, given that manuscript's absence of any other divisions. We have ignored the very few bits of manuscript marginalia; these are prominent only in C, as a record of the Roman emperors in the passage following line 897.

Finally, our record of the readings of P requires some explanation. From 1056 until the manuscript ends at 1143, it is only sporadically legible, even under an ultra-violet lamp. In this portion of the poem, we record the manuscript's reading, so far as we find it decipherable, in every relevant lemma. Non-citation of P here must never be taken as agreement with the text we print: we are only silent about its readings in those loci where the text is illegible or lost. When P agrees with unemended L, we universally cite its presence in the form 'lemma] P; other variants'.

Where we have emended our base-text, we record variation in a slightly different format from elsewhere. For emendations supported in the manuscript tradition, our typical lemma has the form 'emended reading] sigla of those manuscripts with that reading; erroneous reading removed from L; remaining variants, arranged in the customary order'. Where we print a conjecture, the lemma has the form '*emended reading] the exact spelling forms of all witnesses, arranged by the strength of support each gives for the reading we conjecture'. Only in such cases do we cite nonsubstantive variations of spelling (spelling variants in b-verses, because potentially of metrical importance, are substantive).

In preparing our text, we have conceived our responsibility as that inherent in a traditional 'critical edition'. This choice imposes upon us a single explanatory standard, to account for the genesis of every variant in the apparatus. And this standard presupposes, in turn, the identification of anterior readings which we might assign to the *Siege* poet. Our customary procedure for approaching this standard of explanation is that enunciated by the editors of PPA and PPB: that the 'hardest' reading, all other things being equal, will have proven multiply generative in the process of transmission. And the poem we address, the most widely attested in the alliterative tradition besides PP, offers quite ample evidence to facilitate such a procedure. Moreover, we have been both inspired and constrained by the poet's sources, which very often identify for us that variant extant in the corpus most likely to represent the author's response to the Latin or French he was reading. Our Textual Notes offer explanations of the more difficult choices we have made; frequently, where attestation universally speaks against L or where our base-text transmits a *lapsus calami*, we have not burdened our reader by belabouring the obvious.

We recognize that procedures like these we follow have come increasingly under attack on a variety of fronts. To such attacks, we would offer only a few brief ripostes. First, we believe in the responsibility of literary scholars to offer historical explanations, and believe that certain varieties of variation, encountered both in the witnesses to *The Siege* and in other transmissional traditions, are subject to explanation. We do not undertake these in any spirit of scoffing. Variation testifies neither to the stupidity nor the malignity of scribes, but rather to a generally conscientious effort at recording what may often have appeared for various reasons inexplicable; the very possibility of explaining such behaviour will identify it as a rational human pursuit. And the study of any single manuscript version of the poem (the text of E would repay protracted scrutiny) can, so far as we can see, occur within the context of information only a critical edition can supply; the E scribe's behaviour, for example, will be comprehensible only within the context of his exemplar, the lost copy we above call *delta*, constructible by agreements of UDEC.

Moreover, we remain acutely aware of a foundational responsibility which inheres in both editions and, perforce, their makers. Such scholarly works are the tools upon which literary history, however conceived, must rest. Thus, we recognize the poem as the production of an author, uniquely different in his work from all those various persons who have transmitted that work to us.

Further, given those discontinuities and blanks which mark our knowledge of the Middle English literary scene, only a critical edition can elucidate basic historical problems. Without a critical text, we cannot identify linguistic features probably authorial and thus cannot place the poem in any particular Middle English context. Neither can we explain the geography of the text's transmission nor the way in which *The Siege* may have participated in literary activities far removed from the community in which the text was first received. (We applaud such efforts at identifying local literary communities, layered interactions of local and 'imported' texts, as that which Beadle has announced.) And finally, without a critical text, our sense of Middle English lexicon and usage risks serious distortion. For example, there is no Middle English verb *rusken*: at line 731, the only known appearance of the form, it simply represents L's (or his archetype's) conscientious effort to transcribe what he saw in his exemplar, and A, confirmed by UDE, preserves an equally obscure but explicable Middle English word.

Although our edition is 'critical' in the sense that we strive to construct a text selective and eclectic, we are forced to admit that this is an ideal goal, not realizable for every lemma. In many places, we find arguments for competing lections too exactly balanced to allow any compelling decision; in such cases, we in effect elevate L from the status of 'base-text' to 'copy-text' and simply follow its readings. (We discuss a number of these cases in the notes.) And in a smaller, but substantial, number of readings—of which 'Langlandian lines' (see our note to line 165) and line 1333, attested only in L, are outstanding examples—we print in manuscript form lines we suspect of archetypal corruption. Although we can, in many instances, conceive of ameliorative hypothetical reconstructions (and have often argued with each other about them), we cannot convince each other of the efficacy of any such emendation. Thus, in such readings, we allow L to stand as a possibly defective 'copy-text'.

We choose to offer no explanation in our Textual Notes, save occasionally to note alternative readings we might have chosen, for a number of our corrections to L. These broadly concern matters of poetic form, surely substantive variation, and matters which we think should, at this stage of study, be self-evident. We assume that the

Siege poet wrote alliterative verse and consequently, however his scribes chose (or were constrained by their archetypes) to represent him, that he wrote 'proper' alliterative long-lines. Thus, following ample demonstrations by T. Turville-Petre (1980, 1987) and Duggan (1986a), we edit on the principle that the poet wrote lines of four or five stressed syllables of either the form aa(a)/ax or one of the three variants of axa/ax. We have emended L to accord with such patterns, most frequently on the showing of other copies (hypothetical examples below are starred and our logic discussed in appropriate Textual Notes), at:

16 (man > berne);[40] 55 (wode > salt); *118 (world > erþe); *140 (trs. b-verse stresses); 143 (cayftes > chaytyfes); 169 (erþe > grounde); 173 (move emperour to the b-verse); 197 (þou3t > sou3t); 235 (Vasp-); *259 (carieþ > aireþ); 261 (Vasp-); 266 (-holde > -tane); 278 (3euen > geuen); 284 (kyng > gyng); 292 (Sprad > Brayd); 296 (ryued > ioyned); 298 (blonk > wlonk); 304 (?rouke > iouke); *319 (schacked > samned); 329 (Thoppyn > Choppyn); 347 (3af > Garde); 354 (make hem come > brynge Cayphas); 376 (scorned > schorne); 384 (supply to sey); 408 (toun > burwe); 409 (sprad > brad); 471 (closen > chosen); 489 (Vasp-; feld > vale); 490 (-sprad > -brad); 507 (for oþer > wheþer); 532 (supply welter); 553 (Vasp-); *637 (Sone > Rathe); 674 (blowande > playande); 702 (side > half); 716 (supply doun); 879 (supply hunger); 896 (and god > oure Lord); 899 (supply boþe); 925 (chossen > geten); 941 (Vasp-); 949 (man > segge); 978 (doun > toun); 1006 (supply þe walles); 1023 (supply God); 1035 (wende > sente); 1038 (man > freke); 1051 (spred > brede); *1069 (hard > tore); 1077 (platte > flatte); 1112 (3yue > gyue); 1130 (dissed > issed); 1140 (ioyced > reioyced); 1146 (3ouen > gyuen); 1157 (supply to enforme from the head of the next line); 1163 (-3yue > -gyue); 1171 (Toren > Goren); 1173 (vnget > vn3et); 1174 (þou3t > sou3t; toun > cite); 1178 (side > wyse); 1187 (supply fyghtyng); 1219 (a3en > agenes); 1230 (and[1, 2] > voys); *1237 (þey > þe vilayns); 1260 (tende > kende); 1276 (rede > fyne); *1312 (ben worth > fourmed); 1319 (þay > pay).

And on seven occasions, we emend lines technically adequate, ones written in one of the three variants of axa/ax, to lines in aaa/ax:

413 (supply bigly); 454 (þousand > hosed); 526 (felde > stede); 638

---

[40] On such 'lexical substitions', typical of these emendations as a class, see Suzuki.

(anon > on brode); 709 (men > ledes); *1089 (smel > rich); 1327 (do > put).

Similarly, although more controversially, we believe that the poet wrote to the syllabic constraints apparent in b-verses elsewhere in the alliterative tradition. In adopting this position, we follow Duggan's (1986, 1988) extensive discussions. While we admire Cable's study of the problem and find especially provocative his explanation (pp. 41–65) of the development of early Middle English alliterative forms, we remain unconvinced by his demonstration of fourteenth-century technique. Duggan's showing here seems to us superior on four grounds: the size of the visible sample from which Duggan draws relative to that Cable presents; the probable loss of -*e* in the spoken dialects one might associate with alliterative poets from early in the fourteenth century; the specifically syntax-frame bound contexts into which Duggan shows most problematic verses fall; and Duggan's insistence on the poets' use of variational patterns, typical of alliterative technique at large, to achieve metricality.

On the basis of Duggan's findings, we emend L on numerous occasions to present b-verses which meet metrical constraints.[41] While we have disagreed with each other in framing our responses to Duggan's 'rules', these have been limited to two minor questions: the need to emend spellings that are graphemic rather than phonemic in order to ensure that readers supply the required number of syllables; and, since in all cases the application of the rules makes a difference of one syllable only, whether the metrical imperative may have more to do with duration than syllable count (even though a rule expressed in terms of syllable count works well). These are secondary conceptual questions rather than primary or practical ones, and have made no difference to the text on which we have agreed. That text testifies to the usefulness of Duggan's analysis, and, we believe, its superiority in these crucial respects to previous accounts of alliterative metre.

Again, we discuss in our notes only a very few lemmata where we recognize alternative readings (or object to a past interpretation). We add syllables to lines otherwise unmetrical in L at:

---

[41] The consequences of this decision are discussed at slightly greater length in Lawton 1993.

30 (amyd > inmyddis); 48 (supply a); 56 (drof > dryueþ); 62 (supply þe); 78 (supply hem); 106 (supply of); 127 (supply hem); *128 (eche > ilka); 133 (ferre > ferly); 134 (bere > berly); 144 (supply and); 152 (petrus > Pet(e)res); 187 (to > forto); 197 (to > vnto); 343 (serche[n]); *379 (make[n]); 399 (supply he); *411 (rynge[n]); 432 (abide > bide[n]); 510 (regnance > realte); 513 (supply of); 526 (stif > stuffed); 537 (supply here); 581 (diȝten > diȝeden); 584 (supply a); 589 (supply a); 590 (eche > ilka); *641 (spar[en]); 675 (supply many); 686 (kirnel[e]s); 708 (supply þe); *710 (topsail[es]); 743 (supply full); 793 (dryed[en]); 840 (arche[le]rs); *923 (mynde[n]); 929 (mette[n]); 939 (supply þat); 959 (supply and); 1023 (to > forto); 1090 (felde[n]); 1134 (to > forto); 1138 (forsoke[n]); 1149 (supply and); 1153 (supply hem); 1167 (eche > ilka); 1187 (eche > ilka); 1219 (aȝen > agenes); 1221 (þre > al þe); 1228 (supply þe); *1234 (supply ȝit from the head of the line); 1236 (supply a); 1269 (metal[le]s); 1275 (iewels > iemewes); *1276 (supply þer from line 1274); 1295 (seide[n]); 1327 (pyne[n]); 1337 (drow[en]).

On three occasions we retain copy-text in awkward circumstances; for the possibility of reading 199 *grete*[*ly*], 292 *aboute*[*n*], and 477 *coupe*[*n*], see the relevant textual notes. With these lines, two of which suggest retention of *-e* to distinguish otherwise identical OE adjectives and adverbs, one might also compare 559, metrical in the printed text only with retention of L's pp. prefix *y-*.

And we remove hypermetrical syllables from L at:

118 (was bygonne > bygan); 143 (holy > his); 212 (delete was); 264 (delete hit); 575 (delete þe); 724 (delete -es); 932 (delete þe); 989 (whoso > who).

Finally, in addition to explaining our textual choices (and con-comitantly, explicating routine varieties of scribal behaviour), our notes serve a more generally explanatory function. We consider a variety of problems associated with the poet's lexis and the often intricate grammatical frames into which he has cast his narrative. We have attempted to provide extensive references to parallel locutions in other alliterative texts, most particularly in the chronicle poems DT, MA, and WA, secondarily in the works of the *Gawain*-poet. Given past discussions of the relationship of *The Siege* and DT (see 'Dialect and Date' above), we have perhaps erred on the side of lavishness in citing parallels from that poem. And at a number of points, we offer more generally explanatory aid and seek to draw our readers' attention to historical data which we hope will illuminate their experience with the poem.

BIBLIOGRAPHY

Beadle, Richard, 'Prolegomena to a literary geography of later medieval Norfolk', *Regionalism in Late Medieval Manuscripts and Texts: Essays celebrating the publication of* A Linguistic Atlas of Late Mediaeval English, ed. Felicity Riddy (Woodbridge, 1991), pp. 89–108.

Benson, Larry D., 'The "Rede Wynde" in "The Siege of Jerusalem"', *Notes and Queries* 205 (1960), 363–64.

Blatt, Franz, ed., 'The Latin Josephus I. Introduction and Text—The Antiquities: Books I–V', Acta Jutlandica, Aarsskrift for Aarhus Universitet 30, 1, Humanistik serie 44 (1958).

Borroff, Marie, *Sir Gawain and the Green Knight: A Stylistic and Metrical Study*, Yale Studies in English 152 (New Haven, 1962).

Brewer, D. S., 'An Unpublished Late Alliterative Poem', *English Philological Studies* 9 (1965), 84–88.

Briquet, C., *Les filigranes: Dictionnaire historique des marques du papier des leur apparition vers 1282 jusqu'es 1600*, 4 vols. (Paris, 1907).

Cable, Thomas, *The English Alliterative Tradition* (Philadelphia, 1991).

Chism, Christine, '*The Siege of Jerusalem*: Liquidating Assets', *Journal of Medieval and Early Modern Studies* 28 (1998), 309–30.

C[ockayne], G[eorge] E. et al., *The Complete Peerage*, 13 vols. in 14 (London, 1910–59).

[Cross, James E.], 'An Anglo-Saxon Discovery', *Recorder* (University of Liverpool) 106 (February 1991), 14–15.

—— et al., eds., *Two Old English Apocrypha and their Manuscript Source* (Cambridge, 1997).

Day, Mabel, 'Fragment of an Alliterative Political Prophecy', *Review of English Studies* 15 (1939), 61–66.

——, 'Strophic Division in Middle English Alliterative Verse', *Englische Studien* 66 (1931–32), 245–48.

Doyle, A. I., 'The Manuscripts', Lawton 1982, pp. 88–100, 142–47.

Duggan, Hoyt N., 'Alliterative Patterning as a Basis for Emendation in Middle English Alliterative Poetry', *Studies in the Age of Chaucer* 8 (1986), 73–105. [1986a]

——, 'The Authenticity of the Z-Text of Piers Plowman: Further Notes on Metrical Evidence', *Medium Ævum* 56 (1987), 25–45.

——, 'Final -e and the Rhythmic Structure of the B-Verse in Middle English Alliterative Poetry', *Modern Philology* 86 (1988), 119–45.

——, 'The Shape of the B-Verse in Middle English Alliterative Poetry', *Speculum* 61 (1986), 564–92. [1986]

——, 'Strophic Patterns in Middle English Alliterative Poetry', *Modern Philology* 74 (1977), 223–47.

Ford, Alvin E. *La Vengeance de Nostre-Seigneur: The Old and Middle French Prose Versions: The Version of Japheth*, Studies and Texts 63 (Toronto, 1984).

Hamel, Mary, 'Arthurian Romance in Fifteenth-Century Lindsey: The Books of the Lords Welles', *Modern Language Quarterly* 51 (1990), 341–61.

——, '*The Siege of Jerusalem* as a Crusading Poem', *Journeys Toward God: Pilgrimage and Crusade*, ed. Barbara N. Sargent-Baur (Kalamazoo, 1992), pp. 177–94.

Hanna, Ralph, 'Contextualizing *The Siege of Jerusalem*', *Yearbook of Langland Studies* 6 (1992), 107–19.

——, 'Defining Middle English Alliterative Poetry', *The Endless Knot: Essays on Old and Middle English in Honor of Marie Borroff*, ed. M. Teresa Tavormina and R. F. Yeager (Cambridge, 1995), pp. 43–64.

Heawood, Edward, *Watermarks, Mainly of the 17th and 18th Centuries* (Hilversum, 1950).

Hebron, Malcolm, *The Medieval Siege: Theme and Image in Middle English Romance* (Oxford, 1997).

Hulbert, J. R., 'The Text of *The Siege of Jerusalem*', *Studies in Philology* 28 (1930), 602–12.

Jacobs, Nicholas, 'Alliterative Storms: A Topos in Middle English', *Speculum* 47 (1972), 695–719.

Jolliffe, P. S., *A Check-List of Middle English Prose Writings of Spiritual Guidance*, Subsidia Mediaevalia 2 (Toronto, 1974).

Kaluza, Max, 'Strophische Gliederung in der mittelenglischen rein alliterirenden Dichtung', *Englische Studien* 16 (1892), 169–80.

Kennedy, Ruth, ' "A Bird in Bishopswood": Some Newly-Discovered Lines of Alliterative Verse from the Late Fourteenth Century', *Medieval Literature and Antiquities: Studies in honour of Basil Cottle*, ed. Myra Stokes and T. L. Burton (Cambridge, 1987), pp. 71–87.

Kershaw, Ian, *Bolton Priory: The Economy of a Northern Monastery 1286–1325* (London, 1973).

Lawrence, R. F., 'Formula and Rhythm in *The Wars of Alexander*', *English Studies* 51 (1970), 97–112.

Lawton, David A., 'Alliterative Style', *A Companion to* Piers Plowman, ed. John A. Alford (Berkeley, 1988), pp. 223–49.

——, '*The Destruction of Troy* as Translation from Latin Prose: Aspects of Form and Style', *Studia Neophilologica* 52 (1980), 259–70. [1980a]

——, 'The Idea of Alliterative Poetry: Alliterative Meter and *Piers Plow-*

man', *Suche Werkis to Werche: Essays on* Piers Plowman *in Honor of David C. Fowler*, ed. Mícéal F. Vaughan (East Lansing, 1993), pp. 147–68.

——, 'Larger Patterns of Syntax in Middle English Unrhymed Alliterative Verse', *Neophilologus* 64 (1980), 604–18. [1980]

——, 'Middle English Alliterative Poetry: An Introduction', *Middle English Alliterative Poetry and its Literary Background*, ed. David A. Lawton (Cambridge, 1982), pp. 1–19, 125–29.

——, 'Titus Goes Hunting: The Poetics of Recreation and Revenge in *The Siege of Jerusalem*', *Individuality and Achievement in Middle English Poetry*, ed. O. S. Pickering (Cambridge, 1997), pp. 105–17.

The Middle English Prose Translation of Roger d'Argenteuil's Bible en françois, ed. Phyllis Moe, Middle English Texts 6 (Heidelberg, 1977).

Millar, Bonnie, *The Siege of Jerusalem in its Physical, Literary, and Historical Contexts* (Dublin, 2000).

Moe, Phyllis, 'The French Source of the Alliterative *Siege of Jerusalem*', *Medium Ævum* 39 (1970), 147–54.

Oakden, J. P., *Alliterative Poetry in Middle English*, 2 vols. (Manchester, 1930–35).

Pearsall, Derek, 'The Alliterative Revival: Origins and Social Backgrounds', Lawton 1982, pp. 34–53, 132–36.

——, *Old English and Middle English Poetry*, Routledge History of English Poetry 1 (London, 1977).

——, 'The Origins of the Alliterative Revival', *The Alliterative Tradition in the Fourteenth Century*, ed. Bernard S. Levy and Paul E. Szarmach (Kent OH, 1981), pp. 1–24.

Piccard, Gerhard, *Die Wasserzeichenkartei Piccard im Hauptstadtsarchiv Stuttgart: Findbuch*, currently 17 vols. (Stuttgart, 1961–).

Price, Patricia A., 'Integrating Time and Space: The Literary Geography of *Patience*, *Cleanness*, *The Siege of Jerusalem*, and *St Erkenwald*', *Medieval Perspectives* 11 (1996), 234–50.

Samuels, M. L., 'Langland's Dialect', *Medium Ævum* 44 (1985), 232–47, with absolutely necessary corrections at *Medium Ævum* 45 (1986), 40.

Schumacher, Karl, *Studien über den Stabreim in der mittelenglischen Alliterationsdichtung*, Bonner Studien zur englischen Philologie 11 (Bonn, 1914).

The Siege of Jerusalem in Prose, ed. Auvo Kurvinen, Mémoires de la Société Néophilologique de Helsinki 34 (Helsinki, 1969).

Spearing, A. C., *Readings in Medieval Poetry* (Cambridge, 1987).

Suzuki, Euchi, 'Notes on Lexical Substitution in *The Siege of Jerusalem*', *Philologia Anglia Essays Presented to Professor Yoshio Teresawa . . .*, ed. Kinshiro Oshitari (Tokyo, 1988), pp. 184–94.

Thompson, A. Hamilton, *History and Architectural Description of the Priory of St. Mary, Bolton-in-Wharfdale*, Thoresby Society 30 (Leeds, 1928).

Titus and Vespasian, or the Destruction of Jerusalem in Rhymed Couplets, ed. J. A. Herbert (London, 1905).

Turville-Petre, Joan, 'The Metre of *Sir Gawain and the Green Knight*', *English Studies* 57 (1976), 310–28.

Turville-Petre, Thorlac, *The Alliterative Revival* (Cambridge, 1977).

——, 'The Author of *The Destruction of Troy*', *Medium Ævum* 57 (1988), 264–69.

——, 'Editing the *Wars of Alexander*', *Manuscripts and Texts: Editorial Problems in Later Middle English Literature*, ed. Derek Pearsall (Cambridge, 1987), pp. 143–60.

——, 'Emendation on the Grounds of Alliteration in *The Wars of Alexander*', *English Studies* 61 (1980), 302–17.

Van Court, Elisa Narin, '*The Siege of Jerusalem* and Augustinian Historians: Writing about Jews in Fourteenth-Century England', *Chaucer Review* 29 (1995), 227–48.

Waldron, Ronald A., 'Oral-Formulaic Technique and Middle English Alliterative Poetry', *Speculum* 32 (1957), 792–804.

Wilson, Edward, 'John Clerk, Author of *The Destruction of Troy*', *Notes and Queries* 235 (1990), 391–96.

——, 'An Unpublished Alliterative Poem on Plant-Names from Lincoln College, Oxford, MS Lat. 129 (E)', *Notes and Queries* 224 (1979), 504–8.

THE TEXT OF
THE SIEGE OF JERUSALEM

In Tyberyus tyme, þe trewe emperour,   f. 1ᵛ
Sire Sesar hymsulf   seysed in Rome
Whyle Pylat was prouost   vndere þat prince riche
And Iewen iustice also   in Iude[e]s lond[e],

+ Herode vndere his emperie—   as heritage wolde   5
Kyng of Galile + ycalled—,   whan þat Crist deyed
þey Sesar sakles were   þat oft synne hatide,
þrow Pylat pyned he was   and put on þe rode.

A pyler py3t was doun   vpon þe playn erþe,
His body bonden þerto   [and] beten with scourgis: 10
Whyppes of quyrboyle   [vm]bywente his white sides
Til + al on rede blode ran   as rayn [i]n þe strete.

Suþ stoked + on a stole   with styf mannes hondis,
Blyndfelled + as a be   and boffetis hym ra3te;

The introductory rubric: none in LP, Hic InCepit Distruccio Ierarusalem Quomodo Titus
et vespasianus Obsederunt et distruxerunt Ierusalem et vidicarunt mortem domini Ihesu
cristi A, Incipit destruccio de Ierusalem per Titum et Vespasianum U, Here bygynnith (*om.*
C) þe sege of Ierusalem (adds and how it was destroyed E) DEC   1 In][ ]n C   Tyberyus]
tyberies DE   þe] that AU   2 Sire] When P, Sere E   seysed] was cesed (sessede A) PA,
sesed C   3 Whyle] The while þat A   was prouost] profest was P   þat] þe P   *no cesura* C
4 And] An E   Iewen] demed P, Iwyn ('hey' *later*?) D, Iewes C   Iewen . . . also] also Iustece
of I⟨*torn*⟩ A   also] *om.* P   in] of þe P, *torn* A, of UDEC   Iudees] DE, Iudeus LC *Kölbing-
Day*, Iues P, *torn* A, iudee U   londe] UDEC, londis LP *Kölbing-Day*, *torn* A   *no cesura* C
5 Herode] UC, herodes L *Kölbing-Day*, Erode P, And herode ADE   vndere] in DE   his]
om. P, *torn* A, þat DE   emperie] Emperoure P, *torn* A, empire UDE, empere C
6 ycalled] PAUDEC *Kölbing-Day*, was ycalled L   deyed] deyd D, deyde EC
7 þey] If D   sakles were] is sakles D, gyltles were E   þat oft] *torn* A, that myche E, he
þat C   8 þrow]3itt thurghe A, þan D   pyned] peyned E   pyned . . . rode] *torn* A   pyned
he was] hym pynid D   he] has E, *om.* C   9 py3t] phytgh P   py3t was doun] doun was
ypight UDE, was dowun pyght C   was] was thare A   vpon] on PDEC   vpon . . . erþe] al of
grey marble U   playn] plate A   10 body] bodoy C   body bonden] body was bounde E
and] PAUDEC, *om.* L *Kölbing-Day*   11 Whyppes] withe whippes A   quyrboyle]
wirebule P   *vmbywente] bywente LUDEC *Kölbing-Day*, vmbe P, abowte A   sides] sythes C
12 Til] To P   al] PA, he al LUDEC *Kölbing-Day*   al . . . blode] on (al on E) reed blode he
UDEC   rayn] water C   in] PAUDEC *Kölbing-Day*, on L   *no cesura* C   13 Suþ] And
sythen AUC   stoked] strekyn A, sette UDEC   on] PAUDEC, hym on L *Kölbing-Day*
stole] sete C   mannes] men PD, mens AU *Kölbing-Day* n   14 Blyndfelled] And
blyndefelde UDEC   as] PAUDEC, hym as L *Kölbing-Day*   and] *om.* PUDEC   hym] he
UDEC   ra3te] cau3te E

'ȝif þou be prophete of pris,   prophecie', þey sayde,   15
'Whiche [berne] hereaboute   bo[bb]ed þe laste'?

A þrange þornen croune   + þraste on his hed,
Vmbecasten + with a cry   and on + croys slowen.
For al þe harme þat he hadde   hasted he noȝt
On hem þe vyleny to venge   þat his veynys brosten,   20

Bot ay taried on þe tyme   ȝif þey tourne wolde;
ȝaf hem space þat hym spilide,   þey hit spedde lyte,
xl. wynter + as Y fynde   and no fewere ȝyrys
+ Or princes presed in hem   þat hym to pyne wroȝt.

Til hit tydde on a tyme   [on] Tytus of Rome   25
þat alle Gascoyne + gate   and Gyan þe noble

.   .   .   .

Whyle noye n[eȝ]et hym [t]o   in Neroes tyme.
He hadde a malady vnmeke   [in]myd[dis] þe face;   30

15 prophete] profett PU   pris] pryse now A   þey sayde] vs now P   16 berne] PAUD *Kölbing-Day*, man LEC   hereaboute] of þe borde P, at this borde now A bobbed] UE *Kölbing-Day* n, bolled L *Kölbing-Day*, buffett PA, buffetid D, bobette C 17 A] And sythen a A   þrange] strange P, kene A, stronge UDC, scharp E   þornen croune] croune of thorne (thornes E) PAE   þraste] throngon P, was þraste L *Kölbing-Day*, thay thrange A, they thriste UDEC   his] hy E   hed] heued PAU   18 Vmbecasten] Vmkestyn P, They cast UDC, and made E   with] P, hym with LA *Kölbing-Day*, vp UDC, *om.* E   a] a grete UDC, a wel gret E   and] that him UDEC   on] PAUDEC, on a L *Kölbing-Day*   slowen] done P, dede E   19 For] And for C   þe] those A   harme] harmes PA   hasted] yit hasted UDEC   hasted he] he hastede hym A   20 On hem] *om.* E   þe] *om.* P, that AUDC   þat ... brosten] but mekeliche it suffrede E   21 ay] euere DC   taried] tarieth D   on] ouer *Kölbing-Day* (*corr. Kölbing-Day* n), of P, he AD, *om.* UEC   tourne] amende hem E   22 ȝaf] And gaf PE, And lent A   þat hym spilide] of mendement E   spedde] spede A   lyte] litill PAUDC   23 as] PAUE *Kölbing-Day*, was as L, *om.* DC   and] faithly U, feithfully D, trewly C   no] neuer a day E fewere] faere A   fewere ȝyrys] lesse tyme P, lesse UDEC   24 *line om.* P   Or] AUDEC *Kölbing-Day*, Our L   princes] he oghte put A, he (he þe D) prince (veniaunce E, ponyshynge C) UDEC   presed in hem] at that prynce of þat pepill A, on hem put (took E) UDEC   þat ... wroȝt] forsothe y ȝow telle E   hym] hem D   to] þose A, *om.* UDC pyne] paynes A   25 Til] *three-line capital* A, ¶ *precs.* D   tydde] betyde A, tytte E   on] UDE, þat LPA *Kölbing-Day*, þat oon C   26 gate] PAUDEC *Kölbing-Day*, gaten (?) L 27 *line om.* LPAUDEC   28 *line om.* LPAUDEC   29 Whyle] Whilke P, A A Whyle ... hym] He was desesed ful sore E   neȝet] PADC, noyet L *Kölbing-Day*, neght U to in] PUDC, / in to L, nere A, in E *Kölbing-Day*   Neroes] Nero P, nerose (s *an alteration*) A   30 He] That UDC   He hadde] with E   vnmeke] *cesura precs.* L, vnmete A   inmyddis] PUDC, amyd L, in the myddis of A, amyddis E *Kölbing-Day*   þe] his ADEC

þe lyppe lyþ on a lumpe   lyuered on þe cheke.
So a canker vnclene   hit clochced togedres.

Also his fadere of flesche   [a] ferly bytide:
A bikere of waspen bees   bredde [i]n his nose,
Hyued vp [i]n his hed—   he hadde hem of ȝouþe—   35
And Waspasian was caled   þe waspene bees after.   f. 2ʳ

Was neuer syknes sorere   þan þis sire þoled,
For in a liter he lay   laser at Rome:
Out of Galace was gon   to glade hym a stounde—
[Of] þat cuþe he was king,   þey he care þolede.   40

Nas þer no leche vpon lyue   þis lordes couþ helpe,
Ne no grace growyng   to gayne here grym sores.

.   .   .   .

.   .   .   .

Now was þer on N[a]than,   Neymes sone of Grecys,   45
þat souȝt oft ouer þe se   fram cyte to oþer,

31 þe¹] His AUDEC   lyþ] laye PAUDEC   lyuered on] and cleuyd to E   þe²] his
AUDEC   32 So] Als PDEC, with A, *om.* U   hit] *om.* A   hit . . . togedres] enclyned
(enclosyd E) he (hid ? D, it E) had UDEC   clochced] clunchyd P, clotherede A   33 Also]
And also A, *om.* UDC, And E   fadere of flesche] fleschely fader P   of flesche] Vespasian
UDEC   a] PAD, is L *Kölbing-Day, om.* UEC   ferly] wurderlyche E   *no cesura* C
34 bikere] beke P?AUC, swarm E   waspen] waspes PC, waspe A, waspes and (and of E)
UDE   bees] *om.* C   in] PAUDEC, on L *Kölbing-Day*   nose] nese PA, nase UD   *no cesura* C
35 Hyued] þat hewen P, Heued A, and were heuyd E   vp in] UDC, vpon L *Kölbing-Day*, of
P, vp heghe in A, in E   he . . . ȝouþe] oft had he thoght P, while þat he was ȝong E   hem] þam
AU   of] in his D   ȝouþe] thoght C   *no cesura* C   36 Waspasian] Waspasius P, Vespasian
UDC   was] is UC   þe . . . after] bycause of the (his C) waspes UDEC   waspene] waspe PA
no cesura C   37 *lines 37–40 om.* P   *line order 41–44, 37–40* UDEC   Was] Ther was E
neuer] no DE   sorere] so sore UDEC   þan] that UDEC   þis] that A, eny UDE, euer C
sire] man E   þoled] suffrid EC, folwed U   38 in] on UDEC   a] *int.* A   liter] lepir
AUDEC *Kölbing-Day* n   laser at] yit thereto in UDEC   *no cesura* C   39 Out of] Vnto A,
For out of UDC, Of E   was] he was AE, he UDC   gon] kom UDC   gon . . . stounde] *om.,*
line fused with next E   *no cesura* C   40 Of] UDC, for in LA *Kölbing-Day*   Of . . . was] *om.,*
line fused with prec. E   king] lord E   þolede] hadde E, suffered C   *no cesura* C   41 Nas]
Was PD   Nas þer] Thare was AEC   þer] *om.* P   no] *om.* U, non E   leche] lechis A   vpon]
on C   vpon lyue] on the londe E   þis] those A   couþ] to UDC   helpe] hele UDEC
42 Ne] Nor C   no] *om.* PUDEC   grace] gresese P, grise A, gresse UDEC   growyng] appon
grownde A, growyng on grounde / UDEC   to] that UDEC   gayne] graythe A, gayned UD,
vayled C   gayne . . . sores] hem helpe myȝte E   here] for þair P   grym] grete P, *om.* UDC
43 *line om.* LPAUDEC   44 *line om.* LPAUDEC   45 Now] than AE   was . . . Nathan]
of Natan to mene P   Nathan] Nat(h)ane AUDEC *Kölbing-Day*, nothan L   Neymes]
Nayhym A, Naym D   Grecys] grece PAUDE *Kölbing-Day*, greeke C   *no cesura* E
46 souȝt oft] *trs.* UDC, ofte passyd E   souȝt oft ouer] orewent on P   oft] *om.* A   ouer] *om.* E
se] salte see A   fram] fra PA   to] till AUDC

Knewe contreys fele,   kyngdomes manye,
And was a marener myche   and [a] marchaunt boþe.

Sensteus + of Surye   sent hym to Rome
To þe athel emperour   an eraunde fram þe Iewes—   50
Caled Nero by name—   þat hym to noye wroʒt:
Of his tribute to telle   þat þey withtake wolde.

Nathan toward Nero   nome on his way
Ouer þe Grekys grounde   myd þe grym yþes,
An heye setteþ þe sayl   ouer þe [salt] water   55
And with a dromound on þe deep   dr[yueþ] on [swythe].

þe wolco[n] wanned anon   and þe water skeweþ;
Cloudes clateren + on [lofte]   as þey cleue wolde;
þe racke myd a rede wynde   roo[f] on þe myddel
And sone sette on þe se   out of þe souþ syde.   60

---

47 Knewe] He knewe AUEC   contreys, kyngdomes] *trs.* D   fele] full fele AD, manye
E, *add* / and PAUDEC   kyngdomes] kymdomys E, kyndomes C   manye] full Many A,
bothe E   48 And¹] He A   a] *om.* P   myche] of Mighte A   a²] A *Duggan* 1988:127,
om. LPUDEC *Kölbing-Day*   boþe] in fere UDC, also E   49 Sensteus] Sensceus
Kölbing-Day (*corr. Kölbing-Day* n), Cytesens P, Systenis A, Systynes D, Senscyvs C   of]
PUDEC, out of L, of (*expunged and lined*) owt of A   *no cesura* C   50 To] Vnto A   þe
athel] Nero the (þat C) UDEC   athel] hetill P, hath⟨*torn*⟩ A   an . . . fram] *torn* A, in
message (massage C) of UDEC   fram] fra PA   þe²] *om.* PUDEC   *no cesura* C
51 *line om.* E   Caled] That w⟨*torn*⟩ A, That (þei DC) cald him UDC   hym] þaim PUDC,
torn A   to] *om.* PDUC *Kölbing-Day* n, *torn* A   noye] anoye U   52 þey] *torn* A, they
him U, he hem E   withtake] take P, *torn* A, paye UDE, paye it C   wolde] nolde UDEC
53 Nathan] *four-line capital* A, ¶ *precs.* D, This Nathan UDEC   toward] to PUDEC,
vnto A   nome on] takyn hase A, nam the UC, toke þe DE   his] next UDEC   *no cesura* C
54 Ouer] Of D, On C   Grekys] grekissh DEC   grounde] see UDEC   myd] on P, with
UDEC   myd . . . yþes] graythande full ʒerne A   grym] grete E   yþes] waghes PUDEC
no cesura C   55 An heye] and sone E   setteþ] set þai PD, sett he AUC, reysed vp E
þe¹] *om.* P, his C   sayl] ceyl E   ouer] on DC   þe²] those A   salt] PAUDEC *Kölbing-*
Day, wode L   water] watirs A   *no cesura* C   56 And] *om.* PA   on¹] in UDEC   þe]
om. UEC   dryueþ] PC, drof L *Kölbing-Day*, he draue A, dryued UE, drivyn D   on²]
ouer P, in D   swythe] PUDEC, faste L *Kölbing-Day*, full swythe A   *no cesura* C
57 þe¹] þan D   wolcon] AUDEC *Kölbing-Day*, wolcom L, wynde P   wanned anon]
wayned ouer P, wexe full wanne A, wawes onone UD   skeweþ] bolnes P, flowis D,
flowyd E   58 Cloudes . . . lofte] The cloudes al toclaterd (toclateren C) UDEC
clateren] claterd PA   *on lofte] on loude P, one the lande A, gon L *Kölbing-Day*   cleue]
clyue U, toclve DE   wolde] sulde P   59 myd] with PUDEC, and A   a] the ADEC
roof] P, roos LAUDEC *Kölbing-Day*   on] in AUDEC   myddel] myddes PAUDEC
60 sone] sonn P   sette] settes P, sett thaym A   on] ouer U   out of] at P, on UDC, in E
þe²] *om.* E   syde] weste P, clene A, ende E   *no cesura* E

[Hit] blewe on þe brode se, bolned vp harde;
Nathannys naue anon on [þe] norþ dryueþ.
So þe wedour and þe wynd on þe water metyn
þat alle + hurled on an hepe þat þe helm 3emyd.

Nathan flatte for ferde and ful vnder hacchys, 65
Lete þe wedour and þe wynde wor[ch]e as h[em] lyked;
þe schip scher vpon schore, schot froward Rome
Toward [c]ostes vncouþ [kayrande on] þe yþes,

Rapis [o]n radly vmbe ragged tourres.
þe brode sail at o brayd tobresteþ atwynne: 70
þat on ende of þe sschip was ay toward heuen, f. 2ᵛ
þat oþer doun in þe deep as [30] drenche wolde.

Ouer wilde wawes he wende as alle walte scholde,
Stroke stremes þrow yn stormes and wyndes;

61 Hit] PAUDEC, om. L Kölbing-Day on] at P, that U, and DE se] see and AC
bolned] bolmyd E vp] sa A harde] faste PA 62 Nathannys] And Natan P, that
Nathan A, Nathan UDEC naue] nayme son PUDC, hym allone A, þo E anon] om.
PAD, cesura precs. C on] of D þe] PAUDEC Kölbing-Day Duggan 1988:127, om. L
63 wedour] waw P, whedirs A on] and A, an D metyn] walkys D 64 hurled] PA,
hurtled LU Kölbing-Day, hit hurlid DC, it hurtlyd E an hepe] hepis A, hepe UDEC
3emyd] solde 3eme A, kepte E After this line, D repeats line 56 in the same form as previously
65 Nathan] And Nathan UDC flatte] fled P, plate downe A flatte . . . ful] aferd tho /
flewe U, for fere flw (tho / flew E) DE, aferd þanne / and fledde C and ful] om. P
vnder] vndirneth P, vnþur C hacchys] þe heche P, hechis A, þe hacches DC
66 Lete] And lete UEC wedour] water P wedour and þe wynde] wynde and the
wawes UDE, wynde and þe weþur C (last word in margin) worche] PAUDEC, worþe L
Kölbing-Day hem] PA, hit L Kölbing-Day, they UDEC lyked] wolde UDEC no
cesura C 67 scher . . . froward] turned a3enward / and nothyng toward E -on] a- D
schot] and schotte AU, and shete DC froward] fra P, frawardes A, fromward D
68 Toward] To þe P, Vpon UDEC costes vncouþ] PAUDEC (vncouþ] vnknowe E), trs.
L Kölbing-Day *kayrande on] kayrande full A, caried hem UDC, þanne caryed E, yerne
on P, keuereþ L Kölbing-Day þe yþes] he hyes P, swythe A, the wawes UDC, hem E no
cesura C 69 Rapis] Ropes AUEC, þan ropis D *on radly] vnradly LP Kölbing-Day,
ful radly D, full rathely A, ful redely UEC vmbe] apon P, om. AD, thanne UEC ragged
tourres] raschedde in peces A, railed (racyd DE, reyked C) in (on D) sundre UDEC no
cesura C 70 sail] sayles C at] on P o] a PAUDEC tobresteþ] brosten P, brystis
A, in sundre brast U, brast D, brestyth E, brekyn C atwynne] in two PA, atwey U, yn
sundur D, in tweyne E no cesura C 71 of þe sschip] om. PA was] fro A ay] þan
P, þan vp A, euere D heuen] þe heuen PA no cesura C 72 þat] the E doun in]
ende in U, donward to E as . . . drenche] drenche (drowne C) as she (hit DEC) UDEC
30] she U, alle LA Kölbing-Day, he P, hit DEC drenche] droune P wolde] sulde PADE
73 lines 73-74 om. UDEC Ouer] Ouer those A he] thay A wende] went PA alle]
he P scholde] wolde P 74 Stroke] Strake ouer þe P, Starke A Kölbing-Day þrow]
and stronge A yn] cesura fols. L, om. PA

With mychel langour atte laste,   as our lord wolde   75
Alle was born at a by[r]   to Burdewes hauene.

By þat were bernes atte banke;   barouns and kny3tes
And [citezeins] of þe sy3t   selcouþ [hem] þo3t
þat euer barge oþer bot   or berne vpon lyue
Vnpersched passed hadde,   þe peryles were so many.   80

þey token hym to Titus   for he þe tonge couþe,
And he fraynes how fer   þe flode hadde [hem] yferked.
'Sire, out of Surre',   he seide, 'y am come,
To Nero sondisman sent   þe se[ign]our of Rome

Fram Sensteus his seriant   with certayn leteres,   85
þat is iustise and iuge   o[uer þe] Iewe[s al]le.
Me were leuer at þat londe—   lord lene þat Y were—
þan alle þe gold oþer good   þat euer go[me] a[ught]e'.

---

75 langour] anger PUC, desese E   atte] at U   wolde] it wolde C   no cesura C
76 was] is UC   was born] boune P   at] one A   byr] PAC Kölbing-Day, by L, birth
U, brayde DE   to] till P, into D   Burdewes] burdeus P, burdieux AUDE, burdews C
no cesura C   77 By] Bot by A, ¶ precs. D   By þat] Thanne UDEC   were] the A,
were there UDEC   bernes] om. DE, folke C   atte] one the AC, vpon U, on D, on a E
banke] bankes AU   barouns] bothe barouns A   kny3tes] meny oþer biernes D   no
cesura C   E adds line: walkyng vpon strounde / as þey ywunt were   78 And] The
UDEC   citezeins] PAUDC Kölbing-Day, suþ L, peple E   þe] þat AUC   sy3t] Cite
PDE   selcouþ] full selcouthe A, wunder E   hem] AUDC Kölbing-Day Duggan
1988:127, om. LP, they E   þo3t] hadde E   no cesura C   79 berne] beerde U, body
D, man EC   vpon] on P   no cesura C   80 Vnpersched . . . hadde] Passed had
(hath D) vnperisshed UDE   Vnpersched . . . peryles] Passed hadde þo perelles
vnperysched C   passed hadde] trs. A   hadde] om. P   were] om. D, þey were C
many] fele UC, thik DE   no cesura C   81 þey] Till þay A   hym] thaym AUDC,
hym tho E   þe] þair PAU, that E   tonge] tonges A   couþe] knew PAU   no cesura C
82 he] om. P, he thaym AUDC Kölbing-Day, he hym E   fraynes] frayned PAUDEC
flode] flodes C, flode hem U   hem] ADC Kölbing-Day n Duggan 1988:127, om. LU
Kölbing-Day (although cf. prec. U variant), hym P   yferked] wayned P, drevyn A, borne
UDEC   A adds line: That spake Nathan anone for noyede was he mekill   83 Sire
. . . Surre] Out of surry sere E   he] þei D   y am come] / sailed haue we (y E) nowe
(swiþe DE) UDEC   come] sent to Nero A   E adds line: and meche wo in þe water /
þe wynd hath me wrought   84 To Nero] om. A (at end of prec. line)   sondisman]
Sandis by me aren A, om. UDEC   sent] cesura precs. L   þe] to þe PA, am I nowe / the
(om. D) UDEC   seignour] UDEC Kölbing-Day, senatour L, se(nu)r? P, Seny3oures A
no cesura C   85 Fram] Fra PAEC   Sensteus] Sisteus P, Systenis A, Systiens D,
Sencyus C Kölbing-Day (corr. Kölbing-Day n)   seriant] seruant UDEC   certayn] many
straunge U   86 line om. DE   ouer . . . alle] PA, of (of the UC Duggan) Iewen lawe
LUC Duggan 1988:127   no cesura C   87 lines 87–88 om. UDEC   were] hade A
at] with P   londe] om. PA   lene] lenged PA Kölbing-Day   88 oþer] and the A
oþer good] on þe grounde P   gome aughte] A, god made LP Kölbing-Day

þe kyng into conseyl   calleþ hym sone
And saide, 'canste þou any cure   or craft vpon erþe   90
To softe þe grete sore   þat sitteþ on my cheke?
And Y schal þe redly rewarde   and to Rome sende'.

Nathan nyckes hym with nay,   sayde he non couþe:
'Bot were þou, kyng, in þat kuþþe   þer [as] Crist deyed,
þer is a + worlich wif,   a womman ful clene,   95
þat haþ softyng and salue   for eche sore out'.

'Telle me tyt', quod Titus,   'and þe schal tyde better,
What medecyn is most   þat þat may vseþ?
Wheþer gommes oþer graces   or any goode drenches
Oþer chauntementes or charmes?   Y charge þe to say'.   100

'Nay, non of þo', quod Nathan,   'bot now wole Y [telle].
þer was a lede in our londe   while he lif hadde
Preued for a prophete   þrow preysed dedes
And born in Bethleem one by   of a burde schene,

89 þe] ¶ precs. D   into] vnto AU, into his E   calleþ] called PA, thanne called UDEC
no cesura C   90 And saide] Says P   And . . . þou] Kan (kennest C) thow quod he
UDEC   canste þou] can you P, couthe thou A   cure or craft] craft or (of D) cures (cure
C) UDEC   or] thurgh P   vpon] on UDE   no cesura C   91 To] that myghte A
softe] ese C   þe grete] this A, this grym UEC, this ginly D   no cesura C   92 And¹]
om. PUDC   schal] sulde PA, wille UDC   þe redly] trs. PA   þe redly rewarde] redely
rewarde the UC   redly] richely A, radly D, om. E   93 nyckes] nykkede AUDC
nyckes . . . nay] seyde the E   sayde] says P, and sayd A, that UDEC   94 þou] you P
kyng] kyd PA, knowyn UDEC   in þat kuþþe] for a knyghte A   þat] om. P   kuþþe] court
D, lond EC   as] PAUDC, þat LE Kölbing-Day   no cesura C   95 þer] for þere E
*worlich] Kölbing-Day, worthly U, worldlich L, worthy PDEC, wirchipfull A   wif]
wenche A   a²] and a A   ful] om. P   96 softyng and] souerayne P, softyngnynge and
A, a soft thing and UC, a softyng D, a softnyng E   eche] alkyn P, alle A, euery UDEC
sore out] sore P, sare hurtis A, sore on erþe D   no cesura C   After this line, D repeats line
91 in the same form as previously, except here reads þis grymly   97 Telle] Now tell P,
Now tell thou A, ¶ precs. D   tyt] om. PAEC, titely D   þe] you P, thou UE   tyde] fare E
better] þe better PAUDEC   no cesura C   98 medecyn is] Medecyns A   medecyn is
most] is þe mooste medicyne E   is most] trs. UDC   þat²] þe EC   may] mayden C
99 Wheþer] Wheter U   gommes] gom P   graces] grese P, grees U, grasse DC   any]
other P, ells A   drenches] drynkes PAUDEC   no cesura C   100 Oþer] om. AUDEC
chauntementes] Enchauntementz UDEC   chauntementes or charmes] charme or
chauntement P, Charmes or Enchantemetis A   y . . . say] or what maner salues E
101 Nay] om. PE, Noght UDC, ¶ precs. D   non] one UDC   þo] þese PUEC, thase A
wole y] I wille the UDEC   telle] PAUDEC Kölbing-Day, sey L   102 lede] lorde PD,
man E   londe] lawe UC   while] while þat A   lif hadde] lyve (leeue E) myght DE
103 þrow] for his P, thorowe A   þrow . . . dedes] in (and in E) dedes wele (om. E) to (om.
DE) Preise (praysid DE) UDEC   104 And] om. DEC   one] cesura precs. L, vs AUDC,
vs faste E   one by] om. P   burde schene] clene mayde E   schene] clene P

And 30 a mayde vnmarred   þat neuer man touched,   105
f. 3ʳ As clene as clef   þ[at] cristalle [of] sprynges.
Without hosebondes helpe   saue þe Holy Goste
A kyng and a knaue child   30 conceyued at ere;

A [taknyng] of þe Trinyte   touched hire hadde,
þre persones in o place   preued togedres.   110
Eche grayn is o god   and o god bot alle,
And alle þre ben bot one   as eldres vs tellen.

þe first is þe Fadere   þat fourmed was neuer,
þe secunde is þe Sone   of his sede growyn;
þe þridde in heuen myd hem   is þe Holy Goste,   115
Neþer merked ne made   bot mene fram hem passyþ.

Alle ben þey endeles   and eu[en] of o my3t
And weren [inwardly] endeles +   [o]r þe [erþe] + byg[a]n:
As sone was þe Sone   as þe self Fadere,
þe [heye] Holy Goste   with hem hadde þey euer.   120

þe secunde persone þe Sone   sent was to erþe
To take careynes kynde   of a clene mayde;

105 *line om.* E   a] *om.* A   a . . . vnmarred] vnmarred a mayde UDC   mayde] Mayden A
no cesura C   106 As¹] But als UDC, And as E   clene] cleer E   as²] *add* þe PAUDEC
þat] AC, þer LPUD *Kölbing-Day*, þere þat E   of] A *Duggan* 1988:127, *om.* LPDE *Kölbing-*
Day, in UC   adds line E: or as þe `sunne' on þe morwe / whanne it furst schyneth
107 hosebondes] hosbande P   saue] bot PAUC, but of D, but be E   108 knaue] knawe A,
man C   30] *om.* PAUDEC   at] at hir PUDC, at the A, be her E   ere] here E   *no cesura* C
109 A] The E   taknyng] P, touche L *Kölbing-Day*, troche A, trouth UDEC   þe] *om.* E
110 þre] the E   o] a PA   *no cesura* C   111 Eche] Ilke P, And ilke a AU, And eche a DEC
o¹] *om.* P, a AUC   o²] a P, bot a A   god²] greyne U, *om.* C   bot] ere A, is UDC, been E   *no*
cesura C   112 And] *om.* P   And . . . one] this is my beleeue E   þre] *om.* D   ben] nis U,
is C   bot one] o god D   eldres] clerkes UEC   vs] me E   tellen] techen UE   *no cesura* C
113 þe²] *om.* A   114 þe . . . Sone] The (His C) sone is the secund UDC   his sede] hym C
sede] syde PUDE   growyn] sawen A   *no cesura* C   115 þridde] *add* is PUDC   in . . .
hem] *om.* E   myd] / with PAUDC   hem] hym P, thaym A, *adds* þat C   is þe] þe hegh P, the
UD   Goste] *adds* / with hem euere dwellyng E   116 Neþer] Nouther PU, Nother C
Neþer merked] That nowþer Merked es A   ne] no P, nor U   mene] evyn DE   fram] fra
PAUEC   passyþ] passid D   117 endeles] a god A   euen] PAEC, euer L *Kölbing-Day*,
alle UD   o] a PA   *no cesura* C   118 *line om.* P, *line order* 119–20, 118 DE   And] Alle A
inwardly endeles] A, endeles euer L *Kölbing-Day*, *om.* UDEC   or] UDEC *Kölbing-Day*,
byfor L   or þe] was neuer nane A   *erþe] world LUD, *om.* A, wurld E, worlde C   *bygan]
bygonnyne A, was bygonne L *Kölbing-Day*, was (/ was U, was / E) euer bygonne UDEC   *no*
cesura C   119 As¹] Also E   as²] als was A   *no cesura* C   120 þe] And the UDEC
heye] DE, *om.* LPAUC *Kölbing-Day*   Goste] also A   hem] *cesura fols.* L, þaim for soth P,
thaym A   121 persone] *adds* es A   þe Sone] he P   sent] that sent A   to] to þe P, till A   *no*
cesura C   122 take] cacche D   careynes] careman P, carefull manes A, mans UDEC
kynde] *add* here UC   a] that E   clene mayde] *trs.* C   mayde] mayden PADC   *no cesura* C

+ So vnknowen he came   caytifes to helpe
And wroȝt wondres ynowe +   tille he wo driede.

Wyne [o]f water he wroȝt   at o word ene,   125
Ten lasares at a logge   he leched at enys,
Pyned myd [þe] p[a]l[sy]   he putte [hem] to hele,
And ded men fro þe deþ   [ilka] day rered;

Croked and cancred   he keuered hem alle,
Boþ þe dombe and þe deue,   myd his dere wordes;   130
Dide myracles + mo   þan Y in mynde haue—
Nis no clerk with countours   couþe aluendel rekene.

Fyf þousand of folke,   is fer[ly] to here,
With two fisches he fedde   and fif ber[ly] loues
þat eche freke hadde his fulle,   and ȝit ferre leued   135
Of b[att]e[s] and of broken mete   b[erel]e[p]es twelue.

þer suwed hym [o]f [o sor]te   s[euen]ty and twey:
To do what he dempte   disciples were [c]ho[s]en.

123 So] PUDC, and so LAE *Kölbing-Day* came] was comen vs A helpe] helyn DE *no
cesura* C   124 ynowe] PUDEC, ynowe ay LA *Kölbing-Day* tille] to P wo] deth C
driede] suffred UDEC   125 of . . . wroȝt] PAUDEC, he wroȝt of water L *Kölbing-Day*,
adds / al U wroȝt] made E o] a PAUC word ene] woreden P ene] one A, *om.* U, evyn
DEC   126 at] wiþ D logge] loke PAUDEC he leched] *trs.* P leched] helid DC enys]
ones PAUDEC   127 Pyned] thase þat pynede ware A, The pyned UD, peynyng E, The
payned C myd] with P, in AUDEC þe palsy] PUDC, piles L, parilsye A *Kölbing-Day*,
palseye E hem] PA *Duggan* 1988:127, *om.* L *Kölbing-Day*, in- UDEC   128 And ded] þe
dolwyn P fro] from U *ilka] yche a C, euer ilke A *Duggan* 1988:127, eche LPUDE
Kölbing-Day rered] he raysed PAUDC, areysed E   129 Croked and cancred] *trs. sbs.* A
he] *om.* P keuered] cured UDEC hem] he P, also E alle] full clene A   130 Boþ] *om.*
UDEC þe dombe and þe deue] *trs. sbs.* UDEC (dombe] dounbe E), *adds* men U myd] with
PAUDEC wordes] werkes P, worde C   131 Dide] ȝitt did he A, He did of UC, And ded
of D, He dede L mo] PAUDEC, many mo L in mynde haue] haue in mynde UC
132 Nis] þar es (nis U) PUDEC, Es nowþer A no] *om.* UE clerk with countours] counter'
ne (nor UC) clerke PAUDEC couþe] þat couth PA, can DC, that can E aluendel] þaim all
P, the halfe A, hem UDC, *om.* E rekene] rede P, *add* all UDEC, *adds* hem alle E
133 þousand] thowsandez A is] was P, *om.* UE, it is C ferly] PAUDE *Kölbing-Day* n
Duggan 1988:128, ferre L *Kölbing-Day*, meruayle C, *adds* is U, *adds* it is E here] telle A
134 two] thre A he] he þam A berly] PAUDEC *Duggan* 1988:128, bere L *Kölbing-Day*
135 þat] and PC, so þat E eche] ilke a AU, yche a C freke] man EC his fulle] the fulle U,
ynowgh C ȝit] *om.* AUDEC ferre] was P, forthir was A, ferther ouer UDC, more ouer E
leued] lyvid D   136 battes] UDE, brede LPA *Kölbing-Day*, bettes C of²] *om.* PD
berelepes] P, basscketes LU *Kölbing-Day*, basketes full ADC, lepys ful E   137 þer] Sone A
suwed hym] *trs.* A of] PAUDEC, out of L *Kölbing-Day* o] DE, an L *Kölbing-Day*, a PA,
one UC sorte] PE, cite L *Kölbing-Day*, sekte A, sute UD *Kölbing-Day* n, assent C seuenty]
PAUDEC *Kölbing-Day*, sixty L twey] mo P   138 To . . . dempte] þose all till hym his P
what] alle that A, os UEC, þat D (*illeg.*, *perhaps* as?) were] has he P, whare A, *om.* UDEC
chosen] PADC, hoten L *Kölbing-Day*, ichone UE

Hem to citees he sende   his sawes to preche,
Ay by two and by two   til hy [a]twynne were.   140

Hym suwed + of anoþer [sor]te   semeliche twelue,
f. 3ᵛ   Pore men and noȝt prute,   apposteles were hoten
þat of c[h]ay[tyf]es he ches   h[is] churche to encresche,
þe outwale of þis worlde,   [and] þis were her names:

Peter, Iames and Ion   and Iacob þe ferþe;   145
+ þe fifþe of his felawys   Phelip was hoten.
þe sixte Symond was caled,   and þe seueþ [after]
Bertholomewe, `þat´ his bone   neuer breke nolde.

þe eyȝt man was Mathu   þat is myche yloued;
Tadde and Tomas—   here ben ten euen,   150
And Andreu þe elleueþ   þat auntred hym [ofte]
Byfor princes to preche,   was Petr[e]s broþer.

þe laste man was vnlele   and luþer of his dedis,
Iudas þat Ihesu +   to þe Iewes solde.

139 Hem] þat PA, That he UDEC   to] to the A   he] *om.* UDEC   140 Ay]
Euere DE   til . . . atwynne] his wordes to schewen P   hy] alle UC, *om.* E   *atwynne
were] *trs.* L *Kölbing-Day*, ware twelue makede A, were (were all D) disseuered UDC, alle
departyd E   141 of] PAUDEC, out of L   sorte] PDE, cite L *Kölbing-Day*, soyte A,
sute U, sent C   semeliche] semely A, fulliche E   twelue] tweffe P   142 Pore]
Pure A   and] *om.* UDEC   noȝt] nogh C   prute] *adds* þat P   were] they UDEC
hoten] calde P, highten UDEC   143 þat] *om* P, *add* he AU   of chaytyfes] and
þaim P   chaytyfes] D, cayftes L, kaytefes AUE *Kölbing-Day*, pore kynreden C   he]
om. AU   his] UDEC *Duggan* 1986:589, holy LP *Kölbing-Day*, fro holy A   churche]
kyrke PA   to] forto P   encresche] maynetyni P, fell synn A, fulfille UDC, rule E
144 þe outwale] Thurgh vales P, That (these E) wyde walked UDEC   of] in UDEC
þis¹] þe PDEC, *om.* U   and] A *Duggan* 1988:127, *om.* LPUDEC *Kölbing-Day*   þis²]
thus C   were] were UC, ware A   her] he C   145 Iames] Iacob U   Iacob] Iames
UE   ferþe] lasse E   146 þe] PAUDEC, and þe L   fifþe] firste A   his] *om.* P,
the UC, her D, þat E   felawys] folouers P, felawrede UD, felaschipe EC   was hoten]
he hight UDEC   147 sixte] *adds* man A   Symond was] *trs.* A, hiȝte symond E
was] is UDC   caled] *om.* AE   after] UDEC, eke LP *Kölbing-Day*, than A
148 Bertholomewe] Bathillmewe A, barthemew E   his] es PC   bone] boune PA, hest
U, bode E   neuer breke nolde] breke wolde he (*om.* A) neuere PA   nolde] wolde UEC
149 eyȝt] aghtyn PA   was] is UC, hight DE   is myche] *trs.* A   is myche yloued] crist
michul (meche EC) loued UEC, mich crist folwud D   yloued] luffede A
150 Tadde and Tomas] *trs. sbs.* UDEC   ben] is DC   151 And] *om.* PE
þe] *om.* U   elleueþ] elleuynyt AD   auntred] auentured U, auentredde C   ofte]
PAUDEC, myche L *Kölbing-Day*   152 Byfor] Aforne UDE   was] *om.* UDC,
seynt E   Petres] PAUDC, petrus LE *Kölbing-Day*   153 man] *om.* UDEC   vnlele]
a tretour E   luþer] vntrewe C   dedis] tunge U   154 Iudas] And þat was Iudas
(*last word in margin*) A   Ihesu] PAUDC, Ihesu crist LE *Kölbing-Day*   to] vnto A   *no
cesura* EC

Suþ hymsulf he slowe   for sorow of þat dede: 155
His body on a balwe tree   tobreste on þe myddel.

When Crist hadde heried Helle   and was henn[es] passed,
For þat mansed man   Mathie þey chossyn;
3it vnbaptized were boþe   Barnabe and Poule
And no3t knewen of Crist   bot comen sone after.   160

þe princes and þe prelates   a3en þe Paske tyme
Alle þei ha[tt]e + in h[er]te   for his holy werkes.
Hit was a doylful dede   whan þey his deþ caste:
þrow Pilat pyned he was,   þe prouost of Rome.

And þat worliche wif   [whom Y] arst + nempned   165
Haþ his visage in hire veil—   Veronyk 30 hatte—
Peynted pu[r]ely and playn   þat no poynt wanteþ:
For loue he left hit hire   til hire lyues ende.

þer is no gome [o]n þis [grounde]   þat is grym wounded,
Meselry ne meschef   ne man vpon erþe,   170

155 Suþ] And sythyn AU, Afterward E, Aftur C   hymsulf he slowe] slewe he hymselfe A,
he hymself slowgh C   he] om. UE   156 body] adds hynge C   a] an A, om. D   a balwe
tree] om. (blank) E, alther C   balwe] blak P, bal UD   to-] he PC, om. UDE   on] in
PAUDEC   myddel] myddes PAUDC   157 Whan] Then UDC   hadde] om. UDC   and
. . . passed] all haly was turnyd P   was] om. UDC   hennes] henen L, till heuen A, to heuen
UDC Kölbing-Day   passed] turned UDC   scribal line E: Tho oþer apostelys / tokyn
hem togydre   158 For] And for UDC   For . . . man] and in the stede of iudas E   mansed]
cursyd PUC, mased A   Mathie] Matheu P   þey] was A, he UD   159 3it] And 3itt
AUDEC   vnbaptized were boþe] were nat cristenyd E   were] was P, are DU, cesura fols. C
and] ne E   160 And] om. UDC   And . . . Crist] ne ychose for postelys E   no3t] Now D,
noghte ne A   knewen] yknawen UDC   comen] come PADE   161 princes] prince UD
þe²] om. P   a3en] at P, agaynes A, ayeins UD   þe Paske] hym spak þat DE   Paske] pase P
162 Alle þei] and alle E   *hatte in herte] hatede hym in herte A, hatyd hym harde P, hadde
hym in hate LUDEC Kölbing-Day   163 doylful] dolorous UDC, wel fowl E   dede]
deth U   164 þrow] By UDEC   pyned] dampned E   þe] that A, om. UD   prouost]
profest P   of] was of A   165 And] om. PA   þat] þat ilke PA, than this UDC, 3it hath þis E
worliche] worthy PDE, worthily A, wordy C   wif] woman A   *whom] of whom UDEC, þat
LPA Kölbing-Day   Y arst] E, arst was L Kölbing-Day, I are P, I firste AUDC   nempned]
neuende PA, ynempned L Kölbing-Day, tolde UDEC   166 Haþ] om. E   visage] vys D
hire] a AUDEC   veil] adds and A   Veronyk] vernyk P, veronica DEC   hatte] hight
PAUDEC   **AT THIS POINT, C LACKS A FOLIO AND LINES 167–248**
167 Peynted] Pryntyd PU, Enpryntede A   *purely] priuely LP Kölbing-Day, priuely U,
preualy A, privily D   purely and playn] opely þeron E   and] in UD   no] neuer a UDE
poynt] adds ne A   wanteþ] lakketh U, wantid D, fayleth E   168 line om. U   hire¹] with
hir PDE, hir with A   til] vntill A, into D, to E   til . . . ende] all hir lyfe tyme P   169 is no]
nis U   gome] grefe A, withe E   on] PAD Kölbing-Day, in LUE   grounde] PAD Kölbing-
Day, erþe LU, wurld E   þat is] ne gome so A   grym] so gryne D, so sore E   wounded]
wounde? P   170 Meselry] with myselry E   ne¹] nor U, or E   ne²] na P, that A, nor U,
on D   ne² . . . erþe] siknesse or soore E   man] sekenes U   vpon] hase on A, on U

þat kneleþ doun to þat cloþ   and on Crist leueþ,
Bot alle hapneþ to + hele   in [an] handwhyle'.

'[A] Rome re[nay]e[d]!' quod þe kyng.   '[a] riche [emperour],
Cesar, synful wrecche,   þat sent hym fram Rome,
Why nadde þy lycam be leyd   low vnder erþe   175
f. 4ʳ Whan Pilat prouost was made   suche a prince to iugge?'

And or þis wordes were   wonne to þe ende,
þe cankere þat þe kyng hadde   clenly was heled:
Without faute þe face   of flesche and of hyde,
As newe as þe nebbe   þat neuer was wemmyd.   180

'A corteys Crist!'   seide þe kyng + þan.
'Was neuer worke þat Y wroȝt   worþy þe + t[i]lle,
Ne dede þat Y [d]on haue   bot þy deþ mened;
Ne neuer sey þe in siȝt,   Goddis sone dere.

171 þat cloþ] the clay U   on] in A   leueþ] byleues AE   172 Bot] om. P   Bot
alle] That he ne UD   alle . . . hele] þat he be fulliche hool E   hapneþ] hurtes P,
happeth UD   *to hele] Kölbing-Day, to helle L, it heles P, thaym the hele A, be hole
UD   in] within PA   an] AUDE Kölbing-Day, and (i.e., &) L, a P   173 A¹] PA,
At LUDE Kölbing-Day   renayed] PA, reyned LUE Kölbing-Day, regnith D, adds þe
emperour L Kölbing-Day (rejected Kölbing-Day n)   þe kyng] tytus E   a²] U, om. L
Kölbing-Day, þe PD, thou A, þat E   emperour] PAUDE Kölbing-Day n, þan L Kölbing-
Day   174 Cesar] thou Cesare A, adds þat P, adds thou A, add the UE, adds hymself
þe D   wrecche] om. UDE   sent] sette D   hym fram] is in D   fram] fra PA, to UE
no cesura E   175 Why nadde] Whithen had P, AA whyen hade A   nadde] nere D
þy] his D   þy lycam] þai P, thi leghame A, þis cesar E, cesura fols. U   be . . . low] helid
or he 'be' (later) lokyn D, be lokyn E   leyd low] trs. P   low] om. U   vnder] adds þe P
no cesura E   176 prouost] prouest P   was] he E   made] om. P, add / þat PAUDE
a] om. D   prince] lord E   to iugge] Iuged PA, sloughe UDE   177 And] om. UDE
or] vnnethes ware A   þis] thre P, those A   were] war wele PD Kölbing-Day, wele A,
weren al U   wonne] wonnen A, worpen UD, yseyd / fulliche E   178 þe¹] when
the A   þat] om. U   þe kyng] tytus (over erased þe kyng) E   clenly was] clene was UE,
was clene D   heled] yheled UE   179 Without] Withouten PA, '-oute' later D
faute] defawte AE   þe] in þe PA, was his U, on þe D, his E   face] adds was E   of¹]
in P   of¹ . . . hyde] and his flessh als U   and] or PADE   of²] in P   hyde] hewe
(lined) hyde A, hewe E   180 As¹] and as E   newe] clene U   as²] and als A   þe
nebbe] nobill A, a nedle D, a noble E   nebbe] web P   þat] als A   was] hade bene A
wemmyd] wymmede A, yhurt UD, apeyred E   181 A] ¶ precs. D   corteys] comly
curtase A   seide] quod PAUD   þe kyng] tytus E   þan] PAUD Kölbing-Day n, riche
þan L Kölbing-Day, anon E   182 neuer] om. P   worþy] neuer U, wurth E   þe] to
thi UDE   tille] PA, to telle L Kölbing-Day, wille UDE   183 Ne] Na P, Nor U,
adds neuer A   don haue] PUDE, trs. L Kölbing-Day, dide A   bot] but onliche E
deþ] dede PA   mened] rewed UDE   184 Ne] Nor U   þe] I the AD, god U
goddis] god PU   dere] of heuen A

Bot now bayne me my bone,   blessed lord,   185
To stire Nero with noye   and newen his sorowe,
And Y schal buske me boun   hem bale [for]to wyrche
To do þe deueles of dawe   and þy deþ venge.

[Primus passus]

Telle me tit', quod Titus,   'what tokne he lafte
To hem þat knew hym for Crist   and his crafte leued?'   190
'Nempne þe Trinyte by name',   quod Nathan, 'at þries
And þermyd baptemed be   in blessed water'.

Forþ þey fetten a font   and foulled hym þer,
Made hym Cristen kyng   þat for Crist werred.
Corrours into eche coste   þan þe cours nomen   195
And alle his baronage broȝt   to Burdewes hauen.

Suþ with þe sondesman   he [s]ouȝt [vn]to Rome
þe ferly and þe faire cure   his fadere to schewe,

185 bayne] graunte P, be bayne A *Kölbing-Day*   bayne . . . lord] blessyd lord graunte me
my boone E   bayne . . . bone] mon me be boun U, y bowne me to be bysy D   me] to A
Kölbing-Day   blessed] blissed PU, thou blyssedfull A   lord] louerde P   *no cesura* E
186 To stire] Sir P, Stirre thou A, To note D   with] to P   and] to AUD   newen] new P,
newe A   his] hym P, thaym with A, her U   187 schal] *om.* P, wil DE   buske] bese E   me]
and P, and be A, me be D, me and *Kölbing-Day* n   boun] what y may E   hem] her UDE
bale] bales UDE   forto] PA *Duggan* 1988:127, to LUDEC *Kölbing-Day*   wyrche] brewe
UDE   188 To . . . dawe] that dede the this sorwe E   þe] þat P, those AU, þes D   deueles]
deuel P   of] on PU, a- D   deþ] dede PA   venge] avenge DE   followed by inset 'Primus
passus' U   189 Telle] Now telle AUDE, *two-line capital* U, ¶ *precs.* D, *four-line capital* E
tit] *om.* PAUDE   he] þat he AE   190 To] with E   knew] knawes A   knew . . . leued]
hym knowe / and on hym byleeue E   his] in his A, on his U   leued] leuys AD
191 Nempne] Neuyn P, Newyn A, ¶ *precs.* D   þe] þou P   quod] seyde E   quod Nathan]
om. P   at] as P, a U, *om.* DE   192 -myd] with PAUDE, *adds* alle A   baptemed] baptist
PAUDE   baptemed be] *trs.* A   in] wiþ D, in clene E   blessed] blissed P, blyssede A,
yblissed U, yblessid DE   blessed water] *trs.* UDE   193 Forþ] ¶ *precs.* D   fetten] fechede
A, *adds* þere D   font] fatt PUDE, *adds* þo E   foulled] fyllyn P, baptizede A, fylde E   hym]
om. P   hym þer] þat beryn A, it ful of water E   194 Made hym] And made AE   Cristen]
cristenyde that A   for] after PAUDE   for Crist] *trs.* E   werred] serued PAUDE
195 Corrours] Than currous A   into] to P, intill A, in UDE   eche] ilk a A, ilke U, euery DE
þan] þai P, *om.* AU   þan þe cours] *trs.* DE   þe] þair PAUDE   cours] curses A, *add* thay AU
nomen] made PAUDE   196 And] *om.* A   baronage] barnayge sone P   broȝt] to brynge
A, þei broght D   broȝt . . . hauen] to burdeux broght P   Burdewes] buredieux A, Burdeux
UDE   hauen] anone A, in hast UDE   197 Suþ] And sythen sone on A, And sen after U,
And sithin D, And afterward E   with] *om.* UDE   þe] *om.* PD, his UE   sondesman] sondis
ADE, sonde U   he] *om.* PAE   souȝt] A *Kölbing-Day*, þouȝt L, sent PUDE   vnto] PU
Duggan 1988:128, to LE *Kölbing-Day*, towarde A, anone vnto D   198 þe¹] That AU
ferly] sely P   and] *om.* U   and þe] *om.* DE   þe²] that A   to] forto A

And he gronnand glad   grete God þanked
And loude criande on Crist   carped and saide: 200

'Worþy wemlese God   in whom Y byleue,
[As] þou in Bethleem was born   of a bryȝt mayde,
Sende me hele of my hurt,   and heyly Y + afowe
To be ded for þy deþ,   bot hit be dere ȝolden'.

þat tyme Peter was pope   and preched in Rome   205
þe lawe and þe lore   þat our byleue askeþ,
Folowed f[el]e o[f] þe folke   and to þe fayþ tourned,
And Crist wroȝt for þat wye   wondres ynow.

þerof Waspasian was ware   þat þe waspys hadde,
Sone sendeþ hym to,   and [he] þe soþe tolde   210
Of Crist and þe kerchef   þat keuered þe sike,
As Nathan Neymes sone seide   þat to Nero + come.

f. 4ᵛ þan to consayl was called   þe knyȝtes of Rome
And assenteden sone   to sende messageres,
xxᵗⁱ. knyȝtes [þat] were cud,   þe [k]er[che]f to fecche   215
And asked trewes of þe empererour   þat erand to done.

· · · · · · ·

199 And he] tho was his fadur E   he] alle A   gronnand] was P, wundur E   glad] with
gladnes A, *adds* of þat grace and P   grete] gretely P, the grete UD   grete God] and ihesu
crist E   God] he P, *adds* he A   200 And] *om.* A   criande] crid UDE   on] to P, vpon UE
Crist] hym E, *adds* / he U   carped and] and karpand P, carpande and A, and these wurdes E
201 Worþy] Whethir worthlý P, Now thou A, Mercy UDE   wemlese] *om.* P, gracious A
wemlese God] lord myghtful UDE   Y] þat I P, y now D   byleue] leue P   202 As]
PAUDE *Kölbing-Day*, & (*i.e.*, and) L   bryȝt] clene AE   mayde] Mayden A   203 hele]
helpe PADE   hurt] desese E   heyly] here P, hally A, holy U, *om.* E   Y] y to þe E   afowe]
PUDE *Kölbing-Day*, afowne LA   204 deþ] dede PA   be dere ȝolden] yuengyt be E
ȝolden] boght P   205 þat] ¶ *precs.* D   206 þeᵗ] Of þe PAUD   lawe . . . lore] lord . . .
lawe D   byleue] lede P   207 Folowed] He folowede A, Fullid D, cristnede E   *fele]
Kölbing-Day n, faste LA *Kölbing-Day*, fast PUDE   of] PD *Kölbing-Day*, n, on LAU *Kölbing-
Day*, *om.* E   þeᵗ] *om.* E   208 *line order* 209, 210, 208 (*marked for corr.*) U   and] *om.* P   for
þat wye] alday for hym E   wye] wight D   ynow] many P   209 Waspasian] vaspasyane
AD   Waspasian was] is Vespasian P   210 Sone] and anon E   sendeþ] he sendes PD,
sendis he A, he shewed U, sente E   hym to] *trs.* E   he] PADE, *om.* LU *Kölbing-Day*
211 and] and of E   kerchef] cloth E   þat] and D   keuered] cured PUDE   212 Neymes
sone] *om.* UDE   seide] had done P, had saide A, had afor (byfore E) seid UDE   þat . . .
come] as y to ȝow toolde E   to Nero] *trs.* P, was to n A   come] PUD (cf. *Duggan* 1986:589),
was come LA *Kölbing-Day* (was *precs.* to A)   213 *lines* 213–14 *om.* UDE   þan] And P
to] sone A   þe] *om.* P   knyȝtes] knyghthede A   214 And] And thay A   assenteden] sent P
to sende] onone P, *om.* A   messageres] *adds* mony P, *adds* forthe to sende A   215 xxᵗⁱ.]
Anon E   þat] PA, *om.* LUDE   were] ere U   cud] ycald E   þe] that A   kerchef] PAU
Kölbing-Day, clergyf L, kerchifs D, clooth E   to] forto E   to fecche] after P   216 *line om.*
PA   asked] aske D, hadde E   trewes . . . done] of Nero a trewe / (*adds* an U) answere thei
herken (abydyn D, answere thei herken] to gon and to come E) UDE

Ac without tribute or trewes   [by] tenfulle w[a]yes
þe knyȝtes with þe kerchef   comen ful blyue;
þe pope ȝaf pardoun to hem   [and] passed þeraȝens
With processioun and pres   [of] princes and dukes.   220

And whan þe womman was ware   þat þe wede owede
[Of] seint Peter þe pope,   ȝo platte to þe grounde,
Vmbefelde his fete   and to þe freke saide:
'Of þis kerchef and my cors   þe kepyng Y þe take'.

þan bygan þe burne   biterly to wepe   225
For þe doylful deþ   of his dere mayster,
And longe stode in þe stede   or he stynte myȝt
Whan [ȝo] vnclosed þe cloþe   þat Cristes body touched.

þe wede fram þe womman   [h]e + warp atte laste,
Receyued hit myd reuerence   and rennande teris,   230
[T]o þe p[a]lace myd pres   + passed on swyþe
And ay held hit on hey   þat alle byhold myȝt.

217 Ac] *om.* PAUDE   or] to U   trewes] trew PA, be U, trowe D, payment E   by] AUDE, *om.* LP *Kölbing-Day*   tenfulle] tenfull PAU, tene ful D, eny maner E   wayes] PAU *Kölbing-Day* n, wyes L *Kölbing-Day*, dayes D, weye E   adds scribal line E: so þat þey myȝte / go withowte lettyng   218 þe¹] ¶ *precs.* D   kerchef] vernycle E   comen] come P, thay come A   ful blyue] belyue P, agayne sone A, als blyue U, ful swithe D, as swythe E   219 to hem] þerto PAU, *int. later (and then canc.)* E, *om.* E   and] PAUE, þat L *Kölbing-Day*, `þat' (*later*) and (*all canc.*) D   passed] went PE   þer-] it UDE   220 pres] presynge A   of] PAUDE *Kölbing-Day* n, *om.* L *Kölbing-Day*   princes] lordes U   *no cesura* E   adds scribal line E: and with al þe solempnyte / þat he make myȝte   221 And] *om.* PAE   was] is U   ware] comen A   wede] clooth E   owede] aght PAUD, hadde E   222 Of] PUDE *Kölbing-Day*, To L, Byfore A   30 . . . grounde] þar plaght sho hir doune P   grounde] erthe D   223 Vmbefelde] Vmfoldes P, Scho vmbyfaldide A, And (*om.* D) fel doun to UDE   his fete] the erthe U   þe freke] hym E   224 Of þis] þis haly PA, This UDE   kerchef] clothe UDE   and . . . kepyng] *trs. phrs.* UDE   my cors] I P, my body AE   þe¹] þi P, to A, to thi UE, to my D   kepyng] kepe A   Y þe take] es In P   þe²] *om.* UDE   take] bytake AUD   225 þan] Bot than A, Tho U   bygan] gan UD   þe] that A, that blissed U, þe blessid D   þe burne] petur E   burne] beerd U   biterly] full bitterly A   226 doylful] dolorous UD, dispytful E   deþ] dede PA   227 longe stode] *trs.* A   þe] a PA, that UDE   stynte myȝt] *trs.* E   myȝt] wolde P   228 Whan] Bot scho (*canc.*) when that A, *om.* UD, than E   30] sho PA, he LUDE *Kölbing-Day*   30 vnclosed] *trs.* E   Cristes] his A   Cristes body touched] crist forwroght P   body] face AE   229 þe¹] That UD   wede] clooth E   fram] fra PAUE þe²] that U   he] PAUD *Kölbing-Day*, þey L *Kölbing-Day* n   he . . . laste] thanne mekelich he took E   warp] PA *Kölbing-Day*, warpen L, warped UD   atte laste] at ones UD   230 Receyued] and receyued E   myd] with PAUDE   and] and with D   231 To] P?UDE, Out of L *Kölbing-Day*, Towarde A   palace] AUDE, place LP *Kölbing-Day*   myd] with þe P, with AUDE   pres] pees U   passed] P, þey passed LA *Kölbing-Day*, he passed UDE   on swyþe] sone after UE, þereaftre D   swyþe] faste P   232 ay] euere DE   hey] heght PD, lofte A   alle] men U

þan xij. barouns bolde   þe emperour bade wende
And þe pope departe   fram þe pople faste;
Veronyk and þe vail   [V]aspasian þey broȝt,   235
And seint Peter þe pope   presented boþe.

Bot a ferly byfelle   forþmyd hem alle:
In her temple bytidde   tenful þynges.
þe mahound and þe mametes   tomortled to peces
And al tocrased as þe cloþ   þroȝ þe kirke passed.   240

Into þe palice with þe prente   þan þe pope ȝede;
Knyȝtes kepten þe cloþe   and on knees fallen.
A flauour fla[w]e þerfro—   þey felleden hit alle:
Was neuer odour ne eyr   vpon erþe swetter.

þe kerchef clansed hitself   and so clere wexed   245
Myȝt no lede on hit loke   for liȝt þat hit schewed.
As hit aproched to þe prince,   he put vp his hed;
For confort of þe cloþ   he cried wel loude:

---

233 *line order* 237–40, 233–36 A   þan] *om.* PAUDE   xij.] Ten DE, ¶ *precs.* D
bolde] that were bolde A   þe . . . wende] to the kynge went A   emperour] kyng UDE
Kölbing-Day n   bade] bad to UDE   *no cesura* E   234 And] And so U   departe]
departid PA, parted U   fram] fra PA   faste] swythe PAU   scribal line DE: To fette
(fecche E) þe woman wiþ þe wede (clooth / E) þat þe wondris wroght   235 Veronyk
and þe vail] The veyle (clooth E) with Veronica / to UDE   Vasp-] UD, wasp- LPAE
Kölbing-Day   þey] is U   236 And] And to D   seint] sayne A   pope] *adds* / and
U, *adds* þei D   presented boþe] þat presaunt bare P, there present ware thay bothe A,
also in feere E   237 Bot] But then UDE   forþmyd] thare byfore A, forthwith U,
byfor D, anon with E   forþmyd hem] befor þa ledes P   *no cesura* E   238 In] for
in E   her] þe DE   bytidde] *adds* full A   239 þeˈ] *om.* P, thaire AE   þeˌ] thaire
AE   mametes] mawmettry P, Mawmetries A   tomortled] mourlede A, hurtled UD,
altobrast E   tomortled to peces] molt all to pouder P   to] in A, on E   to peces]
togidris D   *no cesura* E   240 tocrased] tocrached A, tothruschede A, toclatrid DE
þroȝ] thorowe A, to UDE   kirke] chirche U, kyng DE   passed] ȝode P?UDE
241 Into] In A   with . . . pope] *trs. phrs.* PUDE   with þe prente] fro (from D) the
puple UDE   prente] prince PA   þan] *om.* PUDE, als A   ȝede] went (*precs.* fro) U
242 kepten] kepes P   and] and þei D   on] on her U   fallen] falles PD, felle AUE
243 A flauour] Ane ayre P, A sauoure A   A . . . flawe] Then sleigh a flavour UDE
flawe] PA, flambeþ L *Kölbing-Day*   þey] þar P   felleden] felden E   alle] Ilkone A
244 Was neuer] There nas UDE   ne] nor U   vpon] on þe D   vpon erþe] vnder
heuen UE   *no cesura* E   245 þe] Te E   kerchef] cloth UDE   clansed] vnclosede
A, clered UDE   wexed] it wax E   246 Myȝt] there myghte A   no] non E   lede]
lad D, body E   on hit] þaron P   schewed] keste P, yaf UD, hadde E
247 aproched] apperide A   þe] that A   put] heeld E   vp] forth D   hed]
heued PAE   248 For] And alle for A, And for UDE   he] *om.* E   cried] cryes P
wel] on PA, ful UD, wol E   **C RESUMES**

'Lo lordlynges, here   þe lyknesse of Crist,
Of whom my botnyng Y bidde   for his bitter woundis'!   250 f. 5ʳ
þan was wepyng and wo   and wryngyng of hondis
With loude dyn and dit   for doil of hym one.

þe pope availed þe vaile   and his visage touched,
þe body suþ al aboute,   blessed hit þrye.
þe waspys w[y]ten away   and alle þe wo after: 255
þat er [w]as lasar-l[ich]e   lyȝtter was neuere.

þan was pypyng and play,   [departyng of stryf];
þey ȝelden grace to God   [alle þ]o grete lordes.
þe kerchef + aireþ fram [hem] alle   and in þe eyr hangyþ
þat þe symple pople myȝt hit se   into soper tyme.   260

þe + vernycle after Veronyk   [V]aspasian hit called,
Garde hit gayly agysen   in gold and in seluere.

---

249 Lo] loo here A, And seyde E   lordlynges] lordes P, lordyngs AUDEC   here]
he sayde PA   250 line om. U   Of] For P   my] y DE   botnyng] bote now
PA, help C   Y bidde] I byde P, abyde DE, I praye C   bitter] betyr E   no cesura C
251 line om. P   þan] ¶ precs. D   was] was bot A, is U   252 loude] grete AE,
loude lowe U   dyn] ˋdyn´ dole (canc.) A, dremyng UD, lamentacyon E, wepynge C
dyn . . . doil] dole and with dyn all P   and dit] all that daye A, om. UE, and dym D,
and noyse C   doil] drede U, sorwe EC   hym one] þe kyng E   one] alone D
253 þe] Te E   availed] vayled P, valid D, took doun E, avaled C, adds with A   þe²]
his UC   vaile] clooth E   his] the U   visage] vice U, vysˋage´ (int. later) D, nose E,
face C   254 þe body suþ] Sythen the body A, and his body E   suþ] aftur C
blessed] and blissed U, blissed C   hit] hym A, he UDEC   þrye] thryse PAUDEC
255 þe . . . wyten] than went the waspes A   wyten] P, wenten LA Kölbing-Day, went
al UDEC   alle] om. UE   þe²] his E   no cesura C   256 er] arst DE, byfore C
was lasar-liche] DE, lasar was longe L Kölbing-Day, laythre was P, lazare was laythe A,
was lazar ful leke U, lazare was lyke C   lyȝtter] so faire U, so light DEC   was] was
he AUDEC   257 þan] þare PUDEC   was] with A   departyng of stryf] P, his
pyne was awey L Kölbing-Day, thay partede at the laste A, partyng (and p. DE) atte last
UDEC   258 þey ȝelden] ȝoledynge P, And gaffe A, Yelde UD, ȝolden C   þey
. . . grace] graces ȝuldyng E   grace] graces UD, thankynges C   to] vnto A   alle
þo] A, þis two L Kölbing-Day, many P, all the UDC, of alle þat E   grete lordes] þere
were E   lordes] lorde P   259 þe¹] þat P, than the A   kerchef] cloth UDEC
*aireþ] carieþ L Kölbing-Day, wente A, caught D, kawȝte C, cauth U, was takyn E
aireþ . . . hangyþ] vp in þe ayre fra þaim al hanged P   *fram hem alle] fro thaym alle
A, fram alle L Kölbing-Day, was (om. E) hem fro UDEC   eyr] chirche UDEC, kirke
Kölbing-Day   hangyþ] hyngede AUDEC   260 þat] om. P, For UDEC   þe]
om. A   symple pople] symple U Kölbing-Day, synful DE, somple C   myȝt] om. UC,
shold DE   hit] om. PD, it to UC   into] to (v [canc.] to A) þe PAU, tul D, tyl þe
EC   261 vernycle] PAUDEC, veronycle L Kölbing-Day   Vasp-] AUDC, wasp-
LPE Kölbing-Day   262 Garde] And garte AUD, and made EC   hit gayly] trs.
PAUD   gayly] graithely UD, worshipfully C   agysen] gyse PA, graith UD, been
arayt E, arayde C

ʒit is þe visage in þe vail   as Veronyk hym broʒt;
þe Romaynes hit [te]ldeþ + a rome,   and for + relyk + holden.

þis whyle Nero hadde noye   and non nyʒtes reste   265
For his tribute was with[tane],   as Nathan told hadde.
He commaundiþ knyʒtes to come   consail to holde,
Erles and alle men   þe emperour aboute.

Assembled þe senatours   sone vpon haste
To iugge who iewes myʒt best   vpon þe Iewys take.   270
And alle demeden by dome   þo dukes to wende
þat were cured þrow Crist   þat þey on croys slowen.

þat on Waspasian was   of þe wyes twey
þat þe trauail vndertoke   and Titus anoþer,
A bold burne on a blonke   and of his body comyn,   275
No ferþer sib to hymself   bot his sone dere—

263 þe¹] *om.* D   visage] vice UD, face EC   in] one A   þe²] *om.* PE   vail]
clooth E   Veronyk] vernyk P, veronica EC   hym] it PAUDEC *Kölbing-Day* n
264 þe] That UC, Alle þe E   hit teldeþ] *trs.* PA   hit] thus A, *om.* UDEC *Kölbing-Day*
teldeþ] P, holdeþ L, telles A, rifly U, rively D, ryfly C, *om.* E *Kölbing-Day*   *a]
om. P, at LAUDEC *Kölbing-Day*   and for] PA, and for a L, a UDEC, for a *Kölbing-Day*   holden] P *Duggan* 1986:589, hit holden LAUDEC *Kölbing-Day*   265 þis] ¶
precs. D   þis whyle] þat wouke P   hadde] hase A   non] na PAUDE   nyʒtes]
nyght P, *om.* U   reste] *adds* myght haue U   266 was] to A, is U   *withtane]
withholde L, vntane P, tell A, tynt UD *Kölbing-Day*, nat payd E, loste C   told hadde]
trs. A, him tolde UDEC   267 *line om.* A   He] tho he E, He *with interlineations to
form* THe kyng C   commaundiþ] somonde PU, commaundid DC, bad E   knyʒtes]
kynges PUE, þe kyng D   to come] *om.* D   come] come / a C   holde] take
(*expunged*) holde L   268 þe] of þe E   emperour] empire UDEC   scribal line
with four-line capital A: Now than the Emperour and his Erlis and alle men abowte
269 Assembled] He sembled P, He callyl also E   sone vpon haste] in rome al abowte E
270 To] Tho to A   iugge] ordeyne E   who] what PUDEC   iewes] iugement UEC,
iuggementz D   iewes myʒt best] solde the Iournaye A   myʒt best] *trs.* P, *om.* UDEC
vpon] on P, *om.* UDEC   Iewys] iugges D   take] be takyn P, shuld haue UDEC
271 alle] *om.* P, alle thay AUDEC   by] it by A   þo] þe PUD, *om.* C   dukes]
princes E   to] forto PU, sholde C   272 cured] couerde A   þrow] in UDC, be E
þat²] whom E   slowen] slynge? P   scribal line added E: and destroye hem vtterly /
for þat wykkyd dede   273 *line om.* U   þat] ¶ *precs.* D   Waspasian was] *trs.*
ADEC   þe] those A   wyes] wyghtis AD, lordes E, dukes C   twey] twyne P
274 þe] *om.* U, þat D, this E   þe . . . anoþer] oþer was tytus / þat þe trauayle
vndertoke C   trauail] iorneye E   vndertoke] to vndertake U   anoþer] þe tother
PAE, *illeg.* D   275 bold] bool E   bold burne] *trs.* U   burne] man E, knyʒte C
on a blonke] for þe nonys E   blonke] hors C   and] *om.* UDC   his] hye UC   his
body] hymselfe A   body] kyn U, blood DEC   comyn] ycome EC   276 ferþer]
ferr P, ferrere A   sib] kyn C   to] fra PA   bot] than U   sone dere] owen sone
PUDEC

Crouned kynges boþe   and mychel Crist loued
þat hadde hem [g]euen of his grace   and here grem stroyed.
Moste þei hadde hit in hert   here hestes to kepe
And here forward[e] to fulfille   þat þei byfor made.   280

þan was rotlyng in Rome,   robbyng of brynnyis,
Schewyng of scharpe,   scheldes ydressed;
Lauȝte leue at þat lord,   leften his sygne,
A grete dragoun of gold,   and alle þe [g]yng [after].

By þat schippis were schred,   yschot on þe depe,   285
Takled and atired   on talterande yþes.   f. 5ᵛ
Fresch water and wyn   wounden yn faste
And stof of alle maner store   þat hem strengþe scholde.

þer were floynes aflot,   farcostes many,
Cogges and crayers   ycasteled alle;   290

---

277 Crouned . . . boþe] Bothe kynges vnder (with C) crowne UC, Boþe were þei
kyngis wiþ crowne D, Bothe were they kynges E   boþe] war þai both PA   and] that
ADE   mychel] myche PDEC   mychel Crist] trs. AUDEC   278 þat hadde] for he
E, That C   þat . . . geuen] om. P   hadde] hase A   hem geuen] trs. E   geuen] A,
ȝeuen L Kölbing-Day, graunted UDEC   of] om. UDEC   his] om. E   grace] adds
gretely P, int. later D   and] om. E   and . . . stroyed] þat þaim of grame broght P, and
owte of grefe broghte A   grem] grame UDC, game E   stroyed] destroied UD, to
destroye E   279 Moste] for moost E   hadde] haldyn P, holde A   hit] om. PEC
here] his DE   hestes] hetes P, highttis A   no cesura D   280 And] om. UDC
here] the A   forwarde] PAUDC, forwardis L Kölbing-Day, auowes E   fulfille] hold D
byfor] aforne UEC   281 þan was] Sone was there A   was] is U   rotlyng]
roghtlynge P, ruschynge A, ruthyng U, rightyng D, rumer E   robbyng] and rollynge A,
and rubbyng UDEC   brynnyis] rust D, harneys E, helmes C   282 Schewyng]
Schymbrynge P, Shimering UC, Shiueryng D, grydyng E   scharpe] add stele PC, add
stele / and AE, adds shelde / and U   scharpe scheldes] sheldis of sharp stele D
scheldes] scheledes P   ydressed] dressen P, to drysse A, dressid D, arayed E
283 Lauȝte] thay tuke thaire (he E) AEC, Toke (To U) her UD   at] of E   þat]
þe PUC, thaire ADE   lord] londe C   leften] and raysed P, and lyftys A, and (om. D)
lifte (reysed E) vp UDEC   his] þair PDE, a C   284 A grete] which was a E   of]
all of P   alle . . . after] forth wente yfeere E   þe] om. D   gyng] UDC Kölbing-Day,
kyng L, gomes P, gentills A   after] PAUDC, folwed L Kölbing-Day   285 þat] that
the AC   schred] shoryd P, redy A, yshrud UD, arayed E, gon C   yschot] and schot
PA, and shuft UD, and put E, and rowed C   on] into P, appon A, in UDEC   depe]
see P   286 Takled and atired] Ytrussed and tired UDEC   on] for E   talterande]
totering UDEC   yþes] waghes PAUDEC   no cesura C   287 wounden] wondyn P,
thay wynde AC   faste] sone PUDEC, full swythe A   288 stof of] stufed with P
maner] kyn P, om. C, adds of A   hem strengþe] trs. UC   strengþe] strenghen U
289 floynes] flewande A, shippes DE, floignes UC   aflot] in þe flode P, in the flete A, on
fˈlʾot U, add / and UDEC   farcostes] farstes C   many] full many A   290 Cogges
and crayers] Cokkes and karekkes C   ycasteled] castelde P, castellid D   ycasteled alle]
Encastelled ylkone A

Galees of grete streyngþe   with golden fanes
[B]ra[y]d on þe brod se   aboute foure myle.

þey ty3ten vp t[op]sail   whan þe tide asked,
Hadde byr at þe bake   and þe bonke lefte,
Sou3te ouer þe se   with soudeours manye,   295
And [io]yned vp at port Iaf   in Iude[e]s lond[e].

Suree, Cesaris londe,   þou may seken euer;
Ful mychel wo m[ou]n be wro3te   in þy [w]lonk tounnes.
Cytees vnder S[yo]ne,   now is 3our sorow vppe:
þe deþ of + dereworþ Crist   dere schal be 3olden.   300

Now is Bethleem þy bost   ybro3t to an ende,
Ierusalem and Ierico   foriuggyd wrecchys:
Schal neuer kyng of 3our kynde   with croune be ynoyntid
Ne Iewe for Ihesus sake   [i]ouke in + 3ou more.

291 Galees] And gales PAUDEC   of] of full A   streyngþe] myght UDEC   golden]
gilden A   fanes] vanys D   292 Brayd] P, Sprad L, Alle abowtte A, The brede UDC
Kölbing-Day, they spredde E, Brad *Kölbing-Day* n   on] ouer P, of UD, in C   on þe brod]
abrod in þe E   four] v. PADEC, seuen U   **AT THIS POINT, A LACKS A FOLIO
AND LINES 293–369**   293 ty3ten] tokyn P, teisen U, tyen DC, gan drawe E   top-]
PUDC, tal L *Kölbing-Day*, her E   þe tide] tydes P   asked] askyn P, axeth UD, wulde E
294 Hadde] Thei hadde the UDC   byr] piry U, pyre C   at] on PUDC   bonke] *illeg. in
crease* P, londe C   lefte] latchyn P   *no cesura* C   scribal line E: and drowyn into deep
water / þat þey my3te seyle   295 Sou3te] Thei saiden and sailed U, þei sailid DC, and
thanne þey seyled E   ouer þe se] *om.* U   se] salte se PDC   soudeours] sawders C
296 And] *om.* PU   ioyned] DC *Kölbing-Day*, ryued L, Rafe P, Right U, took londe E
vp] *om.* UDEC *Kölbing-Day*   at] at þe P, vnto U, into D *Kölbing-Day*, to C   port]
poor`t′ E   Iudees] DE, Iudeis L *Kölbing-Day*, þe Iues P, Iudee U, Iudeus C   londe]
PUDEC, londys L *Kölbing-Day*   297 Suree] Now surry E, Synner (S- *altered from* D-)
C, ¶ *precs.* D   may] mythe E   seken] sygh P, sorough UDEC   298 Ful] *om.* P, Nowe
UDC, For E   moun] P *Kölbing-Day*, men L, worthe UDEC   be] *om.* UE, þe DC   be
wro3te] *trs.* C   wro3te] ywrough E   in] thurgh U, on D   þy] *om.* P   wlonk] UD
Kölbing-Day, blonk L, walled P, fayre E, welthy C   299 Cytees vnder] and cytees in E
Syone] PUDEC *Kölbing-Day*, sene L   now is] newes P   vppe] here P   300 deþ]
dede P   of] PUDEC, of þe L   dereworþ] derworthi U   dere] ful dere U   schal] mon P
be 3olden] ye bye UD, 3e abye E, 3e hit bye C   301 is Bethleem] betheem is C
ybro3t] broght PUDE, brough C   to] till P   an] þe DE   303 of] in D   3our] 3ow E
kynde] kyn UDEC   ynoyntid] anoynt PDEC, enoynted U   304 Ne] Nor UC, ne no E
Iewe] in þe P   iouke] PDC *Kölbing-Day*, rouke (*perhaps* Iouke) L, Iouken U, dwelle E
3ou] UDEC *Kölbing-Day*, 3our L, *om.* P   followed by inset 'Passus secundus' U, marginal
'ij'[us]. passus' by next line P

[Passus secundus]

þey setten vpon eche side   Surrie withyn,   305
Brente ay at þe bak   and ful bare laften—
Was noȝt bot roryng and rich   in alle þe riche tounnes
And red laschyng lye   alle þe londe ouere;

Token toun and tour,   teldes ful fele,
Brosten ȝates of brass   and many borwe wonnen,   310
Holy þe heþen here   hewyn to grounde
Boþ in bent and in borwe   þat abide wolde.

þe Iewes to Ierusalem   þ[er] Iosophus dwelde
Flowen as þe foule doþ   þat faucoun wolde strike—
A cite vndere Syon   sett was ful noble   315
With many toret and toure   þat toun to defende.

Princes and prelates   and poreil of þe londe,
Clerkes and comunes   of contrees aboute
Were sa[mn]ed to þat cite   sacrifice to make
At Paske tyme, as preched hem   prestes of þe lawe.   320

Many swykel at þe sweng   to þe swerd ȝede:
For penyes passed non   þoȝ he pay wolde,

305 þey] one-line capital P, two-line capital U   þey . . . Surrie] Apon Surry þai setyn in
hegyd P   eche] ilk U   Surrie] sorwe C   306 Brente] And brent UDEC   ay] euere DEC   at]
om. P   at . . . laften] as they wente / cytees and townes E   ful] al UDC Kölbing-Day
307 Was] þere was EC   and] cesura precs. E   and rich] om. P   rich] reuth UDC Kölbing-Day,
weepyng E   in . . . tounnes] abowte E   alle] om. P   308 And] And wiþ D, For C   red] light
UDEC   red laschyng lye] rade full raschely P   laschyng] lastyng U   lye] flame C   alle] in al E
londe] cuntre U   ouer] about ovir D, abowte E   309 Token] Takyn P, Thei token UDE,
The C   toun and tour] toures and townes PE, townes and toures / and UDC   teldes] and
castelles E, holdes C   ful] om. PU   fele] many U, riche DEC   310 Brosten] Thei brasten (b.
þe C) UC, and brast E   and] om. P   borwe] townes U, borow DC   borwe wonnen] queynte
gynnes E   311 Holy] All PUDC, and alle E   þe] om. UE   heþen here] faitheles D   here]
folk UEC   hewyn] þai hew (hewen C) PC, thei drowe U, they fill D, þey felde E   grounde] þe
dede P, the deth UDC, foote E   312 Boþ] om. E   in¹] on PUDC   bent] benche UDC, halle E
borwe] bour UDEC   no cesura C   313 þe] ¶ precs. D   þer] PUDEC Kölbing-Day, þat L
Iosophus] iosaphus P, iosephus UDEC   dwelde] dwelleth U   314 Flowen] Fled UDC,
fledde faste E   as þe] and E   foule] folk DE   doþ] om. P   faucoun wolde strike] fomen assaileth
UDEC   315 sett] þat sett P   ful] wol E   noble] fayre P, riche UDEC   no cesura EC
316 many] om. E, manye a C   toret and tour] torrettes and toures PE   þat] þe PUDEC
defende] þefende C   317 lines 317–20 om. PUDEC   319 *samned] schacked L Kölbing-
Day   321 line om. U   swykel] swilke P, swykeful D, a orpyd E, a swykyll C   at þe sweng] at
þat swynge P, swayn D, man E, swayne þen C   swerd] deth E   no cesura E   322 penyes]
peny UD, no peny E, peny nor ‘pownd’ C   passed] passeth U   non] þare none P, noght one
UDC   þoȝ] if P, that UDEC   he] þai PE, þat D   pay] peyne E   wolde] myght UDEC

Bot diden alle to þe deþe   and drowen hem after
With engynes to Ierusalem   þere Iewes were þykke.

f. 6ʳ þey sette sadly a sege   þe cite alle aboute,   325
Piȝten pauelouns doun   of pallen webbes,
With ropis of riche silk   raysen vp swyþe
Grete tentis as a toun   of torke[ys] cloþys.

[C]hoppyn ouer þe cheuentayns   with charboklis foure
A gay egle of gold   on a gilde appul   330
With grete dragouns [and] grym   alle in gold wroȝte
And [t]o lyouns lyk +   lyande þervndere.

Paled and paynted   þe paueloun was vmbe,
Stoked ful of storijs,   + stayned myd armys
Of quaynte colour[es] to know,   kerneld alofte,   335
An hundred stondyng + stage   in þat stede one.

Toured with torettes   was þe tente þanne
Suþ britaged aboute   briȝt to byholde.

323 Bot] Thei UDE, That þey C   diden] did þaim PUDEC   alle] om. C   deþe]
dede P   and . . . after] that thei catche myght U, wiþ dintis of swerd (swerdys E) DEC
drowen] draue P   after] all doune P   324 line om. U   engynes] gynnes PDC   þer
Iewes were] þei chasyn (chased C) ful DC   þykke] comyn P   scribal line E: and thanne to
ierusalem / they priked wel faste   325 þey] om. P, And UDC, Than E   sadly] thei E
alle] om. PE   326 Piȝten] Thei pight doun her (om. D) UDC, and pyȝt vp E, ¶ precs. D
pauelouns] a paviloun DE   doun] om. UDEC   pallen] arras E, sylken C   webbes] wyse P
327 With] The U   riche] rede P, clene E   raysen] raysed PD, thei reiled U, reysed it E,
þey reysedde hem C   vp] ful U   swyþe] hye UEC, on hy D   328 Grete] and grete E
a toun] townes U   torkeys] PDE Kölbing-Day, torken L, turky U, turcheyes C
329 Choppyn] D Kölbing-Day, Thoppyn L, Chippen P, Chopt U, They settyn E, They
chopped C   ouer] on PD, vp on E   þe] þair P   cheuentayns] chiftane PUDC, cheef E
with] om. PUDEC   four] stones P   330 A gay] with an E   of] al of EC   on] stode
on C   gilde] gaye P   331 and] PUDEC, om. L Kölbing-Day   alle . . . wroȝte] grysly
on to loke E   in] of D   332 *to lyouns lyk] lyk (lyke P) to lyouns (lyons P) also LP
Kölbing-Day n, thereto (þerto DE, þerto C) lyons (lyouns E, lyouns C) two (tweyne C)
UDEC Kölbing-Day   þer-] her D   333 and] and paued and C   was vmbe] was P,
about UC   scribal line DE: Pale (The paale E) and paviloun (þe pauylun / was E) peyntid
al (om. E) about   no cesura C   334 Stoked] Stokyn P   Stoked . . . storijs] f. o. stories
(stonys D) ystilled (stikid DC) UDC   stayned] D Kölbing-Dayn, strayned L Kölbing-Day,
and steynyd PUC   myd] with PUDC   armys] army⟨.⟩ D   scribal line E: with storyes of
knyȝthod / and of diuerse aarmes   335 lines 335–37 om. P   quaynte] diuers UDC,
wunderful E   coloures] UDEC, colour L Kölbing-Day, cesura fols. E   kerneld] and
keuerd UDC, ho hem E   a-] vpon C   alofte] outhe E   336 An] And C   *stage] on
stage L Kölbing-Day, in stage UC, on a stag D   in . . . one] on stedis about D   stede one]
place alone C   scribal line E: y trowe nat in þis wurld / were swiche oþer   337 was . . .
þanne] ȝit were þe tentys E   tente] toun U   338 Suþ] And sethen UD, and E, And
aftur C   britaged] bretest P, bright gold U   briȝt] light U

Er alle þe sege was sette   ʒit of þe cite comyn
Messengeres, were made   fram maistres of þe lawe.   340

To þe chef cheuentayn   þey chosen here wey,
Deden mekly by mouþe   here message attonys,
Sayen, 'þe cite haþ [vs] sent   to serche[n] ʒour wille,
To here þe cause of ʒour comyng   [and what] ʒe coueyte wolde'.

Waspasian no word   to þe wyes schewed   345
Bot sendeþ sondismen aʒen,   xij. sikere knyʒtes;
[Garde] hem charge to go   and þe gomes telle
þat alle þe cause of her com[e]   was Crist forto venge:

'Sayþ Y bidde hem be boun,   bischopes and oþer,
Tomorow or [myd]day   [moder-nak]ed alle   350
Vp here ʒates to ʒelde   with ʒerdes an hande,
Eche w[ye] in a white scherte   and no wede ellys,

---

339 Er] and ar E, ¶ *precs.* D   alle] *om.* UE   was] was al E, were C   ʒit] *om.* E   of] fra
P, out of DE   þe²] ʒe C   340 Messengeres were] Mene messengere P   were] *om.*
UDEC   fram] fra P, *om.* U, of C   fram . . . þe] of Moyses DE   maistres] men P
341 chef cheuentayn] *trs.* UDEC   þey chosen] *trs.* U   chosen] chesyn D
342 Deden] And made UDEC   mekly] medely P, meche E   by] wiþ her DE
here . . . attonys] and to hym seyde E   message] messages P   343 Sayen] þai sayde to
P, *om.* UDE, They seyþe C   cite haþ] Ce⟨....⟩he P, Citezeins haue UEC, Citezeins D   vs]
PUDEC *Kölbing-Day*, ʒou L   serchen] U *Duggan* 1988:127, serche LPDC *Kölbing-Day*,
wetyn E   344 To here] and E   here] knowe D   be boun] *om.* E   comyng] com P, kom
UD   and what] PU *Kölbing-Day*, ʒif L, and what þat DEC   coueyte wolde] couet here P,
nowe claymen U, cleyme DEC   345 Waspasian] Walde w. PDE, The while V. U, Now
wold v. C   Waspasian] Vesp- UDC   þe] þase P   wyes] wightis D, messagerys E, men C
schewed] schew PDC, said U, telle E   346 sendeþ] sent PUDEC   sondismen] þe
sawdan P, sondes UC, sodeynliche E   aʒen] *adds* with P   sikere] sik P, wurthi E
347 Garde] D, ʒaf L *Kölbing-Day, om.* P, Made U, and bad E, They made C   hem] He P
charge] chareged þam P, gratthly UD, faste E, redy C   to] forto P   go] gange P   and]
and to UC, *om.* DE   gomes] cyteseyns E, lordes C   telle] to telle D, to seye E
348 alle] *om.* UDEC   her] his PUC   come] UD *Kölbing-Day*, coms L, comyng PEC
was] is UC   forto venge] to avenge UDEC   349 Y] þat I PC, hem y D, hem E
bidde . . . boun] þat þey make hem redy E   be boun] þe P, by redy C   bischopes] the
bisshop U, bisshop DEC   and oþer] all P, and thei all U, and all DEC   350 or] before
E, ere the UC   mydday] UDEC *Kölbing-Day*, vndren of þe day LP   *moder-naked alle]
Kölbing-Day, al (all C) moder (modur D) naked (nakyd D) UDC, to be clene nakyd E,
open-heded alle L, vncled and nakyd P   351 Vp] At E, And vp C   here] þe DE   to
ʒelde] hem to opene E   ʒerdes] ʒeredes P   an] in PD, in her UEC   hande] hondes UE
352 Eche] Ilk a U, Eche a DE   wye] PU, whiʒt L *Kölbing-Day*, bierne D, body E, mon C
a white scherte] his shirt UC, his breche DE   scherte] serke P   and . . . ellys] withouten
wede othir P, without gere more U, bout (*corr. later to* withowte D, withowte EC) oþer
wede (cloth C) DEC

Iewyse for Ihesu +   by iuggement to take,
And [brynge Cayphas] þat + Crist   þroȝ conseil bytrayede.
Or Y to þe walles schal wende   and walten alle ouere,   355
Schal no ston vpon ston   stonde by Y passe'.

þis sondismen sadly   to þe cite ȝede
þer þe lordes of þe londe   lent weren alle,
Tit tolden here tale   and wondere towe made
Of Crist and of Cayphas   and how þey come scholde.   360

And when þe knyȝtes of Crist   carpyn bygonn
þe Iewes token [hem] al[s-tite]   without tale more,
Here hondis bounden at here bak   with borden stauys
f. 6ᵛ And of flo[w]en here fa[x]   and here faire berdis;

+ Nake[ne]d as a nedel   to þe neþer houe,   365
Here + visage blecken with bleche   and al þe body after;

353 Iewyse] The Iewes UDC   Ihesu] PUC, ihesu crist to take L, Iesu sake D, Iesu
Crist *Kölbing-Day*   by] *om*. PC, her U, þe D   *no cesura* C   scribal line E: Iuggement
forto take / for crist whom they slowyn   354 And] *om*. E   brynge Cayphas] PUDC,
make hem come L *Kölbing-Day*, Bryngge also c. / E   þat . . . conseil] *trs. phrs*. U   þat . . .
bytrayede] þe cursyd schrewe E   Crist] PDC, ihesu crist L *Kölbing-Day*, Ihesu U   þroȝ
. . . bytrayede] by iuggement cursidly slow D   355 Or] Ere U   Y] y schal E, *om*. P
walles] wall DC   schal] sall I P, *om*. E   walten] walt P, warpe (*adds* hit D) UD, falle hem
E, caste hit C   alle ouere] to the erth UDC, doun to grounde E   ouere] vnder P
356 Schal . . . vpon] For (þat DC) there ne (*om*. C) shal stik nor (ne DC) UDC   stonde]
ligge E, *cesura fols*. U   by Y passe] ere I hens go U, whan y go (weende E) DEC
357 þis sondismen] The messagers were E, ¶ *precs*. D   sondismen] soudeours U,
messengeres C   sadly] on a sopp P, sent forth (*trs*. DE) UDEC   to þe] and to E   ȝede]
wenten PDE   358 lent] li`n`ggenen U, lengedyn D, iloggyd E, dwelleden C   weren]
war P, *om*. UC, hem D   alle] *om*. E   359 Tit] Alstite U, Anone D, *om*. E, As sone as
þey C   tolden here tale] þis tale toolde E   here] thei this UD, þis C   and . . . made] in
truth os thei shulde UDC, riȝt as þey were bode E   towe made] thoght many P
360 *line om*. U   Crist . . . þey] þat Cyphas cursed was þat he P   Crist, Cayphas] *trs. sbs*.
DC   how] þan DE   361 And] *om*. PUDEC   when] ¶ *precs*. D   þe] þere P, thise
UDEC   of Crist] to P   Crist] cristes C   carpyn] carping UE, spekynge C   bygonn] þus
begunon P   362 þe] *om*. P   token] wentyn E   hem als-tite] PUD (als) *om*. P), alle xij.
L *Kölbing-Day*, anon E, hem as sone C   without] withouten P   tale] eny E, talkynge C
363 Here] And here C   Here . . . bounden] and b. h. h. E   bounden] byndes P   with . . .
stauys] ful (*om*. D, wol E) bitterly thanne UDEC   borden] birdyn P   *no cesura* E
364 of flowen] kytte of E, schoven of C   flowen] P *Kölbing-Day* n, flocken L, flewen UD
here¹] þei þe D, þe E   fax] PUDC *Kölbing-Day*, face L, fayr her E   and] and all C   and
. . . berdis] of þo faire bernes D, of her longe beerdys E   berdes] beredes P
365 *Nakened] Nackynde þaim P, Made hem naked L *Kölbing-Day*, Als naked UDEC
a nedel] a neel U, an heel E   to þe] into her UDE, into þe C   houe] hyde P, hyue U,
coyfe E, gloue *Kölbing-Day* n   366 visage] P, visages L *Kölbing-Day*, face UDEC
blecken with bleche] enbaumed with (in C) blode UDEC   bleche] blek P   al þe] her UE
body] bodys P

Suþ knyt with a corde   to eche kny3tes swere
A chese, and charged hem   here chyuentayn to bere:

'Sayþ vnbuxum we beþ   his biddyng to 3ete
Ne no3t dreden his dom: his deþ haue we atled.
He schal vs fynde in þe felde   ne no ferre seke
Tomorowe pryme or hit passe,   and so 3our prince telliþ'.   370

þe burnes busken out of burwe   bounden alle twelf
A3en message to make   fram þe maister Iewes.
Was neuer Waspasian so wroþe   as whan þe wyes come   375
þat were sc[ho]rne and schende   vpon schame wyse.

þis kny3tes byfor þe kyng   vpon knees fallen
And tolden þe tale   as hit tid hadde:
'Of þy manace ne þy my[n]t   þey make[n] bot lyte:
þus ben we tourned of oure tyre   in tokne of þe soþe   380

And bounden for our bolde speche: þe batail þey willeþ
Tomorowe prime or hit passe—   þey put hit no ferre.
Hit schal be satled on þyself   þe same þat þou atlest.
þus han þey certifiet þe [to sey]   and sende þe þis cheses'.

367 Suþ] And sen UD, and thanne E, And aftur þis C   knyt] knytted P   knyt . . . swer]
trs. phrs. C   with] *om.* P   corde] gret corde C   eche] iche a PC, ilk a U, euery E   kny3tes]
knyght PUDC   swer] a corps D, nekke E, *om.* C   368 charged hem] *trs.* P   chyuentayn]
chefetan PUDE   369 Sayþ] And say UDC, Sey3t E   we beþ] haf we bene P   his] at his P
to] *om.* P   3ete] 3itt P, kepe UDEC   **A RESUMES**   370 Ne] And PDE, We UC   no3t
dreden] drede nothing (noght U) UDEC   his dom his] thay thy domes thy A   deþ] dede PA
we] thaye A, *om.* E   atled] helyd P, ordeynd UDC, cast E   371 *lines* 371–81 *om.* P, 371–79
om. A   ne] *om.* UDEC   ferre] ferther to UDEC   372 or] at E   373 þe] Thise UDC
burnes] men C   burnes . . . burwe] kny3tes turnyd a3en E   busken] busked hem UDC   of]
/ of the UD   bounden] *om.* U, bound D, yboundyn E   374 A3en] *om.* E   to] forto E
fram] fro UDC   fram . . . Iewes] as þey wer chaargyd E   *no cesura* EC   375 was] ¶ *precs.* D
neuer Waspasian] *trs.* EC   Waspasian] Vesp- UDC   wroþe] wo UDEC   wyes] knyghtes
UDEC   376 *schorne and] scorned and L *Kölbing-Day*, yschaue and E, shamed and (*and*
C) UC, shamefully D   schende] yscent E   vpon schame wyse] on (in D) swiche a foule wise
UDEC   377 þis] The UDEC, ¶ *precs.* D   byfor] kome to UDEC   vpon] and (*om.* U) on
(vpon C) her UDEC   fallen] fellen UEC   378 And] And al (*om.* U) thei UDEC   þe]
by U   as hit] that thei U   tid] byfalle C   379 Of] by E   ne] and UDEC   þy mynt] D, þy
my3t LPUC *Kölbing-Day*, thretnyng E   *maken] *Duggan* 1988:142, make LD *Kölbing-Day*,
recche U, sette EC   lyte] a litel UDC, lytel E   380 þus] And thus A, loo how E   ben . . .
tyre] we been arayed E   of our] in UDC   tokne] takynnynge A   381 for] hem by C   our]
om. EC   þe] to AUC, for to D   þe . . . willeþ] as theues we were E   382 passe] passes P
ferre] forthire AUDEC   383 Hit] And seyn it C   be satled] sattell PAUD, falle E, ly3te C
same . . . atlest] sothe as þou says P   þat] tha A, *om.* UD   atlest] Ettillede A, hem myntes
UDE, hem demes C   384 han þey certifiet] thei certifie UC, þei sente DE   þey] we P
þe¹] *om.* PU, 3ow A   to sey] PAUDE, *om.* L *Kölbing-Day*, and seyn C   sende] sendes PAE,
sent DC   þe²] 3ow A   þis] thir A   cheses] chese PUC

Wode we[ll]ande wroþ   Waspasian was þanne,   385
Layde wecche to þe walle   and warned in haste
þat alle maner of men   in þe morowe scholde
Be sone after þe sonne   assembled in þe felde.

He streyȝt vp a standard   in a stoure wyse
B[ygg]id as a belfray   bretful of wepne,   390
Whan oȝt fa⟨u⟩ted in þe folke   þat to þe feld longed
Atte þe belfray to be   botnyng to fynde.

A dragoun was dressed,   drawyn alofte,
Wyde gapande of gold   [þe] go[llet] to s[che]we
With arwes armed in þe mouþe,   and also he hadde   395
A fauchyn vnder his feet   with foure kene bladdys.

þerof þe poyntes were piȝt   in partyis foure
Of þis wlon[k]fulle worde   þer þei werre fondyn;
In forbesyn to þe folke   þis fauchou[n he] hengeþ
þat þey hadde wonnen with swerd   al þe world-riche.   400

385 Wode] *after* welland P, Full wode A   wellande] P, wedande L *Kölbing-Day*,
wylde and A, wepand UDEC   wroþ] *om.* P   Waspasian] Vesp- UDC   þanne] þou? P
386 Layde] He laid UE   wecche] waytes A   walle] walles AE   and] *om.* P
387 þat] Till A   of] *om.* D   in] on PUDEC, that one A   morowe] morne PU, morne
thay A   388 Be] *after* sonne P, By UC   assembled] sembled PUDE, gedered C
389 He] Than thay A   streyȝt] strake PA, sette C   vp] *om.* A   in] on P, appone A
a] an C   stour] sterne UDE, angry C   390 Byggid] UD, bild LC *Kölbing-Day*,
Bellyd P, belde A, ytymbryd E   a] *om.* D   bretful] and britfull P, euen full C
391 Whan] wwhen A, That when C   fauted] *blotched* L, failed UPDEC   in] *om.* PA
folke] felde UDEC   þe²] *om.* EC   feld] fight PAUDC *Kölbing-Day* n, werre E
longed] longeth U   392 þe] þat P   botnyng to fynde] betyd sone P, baynly botede
alsone A   fynde] haue UDC   scribal line E: men schulde to þe belfrey renne / and
there it redy fynde   393 was] was thare A, is UDC   drawyn] and drawen
PAUDEC   a-] appon AUEC, vp a- D   394 of gold] with his mouth E   of . . .
gomes] *trs. phrs.* U   *þe gollet] the gomes UD, gomes LPA *Kölbing-Day*, þe iewes E, þe
lordes C   to] forto U, vnto C   schewe] UDEC, swelwe LPA *Kölbing-Day*
395 arwes] arowes arghely A   armed] and armour C   in . . . hadde] on eche syde E
þe] his AD, *om.* UC   and] *om.* D   *no cesura* E   396 A] and a E   fauchyn]
fawkone AUDEC   feet] fote UC   foure] many E   kene bladdys] kene (kyn D, maner
E) fethers UDEC   397 *lines* 397–400 *om.* E   þerof] Therewith A   were] *om.*
UDC   partyis] partys P   398 Of] And of UDC   þis] þese P, þat D
*wlonkfulle] wlonfulle L *Kölbing-Day*, wankyll P, wankille A, wanton UDC   worde]
folke P, werlde A *Kölbing-Day*, worme UDC   þer] that A   þer . . . fondyn] is wonder
to here UDC   werre] hade were A   399 forbesyn] furbissynge P, schewynge A,
rebukynge C   to] of PAC   þe] *om.* D   þis] þar þe P, the AUDC   fauchoun] P,
fawkon ADUC, fauchouns L   he] UDC, thay A *Duggan* 1988:128, *om.* D. LP *Kölbing-Day*
hengeþ] hangede A, helde UDC   400 hadde] haue P, *om.* UC   wonnen] *om.* D
wonnen with swerd] *trs.* C   with] to P   swerd] werre UDC *Kölbing-Day*   *no cesura* C

[On] a bal of brennande gold   þe beste was [a]s[sised],
His taille trayled þeraboute   þat tourne scholde he neuere   f. 7ʳ
Whan he was lifte vpon lofte,   þer þe lord werred
Bot ay lokande on þe londe   tille þat + lauȝte were.

þerby þe cite myȝt se   no s[agh]tlyng wolde rise   405
Ne no trete of no trewes,   bot þe toun ȝelde
Or ride on þe Romayns,   for þey han + rede take
þer britned to be   or þe [burwe] wynne.

His wynges [b]rad were abrode   boun forto flee
With belles bordored aboute   al of briȝt seluere,   410
Redy whan ouȝte r[a]n   to rynge[n] ful loude
With eche [a] wap of [þe] wynde   þat to þe wynges sprongyn.

Ibrytaged [bigly] aboute   þe belfray was þanne
With a tenful toure   þat ouer þe toun gawged.

401 On a] UDEC, A LPA *Kölbing-Day*   brennande] brent UDEC   þe beste] þe
brest D, þis worm E   assised] UDC, on sette LPA *Kölbing-Day*, yfastnet E
402 trayled] trayles P, takynede A   þeraboute] þarvnder P, to be A, ther doune U,
adoun DE, doun C   he] þai PA   403 Whan] whan þat E   lifte] reysed E   vpon]
on PAUDC   vpon lofte] *om.* E   þer] *om.* UDC   þer . . . werred] þe iewes myȝte it se E
þe] *om.* A   lord] lordis AUDC   werred] aforne UDC   404 Bot ay] Most thei
UDC   lokande] loked PUD, to luke A, looke C   on] to DC   on þe londe] therto U
londe] lane C   tille] to P   *þat] it UC, hit D, þat al L *Kölbing-Day*, all P, alle A
scribal line E: Al þe day longe to feryn hem more (*no cesura*)   405 myȝt] *precedes* þe C
se] se þat D, yse / þat C   saghtlyng] PAUD, setlyng L *Kölbing-Day*, acord E, pece C
wolde] shul U, shold DEC   406 Ne] Na P, Nor UC   no¹] *om.* UDEC   trete]
entrete UD, entre C   of no] ne E   no²] *om.* PAUC   trewes] trew PDE, trewe loue
UC   bot] til UDEC   toun] cite UD   ȝelde] ȝoldyn A, be yolden UDC, were ȝolde E
407 Or] But E   Or . . . þe] And now the Riche A   on] ouur C   for þey] *om.* A   for . . .
take] spede what thei myȝte E   han] PUDC, han her L *Kölbing-Day*, hafe to A   take]
tane PU   408 þer] At thay there wolde A   britned to be] bykere to abyde C   to]
om. A   or] or ells A   burwe] PAUDC *Kölbing-Day*, toun L   scribal line E: or be
kyld as caytyfes / & cowardes be hoolde   409 lines 409–12 *om.* PE, *line om. with
subsequent line-order* 413–16, 410, 412 UDC   *brad] *Kölbing-Day* n, sprad L *Kölbing-
Day*, brighte A   abrode] & brade and A   flee] fly A   410 With . . . bordored]
Brouden (Braydyn D) belles UD, They honged belles C   al . . . seluere] that boldely
(bysyly C) rungen UDC   of] in A   411 *line om.* UDC   *ran] range A, runnen
L *Kölbing-Day*   *ryngen] *Duggan* 1988:142, rynge LA *Kölbing-Day*   ful] appon A
412 With] At UC   eche] ilke AU, a eche D   a wap of þe wynde] AUDC (ʻaʼ D,
wap] waif U, weef D, blaste C), wynde of a wap L, wap of a wynde *Kölbing-Day*   to
þe] his A, þe DC   wynges] wenge UD   sprongyn] touchede ADC, touches U
413 Ibrytaged] Bretist P, brestede A   Ibrytaged bigly] *trs.* A   bigly] PAUDC, *om.* L
Kölbing-Day   was] is UC   scribal line E: The berfrey was britagyd strongliche
abowte (*no cesura*)   414 a] *om.* D   tenful] wounder strong E, dredefull C
toure] turne P, touris D   ouer] to A   toun] Cite D   gawged] glayde P, gaggede A,
gogges U, goggid D, lokyd E, hangedde C

þe b[es]t[e] by [his] briȝtnesse   burnes myȝt knowe   415
Foure myle þerfro,   so þe feldes schonen.

+ On eche pomel were pyȝt   penseles hyȝe
Of selke and sendel   with seluere ybetyn:
Hit glitered as gled-fure—   ful of gold riche
Ouer al þe cite to se—   as þe sonne bemys.   420

Byfor þe foure ȝates   he formes to lenge
Sixt[i] þousand by somme   while þe sege lasteþ;
Sette ward on þe walles   þat noȝt awey scaped,
Sixe þousand in sercle   þe cite alle aboute.

Was noȝt while þe nyȝt laste   bot nehyng of stedis,   425
Strogelyng in stele wede   and stuffyng of helmes,
+ Armyng of olyfauntes   and oþer arwe bestes
Aȝen þe Cristen to come   with castels on bake.

Waspasia[n] in stele wede   and his wyes alle
Weren diȝt forþ by day   and drowen to þe vale   430

415 beste] PAUDC (int. P) Kölbing-Day, batail L ?Kölbing-Day n, dragun E   his]
PAUDEC, þe L Kölbing-Day   burnes] þe beryns P, þe bemes D, men EC   burnes myȝt]
best myght thei U   knowe] kenne UDEC   416 line om. P   so . . . schonen] forsothe atte
leest (atte leest] & no lasse E) UDEC   feldes schonen] felde schone A   417 On]
PAUDEC, And on L ?Kölbing-Day   eche] iche a PDC, a A, ilk a U, euery E   were] cesura
precs. L, was PA, is UDC   penseles] pesalls full A   hyȝe] many D   no cesura E   418 Of]
with A   and] and with A, and of UDEC   sendel] selcouth werke PA, seluer DEC   with]
and P, of A   with . . . ybetyn] semely araied UDEC   y-] in P, En- A   no cesura C
419 gled-fur] þe glede P, gledis of fyre A, red feer E, þe glede of fyer C   ful of] on þe P, or
of A, in the UDC ful . . . riche] þe gold was so fyn E   420 al] om. A   to se] om. E   as]
whan E   þe²] om. C   bemys] schnyned E   421 Byfor] Than byfore A, Aforn UDEC
he] thay AU, þoo C, om. DE   formes] fourmed PAU, fourmyd þan D, ordeyned E,
formede þey C   to lenge] were E   lenge] luge P, liggen UDC   422 Sixti] UDEC,
Sixtene LPA Kölbing-Day   þousand] thowsandes A   by] om. P   while] till A   lasteþ]
lasted PADC, laste E   423 Sette] thay sett A, And set UDC, ȝit was E   ward] wardes P,
sadly A, watche UDEC   on] at P, to AUDC Kölbing-Day, abowte E   walles] wall PUDC
þat . . . scaped] of stong ordynaunce E   noȝt] on U, none DC   scaped] schapid PA, went
UDC   424 line om. D   Sixe] And sex UC   þousand] thowsandes A   in sercle] in a
sopp P, in sercles A, to serche (sh- C) UC   alle] om. P   no cesura C   scribal line E: þat no
wyȝth myȝth awey / in no maner wyse   425 Was] was ther C   noȝt] nat E   nyȝt] sege C
laste] lastede ADC   426 Strogelyng] Strongelynge (?) P, Stering UDC, stowryng E
in] of PUDEC Kölbing-Day n, with A   wede] wedes PD, werke A   and] om. PDC   added
scribal line L: Riȝt so in þe cite / þey schapte hem þerfore   427 Armyng] PAUDEC,
with armyng L Kölbing-Day   arwe] grete PU, stronge DEC   428 with] wþ D   castels]
castell P, strenght U   bake] bakkes PAD, her bak(es?) U, her bakkes E   429 Waspasian]
PAE Kölbing-Day, waspasial L, Vespasian UDC   in stele wede] y-armed C   wyes] wightis
D, knythes E, meyne C   alle] keene E   no cesura C   430 Weren] was P, He U, om.
DEC   diȝt] dight him U, Arayed hem E   forþ] om. PE   by] with the ADC, to the U,
aȝens E   and] om. DE   drowen] dryuen P, drewen AD, drawyng E   to] till P   vale] dale D

Of Iosophat þer Ihesu +   schal iuggen alle þinges,
Bigly batayled hym þer   to + bide[n] þis oþer.

þe fanward Titus toke   to telle vpon ferste
With six[tene] þousand soudiours   assyned for þe nones,
And [as] mony in þe myd-ward   were merked to lenge   435
þer Waspasian was   with princes and dukes.

And sixtene þousand in þe þridde   with a þryuande knyȝt,
Sire Sabyn of Surrie   a siker man of armes   f. 7ᵛ
þat prince was of prouynce   and mychel peple ladde,
Fourty hundred in [an] h[e]r[e   with] helmes to schewe.   440

And ten þousand atte tail   at þe tentis lafte
Hors and harnays   fram harm[es] to kepe.
By þat bemys on þe burwe   blowen ful loude
And baners beden hem forþ—   now blesse vs our lorde!

431 Ihesu] PAUDEC, Ihesu crist L *Kölbing-Day*   iuggen] deme UC   alle þinges]
mankynde E   *no cesura* E   432 Bigly] And bigly PA, And UEC, And boldely D
batayled] Enbatelde AUEC   batayled hym] *trs.* C   hym] thaym AUDEC   biden] A
Duggan 1986:584 1988:127, abide LE *Kölbing-Day*, byde PDC, abyden U   þis] þase PA,
þe E   433 þe] *om* P, ¶ *precs.* D þe . . . toke] Titus toke the vaward UC, Tytus toke
(anon took E) þe vale DE   to] forto C   telle] tolle A   vpon ferst] ȝow forsothe P, the
sothe UDEC   434 sixtene] PUEC, six L *Kölbing-Day*, sexty AD   þousand]
thowshandes A   soudiours] *om.* UDEC   for þe nones] to hymselfe P   *no cesura* C
435 And] *om.* P   as] PAUDEC, *om.* L *Kölbing-Day*   as . . . myd-ward] *trs. phrs.*
UDEC   myd-] medill AUDC   were] was PA, *om.* UDEC   merked] assigned U,
arayed E   lenge] bene UDEC   436 þer] thare als A, the E   Waspasian] Vesp-
UDC   437 sixtene] sexty P, seuyntene A   in] on A   þridde] thirde syde A
þryuande] trew P   scribal line UDEC: And in the rerewarde als fele (meny DE) / with
dukes and knyghtes (with . . . knyghtes] so semely of sight D, with a wurthi [fayre C]
knyȝt EC)   438 armes] harmes E   439 þat . . . was] There (He E) was a Prince
UDEC   and] that UDEC   mychel] mych DEC   ladde] had P, lede A
440 Fourty] Fouretene P   in] on UDEC   an . . . helmes] PAUDEC [an] *om.* P,
here] hepe UDEC), helmes / and harnays L *Kölbing-Day*   to schewe] & scheldis A,
ytyȝed E   441 atte tail] in tale P, of þe tayle A, in the taile UDC, were yleeft E   at]
was at PA   at . . . lafte] to kepe her tentis D, behynde al in tentes E   þe] thaire A
tentis] tent P   lafte] were lafte UC   442 Hors] thaire horse AUDEC   harnays]
thaire hanayse A, her herneys UDEC   fram] fra PAE   harmes] PADEC, harmyng L
Kölbing-Day, harme U   kepe] loke DC   443 By] B *altered from* v L By þat] Bot þe
P, Sone after E   bemys] biernes D, trumpours E, trumpes C   on] in PAUDEC
burwe] town E   blowen] blew A, blewen UDEC   ful] on P, appon A, wel D, wol E
444 baners] beryns A   beden] braude ? P, benten U, bode E, benden C   now] *om.* PD,
þer A, and UEC   blesse] blisses P, blyyse A   blesse . . . lorde] blis vs bytide (þe tyde
C) UDC, penselys manye E   followed by inset 'Passus' A, inset 'Passus tercius' U,
marginal rubric 'Passus ⟨ ⟩' follows line 444 C, marginal 'iijus. passus' by next line P

[Passus tercius]

þe Iewes assembled were sone   and of þe cite come   445
An hundred þousand on hors   with hamberkes atired,
Without folke vpon fot   at þe foure ȝates
þat preset to þe place   with pauyes on hande.

Fyf and twenti olyfauntes,   defensable bestes
With brode castels on bak,   out of burwe come;   450
And on eche olyfaunte   armed men manye
Ay an hundred an hey   an hu[r]d[is]ed withyn.

þo drowen dromedaries doun   deuelich þicke,
[An] hundred [h]os[e]d and yheled   with harnays of mayle,
Eche beste with a big tour   þer bold men were ynne,   455
Twenty told by tale   in eche tour euene.

Cameles closed in stele   comen out þanne
Faste toward þe feld;   a ferlich nonbre
Busked to batail,   and on bak hadde
Echon a toret of tre   with ten men of armes.   460

---

445 þe Iewes] þen *with two-line capital* P, *four-line capital* LE, *three-line capital* A, *two-line capital* U, ¶ D   assembled] sembled UDE, gadered C   assembled were] *trs.* U   of] owt of AUD, fro E   þe²] *om.* U   446 An hundred þousand] thousyndes E   on] appon A   with] in PAUDEC   hamberkes] hawberks PADE, hauberk U, armour C   atired] arayed P, ytired U   448 þat] and E   to] oute at P, forthe A, out to UC, out in D, foorth to E   þe place] with pryde A, the playne UDEC   pauyes] paueschis A   on] in PAUD   on hande] ynowe E   449 Fyf] And fyue UC   fyf and twenti] And xlv. D twenti] fourty E   defensable] fensable DE, fusabull C   450 brode] *om.* E, brothe C on] appon A, on her UE   bak] bakkes AE   of] of þe PUDEC   burwe] town E 451 on] *int.* E   eche] ilke ane AU, eche an C   manye] were E   *no cesura* UEC 452 *line om.* P   Ay] Hase A   Ay an] Nyghe an UC, Nyne D   hey] highte A   an] wiþ D *hurdised] hurdeschede A, hurdist U, hurdys D, hurdes C, hundred L *Kölbing-Day* scribal line E: to fyȝte in hurdys / auoward on here bakkes   453 *lines* 453–55 *om.* D þo] Yit? P, thay A, There UC, Than E   drowen] drafe oute P, 'drewe' A   drowen dromedaries] *trs.* UEC   dromedaries] drewmondaryes A   doun] *om.* P, owte AE deuelich] dulfully A   þicke] fele U, manye C   454 An] PAUE *Kölbing-Day,* And (*i.e.,* &) LC   hosed] A, houshid P, þousand L *Kölbing-Day, om.* UEC *Kölbing-Day* n   and] and alle EC, *om.* U   yheled] y-armed U   with] in PAEC   harnays] helmys A, armes U 455 Eche] Ilke a A, And ilk U, & eche EC   beste with] with UC, baar E   þer] *om.* U, and EC   were] there UEC   were ynne] *trs.* A   ynne] *om.* P   456 told] ytool E   eche] ilke a AU, eche a EC   457 Cameles] *altered from* Clo–? L, Chamelles C   closed] ycloþed E comen . . . þanne] *om., line fused with next* P   458 Faste . . . feld] *om., line fused with prec.* P. þe feld] that fyghte A   a] *om.* D, and a C   ferlich] full felle A, deflich many D, wounderful E, full grett C   459 Busked] thay buskede A, Busk hem U, Buscked hem C   to] towarde the A   and] *om.* UD   on] vpon C   bak] bakkes A, her bak U, her bakkis DEC hadde] ladden UDC, beere E   460 Echon] Ilkane A, Ilk U, Eche DEC

Chares, ful of chosen,   charged with wepne
A wondere nonbre þer was,   whoso wite lyste.
Many douȝti þat day   þat was adradde neuere
Were fond fey in þe feld   [b]e þat [þe] fiȝt endid.

An olyfaunt y-armed   came out, [vpon] l[of]te   465
Keuered 'myd' a castel,   was craftily ywroȝt.
A taber'n'acle in þe tour   atyred was riche,
Piȝt as a paueloun   on pileres of seluere.

A which of white seluere   wal[w]ed þerynne
On foure goions of gold   þat hit fram grounde bare,   470
A c[h]osen chayre þerby   [a]n ch[aun]dele[r]s twelfe
Betyn al with b[ou]rn[d]e gold   with brennande sergis.

þe chekes of þe chayre   were cha[r]bokles fyne
[þ]er, couered myd a riche cloþe,   Cayphas was sette.
A plate of pulsched gold   was piȝt on his breste   475
With many preciose perle   and pured stones.

461 Chares] Choppid P, Chayers A, Charietis DE   chosen] chose men & P, chosen men
AC, choise men U, choys folk D, chose folk E   charged] chareged P, þo com E   wepne]
wapyns A   462 wonder] gret E   so] om. E   wite] will P, wolde A, se D, wiste E
lyste] lysten P, myght UDC, þe sothe E   463 Many] And many PA, For many (mony a
C) UDEC   was] were DE   was adradde] dred was PA   adradde neuer] trs. C
464 Were] om. P, was AUC   fond fey] trs. PA, feld E, fownþen feynte C   þe¹] that A
be] PAUDC, er LE Kölbing-Day   þat] om. E   þe²] PAUDEC, om. L Kölbing-Day
465 y-armed] vnarmed UE, enarmedde C   out] om. P   vpon lofte] P, at þe laste
LAUDEC Kölbing-Day   466 myd] with PAUDEC   was] om. DE   was craftily] þat
craftely was (is UC) PAUC   craftili] craftly E   467 in þe] and a A, wiþin þe D
atyred] tired UC, arayed D   was] is UC   riche] hyȝe C   468 Piȝt as a paueloun] with
a pauylun pyȝt E   as] vp als A, on U, vpon DC   on] xxx. P, of UD   pileres] postes
UDEC   469 line om. P   A] And an U   which] kyste A, arke U, owche C   white] om.
AUC, fyn E   seluere] syluer full schene A   walwed] UDC, walynde L, was sett A,
hanged E, walwynde Kölbing-Day   -ynne] withIn A   no cesura E   470 On foure
goions] And foure graynes P   goions] gargons A, gogeons U, geauntis D   þat . . . bare]
om., line fused with 472 PA, fro (from D, fro þe C) grounde that it bere (bare D, beere C)
UDC, to bere it fro þe grounde E   471 line om. PA   chosen] UDC Kölbing-Day,
chose E, closen L   chayre] chariot U   an] UEC, on L Kölbing-Day, wiþ D
chaundelers] UDEC, charbokeles L Kölbing-Day   472 Betyn . . . gold] om., line fused
with 470 PA   al] and E   with¹] of UDC   *bournde] barne L, bright U, bryght C, brent
D, brende E, barnd Kölbing-Day   with²] and U   sergis] stregese ? P, tapers C
473 þe¹] On þe C   chekes] cheeke AU   were] was A   charbokles] DEC Kölbing-Day,
chabokles L, charebucle PAU   fyne] Kölbing-Day n, full fyn A, stones UE, four DC, fyue
Kölbing-Day   474 *þer] precs. Cayphas LPAUDC (& þer C) Kölbing-Day   myd] with
PAUDEC   a] om. DE   riche] clene U   Cayphas . . . sette] in which cayphas saat E
was] is UD   was sette] solde sytt A   475 plate] plater P   was] om. PA   piȝt] prest P,
put UDE, sette C   breste] hreste P   476 many] many a C   preciose . . . pured] grete
pilar and precious P   perle] perles UE   pured] full proude A, eke (oþer E) riche UE

f. 8ʳ Lered men of þe lawe   þat loude couþe synge
With sawters seten hym by   and þe psalmys tolde
Of douȝty Dauid þe kyng   and oþer dere storijs
Of [Iosue] þe noble Iewe   and Iudas þe knyȝt.   480

Cayphas of þe kyst   kyppid a rolle
And radde how þe folke ran   þroȝ þe re[d]e wa[t]er
Whan Pharao and his ferde   were in þe floode drouned,
And myche of Moyses lawe   he mynned þat tyme.

Whan þis faiþles folke   to þe feld comen   485
And batayled after þe bent   with many burne kene,
For baneres [and beme-worde]   and bestes y-armed
Myȝt no man se þrow þe so[mm]e   ne vneþ þe cite knowe.

[V]aspasian dyuyseþ   þe [va]le alle aboute
þat was with baneres ouer[b]rad   to þe borwe [ȝ]a[t]is.   490
To barouns and bold men   þat hym aboute were
Seiþ, 'lordlynges a londe,   lestenyþ my speche.

477 Lered] þe lerd P, Lernyd DE, And lernede C   couþe synge] gan synge U, myȝte
speke E   *no cesura* E   478 seten] sityn PU and] *om.* DEC   þe] om U   tolde] thei
redde UDC, to reede E   479 kyng] duke UDC   oþer] of U, of his DE, of þe C
480 Iosue] AUDE *Kölbing-Day* n, Ioseph LPC *Kölbing-Day*   þe¹] þat P   Iewe] Ioue P
and] and of D   þe knyȝt] machabeus E, þe kynge C   481 of] oute of PAUDEC   þe] a
PC, *om.* D   kyst] hucche E, cheste C   kyppid] clekis A, cauth vp UDEC   482 And]
om. P   folke] childryn of irael / E   þroȝ] ouer PU   rede water] UD, rerewarde L, brade
water P, rede waters A *Kölbing-Day*, red se EC   483 ferde] folke PUEC, feris AD
were] was P, *om.* DEC   were . . . flode] therein were U   in . . . drouned] drouned
(dronkynede A) in þe flode PA   floode] see C   drouned] drenchid DE   484 he] *om.*
P, thay A   mynned] menyd/meuyd PAUDC, meuyd in E   485 Whan] Bot when A
þis] þe PUDEC, those A   faiþles] fayles P, hethen C   to þe] was in P, were (was U) to the
AUDE   to . . . comen] was komen to þe feelde C   486 And] i- *Kölbing-Day* n
batayled] Embatelde A, þere were enbatayled E   after] by A, aforne UC, byfor D   after
þe bent] *om.* E   þe] þat A   bent] oste C   burne] beryns A   burne kene] bigge (bright
DE, a bygge C) wepyn UDEC   487 For] With UDEC   *and beme-worde] and beme
wode A, and bemewede U, & bemes P, and bright wede D, & trumpes C, þat blased L
Kölbing-Day, & pensellis E   y-] en- PAD   488 þrow] *om.* UDEC   somme] A, sonne
LUDEC *Kölbing-Day*, soyle PC   ne] nor UC   ne vneþ] *om.* P   vneþ] *om.* AUDEC
Kölbing-Day   knowe] to knaw P   489 Vaspasian] UDC, waspasian LPE *Kölbing-Day*,
than waspasiane A, ¶ *precs.* D   dyuyseþ] deuysede AUDEC   þe] de C   vale] PAUDEC
Kölbing-Day, feld L, *cesura fols.* C   *no cesura* E   490 þat was] *om.* UDEC
*ouerbrad] *Kölbing-Day* n, brade P, brode A, ouersprad L *Kölbing-Day*, ouurspradde C, al
(and E) ouersprad (ovirspred D, ouerspredde E) UDE   to] vnto AD   borwe] borowe AD,
town E, cyte C   ȝatis] PAUDE, wallis L *Kölbing-Day*, walle C   *no cesura* E   491 *line*
om. D   To] So P, Til U   barouns] beryns A   and] and to A   hym aboute] *trs.* C   *no*
cesura E   492 Seiþ] He sayde PAUDEC   lordlynges] lordes PUC, lordyngs ADE   a
londe] one lowde A, alowd DE *Kölbing-Day*, all alowde C   lestenyþ] lystyn P, herkeneth C
my] to my AE

Here nys kyng noþer k[ny]ȝt   comen to þis place,
Baroun ne b[achele]re   ne burne þat me folweþ,
þat þe cause of his + come   nys Crist forto venge   495
Vpon þe faiþles folke   þat hym fayntly slowen.

Byholdeþ þe heþyng   and þe harde woundes,
þe [b]yndyng and þe betyng   þat [h]e [on] body hadde:
Lat neuer þis lawles ledis   lauȝ at his harmys
þat bouȝt vs fram bale   with blod of his herte.   500

[Y] quy[t]e-clayme þe querels   of alle quyk burnes
And clayme of euereche kyng   saue of Crist one,
þat þis peple to pyne   no pite ne hadde
[As] preueþ his passioun,   whoso þe paas redeþ.

Hit nediþ noȝt at þis note   of Nero to myn[n]e   505
Ne to trete of no trewe   for tribute þat he askeþ:
[His] querel Y qui[t]-cleyme,   [whe]þer he + wilneþ,
Of þis rebel to Rome   bot resoun to haue.

---

493 Here] There A   nys] es P, is nother C   kyng] *int*. P   noþer] ne PADEC, nor U
kny3t] PAUDEC *Kölbing-Day*, kynȝt L   494 ne¹] nor UC   bachelere] PAUDEC,
burges L *Kölbing-Day*   ne²] nor C   burne] man EC   495 þat] but E, But þat C   þe]
ne the A   þe cause] *om*. P   come] PAUD *Kölbing-Day*, comes L, comyngge EC   nys] es
PAEC, nis but U   forto venge] to avenge UDEC   496 þe] cause þis P, ȝone A, this
UDEC   hym fayntly] hym falsly P, falsely hym AUDEC   497 þe¹] to þe PAD, vnto
U, to his C   heþyng] hethyn P, heuenward U, passyoun C   and] and to PAUDC
scribal line E: Loketh vp to heuynward / & thenkyth on his woundes   498 þe¹] of E
byndyng, betyng] PUDEC, *trs*. L *Kölbing-Day*, buffettynge, betynge A   and] *om*. AUC, of E
þe²] *om*. DE   he on] PAUDC *Kölbing-Day* n, þe L *Kölbing-Day*, he on his E   hadde]
bode D   499 Lat] And lat EC   neuer] noght PE   þis] ȝone A   lawles ledis] helle-
houndes E   ledis] men C   lauȝ] laughen U, leyȝe E   his] hir A   500 bouȝt] dere
boght PAU, so deere bought EC   fram] fra PA, of UD, out of C   fram bale] *om*. E
501 *lines* 501–12 *om*. E   Y quyte-clayme] PAUD, quycke-clayme L, I voyde awey C, I
quycke clayme *Kölbing-Day*   þe querels] all cleymes / and quarelles C   querels] querell
PU   alle] all þe PA   burnes] men C   502 clayme] claymes A, *om*. C   of¹] on P
euereche] euericke a PAU, euery crowned C   saue] but UDC   of²] on P   one] alone DC
503 þat] The whyche C   pyne] pyne hym of hym A, peyne D   ne] *om*. P, þay A, þey
ne C   504 As] PAUDC, þat L *Kölbing-Day*   his] þe P   whoso . . . paas] the pase
(pask D, gospell C) who it (so DC) UDC   -so] *om*. P   þe paas] at paske A   505 at] in
P, to D   þis] our D   note] tym AC   of] *om*. P   mynne] UD, mynde L *Kölbing-Day*,
mene PA, mynge C   506 *line om*. D   Ne] Na P, Nor C   to] forto U   of] for U
507 His] PAUD, þat L *Kölbing-Day*, The C   Y] here I A   Y quit-cleyme] of nero clene I
avoyde C   quit-] PAUD, quik- L *Kölbing-Day*   wheþer] PA *Kölbing-Day*, for oþer L,
quite (queþe D, byqwede C) it where UDC   he] PC, he ne LA *Kölbing-Day*, him UD
wilneþ] wenes P, will AC, liketh UD   508 þis] his UDC   rebel] robberie D, rebelles C
bot] *om*. PC   bot . . . haue] *om*, *line fused with line* 510 D   to²] it wolde U

Bot more þing in our m[o]de   myneþ today,
þat by resoun to Rome   þe rea[lt]e fallyþ,   510
Boþe þe my3t and þe mayn,   maistre [and oþer],
And lords[chip] of eche londe   þat liþe vnder heuen.

Lat neuer þis faiþles folke   with fi3t [of] vs wynne
f. 8ᵛ Hors ne harnays,   bot þey hit hard byen,
Plate ne pesan   ne pendauntes ende   515
While any lyme may laste   or we þe lif haue.

For þei ben feyn[t] at þe fi3t,   fals of byleue,
And wel wenen at a wap   alle + þe wo[r]ld quelle,
Noþer grounded on God   ne on no grace tristen
Bot alle in st[e]rn[e]s of stoure   and in strengþ one.   520

And we ben di3t today   Dri3ten to serue—
Hey Heuen-kyng,   hede to [þyn] owne'!

509 *line om.* D   more þing] murnyng UC   our] my P   mode] UC, mynde LPA
Kölbing-Day   myneþ] moues me P, mene we A, vs mynnes (mynges C) UC, myneþ vs
Kölbing-Day   today] this daye A   510 þat] *altered from* þer ? L   þat . . . Rome]
om., line fused with line 508 D   þe] of D   realte] PUDC *Duggan* 1988:128, regnance L
Kölbing-Day, Rygalite A   fallyþ] longeth C   511 mayn] *om.* A, mayn / and (& þe
C) UDC *Kölbing-Day*   and oþer] P, or ellys L, of all oþer landis A, of (on DC
Kölbing-Day) erthe UDC *Kölbing-Day*   512 lordschip] PUDC *Kölbing-Day*, lord
suþ L, the lordchipe A   of] on D   eche] ilke PU, Ilke a A, euery DC   liþe] ligges
PA   513 *line om.* C   Lat] And lete hem E   þis] 3one A, þe D   þis . . . folke]
be no wey E   faiþles] fayles P   with fi3t] *om.* P   of] PAUDE *Kölbing-Day Duggan*
1988:128, *om.* L   vs] vs to P   514 Hors] Herse A, neyþer hors E   ne] nouther
U, ny C   hard] dere AU   byen] abigge E   *no cesura* C   515 Plate] Plates P,
pate E   ne¹] nor U   pesan] besaunte C   ne²] nor UC   pendauntes] pendande PA
ende] hende P, endes U   *no cesura* E   516 *line om.* U   while] Till A   any
lyme] we C   lyme] lyfe PDE   may] may vs A   or . . . haue] in eny of oure hertis E
we] *om.* C   þe] *om.* P   haue] m⟨aye⟩? P   517 þei ben] thaire A   feynt]
PAUDEC *Kölbing-Day*, feyn L   at] of P, in C   þe] *om.* DE   fi3t] faythe and P,
fyghte / and AUEC   518 *line om.* E   And wel] but 3it þey E   wel] wolde U,
wol DC   at] with A   wap] wayf U, weef DE, lefte C   alle . . . quelle] to wyn all
this werlde A   þe world] UDEC *Kölbing-Day*, þey wold L   quelle] to quelle DC, to
wynne E   519 Noþer] Nouther PU, thay ne are noghte A, Neithir DE, Nor C
on¹] in PAUDEC   God] gud A   ne] nor PU   on no] in his PUDEC, in A
grace] god A   tristen] traysten PA   520 *line om.* U   alle] *om.* E   sternes]
ADEC *Kölbing-Day*, storijs LP, stourness ? *Kölbing-Day* n   of] and C   stour] store
P, hemself E   in²] in her E   one] ouer P, alone DC   521 ben] 'be' P   today]
this daye dere A, in (*om.* U) this day UDEC   Dri3ten] crist for E, allmy3ty god C
522 Hey] Now þou heghe A   Heuen-] heuens A   hede] take kepe A, take hede
Kölbing-Day (*rejected Kölbing-Day* n)   hede . . . owne] has hight vs oure mede P
þyn] A, his L *Kölbing-Day*   scribal line UDEC: To done (brynge C) thise deuels on
dawe (out of lyfe C, To . . . dawe) & þese deuelys to distreye E) / and his deth venge
(avenge DE, to venge C)

þe ledes louten hym alle   and aloude sayde,
'Today þat fleþe any fote   þe fende haue his soule'!

Bemes blowen anon   blonkes to neȝe,   525
Stedis stampen in þe [st]ede   st[uf]f[ed] steil vndere,
Stiþe men in stiropys   striden alofte,
Knyȝtes croysen hemself,   cacchen here helmys.

With loude clarioun cry   and [with cormous] pypys,
Tymbris and tabourris   tonelande loude,   530
Ʒeuen a sch[r]i[k]ande schout;   schrynken þe Iewes
As womman [welter] schal in + swem   whan hire þe water neȝeþ.

[þey] lacchen launces anon,   lepyn togedris;
As fure out of flynt-ston   ferde hem bytwene.
Doust drof vpon lofte,   dymedyn alle aboute   535
As þonder and þicke rayn   þro[b]olande in skyes.

523 þe] om. P, those A, His UDC   ledes] meyne C   louten] louyd P, lowttede A, leued
UC, left D   alle] also P, om. C   sayde] crydyn D   scribal line E: þan seyde his lordes & his
peple abowte (no cesura)   524 Today] this daye he A, He þat þis day C   any] a PA   fende]
deuel UE   haue] feche A   525 Bemes] Beryns A, Trumpores E, Clariouns C   blowen]
blewen AUDC, trumped E   anon] on hye UC, þan on hy D, vpon heygh E   blonkes] and
blonkes A, and horses UC   blonkes to neȝe] and baners vp brayde D, and blewyn vp faste E
to] begonne to C   neȝe] nye PA   526 stampen] staumped UDEC   in] one A   þe] om. U,
þat E   stede] UDE, felde LPA Kölbing-Day Turville-Petre, place C   stuffed] A, stif L
Kölbing-Day, stith P   stuffed . . . vnder] vnder stele-wedes UDE Duggan 1986a:95, vndur þe
stele aray C   527 Stiþe] And styffe A, Stiffe UDEC   Stiþe men] Sithen P   men] man E,
om. C   in] in þair P, vpon U, in þe C   stiropys] stedes U   striden] þai striden P   a-] vpon
UDEC   528 croysen] crossed PAE, & crossen C   cacchen] and tachid P, and caste one A,
and catche UC, & cawthen E   her] hem E   529 With loude] om. UDEC   clarioun] clarions
PAUDEC   cry] þai crye P, cried fast UDEC   with cormous] P, alle kyn L Kölbing-Day,
cormous A, cornmuse D Turville-Petre, curiouses UEC   530 Tymbris] Trompis A,
Tymberers D   and] om. C   tabourris] taboreres AD   tonelande] tutill þai P, tyndillede A,
and trumpes (trompers DC) UDC, & mynstracye E   loude] hye P, one harde A, ful trie UC,
crye D, ynowe E   531 line om. P   Ʒeuen] with A, Thei yaf UDC   ȝeuen . . . schout] whan
þis noyse was ymaad E   *schrikande] shrike (shryke C) in (& C) a UDC, schillande L Kölbing-
Day Turville-Petre, schakande A   schout] shoure U   schrynken] thane (tho U) schrenked
AU, to shame wiþ D, þo tremblyd E, forto shrynke C   532 line om. P   As] And C
womman] women AUEC Turville-Petre   *welter schal] Turville-Petre, weltir solde A, schal L
Kölbing-Day, shrillen U, wepith D, wepeth E, wepyn C   *in swem] Turville-Petre, in a swem
L Kölbing-Day, in swoun A, on hey U, an hey E, on hyȝe C, & waylith D   hire þe water] water
thaym (her D, he C) AUDC Turville-Petre, þat sorwe hem E   533 þey] AUDEC Kölbing-
Day, om. LP Kölbing-Day n Turville-Petre   lacchen] laughte AUDE, kawȝte C   lepyn] and
leppen (lopen U) AUDEC   534 As] Als the A   of] of þe P   ferde] hit ferd DE, thus
faredde C   ferde . . . bytwene] thei hewen on harde U   hem] þai P   535 Doust] the duste A
drof] dryuen P, dref E   vpon] on P, vp a- D   dymedyn] & dymmed P, the dale A, and dryued
UE, drivyng DC   alle] om. PUDEC   536 and] in a P, in UDEC   *þrobolande] Kölbing-
Day n Turville-Petre, and thrymbland P, þrowolande L Kölbing-Day, threpande A, thrilles U,
þirlid D, hurleth E, persheth C   in] the UDC, in þe E   skyes] schoures P, skewes A

Beren burnes þrow,   brosten [here] launces;
Kny3tes crosschen doun   to þe cold erþe.
Fou3t faste in þe felde,   and ay þe fals vndere
Doun swowande to swelt   without swar more.   540

Tytus tourneþ hym to,   tolles of þe + beste,
Foriustes þe iolieste   with ioyn[yng] of werre.
Suþ with a bri3t bronde   he betiþ on harde
[þat] þe brayn and þe blod   on þe bent ornen.

Sou3t þro3 anoþer side   with a s[ad] wepne,   545
Bet on þe broun stele   while þe bladde laste,
An hey breydeþ þe brond   and as a bore lokeþ,
How hetterly doun,   hente whoso wolde.

Alle bri3tned þe bent   as bemys of sonne
Of þe gilden gere   and þe goode stones;   550

537 Beren] thay bere AD *Kölbing-Day* (*rejected Kölbing-Day* n), The bolde (bare E, berne C) UEC   Beren burnes] Beryns borne er P   burnes] barnes EC   þrow] thereaboute UC, þurghout DE   brosten] brysten P, brost D, & burstyn E   here] PUDEC *Duggan* 1988:128 *Turville-Petre, om.* L *Kölbing-Day*, with A   launces] speres UDEC   538 crosschen] croschid P, thruschen A, kneled UDEC   doun] downe thraly A, adoun UDEC   to] vnto A   539 Fou3t] thay fyghte A, Fighten UD, And fow3ten C   in þe felde] on fote U   ay] euur C   fals] iewes E   540 *line om.* PUDC   swowande] sweyande (*altered from* swew-?) A   to] one A   without] withowttyn P   *scribal line* E: þere was non mercy at al / but alle to deth wente   541 tourneþ] turnyd EC   hym] þaim P, *om.* D   to] *cesura precs.* L, onone UDEC   tolles] and tolles PADC, telles U, and kylleth E   beste] PAUDEC *Kölbing-Day Turville-Petre*, bestes L   542 Foriustes] ForIusted of P, Iusters of A, Foriustid D, Forth Iusteth C   iolieste] Ioly kny3te C   with] for P, in U   ioynyng] PAUDEC *Kölbing-Day Turville-Petre*, Ioyned L   543 Suþ] And sythyn AUD, & also E, And aftur C   bronde] swerde C   he] *om.* PAUDEC *Turville-Petre*   betiþ] brittynes A, betheth C   harde] faste PC   *no cesura* E   544 þat] PAUDEC *Turville-Petre*, Tille L *Kölbing-Day*   brayn, blod] *trs.* A   on] appon AC   bent] bronde UDE, swerde C   ornen] lefte AUEC *Turville-Petre*, last ? D   545 Sou3t] He soghte A, And sen (aftur C) UC   Sou3t . . . side] And seth in þe same stede DE   þro3] one AUC   anoþer] þair P, that other UC   side] sydes P   a] many P   sad] PA, sore LUDEC *Kölbing-Day Turville-Petre*   546 Bet] And betis A, smoot E   on þe] appon AUDEC   while] whils þat A laste] lasten P, lastis AU, lastid DC   547 *lines 547–48 om.* P   An] And E breydeþ] areysed vp E, he lefte C   þe] he his A, he the UD, his C   brond] swerde C lokeþ] lokyd E, he loketh C   548 How] hewys AUD, & hewyd E, He hewedde C hetterly] heuyly A   hetterly doun] on (on ful U) hertly UDEC   hente] cacche C wolde] hapyns A   549 *line order* 550, 549 A   bri3tened] bryghtyn P, bretned U, brightnes on D, glisteryd E, shyned C   þe] his E   bent] bentis D, gere E, feelde C as . . . sonne] hew whoso wold D, as þe sunne bemys E   of] of the AUC   550 Of þe] All of P, For the A   gilden] gilten PA, golden UC   gilden gere] prys perre E and] and of PUDEC   þe²] *om.* P

For schy[m]eryng of sche[l]des   and schynyng of helmes   f. 9ʳ
Hit ferde as + þe firmament   vpon + fure were.

[V]aspasian in þe vale   þe fanward byholdeþ,
How þe heþyn here   heldiþ to grounde;
Cam with a faire ferde   þe fals [for]to mete.   555
As gre[m]ed griffouns   [þey] girden in samen.

Spakly here speres   on sprotes þey ȝeden,
Scheldes as schidwod   on scholdres tocleuen;
Schoken out of scheþes   þat scharpe was ygrounde
And mallen metel   þroȝ vnmylt hertes.   560

Hewen on þe heþen,   hurtlen togedre,
Forschorne gild schroud,   schedered burnee.

551 For] What for P, Of DE   schymeryng] AUDE *Kölbing-Day* n *Turville-Petre*,
schyueryng LPC *Kölbing-Day*   ofᵗ] *om.* E   scheldes] PAUDEC *Kölbing-Day*
Turville-Petre, schendes L   of²] *om.* UEC   552 ferde] fore P   as] PAUDEC
Turville-Petre, as alle L *Kölbing-Day*   firmament] firment P   vpon] al on U, on DEC
fure] PAU, a fure LDEC *Kölbing-Day Turville-Petre*   553 Vaspasian] UDC, wasp-
LPAE *Kölbing-Day Turville-Petre*, ¶ *precs.* D   fanward] vauarte PUC *Turville-Petre*
554 How] And howe U   here] hopped UEC, hepid D   heldiþ] heledes P, hedeles
UDC, heuydles E, *cesura fols.* C   to] to þe AUC   555 Cam] he come AU, And
come DE, And he come C   a faire] his D, meche fayr E   ferde] felde P, folke AE,
feris D   þe] those A   fals] ADEC *Turville-Petre*, fals men L *Kölbing-Day*, folke P,
fals folk U   forto] PAD *Turville-Petre*, to LUEC *Kölbing-Day*, vnto C   mete]
maynteine P   556 As] And als AE, Right os UDC   *gremed griffouns] greued
griffouns L *Kölbing-Day*, þe grimly griffons P, Gryffons (-nes E) wiþ (with E) grame DE
Turville-Petre, gryffones (-ons U) one (on UC) grownde (grene UC) AUC   þey]
AUDEC *Turville-Petre*, *om.* L *Kölbing-Day*, *after* girden P   in] *om.* P, all A   in
samen] togeder UDEC   557 Spakly] Full spakly A, Spedely UDEC   on sprotes]
in spildirs A, on men E, on peces C   þey] *om.* P, gun (gunne to E) UEC   ȝeden]
springe UEC, sprungyn D   558 scholdres] sound*ur* C   to-] þai PDE, dede C
559 Schoken] than thay schoke A, And shoten U, Swerdis shokyn DC, schottyn E   of]
of þair P, *om.* E   scheþes] schetes P, arwes E, shede C   scharpe] schrape A   was]
war PAUDEC *Kölbing-Day Turville-Petre*   ygrounde] gronden PDC   560 And]
om. P   mallen] melyn A, malle (mallede C) with that UC, mette wiþ þe D, smete with
þat E   þroȝ] thorowte A   vnmylt] with vnmaght P, maltyn A, mens U, mennys DC,
many mennys E   hertes] herte E   561 *lines* 561–62 *om.* P   Hewen] thay hewe
AUDEC *Turville-Petre*   on] appone A   þe heþen] harde stele A   heþen] he't́hyn D
hurtlen] and hurtles AUD *Turville-Petre*, and hurtlyd E, and fowȝten C
562 Forschorne] For schire A, Forshere U   gild] gyltyn A   gild schroud] shroudes
ful shene UD   schedered] schodires A, on shiderand UD, schodered *Kölbing-Day*
(*rejected Kölbing-Day* n)   burnee] those beryns A, beerns UD *Kölbing-Day* (= *byrnes*
Kölbing-Day n)   scribal line E: Hors wox al blody / so thei were ywoundyd   scribal
line C: They hewen þe armour full shene / on shynynge barnes

Baches woxen ablode   aboute in þe vale,
And goutes fram gold wede   as goteres þey runne.

Sire Sabyn setteþ hym vp   whan 'hit' so ȝede,   565
Rideþ myd þe rereward   and alle þe route folweþ,
Kenely þe castels   came to assayle
þat þe bestes on here bake   out of burwe ladden.

Atles on þe olyfauntes   þat orible were,
Girdiþ out þe guttes   with grounden speres;   570
Rappis rispen forþ   þat [rydders] an hundred
Scholde be busy to burie   þat on a bent lafte.

Castels clateren doun,   cameles brosten,
Dromedaries to þe deþ   drowen ful swyþe;
þe blode fomed hem fro   in + flasches aboute   575
þ[at] kne-depe in þe dale   dascheden stedes.

563 Baches] Bankes PDC, Alle A, Bank U   woxen] wexen PA, blowen UD, flowen C
a-] with U, of C   blode] floode C   aboute] abouten U   in] all that brode A   scribal line
E: manye stremes in þe vale / of blood faste runne   564 And goutes] Blode P, And
UDC   fram] oute of PAUDC *Turville-Petre*   gold] gilten A, gay (þe gaye C) golde UC,
gay goldyn D   wede] clathes P, gere D, *om*. C   as] *om*. UDC   þey] there UDC   runne]
ranne A, yede UDC   scribal line E: for there was meche more ysched / þan eny man can
telle   565 Sire] ¶ *precs*. D   Sabyn] Sabyr C   setteþ] sett PC, sees A   hym vp]
hymselfe A   hit so ȝede] he sawe tyme UDEC   566 Rideþ] And rydis A, And rode
UDEC   myd] with PAUDEC   þe¹] a P   folweþ] after UDEC   567 Kenely] And
full kenly A, & kenely E   þe] her D   þe . . . came] thay come the castells A   came] he
come P *Turville-Petre*, thei kome UD, he caste hym E, þey gan C   568 *lines* 568-72
om. P   here] *om*. C   here bake] bakkes AD   of burwe ladden] fro towne beryn E
burwe] borowe AD, þe cyte C   ladden] ledith D   569 Atles] Thay Eghtillede A, *om*.
UDEC   on] to A, Than UE, Vpon DC   þe] those A   þat] he (thei E) hit / that UDEC
570 Girdiþ] And girdes A *Turville-Petre*, And gurt UDEC   þe] thayre AE   grounden]
scharpe growndyn A   571 Rappis] Here ropes C, Roppis *Kölbing-Day Turville-Petre*
rispen] breken C   forþ] owte A, aright UD, down ryght C   rydders] A ?*Kölbing-Day* n
Turville-Petre, redles L ?*Kölbing-Day*, redely UDC   scribal line E: & ropes al toburste /
and rente on smale peeces   572 burie] bere A   on a] oon on C   a] the AD   bent]
bank UDC   lafte] leuyde A, lastyn D   scribal line E: þer myȝt non hors bere / þat in þe
feeld lafte   573 Castels clateren] Claterd castels UEC, þere clatrid castels D   clateren]
claterd PA   doun] þai doune P, adoun UDEC   cameles] camels PA, the camels (-es C)
UC, and camelis DE   brosten] thay brustyn A, tobrostyn D, toburste E
574 Dromedaries] And dromedaries UDC   drowen] drouen P, drivyn D   ful] *om*.
PD, als A, wel U   swyþe] fast DC   575 þe] tha the A   in] PAUDEC *Duggan*
1986:584 *Turville-Petre*, in þe L *Kölbing-Day*   flasches] slowes P, flattis A, flodes al (*om*.
DC) UDC, feeldes E   576 þat] PAUDEC *Kölbing-Day Turville-Petre*, þe L   kne-]
kene P   dale] vale EC   dascheden] daschen doune P, dasschyne thaire A, dasshed the
UC, dasshid D, stopen þe E

þe burnes in þe bretages   þat aboue were
For þe doust and þe dyn,   as alle doun ȝede
[W]han hurdizs and hard erþe   hurtled togedre,
Al forstoppette in stele   st[a]r[k]e-blynde wexen   580

And vnder dromedaries +   diȝ[ed]en + sone.
Was non left vpon lyue   þat alofte standeþ
Saue [an an]lepy olyfaunt   at þe grete ȝate
þer as Cayphas þe clerke   in [a] castel rideþ.

He say þe wrake on hem wende   and away tourneþ   585
With twelf maystres + ma   of Moyses lawe;
An hundred helmed men   hien hem after   f. 9ᵛ
Er þey of castel myȝt come,   cauȝten hem alle.

Bounden þe bischup   on [a] bycchyd wyse
þat þe blode out barst   [ilka] band vndere,   590
And broȝten [to] þe b[erfray]   + alle [þe] bew-clerkes
þer þe standard stode   and stadded hem þer.

577 burnes] men E, mayne C   bretages] bretage PU, bretace A, bastyles C   aboue]
aboute PD, abowne A, abouen UC   578 doust] dyntis DE   and] of E   as alle] alle a-
UDEC   579 *line order* 580, 579 L *Kölbing-Day, line om.* P   Whan] Thenne C
hurdizs] þe hurdis D   erþe] herthe E   hurtled] hurtlyn D, hurtledyn E, Iusted C
togedre] op hepe E   580 -stoppette] -stuffyd E   in stele] for hete E   starke-]
PUDEC *Turville-Petre*, storte- (*a corr., orig.* strrte?) L, stane- A   wexen] þey wuxe E
581 *line om.* P   And vnder] An (And DE) hundred of UDEC   diȝeden] AC, doun /
diȝten L *Kölbing-Day,* dyed UDE *Kölbing-Day* n, doun dyede *Turville-Petre* *sone] hem
sone L *Kölbing-Day,* full sone A *Turville-Petre,* in that (a DEC) stounde (whyle C) UDEC
Kölbing-Day n   582 Was] *om.* P, thare was A   non] no beste A   vpon] on D   alofte]
on grounde U, on foot E   standeþ] stode PAUDEC *Turville-Petre*   583 Saue] but E
an anlepy] A *Kölbing-Day (rejected? Kölbing-Day* n) *Turville-Petre,* olepy L, anely ane P, an
UD, on EC   at] allone atte UDEC   grete ȝate] brode ȝatis A   584 as] þat E   a]
UDC *Duggan* 1988:128, þe E, *om.* LPA *Kölbing-Day Turville-Petre*   rideþ] houyd E
585 wrake] werke C   wende] vendes P   away] aȝeyn C   tourneþ] turned UE   *no
cesura* C   586 twelf] alle þe grete E   ma] P, made LAUDC *Kölbing-Day Turville-
Petre, om.* E   *no cesura* C   587 An] And than an A, And an C   hundred] hundred of C
hien] hyed PAUDEC *Turville-Petre*   hem] hym A   *no cesura* E   588 Er] And or
þat A   of] in þe P, to þe A, to her D, of þe C   myȝt] *om.* P, may U   cauȝten] þai cached
P, to cacch D, and cawȝten C   scribal line E: & toke hem alle ar thei myȝte / out þe castel
come   589 Bounden] Bandyd P, thaye bonde A, And bowndyn E   þe bischup] þis
cayfas E   on] besyly one A, in DE   a] PUEC *Duggan* 1988:128 *Turville-Petre, om.* L
Kölbing-Day, ane A, þe D   bycchyd] byter E, sory C   590 þe] *om.* P   ilka] A *Duggan*
1988:128, eche LUD *Kölbing-Day,* iche a PEC *Turville-Petre*   band] bone C   band
vnder] veyne aboue other U   *no cesura* E   591 And] *om.* P, Thei UDC   broȝten]
ledde E   to þe berfray] PAUDEC (to) vnto A, berfray] bastyle C) *Kölbing-Day Turville-
Petre,* þe bischup / and L   þe²] PUDEC *Turville-Petre,* his L, those A *Kölbing-Day*
bew-] bolde P, bone A, benche UD, grete E, sorye C   *no cesura* U   592 þer¹] Whare
PUDC, where þat E   stadded] stedde PA, stokked UEC, stowid D   hem] thaym alle A

þe beste and þe britage   and alle þe briȝt gere,
Chaire and chaundelers   and charbokel stones,
þe rolles þat þey redde [o]n   and alle þe riche bokes   595
þey broȝte myd þe bischup,   þou hym bale þouȝte.

Anon þe feyþles folke   fayleden herte,
Tourned toward þe toun   and Tytus hem after:
Fel[d]e of þe fals ferde,   in þe felde lefte,
An hundred in here helmes   myd his honde one.   600

þe fals Iewes in þe felde   fallen so þicke
As hail froward heuen,   hepe ouer oþer.
So was þe bent ouerbrad,   blody byrunne,
With ded bodies aboute—   alle þe brod vale—

Myȝt no stede doun stap   bot on stele wede   605
Or on burne oþer on beste   or on briȝt scheldes.
So myche was þe multitude   þat on þe molde lafte
þer so many were + mart,   mereuail were ellis.

593 and¹] of PC   britage] bretace A, castell C   594 Chaire] Chayers PD, charyer E
chaundelers] chaunlabres P, þe candelstykkes C   and²] with E   charbokel] scharbokill P
595 þe¹] om. P, And þe C   rolles] rolle AUDEC   þey] he UDEC   redde on] PAUDEC
Kölbing-Day Turville-Petre, redden L   þe²] þair P, those A   riche] fayr E   596 myd] forth
P, with AUDEC   þou] þof P Turville-Petre, þoghe þat A   hym] he U   bale] heuy C   þouȝte]
thoughten P   597 lines 597–98 om. P   Anon] than onnone A, ¶ precs. D   fayleden] faylede
the A, faylid D, fayled her C   herte] hertes UDEC   598 Tourned] thay tournede A, &
turned E   toward] homward to E   hem] sone U, faste E   no cesura C   599 Felde of] U
Kölbing-Day Turville-Petre, Fele of LD, Felles þe P, He fellide A, And felde C   þe¹] those A
fals] faithles U   ferde] þat ferd P, folke AUDC   in] whils that A, and thei UC, on D   in . . .
lefte] als þai fle walden P   lefte] laste A, fledde C   scribal line E: & chasyd hem abowte / as
houndes dooþ þe hare   600 An] And C   in her helmes] in þat haste P, of those haythyn
men A, of hethen UDC   myd] with PAUDC   his] his owene C   honde] handis AD   one]
allone UDC   scribal line E: and felde an vndryd hymself alone / ar þat he stynte   scribal line
added D: He britnyd with his bronde & broght to þe deþe   601 Iewes] folk UDEC   in]
on A   in . . . fallen] trs. phrs. UE   fallen] om. P, ware fallyn A, fellen UEC, flowyn D   no
cesura C   602 froward] fro A, from UD, doth from E, fro (expunged) þat cometh fro C
heuen] þe heuen PA, heuenward UDEC   hepe] in hepes PA, ilkone U, eche hepid D, eche E,
hoppeth C   ouer] on U, from D, vpon E, vp & C   oþer] vndur C   603 lines 603–06 om. P
was] were D   bent] banke UC, bankis D, vale E   ouerbrad] -b- a later? correction over erasure
L, ouer alle A, al aboute UDC, om. E   blody byrunne] baumed (ybawmyd E) al (om. E) with
blode UE   604 line om. D   ded] those dede A   aboute alle] trs., cesura fols. UC   alle . . .
vale] ywis on euery syde E   þe] that A, by the U   no cesura E   605 Myȝt] there myghte
AEC   Myȝt no] Ne myght U   doun stap] trs. UDEC   on] all vpon C   stele] schene A
wede] wedis D, om. C   606 Or] Othir AE   burne] brene A, beerns UD, men EC   burne,
beste] trs. UDEC   oþer] or AUDEC Turville-Petre   beste] breste A, beestes UDEC   or²] or
ells A   scheldes] heuedis A   607 So . . . multitude] M. w. þare myche P, þe m. w. (is U) s.
mekill AUDEC Turville-Petre   þat] om. P, that thare A   þe²] om. AU   molde] mosse DE,
grownde C   lafte] last? D   608 mart] Turville-Petre, mart`red′, int. later L, morte P,
merrede full A, marred UDEC Kölbing-Day   mereuail] veruayl E   were²] war P, hadde be E

ȝit were þe Romayns as rest   as þey fram Rome come:
[Vn]r[i]ue[n] eche a renk   and noȝt a ryng brosten,   610
Was no poynt perschid   of alle here pris armure.
So Crist his knyȝtes gan kepe   tille complyn tyme.

An hundred þousand helmes   of þe heþen syde
Were fey fallen in þe felde   [and noȝt a freke skaped],
Saue seuen þousand of þe somme   þat to þe cite flowen   615
And w[onn]en with mychel wo   þe walles withynne.

Ledes lepen to anon,   louken þe ȝates,
Barren hem bigly   with boltes of yren;
Brayden vp brigges   with brouden chaynes
And portecolis with pi[nn]e   picchen to grounde.   620

þei wynnen vp whyȝtly   þe walles to kepe,
Frasche vnfounded folke,   and grete defence made;

609 *lines* 609–11 *om.* P   were þe Romayns] the R. w. UE   as¹] also A, *om.* UDC
rest] ristede A, sounde UDC, hool E   as²] os when UDEC   fram] fro A   fram Rome]
first UDEC   comen] con⟨torn⟩ D   610 Vnriuen] A *Kölbing-Day Turville-Petre*,
Ronnen ouer L, Wele araied UDEC   eche] eueryche AE, ilk U   a¹] *om.* DE   renk] man
EC   and] *om.* UDC   noȝt a] no A   a] o EC   ryng] ryengne A, thing D   611 *line*
om. AC   scribal line UDE: May (Might DE) no beern (body E) on hem breke / so bigly
(boldely DE) thei stonde (stode DE)   *Turville-Petre*: Myȝt no berne on hem breke better
was neuere   612 *line om.* DE   So] thus A   his . . . gan] gan his men UC   gan kepe]
kepyn P   tille] to PU   complyn] complynes UC   scribal line after 612 P: Might noght
þaire brayne bresten better was neuer   scribal line after 612 UDE: For (so E) there (*om.*
DE) nas segge (þer man E) of the sege / that of sore wist   scribal line after 612 C: Ther
was no bone broken / better were þey neuur   613 þousand] thoused E   helmes] of
helmys A   of] on PUDEC   þe] *om.* A   syde] Iewes A   614 fey] for- P, *om.* E,
faynte C   fey fallen] *trs.* UDC   fallen] fownden AUDC, feld E   and . . . skaped]
PAUDEC (and) that A *Kölbing-Day, om.* DC   noȝt a] no A *Kölbing-Day*   a] o DEC   a
freke] one U, o man C   skaped] shapid P, yskaped U, stopid D, lasse E) *Kölbing-Day
Turville-Petre*, or þe fiȝt ended L   615 of þe somme] *om.* UDEC   somme] same P
þat] *om.* P   þe cite] toun E   flowen] ȝode P, flede AC, flewe U   *no cesura* C
616 And] They C   *wonnen] *Turville-Petre*, wan P, wane A, wanne C, wan (*after* wo)
UD, wymmen L, *om.* E, wynnen *Kölbing-Day*   mychel] wunder meche E   þe] kepten
þe E   withynne] *om.* E   617 Ledes] þe ledes P, Men EC   lepen] lightely P, lopen UE
to] *om.* PA, vp E   louken] lokked PD, and I⁀o⁀ukes to A, and lokked UE, and lokkeden C
ȝates] ȝate P   618 Barren] Barryd PAUDC, And barryd E   bigly] full bygly A
boltes] barres C   619 Brayden] thay brayde A, And brayde C   vp] vpon D   brigges]
the brygge A, the brigges UDEC   with] and P   brouden] berres and P, bygly A, the
bolde U, þe brode D, her stronge E, þe bownden C   620 And] þe P, And the A
pinne] DE, pile L *Kölbing-Day*, pynnes P, pyne AUC *Turville-Petre*   picchen] perched P,
thay putt it A, pight UD, putte E, pyȝten C   to] þe P, to the AUDEC   grounde] erthe U
621 wynnen] wan PA, wenten UDEC   whyȝtly] lightely P, full wyghtly A
622 Frasche] Fell D   Frasche . . . folke] brought forth fressch men E   vnfounded]
vnfonded P *Kölbing-Day*, and vnfandide A, vnwonded C   and] þat A, a UC, *om.* D

Tyeþ into tourres   tonnes ful [þykke]

f. 10ʳ With grete stones of gret   and of gray marble.

Kepten kenly with caste   þe kernels alofte,   625
[Wh]a[pp]en [o]ut querels   with + quartes attonys.
þat oþer folke at þe fote   freschly assayled
Tille eche dale with dewe   was donked aboute.

Withdrowen hem fro þe diche   dukes and oþer—
þe caste was so kene   þat come fram þe walles—   630
Comen forþe with þe kyng   clene as þey ȝede,
W[ant]ed noȝt o wye   ne non þat wem hadde.

Princes to here pauelouns   passen on swyþe,
Vnarmen hem as-tyt   and alle þe nyȝt resten
With wacche vmbe þe walles   to many wyes sorowe.   635
þey wolle noȝt þe heþen here   [þu]s harmeles be lafte.

623 Tyeþ] þai titt P, thay tuke AC, Token UDE   into] to the U   tourres] þe toure P,
torettis A   ful] om. P   þykke] PAUDEC Turville-Petre, manye L Kölbing-Day
624 With] ful of E   of gret] om. DE   gret] gete P, greke A   and] all D   and . . .
marble] of marbel and oþer E   625 Kepten] thay kepe A, Thei kepte EC   kenly] kyndely
P, sharpely C   with, þe] trs. P   kernels] corners UDEC   alofte] aboute UE   626 lines
626–28 om. U   Whappen] P Turville-Petre, Quarten L, warppis A, Quattid (and q. E) DE,
They shette C, Quarren Kölbing-Day   out] ADEC Turville-Petre, after querels L Kölbing-
Day, doune P   with] be PAC Turville-Petre, om. DE   *quartes] quarters (-eres C) LPADEC
Turville-Petre, quartots Kölbing-Day   attonys] many P   627 þat] þe DE   at þe] att D,
vpon C   at þe fote] withowte E   freschly] bysyly E   assayled] assayles PAD   628 Tille]
To P   eche] ich a PDE, ilke a A   dale] diche DE   with . . . aboute] were ful / of dede
mennys bodyes E   dewe] the dewe AC   629 Withdrowen] Withdrawes P, than thay
drewe A, Tho withdrowe UDEC   hem] om. UEC, þei D   fro] for P   diche] derke P, dikes
A, dike U   dukes] bothe dukes U   no cesura C   630 þe¹] For þe PAUDEC Kölbing-Day
Turville-Petre   caste] schot E   kene] scharp EC   fram] fra PAUDEC   walles] wall PC
631 Comen] thay cone (comen C) AC, and comyn E   forþe . . . kyng] w. þe k. forth aȝeyn C
with] to E   clene] ryght P   þey] þe C   ȝede] forth ȝodyn P   632 Wanted] PA Kölbing-
Day Turville-Petre, wounded L, Wanted hem UD, lakkyd hym E, They wanted C   noȝt]
neuer EC   o] a PUDEC, on A   wye] wyghte AD, man EC   ne non þat] ne (nor C) no AC,
that a U, not one þat D   þat] om. E   wem] wounde PAU Turville-Petre, harme DE,
woundes C   hadde] h⟨gutter⟩ D   633 Princes] Thanne princes C   here] om. DE
pauelouns] palace P   passen] passed PUD, presede AC, passyde E   on] om. DE   on swyþe]
forth harde U, full thykke C   634 Vnarmen] Vnarmed P, And araied (vnarayde C) UDEC
as-tyt] all P, sone AC, rathe U, þere DE   alle] om. P   resten] ryste A, rested UDEC   no
cesura C   635 wacche] waches PA, gode wayte U   vmbe] att P, abowte AUDC, abowte
withoute E   walles] wall PUDEC   to] om. AUDEC   wyes] wyfe P, wyghtis to A, wye to U,
wight to D, on to E, manye a man to C   sorowe] sore ? (in gutter) D   636 þey] om. P, Bot
A, For thei U   wolle] nolde U, wulde E   þe] this A, þese C   heþen] false E   here] om.
UDE, houndes C   þus] PAUDEC Turville-Petre, so L Kölbing-Day   be lafte] shuld passe
U, passe DC, passed E   followed by inset 'Quartus passus' U, marginal 'iiii. passus' by next
line P, followed by inset 'Passus' A, quire end with awkward cast-off D, cf. marginal 'Passus
iiijus.' by line 639 (at head of the next page) C

[Quartus passus]

[Rathe] as þe rede day   rose [o]n þe schye
`Bemes blowen + on [brode]   burnes to + ryse.´
þe kyng comaundeþ acry   þat comsed was sone,
þe ded bodies on þe bonke   bare forto make: 640

To spoyle þe spilt folke   spare[n] scholde none,
Geten girdeles and gere,   gold and goode stones,
Byes, broches bry3t,   besauntes riche,
Helmes hewen of gold,   hamberkes [nobl]e.

Kesten ded vpon ded,   was deil to byholde.   645
[W]eyes made [þey] wide   and to þe walles comen;
Assembleden at þe cite   saut to bygynne
Folke ferlich þycke   at þe foure 3ates.

þey bro3ten toures of tre   þat þey taken hadde
A3en euereche 3ate,   3arken hem hey.   650

637 *Rathe] As rathe D *Turville-Petre*, Sone LA *Kölbing-Day*, Alsone U, As sone EC,
Onone P, *two-line capital* PU, *three-line capital* A, ¶ *precs*. D, *four-line capital* E   as] after A
þe¹] *om*. P   day] day rawede A   rose on] PEC *Kölbing-Day Turville-Petre*, rosen L, and rase
one A, gan rise on U, ros yn D   schye] skyes UDE   638 *line added in margin* L   Bemes]
Beerns U, Claryones C   Bemes blowen] trumpores trumped E   blowen] blewen PAUC
Turville-Petre   on brode] PAC *Turville-Petre*, anon L *Kölbing-Day*, her bemes U, on brode
and D, vp E   burnes] berenes P, the host UE, þe lordes C   to] forto UE, gan DC   ryse] AD
Turville-Petre, aryse LC *Kölbing-Day*, rayse PUE   639 comaundeþ] comaunde PU, hase
comandide A, comaundid DC, anoon made E   comsed] counsayle P, conscent A, knowen
UDEC   sone] *om*. P   640 þe¹] That þe C   on] to P, in E   þe²] *om*. U   bonke] bent PA
Turville-Petre, feeld E   forto] vnto C   641 To] And E   spoyle] dispoyle DE   þe] that A
spilt] sleyne C   *sparen] spare LPA *Kölbing-Day Turville-Petre*   sparen ... none] and spare
(s. hem E) no lenger UDEC   none] no man A   642 Geten] thay gatt AC, Grete D   and
gere] of UDEC   gere] gay gere P, gere of A   gold] *cesura fols*. UEC   and²] with E   goode]
many gode UDEC   643 *line om*. P   Byes] Ryngis A, Bedes and UDEC   bry3t] full
bryghte and A, / and UDEC   riche] full riche A   644 hewen] hewyd D, helyd E   of]
with ADE   gold] golde / and AUEC   hamberkes] hauberks PU, haburgones C   hamberkes
noble] perre wol riche E   noble] PUDC *Turville-Petre*, manye L *Kölbing-Day*, full nobylle A
645 *line om*. U   kesten] Lefte P, thay keste AC, And caste E   was] þat PEC, *om*. D   deil]
ruthe D, heuy hit C   to] was to PEC   byholde] holde P, se EC   646 Weyes ... wide] P,
Made wide weyes L *Kölbing-Day*, Made (They made C) wayes full w. AUDC *Turville-Petre*
walles] wal U   comen] wente C   *scribal line* E: thanne þey tooke hem togidre / and to þe
town come   647 Assembleden] And a. C   at] to AUDEC   cite] walles E   saut] asawte
PAUC *Turville-Petre*, and assaute DE, *cesura fols*. C   to bygynne] bygunne D, made E
648 Folke] Fresche folke AC   Folke ... þykke] and faste felde doun þe folk E   ferlich] full
AC, fresshely D   þycke] felle U, fele D   at] byfore A   649 þey] *om*. PUD, And E
bro3ten] Braste P   toures] torettis A   þat ... hadde] & tokyn þaim all P   þey²] þat A   þey
taken] *trs*. DC   650 A3en] And a3ens C   euereche] euer a P, ilke a A, euery a U, eche C
3arken] 3arkynde P, 3erkede AUD, and reysed E, reysed C   hem] þai P, thaym full A

Bygonnen at þe grettist   a garrite to rere
Gr[ei]ded vp fro þe grounde   on xij. grete postes.

H[it] was wonderlich wide,   wroȝt vpon hyȝte,
Fyue hundred in frounte   to fiȝten at þe walles.
Hardy men vpon h[yȝ]te   hyen at þe grecys   655
And + bygonnen with bir   þe borow to assayle.

Quarels flambande of fure   flowen out harde
And arwes [vn]arwely   with attyr enuenymyd.
Taysen at þe toures,   tachen on þe Iewes;
þroȝ kernels cacchen here deþ   many kene burnes.   660

f. 10ᵛ   Brenten and beten doun   + b[e]ldes wel þycke,
Brosten þe britages   and þe brode toures.
By þat was many bold burne   þe burwe to assayle,
þe hole batail boun   aboute þe brode walles

þat were byg [at a] b[i]r   and bycchet to wynne,   665
Wondere heye to byholde   with holwe diches vndere,

    651 Bygonnen] *stroke over* o L, thay bygan AC   grettist] gretteste ȝate C   rere] arere
DE   652 Greided] PUD *Turville-Petre*, Groded L *Kölbing-Day*, Getyn AC, deepe
ypyȝt E   vp fro] in E   on] of P, wiþ D   grete] stronge E, sykur C   653 Hit]
PAUDEC *Kölbing-Day Turville-Petre*, he L   wonderlich] wonder P   wide] wyed E
wroȝt] and wroght PAC *Turville-Petre*, and ywrought U   vpon] on U   hyȝte] hye UDE,
hyethe C   654 Fyue] Foure P   in] on PU, on a AEC, a D   to fiȝten] faght P, fight D
at] on PUC   655 Hardy] Armed U   vpon] vp C   hyȝte] PA *Turville-Petre*, haste L
Kölbing-Day, hye UDE, hyed C   hyen] hyed P, hewed UE, hewen DC   at] to A
656 bygonnen] *additional mark of abbreviation* L, bygynnes A, bigan tho UC   bir] a bir
PA, birth U, myȝt E, strengthe C   þe] to E   borow] burgh PAU, cyte EC   657 *lines*
657–63 *om.* U, 657–68 *om.* E   flambande] flaumand PAC, flaummyd D   of] one A, in DC
flowen] flappid D   out] in PADC *Turville-Petre*   harde] herde P, faste A, full þykke C
658 And] With P, *om.* A   vnarwely] A *Kölbing-Day Turville-Petre*, arwely L, egrely P, ful
hastily D, full smertelye C   with attyr] attirly A   659 Taysen] þai taysed P, thay
schotte A, They tachen C, þey taysen *Turville-Petre*   toures] torettis A   tachen] and
tachid PA, and tachyn D *Turville-Petre*, and chasen C   on] *om.* PDC   660 þroȝ
kernels] With care DC   cacchen] cachede AC   here deþ] þai (thaire A) dede PA   kene]
bolde A, a sharpe C   burnes] men P, beryn A, baroune C   661 Brenten] Brayded P,
thay brynte ADC   beldes] AD *Turville-Petre*, þat bilde was L *Kölbing-Day*, bretage P,
byggynges C   wel] *om.* P, full A *Turville-Petre*, so DC   þycke] stronge C
662 Brosten] thay brast of A, They brake C   þe¹] all þe P, thaire A   britages] belde
P, bretace A, bastyle C   þe²] of thaire A   brode] brede A, stronge C   toures] wallis D
663 *lines* 663–64 *om.* D   was] were C   bold burne] beryn P, bolde menne C   burwe]
burgh PA, cyte C   *no cesura* C   664 þe hole] Thei held the U   boun] bouned P, full
bown A   þe²] those A   walles] wall P   665 were] was PAU   byg] bygged P, bitter U
at a bir] UDC (at) os U, a] þe D) *Turville-Petre*, and brode L *Kölbing-Day*, *om.* P, and bare A
bycchet] bygge U, bittir DC   to] forto U   666 Wondere] Right D   heye] es P
with] and AU   holwe] holl P, holle A   diches] dykes PA, diche U

Heye bonked aboue   vpon boþe [halu]es,
Riȝt wicked to wynne   bot ȝif wyles helpe.

Bowmen atte bonke   benden here gere,
Schoten vp scharply   to þe schene walles   670
With arwes and arblastes   and alle þat harme myȝt
To affray þe folke   þat defence made.

þe Iewes werien þe walles   with wyles ynowe,
Hote [play]ande picche   among þe peple ȝeten;
Brenn[and]e leed and brynston   [many] + barel fulle   675
Schoten schynande doun   riȝt as schyre water.

Waspasian wendeþ fram þe walles   wariande hem alle.
Oþer busked were boun,   benden engynes,
Kesten at þe kernels   and clustred toures,
And monye der daies worke   dongen to grounde.   680

667 Heye] Y- U, And hyȝe C   bonked] bankis D   aboue] aboune P, abowte AUDC
Kölbing-Day Turville-Petre   vpon boþe halues] alle the brode walles U   boþe] foure P
halues] PADC *Turville-Petre*, sydes L *Kölbing-Day*   668 Riȝt] And wonder PAUDC
Turville-Petre   ȝif] *om.* U   helpe] helped PA, hem myght helpen U, help⟨torn⟩ D
669 Bowmen] than bowmen A   atte] to þe P, *om.* E   bonke] bankes A, benethe E
benden] bended P, thay benden A, benten UDE, benden vp C   gere] bowys E
670 Schoten] And shoten UC, shettyn D, schottyn E   vp] vp full A   to] at PADC
Turville-Petre, vnto U   þe schene] the brode U, folk on þe E   671 arblastes] arblast
DC   þat] þat þat C   672 To] Forto A   þat] that the A, þat hem C   *no cesura* E
673 werien] weryn P, weryde AUD, kepten E, wroȝte on C   walles] wall D   with]
om. C   wyles] gynnys E, whyles C   674 Hote] And hoot E, *om.* U   playande] PA
Kölbing-Day Turville-Petre, blowande L, Boyland UDC, *om.* E   picche] pyk PA, piche
and ter UE   among] at P, amanges A, ouer U   peple] folke P, wal U   ȝeten] ȝettes P,
ȝett A, thei throwe U, cast DEC   675 Brennande] PAUDEC *Kölbing-Day Turville-
Petre*, brennen L   leed] pyk A   leed and brynston] *trs. sbs.* UDEC   and] *cesura fols.* E
many barel] UDC (many a b. C), barels LPA *Kölbing-Day Turville-Petre*   many barel
fulle] hoot ymolte E   full] staffulle A   676 Schoten] thay schotte A, Shetyn D,
They shoofedde hit C   Schoten schynande] faste threwyn E   schynande] sheluyng U,
shelmyng D, *om.* C   doun] adoun UDE   riȝt as schyre] as it hadde be E   schyre] þe
bright P, shere D   677 Waspasian] than w. A, Vesp- UDC   wendeþ] went
PUDEC (*after* walles E)   fram] fra PAUDEC   walles] wall PUDC   wariande] and
waried UD, *om.* E, and cursed C   hem alle] a lytel while E   alle] harde PAD *Turville-
Petre*   678 Oþer] bot oþer AUDE, And oþur C   busked] busken P, þan buskyd D,
om. E   were] and P, were and A, her U, are D, hem C   boun] bowes U, wunder bysy
E, redy C   benden] and bendide A, and bent her U, and bentyn D, to beende EC
679 Kesten] thay keste AUC, To cast DE   at þe kernels] faste to þe townn C   þe]
om. P   kernels] corners UDE   and] *om.* PD, þey C   clustred] clatered AUC, þe
cursid D, clatere E   toures] þe towres AUE, caitifs to quelle D, her towres C
680 And monye] Many a C   der] *om.* A   daies] day- PAUDE   dongen] thay dange
AE, thei dungen U, þey casten C   to] to the AUEC

By þat wriȝtes han wroȝt   a wonder stronge pale
Alle aboute þe burwe   with bastiles manye
[þat no freke myȝt vmfonge   withouten feþer-hames],
[Ne] no segge vndere sonne   myȝt fram þe cite passe.

Suþ dommyn þe diches   with þe ded corses,   685
Crammen hit myd karayn   þe kirnel[e]s vnder
þat þe stynk of þe ste[w]e   myȝt strike ouer þe walles
To coþe þe corsed folke   þat hem kepe scholde.

þe cors of þe condit   þat comen to toun
Stoppen, euereche a streem   þer any str[and]e ȝede,   690
With stockes and stones   and stynkande bestes
þat þey no water myȝt wynne   þat weren enclosed.

Waspasian tourneþ to his tente   with Titus and oþer,
Commaundeþ consail anon   on Cayphas to sitte,

681 þat] þenne C, *add* the UDC   wriȝtes] wretches withinne / U   han] had AEC
a] *om.* PD   wonder] *om.* U, meny D   stronge] strange P   *no cesura* C
682 burwe] burght E   bastiles] bastels PU   manye] full manye A   683 *line om.* L,
supplied largely from P   freke] manne C, *adds* in U *Kölbing-Day*   myght] *om.* AC
vmfonge] P, vnfongede A, *om.* U, found D, fonde E *Kölbing-Day*   out wente C
withouten] without UD   fethyr-hames] A, fele harmes P *Turville-Petre*, fressh
harmes ('h'armes E) UDEC   684 Ne] PAUD *Kölbing-Day Turville-Petre*, þat
L, Nor C   segge] manne C   myȝt] *om.* UD   fram] fra PAC   cite] toune U
scribal line E: thorw þe segge passe / for auȝt þat he cowde   685 Suþ] thay A, And
sen U, And thanne þey E, Aftyr þey C   dommyn] demmyd PA, fille thei UD, fylled EC
diches] diche PUDE, dikis A   ded] dede PADEC   corses] cors P, bodys UDC   *no
cesura* E   686 Crammen] Crommyd PD, And kramede AEC, Fillen U   hit] þam
AU, *om.* DE   myd] with PAUDEC   karayn] caryons A   *kirneles] kirnels L *Kölbing-
Day Turville-Petre*, kyrnels P, kirnells A, corners (-res C) UDEC, *adds* alle U
687 stynk] stythe stynke A, stynche U, steme DE   of] and AUDEC   þe¹] þat P
stewe] PAC *Turville-Petre*, steem LU *Kölbing-Day*, stench DE   myȝt] may U, *mark over
m* E   strike] carie U, stynk D   walles] wall P   688 To] *om.* AC   coþe] *om.*
PAC, coren UD, poysen E   corsed] fals E   folke] *adds* forto care A, *adds* vnto greue C
þat . . . scholde] and (to D) catchen her bane UD, and so her deth cacche E   hem] þai P
scholde] wolde P   689 cors] curses A   þe²] *om.* UC   condit] condites AC
comen] come PAUDEC   to] fro UD   toun] þe toune PAUEC *Kölbing-Day Turville-
Petre*, þe wellis D   690 Stoppen] Stoppid P, And stoppede A, Thei stopped UDEC
(s. on E)   euereche] euerylke A   a] *om.* DEC   streem] strande P, syde E   þer] ȝare
P, wher D   strande] A *Kölbing-Day Turville-Petre*, strem LP, cours U, spryng DEC
ȝede] were D, was E   691 With] Both with P   stockes] stakis AC   and] and
with P   stynkande] stynkand PAU, stynkyng D   bestes] bodyes E   *no cesura* C
692 *line om.* P   þat¹] *om.* C   þey] *adds* myȝte to C   myȝt] may U, *om.* C   wynne]
come C   þat weren] in (into D, þat in E) the toun UDE   en-] within AC, *om.* U, y- D
enclosed] were E   693 Waspasian] ¶ *precs.* D, *adds* þan D   tourneþ] *om.* E,
turned C   tente] tentis A   and oþer] hym turned E   694 Commaundeþ]
Comande P, Commaundid D, and comaundyd EC   consail] a c. UDC, his c. E   anon]
om. UDEC   *no cesura* E

W[ha]t deþ by dome   þat he dey scholde   695
With þe lettered ledes   þat þey lauȝte hadde.

Domesmen vpon de[y]es   demeden swyþe
þat ech freke were quyk fleyn   þe felles of clene;
[Firste] to be on a bent   with blonkes todrawe
And suþ honget on an hep   vpon heye galwes,   700

þe feet to þe firmament,   alle folke to byholden,   f. 11ʳ
With hony vpon ech [half]   þe hydeles anoynted;
Corres and cattes   with claures ful scharpe
Foure kagge[d] and knyt   to Cayphases þeyes;

Twey apys at his armes   to angren hym more   705
þat renten þe rawe flesche   vpon rede peces.
So was he pyned fram prime   with persched sides
Tille þe sonne doun s[yed]   in [þe] somere tyme.

695 What] PUDEC *Kölbing-Day Turville-Petre*, whatekyns A, with L   deþ] dede PA
by] by her UDEC   dey] haue E   696 With] And D, And also with C   þe] those
AUD, alle his E   lettered ledes] grete clerkys E   ledes] menne C   þey] þe PC   lauȝte]
lawe P, loght D, cawȝt E, lawes C   hadde] ledde C   697 Domesmen] than d. A, The
d. C   vpon] her C   deyes] PADE *Kölbing-Day Turville-Petre*, deþes LC, dayes U
demeden] demed PU   swyþe] full swythe AU, full sone C   698 þat] When P, whils
AC   ech] ilk a A, ilk U, eche a E, euery C   freke] man C   were] was PC   quyk] *om*.
PUDE   fleyn . . . clene] / þe skynnes of to be flayne C   felles] fell PU, flesche A   of] *om*.
A, of ful U   699 Firste] PADC *Turville-Petre*, þen L *Kölbing-Day*, And than U, Bot
feerst E   to be] *om*. UDE   on a bent] with bondes ybounden / and U   on] *blotch* D   a]
þe PAC, *om*. DE   bent] bankes P, tentis to be DE, erþe C   blonkes] hors U, houndis D,
ropes E, horses C   todrawe] drawen PU, ydrawen ADEC *Turville-Petre*   700 And]
om. D   suþ] thanne E, aftur C   honget] hongen U   on an] appone A, *om*. U, on DC, in E
hep] heghte A, hye UDC, haste E   vpon] on þe P   galwes] gawes E   701 feet] fette
A, fote U   to] towarde C   alle] the UDC, þat E   folke] men P   to] myȝte E
702 vpon] on PUDEC   ech] ilke PU, Ilke a A, euery E, eche a C   half] PAUD *Kölbing-
Day Turville-Petre*, side LE, parte C   þe] þair PC   hydeles] sydes P, hiddills A, bodys
UDC, body E   anoynted] to enoynt U   703 Corres] With curres UD, and dogges E
Corres and] And clauerand A, And currys with C   with] and D, þat C   claures] clowes
AUDEC   ful] *om*. P, hadde full C   704 Foure] Fourty D   Foure kagged] To 'be'
bounde E   *kagged] *Kölbing-Day*, kagges L, cacchyd P *Turville-Petre*, catched U, cacchid
D, chachede A, were kawȝte C   and knyt] with a corde A   to] till A, *om*. DC
Cayphases] Cayphas PAUDEC   þeyes] sydes PU, about DEC   705 Twey] And two
UEC, And xx. D   at] to A   at his armes] also UDEC   to] *om*. P   more] þe more C
706 þat] To UDE, Forto C   renten] ryuen P, ryve scholde A, rende UEC, rente D   þe]
his AE   rawe] *om*. P   vpon] all on C   rede peces] bothe sydes U, euery syde E
707 *line om*. U   So] And thus E   pyned] peyned E   fram] fra P, fro þe A   fram . . .
sides] / þat cursyd schrewe E   prime] *adds* tyme C   persched] perched P   sides] syþes C
708 Tille] To P   doun] adoun U, was down C   syed] D, souȝt L *Kölbing-Day*, sett
PAUC *Turville-Petre*   þe²] PAUDC *Duggan* 1988:128 *Turville-Petre*, *om*. L *Kölbing-Day*
somere] somers PUC   tyme] tyde AUC   scribal line E: al þe longe somer day / fro
morwe tyl euyn

þe lered [ledes] of þe lawe   a litel bynyþe
Weren tourmented on a tre,   topsail[es] walten—   710
Knyt to euerech clerke   kene corres twey—
þat alle þe cite myȝt se   þe sorow þat þey dryuen.

þe Iewes walten ouer þe walles   for wo at þat tyme;
Seuen hundred slow hemself   for sorow of here clerkes.
Somme hent he[m by þe] heere   and fram þe hed pulled   715
And somme [doun] for deil   + dasch[e]n to grounde.

þe kyng lete drawen hem adoun   whan þey dede were,
Bade, 'a bole-fure betyn   to brennen þe corses,
Kesten Cayphas þeryn   and his clerkes [alle],
And bren[n]en euereche bon   into + browne askes.   720

Suþ wen[de] to þe walle   on þe wynde syde
And alle abrod on þe burwe   bl[o]wen þe powdere.

709 lered] lernyd DEC   ledes] PUD, men LAEC *Kölbing-Day Turville-Petre*   þe²]
om. E   bynyþe] besyde E   710 Weren] thay were A, Ere U, Are D   tourmented]
turment PAU, also yhongyd E, turned C   on a tre] *om.* E   *topsailes] *Duggan*
1988:144n61, topsaile A, topsayle PC, topsail L *Kölbing-Day Turville-Petre*, topseyl E, and
topsaile U, and topsayle D   walten] tumbled U, yturnyd D, y wene E, waltur C
711 Knyt] And knytte (k. were C) AC   euerech] eueriche a PAU   kene] *om.* PAUDC
corres] cattis A, curdogges UDC   scribal line E: with dogges and cattys also ybounde (*no
cesura*)   712 þat¹] Til D   þe cite] men E   myȝt] may U   sorow] wo U   þat²]
om. E   dryuen] drow P, hade ADEC, fele U   713 þe¹] Manye E   walten] waltrid
D, *om.* E, tombledde C   þe²] *om.* AD   walles] wal DC   wo] sorow PUC   at] *om.*
PU, in DC   at þat tyme] þan þei fyllyn E   714 hundred] score UDE   slow
hemself] *trs.* P   sorow] wo C   here] þe P, þat E   clerkes] syȝte E   715 Somme]
Thei UDE   hent] toke C   hem by þe] A, here LP *Kölbing-Day Turville-Petre*, hemself
by the UDEC   fram] fra PAUC   fram . . . pulled] pullyd it of faste E   hed] heued P
716 doun] PAUDEC *Kölbing-Day Turville-Petre*, *om.* L   deil] sorowe C   daschen] P,
daschande L, daschede AUDEC *Kölbing-Day Turville-Petre*   to] to the ADEC
717 lete] garte A, bad UEC, hem hete þan D   drawen hem] hem hem be drawe E
hem] *om.* D   adoun] doune PAUDEC *Turville-Petre*   whan] fra P, for A   dede were]
were sone dede A   718 Bade] And ADE, And bad U, He badde C   a] *om.* U
bole-] bale PA, *om.* UDC, gret E   betyn] to be fet UD, be maad faste E, to make faste C
to . . . corses] be þe galwys E   brennen] bren U   þe] thaire A, alle the U, with þe D, in
þese C   corses] clerkes UDC   *no cesura* E   719 Kesten] Thei casten UC, And
cast D, and þanne E   and] and al D   clerkes alle] cursid clerkis D   alle] PAUC
Turville-Petre, twelf L *Kölbing-Day*, caste E   720 And] to be E, & þer þey C
*brennen] brenten L *Kölbing-Day Turville-Petre*, brynd P, brynte A, brent UDE, brente
C, *adds* þaim P   euereche] eueriche a PAU, vp eche D   into] to U, al to E   browne]
PAEC *Turville-Petre*, þe browne LUE *Kölbing-Day*   browne] smale E   721 Suþ]
And sythen AUD, And thanne þey E, And aftur C   *wende] wente AEC, went LPUD
Kölbing-Day Turville-Petre   walle] walles PE   722 And] *om.* C   alle] *om.* UDE
on] in PAD, into C   burwe] burgth E, cyte C   blowen] P, blewen LDE *Kölbing-Day
Turville-Petre*, blewe thay AU, þey blewen C

"þer is doust for ȝour drynke",   adoun to hem crieþ
And b[id]de hem bible of þat broþ   for þe + bischop soule'.

þus ended coursed Cayphas   and his clerkes [twelf],   725
Al tobrused myd bestes,   brent at þe laste,
In tokne of tresoun   and trey þat [þ]e[y] wroȝt
Whan Crist þrow h[ere] conseil   was cacched to deþ.

By þat was þe day don,   dym[m]ed þe skyes,
Merked montayns   and mores aboute,   730
Foules fallen to fote   and here feþres r[y]s[t]en,
þe nyȝt-wacche to þe walle   and waytes to blowe.

Bryȝt fures [a]brode   betyn in þe oste.
þe kyng and his consail   carpen togedre,
Chosen chyuentayns out   and chiden no more   735
Bot charged þe chek-wecche,   and to chambre wenten

723 is] *om.* P   for] to AUDEC *Kölbing-Day*   -doun] duke PAUDEC *Kölbing-Day*
Turville-Petre   to] on U   to hem] þo C   hem] hym P   crieþ] cryed P, sayde AEC
724 And] He C   *bidde] bade LA *Kölbing-Day Turville-Petre*, bad PUDE, badde C
hem] hym P   bible] bibe PAD *Turville-Petre*, drynke EC   of] *om.* D   of þat] it in UC
of þat broþ] alle abowte E   þat] þe P   broþ] beuerache D   bischop] PAU *Duggan*
1986:592 *Turville-Petre*, bischopes LEC *Kölbing-Day*, bisshops D   725 þus] And
thus U, ¶ *precs.* D   ended] endes PU   coursed] *om.* UDE   twelf] PUDEC *Turville-*
Petre, alle LA *Kölbing-Day*   no cesura E   726 *lines* 726–27 *om.* P, *line om.* UDEC
scribal line A: those gylefull bestis with bale were one thaire bodyes hangede
727 tokne] the tokynnynge A   of] of the AE, of her UC   and trey] *om.* AC
þey] AUDEC *Turville-Petre*, he L *Kölbing-Day*   wroȝt] brewede hade A, to Ihesu
wroȝte C   728 whan] when þat A   whan Crist] þat P   þrow] at UD, in E, by C
here] PAUDEC *Turville-Petre*, his L *Kölbing-Day*   was] criste P   cacched] demed E
to] and put to C   deþ] dede P, the dede A, þe *(torn)* D   729 þat] þen C
dymmed] D *Kölbing-Day*, dymned L, and dryuen P, and dynnede A, and dymmed U, &
þenne dymmedde C   þe skyes] to þe ende P   skyes] skye A   scribal line E: And so
þe day be þat tyme / was brought to þe hende   730 *lines* 730–33 *om.* E   Merked]
And Mirkenede the A, *add* the UD *Kölbing-Day*, Then wax dirke þe C   and] and þe C
mores] marreis U   aboute] al about D   731 Foules] And fowles C   fallen] fellen
UC   fote] the grownde A   and] *om.* UDC   rysten] PA *Kölbing-Day*, rusken L, to
reste UDC   732 nyȝt-] *om.* PC   -wacche] watches PA   to¹] on UD, went to C
walle] wallis AC   and] þe C   to²] gun UC   to blowe] abowte P   733 fures]
fyre U   abrode betyn] on brade bette PA, aboute betyn / abrode L *Kölbing-Day*, al
obrode / is brent U, and brood ar bette D, and brode / were made C   734 carpen]
carpyd PE, speken C   735 *line om.* P   Chosen] Full gude A, and chosyn E, They
chosen C   chyuentayns out] *trs.* UDEC   out] þay chese owte A   and] *om.* D
chiden] chyde þay A, chidden UC   chiden no more] manly man of harmes E
736 Bot] *om.* P   charged] chargen A   chekwecche] chief-watche UC, chefteins D
and] *om.* P   to] to her DC   chambre] chambirs A   wenten] to wende P, ȝoden A
scribal line E: to kepe þe wacche al þe nyȝt ouer *(no cesura)*

Kynges and knyȝtes   to cacchen hem reste.
Waspasian lyþ in his logge,   litel he slepiþ
Bot walwyþ and wyndiþ   and waltreþ aboute,
Ofte tourneþ for tene   and on þe toun þynkeþ.   740

Whan + schadew and schire day   scheden attwynne,
f. 11ᵛ Leuerockes vpon lofte   + lyften here steuenes;
Burnes busken hem out of bedde   with bemes [full] loude,
Boþe blowyng on bent   and on þe burwe walles.

Waspasian bounys of bedde,   busked hym fayre   745
Fram þe f[r]o[n]te to þe fourche   in fyne gold cloþes;
Suþ putteþ þe prince   ouer his pal[l]e[n] wedes
A brynye browded þicke   with a brestplate,

---

737 *line om.* U   Kynges] Kynge P, ⟨*torn*⟩yngis D, Bothe kynges C   knyȝtes]
princes C   to] *om.* A   cacchen] take PC   hem] thaire AD, hem somme C   scribal
line E: And tho he took his reeste / as reysown wulde   followed by inset 'Quintus
passus' U, marginal 'Passus vᵘˢ.' by this line C   738 Waspasian] *two-line capital* U,
three-line capital E   lyþ] *om.* E, lyȝte C   his] *om.* UDE   litel] and littill AC
739 walwyþ] walowedde C   wyndiþ] wrythis A, wendith D, walkeph E, turned C
and²] and vmwhile U   waltreþ] walkes UD, turyȝt E, meued C   740 Ofte] And
ofte PE, And oftetyme UD, And euermore C   tourneþ] *om.* UDEC   for] hym for
PA, in a D, in gret E   for tene] bytwene U, bytwene tymes C   and] *om.* UDEC
þynkeþ] he þenketh C   added line E: how he myȝt it wynne / with eny maner while
741 Whan] Till A   Whan . . . day] Tyll þe daye and þe nyȝte C   schadew] PAUDE,
schadewes L *Kölbing-Day*   scheden] schauen P, schewed U, departyd EC   attwynne]
in twyn PAC   742 Leuerockes] And l. AU, Then l. C   vpon] sone apon P, lepis
one A, on E   lyften] PUE *Kölbing-Day*, lyfteneþ L, to newen A, lyft vp D, sone leften
vp C   steuenes] steuen PAE, steuys D, voys C   743 Burnes] And Beryns A,
barnes E, And lordes C   busken] busked PD, dressede C   hem] *om.* PAUD   out]
om. P   out of] fro E   with . . . loude] and into feeld ȝede E, and claryones blew vp
lowde C   full] UD *Duggan* 1988:128, *om.* LP *Kölbing-Day*, one A   744 blowyng]
blew PU, þan blew D, blewe þay C   on¹] at þe P, on the A, in the UDC   bent]
felde C   on²] at P   burwe] borowe AD, cyte C   walles] wal U   scribal line E:
trumpyng and claryonyng / and meche noyse made   745 bounys] buskes PAU,
buskid D, busked hym / E, dressede hym C   of] of his A, out of UD, owt fro E, fro
his C   busked] and bounes PA, and raies U, bounyd D, & arayde C   busked hym
fayre] blyue E   hym] *om.* P   fayre] to ryse A, ful faire U   *no cesura* C
746 Fram] Fra PUDEC, And fro A   *fronte] face P, fote LU *Kölbing-Day*, foot DE,
foote C, fourche A   fourche] fote PA, frount UD, heed E, forhedde C   in . . .
cloþes] arayed hym thanne ¶ (746a) in fyn gold weede E   fyne] fayre P, fyve D   gold
cloþes] cloth of golde C   cloþes] hym clothis A, wede U   747 *line om.* UE
Suþ] And seth D, And aftur C   putteþ] putt PD   þe] that AC, on þat D   ouer] on
P, aboue DC   pallen] AD *Kölbing-Day*, pale LP, gay C   wedes] aray C   748 A
. . . þicke] *om., remainder fused with line* 746a E   brynye] bright bye D, haburioune C
browded] browden P, browdirde AC, braden U   þicke] full wele A, al thik U, ful
thik D

[þe] gra[t]e of gray steel   and of gold riche.
þerouer he casteþ a cote,   colour of his armys;   750
A grete girdel of gold   without gere oþere
Layþ vmbe his lendis   with lacchetes ynow.

A bryȝt burnesched swerd   he belteþ alofte,
Of pure p[olisch]ed gold   þe pomel and þe hulte;
A brod schynande scheld   on scholdire he hongiþ   755
Bocklyd myd briȝt gold,   aboue at þe necke

þe glowes of gray steel   þat were with gold hemmyd.
Hanleþ harnays   and his hors askeþ;
þe gold-hewen helme   haspeþ he blyue
With viser and + avental   deuysed for þe nones.   760

A croune of clene gold   was closed vpon lofte
Rybaunde vmbe þe rounde helm,   ful of riche stones,

749 þe grate] UDC, Grayþed L, þe grace P, the grate was A *Kölbing-Day*, with a
grate E   of] of þe PU, on þe DC   steel] ⟨..⟩ld P   and] was PUDC   and . . . riche]
ygrounde wol scharpe E   750 þerouer he casteþ] And thanne dode on E   -ouer]
-on PUC   he casteþ] *trs.* AUDC   casteþ] keste PAUD, castede C   colour] to couer
P, colourede A *Kölbing-Day*, of c. UDC, with colours E   of] *om.* P   added line E: þe
whiche were riche / and dredful on to looke   751 A] And a C   without] withouten
PAU   oþer] more AUDC   scribal line E: þanne gurt hym with a gurdyl / ful of riche
stones   752 Layþ] He laid UDC   vmbe] vp be P, abowte A, on UDC   lacchetes]
lacches PU   ynow] many UD, full monye C   scribal line E: with dyamaundes and
perre / richelich arayed   753 A] with a A   swerd] brande AD   he] *om.* P, and A
belteþ] bested? P, girdis hym AC, girde him UD, putte on E   alofte] about UDC,
aboue E   754 polisched] PAUDEC, purged L *Kölbing-Day*   þe¹] *om.* P, bothe C
þe¹ . . . hulte] *om., fused with line* 756 A   þe²] *om.* PDC   hulte] hyltes PEC, alle D
no cesura E   755 *line om.* A   schynande] scynand P   on] on his UDEC   he] *om.*
UDE   hongiþ] hep⟨..⟩rs P, honged EC   756 bocklyd] And bokeled C   bocklyd . . .
gold] *om., fused with line* 754 A   myd] with PUDC   briȝt] fyne UD   aboue] abowte A
Kölbing-Day, al about U, cast about D, abouen C   at] in P   at þe] his UD   necke]
crek? P   scribal line E: Al yclosyd in steel / hard for þe nonys   757 þe] His PE,
with A   of] of the U   gray steel] plate E   þat] *om.* PUDEC   were] *after* gold
UDEC   758 Hanleþ] than hendely A, Hauleþ ouer *Kölbing-Day*   Hanleþ harnays]
And (*om.* E) then (*om.* D) he hyed him in hast UDE, When he was arayde thus C
harnays] and has on P, I ȝowe hete A   and] he A, *om.* C   hors] *om.* E   askeþ] asken?
P, asked UDE, sone he asked C   759 þe] And the A   haspeþ he] claspyd P, he
asked UD   haspeþ he blyue] one his hede hespis A, hym was browȝte þenne aftur C
blyue] also U, in hye D   scribal line E: And leep vp lyȝtliche / as a knyȝt schulde
760 viser] vyserne P   and] PAUDEC, and with L *Kölbing-Day*   avental] ventayle
PDEC   deuysed] auised UDEC   761 A] And a C   of] of full A, of the U, al of
DE   vpon] one A   vpon lofte] abouue PC   762 Rybaunde] Reyled PC,
Enverownde A, Ynailed U, Rayed D, and set E   vmbe] aboute P, all one A, rounde on
UD, vpon E, rounde aboute C   þe] *om.* A, his E   rounde] *om.* UDEC   helm] *om.* A
ful] all P, with full A   stones] tounes? P

Pyȝt prudely with perles   into þe pure corners
And so with saphyres sett   þe sydes aboute.

He strideþ on a stif stede   and strikeþ ouer þe bente   765
Liȝt as a lyoun   were loused out of cheyne.
His segges sewen hym alle   and echon sayþ to oþer,
'þis is a comlich kyng   knyȝtes to lede'.

He boweþ to þe barres   or he bide wolde,
+ Bet on with þe brond   [þat] þe bras rynges: 770
'Comeþ caytifes forþ,   ȝe þat Crist slowen;
Knoweþ hym for ȝour kyng,   or ȝe cacche more!

Wayteþ doun fro þe walle[s]   what wo his on hande:
May ȝe fecche ȝou no fode   þoȝ ȝe fey worþe.
And þoȝ ȝe waterles wede,   wynne ȝe [hit neuer]—   775
O droppe þoȝ ȝe de[y] scholde +   daies in ȝour lyue!

    763 Pyȝt] And pyghte A   prudely] e *expunged?* L, *om.* UDE   perles] peryll P, perle
A, perles of pris UDE   into] vnto A   into . . . corners] playnly aboute P, and prudly
araied UDE, þe helme rounde abowte C   pure] prowde A   764 so] all P, also A,
þan E, *om.* C   sett] *om.* A   sydes] syde E, syþes C   aboute] all ouer P, all abowte
AUE, to and fro C   765 on] of D   stif] stythe PA   strikeþ] strakes P, strekis A,
shrikes? U, styred C   ouer] on PUDC   bente] grounde UDC   scribal line E: Thanne
prikeþ he forþ / stefly on his steede   766 *line om.* P   Liȝt] Righte A, Lightly UD,
As lyȝtly E   a] any A   lyoun] *om.* C   loused] *after* cheyne A, launcid D, lete E, lesed
/ C   out of] from his U, of his C   cheyne] chene A   767 segges] lordes E,
menne C   sewen] saw PC, seese A, syen U, seyen D *Kölbing-Day*, seen E   alle] eche
oone C   echon] ilkone AU, eche DE, euery manne C   sayþ] said UDC   sayþ to
oþer] other (to oþer E) sayde PE   to] till AU   768 followed by added line A: And
boldly may þay byde þat swylke a beryn folowes   769 He] than he A   boweþ] hyes
P, hies hym A, rood E, pryked C   barres] barrers AUD   or] there U   bide] abyde
DEC   770 Bet] P, betynge L *Kölbing-Day*, And bet UDE, And beteth C   þe¹] his
PDEC   brond] swerd EC   þat] UDC, on L *Kölbing-Day*, þat all P   þat . . . rynges]
and seyde to þe false E   bras] bras*ser* ? P   rynges] ryngid DC   scribal line A: Owte
braydis he his brande and bett appone harde   771 Comeþ] Sayde commys A
caytifes forþ] out (out ȝe C) keitifs UC   forþ] owt A   ȝe] all ȝe P, he crieþ þe D, he
seyde / C   772 Knoweþ] And knowes AUDEC   kyng] god C   or] *illeg.* P, ere U,
ar E   773 *line om.* UDEC   walles] PA, walle L *Kölbing-Day*   on] in P
774 May ȝe] *trs.* AUDEC   fecche] foche A, fet DEC   þoȝ] ȝif þat A   þoȝ . . . worþe]
wulde ȝe neuer so fawe E   fey worþe] dye shulde C   775 þoȝ] of? P, ȝif A   þoȝ . . .
wede] also to ȝour watyr C   waterles] watles? P   wede] ben U, wone D   wynne] ȝit
wynn A, wynne shul UD   hit neuer] PA, noȝt o droppe L *Kölbing-Day*, neuer UD,
maye neuur C   scribal line E: And also waterles ȝe be / how wulde ȝe leeue
776 O droppe] PUDC (O) A PUC), *om.*, *but at end of prec. line* L *Kölbing-Day*, A dope A,
for o drope E   þoȝ] if PA   þoȝ . . . scholde] ne gete ȝe E   dey scholde] PAUDC, deþ
scholde dey L *Kölbing-Day*   daies] þe dayes PA   in] of PADE   *no cesura* E   added
line E: for y haue stroyed alle þe stremys / þat to þe town runne

þe pale þat I piȝt haue—   passe hit who myȝt?—
þat is so byg on þe bonke   and haþ þe burowe closed,
Fourty to [de]f[end]en   aȝens fyue hundred: f. 12ʳ
þoȝ ȝe were etnes echon,   in scholde ʼ[ȝ]eʼ [tourne]!   780

And more m[e]ns[ke] were hit ȝit   mercy [to] byseche
þan metles marre   þere no myȝt helpysʼ.
Was non þat warpiþ a word   bot waytes here poyntes
Ȝif [any] stertis on st[r]ay   with stones hem to kylle.

þan wroþ as a wode bore   he wendeþ his bridul: 785
ʻȜif ȝe as dogges wol dey,   þe deuel haue þat recche!
And or I wende fro þis walle   ȝe schul wordes schewe
And efte spaklokere speke   or Y ȝour speche oweneʼ.

By þat a Iewe Iosophus,   þe g[y]n[fu]l clerke,
Hadde wroȝt a wondere wyle   whan hem water fayled;   790

777 piȝt haue] hafe pighte down A, *trs.* E, here pyght is C   haue] *om.* P   passe]
pall? P   hit] *om.* C   hit who] ȝe ne D, ȝe E   who] woso AUC   myȝt] maye PC, mowe
D, neuere E   *no cesura* C   778 þat] It PAC   so] full AC, *om.* U   byg . . . bonke]
long and so brood E   on] ouer P, appon A, atte UDC   þe²] ȝour PAC   burowe] burgh
PU, town E, cyte C   closed] enclosyd E   779 Fourty] twenty E, For fowrty menne C
defenden] P, fyȝten LC *Kölbing-Day*, fende off AUD *Kölbing-Day* n, defende / and hold
of E   aȝens] agaynes A, *om.* E   fyue] sixe E   780 þoȝ] If A, for thow E   etnes]
gyauntes A, ethnes D, deuelles C   echon] Ilkone A   in] aȝayne PAC, out E   scholde]
shul UDE   scholde ȝe tourne] turne ȝe shull C   ȝe] PAUDEC *Kölbing-Day*, ʻweʼ L
tourne] PAUDC *Kölbing-Day*, wende L, neuere E   781 And] A P, *om.* E, And ȝette C
menske] PA, manschyp LD *Kölbing-Day*, wirship UC, wysdom E   were hit] it is UD, *trs.*
EC   ȝit] *cesura precs.* L, *om.* PUDEC   to] PAUDEC, *om.* L *Kölbing-Day*   byseche]
seche PD, craue A, crye E   782 metles] for the mette A   metles marre] forto marre
(deye E) meteles UDEC   þer] *om.* P   þer . . . helpys] beestes as ȝe were E
783 *lines* 783–88 *om.* P   Was] Bot was there A, Ther were C, ¶ *precs.* D   þat] to C
warpiþ] warpede agayne A, warpen U, warpid D, spak E, speke C   a] o DE, on C
waytes] wayten U, waytid DEC   here] his E   poyntes] poynt AU, tyme DEC
784 any] AUDC *Kölbing-Day*, *om.* L   stertis] stirrede A, styrte out C   stray] AUDC
Kölbing-Day, stay L   hem] *om.* ADC, for U   *scribal line* E: How he myȝt pryuyly with
stonys eny kylle (*no cesura*)   785 þan] *om.* C   a] the AE   wode] wylde AUDC
wode bore] wynd E   he . . . bridul] waspasyan seyde E   wendeþ] weyndis A, wyndes U
786 Ȝif] Thogh C   as . . . dey] dye as dogges C   wol] wel E   dey] dy he sayd AD
þat] wo A   recche] re⟨torn⟩ D, rekketh C   787 or] *om.* A, thei UDC   wende]
fonde U   þis] the AUDC   wordes schewe] abyde there (me here C) UC, wone stille D
scribal line E: for ȝif y leeue and y may / fayn schal schal y ȝow make   788 And efte]
om. E   efte] oft UDE   spaklokere] spedlier UDEC   speke] forto speke E   ȝour]
om. A   owene] profire A, here UDEC   789 By þat] þan P   a Iewe Iosophus]
Iosephus the gentyll (iewe UDEC) PUDEC   a, þe] *trs.* A   þe] þat PUDE, þat was a C
gynful] UD, gentyl LAEC *Kölbing-Day*, gynnes P   clerke] couth many P, was euer UDE
790 Hadde] *om.* PD   Hadde wroȝt] *trs.* U   wondere] wonderfull PA   whan] when
þat A   hem] þair P   hem water] *trs.* U   fayled] wanted UD   *scribal trs.* C: whenne
þat þey water fayledde / wroght a wondur wyle

Made wedes of wolle   in wete forto plunge,
Water-waschen as þey were,   and on þe walle hengen.

þe wedes dropeden doun,   d[r]yed[en] ȝerne,
Rich rises hem fro,   þe Romayns byholden,
Wenden wel here wedes   hadde wasschyng so ryue   795
þat no wye in þe wone   water schold fayle.

[Bot] Waspasian þe wile   wel ynow knewe,
Loude lawȝþe þerat   and lordlynges byddis,
'No burne abasched be   þoȝ þey þis bost make:
Hit beþ bot wyles of werre   for water hem fayleþ'.   800

þan was noþyng bot [n]ote   anewe to bygynne,
Assaylen on eche a side   þe cite by halues,
Merken myd manglouns   ful vnmete dyntes,
And myche of masouns note   þey marden þat tyme.

791 Made] He made AC   wolle] welle? P   wete for-] water AD   wete ... plunge] þe
reyn leet legge hem E   792 water-] with water E   on] ouer U   walle] wallis ADEC
hengen] hangede AC, hangeth U, hem hongyth E   793 þe] ⟨..⟩ þe P   dropeden]
droppen PD   doun] *cesura precs*. L, adoune PDEC, *added marg*. A   *dryeden] dryed
Kölbing-Day, and dryede A, and dried U, and dryed C, deyed L, dryen P, and dryen D
dryeden ȝerne] and gunne faste to drye E   ȝerne] full ȝerne A, anone C   794 Rich] the
reke AC   rises] rose AC, aryseth E   hem] þer PUD   fro] from D   þe] *om*. P
byholden] behylden C   795 Wenden] Thei wende UDE   Wenden wel] And wele
wende thay that A, And hadde wonder C   here] those A   here wedes] in her wit UDEC
hadde ... ryue] waschen had bene PA, no (þat no E) wantyng thei hadden UE, no watir
hem wantyd D, how þat þey were wete C   796 *line om*. A   þat] Ne UD   no wye]
noght D   wye] wight U   þe] that UD   wone] wonne that U   fayle] tharue P   scribal
line E: but greet plente of water / eche of hem alle   scribal line C: And no manne wente /
þat þer were watyr withInne   797 Bot] PAUDEC, *om*. L *Kölbing-Day*, ¶ *precs*.
(*later?*) D   Waspasian] Vesp- UDC   þe] that A   wel ynow] of þe wer (werres E)
PAUEC, of werre wele D   knewe] knewen P   *no cesura* E   798 Loude] And lowde to
A, And lowde E   lawȝþe] laughe A, laught U, lawȝed E, he lawȝede C   þerat] he bygane
A, he therof UD, þerof E   lordlynges] lordynges P, ledis A, to his lordes UDEC   byddis]
he badde A, seyd UDEC   799 No] Ne P, Nor U   No burne] And saide beryns A,
Syres C   burne] body E   abasched be] ben bayste P, beese noghte abassched AC, basshen
nor bowe U   þoȝ] gif A   þey þis] yn? ȝon P   þis] þus E   800 bot] *om*. C   of] in P
fayleþ] wantes PUDE   801 þan] Tho UDE   was] nas UD   noþyng] þare P, there
noghte ells anone A, *om*, UDE, þer non C   bot] *cesura precs*. L, man P, *om*. E   *note
anewe] note newe P *Duggan* 1986:589, *trs*. L *Kölbing-Day*, newe note / AUDC, newe werk
/ E   to] onone to UDE, aȝeyn to C   802 Assaylen] Assemblede A, Assailed (He a. E)
UE, To assaile DC   on] by D   on ... halues] þe cyte / faste on eche a syde E   eche a]
the P, Ilke a A, ilk U, eche DC   side] halfe P   by halues] abouten P, to byholde U
803 Merken] Thay merken A, Marked UDC   myd] with PAUDC   manglouns]
Mangonells AC, magnels U, machenelles D   ful] *om*. PAD   scribal line E: And brak
doun with engynes / and sparyd nere a place   804 of] *om*. PUD, of the A   masouns]
mason P   note] werke C   þey] *om*. PU, thaire A   þat tyme] by tymes U   scribal line E:
þat masones and many men / wrought in many ȝeres

þerof was Iosophus ware   þat myche of werre couþe   805
And sette on þe walle side   sakkes myd chaf
Aȝens þe streyngþe of þe stroke   þer þe stones hytte
þat alle dered noȝt a dyzs   bot grete dyt made.

þe Romayns runne to anon   and on roddes knytte
Siþes for þe sackes   þat selly were kene,   810
Raȝten to `þe´ ropis,   rent hem in sondere
þat alle dasschande doun   into þe diche flatten.

Bot Iosophus þe gynful   here engynes alle
+ Brente with brennande oyle   and myche bale wroȝt.
Waspasian wounded was þer   wonderlich sore   815
þrow þe hard of þe hele   with an hande-darte

þat boot þrow þe bote   and þe bone nayled
Of þe frytted fote   in þe folis syde.   f. 12ᵛ
Sone assembled hym to   many sadde hundred
þat wolden wrecken þe wounde   oþer wo hab[id]en.   820

805 þerof] ¶ *precs.* D (*later?*)   was] is U   was Iosophus] *trs.* AUDEC   myche] mekill A
806 And] He AC, *om.* UD   sette] seker P, fylde E, hengede C   on] to A, vpon U, & on E   on
... chaf] *trs. phrs.* UDE   walle] wallis A, walles hem hongyd E   side] *om.* AEC, sydes UD
sakkes] was sett P   myd] with PUD, of A, ful of EC   807 þe³] *om.* P   stones] stone AU,
gonnes C   hytte] hittes U   808 dered] dened P   noȝt] not DEC   dyzs] dissh U, del E
grete] *om.* P   dyt] dyn PAUDC, noyse E   809 þe] þo P   Romayns] ramaynes A   runne]
rane AUC   to] þerto C   anon] *om.* P   on] apon PUC   roddes knytte] poles fastnyd E
810 for þe sackes] *om.* E   selly] ferly A, sharp DE, *om.* C   kene] and kene D, / þe ropes for
kytte E, bothe fell & kene C   811 Raȝten] And raughte AE, They rawȝte C   to] *om.* E   þe]
om. P   ropis] sakkes and þe ropes E   rent] and rent PAUDEC   in] a- E   812 dasschande]
daschyn P, daschede AE, thei dasshen U, þei dasshid DC   doun] adoun UDEC   into] and to
P, and in AUDEC   diche] dykes A   flatten] fallyn PU, flowe A, fellyn DEC   813 Bot]
Than EC, ¶ *precs.* D   gynful] gentill AE, Iewe C   her] thise UE, þe D   her ... alle]
ordeynede wyles moo C   engynes] gynnes PUDE   alle] aspied UDE   814 Brente] PA
Kölbing-Day, brenten L, men he brent UD, he hem brente C (*the verb after* oyle UDC)   with]
with a A   brennande] boylyng D   and] *om.* P   myche] mekill A   wroȝt] thaym wroghte A
scribal line E: And hoot boylyng oyle / on hem he leet caste   815 Waspasian] Vesp- there
U, Vasp- D, W. þanne / E, And Vasp- C   wounded was] *trs.* AUE   þer] *om.* PAUE
wonderlich] *om.* E   816 hard] herte PU, myddel E   þe] his E   hande-] scharp E
817 *line om.* P   þat] It A, That he D   boot] the bitte U, þe poynte C   þe¹] *om.* UDC   and ...
nayled] *om., line fused with next.* U   scribal line E: So þat his boote and his heele / were nayled
togydre   818 *line om.* PA   Of þe frytted] And þerto (*also* E) fastnyd (fetered C) þe (*om.* E)
DEC   Of ... fote] *om., line fused with prec.* U   fote] *om.* E   in] to DEC   in ... syde] rennyng
bothe sydes U   þe²] his E   folis] steedes E, hors C   819 Sone] Bot sone A   assembled]
assemblis P, þer kome C   assembled hym to] him sembled to U, to hym semblyd D   many]
many a C   sadde] bolde U   hundred] segge U, seggis D   scribal line E: tho were besy
wounder sone / many wurthi knyȝtes   820 þat wolden] to E   wolden wrecken] *trs.* A
wrecken] awreke E, avenge C   þe] þat AUDEC   oþer] or elles PAEC, or muche UD   wo]
ioye U, sorowe C   habiden] AUDEC, habben L *Kölbing-Day*, hab? P

þey b[rayd]yn to þe barres,   bekered ȝerne,
Fouȝt riȝt fel[ons]ly,   foyned with speres,
Io[u]ken Iewes þroȝ.   Engynes by þanne
Were manye bent at þe bonke   and to þe burwe þrewen.

þer were selcouþes sen,   as segges mowe here.   825
A burne with a balwe ston   was þe brayn cloue:
þe gretter pese of þe panne   þe pyble forþ strikeþ
þat hit flow into þe feld   a forlong or more.

A womman bounden with + barn   was on þe b[el]y hytte
With [a] ston o[f] a sta[yre],   as þe storyj telleþ,   830
þat þe barn out brayde   fram þe body clene
+ Born vp as a bal   ouer þe burwe walles.

Burnes were brayned   and brosed to deþ,
Wymmen wide open   walte vndere stones;

---

821 þey] þat P   braydyn] AUDEC, bowyn L *Kölbing-Day*, brayed þan P   barres]
om. P, barers AUDEC   bekered] byker P, and bekirde AUDE, and fowȝten C
ȝerne] full ȝerne PAUE, in iryn D, well ofte C   822 Fouȝt] with foynynge C
Fouȝt, felonsly] *trs.* UDE   riȝt] in P, with A, thei UDE   felonsly] U, felly LDEC
Kölbing-Day, felony PA   foyned] and funyde AUDE, and spendeden C   with] her C
823 *Iouken] Iolken L, Iugkyn P, thay Iusken at those A, And the U, Iollid D, & beryn
E, Ther þey Iolledde C, Jokken *Kölbing-Day*   þroȝ] throwen out U, þurghout DE
Engynes] ⟨..⟩innys P, with e. D, and e. C   Engynes by þanne] into þe harde walles E
by þanne] with P, bydene U   824 *line om.* P   Were] that were A   manye] *om.*
UDC   at] one A   to] at A, into C   burwe] borow D, cyte C   þrewen] thrawen
AU, drewenn C   scribal line E: so angry þey were thanne / for hirt of here kynge
825 *lines* 825–28 *om.* E   þer] For there A   selcouþes sen] selcouth signes P,
meruayles mony C   selcouþes . . . here] segges many / sey selkouthe thinges U
segges] men C   mowe] may PAC, myght D   here] sene D   826 burne] barne
A, manne C   balwe] rounde UC   was . . . cloue] ythrowen was to grounde U   þe]
to þe DC   brayn] hed A   827 *line om.* P   þe gretter] A (The U) grete AUC
þe pyble] with þe brayne C   pyble] stone A, polel U, pomel D   forþ strikeþ]
owtestrake A, out started C   828 *line om.* PC   hit] *om.* U   hit . . . feld] *trs. phr.*
UD   or] and AUD   829 womman] beern U, bierd D   bounden] grette C
barn] PAU, a barn LD *Kölbing-Day*, chylde C   on] in D   bely] PUC, body LAD
Kölbing-Day   scribal line E: A womman with chylde / was smeete on her woombe
830 a] PAUDEC, þe L *Kölbing-Day*   *of]* out of U, on LPAC *Kölbing-Day*, in DE
a] þat E   stayre] PAC, staf L, toure U, stound DE, staf-slyng *Kölbing-Day*   telleþ]
tell P   831 *line om.* A   barn] chyld EC   out . . . body] fro þe body / fell out C
brayde] went UE   fram] fra PU, of DE   832 Born] PUDE, And was born L
Kölbing-Day, And borne AC   vp] *om.* A   burwe] burgh PAU, town EC
833 Burnes] Chyldryn E   Burnes were] Ther were menne C   brayned and
brosed] brynt P   and . . . deþ] pleyȝyng in þe stretes E   brosed] birssede A   deþ]
dede and allso brytyned P, dede A, the deth UDC   *no cesura* E   834 Wymmen]
And women AC   walte] w⟨....⟩ P, went / UD, laye E, fell / C   stones] þe stones
PUDC

Frosletes fro þe ferst   to þe flor þrylled   835
And many toret doun tilte   þe temple aboute.

þe cite had ben seised   myd saut at þat tyme
Nad þe folke be so fers   þat þe fende serued,
þat kilden on þe Cristen   and kepten þe walles
With arwes and arblastes   and arche[le]rs manye.   840

With speres and spryngoldes   sponnen out hard,
Dryuen dartes adoun,   ȝeuen depe woundes
þat manye renke out of Rome   [by] rest[ing] of + s[o]nne
Was mychel leuere a leche   þan layke myd his to[les].

Waspasian stynteþ of þe stoure,   steweþ his burnes   845
þat were forbeten and bled   vndere bryȝt yren;
Tyen to here tentis   myd tene þat þey hadde
Al wery of þat werk   and wounded ful sore.

835 *line om.* PU   Frosletes] That fylettes C   Frosletes . . . to] thorowe forsoure
and forcelett was A   þe¹] her C   ferst] front D, forhedes C   to . . . þrylled] all
abowte flowen C   scribal line E: with childryn in here wombes / brosyd to þe grounde
836 And] *om.* P   toret] torettes C   doun . . . temple] of the toun / tilt al U   tilte]
tirled PA, fell C   temple] town al A, temple al D, cyte all C   scribal line E: þat gret
dool was to se / in many dyuers place   837 þe] So þe C   þe cite had] they had
sothely A   ben] *om.* E   seised] cesed P, takyn E   myd] be PAU, with DC, at þat E
saut] saynte P, assawte AD, than U   þat tyme] thenne DE   tyme] assaute U
838 Nad] Hadde noght C   fers] stronge C   fende] deuyl EC   839 þat] thay A,
wich E   on] *om.* A, of UDEC   þe¹] *om.* P   Cristen] c. men A   and] that U
840 arblastes] alblasters PA, arblast DC   *archelers] *Kölbing-Day* n Duggan 1988:128,
aschelers (assh- C) PC, achillers A, archers LUD   archelers manye] many maner
schottys E   manye] grete PA   841 With] And with A, *om.* UDEC   speres and]
gud A   and] out of UEC   sponnen] spynen PA, sprongen UDE   out] full CE
hard] faste P   842 Dryuen] Drywen P, thay dreuen owte A, Driued U, They
drewen C   Dryuen dartes] *trs.* E   adoun] doune PA   ȝeuen] and gyffen A, and
deled UE, and dele D, and made C   depe] grete AC, many U   woundes] dyntes U
843 manye] many a C   renke] *om.* P, renkes A, on E, manne C   out] *om.* EC   by]
resting] PAUDEC *Kölbing-Day*, reste L   sonne] PD, þat synne L, the sonne AUEC
Kölbing-Day   844 Was] were AC   þan] & P   layke . . . toles] any thing (layke
D, pley E, body C) elles UDEC   myd] with PA   toles] P, ton L *Kölbing-Day*, toose A
845 Waspasian] ¶ *precs.* D   stynteþ] stynt UD, stynted EC   of] *om.* C   of þe stour]
þanne E   þe] that UC   steweþ] and strengtes P, and stemmys A, and stowed UD,
and bestowyd E, and kome to C   burnes] men P, knyghtis AC, peple E   846 *line*
om. U   forbeten] betyn ADEC   bled] brent D, bybled E   vnder] thorowe thayre A
bryȝt] þe b. C   yren] Iryns A   847 Tyen] Tyghtis P, thay tournede AC, Turned
UD, and turned E   to] *om.* P, toward D   her] his E   myd] with PUDEC, with
the A   hadde] has P   848 Al] Wonder PUDEC, And were A   þat] þair PA, þe
D, *om.* UE   werk] werre DE   wounded] wrethed P, wonderly A   ful] *om.* PA
sore] bothe P

Helmes and hamberkes   hadden of sone:
Leches by torche-liȝt   loken here hurtes,   850
Waschen woundes with wyn   and with wolle stoppen,
With oyle and orisoun   ordeyned in charme.

Suþ euereche a segge   to þe soper ȝede;
þeȝ þey wounded were   was no wo nempned,
f. 13ʳ Bot daunsyng and no deil   with dynnyng of pipis   855
And þe nakerer noyse   alle þe nyȝt-tyme.

Whan þe derk was don   and þe day spr[o]ngen,
Sone after þe sonne   sembled þe grete;
Comen forþ with þe kyng   conseil to here
Alle þe knyȝthod clene   þat for Crist werred.   860

Waspasian waiteþ awide,   his wyes byholdeþ
þat were freschere to fiȝt   þan at þe furst tyme;
Prayeþ princes [ȝ]ernest   and alle þe peple after
þat eche wye of þat werre   schold his wille s[ch]e[w]e,

849 Helmes] than helmys A, Here helmes C   hamberkes] here armour C   hadden] þai
haden PAUD, þey dodyn E, þey kaste C   sone] full sone ADC   850   line om. P   Leches]
And leches AC, thanne leches E   by] with A   torche-liȝt] torches UE, light torches D
loken] loked to UC, lokyd DE   hurtes] woundes C   no cesura U   851   Waschen] they
wesche A, Wassh her U, Wasshe þe D, wusschen her E, They wasshedde here C   woundes]
þair woundes P   stoppen] hem stopped E, stoppede C   852   With] þanne with E   oyle]
woll P   and] and with PAUDC   orisoun] Orysons AUDEC   ordeyned] ordaynd PU, þei
ordeyned E, and with other C   in] om. UDEC   charme] charmes AUDEC   853   Suþ]
And sythen AUD, And after þat C   euereche a] iche P, Ilke a A, euery C   segge] manne C
to] vnto A   ȝede] ȝoden P   scribal line E: Thanne to þe sopeer eche man wente (no cesura)
854   þey . . . were] the woundes be (were DC) sore UDC, her woundes sore were E   was]
there was (is U) AUC   was no wo] þai no wounde P   no] none U, none þat (þat of C) DEC
nempned] mened PDC, neuennede A, meneth U, made E   855   daunsyng . . . deil]
daunsed delles UD, daunsyd and sunge E   deil] sorow C   dynnyng] noyse C   856   þe¹]
om. P, with UDEC   nakerer] nakyr P, nakirrers AD, nakeris UC   nakerer noyse] noyse of
nakers E   noyse] nysely C   nyȝt-tyme] nyghtis tyde A, nightis tyme DE   857   lines 857-
62 om. UDE   derk] nyght PC (marg. C)   sprongen] PAC Kölbing-Day, spryngen L
858   þe sonne] þen (illeg. blot) P, the sone rysynge A   sembled] assembled PA, were gedered C
no cesura L   859   Comen] thay come AC   forþ with] byfore A   conseil] þe (int., then
canc.?) concelle A   here] holde C   860   knyȝthod] knyghtis full A, knyȝtes C   clene]
keene C   werred] werrayede A   861   Waspasian] than w. A, Vasp- C   waiteþ] om. P
awide] abowte C   his] and his A   wyes] mayne C   byholdeþ] beholde P, to byholde C
862   were frescher] fresschere were þanne C   at . . . tyme] þay byfore were A, euur þey were C
863   Prayeþ] He prayes PA, Vespasian praies U, Vaspasyan prayed DE, He prayde C, ¶
precs. D   princes] the prynce A, the princes UD, his his lordes E   *ȝernest] on ernest L
Kölbing-Day, fyrste C, firste P, in haste A, om. UDE   and . . . after] al abowte E   alle] om. D
no cesura E   864   eche] ich a P, Ilke a AU, euery C   wye] wyght PUD, man EC   of þat
werre] one his beste wiese A   of . . . schewe] schulde schewe / his wille of þe werre E   þat²]
the UD   wille] avyce A, wyle U, wytte C   schewe] PAUDC, specke L Kölbing-Day

'For or þis toun be tak   and þis toures heye,   865
Michel tor[fere] and tene   vs tides on hande'.
þey tourned alle to Titus   and hym þe tale [graunten]
Of þe cite and þe sege   to seyn for hem alle.

þan Titus tourneþ hem to   and talkyng bygynneþ:
'þus to layke with þis + lese   vs lympis þe worse,   870
For þey ben fele of defence,   ferce men and noble,
And þis toured toun   is tenful to wynne.

þe worst wrecche in þe wone   may on walle lygge,
Strike doun with a ston   and stuny many kny3tes,
Whan we schul hone and byholde   and litel harme wirche   875
And ay þe loþe of þe layk   li3t on vsselue.

Now mowe þey ferke no ferre   here fode forto wynne:
Wolde we stynt of our strif   whyle þey here store ma[r]den,

---

865 For] *om.* P   or] *om.* U   be] to be U   tak] tane PUDC   and] or A, and al
DC   and þis] with alle þe E   þis] þere P, thire A, thus U   toures heye] many
toures U, *trs.* DEC   heye] 3oldyn A   866 torfere] PA *Kölbing-Day*, torsom L,
tray UD, schame he seyde / E, tormente C   tene] angur C   vs tides] we moste E,
vs falleth C   on hande] to (*om.* DE) abyde UDE, to haue C   867 þey] than
thay A   þey . . . alle] Then turned he UDE   tourned] turne PA   graunten] A,
grauntede PUDEC, scheweþ L *Kölbing-Day*   868 and] and of EC   sege] segge A
869 þan] And A   Titus tourneþ hem to] Titus hym 'turnes' P, turned him (*om.* DC)
Titus UDC   and talkyng] and talkyn P, talke he A   scribal line E: þan answeryd
tytus / wyslyche y weene   870 þus] Sayse thus A   layke] byker C   þis] 3one
A, þe D   *lese] lese folke A *Kölbing-Day*, losse D, lesne L, ledes PU, folk C   lympis]
lent is D, falleth C   þe] ay þe A   worse] werre C   scribal line E: it is good wurche
be auys / who schal dele with schrewys   871 *line om.* D   fele] fell men P, felle
Kölbing-Day   of] at E   ferce] and feers U   and noble] at nede U, and boolde E
872 is] full A, *om.* E   tenful] trowbelous C   *no cesura* E   873 wrecche] wight
U, *om.* D   in þe] of 3one A, of the UC, in her D   wone] wonne U, wonys D, town C
on] on þe PUC, one 3one A, in her D   walle] wallis D   lygge] *om.* P, stonde U
scribal line E: þe leeste boy among hem / may ligge on þe walles   874 Strike] And
kaste C   with] *om.* C   a ston] stonys A   and] *om.* PD   stuny] stunne U   stuny
. . . kny3tes] many men stonye E   875 Whan] Wende P, whyle C   hone] on
roume P, hovere D   litel harme] *trs.* P   litel . . . wirche] no stroke smyte C
wirche] *om.* P   876 *line om.* P   And] Bot A, *om.* D   ay] all A, Euere DC
loþe] lesse U, losse D, hurte C   of] and C   layk] losse C   li3t] 'to' lyghte A, lighten
U, shall ly3te C   li3t . . . selue] shal on ourself light D   scribal line E: And þe wo on
vs seelf / euyr more schal reste   877 Now] þat P, And now D   mowe þey] *trs.*
PC   þey] þe E   ferke] fare PA, freke U, fook E, goo (*after* ferther) C   ferre] ferther
PUDEC, Forthire A   here] *om.* PD, hem E   fode] mete C   forto] to D   wynne]
gete P   878 Wolde] Bot walde AE   we] we now A   we, our] 3e, 3oure PUE
whyle þey] to A, wil þei D, tyll þey C   here] þe P   store] stoour P, vitailes U, *om.* E
marden] A *Kölbing-Day*, maden LP, spende UE, spendid D, haue spended C

We scholde with [hunger] hem honte   to hoke out of toun
[Without weme or wounde   or any wo elles.]   880

For þer as fayleþ þe fode   þer is feynt strengþe
And þer as hunger is hote   hertes ben feble'.
Alle assenteden to þe sawe   þat to þe [seg]e longed,
Apaied, as þe prince   and þe peple wolde.

To þe kyng were called   constables þanne,   885
Marchals [and] maser[s],   men þat he + tristiþ;
He chargeþ hem chersly   for chaunce þat may falle
With wacche of waled men   þe walles to kepe:

'For we wol hunten at þe hart   þis heþes aboute
And hure racches renne   amonge þis rowe bonkes;   890
Ride to 'þe' reuer   and rere vp þe foules,
Se faucouns fle,   fele of þe beste—

879 *line om.* U   scholde] shul DEC   hunger] PADEC *Kölbing-Day, om.* L   honte]
hent PDE, hurte A   to] and PADEC   hoke] holke A, holy D, hunte E, hurle C   out of
toun] hem shende D   880 *line om.* LP, *supplied from* A   weme or wounde] wounde or
werk (eny hurt E) UDE   or . . . ells] with want (wantyng DE) of her (*om.* DE) fode UDE
881 þer as] where E   fayleþ] fawtis A, lakketh C   þe] *om.* EC   fode] mete C   þer is
feynt] feble es þe P   feynt] littill A   strengþe] herte E   882 as] þare P, þat E
hertes] hurtis A, þe hertis D, strenght E   ben] arn ful U, is but E   feble] faynte P
883 *line order* 884, 883 A   Alle] And alle A   assenteden] assent U   to¹] till P   þe¹] his
PAC, that UD, *om.* E   sawe] segge UD, hym E   to²] *om.* P   sege] PAUDEC *Kölbing-
Day,* cite L   longed] harde P, lasten U   884 *line om.* P   Apaied] The kynge was (is
UD) payede (plesed C) AUDEC   as] and A, with C   as . . . wolde] with his wurdes and
his princes alle E   þe¹,²] his U   and] if A, and os U   wolde] alle C   885 *line om.* U
To] ¶ *precs.* D   To . . . called] Than (*om.* C) the kyng callede hym to (to hym / his C) AC
þanne] tene A   *scribal line* E: And leet calle cunstaples / and kepers of þe peple
886 *line om.* P   and masers] AU, maser L, and Marcers D, and masons E, and bedelles C,
masers *Kölbing-Day*   men] *cesura fols.* L, and men AUC   men . . . tristiþ] *om., fused with
next* DE   he] AUC, he to L *Kölbing-Day*   tristiþ] traystis A, troisteth U, trystedde C
887 He] And A, *om.* U   He . . . chersly] *om., fused with prec.* DE   chargeþ] schareged P,
chargede AUC   chersly] *om.* P, chefly A *Kölbing-Day,* ful styfly U, styfely C   for] for all P
chaunce] chances A, charge U   þat] *om.* E   þat may falle] als a chyftan sulde P   may]
myghte AE   falle] happe UD, befalle E   888 With wacche] To make þe watches A
wacche] watches UDE   of] and with PE, with A, and UD   waled] welyd P, witty A,
wyles UDE, waker C   men] *om.* UDE   walles] wall for- P   to kepe] abowte A
889 we] y E   þe] thir A   hart] hertes PA   þis] in P, the C   heþes] heghes A, hatthes U
890 And] *om.* A   And hure] with C   hure] se PUD   racches] þese rose P, thire raches
A, the ratches UD   renne] yrenne U, *om.* C   amonge] in P   þis] þe PUDE, hem in þe C
bonkes] bowys E   891 Ride] They ridyn þen D, and ryden E, And þenne ryde C   to]
on E   þe¹] *om.* P, thiese A   reuer] reuers AC   and] *om.* PD   rere] rayse PAUC,
reysid D   rere . . . foules] foules vp reyse E   þe²] *om.* PUDC   892 *line om.* PE   Se]
See the AUD, To se C   fele] and felle A, and fallen UD, and sle C, fole *Kölbing-Day*   of
þe beste] on her prayes UD

Ech segge to þe solas   þat hymself lyke[þ]'.
Princes out of pauelouns   presen on stedes,
Torn[ei]en, trifflyn,   and on þe + toun wayten.   895 f. 13ᵛ
þis lyf þey ledde longe: [oure Lord] ȝyue vs [ioy]e.

[Quintus passus]

In Rome Nero haþ now   mychel noye wroȝt:
To deþ pyned þe pope   and mychel peple quelled,
Petre, apostlen prince,   and seint Poule [boþe],
Senek and þe senatours;   and alle þe cite fured;   900

His modire and his my[l]de wif   murdred to deþe,
Combred Cristen fele   þat on Crist leued.
þe Romayns resen anon   whan þey þ[i]s rewþe seyen
To quelle þe emperour quyk   þat hem vnquemed hadde.

---

893 Ech] than Ilke a A, Ilk a U, Eche a DE, And eche C   segge] frek E, man C   to
þe solas] *om.* UDE   þe] his C   þat] by UDE   hymself] hym PC, *cesura fols.* UE
lykeþ] P, lyked L *Kölbing-Day*, wolde A, os him best semeth (semyd D, lykyd E) UDE,
beste pleseth C   894 Princes] And prynces A, Thenne princes C   presen] presed
UDC, prikyd E   presen on stedes] prasyd þai wer P   on] owt one A, on her UDE
on stedes] full thykke C   *no cesura* C   895 *Torneien] *Kölbing-Day*, Tornen L,
with tournaye and A, And turned (turnyd D) with UD, and wente withowte E
Torneien trifflyn] with sterne menne & stronge C   trifflyn] truffelynge A, tariyng
UDE   and on] and AUE, *om.* D, þat to C   þe] AUDEC *Kölbing-Day*, þe þe L
toun] touris to D   wayten] kepte E, waytedde C   *scribal line* P: Passid forth ouer þat
place and þaim playe wolde   896 þis] þat P, And this A   þey ledde] *trs.* PAUDC
ledde] lede A   longe] full lange A   oure Lord] PAC, and god L, and lord UD *Kölbing-
Day*   ȝyue] grante A   ȝyue vs ioye] he vs blesse C   ioye] PUD, grace L *Kölbing-Day*,
heuen A   *scribal line* E: þat non of þe fals foolk / fle awey myȝte   marginal
notation 'vᵗᵘˢ. passus' P, inset 'Passus' A, inset 'Sextus passus' U, marginal notation
'Passus vjᵘˢ.' by this line and 'nota' at head of next C   897 In] *five-line capital* L,
four-line capital PA, *six-line capital* U, ¶ *precs.* D, *eight-line capital* E   Nero, now] *trs.* A
Nero haþ] *trs.* UDE   haþ now] was / and C   now] by nowe U, be now / and E
mychel] myche PUDE   noye] wo EC   898 deþ] dede PA   pyned] putt Petir A,
putte E, pyned he C   mychel] myche PUDEC   899 *line om.* A   apostlen] of
apostels þe P, posteleyn (þe p. D) UDE   apostlen prince] prince of posteles C   seint]
om. UDE   boþe] P, *om.* L, yit (eek E) therto UDE, also C *Kölbing-Day*
900 Senek] Seneca C   þe'] *om.* P   and alle] of P, and DC   fured] free P,
peired UDE   901 mylde] PADC *Kölbing-Day*, myde LUE   murdred] muchyd P,
he morthirrede AC, ymurdred U, motheryd E   to] to þe D   deþe] dede PA
902 Combred] And cumberd UDC   Cristen fele] mony cristen C   fele] full fele A
leued] lyued P, beleuyd E   903 þe] þo P, than thiese A, *om.* UDE   resen] rysyn
PUDC, *om.* A   whan] fro A   þis] PADEC *Kölbing-Day*, þus L, the U   seyen] sene
P, herde AD   904 To] Tuke to A   þe emperour] hym E   quyk] all qwyke AE
vnquemed] vnqwyete A, quelled U, desesyd EC   vnquemed hadde] *trs.* C

þey pressed to his paleys,   porayle and oþer,   905
To br[yt]ten þe bold kyng   in his burwe riche.
þe cite and þe senatours   assented hem boþe
Non oþer dede was to don: þey han his dome ჳolden.

þan flowe þat freke   frendles alone
Out at a pr[iu]e posterne—and alle þe peple folwed—   910
With a tronchoun of tre: toke he no more
Of alle þe glowande gold   þat he on grounde hadde.

On þat tronchoun with his teþ   he toggeþ and byteþ
Tille hit was piked at þe poynt   as a p[rik]kes ende.
þan abideþ þat burne   and biterlych spekeþ   915
To alle þe wyes þat þer were   wordes aloude:

'Tourneþ, traytours, aჳen: schal neuer þe tale rise
Of no karl by þe coppe   how he his kyng quelde'!
Hymself he + stykeþ myd þat staf   streჳt to þe hert
þat þe colke toclef   and þe kyng deyed.   920

905 *line om.* D   pressed] presen PAU   his] þe PAUC   paleys] Palessewardes A
porayle] poueryl P, pore A, pore peple C   and] and alle A   906 brytten] PAD *Kölbing-*
Day, brenten L, birten U, cacche E, murder C   þe bold] þis cursyd E   in] and all U in . . .
riche] ჳif þat they myჳte E   his] the D   burwe] burgh PAU   907 cite] comyns E
assented] assentes P   assented hem boþe] of one assent werne UDEC   hem] hade A   *no*
cesura E   908 was] es PD, for E   þey . . . ჳolden] thei haue him demed U, but deme hym
to dethe E, his deth þey haue dyჳte C   his] the A   ჳolden] ჳoledyn P   909 flowe] fled
PADEC, fledden U   þat] þe PDE, this U   freke] wrecche C   freke frendles] *trs.* A
frendles] *adds* hymself all C   frendles alone] is (it is D) ferly to here UD, as ferly is to telle E
alone] oute P, frekly anone A   910 Out] *om.* PE (*at end of prec. line* P)   priue] PAUDEC,
pore L *Kölbing-Day*   þe] *om.* E   folwed] sewes PA, after UDEC   911 With] Bot P, With
him U, Safe C   of] of a PAC   toke . . . more] *om., fused with line* 913 A   912 *line om.* A
glowande] gleterand PC   grounde] erthe PC   913 On . . . teþ] *trs. phrs.* P, *om., fused with*
line 911 A   þat] þe P, this UDE   þat he A   toggeþ] gnawyd E   and byteþ] ful fast U
byteþ] bytyd E, bytheth C   914 was piked] is prikked U, is pytte D, was prykked C   a
prikkes] AUD, a pokes L *Kölbing-Day,* pryk P, a prikke C   scribal line E: til it were scharp at
þe ende / ryჳt as prykke   915 abideþ þat burne] he bydes þe berynes P, byddis he those
beryns A, abydeth he þe barones C   þat] the UD   þat burne] he a while E   biterlych]
baldely he P, bittirly he AD   spekeþ] sayde UDE   916 *line om.* A   To] Till P, And to C
wyes] wyse U, wightis D, folk E, comens C   þat] *om.* U   were] was / þese E, were / these C
aloude] on hye D   917 schal] þer shall C   neuer] no C   þe] *om.* UDEC   tale] worde P
rise] arise UDEC   918 Of] þat PC   no] any C   karl] capped (coysid D, cursyd E) carle
UDE   by þe] make his P, at the A   by þe coppe] *om.* UDE, of ჳour kynde C   coppe] cope P,
couppe A   how] þat PUDE   how he] hath C   quelde] slewe A   919 Hymself] *after*
stykeþ AC   *stykeþ] styked P, stekide A, stikyd D, strykeþ L *Kölbing-Day,* strike U, smote C
myd] with PAUDC   þat] the AUC   staf] stake AC   streჳt to] strake to P, thoroweowte A,
rith vnto U   scribal line E: with þe trunchun þanne hymseelf / he smoot to þe herte
920 þat] And E   þe colke] it vnclenly UD, atwo E, hit C   toclef] gon cleue P, all tocleue A,
cleuyd it E, toclefe asounder C   and] and so UDEC   kyng] schrewe E

Six monþe after and no more   þis myschef bytydde
þat Waspasian was went   to werry on þe Iewes—
Foure mettyn myle out of Rome   to mynde[n] foreuere
þat erst was emperour of alle   þus ended in sorow.

þe grete togedres [g]an,   [get]en hem anoþer,   925
On Gabba, a gome   þat mychel grem hadde
þroȝ Othis L[ucy]us, a lord   þat hym longe hated;
And at þe last þat l[e]d[e]   out of lyf hym broȝt.

Amydde þe market of Rome   þe[y] mette[n] togedres;   f. 14ʳ
Othis falleþ hym fey,   ȝaf hym fale woundes   930
þat foure monþes and more   hadde mayntened þe croune.
And þo deyed þe duke   and + diademe lefte.

+ Whan þat Gabba was gon   and to grounde broȝt,
Othis entriþ [ȝ]ernest   and emperour was made;
þ[at] man in his maieste   was monþes bot þre   935
+ An + ȝeldeþ Sathanas þe soule   and hymself quelled.

921 Six] Seuene C   after] om. AU   and] om. UD   and no more] om. E   more] mo D   þis]
þat þis DE   myschef] turn E   bytydde] bifell DC   922 þat] om. E   Waspasian] Vesp- UDC
was] is U, om. E   went] gone C   werry] wer P, werre ADEC, weren U   no cesura E
923 lines 923–24 om. UDE   to . . . euere] þe sothe forto telle E   *mynden]
Duggan 1988:127, mynde L, mene P, menyn A, mynne U, myn D   924 þat] He þat A   erst]
firste P, om. AUDE   alle] alle Rome A, om. D   þus] þat D   ended] endeth U, endyd he D
925 *togedres gan] togeder er gone P, togeder gan gone / to U, gan togidir (togydre E) gon
DE, togedres þan L Kölbing-Day, gadirde þam togedire and A, gedered togydur / & C   geten]
PUD Kölbing-Day, chossen LE, gatt AC   926 Gabba] gabaoo A   a] om. D   a gome] a gode
grome U, be name E, a werche C   mychel] myche PAUEC, mych D   grem] gram AUDE
grem hadde] sorowe wrowȝte C   no cesura E   927 þroȝ] To UDC, of E   Othis] Othe⟨.⟩ P,
Otus AUD, on E, sir otus C   Lucyus] AUDEC Kölbing-Day, lyous L, Lustius P   a lord]
om. C   þat] þat had PD, þat lange tym had A   longe] om. A, longe hadde C   928 And]
om. C   at . . . lede] trs. phrs. A   þe] om. D   þat] þe PD, þis E   lede] PAU Kölbing-Day, lord
LDEC   out . . . hym] hym on lyfe P, hym of lyte A   hym] om. U   broȝt] broughe E
929 Amydde] In myddes PAC   þey] PAUDEC Kölbing-Day, þe L   metten] PAUDC
Duggan 1988:127, mette LE Kölbing-Day   togedres] in fere PA   930 Othis] Otus A, There
Othus (sir otus C) UDEC   falleþ] felde PAUDEC   fey] in fey EC   ȝaf] and gaf PAUDEC
fale] fele PDE, felle A, ded U, many C   931 foure] foure of P   and] om. U   more] no more
AUC Kölbing-Day   hadde] he D   mayntened] bore E   932 And] om. PAC   þo] þan PE,
thare AUD, Thus C   þe] þat PADEC   duke] prince C   and] PAE Duggan 1986:584, and þe
LC Kölbing-Day, and his U, þe D   diademe] lyfe C   933 Whan] PUDEC, And whan L
Kölbing-Day, than whan A   þat] om. AC   Gabba] gabaoo A   to] to þe D, in E   to grounde]
oute ⟨ ⟩ome P, to þe erthe C   broȝt] ybrowht E   no cesura C   934 Othis] Otus AUDEC
Othis . . . ȝernest] In er. en. O. UD, þanne e. O. E   entriþ] entred UDEC   *ȝernest] on ernest
L Kölbing-Day, In ernest UD, in areste A, In P, aftur C, om. E   was] is UD   935 þat]
PAUDC, þe L Kölbing-Day   þat man] And he E   in] leuede in A   was] om. A, nys U
monþes bot þre] but monethes thre (trs. E) UE   936 An] PAUDE, þan L Kölbing-Day,
He C   ȝeldeþ] ȝelde PAUDEC, he ȝeldeþ L Kölbing-Day   Sathanas þe soule] his (þe D) s. to
s. UDE   þe] his AC   and] for he EC   -self] marg. C

þe Romayns r[a]isen + a renk   Rome forto kepe,
A kny3t þat Vitel was calde,   and hym þe croune rau3te.

. . . .

Bot for Sire Sabyns sake,   a segge [þat] was noble,
Waspasian broþer of blode   þat he brytned hadde . . .   940

[V]aspasian vpon Vitel   to vengen his broþer
S[en]t out of Surrie   segges to Rome.

. . . .

þat [a]s naked as an nedul   þe newe emperour
For Sire Sabyns sake   alle þe cite drowe +;

Suþ gored þe go[r]e[l]   þat his guttes alle   945
As a bowe[l]ed beste   into his breche felle.

Doun 3er[m]ande he 3ede   and 3eldeþ þe soule;
And [þey] kay3t þe cors   and kast into Tybre.

Seuen monþes þis [segge]   hadde septre on hande
And þus loste he þe lyf   for his luþer dedes.   950

937 þe] Than the A   raisen] PUD, risen vp L *Kölbing-Day*, rayssede AC, resyn þo E   a
renk] anon E, a lorde C   forto] vnto U   938 Vitel] vytale PADC, Vitaill U   Vitel was
calde] hy3t vytayle E   was] is UD   and] þat D, þanne E, þey C   hym] *om.* UDE   rau3te]
yemyd D, caw3te E, 3afe C   939 for] *om.* PDE, that U   Sabyns sake] sabyn soght P, Sabyn
sye U, Sabyn hit sees D, sabyn of surry E   a . . . noble] þerwith was displesyd E   segge] sege
P, kny3te C   þat] PAUDC *Kölbing-Day*, om. L   was] than was A, is U   noble] *om.* A
940 of blode] *om.* PUDE   brytned] betrayde P, blenkede A, yhurt E, murthered C
941 *line om.* A Vaspasian] UDC, wasp- LPE *Kölbing-Day*   vpon] on UDE, roose on C
Vitel] vytale PDC, vitaill UE   broþer] brother (-eres C) deth UC   *no cesura* E   942 Sent]
PUDE *Kölbing-Day*, Sou3t L, Sendis A, He sente C   segges] meche folk E, kny3tes C
943 þat] *om.* P, that made A, and they E, They made hym C   as] PDE *Kölbing-Day*, is L, al
U, *om.* AC   an] *om.* P   þe] þat A   newe] new PD   944 Sire] *om.* C   alle] in al E   drowe]
UDE, drowe hym L, was drawen P, drawen C   scribal line A: And his bolde beryns one the
bent brittenede to dede   945 Suþ] And sythen AUDE, And aftur C   gored] *om.* A, *after*
gorel E   þe] þat C   gorel] E, gome LPUD *Kölbing-Day*, gome hymselfe A, prince C
946 As . . . beste] Hastly (Brothely D) at a braide UD, gurd out at a breyd E   boweled] PC
Kölbing-Day, bowewed L, boluede A   into] in UD, and in E   into his breche] of (out of C) his
body AC   felle] hange P, fallyn D   947 Doun] Dawe U, þanne E, All downe C   Doun . . .
3ede] And þus þere he died D   *3ermande] *Kölbing-Day*, 3ernande L, yemerand U, 3arande
A, heledand P, stumbling E, gronynge C   and] *om.* C   3eldeþ] 3eledes P, 3aldide A, yelde vp
UDE, 3olde out C   þe] his E   soule] gaste A   948 And þey kay3t] Thenne toke þey C
þey] PA *Kölbing-Day*, *om.* L, then thei UD, þo þei E   kay3t] caght PAD, catchen vp U,
tookyn E   cors] corpse ADU, body C   kast] casten U   into] it in PADEC   949 þis] þat
PC, the UD   þis segge hadde] and no more A   segge] PUD *Kölbing-Day*, man LC, vityal E
hadde] *before* þis P, *after* septre UDE   septre] the septre AUDE   on] in PUDEC, he A
hande] hade A   950 þus] þan PA, so UDEC   loste] lefte PAUC   he] *om.* P   þe] his DE
luþer] euell C   dedes] dede U   *no cesura* E   line added UE: And (*om.* E) then (þo E) alle the
(*om.* E) grete of the toun / togedir gun gone (t . . . . g.] besid hem faste E) (*no cesura* E)

Anoþer segge was to seke   þat septre schold haue,
For alle þis grete ben gon   and neuer agayn tournen.

Now of þe cite and of þe sege   wolle Y sey more,
How þis comelich kyng   þat for Crist werreþ
Haþ holden yn þe heþen +   þis oþer half wynter   965
þat neuer burne [of] þe burwe   [s]o bold was + to passe.

As he to dyner on a day   with dukes was sette
Comen renkes fram Rome   rapande swyþe
In bruneys and in bryȝt wede   [and] with bodeworde newe,
Louten alle to þe lord   `and´ lettres hym rauȝten.   960

Sayn, 'comelich kyng,   þe knyȝthod of Rome
þroȝ þe senatours assent   and alle þe cite ellis
Han chosen þe [fo]r chyuentayn   here chef lord to worþe
And riche emperour of Rome: þus redeþ þis lettres'.

þe lord vnlappeþ þe lef,   þis lettres byholdeþ,   965
Ouerlokeþ ech a lyne   to þe last ende.   f. 14ᵛ

951 Anoþer] For other U   segge] segges U, prince C   was] *om.* U, is D   was to seke] þey
sowȝte C   þat] þe PUD   septre] the septire AC   schold] to U, forto D   scribal line E:
Anoþer emperour to haue / whan þey myȝt hym fynde   952 *line om.* E   For] thus AC
þis] þere P   grete] *om.* P   and] þat P   neuer] none U   agayn] aȝayne PUDC   tournen]
turned PAC, turnith U   953 Now] ¶ *precs.* D, *three-line capital* E   þe] þis D   cite] sege
UE, segge D, kynge C and] *om.* UDEC   of²] *om.* PA, in U   þe²] ȝe P, *om.* UDEC   sege] *om.*
P, Surre UDC, ierusalem E   Y] þat I P, we D   sey] talke E   954 How] And how A   þis]
the E   werreþ] wered UDC, werre E   955 yn] *om.* AC, on UDE   þe] thire A   heþen]
PDE, heþen men LAUC *Kölbing-Day*   þis] *om.* PDU, now E   wynter] ȝere PUDE
956 neuer] no AC   burne] *om.* D, boy E, manne C   of . . . was] PAUDC (of] oute of PUDC,
þe] *om.* U, was] is UD), was so bold / þe burwe forto L *Kölbing-Day*, was so boold / out of þe
town E   burwe] cyte C   *no cesura* C   957 to] to the A   dukes] renkes U, loordes E
sette] yset E   958 Comen] þare come PC   renkes] messagers E, knyȝtes C   fram] fra
PAUEC, out of D   rapande] raykande P, Rydande full A, respand UD, rennyng E, rydynge
on C   swyþe] faste C   959 In] With U   In . . . wede] woundeliche weel arayed E, All
armed in clene steele A   burne] *om.* D, boy E, manne C   of . . . was] PAUDC (of] oute of PUDC,
wedis A   and²] AC, *om.* LPUDE *Kölbing-Day*   with] broghte AC   bodeworde] tydynges
EC   newe] goode C   960 Louten] thay lowte A, And lowtyd E, They kneled C   and]
om. P   hym] þey hym C   rauȝten] brought U, schewyd E, toke C   961 Sayn] Sayde P,
And sayde AE, Seying U, And seyn D, They seyde C   comelich kyng] semliche A
knyȝthod] knyghthede P, knyghode A   962 þroȝ] With UDEC   þe¹] *om.* D   alle] *om.* P
þe²] *om.* E   ellis] als P, aftur C   963 þe] ye P   for] PAUC, her LDE *Kölbing-Day*
chyuentayn] chief U   here] oure P, and E   here . . . worþe] *trs. phrs.* PADC   chef lord]
chiuetaigne U, emperour EC   worþe] be PAUDEC   964 And] þe P, thou A   þus] *om.* P,
now A   redeþ] reden A   þis] þare P   scribal line UDEC: Os ye may (þow mayst E) se by the
(þis E) seal / assay yif (howe C) ye (ȝow D, þe E) liketh   965 *line om.* P   þe¹] than the A
vnlappeþ] liftes vp U, left vp DC   þis] and the AC, the UD   lettres] letter C   byholdeþ] to
byholde D   scribal line E: He took þe lettres in his hond / and on hem he loketh   966 V
BEGINS Ouerlokeþ] He ouerlokes in P, He loked U, And lokith D, & radde ouer E, He
loketh C   ech a] euerIlke a A, euery VDEC, euery a U   to] vnto V, til D   *no cesura* V

Bordes born were doun   and þe burne riseþ,
Calleþ consail anon   and kyþeþ þis speche:

'3e ben burnes of my blod   þat Y best wolde,
My sone is next to myself,   and oþer sib manye—   970
Sire Sabyn of Surrie,   a segge þat Y triste,
And oþer frendes fele   þat me fayþ owen.

Now is me bodeword [b]ro3t   of blys froward Rome
To be lord ouer þat l[e]d[e],   as þis lettres spekeþ.
Sire Sabyn of Surrie,   sey þe byhouyþ   975
How Y my3t sauy myself   and I so wro3t.

For Y haue heylych hey3t   here forto lenge
Tille I þis toured [t]oun   ha[ue] taken at [my] wille
And me þe 3ates ben 3et   and 3olden þe keyes
And suþ honshed on hem   þat þis hold kepyn,   980

967 Bordes] than burdis AE   born] take E   born were] *trs*. PAVC, were take E
doun] all doune P, adowne VE   þe] *om*. A   burne] bernys PA, lord U, kyng EC
riseþ] to rysse A, ariseth UE   968 Calleþ] Callid D, and calleth E, He kalled his C
consail] þaim P   and] *om*. VD   kyþeþ] kythid D, chaunged C   kyþeþ þis speche]
þis mateer meuyth E   þis] þe PA, his VUDC   969 ben] *om*. C   burnes] *om*. P,
borin V, barnes E, lordes C   þat] and that U, þe whyche C   Y] me V   Y best] my
blysse A   best] moste C   wolde] trayste P, loue UDE, truste C   970 sone . . .
myself] nemys and myn sonnys A   is] here P, *om*. E   next] sib DE   to] *om*. V
oþer sib manye] our seggisman D   sib] of 3ow E   971 segge þat] kny3t in whom
E, manne þat C   triste] trayste A, trust VUDC   972 *lines* 972–75 *om*. D   fele]
full fele AV, ere fele here U, here fele E, mony C   me fayþ owen] feithe owen to me V
973 Now . . . blys] Here ben tydyngdes brought to me / E, Ioyfull worde is me brow3te
/ C   me] *om*. A   bro3t of blys] V, *trs*. LPAUD   froward] from PV, me fro A, out of
U, ry3t now fro E, fro senatours of C   974 *line om*. P   To] Forto A, þat y shal E
ouer] of AVUEC   þat] the U   lede] AV, lond LUEC *Kölbing-Day*   as þis] þe V,
thises U, as the E, these C   spekeþ] tellis A, it seyen U, sygge E, þus seyn C
975 sey] to say UC   sey þe byhouyþ] y preye þe to seye E   976 Y my3t] *trs*.
AUDEC   my3t] may AV   sauy myself] *trs*. D   and] if DEC   wro3t] were E
977 heylych] ⟨*torn*⟩ly P, holly A, holy VUD, fully C   hey3t] byhight UE   forto] to C
lenge] lende V, ligge E, abyde C   978 *line order* 979, 978 PAVUC *Kölbing-Day*
Tille I] And A, Sithen V, And forto haue C, And I *Kölbing-Day*   toun] PAVUDEC
Kölbing-Day, doun L   haue] PUDE *Kölbing-Day*, han L, *om*. AV   haue taken] ry3t C
taken] tan U, *om*. EC   my] AVUDEC, *om*. LP *Kölbing-Day*   979 And] To PA,
Til VUC *Kölbing-Day*   me] *om*. PVDEC   þe[1]] thir A, þis VU   3ates] *torn* P, gates V
ben] *om*. E   3et] gate V, yolden U, yevyn D, openyd EC   3olden] 3oleden P, *after*
keyes AEC, yeuen U   þe[2]] *om*. E   keyes] kayes to me E, town C   980 suþ] *om*.
AV, also E, forto C   honshed] venged P, vengede be A, venge me V, hongen U,
hongyd DE, venge god C   on] of AC   hem] thies heythen men (*om*. VC) AVC, hye
UDE   þat] that haue U   þis] þe PUDE   holde] town EC   kepyn] kepte UE

[B]etyn and brosten doun þis britages heye
þat neuer ston in þat stede stond vpon oþere.
Kyþe þ[y] consail sire kny3t', þ[e] kyng to hym sayde,
'For Y wol worche by þy witt 3if worschip may folowe'.

þan seiþ Sire Sabyn anon, 'semelich lord,   985
We ben wyes þe with þy worschup to furþer,
Of longe tyme bylafte and ledes þyn owen:
þat we don is þy dede, may no man demen elles'.

þe dom demed was þer + who doþ by anoþer
Schal be soferayn hymself + sein in þe werke.   990
For as fers is þe freke atte ferre ende
þat + of-fleis þe fel as he þat foot holdeþ.

'Bytake Tytus þy sone þis toun forto kepe
And to þe dou3ti duke Domyssian his broþer.
Here I holde vp myn honde myd hem forto lenge   995
With alle þe here þat I haue while my herte lasteþ.

981 Betyn and brosten] PAV (brosten] brayde P), *trs. verbs* L *Kölbing-Day*, Brent and brusten (broke D, bete E) UDE, And beten and breken C þis] þe PE, thaire A britages] bretage PU, bretasynges A, torrettes C heye] alle A, so hye U, abowte E 982 þat¹] Tyll þat C neuer] no AVC, nouther U, neiþer DE ston . . . stede] ston nor (ne E) styk / ne (*om.* E) UE, stik nor stone shal D in þat stede] appon stone AC þat²] *om.* P, þis V stond] ligge (*after* oþer) E stond vpon oþere] in þat place be lafte C oþere] lofte A, erthe U 983 *lines* 983–84 *om.* C Kyþe] Now kythe A þy] PAVUD *Kölbing-Day*, þe L þe] PAVUD, þis L *Kölbing-Day* scribal line E: And þerfore tel me þy wyt / y preye þe blyue 984 witt] wille VDE may] it UDE folowe] be P 985 Ex **FRAGMENTARILY PRESENT THROUGH 1017** seiþ] sayde *after* Sabyn A, said V anon] *om.* PV, to that A semelich] semelyche PAV scribal line· UDEC: The knyght kneled onone (adown EC) / and to the kyng said 986 We] Here C wyes] wightis D, meyne C wyes þe with] alle thyn owne E þe with] with þe / þat C wolde C furþer] folwen U, willyn D, saue E, *om.* C 987 *line om.* P Of] OF a A bylafte] with þe lafte C and . . . owen] thy legemen ilkone (echone DC) UDC scribal line E: þy leege men and sogettys / euyr at þi wille 988 þat] And þat P don] deme U þy] þe E may] þere may VC elles] other UDEC 989 *lines* 989–92 *om.* E who] AV *Duggan* 1986:590, whoso LUC *Kölbing-Day*, þat who P, þat whoso D 990 Schal] He sall PA, He shall V be] *om.* Ex sein] PAV *Kölbing-Day*, seint L, yseyn U, set D, *om.* C in] by D þe] þis V, that UC werke] dede UD, same dede C *no cesura* V 991 *lines* 991–92 *om.* UD as] els P, also C fers] faye P, foule A, ferfurthe VC, Ferre Ex þe freke] he C ferre] ferrere A, ferther C 992 of-] PACEx *Kölbing-Day*, ofte L, *om.* V fel] skynne C he] *om.* V þat²] that the AC adds scribal line E: Therfore my leege lord / y telle the owre wille 993 Bytake] to take E þy] youre V forto] now to UDC *no cesura* E 994 þe] that U dou3ti] *om.* A Domyssian] Damacian V, domyan E his] that es his dere A adds scribal line E: for thei beth best wurthi / after þe in sothe 995 Here] And here AVUDEC vp] 'vp' A myd] with PAVUDEC hem] þaim PA, 3ow D lenge] lende AV, abyde EC 996 here] herte V, help UDEC while] þerwhilles A, whiles UP herte] lyfe AVUDEC

And þou schalt ride to Rome   and receyue þe croune,
In honour emperour to be,   as þyn eure schapiþ.
So may þ[e] couenaunt be kept   þat þou to Crist made:
þyself dest þat þy soudiours   by þyn assent worchen'.   1000

þan with a liouns lote   he lifte vp [his] eyen,
To Titus tourneþ anon   and hym þe tale schewed.
And as Sire Sabyn hadde seid,   he hym sone granteþ
With his broþer and þe burne[s]   as he hym blesse wolde:

'+ I wol tarie at þis toun   til I hit taken haue,   1005
Made weys þrow [þe walles]   for wenes and cartes
f. 15ʳ Oure boþere heste to holde,   ȝif me + hap tydiþ,
Or here [t]ohewen be   or I hennes passe'.

A boke on a brode scheld   was broȝt on to swere:
+ Burnes boden [to] þe honde   and barouns hit kyssen   1010

997 to] vnto AUC   and²] om. P, to UEC   and² . . . croune] thi c. to rescheyue A   þe]
þer þi P   croune] corowne U   998 In honour] An U, And D, And there E, with
honour C   to] new to U, now to D, om. E   be] be made UE   as . . . schapiþ] to þi lyfes ende
P, als now the tym askes A, os the is now (om. DE) shaped (happid D, behote E) UDE   eure]
om. V, kynde C   schapiþ] asketh C   999 So] For so C   þe] PAVUDEEx, þy LC
Kölbing-Day   be] by C   kept] kep V   to] with A   made] madest VUE   no cesura V
1000 dest þat] hit does V   þy soudiours] thine UDC   by] doon be V, dos / and UD, doth
yf C   þyn . . . worchen] þy wyll assente C   scribal line E: and þe holde a trewe kyng /   for
ellys were gret schame   1001 lote] look VUDEC   his] PAVUDEC, þe L Kölbing-Day
1002 To . . . anon] Tornes (Turned V, and turnyd E, He turned C) hym (marg. A, om.
VCEx) to (toward C) T. AVECEx   tourneþ anon] trs. U   anon] hym onone P, om. EC
tale] om. A, staat E   schewed] schewes PAUD, grauntyd E, tolde C   1003 Sabyn]
sablyn' Ex   hadde] has PAUD   he hym] be it P   he hym sone] onone he it U   granteþ]
graunted PC   scribal line E: Thanne answered tytus / and þe auysement seyde
1004 With] Forto (To VC) byde (abyde C) with AVC   and þe burnes] om. AVC   þe]
om. UD   burnes] UD Kölbing-Day, burne LP   as he] þat PAUD, what so C   as . . . wolde]
till þe burgh be yolden V   hym] om. C   blesse] blysse PAU, betythe C   wolde] wolden
UD   scribal line E: þese wurdes þat folwyn / and avow maade   1005 I] PAVUDEEx,
And I L Kölbing-Day, For I C   wol] sall AVUDCEx, weele E   tarie] abyde E   at] on V
hit . . . haue] haue it take E   1006 Made] And maad V, And þenne made he C   Made
weys] trs. UD, and weyes make E   þe walles] PAE Kölbing-Day, om. L, þe wall VDC, wal U
for] with P   1007 Oure] Sure V, My E   boþere] fader PE, om. VC, bothe U, other D,
brother Ex   heste] hete P, hightis A, heestes VUDEx, hostes   to] forto E   ȝif . . . tydiþ]
þat we to criste made C   me] vs V, y D   hap] PAVUE, þe happis L, hele D, þe happ
Kölbing-Day   tydiþ] tyde PAU, have D, betyde E   no cesura V   1008 here] ellis D, elles
here C   tohewen be] PEx, trs. L Kölbing-Day, hewen forto (om. V, to UC) be AVUC,
britnyd to be D, deed forto be E   or] if D   hennes] hythen PA, hens UDC   1009 on']
and PUE   was] were E   was broȝt] trs. D   on²] for- AV, after swere D   1010 Burnes]
AUDEx, Alle burnes LP Kölbing-Day, Barnes V, þe peple E, The dukes C   boden to þe
honde] þan handes helde P   boden] bedyn AUD, leyde E, putte C, byden Ex   to] AVUDC
Kölbing-Day, om. LEx, on E   þe honde] thaire (he V) handis AVUDEC   and] om. D
barouns] boldely P, þe E, lordes C   hit] to PUD, om. E   kyssen] kysten VEC   no cesura V

To be leel to þat lord   þat hem lede scholde,
Sire Titus þe trewe kyng,   tille þey þe toun hadde.

Fayn as þe foul of day   was þe freke þanne,
Kysseþ knyȝtes anon   with carful wordes:
'My wele and my worschup   ȝe weldeþ to kepe,   1015
For þe tresour of my treuþ   vpon þis toun hengyþ.

I nold þis toun were vntake   ne þis toures heye
For alle þe glowande golde   vn[der] + God-riche,
[N]e no ston in þe stede   stond[ande] alofte,
Bot alle ouertourned and tilt,   temple and oþer'.   1020

þus laccheþ h[e] leeue   at his ledes alle,
Wende wepande away   and on þe walles lokeþ,
Praieþ [God] as he gooþ   hem grace [for]to sende
To hold þat þey byhot han   and neuer here herte chaunge.

Now is Waspasian went   ouer [þe] wale stremys,   1025
Euen entred into Rome   and emperour maked;

1011 leel] trewe EC, leue Ex   þat¹] thaire A, þe VUDEC   1012 Sire] To DC, Anon E
trewe] om. E   kyng] knyȝte C   tille] to PE   þey] after toun E   1013 line om. E   þe¹] om.
AVUDCEx   foul] folowe C   of] of þe PAVUDC, with t- Ex   freke] kyng VC
1014 Kysseþ] torn P, kysses his AV, He kissed (k. þe D, k. his CEx) UDCEx   anon] þan P,
sone C   with] and saies with V   carful] komeliche UDC   scribal line E: And his knyȝtes
togydre / gadrid and seyde   1015 My] Sayse my A   My wele] ⟨torn⟩ll P   worschup]
welfare C   weldeþ] woleden P, weleden A, weld UD, haue C   to] and AV   to kepe] in youre
hondes UDEC   1016 tresour] trust U   treuþ] trowȝthe CE   vpon] on PVDEC   þis]
ȝondur C   1017 nold] nolde but U, wolde not but C   þis toun] þe toures P   vntake] vntane
PVD, tane UC   ne] and PAVUC, and al D, with E   þis] his E   toures] toune P   toures heye]
trs. D, grete toures E   Ex ENDS   1018 glowande golde] golde and þe gode P, schynyng
gold EC   vnder God-] PAVUDC, vpon grounde L Kölbing-Day, vnder the cope UE   -riche] of
heuen UDEC   no cesura V   1019 Ne] PAVUDE Kölbing-Day, be L, Nor C   no] om. U
þe] this A, that ilk U, no DE, þat C   stede] place C   stondande] PAVUDC Kölbing-Day,
stonden L, laft E   alofte] were lefte AV, vpon oþer EC   1020 alle] om. UDC, þei were E
-tourned and] om. AE   and] cesura precs. L   tilt] tirlled PA, tild DE, tumbled C   temple] the
temples U   temple and oþer] and partyd atwynne E   1021 þus] So P, Tho E, Thenne C, ¶
precs. D   laccheþ] laughte AD, laughten V, took E, taketh C   he] PV, his L, he his AC
Kölbing-Day, the kyng UD, waspasyan / E   at] of E   ledes] lordis AUEC   alle] om. E
1022 Wende] after away U, And wente E, He wente C   on] om. E   walles] wall PV   lokeþ]
lokyd PAUEC, waytid D   1023 Praieþ] And (And he C) preyde EC   God] PVUDEC
Kölbing-Day, om. L., to god A   as he gooþ] of his godenesse C   gooþ] ȝede E   hem] hym P,
om. A, þat he hem E   forto] AU, to LPVDC Kölbing-Day, om. E   1024 hold] help D
byhot] heght PAVUEC, hit D   han] om. VE   and] þat C   neuer] noghte A   here] om. U   her
herte] after and A   herte] hertis AVDEC   chaunge] 'to' change A, turne C   no cesura V
1025 Now] four-line capital V   Now . . . went] Anonryȝt he wente forth E   Waspasian]
Waspasius P, Vasp- VUDC   went] Igone C   þe] PAVUDEC, om. L Kölbing-Day   wale] vale
PV, wane A, wyde U, wild DE, bygge C   stremys] wawys E   no cesura V   1026 Euen]
And E   entred] Entirs A   into] to PD   maked] es makede A, ymaked UD, was maad EC

And Titus for þe tydyng   ha[þ] take [so] mychel ioye
þat in his synwys soudeynly   a syknesse is fallen.

þe freke for þe fayndom   of þe fadere blysse
With a cramp and a colde   cauȝt was so hard   1030
þat þe fyngres and feet,   fustes and ioyntes
Was lyþy as a leke   and lost han here strengþe,

+ Becroked aȝens kynde   and as a crepel woxen.
+ Whan þey sey hym so   many segge wepyþ;
þey [s]en[t]e to þe cite   and souȝten a leche   1035
þat couþe keuere þe kyng   and condi[t] delyueryn.

Whan þey þe cyte hadde souȝt   with seggys aboute,
Fynde couþe þey no [freke]   þat on þe feet couþe
Saue þe self Iosophus   þat surgyan was noble,
And he graunteþ to go   [þe gome forto hele].   1040

Whan he was comen to þe kyng   and þe cause wyste
How þe segge so sodeynly   in syknesse is fallen,

1027 for þe] of that UD, of E, for þat C   tydyng] tytynges P, tyȝandes A, tithandes V
haþ] AVUDC *Kölbing-Day*, han L, *om.* E   haþ . . . ioye] so myche noy had P   take] takyn
AC, made V, took E   so] AVUC *Kölbing-Day*, *om.* L, such DE   mychel] muche U, a DE
1028 his] *om.* D   synwys] syns P, syde was U   soudeynly] *after* syknesse P   is] y- U,
was E   1029 þe¹] þat V   þe freke] So E, That prince C   þe²] greet E, his C
fayndom] fantom P, faynnes AVC, faynhede (-hode DE) UDE   þe³] his PVUDEC
fader] faderes CA   blysse] worshyppe C   1030 cauȝt was] kankers P   was] is UD
so] full P, he A   *no cesura* V   1031 þe¹] his AVUEC   fyngres] fetures U   fyngres,
fustes] *trs. sbs.* PAVDEC   and¹] and þe P, and his AVEC   fustes] handis A   fustes and
ioyntes] ioynte and handes U   ioyntes] other P   *no cesura* V   1032 Was] Wex P,
weryn VDE, waxen U   lyþy] laythly P, lene A, letchy V, litel U, lithe D   leke] leef UDE
lost] lorne AV, lefte C   han] had PAEC, haddin V   here] þe PA   1033 *Be-] ben L,
He PAVUDEC *Kölbing-Day*   aȝens . . . crepel] as a crepel / al aȝens kynde E   as] *om.* V
woxen] waxen P, wexe AVC *Kölbing-Day*, waxeth U, wexid D, *om.* E   1034 Whan]
PAVUDE, And whan L *Kölbing-Day*, But whenne C   sey] se P   so] so bynommen A, so
byset D   many] many a VUDC   segge] man EC   wepyþ] wepyn P, wepide AVUDEC
1035 þey] And AE   sente] PAVUDEC, wende L, sende *Kölbing-Day*   souȝten] soughte
thare A, sowȝte hem C   *no cesura* V   1036 keuere] kepe P, cure UDE, hele C
condit] PA *Kölbing-Day*, condis L, condit hym (hem E) VUE, conduyt þei D, a condyte C
delyueryn] delyuerede AVUDC, ȝeue E   1037 hadde] hafe P   with] the U   seggys]
segges al U, wyse men E, herowdis all C   aboute] ynow DE   1038 Fynde . . . man]
thei non cowde fynde E   couþe¹] kan UD   freke] PAVUD *Kölbing-Day*, man LC   on]
of PVUC   þe] that A   þe feet] surgery V   couþe²] knewe C   1039 þe self] one V,
himself UD, þe knyȝt E, only C   þat] *om.* V   þat surgyan] þe freke þat P   was] is U   *no
cesura* V   1040 And] *om.* C   graunteþ] graunted PAVUDEC   to go] forto come V
þe . . . hele] UDE (gome) kyng E), with a goode wylle LPAVC *Kölbing-Day*   *no cesura* VC
1041 Whan] ¶ *precs.* D   was comen] com EC   and] and al UDE   cause] case PUDEC
1042 *line om.* C   How] Why PAV, How þat E   þe segge] he E   so] 'so' P, *om.* VUDE
is] was PAVE   *no cesura* V

Tille he haue complet his cure   condit he askeþ
For what burne of þe burwe   þat he brynge wolde.

þe kyng was glad alle to graunte   þat þe gome wylned,   1045
And he ferkiþ hym forþ,   fettes ful blyue
A man to þe mody kyng   þat he moste hated
And yn bryngeþ þe burne   to his beddes syde.

Whan Tytus saw þat segge   sodeynly with eyen,
His herte in an hote yre   so hetterly riseþ   1050
þat þe blode bygan to [b]red[e] abrode in þe vaynes
And þe synwes resorte   in here self kynde.

Feet and alle þe fetoures,   as þey byfore were,
Comyn in here owen kynd,   and þe kyng ryseþ.
þonkeþ God of his grace   and þe goode leche,   1055
Of alle saue þat his enemy   was yn on hym broȝt.

1043 Tille] To P   haue] had PAVUDEC   complet] kythede A, kithe V, done C
complet his cure] his cure ydoon E   cure] dede and cure / a C   askeþ] askyd PDEC
1044 For what] And for a V   burne] man EC   of] withinne C   þe burwe] town E,
þe cyte C   1045 was] is UD   alle to graunte] and all graunted P, and grantede /
all (om. C) AVC, forto graunt al U   þat þe gome] his C   þe gome] iosephus E
wylned] askyd PAE, desires V, wolden U, wilnith D, askynge C   no cesura C
1046 he] anon he E   ferkiþ] foundes P, ferkede AV, wente E, hertyly wente C   hym]
om. PEC   forþ] before P   fettes] and serchys P, and fechede AVE, to fette C   ful]
him U   ful blyue] belyue PV, anoþer A, a beerne D, hym a leche E, hym anone C
1047 þe] that A   mody] sykke E, dowȝty C   hated] hoted P   1048 yn] sone A,
om. UDEC   bryngeþ] browȝte C   þe] þat P, he the A, forth that U, bysily þe D
þe burne] hym euyn foorth E, þat man sodenly C   beddes] bed PU, bedde A   no
cesura V   1049 saw] sodanly se P, sees A, after segge UDE   þat] þe VDC, þis E
segge] sight P, man EC   sodeynly] om. P, so s. DE   with eyen] hym by E, in sight U
eyen] eghe AV, sight DC   1050 His] In his PUDE   in] om. PUDE, and A   an]
his A, om. V   hote yre] hete UDE   so] om. AVUC, for E   hetterly] hertly P, O
(canc.) Etterly A, sodainly VUDC, teene E   riseþ] arises VUD, anon aryseth E, arose C
1051 þat] om. PAVC   bygan] al bygan UE   *to brede] Kölbing-Day, to spred L, with
þe hete PAVC (with) with A, in C   þe] om. P, the A, þat C   hete] heete V), om.
UDE   abrode] to brede PAVUC, to blede D, to wurche E   þe] his PUDE
1052 þe] om. P, his E   synwes] synours P, rody U, rode D, colour E   resorte] to r.
PA Kölbing-Day, to comforte VC, to restore UDE   here] the AV, his UDEC   self]
selfe PAV, right U, owne DE, owene C   kynde] wise V   1053 alle þe fetoures]
fetures ichone UDE   þe] om. PAC   byfore] ere U, afor D, afore E   no cesura V
1054 Comyn] They come C   in] till V, to UDEC   here] the A   owen kynd] kynde
aȝen E   and] and þenne C   ryseþ] ariseth UDE   1055 þonkeþ] Thanked UD,
thankyng E, He thanked C   þe] his AC   1056 from this point, the head of
f. 110ᵛᵃ, P ONLY FRAGMENTARY TO LINE 1143, then all lost, collations
henceforth record all extant P readings in contested lemmata   line om. P
saue] but of E   þat] om. AUDEC, only V   was] that was UD, þat stood E   yn on]
so to VC, to UD, om. E   broȝt] besyde E

þan sayþ Iosophus,   'þis segge haþ þe holpyn
And here haþ be þy bote,   þoȝ þou hym bale wolde.
þerfor graunte hym þy grace   aȝen his goode dede
And be frende with þy foman   þat frendschup haþ serued'.   1060

þe kyng sa[ȝ]tles with þe segge   þat hym saued hadde
And + graunted hym grace   to go where h[ym lyke]de.
With Iosophus he made ioye   and iewels hym rauȝte,
Besauntes, byes of gold,   broches and ryngys.

Bot alle forsakeþ þe segge   and to þe cite ȝede   1065
With condit as he come—   he kepiþ no more.
[And] Tytus segyþ þe toun   þer tene is on hande
For hard hunger and hote   þat hem is bylompyn.

[Now] of þe tene in þe toun   were [tore] forto telle,
What moryne and meschef   for mete is byfalle.   1070

1057 sayþ] sayde AVDEC, said him U   Iosophus] *adds* þe gentill sir A, *adds* sir V,
adds thoo / syr C   segge] P, *om.* U, man E, wreche C   haþ þe holpyn] P, is (*om.* E)
thin owen (t. o.] þe D, þy E) leche UDE   1058 And . . . bote] And (And he is C)
bote of al (*om.* DE) thi bitternes UDEC   here] he V   haþ] *om.* A   bale] P, sle C
wolde] woldist VE   1059 þerfor] And therefore AC, Forthy U, For D   þy] *om.*
VC   aȝen] P, for AVUDEC   dede] P, will A   1060 And] *om.* UD   be] *om.* AV
frende] fayn D   with] to E   foman] foo C   serued] P, shewed VU, deseruyd E   *no
cesura* V   1061 þe¹] Thanne þe C   þe kyng] He P   saȝtles] D, satles L *Kölbing-
Day*, saght- P, saughtled VAU, acordyd E, sawe how C   þe²] þat D   segge] man EC
þat] *om.* C   saued] heled P   1062 And] AVUDEC, And þer L *Kölbing-Day*
graunted] grauntis A, gaf U, yaf DE   grace] gudly A   to] forto UD   go] *cesura fols.*
UE   wher] thare A   hym] V, he LC *Kölbing-Day*, hym beste PA, him gode UD, þat
he E   lykede] PAVUD, wolde LEC *Kölbing-Day*   1063 With] OF AVC   With . . .
ioye] He ioied with Iosephus UDE   iewels] Iewelles VC, iewes E   rauȝte] raghten P,
ȝaue EC   *no cesura* V   1064 Besauntes] Bothe besantes C   byes] bedis A, *om.* EC
gold] clene gold E   1065 Bot] Thanne E   forsakeþ] forsoke UDC, lefte E   þe¹]
that AU, þis E, he C   segge] man E, thanne C   ȝede] P, he ȝede L, turnedde C
1066 With] Bot with AV, With sauf UE, Wiþ saser D, Safe with þe C   as] þat C   he]
thei U   come] hadde C   he kepiþ] and kepys P, *trs.* AV, kept thei (he D) UD, he kepte
E, he asked C   no more] P, noghte ells A   1067 And] PAUDE *Kölbing-Day*, Now
L, *om.* V, Thanne C   segyþ] seget P, beseggede C   þe] P, þan þe D   þer] þaire PV,
om. U, where E, and þer C   tene] P, wo E, sorowe C   is] P, was C   is on hande]
begynneth E   on] P, in UD   1068 For] with A, Thorow C   hard] P, gret E
hote] P, heete VUD, scharp E   hem] þaim PA, þey C   is] P, now E   is bylompyn]
withInne hadde C   bylompyn] P, bystadde A, bewarpen V, byfalle UD, befalleth E
1069 Now] AVE *Kölbing-Day*, And L, *om.* UDC   tene] sorwe C   in] P, of AUEC,
and of D   were] is UDC, it is E   were tore] *trs.* AEC   *tore] *Kölbing-Day*, hard L,
-to? (?-re?) P, tym A, tyme UDEC, *om.* V   forto] P, to AEC, now to D   telle] saye
PAV   1070 mete] meteles D   is byfalle] P, therein groweth UE, þer is growyn D
byfalle] bytyde A

For four[ty] dayes byfor   þey no fode hadde,
Noþer fisch ne flesch   freke on to byte—

Bred, browet ne broþe,   ne beste vpon lyue,
Wyn ne water to drynke   bot wope of hemself.
Olde scheldes and schone   scharply þey eten: 1075
þat liflode for ladies   was luþer to chewe.

Fellen doun for defaute,   [f]latte to þe grounde,
Ded as a dore-nayl,   eche day many hundred.
Wo wakned þycke: as wolues þey ferde—
þe wy[ght] waried on þe woke   alle his wombe-fille.   1080   f. 16ʳ

On Marie, a myld wyf,   for meschef of foode,
Hire owen barn þat 30 bare   + brad on þe gledis,
Rostyþ rigge and rib   with rewful wordes,
Sayþ, 'sone, vpon eche side   our sorow is alofte:

1071 For] *om.* UD   fourty] DE, foure LAVUC *Kölbing-Day*   byfor] aforne UD   þey
no fode] P, fode (bote D) thei ne (non E) UDE   fode] mete C   1072 *line om.* U   Noþer]
Nowthir A, Neþer DE, Nor C   fisch, flesch] P, *trs.* DE   ne] nor C   freke] no freke A, þat
freke D   freke . . . byte] þat hem releue my3te E, þat þey my3te on byte C   on] for- PAV
on to] might D   byte] bye PD, bytte A   1073 Bred] Nother brede C   browet] beste P,
om. AVC, brothe UDE   ne¹] nor P, nouther U, neiþer DE, nor C   broþe] ⟨..⟩de P, beste
UE, befe D   ne²] *om.* P, ne no A, nor C   beste vpon lyue] þat þa⟨.⟩ by couthe P, thing (beste
C) that beres lyf (vpon erthe DEC) UDEC   1074 *line om.* A   Wyn ne] *om.* V   ne] nor C
Wyn, water] *trs.* PUDE   to drynke] ne windregges V, drunken U   wope] wete P, wepyng
VUC, wepe D, þat com E   of] P, for D   1075 scheldes] schetis A, shepe U, schepes E
and schone] fete hornes and shone U, feet E   scharply] P, Full scharpely A   þey] P, þe C
1076 *line om.* PU   þat] Swiche AC, Suche was V   liflode] mete E   for] to A   was . . .
chewe] þat somtyme were shene V, þat tyme was wol swete E   luþer] lethir A, heuy C   to]
forto A, vnto C   chewe] schewe AC   1077 Fellen] And fele V, Thei felle UDEC
doun] dede down A, *om.* V   flatte] UDE *Kölbing-Day*, platte L, faste P, fellen V   flatte . . .
grounde] P, ilke a daye many hundrethe A, on þe colde erthe C   þe] *om.* V   grounde]
erthe U   *no cesura* V   1078 Ded] Als ded UDE   eche] Ilke A, ilk a U, echee C
hundred] P, hundrethe (*canc.*) thowsande A, *om.* UDE, a hondred C   1079 Wo] the woo
A, Sorowe C   wakned] wakkynnys so A, waked VUDE, awaked C   þycke] þerewith
UDC, þerwith / for E   *no cesura* V   1080 wyght] AUD *Kölbing-Day*, wye L, grete F,
feble C   waried] werreyde AU, wyries D, eete E   on] *om.* UDEC   woke] wayke AUD
(-yke P), smale E, full C   alle] P, and UD, and so E, for he C   alle his] thaire A   his] P,
her E   wombe] P, wombes E   fille] P, forto fill A, filled UEC, fillis D   scribal line V: þey
had nought in viij. daies / ones þeire womfull   1081 On] O saynt A, And one V, Ther
was on E   Marie] Marion VUDE   myld] myd- E, good C   for] P, þat for E   meschef] P,
defaute VE   1082 barn] child UEC   brad] D, 30 brad L *Kölbing-Day*, brynt it P, Made
brede A, brad hit V, braid U, leyde E, leyde hit C   on] P, vpon E   þe] *om.* P   gledis] P,
coles UDEC   1083 Rostyþ] Scho ruschede owte A, Rosted UD, and roostyd bothe E,
She rostedde C   rigge, rib] *trs. sbs.* AV, ribbes, rigge UD, rybbe, syde C   rewful] P, rewely
UD, wol rewely E   adds line (a version of 1088, also included below) A: Sayse Enter thare
þou owte come and Etis the rybbis   1084 Sayþ] And A, And said V, Said UD, 3he
seyde E   Sayþ sone] Dere sone sche seyde C   vpon] on VUDEC   eche] Ilke a A, ilk U,
echee a C   our] *om.* UDEC   is] comes V   alofte] newe A, on hande PVUDEC

Batail aboute þe borwe   our bodies to quelle;   1085
Withyn h[u]nger so hote   þat neȝ our herte brestyþ.
þerfor ȝeld þat I þe ȝaf   and aȝen tourne,
+ Entre þer þou [o]ut cam',   and etyþ a schouldere.

þe [rich] roos of þe rost   riȝt [in]to þe [strete]
þat fele fastyng folke   felde[n] þe sauere.   1090
Doun þei daschen þe dore,   dey scholde þe berde
þat mete yn þis meschef   hadde from men l[a]yned.

þan saiþ þat worþi wif   in a wode hunger,
'Myn owen barn haue I brad   and þe bones gnawen,
Ȝit haue I saued ȝou som',   and + a side feccheþ   1095
Of þe barn þat ȝo bare,   and alle hire blode chaungeþ.

[Forþ] þey went for wo   wep[ande sore]
And sayn, 'alas in þis lif   how longe schul we dwelle?

1085 Batail] Alle A, after borwe UDE, And sore batayle C   aboute] withowttyn AV
aboute þe borwe] withouteforth C   þe] P, om. V   borwe] P, town is E   our bodies] oure
body⟨e⟩ P, vs all for- U   1086 Withyn] And withIn es A, withynne is V   hunger] AVUDE
Kölbing-Day, hinger L, hongur is C   neȝ] nere PA, om. DE   our] oure PAV, the U, myn DE
herte] hertes PAV   brestyþ] bresten VPA, breketh C   1087 þerfore] And therefore AC,
Now UDE   þat] me (to me C) that UDEC   I þe] -I P, þou A   aȝen] P, againe V
1088 Entre] AVUDC, And entre L Kölbing-Day, into my body E   out cam] AVUDC (cf.
oute ⟨....⟩ P), trs. LE Kölbing-Day   etyþ] etyn P, eet faste of E, þanne eete sche C   a] P, the
AD, his E   schoulder] P, childe A   1089 *rich] smel LVE Kölbing-Day, smelle AUD,
smell C   roos] after rost P, arose VU   of þe rost] sone olofte U   þe²] þat E   riȝt] sykes? P, al
U, anoon E, abowte C   into] UDE, to L Kölbing-Day, in PAVC   strete] PAVUDEC, walles
L Kölbing-Day   1090 line in margin A   þat] There UD, and E   fele] many EC   felden] V
Duggan 1988:127, felde LPUE Kölbing-Day, felide A, þer felede C   felden þe sauere] fastyd
had longe D   þe sauere] P, it sone UE   1091 Doun] And downe AE   þei] om. E   þei
daschen] trs. DC   daschen] dasshedin VDC, casten U, dryuyn E   dore] dores C   dey] and
said dien V, dyen U, and deye E   dey . . . berde] sayd sho dy sulde P, and hastely thay askede
A, dye þat womman schulde C   scholde þe] she shuld UE   berde] barin V, om. UE   no
cesura V   1092 þat] why that þat A, for E   mete] good mete (after men) V   þis] þat
AUDEC, om. V   hadde] was A, after men UDC   hadde . . . layned] fro hem dode keepe E
from] fra PAU   men] þa men P, hem U   layned] PAV, loyned L Kölbing-Day, ykept UDC
no cesura V   1093 þan] And þanne C   saiþ] sayde AVDEC, saiden U   þat] þe VU, this D,
om. E   worþi] worthiliche A, om. UDE, wofull C   a] P, om. V, þat D, her E   no cesura V
1094 barn] child EC   haue I brad] es my brede A   brad]-ttynd P, brend E, roste C   and] and
I A, om. U   bones] body E   gnawen] gnawe A, al tognauen U   no cesura V   1095 ȝit] but
ȝit E   I, ȝou] om. E   and . . . feccheþ] to parte with ȝow þis tyme E   a] AVUD, forþ a L
Kölbing-Day, ⟨f..⟩th a P, þe C   feccheþ] ⟨..⟩tch- P, fechide AVUDC   1096 barn] chylde C
and alle] bot than A, þanne all C   alle] then U, om. D   blode] ble A   chaungeþ] P, chaungede
AVD, turned C   scribal line E: And fette forth of here child / a gobat red yroosted
1097 Forþ] VUDEC, Away L (later in line P) Kölbing-Day, And furthe A   þey went] trs. AV
for] with A, þan for D   wepande] AVU, wepyng LDE Kölbing-Day, wepynge C   sore] V,
echone L Kölbing-Day, full sore AUDEC   1098 And] om. U   And sayn alas] Alas þey
seyde C   sayn] sayde AVUDE   dwelle] P, lenge A, duren UDE, lyfe C

ȝit beter were at o brayde   in batail to deye
þan þus in langur to lyue   and lengþen our fyne'.   1100

þan þey demeden a dom   þat deil was to hure
To voiden alle by vile deþ   þat vitelys destruyed—
Wymmen and weyke folke   þat weren of + [e]lde
[þat] myȝt noȝt stonde in stede,   bot here store mardyn;

After to touche of trewe,   to trete with þe lord.   1105
Bot Titus graunteþ noȝt for gile   þat þe gomes þenke,
'For he is wise þat is war   or hym wo hape,
And with falsede afere   is fairest to dele'.

To worchyn vndere þe wal   w[a]yes þey casten
Whan Tytus nold no trewe   to þe toun graunte.   1110
With mynours and masouns   myne þey bygonne,
Grobben faste on þe grounde,   and God [g]yue vs ioye.

1099 ȝit] It UE   beter were] were it (vs D) better ADC, *trs*. VUE   o] a AVUDEC
1100 langur] sorowe C   lyue] ly A, leve VE   lengþen our] in lasse U, mych lasse DE
fyne] pyne AVUD *Kölbing-Day*, peyne EC   1101 þey demeden] P, *trs*. C   þat deil
was] was (is U) dolefull AU   deil] P, pyte C   scribal line E: Than was ymad a cry / þat
sorwe was to heere   1102 To . . . deþ] þat alle schulde voyde þe town E   by] with PD,
the A, to V   vile] P, wild D, *om*. C   deþ] dede P, *om*. A   vitelys] vitaille V, vitails U   *no
cesura* V   1103 Wymmen] As wommen EC   weyke] werke VD, wayker U   þat] and
those þat A, þat fallen C   weren of] were in UDEC   elde] AVC, olde age L *Kölbing-Day*,
grete elde UD, gret age E   1104 þat] AVUD, *om*. L *Kölbing-Day*, þo þat E, And C
myȝt noȝt stonde] noghte ne (*om*. V) stude AV, ne (*om*. DE) stode UDE, alle swych þat
stode C   in] in no UDEC   here] þe VE   mardyn] spended U, dispendid D, destroyed
E, wasted C   *no cesura* V   1105 After] P, And aftir ADC, And afterward U, And
thanne E   to] thay A *Kölbing-Day*, *om*. VUDE   touche] touchede V, touchin D, tretyn
EC   of] of a PAVDE, to U   to] and U, a D, *om*. C   to . . . lord] whan þey sey tyme E
trete] entrete U, *om*. C   lord] lordes UD, grete lordes C   1106 Ex
FRAGMENTARILY PRESENT THROUGH 1138 AND AT 1196   Bot] ¶ *precs*. D
graunteþ noȝt] wolde noght graunte / V, graunte (-ed EC) hem (hit C) noght (nat E) DEC
noȝt] noghte thareto A   for gile] *om*. UDEC   þat . . . þenke] for all here queynte gynne C
þe] *om*. V   þe gomes] þei þanne E   þenke] thoghte AVD, desyred E   1107 hym] he
U, he hym E   hape] happyn ACEx, happes VU   1108 And] For aye A, Ay V, And is
UDE, Euur C   with] of E   afere] on fare A, on feere V, aferde UE, afelde D   is] *om*. UD
is . . . dele] and putte it at þe wurse E   fairest] faire for- VC   dele] delle (*with* l'
expunged?) U, melle C   1109 wal] wallis AVEC, wall þan D   wayes] AVUDEC
Kölbing-Day, wyes L   þey casten] forto make U, -to cast Ex   1110 Whan] P, *om*. D
Tytus] þay A   nold] wolde VD, *om*. E, to þe Iewes / C   to] vnto A   to þe toun] wolde C
graunte] grauntyd E   1111 mynours, masouns] *trs. sbs*. PAVUDEC   myne] to Myne
AVUDEC   bygonne] bygynne CEx   1112 Grobben] And grobbis APV, And grubbed
UDE, And dyggedde C   faste] *om*. ? P   on] in PA *Kölbing-Day*, vndir VUDEC   þe] *om*.
UDC   and] there A, *om*. D   and . . . ioye] speede what they myȝte E   God] lorde V,
marg. C   gyue] AVUEx, ȝyue LDC *Kölbing-Day*   ioye] ioyes P

[Sextus passus]

As Tytus after a tyme   vmbe þe toun redeþ
Wyþ sixty speres of þe sege,   segges a fewe,
Alle outwith þe ost,   out of a kaue   1115
f. 16ᵛ Vp a buschment brake   alle of briȝt hedis,

Fyf hundred fiȝtyng men,   and fellen hem aboute
In iepouns and iambers.   Iewes þey were,
Hadde wroȝt hem a wey   and þe wal myned,
And Titus tourneþ hem to   without tale more.   1120

Schaftes schedred were sone   and scheldes yþrelled,
[+ Many schalke þrow-schot   with þe + scharpe ende,]
Brunyes and briȝt [yren]   blody byrunne,
And many segge at þat saute   souȝte to þe grounde.

Hacchen vpon hard steel   with an het[ter] wylle   1125
þat [þe] fure out + flowe   as of flynt-stonys.

marginal rubric 'vj pa-' P, inset 'Passus' A, marginal rubric 'Septimus passus' V, inset 'Septimus passus' U, marginal rubric 'Passus vij^{us}.' C   1113 As] Now P, *three-line capital* LAVE, *two-line capital* PU   *after*] after one AVDE, *om.* vmbe] abowte AUDECEx, abouten V toun] Cete A redeþ] rode C, rideþ *Kölbing-Day*   1114 *line om.* P sixty speres] *trs.* UDE segges] and other (*om.* D) segges UD, and archers E, and ȝemen C a fewe] many U   1115 Alle] And alle A Alle . . . ost] by þe dike as he rode V, At þe sowth-est syde C outwith] -of P, withowte the Owttyn A, awey from (fro DE) UDE out of] vnder P   1116 vp] P, *om.* VDE, Out U brake] P, bruschede (*after* vp) A, brake oute V, vp brak DE briȝt] white D hedis] heuedis APV, helmes UDEC   1117 fiȝtyng] fiȝtyng] *om.*? P, of fyȝtynge C men] folke ADE and] *om.* AVUE *Kölbing-Day* fellen] fil D, Felle Ex hem] hym PAUDECEx aboute] aboute ⟨..⟩me P   1118 In] Ane P iepouns] lernes? P, Iope C iambers] in Iambyse A, hauberkes V, iambes U, iambews DE, in Iambewes C Iewes þey] all þe Iewes C *no cesura* V   1119 Hadde] P, that hade AUD, þey haddyn VC, that E wroȝt] wrokyn A hem] *om.* AVC and] and vndir VU þe] *om.* U wal] P, wallis AVC *no cesura* V   1120 And] *om.* P, but E, Thenne C tourneþ] turned to (*om.* C) EC hem] hym VU to] tho E without] withouten PAVC, withoute UE tale more] *trs.* C *no cesura* V   1121 Schaftes] P, And þer was schaftis A schedred] shyuerde PVUDEC, sondirde A were] P, full A sone] *om.* PA and] P, *om.* V scheldes] þe wy- P, many schelde A, sheldes were V, scheldes thorow C yþrelled] -ko⟨...⟩ P, thirllede AVCEx, yhurled U *no cesura* V   1122 *line om.* L, *supplied from* A Many] VUDEC, and many PA *Kölbing-Day* schalke] *om.* PE, a segge V, segge D, a legge was C þrow-] P, þroug- V with the] P, was with E scharpe] VUDCEx *Kölbing-Day*, scharpere A, wol scharpe E ende] P, arwes E   1123 Brunyes] P, Bernes VD Brunyes . . . yren] Haburgynes and hauberkes (armour C) EC yren] PV, wede LUDC *Kölbing-Day*, Iryns A blody] P, al blody U, blody were E, was blody C   1124 *line follows* 1195 AVC (*not in* PEx) And] That C many] many a V segge] segges U, man EC at þat] at þe VU saute] assawte A souȝte] soughten U, fell C to] *om.* E þe] *om.* U *no cesura* V   1125 Hacchen] Hewen PUD, thay hewe AVC, The hewen E an] full AVC, so U (Ex?), *om.* E hetter] A, herty LD *Kölbing-Day*, -hetty-? P, hettill V, hertly UE, byttur C, herter Ex   1126 þat] *om.* P þe] PAVUDEC, *om.* L *Kölbing-Day* out flewe] *trs.* E flowe] flowen L *Kölbing-Day*, flewe AVUDEC (fle- P) of . . . -stonys] it dooth of flyntes E flynt-] the Flynt Ex

Of þe helm and þe hed   hewen attonys;
þe stompe vndere stede feet   in þe steel leueþ.

þe ʒong duk Domycian   of þe dyn herde
And + issed out of þe ost   with eʒte hundred speres,   1130
Fel on þe fals folke,   vmbefeldes hem sone,
As bestes bretnes hem alle   and haþ his broþer holpen.

þan Titus toward his tentis   tourneþ hym sone,
Makeþ mynour[s] and men   þe myne [for]to stoppe;
After profreþ pes   for pyte þat he hadde   1135
Whan he wist of here wo   þat were withyn stoken.

Bot Ion þe ienfulle   þat þe Iewes ladde,
An oþer Symond of his assent,   forsoke[n] þe profre;
Sayn leuer in þ[at] lif   lengen hem were
þan any renke out of Rome   [re]ioyced here sorowe.   1140

1127 *line om.* P   Of] Bothe AC   þe¹] her E   helm, hed] *trs. sbs.* A   helm] helmys E
þe hed] hedis D, her heuedys E   hewen] þay hewen AUEC   attonys] togedirs AVC
1128 *line om.* PD   þe¹] That þe C   þe stompe] thay tombill A   stompe] stompes U
vndere] vndir þe V   stede] stedis AE   in . . . leueþ] and stampes one stele wedis A
steel] stede Ex   leueþ] lafte VE   1129 ʒongl] *om.* P   þe²] that AC, this UDE   dyn]
dede P, *om.* E, noyse C   1130 And] He C   issed] UDE *Kölbing-Day*, dissed L, hyes P,
faste hyes A, Issues V, houede C   out . . . ost] P, withoute þe chase C   eʒte] P, *om.* V,
an U   hundred] score P   *no cesura* V   1131 Fel] Felled P, than thay felle A, þey fellin
V, Falles U, And falliþ D, and fallen E, They fellede C   on] of PAC, *om.* V   folke] folke /
and AUDEC, folke abouten / and V   vmbefeldes] felden V, felles UD, felde E, slewe C
hem] P, hem ful U, hem doun E   sone] P, euerychone C   1132 As] P, And als A
bestes . . . alle] þei hadde be beestes E   bretnes] P, bretynede AV, he murthered C   alle]
P, *om.* C   and] *om.* ? P   haþ] *om.* PAUD, helpyd E   his] her P   holpen] helpede A,
helpes UD (-ys⟨e⟩ P), *om.* E   *no cesura* V   1133 toward] to EC   tentis] tent AVUDE
tourneþ] turnede AEC   hym sone] -so- P, belyfe AV, anone C, blyue Ex   *no cesura* C
1134 Makeþ] P, And makes V, Made U, and made E, He made C   mynours] AVUDEC
Kölbing-Day, mynour L, mason P   and men] P, anoon E   þe] P, that AC   forto]
PAVUDEEx *Duggan* 1988:128, to LC *Kölbing-Day*   1135 After] P, And then UDE,
Thanne he C   profreþ] P, proferde AC, thei preyde E   pes] þaim pese PAVUC, he pees
D, hym of pees E   þat he hadde] P, of his sowle E   1136 Whan] P, when þat A   of]
P, *om.* A   were] weren UD   stoken] closede AVCEx, *om.* UDE   1137 Ion] ʒone P,
Iosaphus AUDE, sone V, Iona C   ienfulle] gynful man P, gentill A, sinfull man V,
gylefulle C   þe²] all þe PAV   1138 An oþer] And another PAC, And UDE   of] at
UDE, by C   his] *om.* PAVC   forsoken] VUE *Duggan* 1988:127, forsoke LADCEx
Kölbing-Day   þe] þan þat A   Ex ENDS   1139 Sayn] P, And sayde thaym were A,
And seid V, Thei said UDEC   leuer . . . were] in that lyf longe / leuer hem were to ligge E
leuer, lengen] P, *trs.* UDC   þat] PAVUDC, þis L *Kölbing-Day*   lengen] longer P, lyngen
V, byde C   lengen hem were] langare to lenge A   hem] þa- P, thei U   1140 renke] P,
wiþt E, manne C   out] P, *om.* AE   reioyced] D *Kölbing-Day*, Ioyced L, rewede of A,
shulde reioisse of (*om.* C) VC, renewed UE   here] þaim ? P

Sale in þe cite   was cesed [by] þanne;
Was noȝt for besauntes to bye   þat men bite myȝt.
For a ferþyng-worþ of fode   floryns an hundred
Princes profren in þe toun   to pay in þe fuste.

Bot alle was boteles bale   f[or] whoso bred hadde   1145
Nold a gobet haue [gy]uen   for goode vpon [erþe].
Wymmen falwed faste   and here face chaungen,
Feynte and fallen doun   þat so faire were,

Swounen, swallen as swyn,   [and] som swart wexen,
Som lene on to loke   as la[n]terne hornes.   1150
þe morayne was so myche   þat no man couþe telle
Where to burie in þe burwe   þe bodies þat were ded,

Bot wenten with hem to þe walle   and walten [hem o]uere.
Into þe depe of þe diche +   þe ded doun fallen.
Whan Titus told was þe tale,   to trewe God he vouched   1155
þat + he propfred hem pes   and grete pite hadde.

1141 Sale] P, Bot seknes A   þe] om. P   cesed] seson V, cesura fols. C   by] PAVUDEC,
with L Kölbing-Day   no cesura VE   1142 Was noȝt for] Myght none to P   besauntes]
beisaunt VDE, a besaunte C   men] P, man E   bite] bytt A, bye UD, ete C   no cesura V
1143 a] P, o E   fode] P, mete C   an hundred] C V   no cesura V   This line is the last on P
f 110vb, P ENDS   1144 profren] profirde AUEC   pay] paien V   þe fuste] hande E
1145 bale] wo U   for] AVUDEC Kölbing-Day, fro L   whoso] he þat A, who that UC, so E
1146 Nold] Ne wolde noght U, wolde not C   a . . . gyuen] trs. phrs. DE   haue gyuen] gyuen
U, ȝyue E   gyuen] AVDC Kölbing-Day, ȝouen L   goode] golde VUDEC   vpon] that was
on U   erþe] AVUDEC Kölbing-Day, lyue L   1147 Wymmen] Femels UD   falwed] fadyd
EC   faste] full faste A   here] al the UD   face] faces EC   chaungen] changede AVDE,
chaungeth U, wannede C   no cesura V   1148 Feynte] For fayntnes A, For feinte þey V,
Feynted UE, Fayntyn D, For þe fawte C   and] thay AV, some C   fallen] felle AVEC,
feyned U   doun] doun / alle U, adowne C   so] full A, ere so D   so fair were] arst were wol
fayre E, fayre before weren C   1149 Swounen] Some AE Kölbing-Day, Sum men V,
Swollyng U, Swonyng C   swallen] swelling U, swellyn D   as] als a A   and] AVUDEC
Duggan 1988:128, om. L Kölbing-Day   swart] pale C   swart wexen] waxen worthe U   wexen]
were A, waxen C   1150 Som] And some was (were C) AC, Summe were V, For U, Ful D
on to loke] als a leke or A   as] als a A   lanterne] AVUDEC Kölbing-Day, laterne L   hornes]
horne A   1151 þe morayne, so myche] trs. UDE   was] wax AV   couþe] myght D
1152 burie] bere A   burwe] town E, cyte C   þe²] om. V   were ded] there dyed U, deyde DE
no cesura V   1153 wenten] after hem UD   with hem] om. C   walle] wallis AC   walten]
warpen V, walwed U, waltryn D, tumblede C   hem ouere] VUDC Kölbing-Day Duggan
1988:128, euere L, þam alle ouer A   scribal line E: But drowe hem ouer þe walles / whan they
sey tyme   1154 Into] In AV, and so into E   depe of þe] om. E   diche] UDEC, diche depe L
Kölbing-Day, dikis A, dyke V   þe ded doun] doun (adown E) gun thei UDEC   fallen] felle
AV   1155 Whan] whanne 'to' V, & whan þat E, ¶ precs. D   told . . . tale] trs. phrs. V, was this
tale tolde U   told was] wiste E, herde C   þe] this DEC   tale] om. E   to] of AVC   trewe] om.
VC   vouched] witnes A, tas witnesse V, vowed UD, seyde E, toke recorde C   1156 line
om. U   þat] How þat C   he] AVC, hadde L Kölbing-Day, he had DE   and] he D   and . . .
hadde] it greuyd hym sore E   grete] om. V   hadde] on hem hadde V

þo praied he + Iosophus to preche   þe peple [to] | enforme   f. 17ʳ
[For]to saue hemself   and þe cite ӡelde.
Bot Ion forsoke þe sawe   so forto wyrche,
With Symond þat oþer segge   þat þe cyte ladde.   1160

Myche peple for þe prechyng   at þe posterne ӡatis
Tyen out of þe toun   and Tytus bysecheþ
To for[g]yue hem þe gult   þat þey to God wroӡt,
And he graunteþ hem grace   and gaylers bytauӡt.

Bot whan þey metten with mete,   vnmyӡty þey were   1165
Any fode to defye,   so faynt was here strengþe.
Ful þe gottes of gold   [ilka] gome hadde;
Lest fomen fongen hem schold,   here floreyns þey eten.

Whan hit was broӡt vp abrode   and þe bourd aspyed,
+ [With]outen leue of þat lord   ledes hem slowen,   1170
[G]oren euereche a gome   and þe gold taken,
Fayn[er] of þe floreyns   [þan of] þe frekes alle.

1157 þo] than AVC, om. UDE   praied] om. UDE   he] AVC, he he hadde L Kölbing-
Day, He bad UDE   to preche] cesura precs. L, the iewe UD, þanne E, om. C   þe] & the A,
'to' þe V   to enforme] AUC Kölbing-Day, om. L (enforme at head of next line), / and hem
forto lerne V, enfourme DE   1158 Forto saue] AVC Kölbing-Day, enforme hem to saue
L, In sauyng of UDE   hem-] him- UE   and] om. UDE   cite] towne U   ӡelde] to ӡelde AE,
forto yelde U, vp to to yeld D   1159 Ion] Iosaphus AUDE, sone V, all C   forsoke]
forsakis A, folkes V   þe sawe] om. A, þey sawe V, tho UDE, Iosephus C   1160 with]
And C   þat oþer segge] his sergeant UC, his seruant DE   þe] alle the AVUDC   ladde] lede
A, laddyn V   no cesura V   1161 Myche] Bot mekill A   Myche . . . prechyng] For al his
preching (talkyng E) the (of þe D, to þe E) puple UDE   þe¹] þat C   at þe] atte a E   ӡatis]
gate UE   1162 Tyen] Turnes A, Turned VC, Ten turnid D, ten went E   of þe toun]
priuyliche E   þe] om. D   bysecheþ] bysechid DE, þey besechynne C   1163 forgyue]
AVU Kölbing-Day, forӡyue LDEC   God] criste V   wroӡt] dyde C   1164 And] om. C
he] Titus A   graunteþ] graunted UDEC   graunteþ hem] trs. UD   grace] his grace UD
gaylers] Iaolers A, gailer V, to gaylers D, to þe Iaylers C   bytauӡt] hem betook E, he hem
bytoke C   1165 Bot] om. V   with] with the A   1166 fode] mete C   was] were AUDE
strengþe] strenghis AUDE   1167 Ful] For ful UDC   ilka] U, eche L Kölbing-Day, iche a
A, eche a DC   ilka gome] þe gomes echon V   gome] manne C   scribal line E: And her
guttes yschronke / and her stomak boþe   no cesura V   1168 Lest] Or thaire AV, Leste
he'r' C   fongen] founden U, fynd D, haue C   fongen, schold] trs. AV   hem] om. U   here]
om. U   eten] frette U   scribal line E: þat for al þe wyde wurld / þey myӡte no mete brokke
1169 lines 1169-72 om. E   Whan] Bot when A   hit] that Iape A, þei D   was broӡt, abrode]
trs. A   was] were D   vp] om. AD, out UC   a-] on AVD   and] and al U   and . . . aspyed]
om., line fused with next VC, þe bernes of þe sege D   aspyed] knawen A, sene U
1170 Withouten] AUD Kölbing-Day, Souӡten L   Withouten . . . lord] om., line fused with
prec. VC   leue] 'lefe' A   þat] the AUD   ledes] þe meyne C   1171 *Goren] Kölbing-Day,
thay gorrede A, Thei gored U, They gorid D, Ther þey gorede C, þey slitten V, Toren L   a]
om. VDC   gome] manne C   and] and al D   taken] tuke AVD, rauthen U, þey toke C   no
cesura V   1172 Fayner] VUD Kölbing-Day, Fayn LC, And faynere A   floreyns] golde A
þan of] AVUD Kölbing-Day Duggan 1988:128, were L, and þenne of C   frekes] Iewes C

Ay were þe ӡates vn[ӡ]et   tille two ӡeres ende,
So longe þey [s]ouӡt hit by sege   or þey þe [cite] hadde.
Eleuen hundred þousand Iewes   in þe mene whyle   1175
Swalten while þe sweng last   by swerd and by hunger.

Now Titus conseil haþ take   þe toun to assayle,
To wynne hit on eche [wyse]   of warwolues handes,
Neuer pyte ne pees   profre hem more
Ne gome þat he gete may   to no grace taken;   1180

Armen hem as-tyt   alle for þe werre,
Tyen euen to þe toun   with trompis and pypys,
With nakerers and grete noyce   neӡen þe walles
þer many styf man and stoure   stondiþ alofte.

Sire Sabyn of Surrye   on a syde ӡede;   1185
þe ӡong duke Domycian   drow to anoþer.
XV. þousand [fyghtyng] men   [ilka] freke hadde
With many maner of engyne   and mynours ynowe.

1173 Ay] ӡit AVE, Euer D, And ӡette C   ӡates] gates UE   vnӡet] A *Kölbing-Day*,
vnget LUEC, vnshette V, yemyd D   tille two] vnto the A, til þe D   *no cesura* V
1174 So] for so E   þey] *om.* DE   þey souӡt] *trs.* C   souӡt] V *Kölbing-Day*, þouӡt L,
bysoughte A, setten U, set DC, laste E   hit by] the UEC, was þe D   by] with A   or]
tul D   cite] AVUDEC *Kölbing-Day*, toun L   hadde] wan UE   1175 þousand] *om.* A
Iewes] of Iewes V, *om.* UDEC   mene] same V   whyle] tym AVUC   1176 Swalten
while] deyde in tyme E, Dyede whyle C   sweng] sege AUDE, swyng V, labour C   by¹,²]
with DE   swerd] thrist U   and] or E   1177 Now] ¶ *precs.* D, *three-line capital* E
Titus . . . take] tuke Titus 'to' consaylle A, tytus aӡen gooth E   take] tane VU   to] forto E
1178 To] And þe town to A, and it to E   hit] *om.* AE   on eche wyse] ӡif he may E
eche] alle AVC, ilk U   wyse] AVC *Kölbing-Day*, side L, half U, way D   of] owt of þe AE,
or V   warwolues] warlawes AVD, false E   1179 Neuer] Nowthir A, And neuer
VUEC, And D   ne] nor UC   profre] to profire AUC, proferen V   profre hem] hem to
profre E   *no cesura* V   1180 Ne] Ne no A, No D, Nor C   gome] man E, Iewe C   he]
thay A   gete] take E   may] þay sall A   to] his UDE, *om.* C   no] *om.* AUDE   taken] ne
wynneth UD, forto graunte E, shall haue C   1181 Armen] than thay armede A, þey
armed VUEC, þan armyd D   as-] also A, al þat D, alle in þat E, ryth C   -tyt] tyde DE,
sone C   alle for] and streight to UD, full bryӡte to C   alle . . . werre] boþe hond and
foote E   1182 Tyen] And tournes A, Turned V, They turned C   Tyen euen] And
euen turned (wente E) UDE   euen to] towarde C   1183 nakerers] Nakirs AUDEC,
Nacornes V   neӡen] thei neghen U, þei ny D, euyn E, þey nyӡede C   þe] to þe AUDE
1184 þer] where E   many] many a VC   man] men ADE   and] in VC   and stoure]
om. E   stoure] stronge U   stondiþ] standis A, stondyn D, stoodyn E   1185 *line om.* U
Sire] and sir V   on] till AVC, of D, in þet E   a] o E   ӡede] went DE   1186 þe] And
þe C   þe . . . Domycian] and domycian þe deuk E   drow] droughe hym A, yede V,
went D   to] till AVC   *no cesura* V   1187 XV.] Fyve AV, Fyfty UDEC   fyghtyng
men] A *Kölbing-Day*, men L, of fyghtande men VC, of men U, of folk DE   ilka] U, eche
LEC *Kölbing-Day*, aythir AV, eche a D   freke] of hem EC   hadde] ladde E
1188 maner] maners AV   of] *om.* UDE   engyne] Engynes AV, gynnes E   *no cesura* V

Tytus at þe toun-ȝate   with ten þousand helmes
Merkeþ mynour[s] at þe wal   where þey + myne scholde,   1190
On ech side for þe assaute   setteþ engynes
And bold br[eny]ed men   in belfrayes heye.

Was noȝt bot dyn and dyt   as alle deye scholde,
So eche lyuande lyf   layeþ on oþere.
At eche kernel was cry   and quasschyng of wepne   1195   f. 17ᵛ
And many burne atte brayd   br[os]ed to deþ.

Sire Sabyn of Surrye   whyle þe saute laste
Leyþ a ladder to þe wal   and alofte clymyþ,
W[y]n[n]eþ wyȝtly þeron   þoȝ hym wo happned,
And vp stondiþ for ston   or for steel-[wa]re.   1200

Syx he slow on þe wal   Sire Sabyn alone;
þe seueþ hitteþ on hym   an vnhende dynte

   1189 Tytus] And Titus AVC   at] to DE, ȝede to C   toun-] grete V   -ȝate] ȝatis AC,
set U, yede DE (after þousand E)   helmes] om. E, menne C   1190 Merkeþ] Merked
UD, He markede C   Merkeþ mynours] and mynours toolde E   mynours] AVUDC
Kölbing-Day, mynour L   at] to AC, in UD   at þe wal] rediliche E   þe] om. U   wal]
wallis A   where] þere VC   myne] AVUDEC Kölbing-Day, mynde L   myne scholde]
trs. E   1191 lines 1191–93 om. U   ech] Ilke a A, eche a C   þe] om. AVD   assaute]
saut EC   setteþ] thay settyn AV, þey sette her C   setteþ engynes] engynes he sette E
1192 brenyed] AV, brayned LDE Kölbing-Day, armedde C   men] meen V   in] one A
in . . . heye] an hyȝ in britages E   belfrayes] belfreis V, britages D   heye] full heghe A
1193 was noȝt] than was AVC, Tho were E   bot] om. E   dyn and dyt] dole (þole C) and
dyn AVC, dyngis & dyntis D, dasschynges & dyntes E   deye scholde] down ȝede A,
adowne (down C) shulde VC   1194 eche] Ilke a AU, euery EC   lyuande] leueande? A,
adds in U   lyf] lede AV, man EC   layeþ] layde AUDEC, lasshes V   on] appon AUDEC
1195 At] In V, On C   At . . . kernel] oueral E   eche] Ilke a AU, eche a C   kernel] corner
VU   was] was a D, was meche E   and] om. V   quasschyng] crassynge A, cratching V,
catching UDEC   of wepne] and wepyng V   wepne] wapyns A   1196 line follows
1123 PAVCEx   And] Any P, om. C   burne] P, beryns AD, a barin V, barnes E, a manne C
atte] at þat PAC, at a VUDE   brayd] fyȝte C   *brosed] -brusyd Ex, birssede A, brusshed
V, brayned LUE Kölbing-Day, braynid D, fell C   to] til- P, to þe VUD, doun C   deþ]
dede AVC   1197 Sire] than sir A   þe] þat C   saute] assawte AD, sege U   laste]
lastes AU, lastedde C   no cesura V   1198 Leyþ] layde AVUDC, sette E   wal] wallis A
and] vp E   alofte clymyþ] trs. A, forto clymbe E   1199 Wynneþ] D, wendeþ L
Kölbing-Day, wane vp AV, He wynnes U, And wanne vp C   Wynneþ wyȝtly] and faste vp
went E   wyȝtly þeron] to þe walle V   þeron] om. C   -on] -appon A   þoȝ] þofe þat A,
thouȝth E, þat C   happned] happed VUDEC   1200 And] And there UC   stondiþ]
stondis he A, stood E   for ston] for stones A Kölbing-Day, on þe walle VC, on (on a DE)
stone UDE   or for] in his AV, al in UDE   or . . . gere] all armedde in stele C   ware] U,
gere LA Kölbing-Day, weede VDE   1201 Syx] after slow UDEC   wal] walles A
Sire Sabyn] om. U, anon E   alone] hym allone A, hymsilven V, hymseluen (-self E)
allone UE   1202 hitteþ] hitt AVDE, hitten U   on hym] hym one the hede AE, apon
hym V   an] ryȝte a C   an . . . dynte] wol sore as y ȝow telle E   vnhende] vnmete A,
hydous D, sore C   no cesura V

þat þe brayn out brast   at boþ noseþrylles,
And Sabyn ded of þe dynt   into þe diche falleþ.

þan Tytus wepyþ for wo   and warieþ þe [stounde]   1205
Syþ he þe lede haþ lost   þat he loue scholde:
'For now is a duke ded,   þe douȝtiest Y trowe
þat euer stede bystrode   or any steel wered'.

[Than] Tytus on þe same side   setteþ an engyne,
A sowe wroȝt for þe werre,   and to þe wal dryueþ   1210
þat alle ouerwalte þer h[it] went,   and wyes an hundred
Were ded of þat dynt   and in þe diche lyȝten.

þan Tytus heueþ vp þe honde   and Heuen-kyng þonkeþ
þat þey þe dukes deþ   han so dere bouȝte.
þe Iewes preien þe pees—   þis was þe Paske euene—   1215
And þe comelich kyng   þe keyes out rauȝten.

'Nay traytours', quod Tytus,   'now take hem ȝourselfen,
For schal no ward on [þe] wal   vs þe way lette:

1203 þe] al the U   brayn] braynes A, brayd D   out brast] on ('t the' *later*) brayn D   brast]
brayd E   at] aboute U   boþ] bothe his A, bothe VC, the U, his DE   nose-] nesse- A, nase- V,
nese- U   1204 And] And sir A, Syr C   ded] was dede A, dyedde C   of þe dynt] at þat
stroke C   þe¹] that UE   into] and in AC, in V   þe²] *om.* E   diche] dyke AV   falleþ] felle A,
fallyd E   1205 wepyþ] weep EC (*after* wo C)   wo] sorowe C   warieþ] werwyth E, cursed C
þe] þat C   stounde] AVUDE, tyme LC *Kölbing-Day*   1206 þe] þat VUD   lede] lorde AV,
lyf D   lost] forlorne A, lorin V   he] euer he AV, neuer U   loue] lese A, love V, lyue UD
scribal line E: for he sey þe knyȝt deed / þat he moost louyde   scribal line C: Syns þey thus
haue 'hym' sleyne / pyte it were þey lyue shulde   1207 For] And seyde E   a] the A   a
duke] *after* ded C   Y trowe] of erthe U, on erþe I trowe C   1208 bystrode] vmbystrade A
or any] oþer V   any] euer A   steel] armour C   1209 Than] AVUDEC, *om.* L *Kölbing-Day*
þe] that UDE   same] *om.* UD   setteþ] setten U, sette E   an] *om.* D, to an C   1210 A sowe]
Wele UDE   A . . . werre] wode nyȝe he was for wrothe C   sowe] sewe A   wal] wallys A
dryueþ] caste E   1211 alle] *om.* UD, hyt all C   -walte] welterde A, *prec. by erasure* V,
drewe C   þer] whereso V, where U   þer hit went] *om.* C   hit] VUD, he L, scho A   went]
hent D   wyes] wyghtis D, Iewes C   wyes an hundred] weies made C. V   scribal line E: And
oueral where it hitte / were þey neuer so stroonge   1212 Were . . . dynt] topseyl
ouerthrowyd E   of] with C   þat] the AVC, his D   dynt] stroke C   diche] dykes A, dike V
lyȝten] flowe A, laften V, dasshen U, dasshid D, fyllyn EC   1213 heueþ] hewys A, lifte E,
holdeth C   þe] his AVUDEC   honde] handis AUC   Heuen-kyng] allmyȝty god C   þonkeþ]
he thankis A, thankyd E   1214 þey] *om.* U, he D   þe dukes] sire Sabyns UDE   han so
dere] so dere now (*om.* VDEC, thei U) hase (hath D) AVUDEC   bouȝte] ybought V, aboght
D, ybough E   1215 þe¹] þan þe E   preien] prayede þat prynce A, þanne praied V, preyde
E, Prayde hym C   þe pees] of pesse A(*marg.*)DEC, for pees V, a pees U   þis . . . euene] to
passen fro the (*om.* D) deth (pyne D) UD, for so yhurt þei were E   þe³] at the A   Paske]
estur C   euene] tyme A   1216 And] And to AVUDEC   þe¹] that A   out] thei UC   out
rauȝten] delyueryd E   rauȝten] kasten C   1217 Nay] False C   now] *om.* U   take] kepe E
ȝour-] *marg.* A   1218 For] *om.* V, There C   ward] wardis A   on] of DE   þe¹] AVDC, ȝour
L *Kölbing-Day*, this UE   wal] walles A   vs þe way] the wayes vs U   way] wallis A

We han geten vs a gate   a[g]en[es] ȝour wille—
þat schal ben satled soure   on ȝoure sory kynde'.   1220

Or þe ȝates were ȝ[et]e   [al þe ȝeres tyme]
Ouer þe cyte were seyn   selcouþe þynges.
A bryȝt bren[n]yng swerd   ouer þe burwe henged
Without ho[l]d oþer helpe   saue [of] heuen one.

Armed men in þe ayere   vpon ost-wyse   1225
Ouer þe cyte were seyn   sundrede tymes.
A calf aȝen kynde   calued in þe temple
And eued an ewe-lombe   at [þe] offryng tyme.

A wye on þe wal   cried wondere heye,   1229
'Voys fram est, [voys] fram west,   [voys] fram þe foure wyndis'!
And sayd, 'wo, wo, wo,   worþ on ȝou boþe,
Ierusalem þe Iewen toun   and þe ioly temple'.

1219 We] for we E   geten] hotyn D   a] *om.* DE   gate] way C   *agenes] *Duggan*
1988:144n61, agains V, ageyns U, aȝens DC, al aȝens E, aȝen L, Mawgrethe A   wille]
wills A, owen wille U, good wylle C   1220 þat] & þat E   schal] sall A   ben
satled] sattel UD, ȝow reewe E, sytte C   soure] one ȝoureselfe and A, forsothe V, ful
sore (sour D) UDC, sore E   on . . . kynde] and al ȝowre kynde after E   *no cesura* C
1221 Or] ȝitt or AV, And ere UDC   were ȝete] *trs* V   ȝete] A, ȝolden LUD *Kölbing-*
Day, vnshette V, geten C   al . . . tyme] AVC (al] was all A, þe] þe thre C) *Duggan*
1988:128, þre ȝer byfore (aforne UD) LUD *Kölbing-Day*   scribal line E: Thre ȝer before
/ þe town was yȝuldyn   *no cesura* V   1222 þe cyte] it E   were] was A
selcouþe] sere s. A, many s. U, wondurful E, meruelous C   þynges] sightis DE   *no*
cesura V   1223 brennyng] AVUDEC *Kölbing-Day*, brendyng L   burwe] burgh VU,
town E, cyte C   henged] hange A, hanges U   *no cesura* V   1224 hold] AVU,
hond L *Kölbing-Day*, holdyng DEC   hold, helpe] *trs.* A   saue] but E   of] AUDEC
Kölbing-Day, þe L, *om.* V   heuen] godis V, god UE, hem D   one] owne V, allone
DEC   1225 Armed] Also armedde C   vpon] in the UDE, on þe C   ost-] wondir
V, beste UDEC   -wyse] wyes A   1226 Ouer] was ouer A, werin ouer V   were]
om. AV   sundrede] sere Certayne A, many sundry V, in sundri UD, in many dyuerse E,
at certeyne C   tymes] tyme UE   1227 aȝen] al agayn D   þe] thaire A
1228 And] An ewe V, And there UDE, And an ewe C   eued] had A, yemed U, was
euedde C   ewe-] *om.* VC   -lombe] *om.* UDEC   at] in UE   þe] AVUEC *Kölbing-*
Day Duggan 1988:128, *om.* LD   offryng] Offerande A, offerynge C   1229 A] And a
U, Also a DE   wye] wight D, man EC   on þe wal] *after* cried AV   wal] wallis AE
cried . . . heye] was walkyng (weylyng E) that tyme UE   wonder] wondirfully A,
wondirly VC (*cesura precs.* V), wel D   heye] lowde AVC   1230 *line om.* UDEC
fram[1,2,3]] fro (fra *in third use*) A, of V   voys[2,3]] AV, and L *Kölbing-Day*   þe] *om.* AV
wyndis] halues A   1231 sayd] *om.* A, cryed E   wo wo wo] wo be to ȝow alle A, woo
woo V   worþ] wurgh E, lyȝte C   worþ . . . boþe] and wo appon ȝowe worthe A   on
ȝou] vppon V, to yow UDE   boþe] all at ones C   *no cesura* E   1232 Ierusalem]
The gentil I. U, To setle I. D   þe Iewen] and the Iewes the A, þe Iewes VC, þe gentyl E
þe Iewen toun] *om.* UD   toun] *om.* E   ioly] *om.* A, fayre E

[þe same tyme þe toun   was taken and [wonnen]]
[S]ayþ þe wye on þe walle   ȝit o word more:

f. 18ʳ 'Wo to þis wor[þ]ly wone   and wo to myselue'!   1235
And deyd whan he don hadde   þrow dynt of [a] slynge.

And þan þe [vilayns] deuysed hem   and vengaunce hit helde
And wyten her wo   þe wronge þat þey wroȝte
Whan þey brutned in þe burwe   þe byschup seint Iame;
Noȝt wolde acounte hit for Crist   þe care þat þey hadde.   1240

Bot vp ȝeden here ȝates,   and ȝelden hem alle
Without brunee and briȝt wede   in here bare chertes.
Fram none tille þe merke nyȝt   neuer ne cesed
Bot [ay] man after man   mercy bysouȝt.

Tytus into þe toun   takeþ his wey.   1245
Myȝt no man st[y]ken on þe stret for stynke of ded corses.

1233 *line om.* LUDE *Kölbing-Day, supplied in the form of* V   þe¹] In þe C   þe²]
þat the A   *taken and wonnen] wonnen and tane A, taken and graunted V, taken and
ȝolden C   1234 Sayþ] sayde AVUDC   wye] wight DC   walle] walles A   *ȝit]
appears at head of line LAVUDC *Kölbing-Day*   o] a A, one V, thyes U, þis ilk D,
another C   word] wordes U   scribal line E: And ȝit oftetyme he seyde / þese wunder
wurdes more   1235 worþly] A, worldly L *Kölbing-Day,* worthy VUDE, wordy C
wone] town E, place C   my-] hym- V   1236 And] He C   deyd] dede V, deyde
anon E   don hadde] had said V, *trs.* E   þrow] thorowe þe A, with UDE, with þe C
dynt] strook EC   a] AVUDEC *Kölbing-Day Duggan* 1988:128, *om.* L   add scribal line
LUDEC *Kölbing-Day*: And haplich was had away / how wyst I neuere (haplich) *om.*
UDEC   was] was in hast UDC, was anon E   had] ybore E   how . . . neuere] how
(but hoow E) no man wyst UE   I] þey C)   1237 *lines* 1237–40 *om.* AVC
And¹] *om.* UDE   þan] ¶ *precs.* D   *þe vilayns] þey LE *Kölbing-Day,* thei U, þei D
deuysed] auised UD, supposyde E   hem] hem thereof U, hem wele D, *om.* E   and²]
þat E   hit helde] schulde falle E   1238 *lines* 1238–40 *om.* UDE   1241 Bot]
Than A, *om.* VC, And UD, Thei E   vp ȝeden] vp yelden U, vpheld D, dode vp E, Vp
wente C   here] the AVDEC   and] anone / thay AVC, þanne and E, þey *Kölbing-
Day*   ȝelden] ȝolden AVUEC   1242 Without . . . wede] and owte comyn naked E
brunee] brenyes A, any UDC   and] or AV, *om.* UDC   in] but in C   briȝt wede] armour E
wede] gere A   in] but in C   in her bare] al bare (*om.* E) in (to D) her UDE
chertes] serkes AC   *no cesura* V   1243 Fram] Fro þe A, From þe V, Fro UEC
none] morne U, morow DE   tille] to AVUE, into C   þe] *om.* UDE   merke] *om.*
AV, derke C   neuer ne cesed] cesed thei neuer UDE   ne] thay ne A, þey VC
1244 ay] VUE, *om.* LA *Kölbing-Day,* euere DC   bysouȝt] besoughten VDC   *no
cesura* V   1245 Tytus] And Titus AUD, Titus þanne V, Than tytus EC   takeþ]
anon took E   his] the AVDE, the right UC   1246 Myȝt] Ne myght U   no
man] he UD   *styken] steken *Kölbing-Day,* stoken L, stynt UD, stande A, stonde VC
on] in AVUDC *Kölbing-Day*   þe stret] no stede D   stret] stretes V, stoure U
stynke] stynkyng D   ded] dede AV, the UC, *om.* D   *no cesura* V   two scribal lines
E: but in no stede myȝt he longe abyde (*no cesura*) // for stench of dede bodyes / þei
laye so thikke

þe peple in þe pauyment   was pite to byholde
þat were enfamy[n]ed [and] def[e]te   whan hem fode wanted.

Was noȝt on ladies lafte   bot þe lene bones
þat were fleschy byfore   and fayre on to loke;   1250
Burges with balies   as barels or þat tyme
No gretter þan a grehounde   to grype on þe medil.

Tytus tarieþ noȝt for þat,   bot to þe temple wendiþ
þat was rayled þe roof   with rebies grete;
With perles and peritotes   alle þe place ferde   1255
As glowande gled-fure   þat on gold [fl]ik[r]eþ.

þe dores ful of dyemauntes   dryuen were þicke
And made merueylous lye   with mergeri perles,
[þat a]y lemaunde lyȝt   + as a lampe schonen:
Derst no candel be [k]ende   whan clerkes scholde rise.   1260

    1247 *line om.* E   in] one AVUC   *no cesura* C   1248 were] was AUD   enfamyned]
VU *Kölbing-Day*, enfamyed L, Enfameschede A, with famyne D, famyssched C   and
defete] U, for defaute (þe f. C) LAC *Kölbing-Day*, for faute V, defetid D   hem] þey VDC,
the U   fode wanted] mete lakkede C   scribal line E: þat for hungur sturue / for wantyng of
foode   1249 noȝt] not D, no flessch E, þer noȝte C   on] of the A, on no C   ladies] lykam
(þe l. D) UD, hem E   lafte] beleft VU   þe] thaire A, *om.* D, only E   lene] hide and V, dede
D, bare EC   bones] chekes A   *no cesura* V   1250 were fleschy] *trs.* UDEC   fleschy]
fleschely A, fresshe VUD, fressch foolk E, fayre C   byfore] tofore V, aforn UDE   fayre]
fresshe C   on to loke] to beholde VDEC   1251 Burges] And burgeys UC, The burgeys
D, burgeyse`s′ E   with] and A, with her U   balies] baylȝes A   barels] beralles AEC, barell
V, *om.* U   or þat tyme] þay lukede A, aforn that U, bifor D, þat hadde E, sommetyme C
1252 No] were no V, were as E   gretter] smal E   þan] as E   grehounde] grehoundes E
to] þan to D   on] in AVUDEC   medil] myddis AUDE   1253 Tytus] Then Titus UDE
tarieþ] tarid UDEC   noȝt] nat E   for þat] *om.* UDE   wendiþ] went UDE, ȝode C
1254 was] was alle AV   rayled] arraied U   þe] in þe C   grete] full grete A, ryche C
scribal line E: of which þe roof al was / with rubyes arayed   1255 and] and with AC
peritotes] precyous stonys A, baleis V, petitotes E   alle] þat all V   alle … ferde] and many
bryȝte stones E   ferde] ouer A, ypight U, pight D, sette C   1256 As] The D   As …
gledfure] that schyned as þe sunne E, That glystered as coles in þe fyre / C   glowande] þe
glemande A, glemende as V   gled-] golde V   þat] whan it E, *om.* C   on] on þe DC
*flikreþ] flikeþ V, stikeþ L, strykes A *Kölbing-Day*, strikes U, strikis D, striketh E, ryche C
1257 ful of] with EC   were] were full A, ful U   þicke] fast U   1258 And] *om.* V, Y- D
made] made also C   made … lye] full Mervellously made A, Made full gynfully V,
meruelyche ywrought E   *no cesura* C   1259 *lines* 1259–60 *trs.* L *Kölbing-Day*   þat ay]
V, So were þey L *Kölbing-Day*, þat one ane A, That ouer U, þat euere with D, and euermore
E, That euur C   lemaunde] lemed V, lemnand U, ȝaue E, lemede þe C   as] AVUDE, and
as LC *Kölbing-Day*   a lampe] lampis þay AV   a lampe schonen] it were a launpe E
schonen] shyne V, shewed C   1260 Derst] þurt V, There thurt U, it nedyd E   be kende]
lyȝt E   *kende] kynde U *Kölbing-Day*, kindelled (-elid D) VD, tende L   whan clerkes
scholde] clerkes see to V, to clercs forto U, clerkis to D   rise] areyse D, aryse E   scribal line
A: thurghe thase kanells of kynde clerkes to ryse, scribal line C: The clerkes hadde none oþur
lyȝte / whenne þat þey dede ryse

þe Romayns wayten on þe werke,   warien þe tyme
þat euer so precious a place   scholde per[i]sche for + synne.
Out þe tresour to take   Tytus commaundyþ,
Doun bete þe bilde,   brenne hit into grounde.

þer was plente in þe place   of precious stonys: 1265
Grete gaddes of gold   whoso grype lyste,
Platis, pecis of peys,   pulsched vessel,
Bassynes of brend gold   and oþer bry3t gere;

Pelours masly made   of metal[le]s fele
f. 18ᵛ   In coppe[r] craftly cast   and in clene seluere;   1270
Peynted [with] pure gold   alle þe place + ouer.
þe Romayns renten hem doun   and to Rome ledyn.

Whan þey þe cyte han sou3t   vpon þe same wyse
Telle couþe no tonge   þe tresours þat þey + founden:
Iewels for ioly men   [and] ie[me]wes riche;   1275
Floreyns of [fyne] gold   [þer] no freke wanted,

1261 wayten] beheelde E, wayted C   on] *om.* UDE   werke] wallis A, *add /* and
AVUDEC   warien] wary U, cursyd EC   tyme] Iewes AVC   1262 euer] *om.* EC
perische] AVUDEC (*after* synne A), persche L *Kölbing-Day*   synne] VUDEC, here synne
LA *Kölbing-Day*   1263 Out] Then out UD, *om.* C   to] away to C   commaundyþ]
comaundyd EC   added scribal line D: And ouertilt the temple tytly at onys   1264 *lines*
1264–65 *om.* C   Doun] And down A, And downe to V, Adoun UD   bete] brayd þei D
þe] that A   bilde] beldynge A, bolde U   brenne] and brenne V, and adoun brenne U, and
bete D   brenne hit] *om.* A   hit into grounde] *om.* U   into] to D   into grounde] to the
bare erthe A, to þe erthe V   scribal line E: And þe temple to þe ground / anon to be bete
1265 þer] The E   was] were A, was grete U   in þe place] *om.* UE, of perlis D   þe] that A,
om. V   of] of many V, and D   precious] precyouse AV, preciouses U   *no cesura* E
1266 gaddes] goddes EC   whoso grype lyste] *om.*, *fused with next line* A   lyste] luste VEC,
myght U   1267 *line om.* C   Platis . . . peys] *om.*, *fused with prec. line* A   peys] price
VUDE   pulsched] and poleschede AV, pulisched *Duggan* 1988:127   pulsched vessel] v.
(and v. E) ypol. UDE   1268 Bassynes] Besauntis byes DE   brend] full bryghte A, *om.*
DE, clene C   oþer] mekill AV   bry3t] ryche EC   gere] thynges E   1269 masly] full
Massally A, massy VE, massely UDC   metalles] V, metals L *Kölbing-Day*, metalle AUDC,
marbul E   fele] full fyne AUC, ful riche DE   1270 In] *om.* UDEC   copper] AV
Kölbing-Day, coppe L, Cuppes UDEC   cast] coruen AC   and in] os of U, al of DEC
seluere] golde C   1271 with] AVUDEC *Kölbing-Day*, as L   pure gold] perry UDEC
ouer] VUDEC, was ouer LA (was *after* gold A) *Kölbing-Day*   1272 renten] renden C
hem] it V   doun] adoun UD   ledyn] led AVUDEC   1273 þey] *om.* E   han] had
AVDC, was E   vpon] in VDE, on UC   þe²] this A   same] selfe AV   wyse] wyes A
1274 Telle] *after* tonge E   tonge] tongez A   þe] *cesura fols.* V   tresours] *cesura fols.* L,
tresoure AVUDEC   þey] AUDEC, þey þer L *Kölbing-Day*, þe V   founden] hadde C
1275 and iemewes] UDEC, Iewels L, and (*om.* V) gemmys AV, Iemewes *Kölbing-Day*
riche] full riche AVU   1276 Floreyns] And florence AV   fyne] VUDEC *Kölbing-Day*,
rede L, full fyne A   *þer] ywis E, *om.* LAVUDC (cf. L line 1274) *Kölbing-Day*   no] non E
freke] man EC   wanted] ne wanttide AU

[Ne r]iche peloure and pane　princes to were;
Besauntes, bies of gold,　broches and rynges,
Clene cloþes of selke　many carte fulle—
Wele wanteþ no wye,　bot wale what hym lykeþ.　　　　　1280

Now masouns and mynours　han þe molde souȝte,
With pykeyse and ponsone　persched þe walles;
Hewen þrow hard ston,　h[url]ed hem to grounde
þat alle derkned þe diche　for doust of þe poudere.

So þey wrouȝten at þe wal　alle þe woke tyme　　　　　1285
Tille + þe cyte was serched　and souȝt al aboute,
Maden wast at [a] wappe　þer þe walle stode
Boþe in temple and in tour　alle þe toun ouer.

Nas no ston in þe stede　stondande alofte,
Mortere ne m[u]de-walle　bot alle to mulle fallen;　　　1290
Noþer tymbre ne tre,　temple ne oþer,
Bot doun betyn and brent　into blake erþe.

1277 Ne] UDEC, *om.* LAV *Kölbing-Day*　riche] *om.* UE　　pelour] pelewes C
and] ne UE, of D　pane] palle AVDE　princes] for pryncys AC　　1278 Besauntes
. . . gold] bedes of fyn goold E　bies] bedis A　　1279 Clene] loonge E　selke]
golde AC　many carte] cartes to V　carte] cartes UC　　1280 Wele] wherof V, Wel
D, welthe C　wanteþ] wanttide AVDE, lakkedde C　wye] wight D, man EC　wale]
wele A, chese V, welde UD, hadde E, toke C, waleþ *Kölbing-Day*　what] þat D　what
hym lykeþ] of þe beste C　hym] hem D, he E　lykeþ] lykede AVD, wulde E
1281 han] *om.* UDE　molde] erthe C　souȝte] haue ysought UDE　　1282 *line*
om. C　pykeyse] pykes A, pounsons U, poncys DE　ponsone] with pecas A, oþer
crafte V, pikeis UDE　　1283 Hewen] Hewyd E　þrow] down the A, þurgh þe DEC
hard] *om.* E　ston] stanys AE　hurled] U, hadde L *Kölbing-Day*, and had AC, and
drof V, hurtlid D, and hurlyd E　hem to] to U, to þe D　　1284 *lines* 1284–87 *om.* C
þat] For U　derkned] derked VUD, *om.* E　diche] dike AVU, diches derk were E
for] of AV　of þe] and of AV　　1285 at] al D　wal] wallis AE　woke] weke V,
wlonk UD　　1286 Tille] DE, Tille alle LAVU　cyte] riche Cite V　was serched]
is serched U, is cerclid D, were yseergyd E　serched and souȝt al] so seruede AV　*no*
cesura V　　1287 Maden wast] thay wastede clene A　Maden . . . wappe] All þey
made pleine V, The wyes (wightis D) made al wast UD, oueral þey made waast E　a] A
Kölbing-Day, þe L　walle] wallis AUE　stode] stonden U　　1288 Boþe] *om.* E
in[1,2]] þe AD, *om.* VC, in þe E　tour] town E　alle] and all AV, and in E　toun]
toures E　ouer] after A, ek E　*no cesura* V　　1289 Nas] thare was AVC, Was
UDE　þe] that UC, no DE　stede] place C　stondande] *after* ston A, liggyng E
alofte] lefte A, on (vpon E) other DE, ylafte C　　1290 *line om.* UC　mude-] AVE
Kölbing-Day, made LD　alle] *om.* V　mulle] mukke V, mold D, þe moolde E　fallen]
ȝode AE, fellin V　　1291 *line om.* C　Noþer] Nowthir AU, Neþer in D, neyther E
ne[1]] nor U, nor in D　temple] on temple V　temple ne oþer] of town ne of temple E
1292 brent] brynte A, ybrent E　into] to the AUC, all to VD, into þe E　blake] bare
DE, harde C

And whan þe temple was ouert[ilt]   Tytus commaundys
In plowes to putte   and alle þe place erye;
Suþ [þey] sow hit with salt,   and seide[n] þis wordes: 1295
'Now is þis stalwourþe stede   distroied foreuere'.

Tytus suþ sett hym   on a sete riche
A[lle] Iewes to iugge   [as] iustice hymself.
Criour[s] callen hem forþ   as hy þat Crist slowen,
And beden Pilat apere   þat prouost was þanne.   1300

Pilat proffriþ hym forþ,   apered at þe barre.
And he frayneþ þe freke   alle with faire wordis
Whan Crist of dawe was don   and to þe deþ ȝede
Of þe he[þ]yng þat he hadde   and þe hard woundis.

þan melys þe man   and þe matere tolde   1305
How alle þe ded was don   whan he deþ þoled
f. 19ʳ For þritty penyes in a poke   his postel hym solde:
So was he bargayned and bouȝt   and as a beste quelled.

1293 And] om. AVUDEC   temple] town E   was] is U   -tilt] UD, tourned L Kölbing-
Day, tytt A, tekte V, throwe E, kaste C   commaundys] comandide ADEC   no cesura V
1294 to] forto A   alle] om. C   erye] to Erye A, erith U, eryed E   1295 Suþ] And
sythen AUD, And thanne E, And aftur C   þey] AV, om. LUDEC Kölbing-Day   sow] sewe
AVUDEC   seiden] VU Duggan 1988:127, seide LADEC Kölbing-Day   þis] thies same A
1296 is] after distroied V   þis . . . stede] þe temple and þe town E   stalwourþe stede]
worthy place C   distroied] stroyede AUDC   1297 Tytus suþ] trs. A, And s. T. V, Then
T. UDC   sett hym] was sett AVC   hym] himself UD   on a] in A, in a VC, on U   sete]
setill full AU, seege V, cheyre full C   scribal line E: Thanne tytus hymseelf / sat as a iugge
1298 *Alle] Alle þe E, Os alle the U, And al þe D, As Iuge L Kölbing-Day, To Iuggen thase
(iuge þe V, Iuge the C) AVC   to iugge] om. AVC, forto deeme E   as] ADC, om. LU
Kölbing-Day, a V   as . . . hymself] þat laaft were alyue E   1299 Criours] VUDC
Kölbing-Day, Crioure L, And Bedells A, And E   callen] callede AVUDEC   hem] hym D
hem forþ] afore hym E   as hy] tho EC   1300 line 1302 precs. line 1300 D   beden] om.
AU, bade VDE, that C   apere] apperide AU   prouost was] trs. UC   þanne] þat tyme E
1301 proffriþ hym] com E   apered] apperis AVUD, þo (om. C) / and peerid EC   þe]
om. D   1302 he] Titus AVEC   frayneþ] fraynid D, apposyd E, askedde C   þe freke]
hym EC   freke] folk D   with] in UD   no cesura V   1303 Whan] How when A, How
UDE, Howe that C   of] on UD   of dawe] om. E, to þe deth C   don] doon on þe cros E
and] and how C   and . . . ȝede] and thervpon yslawe E   þe] om. AUD   deþ] dede AV
ȝede] þede D, he 3ode C   1304 Of] And of E   heþyng] VUD Kölbing-Day, heuyng L,
hethynges A, betyng E, rebukynge C   þat] om. UDE   and and of UDEC   þe²] his EC
hard] depe E   added scribal line L: And of þe tene þat hym tidde / telle hym þe soþe
1305 þan] ¶ precs. D   melys] mened UC, mynnys D   þe¹] that AUC   þe²] alle þe C
matere] manere AVUD   tolde] tellis D   scribal line E: Tho answeryd pylat / and toolde
þe sothe   1306 alle] om. D   whan he deþ] and how that crist U, whan þat Crist D
deþ] the dede A   deþ þoled] was ytake E, deth suffrede C   1307 poke] purse ADE,
bagge C   postel] apoostel EC   1308 So] Thus C   quelled] sleyne C   scribal line E:
And thanne was he take / and to þe deth ydemyd   no cesura V

'Now corsed be he', quod þe kyng   'þat þe [a]cate made;
He wexe marchaunte amys   þat þe money fenged,   1310
To sille so precyous a prince   for penyes so fewe
[þey eche a ferþyng had [fourmed]   floryns an hundred.]

Bot I schal marchaundise make   in mynde of þat oþer
þat schal be heþyng to hem   or I hennes passe—
Alle þat here bodyes wol by   or bargaynes make   1315
By lowere pris forto passe   þan þey þe prophete solde'.

He made inmydde[s þe] ost   a market to crye,
Alle þat cheffare wolde chepe   chepis to haue;
Ay for a peny of pris,   whoso pay wolde,
þrytty Iewes in a þrom   þrongen in ropis.   1320

So were þey bargayned and bou3t   and bro3t out of londe:
Neuer suþ o[n] þat syde   cam segge of hem after,
Ne non þat leued in here lawe   scholde in þat londe dwelle
þat tormented trewe God.   þus Titus commaundyþ.

1309 Now] om. VUDEC   corsed] Acursed UE   quod þe kyng] seyde (quod C) tytus EC
þe¹] that A   þe²] that AUE   acate] U, cate L Kölbing-Day, bargaun A, achat V, acade E,
countes C   made] wrought UD   1310 wexe] wexe a AC, was U, was a DE   a-] of V   þat]
when he AVDEC   þe] that AD, om. VE   fenged] tuke AC   1312 line om. LUDE, supplied in
the form of A   eche a] Ilke a A, euery VC   *fourmed] ben worth VC, bene A, bene ful Kölbing-
Day   hundred] M¹. V   1313 Bot I schal] I wyll no`w´ C   Bot . . . make] A marchandise wil
(now weele E) I make UDE   schal] sall a A   1314 þat . . . hem] And þat schal the iewes
reewe E   heþyng] a fowle rebuke C   to] tille V   hem] thaym A, hem alle U, 3owe C   hennes]
hythen A, hens UDC   passe] wende V   1315 Alle] who E   wol] marg. A, after þat E, after
here C   wol by] trs. D   or . . . make] y graunte hem þis tyme E   bargaynes] bargaine V,
bargayns U, marchaundyse C   make] of þam make A   1316 By] By a A, for E, To C   lower]
lasse E   forto] or I A, to U, on to D, hem to E   passe] haue E   þey] om. V   þe prophete] oure
Prince UD, oure god E   solde] om. V   1317 line om. U   He made] Thanne made he E   in-]
a- C   -myddes] VC, myddel L Kölbing-Day, the myddis AD, þe mydde E   þe] VC, of L, / of
the ADE Kölbing-Day   ost a] om. DE   market] town E   to] a D, om. E   1318 Alle] that
alle A   cheffare] at that faire A   wolde] wille U   chepe] be A   chepis] chepen U, grete chepe C
to] forto U   scribal line E: who wulde eny iewes bygge / þat he come anon   1319 Ay] om. A,
Euere DC   a] on CV, o D   of] om. U   whoso] chaffer whoso U   whoso pay] trs. C   pay] om. U
scribal line E: And haue for o peny alone / 3if he paye wulde   1320 þrytty] Alwey thrytty E
in¹] on UD   in a þrom] om. E   þrom] thome A, rope C   þrongen] ythrungen U, ybounde
togydre EC   in²] with DE   in ropis] om. C   1321 So] Thus E   were þey] trs. U, they hym D
bargayned and bou3t] bought and soold E   and bro3t] with bale A, and dreven V   of] of þat E
londe] lyfe C   no cesura E   1322 line om. U   Neuer] And neuer AEC, þat neuer V   suþ] om.
A, aftur C   on] VC Kölbing-Day, out of L, of A, in D, om. E   þat syde] there a3en E   syde]
sede A   cam] come thare A   segge] non E, manne C   hem after] ther kynde E   after] more VC
1323 Ne] Nor C   non] man V   leued] lyueth U, lyvid D, leueth E   in] one AVC
her] þat VUD   lawe] laye AV   scholde] shul UDE   1324 þat . . . God] Man
womman ne childe V   tormented] torment A, turnementyd E   God] cryst E   þus] and
so AE, om. V, so D   commaundyþ] comauundid DEC

Iosophus þe gentile clerke   + aiorned was to Rome   1325
þer of þis mater and mo   he made fayre bokes.
And Pilat to prisoun was [put]   to pyne[n] foreuere
At Vi[enn]e, þer [v]eniaunce   and vile deþ he þoled.

þe wye þat hym warded   wente on a tyme
Hymself fedyng with frut   and feffyt hym with a pere.   1330
And forto paren his pere   he praieþ hym ȝerne
Of a knyf, and þe kempe   kest hym a trenchour.

And with þe same he schef   hymself to þe herte
And so, + kaytif as his kynde,   corsedlich deied.

.   .   .   .
1335
.   .   .   .

Whan alle was demed and d[on]   þey drow[en] vp tentis,
Trossen here tresour   and trompen vp þe sege.
Wenten syngyng away   and han here wille forþred
And hom riden to Rome;   now rede ous oure Lord.   1340

Hic terminatur bellum Iudaicum apud Ierusalem.

1325 Iosophus] Saue iosephus E   gentile] gynful D   clerke] iewe UE, *om.* D
aiorned] UDEC, aIorneyd L *Kölbing-Day*, aIoynede A, Ioyned V   aiorned was] *trs.* V
1326 þer] And thare A, þat V, *om.* DC, and E   mater] maters AD   mo] more C   he]
om. V, there he E, to C   made] make C   fayre] many D, *om.* E   1327 to] into V   to
. . . put] putt was to (in D) presone AD, to (was to E) prison put UE   was] *om.* VC   put]
AUDEC, do L *Kölbing-Day*, *om.* V   pynen] A *Duggan* 1988:127, pyne LVUDEC *Kölbing-
Day*   for-] ther for- EC   *no cesura* V   1328 At] And DE   Vienne] UDEC, viterbe L
Kölbing-Day, vittern A, vettury V   þer] *om.* UDEC   veniaunce . . . deþ] a vile (fowle C)
deth / and vengeance UDC, a vyl deeth / for his synnes E   deþ] dede A   he] UDC,
precs. veniaunce LV, *om.* A   þoled] tuke A, suffred EC   1329 *lines* 1329–34 *om.*
AVUDEC   1334 *kaytif] þe kaytif L *Kölbing-Day*   1335 *line om.* LAVUDEC
1336 *line om.* LAVUDEC   1337 Whan] And when A   was demed and] these doomes
were E   don] AVUDEC *Kölbing-Day*, dempte L   drowen] VU *Duggan* 1988:128, drow
LD *Kölbing-Day*, tuke A, drewe EC   vp] vp thaire AUDE   1338 Trossen] Trussed
UDE, They trussede C   here] vp thaire AUDE   trompen] trumped UDEC   þe sege]
her segges U   1339 wenten] And wente C   and han] whanne þey V   han . . .
forþred] left wo there (byhynde C) UDEC   wille] wills A   forþred] haddyn V
1340 And hom] Home þey C   hom] *om.* A   hom riden] hool reedyn E   now] thare A
now . . . Lord] yblessyd be god almyȝty E   rede] helpe C   Lord] *adds* Amen Amen Amen
A, *adds* AmeN E   Added lines UDC: Ihesu ioyne (Ioye C) hem and vs / with ioye in
his blisse   And to wele (welthe C) hem wysse / that reden (wryten C) this geste (That
wrote þis geest to his wele he hym wisse D)   The colophon: Explicit la sege de
Ierusalem (with Robert Thornton's signature colophon) A, Destructio Ierusalem per
Vaspasianum et Titum V, amen U(*later?*)E, Explicit þe sege of Ierusalem D, Explicit C

TEXTUAL COMMENTARY

1–6 The source, VS 1–2, here imitates such biblical loci as Luke 3:1 and the introduction to the apocryphal Nicodemus: 'Factum est in anno XVIII imperatoris Tyberii Caesaris, imperatoris Romanorum, et Herodis filii Herodis imperatoris Galileae, anno XVIIII principatus eius' (the latter figure is inaccurate; see 5 n).

1 *Tyberyus tyme*: He reigned 14–37 C.E.

trewe: This identification (see further 7 n) probably looks ahead to the criminality of Nero and to the civil wars which follow his reign (see lines 897 ff. below). Possible relations to the opening of GGK, and Aeneas's 'tricherie, þe trewest on erthe', may be purely fortuitous.

2 The first two quatrains form a single sentence, nearly all of it parallel time-marking, following the syntax of VS.

3 *whyle Pylat was prouost*: His rule as procurator of Judea was 26–36 C.E.

4 *Iudees*: L (here joined by C) overextends the evocation of the Latin tradition by putting most names into Latin forms.

5 *Herode*: Herod Antipas, who ruled the tetrarchy of Galilee from the death of Herod the Great (4 B.C.E.) until his exile (39 C.E.). See Luke 23:6–12 for his responsibility for the Galilean Jesus.

his: i.e. Tiberius's. The scribes confuse MED *empire* and *emperie*; the latter is probably confirmed by VS 1 'imperii'.

as heritage wolde: Poly 4.2 (4:280–90), Higden's account of Herod, is primarily concerned with what Trevisa calls 'þe heritage of þe kyngdom' (Higden's *successi[o] regni*). Poly identifies Herod Antipas's kingdom as Galilee at 4:290.

7 *þey*: L's usual Oxford form, but apparently archetypal *þof* (the reading of PU), *yof*, or *of* lies behind D *If* (the remaining copies have some form of *though*). Similar errors recur; cf. the cluster at A 774, PA 775, PA 776, A 780 (and C 786, A 799).

oft synne hatide: Perhaps depends upon the account of Tiberius's youth in Poly 4.4 (2:310–12): 'Hic primum cum magna modestia reipublicae praefuit. . . . Hic primo satis prudens et fortunatus in armis'.

9–16 Cf. Matt. 26:67–68.

9 *vpon*: We retain L's reading following Greg's rule of copy-text; many scribes clarified the sequence *doun vp-*.

11 *vmbywente*: We emend on the basis of PA, which imply that the archetype read *vmbe*; these mss. may be grammatically preferable in taking 11b in conjunction with *bonden* 10. However, we fuse PA with the variant of other copies and read the verb *umbegon* 'encircle'; the usages cited at MED *bigon*, sense 1c, seem considerably less specific ('surround, beset, engulf'). *white* provides the third stave, and the line cross-alliterates /hw/ and /kw/, as do 507 and 626.

12 *al*: i.e., Jesus's sides. We emend L *on*, echoic of the first use in the line, to the reading of the other mss.

   ran as rayn in þe strete: For the proverb 'blood running like rain', see Whiting R 17; *in þe strete* perhaps suggests an overflowing gutter, as in WA 4923–24 (see 564 and n.).

13–14 L adds two uses of *hym* to indicate the obvious object; similarly fastidious grammatical clarifications, which we recognize as typical of the scribe, occur in lines 17 and 18.

14 *blynd(felled) as a be*: For 'blind as a bee', see Whiting B 163, with but a single late parallel; Kölbing and Day's note cites a further example from Maidstone.

16 *bobbed*: Cf. Matt. 26:68: 'Prophetiza nobis Christe, quis est qui te percussit?' L *bollen* is simply a homeograph (cf. MED *bollen* v.1, sense 3); *bobben* is virtually conventional to describe the blindfolded Christ at the buffeting.

20 *vyleny to venge*: The Jews establish the terms of their own guilt at Matt. 27:25 (repeated at Nicodemus 9:4 and 12:1): 'Sanguis ejus super nos et super filios nostros', a prophecy fulfilled in the death of Mary's baby at 1081 ff.

21 *taried on*: Cf. OED *tarry* v., sense 3b, with later Scots citations of *tarry (up)on* 'linger in expectation of an occurrence'.

23 The entire line is an appositive to 22 *space*.

24 *worchen to pyne*: A variation of the commoner *putten/done to pyne* 'torture, torment'; the construction occurs again in line 51.

   in hem that hym: 'upon those who [tortured] Jesus'.

25 *on*: This UDE reading is confirmed by VS 3 'quidam'; other mss. dissimilate from earlier *on*. C also reads *on*, but the scribe's effort to clarify the grammar is unmetrical.

27–28 Here quatrain divisions fail, but we find this failure a product of transmission, not a challenge to the theory of composition by four-line units. The surviving text lacks any main clause verb. At this point, two lines have been dropped—either one here and one after our line 32 or else (the solution we adopt) two lines at this point. Cf. VS 2–4: 'In diebus illis erat quidam Titus . . . in regno Aquitannico in ciuitate que dicitur Burdegala'. If 29 *whyle* in fact is correct, and if it means 'until', one might propose a one-line loss on the order of 'Bode in a burwe þat Burdegala hatte'. But the absence of the line(s) makes it impossible to determine whether line 29 began with the conjunction or with P *whylke* (in which case, two lines could easily have been dropped here). A is the most successful of the manuscripts at negotiating the disruption.

30 *unmeke*: A *unmete* 'severe' is a promising reading, but is probably a *facilior* homeograph. In any event, it lacks the strong attestation of the use at line 803.

32 *So*: L's dialect replacement for archetypal (and presumably authorial) *Als*. The durior reading, L *cloched*, represents the pa. p. of *clicchen* 'clutch' used metaphorically and paralleling 31 *lyuered* 'coagulated'. P *clunchyd* probably should be connected with the rare MED *clonch* sb. 'a lump'; A substitutes MED *cloddred* 'clotted, lumped', a word which virtually always describes clotted blood.

33 *a ferly bytide*: 'A wonder befell'; the on-verse forms the object.

33–40 This material comes, not from VS 2, but from LA, ch. 67 (p. 298): 'Eo autem tempore Vespasianus monarchiam in Galatia a Tyberio Caesare tenebat; nuntius igitur Pylati [i.e. the Nathan of VS] a ventis contrariis in Galatiam pellitur. . . . Vespasianus enim quoddam genus vermium naribus insitum ab infantia gerebat, unde et a vespis Vespasianus dicebatur'.

34 *bikere*: We find no grounds for choice between rare MED *bike* n.1 'a nest of bees' and the hapax MED *biker* n.3, with same sense.

37–44 The omission in P and disrupted line-order of UDEC reflect different handlings of the same generative error. In all cases, scribes returned to copy a quatrain too far along under influence of similar openings: cf. 37 *was ne(ue)r*, 41 *was/nas ther*. In P the result is simple homeoarchy with the loss of four lines; the archetypal scribe behind UDEC recognized the omission and then copied out what he had previously skipped—although if he left any note to restore the archetypal line-order, it was lost in all the descendant mss.

38 *liter*: We follow L, supported by such visualizations of Vespasian's illness as BF 134 'iesoit' and 168 'se leva'. AUDEC respond to *laser*, which they take in the narrow sense 'afflicted with leprosy,' not the poet's 'grievously ill' (cf. the distinction of Cln 1093–94 and see 256 below).

39–40 E skips on caesural *was* +.

40 *Of*: LA are contaminated from line 38.

42–44 In line 42, as the scribes perceived, the placement of the caesura is problematic. L, which divides growyng / to, is marginally acceptable (see Duggan's discussions of lines with the form aa/aax, 1986a:94–97 and 1987:34–36). But given, not simply the problematic line but the simultaneous failure of quatrains here, we prefer to see the line as a fusion of two distinct verses—'her grym sores' appears a docked b-verse, short a syllable at the head—the result of an eyeskip. Presumptively, the lines fused were the second and fourth of the quatrain 41–44 and shared the same stave letter. Such skips from one caesura to a neighbouring one occur occasionally in individual copies; see 1233 n for an example involving LUDEC; P at 457–58; A at 754–56 and 911–13; U at 817–18; D at 662–64; E at 39–40; DE at 886–87. The original is beyond our power to offer with any certainty; but some sequence like the following might well lie behind the difficulty:

> Ne no gome vpon ground   to gaynen hem there
>
> .   .   .   .
>
> Ne no grace growyng   for her grym sores.

45 *of Grecys*: VS 8 here reads 'Ysmaelita' (i.e. a Levantine, and not apparently Christian), but cf. VS 21, 'de gente Grecorum'. Majority *Grees* 'Greeks' simply offers the French form for L's reading, modern 'Greeks'.

46 *salte se* (A): Echoes line 55 below: Thornton has absorbed the text before copying it.

49 (cf. 85) *Sensteus*: Cf. Poly 59–61: 'Nerone aliquando inquirente de numero Iudaice plebis apud Iersolimam existentem, . . . rescripsit Cestius preses . . .'. This passage may well be the basis for the identification of *Se(n)steus* as being from or ruling in Syria, misunderstood in L, but see our discussion of Jos at p. xlv above.

50 *þe athel emperour*: In VS 10 the reigning emperor is Tiberius. But for the exact dating (cf. 23 *xl. wynter*) and emperor, the poet relies upon Jos and Poly 15–16, which describe events of *c*. 66 C.E.

50–51 The poet's ornate construction places grammatically related items in on- and off-verses, respectively: 51a modifies 50a *emperour*, and 51b modifies 50b *eraunde*, the whole defined in 52: 'on an errand which harmed the noble emperor named Nero, viz. to tell that they (the Jews) wished to withhold his tribute'. The difficult construction is responsible for some of the variation in 51b.

51 *wroȝt to noye*: Cf. the same construction in line 24.

52 *withtake*: The recasting of the narrative of VS 10 ('ad portandum ei magnam pecuniam') to insist upon withheld tribute may reflect either the implicit narrative of BF (see 216–17 n) or the CD variants for Poly 67–68 'in isto conflictu' (4:426 n 11): 'propter Iudaeorum rebellionem sedandum et tributi negationem missus est dux Vespasianus cum Tito filio suo a Nerone ad expugnandum Iudaeum'. But see the discussion of Jos at pp. xlv–vi. The issue of withheld/demanded tribute forms, of course, one of the great motives of the alliterative historical tradition, a theme of national destiny prominent in MA, WA, and DT.

54 *the Grekys grounde*: The Mediterranean; cf. MA 594 'the Greekes Se'. The b-verse, with *ypes* in fourth position and alliterating adj., is conventional; cf. MA 747 and 763, Pat 147 (but contrast Pat 233, Cln 430).

55 The off-verse provides variation parallel to line 54a; both halflines modify 53b.

56 *dryueþ*: L *drof* is unmetrical; the present follows on 55 *setteþ*. In both cases, of course, L's *-eþ* represents the scribe's dialect, not authorial *-es* or *-en*. 'Drive over the deep', occasionally in forms with three alliterating staves, is a stock a-verse; cf. WA 64; MA 761 and 816; Cln 416. At Pat 235 the elements are split between halflines (and the construction differs from that here).

57–75 These lines expand, in a traditional alliterative seastorm topos, upon VS 14–15. See Jacobs's discussion.

58 *on lofte*: L *gon* appears to echo *anon*, analogously placed in line 57. Moreover, parallel lines like Cln 951, GGK 2001 (and the b-verses of WA 555, DT 4626 and 5787, more distantly DT 12501 and line 573 below) suggest that the traditional construction would include an adverb or adverbial phrase here. We thus follow PA, although *aloud*, the reading of both copies, appears to us scribal.

59 *roof*: We adopt the harder reading of P: the cover of cloud broke. Another scribal failure to recognize the verb *riven* occurs in line 610.

rede: Cf. the very similar DT 1984: 'A rak and a rayde wynde rose in her saile'; as Kölbing and Day's note indicates, the adjective there suggests that *rede* may represent *roide* 'violent' (so MED, sense 1d), and not the adjective 'red', which nonetheless might describe the hot southern wind Nothus. L. D. Benson's suggestion, *rad*, strikes us as a facilior reading.

60 *syde*: L here is confirmed by VS 14 'ventus qui dicitur Auster.' Thus this off-verse modifies *wynde* 59.

61 *It*: I.e., the *rede wynde* 59; this is the subject of 62 *dryueþ*: '(and) drives Nathan's fleet to the north'.

63 *So*: Coordinated with 64 *þat*. With the full line, cf. Cln 371, more distantly Pat 141.

64 *hurled*: For *hurl/hurtle* alternation, see MED *hurlen* v., sense 1b(c); LU appear a unique usage. In spite of numerous omissions, *an* is not dittography; cf. Cln 1211, Pat 149 (a nearly parallel line), PTA 57.

66 *worche*: We supply the more pointed verb, universal outside L. But the variation here may represent an example of split transmission, double and diverse haplography: the original may have read 'worþe / worche as hem'. In the b-verse, we believe that L has ignored an impersonal usage.

67 *scher vpon schore*: 'Swerved aslant', following MED *sheren* v., sense 5c (cf. MA 3600) and *shore* n.1, sense c (a unique usage distinguishable from the four examples from the Gawain-poet there cited). The b-verse (a similar construction appears in 285) has abundant parallels in DT; cf. 1044, 1994, 2744, 2966 etc.

69 The line is in fact parallel to 68b and a fifth line in that 'quatrain', balanced by the immediately following group of three lines. We doubt that *vn-* here is an intensive prefix, and read the common adverb *radly* (cf. 'rise radly' WP 41 and 810, WA 430 and 1354; 'run radly' Erk 62) with this verb of motion (also used for sailing at DT 4620). The towers (which most scribes avoid by intruding a paraphrase of 70b) are billowing waves, as at DT 13489 ('o the torrit ythes') or 1983 ('There a tempest hom toke on þe torres hegh'); cf. also the 'hill-like sea' of DT 4633 and 12504, as well as the towering clouds of Cln 951. They are presumably *ragged* 'rugged' because they look like heaps of stones; cf. most pregnantly, DT 12559.

72 In the mss., the b-verse has been variously influenced by 73b. We read: 'as if it would drown/founder', following UDEC. For a similar locution, cf. DT 1996; a similar description, if couched in different language, occurs at Cln 423.

73–74 UDEC skip on line-ending *wolde*.

73 Translate: 'He travelled over waves so wild that everything appeared to gush forth'. Cf. the uses of *walten* at Cln 364 and 1037.

74 *stroke*: parallel to *wende* 73.

76 *at a byr*: A *one* preserves the more usual proposition (cf. DT 1982), and the majority reading may come from *atte* in the following line. But cf. line 665 below and *at a bir* 'immediately' (MED *birre* n.1, sense 3c): the construction may not be the simple 'in a gust of wind' which Thornton assumed.

82 *yferked*: MED *ferken* v., sense 2 'to drive someone' (the verb also means 'carry,' as U sees). Transitive uses also occur at Alexander A 67, 1219 (cf. the reflexive at 1042 below).

83 *seide*: For *say* as a word frequently chosen for alliterative rhyme and capable of b-verse stress, see Michael Peverett, '"Quod" and "Seide" in *Piers Plowman*', *Neuphilologische Mitteilungen* 87 (1986), 117–27. UDEC apparently prefer a more substantial word in this position.

86 *ouer þe Iewes alle*: As Duggan (1988:127) notes, L's b-verse is not metrical; he suggests inserting *þe*, as do UC. But that reading probably represents secondary scribal adjustment of the metre, and the identification of *Se(n)steus* as a Roman official would seem to remove him from legal actions specifically Jewish. We thus follow the metrical reading of PA.

87 *lene*: PA err, since they probably imply 'I wish I were still with Cestius'. But following VS 22–24, Nathan wishes he were in the Tiber at Rome, rather than in a place he did not intend to visit.

88 *gome aughte*: LP might reflect a reading like 'gome hadde', and the UC eyeskip probably runs *lawe/aw(ght)e* (DE skip independently on line-openings in *þ*-).

92 *redly*: Like D's *radly*, a fairly direct translation of VS 27 'statim'.

94 *kyng*: PA *kyd* and UDEC *knowen* only echo *kuþþe*; VS 30 'fuisses' suggests this line should describe a state and thus confirms L's vocative *kyng*, as does the general rhetorical context. Titus asks, 'Can you heal me here and now?' Nathan answers, 'No, but *were you there* someone else can/could'.

96 *out*: MED *oute* a., sense 4 'extant;' the word always occurs at the ends of b-verses, e.g. PPB 12.145, 267; Cln 1046; DT 1541, 2175, 7062; WA 598, 2574.

97 *better*: The majority *þe better* echoes earlier *þe* 'thee'.

99 *graces*: As VS 25–26 'aut pigmentorum aut *herbarum*' indicates, 'grasses, medicinal herbs'.

101 *telle*: L *sey* has intruded from the preceding line.

102 *while he lif hadde*: Grammatically ambiguous and could modify either *lede* or (more pointedly?) *preued*.

103 *þrow*: Duggan (1988:128) suggests constructing a metrical b-verse on the basis of the disyllabic readings of either P or A. However, we take the line as a normal metrical example of a plural adjective following a preposition and let our copy-text L stand.

104 *one by*: 'In a byre, a cowshed'.

105 *man*: See 170 n below.

106 *þat cristalle of sprynges*: The AC grammatical structure provides a metrical b-verse and probably the better sense 'that crystal grows out of' (cf. *Pearl* 453). 'Clean/Clear as crystal' is, of course, proverbial; see Whiting C 588–89. Here the statement may gain additional force as an allusion to conventional depictions of the Annunciation as a light shining through glass.

107 Translate: 'without the help of any husband except the Holy Ghost'.

108 *30*: The omission in PAUDEC is metrically driven, and presumes second syllable stress on *conceyued*. In fact, the line scans with the alliterating prefix stressed, and *30* is grammatically necessary, following on the preceding line.

at ere: An allusion to the Annunciation, Mary's oral 'impregnation'; cf. Luke 1:28–38, esp. verse 29. See further Kölbing and Day's note. The a-verse precisely states the glorious nature of this birth, the Incarnation.

109 *taknyng*: It is possible that the reading we adopt from P is a substitution, just as the readings of the other mss.; they all contain efforts at undoing an anticipatory reading like that in L (but presumptively in O'). For *token* as 'sign' or 'evidence', see Erk 102, WA 4577, and the several uses in GGK (most notably 2507, 2488).

111 *bot*: In spite of placement, this apparently means the same thing as would the equally metrical *bot o god alle*. This is distinguished from the following line as saying 'only one God total', as opposed to 'the one god is the combination of the three'.

116 *mene fram hem passyþ*: The doctrine of the procession of the Holy Spirit; cf. DPR 46/10–11: '*Processio* longith to þe holy goost in þat he cometh forth'; and 45/18–20: 'And so oone and þe same þing is þe fadir gendringe and þe sone igendred and þe holy goost þat cometh forþ of eiþir' (see further 44/19–21, 45/30–32, and PPB 10.244). The spirit is *Neþer merked ne made* 'not created' because eternal; contrast PPB 9.31, where man's resemblance to divinity is 'of marc and of shafte'. The same doublet 'marked ne made' appears at MA 1304 to describe God's power and majesty.

117 *euen*: 'Equally' is probably correct (L *euer* has slipped in from the next line), if perhaps theologically objectionable.

118 The omission in P and the line order problem of DE are independent. The line's alliteration is unclear, and the form we present rhymes on vowels. After much consideration, we adopt A *inwardly*, which seems unmotivated, since A lacks the noun *world* in the b-verse (and weakly tries to emphasize *was* for rhyme). We assume the point to be that Creation is an exfoliation of power within time (cf. PPB 9.26–39). We provide a clearly alliterating synonym in the b-verse, following Duggan's discussion (1987:36, 38–39) of *erþe/world* alternation. But such an adjustment may be unnecessary, since there are certainly ME (and modern) dialects with '*orld* forms, which might rhyme vocalically; cf. such a reading as WA 18 ('all þe (w)erd' ouire', not '*all'* þe werd ouire'?). L *byfor* is another bit of scribal fastidiousness, an effort to preserve *er/or* from haplography after *euer*. To meet b-verse metrical constraints, we read simple past, rather than pp.: indeed the universally-attested *was* may be in all cases of the same origin as A's use, an effort to shore up alliteration.

120 *hye*: We follow Duggan 1988:129; with the a-verse, cf. PPB 12.139. L has misplaced the caesura, which appears in its correct position in UEC; thus *hem* provides the alliterating stave of the b-verse. To repair the line so that it conforms to the expected aa/ax alliterative pattern, we insert the adjective *hye* from DE, although we remain conscious that this may represent a stopgap and that we may merely follow a scribal solution to the problems which we perceive (cf. P's similar reading in 115).

122 Esp. with the scribal UDEC version, cf. DT 4300.

123 *so*: LAE *And* arguably has been imported from the next line.

124 *ynowe*: LA *ay* appears to us a simple scribal intensifier, an effort at rendering explicit the litotes of *ynowe*.

125 *ene*: Should mean 'once', but VS 34 and VS verse 29 (following John 2:11—all these miracles are, of course, derived from the gospels) suggest the sense 'first of all': '*Primum* fecit de aqua vinum'. The poet, in composing this antigospel, contrasts Jesus's superabundance with the dearth the Jews receive as punishment for their stiffneckedness.

126 *logge*: *loke* probably responds to *at enys* (L's form perhaps contaminated from the preceding line). The extended sense of *logge* depends upon Luke 17:12 'quoddam castellum'.

127 See Matt. 9:1–8.

132 *clerk with countours*: PP is revolutionary within the alliterative tradition in imagining that *clerkes* should be those learned and in orders. Most other poems consider *clerkes* those domestic servants most useful for keeping accounts; cf. PTA 148; the insulting 'cowntere' of MA 1672 (see the probably indifferent majority reading here); and, more distantly, WA 5045–46. The sentiment, although basically from VS 41, depends on such biblical loci as John 20:30, 21:25.

coupe aluendel: The past tense *coupe* 'could' belongs to a word-class capable of metrical suppression or elevation ad lib. (cf. 90 but contrast 41), and its stress here is probably unexceptionable. P *hem all*, with support from UDC, may be preferable to L *aluendel* and perhaps even confirmed by the passages we have cited in the preceding note.

133–36 See Matt. 14:13–21 (that the loaves were of barley-bread depends on the version of John 6:9, 13).

136 *battes*: Especially in the southern mss., this form appears to us *durior*. The sense 'lump (of bread)' occurs only at WA 4295, PPA 7.195, PPC 18.91, and in ms. J (south Lincs.) at PPA 12.70 'Of battys and brokyn bred'. Similarly, although we remain uncomfortably aware of possible interference from 134 *berly loues*, we choose P's harder reading, partly supported by E, in the b-verse.

137 *sorte*: 'Group, company, troop'; the reading is not clearly superior to *sute* (cf. PPB 5.487, 490 and Skeat's note). Translate: 'seventy-two of one group followed'. Lines 137–38 (and the parallel 141–42) may construe as a-verse + a-verse, b-verse + b-verse: 'There followed him in one company to do what he commanded seventy-two chosen as his disciples'. Further, VS 51 'predicare mandauit' perhaps implies that lines 139–40 are an appositive expansion of *what he dempte*, rather than a separate sentence (more clearly so in all mss. save L, which have *That* at the head of line 139).

138 *chosen*: L imports the end of the parallel line 142.

139–40 *to citees . . . ay by two and by two*: Cf. Luke 10:1; the parallel sending of the apostles occurs in Luke 9:1–6.

140 *atwynne*: As is implicit in the UDEC substitution, a pp.

141–54 Cf. Matt. 10:2–4 *et seq.*

144 *outwale*: An MED hapax legomenon. To achieve b-verse metricality, we follow A *and*. But this reading may be scribal, testimony to Thornton's sensitivity to verse requirements, and fully inflected *weren* an equally plausible reading (as in 358 and 692; but contrast 435 and 473 where it would be unmetrical). Both syntactically parallel nouns, *chaytyfes* and *outwale*, refer to the humble professions the apostles followed before their various callings; see e.g. Matt. 4:18 ff. (where Andrew appears as Peter's brother, as in 152) and note Acts 4:13.

147 *after*: This persuasive UDEC reading connects the line with the next: 'the sixth was called . . . and next the seventh was called'.

148 *his*: 'Jesus's'.

149 *yloued*: UDEC substitute the commoner *loven* for *lowen* 'to praise'.

151–52 *ofte Byfor princes to preche*: So far as we can tell, this claim serves merely to fill out the quatrain. LA ch. 2 (12–22) centres on the occasion of Andrew's martyrdom, his *conflictus* with the Achaian magistrate Aegeas, and the derived Middle English versions (*South English Legendary*, *Scottish Legends*, Mirk's *Festial*) do not expand this account.

152 *Petres*: L takes the name, which scans as a trisyllable, as Latin.

154 *Ihesu*: *Crist* is a scribal supply, probably to fill out an a-verse thought too short. L frequently provides the full *nomen divinum* against the evidence of the other mss.; see also 353, 354, 431.

156 *myddel*: We find the variants *myddel* and *myddes* indifferents and follow L as copy text. The poet here translates, not the narrative of Matt. 27:5, but Peter's locution at Acts 1:18: 'et suspensus crepuit medius'.

157 *hennes*: Rather than *heuen*, we read L's ambiguous form as in fact representing *henen* 'hence'; see lines 1008 and 1314 for similar b-verses. We print, however, L's usual form.

157–58 Cf. Acts 1:20–26.

159–60 *noȝt knewen of Crist*: Answers the rule for apostolic election Peter enunciates at Acts 1:21–22; see further 184 n. Paul once explicitly admits that he never saw Jesus but *c[a]me sone after*; see 1 Cor. 15:8. For the conversion of Barnabas, see Acts 4:36–37; for that of Saul/Paul on the Damascus road, Acts 9.

160 *knewen of*: Simple past: 'and they knew nothing of Christ (personally)'; UDC have pp. *yknawen of* 'not known to Christ', probably to make this line parallel to the preceding.

162 *hette in herte*: We emend this line, particularly vapid in LUDEC, on the basis of VS 42 'inuidia accensi', in conjunction with PA. Cf. the formula 'All hatnet his hert', to describe both love and wrath and widely dispersed in DT (e.g. 9153, 9304, 9958, 10202, 10247).

163 *dede*: 'Deed'; but *deþ* has the northern dialect form *dede*, routine in PA (as in this b-verse) and the source of U's misinterpretation here.

165–72 VS 54–57, as does Nicodemus 7:1, identifies Veronica with the woman cured of a running sore after twelve years (Matt. 9:20–22).

165 *whom*: The word clearly bears alliteration at 201. But the line none-theless appears one of a small number of 'Langlandian' lines with third position alliteration on a 'mute stave' (for examples with *who(m)*, see Mum 297, 574, 736). These occur to some extent in all alliterative poems; see Turville-Petre 1980:306 and Duggan's discussion (1986a:91–92) of the b-verse formula of authority *'as' þe boke tell'es'* (PTA 306, 423; WA 2360, 3500), not *'as þe boke' tell'es'*, or *'as tell'es þe boke'*. Such verses, although we consider several of them very likely archetypal O' corruptions, resist any treatment short of the conjectural cautery, and we have allowed them to stand. See further such fairly clearcut examples as 292, 436, 583, 634, 671, 681, 797 (with which cf. GGK 477 and 803), and 1175.

167 *Peynted*: The variation *peynt/prynt* is not resolvable: note VS 57 'figurauit', but also Poly 4.4 (4:322): 'ut eam cum panno suo lineo *impressionem* Dominici vultus habente ad Cesarem Rome [Velosianus] perduceret'. And note 241 *prente*, unique to L.

purely and playn: The universally attested reading *priuely* is senseless; it has been produced by misexpansion of an *r*-suspension. The reverse error, in which 'privy' appears for 'poor', occurs in line 910. Although Kölbing and Day offer a great many citations to establish the sense *privy* 'manifest', most in fact testify to other, well-recognized usages, esp. 'private, one's own' (see Anderson's note to Cln 1107).

169 *grounde*: LU *erþe* has intruded from the following verse.

169–70 The sense is 'there is no man . . ., nor (a man with) any disease or mischance at all who kneels . . . without all becoming immediately healed'. *man* 'crime, misfortune', which we believe also occurs in line 105, is last

cited by MED from *Cursor Mundi*; but the compounds *mon-sworn* 'crimin-
ally forsworn, perjured' and *man-swering* 'perjury' were still in use in the
fifteenth century (the latter appears at DT 734 and Cln 182) and suggest
that the word had a longer life.

172 *in an handwhyle*: A common b-verse; cf. WA 632, DT 1825, Erk 64,
PTA 267.

173 *A Rome renayed*: PA are clearly more satisfactory than L (and their
rhetorical form supported by VS 60 'Ve, ve tibi Tyberi'), and the general
agreement of other mss. against L supports them. *Rome* here is metonymy
(as 'France' for 'Louis XIV'). This verse and the next form emotive
vocatives.

176 *iugge*: VS 62 'qui occiderunt' probably implies that the word here
means 'condemn to death', overspecified in UDE *slough*. At this point, VS
63–64 has a sentence not reproduced in the poem but plainly the inspiration
both for the punitive expedition to Jerusalem generally and specifically for
Caiaphas's later torments (697–712), in *The Siege* derived from BF:
'Verumptamen si fuissent ante faciem meam, ego eos occidissem in ore
gladii, et aliquos in ligno suspendissem'.

177 Cf. DT 5053.

179 Translate: 'the face, faultless in flesh and skin (i.e., inside and out?),
(was) as new'. The most interesting variants in the line arise from
grammatical misunderstanding: the off-verse modifies the appositive adj.
phrase *withoute faute*.

181 *seide*: *quod* probably has been attracted by the alliteration, and the stave
falls on *kyng*. L inadvertently supplies *riche* to put the line into the form of
common b-verses like that of line 3; here the copyist has been attracted to
his scribal version of 173.

184 Cf. Heb. 11:1 and John 20:29; and recall line 160.

185 *bayne*: A verb; cf. VS 69 'Iube'.

186 *his*: AU *thaym/her* attempt to connect the verse with the following line,
but only Nero (whose first sorrow is withheld tribute) has had a previous
sorrow to renew. The whole line forms an appositive to *bone* 185.

189 *Telle*: The AUDE supply of *Now* is apparently related to these mss.'s
omission of *tit*, as a way of adjusting the syllable count. A similar omission
in the same halfline form occurs earlier at 97.

191 *at pries*: Modifies *Nempne*.

192 *in blessed water*: Although the verse represents the syntactical frame
prep. + adj. + sb. (Duggan 1988:133), it is probably not metrical, and
Duggan refers to it as 'an anomaly' (134).

193 *font*: A font-stone, as in JA 7, rather than a stationary vessel. This sense may be responsible for the rationalizing variant *fatt*—where in a non-Christian country could one find such an implement?

194 *werred*: The scribes responsible for the majority reading, *after Crist serued*, appear not to understand the past subjunctive 'would go to war for Christ'. They seem originally to have introduced a temporal specification to clarify that the verb does not simply refer to past conduct. However, this substitution reduced the b-verse to nonsense, 'who later made war on Christ', and required further adjustments.

195 *into eche*: We follow copy-text, but other mss. with *in ilk(e) a* probably reflect authorial dialect more closely. With the a-verse, cf. DT 3648.

197 LA mean 'Afterwards with Nathan he went to Rome', misunderstood in most copies as 'He sent to Rome by messengers'. The L error, *souȝt* reproduced as *pouȝt*, appears again at 1174.

199 *he*: I.e., *his fadere* Vespasian, who is *gronnand glad* because still unhealed yet presented with the possibility of his health.

   grete: The b-verse is only metrical in L by reading *gret-e* adv. (cf. the possible *loud-e* 477 and *scharp-e* 559). Both P *gretely* and UD *the grete* appear scribal efforts at constructing a metrical b-verse. We suspect that *gret-* might represent the remains of a verb, either *greten* 'lament' or *greden* 'cry out'. Perhaps the poet wrote 'grette to grete God', a reading lost by haplography and filled out with a line-ending verb in O'. We simply present copy-text, although we are reasonably certain that it is corrupt.

204 *hit*: I.e., your death; thus translate: 'unless it is paid for to the limit (lit. expensively)'.

205 *pat tyme Peter was pope*: Conventionally, Peter was martyred by Nero, perhaps in the company of Paul (see 899), *c.* 64–66 C.E., after a twenty-five-year papacy. For his election by Jesus, see Matt. 16:16–19, 18:18.

207 *folowed fele of*: *Follow on* means 'to pursue', but the form should be construed as DE do, 'to baptize', confirmed by BF 23 'et baptiza'. Other copies describe Peter harrassing Romans until they all convert. The universally attested *faste* then represents smoothing with an ostensible verb of motion: BF 23 reads simply 'le pueple', and does not support the alliterating *fele*, which we supply, as Kölbing and Day suggest.

209 *pat pe waspys hadde*: Continues the characterization derived from LA (see 33–40 n); in BF 29–31, Vespasian is brother of the emperor and is simply leprous.

210 *he*: The pronoun indicates a change of speaker: Vespasian commands Peter to appear, but the expertise is the apostle's.

212 *come*: Simple past; L's perfect tense is unmetrical (although in the word-order of A not so).

214 *messageres*: Chaucer scans the word mess'a·ger', and we assume that the fourth stress falls on *-ger-*. Cf. the routine scansion of *emperour* in line 1 etc.

215 *cud*: PA are preferable in construing the a-verse as parallel to 214 *messageres*. Thus, they read, not as pp. 'chosen', but the adjective 'courteous', answering BF 87 'chevalers des plus sages de sa meson'.

216–17 *trewes*: Kölbing and Day thought correctly that a portion of text had dropped out here. Indeed, the repetition of the word *trewes* in both lines may be the remains of an eyeskip which stimulated a substantial loss (about a ms. page in BF) at this point. Line 216 answers BF 87–88 'manda a Pylate le prevost que il li enuoiast son *treuage* que li juis li devoient'. Subsequently, in BF 117–18, the messengers apparently do bring the tribute—'Pylates manda aus princes et aus mestres que il apareillassent *le treü* l'empereor'. One should note in 217 D *trowe*, E *payment*, closer to the source: OF *treuage/trouage* and *treu* both mean 'tribute' (MED *treuage*); these seem to have been confused with ME *trew(es)* 'truce' in the other copies. We limit our reconstruction to an indication of the textual lacuna: in the circumstances, even the emendation 217 *trewes* > *trewage* seems incapable of improving much upon an O' corruption.

219 Translate: 'The pope gave them pardon and then came to them with procession. . .'. He pardons because they have performed their religious duty, returned with Veronica, even if they could not perform their civil duty, bringing tribute. PAUD *perto* is echoic of the line end, but this reading may point to a possibly original *hem to*.

222 *Of*: Completes the construction *war of*, with 221b a relative clause modifying *womman*.

223 *vmbefelde*: The first use of this L dialect form (see also 1131), presumptively from West Saxon *fealdan*.

224 *cors*: Not parallel to the infamous GGK 1237, but directly from BF 129 'mon cors et cest saint cuevrechief'; *cors* appears as the English *body* in 254.

Most variation in this line is predicated on the fact that the a-verse is a prepositional phrase dependant on *þe kepyng*. Scribes have anticipated a different grammatical form, then had to improvize.

225 *full biterly* (A): The intensifier probably only accidentally corresponds to BF 132 'moult durement'.

227 *in þe stede*: We retain our copy-text, although we find it vapid. But note PA *a stede*, which may imply a lost reading in *a-/on st-*, e.g. *in a study* (DT 9263), *astound/astonied* (DT 2520, 9488, 11806), less likely *and stotayed* (MA 3467). There is no parallel in BF 132.

228 *whan*: Depends on *stode* in the preceding line, and answers 225 *þan*. We follow PA *scho*, since the rest of the mss. may have *he* from West Midland forms for *she* (the action is again unparalleled in BF).

229 *he warp*: The majority reading accords with BF 132 'le prist entre ses mains' and earlier singular weeping references. L provides the plural here and again in line 231, while UDE insert an explicit singular there to achieve the same accord of reference.

230 *rennande*: The poet may have written *remande* 'lamenting'; cf. the same error at PPB 18.100. As Duggan (1988:143) points out, like other alliterative poets, the author avails himself of the trisyllabic pres. p. (< ON -andí) to construct a metrical b-verse; cf. the similar 472 but contrast 437. The same a-verse occurs at WA 1247, 1305, 1770, 3338.

231 *To þe palace*: BF 133–34 'et s'en vint tout droit el grant palés l'empereor' confirms AUDE (and cf. line 241 below).

234 *departe*: An infinitive parallel to *wende* (cf. BF 143–45 'envoia . . . et li manda que il se despeeschast du pueple'). The majority reading *swythe* may well have intruded from line 231.

235b-36 As we print the text: 'They brought to Vespasian and Peter presented both to him'. But the parallelism of BF 144–45 'despeeschast . . . et se hastast de venir a lui' might support U; moreover, this ms. more nearly resembles poetic grammar, since it joins 235a and 236a, 235b and 236b: 'They brought and presented both Veronica, with her veil, and Peter to Vespasian'.

239 Cf. DT 4312 (and more distantly 4301).

241 *prente*: I.e, the image on the vernicle (cf. 167 n).

242 *kepten*: 'Worshipped', a specification of BF 156 's'agenollierent'.

243 *flawe*: L *flambeþ* anticipates lines 245–46 and apparently misrepresents *fleweþ* 'flies' or *floweþ* 'flows'; we follow the majority reading, the past tense of the first of these verbs.

felleden: L's spellings for *-el(e)* and *-ell-* show some coalescence; cf. 172 *helle* 'health', 871 and 892 *fele* 'fell' adj. and 'fell' v.

246 *schewed*: Although the variant readings might imply an original *schedde/schadde* (which P and UD would then gloss variously), the locution *show light* 'shine' is widely attested (MED *sheuen*, sense 11c).

248 *for*: The grammar is ambiguous, either verbal 'cry for' or Verb + prep phr. ('because'). BF 159 reads only 'cil Vaspasiens commença a crier a haute voiz'.

249 *lordlynges*: We preserve L's reading as copy-text; the word is not specifically diminutive in ME. Duggan (1987:37) identifies *Lo* as a unique example of such light alliteration; but cf., among many other instances, 421 *By for'*, *853 Sup*, and 929 *A·mydde'*.

250 Translate the on-verse: 'from whom I pray for my health'; *bidde* is confirmed by BF 161 'je requier'.

252 *dyn and dit*: Although with some doubts, we retain the copy-text. Beyond 808 and 1193 below, the only parallels for OF dit in MED are DT 1347 and 11946, both with *dyn and dyte*, but in fact lines which agree with this one in all three alliterating staves also occur at 5788, 8675, 8680. But we remain uncomfortable in the face of DU *dremyng* and the potentially related C *wepynge*. Such readings may support a pres. p. + sb. (*dynnande dit? dreuande dit?*). BF 162–63 contains no parallel.

253 *availen*: i.e., *avalen* 'lower', but the form has perhaps been attracted to that of the following noun. *Visage* directly translates BF 164 'visage'.

254 The line has nearly a full stop at the caesura—'and afterward touched his body all over; he blessed it three times'. Variation in the off-verse reflects a scribal effort at writing the line into a single statement.

255 *wyten*: We take this P reading 'depart' to be *durior*.

256 *was lasar-liche*: DE surely point the right way, toward a compound *lazar-liche* 'sickly corpse'. But possible readings might also include *lazarly* adj., which would explain the related UC variants. Cf. the similar reading in 332. *layth(er)* forms have been generated from misinterpreting *lazer* (i.e. *laʒer*) as if it were *lay(y)er*.

257 *departyng of stryf*: P is attractive and antecedent to AUDEC; moreover, it lacks the jingly internal rhyme of L. However, one has considerable difficulty explaining the derivation of either L's or P's reading from the other; but BF 169 'ot si grant joie'; 170 'si grant joie'; 171 'en joie et en leesce' support an appositive b-verse and the general sense 'an end to their anxiety'.

258 *ʒelden grace*: A gallicism, derived from BF 169 'rendirent graces a Deu'.
    alle þo: We follow A, supported by a rash of secondary variation and BF 168–69 'li empereres et touz li pueples'.

259 Because LPA *eyr* has the support of BF 178 'en l'air en haut', we assume that this line originally alliterated on vowels. Thus the UDEC provision of *chirche* (< *kirke* with alliteration in /k/) is probably wrong. If this is the case, then *kaireþ* is likewise erroneous, but may easily be corrected to another common alliterative verb of motion rhyming on a vowel and answering BF 178 'se leva'.

260 *pople*: In spite of attestation both in LPA and BF 178 'li pueples', the noun may well be scribal filler, intruded out of distaste for the absolute adjectival sb. (see further 461 n). The widely attested *þe* makes sense with the adjective, less so with adj. + noun, and the form we print may blend two different developments of the text.

261 *vernycle*: L again overetymologizes and follows a Latinate form absent in the other mss.

262 *gayly*: UD greithly 'nobly' might be anterior, but the form may simply echo the mss.'s substitution for the following difficult verb. *agisen* appears in MED as a hapax legomenon, and the simplex *gisen* is rare (although cf. RR 3.159, where it may be a nonalliterating scribalism). BF 183 has only 'fist metre'.

264 Most mss. include substantial anticipations (or echoes) of one halfline in the other. L *holdeþ* anticipates the fourth stave, and P *teldys* (with confirmation in A's homeograph) is the hardest reading; BF 183–84 'le fist metre en une fort tour pres de son palés', would support this verb, 'pitch a tent, build, raise'. C reads *hold* for *teld* again at 309. On the basis of BF and of P's construction, *teldys it Rome*, we perform the minimal surgery on a line perhaps beyond repair: 'the Romans build it a room'. Following such a reconstruction, the scribes read the common noun as the name of the city and provided a preposition to smoothe the construction. We attempt also to remove importations from the a-verse which have swollen the second halfline; again we have relied on P as our model.

266 *withtane*: In L (and the certainly secondary substitutions of EC), alliteration fails. *tynt* surely represents the UDEC exemplar, but was conceivably a scribal emendation there. L and P suggest rather *withtane* pp., a return to the locution and subject-matter of line 52.

268 *emperour*: UDEC *empire* reflects the archetypal scribe's inattention to the poet's placement of grammatically related materials in parallel on- and off-verses: 268a elaborates *knyȝtes* in 267a, 268b *consail* in 267b.

270 *iewes*: Most scribes emend out the pun *iuwise/Iewes* (which also occurs at WA 1314), and thus miss the point—that Jews deserve only justice, and a justice administered by those committed to their victim Jesus (272 *þey* has 270 *Iewys* as antecedent).

278 *grem*: The mss. provide essentially dialectical variants of the same word. We print the derivative of ON *gremi*; *grame* represents the cognate OE *grama*.

280 *forwarde*: The isolated L *forwardes* pl. has probably been attracted to *hestes* in the preceding line. *byfor* recalls Titus's promise at 185–88, Vespasian's at 201–4.

281 *rotlyng*: I.e., *rattleing* 'disturbance', probably the best reading. Cf. WA 1067, with variant 'rastelyng', the only parallel and translating Latin 'turbacio'. All other readings appear homeographic approximations except the synonymous U *ruthing* 'stirring', to be associated with the verb *ruþen* (unrecorded as a gerund) at Cln 895 and 1208, GGK 1558, twice collocated with *rise*.

282 *schewyng*: 'Muster', as in WA 2794 (and cf. MED *sheuinge*, sense 1a, esp. the citations from the Berkeley Vegetius and 1430 *Brut*). The French 'muster', after all, is a derivative of Latin *monstrāre* 'show.' The other readings seem responses to archetypal *schiuyng* or *scheuyng*, interpreted as a form of the verb 'to cut'.

scharpe: Typically in alliterative poetry, the word refers to war-imple-ments (see not just GGK 424 etc. but MA 3841, JA 513, and 559 below). The intruded noun *stele*, which again reflects distaste for the absolute adjective, shows that the scribes all interpret the adjective in this way. But the sense might be improved were one to take the word as 'violent (men)'.

284 *after*: Probably the anterior reading: L seeks an unequivocal verb of motion. The off-verse should be construed with line 283a: 'they (Titus and Vespasian) took leave, as did the whole troop behind them'.

285 *schred*: Presumably a dialect form (from OE scrȳdan, not *scrūdan) of the more familiar UD reading, 'shrouded, equipped with sails'.

286 *talterande*: From OE tealtrian 'toss about', and predating the earliest OED citation of the root (the adj. and adv. at *Kingis Quair* 57 and 1145, respectively).

288 Cf. the virtually identical line at DT 5385.

289 *floynes* and *farcostes* also appear in conjunction at MA 743.

292 *Brayd*: L *sprad* does not alliterate; *bradde* pa. p. 'spread' would, as would the P reading we insert, presumably *breyden* 'scattered'. L's error recurs; see further 409, 490, 1051, but contrast 603.

aboute foure: The b-verse probably is metrical on the supposition that *four-e* is disyllabic after the preposition. But one might equally read the full form *aboute*[*n*].

293 *tyȝten*: Probably pt. of *tyen*, L's usual form for OE tēon. For parallel sense and collocation, see MA 744; but cf. also the present *Tittez* 'pulls?' at MA 1801.

294 Cf. the identical line at DT 12490 (and many uses of the parallel a-verse, e.g. 4622).

296 *ioyned vp*: 'Came ashore', i.e. the same sense as the substitution *ryued*. We take *joinen* in a sense unrecognized in MED, as a verb of motion; cf. WA 1407, 1577 (in both cases reflexive). The complement *vp* then describes the army leaving its ships.

port Iaf: Jappa was the normal landing place for Palestinian pilgrimages in the later Middle Ages. Cf. the Cotton *Mandeville's Travels* (EETS 153, 18/ 32–34): 'And whoso wil go lenger tyme on the see and come nerre to

Ierusalem, he schal go fro Cipre be see to the Port Iaff, for þat is the nexte
hauene to Ierusalem.'

297 *seken*: I.e., *siken* 'sigh'.

303 Translate, taking *kyng . . . with croune* as pleonastic: 'a king of your
race/lineage shall never again be anointed'.

   ynoyntid: We retain L following the rule of copy-text. Cf. with the line,
PPB 18.103–9 and esp. 109a 'Cum veniat sanctus sanctorum, cessabit unxio
vestra' (a version of Dan. 9:24). Like the apocryphal gospels, esp.
Nicodemus, *The Siege* imitates Matthew in its demonstration that biblical
prophecy (and its promise of a new age) has been fulfilled through
destruction; for the most powerful of these echoes, see 356 n. The locus
in Daniel is seminal in this treatment; cf. Daniel 9:26: 'Et civitatem et
sanctuarium dissipabit populus cum duce venturo; et finis ejus vastitas, et
post finem belli statuta desolatio'. And echoes of Daniel recur in the gospel
narratives and underwrite many aspects of the poet's portrayal; see further
Matt. 23:37–38, Luke 19:42–44 and 21:20–24, Acts 1:20. But other
prophetic utterances not repeated by the evangelists also shape the account:
thus 'þe wye on þe walle' (1233) may answer Isa. 62:6; the encircled city,
Jer. 4:16–18; the desolation and the site of the temple ploughed, Jer. 9:11
and 26:18 (the latter explicitly from Micah 3:12); Mary and her child, Lam.
2:20 (the whole chapter, a lament for the destruction of the First Temple, is
relevant).

304 *for Ihesus sake*: 'On account of his enmity toward (or resistance to?)
Jesus', an objective genitive. See MED *sake* n., sense 4e.

   iouke: The same confusion of anglicana *r* and *I* occurs in many copies
at 296.

306 *at þe bak*: 'Behind them', to be construed with *laften*; cf. E's paraphrase.

307 *rich*: L's form for *reke* 'reek, smoke' (again at 790 and 1089).

308 *laschyng*: 'Flashing, burning', a sense recorded elsewhere only at Cln
707, WA 553, Erk 334.

311 *to grounde*: Although PUDC *to the deth* corresponds to BF 202: 'touz les
juis que il trouvoit metoit a l'espee a ocision', that clause is in fact
translated in 321–24.

312 *Boþ in bent and in borwe*: As the later account indicates, both those who
will risk open fight and those who must be besieged.

   þat abide wolde: Modifies *here* 311.

314 *flowen as þe foule*: Whiting F 578 provides the closest parallel, only
recorded in Lord Berners; but cf. the related F 569, F 579–81.

315 *A cite*: As Kölbing and Day suggest, probably appositive to 313
Ierusalem. Then, *vnder Syon* must modify *sett*. Translate: 'The Jews fled

to Jerusalem, a noble city which sat beneath Mt. Zion and was defended by many a tower', although perhaps the poet distinguishes the *cite* Jerusalem from the *toun* 'arx' Zion.

317–20 The omission outside L apparently reflects homeoarchy: the archetypal scribe remembered he should start copying at the head of a quatrain with a line of *p*-alliteration, but instead looked for a line after *p*-alliteration and resumed at the wrong quatrain head.

319 *samned*: As Schumacher (xxx) noted—and Hulbert (p. 605) confirmed—, in this poem crossrhyme of /s/ and /ʃ/ is virtually limited to lines unique to L—here, at 426a, and at 1333. (At 376, L erroneously crossrhymes /s/ and /sk/.) Examples occur very infrequently elsewhere, e.g. U 210, A 469, DE 545 (s:st), VD 1122, possibly UDE 714 (s:sk) and E 866. Given the tendency to rhyme the sounds apart elsewhere, we provide an alliterating verb which answers the source, here probably Poly 56–58: 'Iccirco tanta multitudo Ierosolimis tunc erat, quia in diebus Azimorum ex omni Iudea ad templum *confluxerant'*.

319–20 *sacrifice . . . At Paske tyme*: For the original sacrifice, the lamb, see Exodus 12; and for the holiday sacrifices in the temple, Num. 28:16–25. Traditionally, the siege began *c*. 31 March 70 C.E. and lasted just over 140 days; see further 1215 n and 1281 n. The onset, of course, corresponds to the opening of Jesus's Passion proper, the Last Supper, a Pesaḥ seder (see Matt. 26:17–30).

321 The narrative returns to the Roman army and its depredations (dropped at 312 above).

322 *passed*: 'Passed unscathed', and not 'passed pennies'.

323 *drowen hem*: I.e., the Roman army drew itself.

328 *torkeys*: MED presents L *torken* as a hapax legomenon, *Turkein* adj. (OF turquin 'Turkish'). But the word has likely been generated from a combination of minim confusion and the analogously placed *pallen* 326. We follow the other mss., in MED as the synonymous *Turkeis* adj., most commonly used of bows (cf. BF 387).

329 *Choppen*: L's erroneous *T-* is paralleled at 1171, where the scribe writes *Toren* for correct *Goren*; and a form like *Choppen* both answers alliterative requirements and is confirmed by all mss. save E. We take this verb as having 330 *egle* as its direct object, and thus retain L *with* in the b-verse; BF 264 'sus' also supports a preposition here.

However, *Choppen* remains obscure: it corresponds to BF 265 'tresjetes' 'founded, made', often of golden objects (but ms. C and Ford 'treciee' 'interwoven?'). MED *choppen* v.1, sense 3a, cites this reading as a hapax legomenon 'put up (a coat of arms)'. But Kölbing and Day seem to us more persuasive: in their note, they interpret the word as a nonce-derivative of

MED *chape* n., 'a metal plate, mounting, or trimming'. The only parallel use as a verb occurs at Chaucer, *General Prologue* 366–67. Thus translate: 'They mounted (a piece of metal,) a golden eagle'.

The poet, of course, expects his audience to recognize the symbol of the Roman legion. This, following his sources, he inflects toward contemporary heraldic notions of the imperial through juxtapositions with the regal lion and dragon.

332 *to lyouns lyk*: The poet here translates BF 265–66: 'ou li lions et li dragons estoit d'or entailliez'. We take LP 'and (a)like two lions as well' to be the closest representation of O'. The UDEC archetype found the construction, interpreted as 'like to', difficult, since dragons and lions should not look alike; the resulting mss. reading attempts to combine both possibilities, *to* 'to' and 'two'. But LP *also* is surely otiose, and we believe these mss.' reading reflects the intermediate version *lyk to lyouns* with padding. Translate our hypothetical reading: 'And two lions of a like sort (i.e., golden)'.

334 *stayned*: Presumably refers to decoration, and parallels references to painting in the preceding line and to *coloures* in the next; cf. BF 266–68. One should probably understand these as tapestries depicting Roman triumphs (answering the *dere storijs* of 479) and tricked coats of arms.

336 *stage*: We emend to the form suggested by BF 269: 'cinquante estages'. *on* preserves the usual ME sense of *stage*, but the poet intended the French 'rooms'.

338 *briȝt to byholde*: On this b-verse formula, see Turville-Petre 1977: 88.

340 *made*: BF 206 'que il envoieroient a Vaspasien mesages' implies the word means 'sent'. The a-verse is formulaic; cf. DT 1797 and MA 2322 (where ms. *doo* is a substitution for alliterating *make*).

343 *cite*: We simply retain our copy-text.

vs: L has very likely been attracted by the *ȝour* of the b-verse, although its sense *haþ ȝou sent* ('has sent to you') perhaps is slightly superior.

344 *comyng*: Given the attestation, we retain copy-text, but note the parallel variation at 348 and 495.

wolde: The word provides a necessary fourth stress in L (and cf. P *here*). In the archetype of the other copies, the word has been attracted to the head of the following line, which rhymes on /w/, with secondary adjustment of the line-ending verb *schewed*.

345 BF 209–23 here includes a very long speech, which the poet withholds and transforms into Vespasian's instructions to his messengers. Similar transpositions of BF material typify the section of the poem leading up to the great battle.

347 *Garde hem charge*: 'Had them instructed'.

350 LP have vocalic alliteration, in which *or* must carry stress. L's rendition of the archetype, *open-heded*, writes the line into the fullest conventional directions for suppliants; cf. MA 2308, where the Romans appear hoodless, barefoot, and kneel 'in kyrtilles allone'. But the UDEC b-verse is confirmed by BF 219–20 'demain . . . tuit nuz en chemises'. In such a reading of the evidence, the line alliterates on /m/, and LP *vndren of þe day* offers a specifying substitution for the alliterating *mydday*. For *moder-naked*, see MED *moder*, sense 8f, and Whiting M 721.

352 *and . . . ellys*: We find the variation of L and P unresolvable and retain our copy-text.

354 *proȝ conseil*: Alludes to Matt. 26:3–4, 57–66 and the more explicit John 18:14 (cf. 161–66), as well as to Caiphas's central role in such texts as Nicodemus.

356 Echoing Matt. 24:2, cited LA ch. 67 (p. 298), the most widely disseminated of the prophecies in the poem (also at 982, 1019–20, 1289); cf. 303 n.

357 The poet takes up the narrative line dropped at 346.
 sadly . . . ȝede: 'Went directly'.

360 The line modifies *tale* 359; translate: 'their account of Christ and Caiphas and how Vespasian directed that the Jews should come'.

364 *flowen*: We follow Kölbing and Day's suggestion and provide the reading of PUD, the past of MED *flen* v.2 'to shave' (see sense 1c). Cf. Arthur's similarly contemptuous shaving of the Roman messengers at MA 2330 ff., 'To rekken theis Romaunes recreaunt and ȝolden' (2334); and, perhaps the ultimate source, 2 Reg. 10:5.

365 At the line head, we adopt P's verb *nake(ne)n* (cf. the past tense *naknet* DT 2427), in all other copies converted into an adjectival proverbialism (see Whiting N 64, also at PPB 12.162, WA 4155, and 943 below).
 neþer houe: We hope this form, literally 'lower hood'—D has the more explicit spelling *houve*—answers BF 243 'et firent despoillier les douze chevaliers Vaspassien tous nus *en braiez*', i.e. stripped them to their underwear or breeches. Many such constructions—MilT 3582 'nether ye', WBP 44b 'nether purs', DPR 300/19 'neþir berd her'—are simply euphemistic (and might support a *neþer hole* 'anus' here). But they display a general pattern of associating an upper body feature with an analogous structure near the loins. And Kölbing and Day, who approvingly cite WA 2892 and 5086 *nethirgloues* 'shoes', is also to the point in providing another example involving clothing.

366 *blecken with bleche*: Equivalent to MED *blacchen with blacche* 'blacken with ink/black pigment', to translate BF 245–46 'lor nercirent les joes de charbon'. The b-verse, like 365b, depends upon the verb *Nakened*.

368 *A chese*: The cheeses initially appear without explanation at BF 246, and the Jews taunt Vespasian's messengers as 'liez et atirez conme fol' (248), of which they may be such an example. But one should also understand the cheeses as smelly globes, and thus mockery of the imperial orbs prevalent in Roman decoration.

371–82 The PA omission is apparently motivated by the identical on-verses of 372 and 382, although neither ms. has an exact homeoarchic skip.

376 *schorne*: L cross-rhymes /ʃ/ and /sk/ while E has a helpful gloss. We emend to the past participle of the verb *shear*.

379 *mynt*: This D reading, supported by a gloss in E (and cf. UDE 383), is probably *durior*; see MED *mint* n. 'intent to strike' (cf. GGK 2345, 2352). The other mss. substitute an obvious reading for 'mȳt.' To assure a metrical b-verse, one could equally, as Duggan (1988:127) suggests, insert UDC *a*.

380 *tourned of our tyre*: 'Taken out of our clothes', parallel to 381a. The b-verse introduces lines 381b–82, the conclusion of the 'quatrain'; translate: 'to signify the truth we tell—that they wish for battle no later than tomorrow'.

383 *schal*: Although not necessary to fulfil alliterative requirements, the line possibly suggests alliteration on /s/ as *sall* (see also 990, 1220).

be satled: Here, as in line 1220, we take L's passive form as the harder reading; cf. MED *setlen*, sense 8b, for the phrase *ben setled on* 'befall'. Active uses of the verb in ME have the purely physical sense 'fall, drop'. For other difficulties involving this verb, confusion with *saʒtlen*, see 405 and 1061.

384 *certifiet*: 'Instructed'.

386 *in haste*: This grammatically ambiguous phrase may simply vary on 385a.

389 *streyʒt*: We retain L as copy-text: *stretch* and *strike*, the PA reading, overlap in the sense 'rise, raise'. For *stretch*, cf. WA 3204, DT 3841; for *strike*, WA 1509, MA 1229.

390 *byggid*: This UD reading is attractive, particularly since U's (and probably E's) support of D, fully capable of having intruded such regionalized diction independently, indicates that it is likely from the UDEC archetype. MED cites only two uses of *belfrey* 'siege tower' outside this poem; the poet's diction is not here constrained by BF 299, which has only 'son estendart'.

391 The b-verse modifies *oʒt*. We retain *fauted* and *feld* as copy-text. UPDEC *failed* does exactly answer BF 321 'failloient' but might well be an English substitution for the synonymous LA reading. In the second disputed lection, we suspect that PA and UDEC independently substitute and that UDEC's use of *feld* earlier in the line suggests their archetypal scribe in fact saw a reading like L's.

394 *of gold*: Modifies *dragoun* 393.

þe gollet to schewe: Majority attestation would put *gomes* in O' (E *þe iewes* might represent 'jaws', not 'Jews'). But BF 301 reads 'Et avoit en sa golle doze saetes', partially rendered in the particularly vapid 395. Translate LPA 'as if he would swallow men'; UDEC, 'in order to show his gums'. We find the general structure of UDEC preferable, but believe that the poet in fact, as frequently, translated with French lexis. In this case, 395 *in þe mouþe* may simply be an O' intrusion and 395a clearly dependent on *gollet*. But we suspect that this pair of verses may be corrupt beyond our power to detect, much less repair.

396 *fauchyn*: Although the A spelling *fawkone* may be a legitimate dialect variant of 'falchion' (translating BF 301 'une espee'), this reading, also in the UDEC archetype, created considerable confusion there. The spelling allowed misprision as a reference to a bird and thus generated the erroneous b-verse reading *fethers*.

397–400 Translate: 'The points were fixed in/upon the four parts of this wonderful world (398a modifies 397 *partyis*), indicating where they had waged war; he hangs this falchion (or this falchion [= *he*] hangs) as an indication to the people that they had conquered all the kingdoms of the world' (400 depends on 399 *forbesyn*).

398 *wlonkfulle*: PA *wankyll*, a reflex of OE wancol 'wavering', seems exactly opposite to the expected sense (and the adjective has no parallel in BF 302 'quatre parties du monde'). But the form in -*k*- confirms original *wlonk*-; this line is cited as a unique usage in OED.

400 *swerd*: The UDC substitution *werre* is scribal, in part echoic of 388, in part another refusal (cf. 391) to heed a metonymic usage. The line in fact contains adequate alliteration, since *with* carries the ryme.

401 *assised*: The UDC variant for the final stave is authorial, directly from BF 303 'seür quoi il estoit assis'. The other mss. have substituted the monosyllabic English equivalent for the verb and advanced *on* from the line head to eke out a metrical b-verse.

402 Following BF 321–25, the statement is completed in 404 (403b modifies *londe* 404). The dragon's head faces the enemies of Rome until they are defeated.

404 *lokande*: PUD *loked* is perhaps preferable. We emend the b-verse to clarify the construction: *þat* (= *þe londe*) is the subject of *lauȝte*, not—as L interprets it—part of an extended conjunction *tille þat*.

409–12 All mss. but LA apparently skipped on the line endings *wynne . . . wynges*, with some partial restoration (what we collate as line 410 seems partly fused with 409) in UDC. But there may be deeper disruptions involving line order and extending to the end of the description at 420.

411–12 The basic construction is 'ready to ring with each blow'. However, only comparison with BF 313–14 shows that the *whan*-clause of line 411a essentially restates 412. And the verb of BF, *feroit* 'struck', corresponds to a well-attested sense of MED *rinen* (OE hrīnan). LA have assimilated it to the commoner verbs *ring* and *run*. Off-verse metrical constraints require either the full infinitive form or, as Duggan (1988:128) suggests, inserting A *vpon*.

414 *gawged*: 'Projected?' a unique usage of MED *gauge* v. (usually 'gage, measure'). The other mss. offer homeographic substitutions.

419 (cf. 1256) *glitered as gled-fure*: See Whiting G 148–52; and for the sunbeams of the following line (a similar locution occurs at 549), Whiting S 897. In the b-verse variants, the scribes all strive to remove grammatical discontinuity.

420 *as*: Parallels 419 *as*: '(the silver, mixed with rich gold,) shone like a fire or like the sunbeams'. This material is parenthetical yet intermixed with the core of the sentence 'There were pensels . . . visible over the whole city'.

421 *þe foure ȝates*: This is not an historical description of Jerusalem, but an alliterative formula (although note BF 295 'les quatre mestres portes'). Cf. WA 2259, 2344, 2357, which in no case reflect the source (and in the first, *foure* does not rhyme). The locution apparently reflects the normal form of Roman military towns, constructed as rectangles along two transverse streets, with gates at their extremities. Cf. Jos's admiring description of the Roman *castra* at 3.3, fol. 272^r (3.81–82, 2:601): 'Ex omni autem muri parte, quatuor portas aedificant, tam iumentes aditu faciles quam ipsis, siquid urgeat, intro currentibus latas. Intus autem castra uici spatiis interpositis dirimunt, mediaque tectorum tabernacula collocant, et inter haec duci maximi diuum templo simillimum prorsus'.

422 *Sixti*: The correct numeral is confirmed by BF 234–35 'Vaspasien n'avoit mie plus de soixante mile homes a armes'.

423 *on*: Most scribes assumed this preposition means 'on top of' and thus substituted the in fact synonymous *to* 'toward'.

426 *strogelyng*: Although MED *strogelinge* typically means 'contention, wrestling' only in the gross physical sense, we hope the poet anticipates the modern 'struggle into one's clothes'. Kölbing and Day suggest connection with OED *straggling* vbl. sb.2 'rub loose bits of metal from', but this would seem more applicable to sharpening weapons, and the word occurs only in two nineteenth-century citations. Emendation to MED *stragelen* will neither support Kölbing and Day nor resolve difficulties; the word has only senses comparable to modern 'straggle'.

426a L crossrhymes /s/ with /ʃ/, and the b-verse is unusually vapid. Moreover, this extra line creates a five-line quatrain and overspecifies a transition, based on knowledge of later events. And further, L's *with* at the head of the following line is a unique connective provided by the scribe to facilitate the return to copy.

430 *day*: I.e. 'dawn'.

430–31 *þe vale of Iosophat*: On the basis of Joel 3, the site of Last Judgement (cf. also PPB 18.369), usually associated with the Valley of Cedron in Jerusalem. The vale is also the site of another famous alliterative battle, the 'Fuerre de Gadres' narrated at WA 1320 ff. (and cf. MA 2876–77, PTA 339–52).

433–41 The poet reduces (only once, in line 441, even conceivably in response to alliterative necessity) the more extensive structured description in BF 294–99—ten apparently equal troops. This revision, together with the strongly attested *sixtene* 437, emboldens us to emend to majority PUEC *sixtene* in line 434.

436 One of a series of 'Langlandian' lines, typified by 'mute stave' alliteration in the b-verse, which we have allowed to stand; see 165 n.

439–40 The lines distinguish Sabin's personal force, the troop from his province Syria, from the full contingent assigned to him. For Sabin's identity, see the discussion of the quatrain and its Josephan resonances at pp. xlvi–ii above.

441 *atte tail*: Given the spellings, the various prepositions supplied by the mss., and BF 297 'demorer en l'arieregarde pour le hernois garder', we construe the phrase as 'in the rear'.

442 *hors*: We follow copy-text (here L is supported by P, and the a-verse recurs at 514); although this on-verse may appear bobbed, it is equally likely that precisely such a perception has stimulated AUDEC to increase the number of syllables.

444 *baners*: I.e., *banyers* 'banner-bearers'.

445 *come*: The construction is ambiguous. One could read as either 'The Jews assembled and came', with 446 appositive to *Iewes*; or as 'The Jews assembled, and 100,000 came'.

449 Rhyme is carried by the syllables *fyf*, *-faunt-*, and *-fens-*. BF 333–35 has probably inherited this description from the elephant-mounted Asiatics in accounts of Alexander; cf. WA 3720 ff. and 3947–50 (and esp. cf. line 450a with WA 3730). A similar array of oriental warbeasts appears in MA 2283–89; at MA 615 witches and warlocks ride camels because they are 'bustous churles', too heavy for horses.

450 *with*: Perhaps the instrumental 'by means of', modifying *defensable*, not *bestes*; cf. BF 333 'les chastiaus deffensables'.

453–55 D skips on line-ending *yn(ne)*.

454 *hosed*: Not only is L *þousand* facilior, it does not correspond to BF 385 'i avoit bien cent dromadaires'. Further, *and*, which only U does not transmit, suggests that the line originally included a pp. parallel to *yheled*. P *houshid* '?supplied with houses' appears a unique usage, but probably anticipates 455 (and may recall 452, although that line does not appear in P). We follow the probable hardest reading, A *hosed* 'supplied with (armoured) leg coverings'. The phrase is unparalleled in BF.

457–58 P skips on the similar midline words *stele / feld*.

458 *a ferlich nonbre*: This b-verse has only two monosyllabic dips and is taken by Duggan (1988:134) as an anomaly, one we allow to stand. We punctuate to emphasize the potentially harder sense in an ambiguous construction: rather than appositive to 457 *Cameles*, *nonbre* may be the subject of *busked*. Similar enjambment occurs in the next lines, where *Echon* is the subject of *hadde*.

460 *ten*: Perhaps only an alliterative convenience; BF 357–58 reads 'dis huit'.

461 *chosen*: Once again (see 260 n, 555, 870, 955), most scribes object to the absolute adjective. But contrast such widely attested uses as *douȝti* 463 and *wyght* 1080.

462 Translate the off-verse: 'Whoever was pleased to know it'.

463 *was*: Perhaps a relict plural form from a northern exemplar.

464 *be þat þe*: L 'translates' a northern form into his own dialect and loses *þe* through haplography.

465 *vpon lofte*: P's reading is arguably anterior on the basis of BF 352–53 'et tendirent lor tabernacle en haut sus ung des chastiaus des olifans' 'and they drew forth the Jewish ark, mounted on high on one of the elephants' castles'. In such a reading, the distich is enjambed, and this phrase modifies 466 *keuered*; the awkwardness of this syntax has probably produced the substitution *at þe laste*. To fully correspond to BF, one would need to replace the O' reading *A* 467, probably with *Here*: this is not just any tabernacle, but the ark of the covenant.

468 *pilers*: Directly from BF 354 'doze pilers d'argent', as UDEC *postes* is not.

469–73 Allusions to twelve provide a negative version of the purified New Jerusalem of Apoc. 21 (and cf. the numerous other twelves and multiples of twelve in that text, all of which reconstruct the world of the twelve Jewish tribes). The description may rely, at some distance, on that of the ark of the covenant in Exod. 25 (note 467 *tabernacle*, a direct borrowing from BF); cf. for example, 471–72 with the golden candlestick and seven golden lamps of

Exod. 25:31–39. But the general description probably owes most to the rich howdah of 1 Macc. 6:43.

469 *which*: As both spelling and rhyme indicate, this is not the word *hutch* (BF 355 'huche') but the synonymous OED *whitch* (OE hwicce). The word recurs in /w/-lines at Cln 362 and perhaps JA 237 (b-verse alliteration only?). A's *syluer full schene* has been imported from Thornton's copying of AA (see AA 307, 384, 455).

470–72 PA here eyeskip on *gold* at the caesura.

470 *goions*: Cf. BF 355–56 'asise sus quatre lions d'or', which probably implies that the poet is translating a scribal error in his source manuscript. The English text requires a sense like that of the French etymon 'peg, block of metal', and not the usual ME sense 'ring or hinge'.

471 *chayre*: BF 355 has merely 'vne chose', but later in 358 'une chaere doree ouvree a pierres precieusez'. In the b-verse, UDEC *chaundelers* is confirmed by BF 394; L anticipates 473.

472 *bournde*: LDE are attracted by the b-verse. The reading again responds to alliterative context; in BF 356 the candlesticks are 'd'argent', which cannot be burnished.

473 *cheek*: 'Side' (MED sense 5), with but a single parallel citation (Palladius). We interpret the ambiguous final word of LP as *fyne*; in the archetype behind DC, the same form was read as *fyue*.

474 *per*: The a-verse, as BF 358–59 'estoit afublez d'un drap d'or fet en guise de mantel' indicates, in fact modifies *Cayphas* and describes the ephod of Exod. 28:6–12. Thus translate: 'The sides of the chair, where Caiphas, clad in a rich cloth, sat . . .'. On this basis, we move *per* from the head of the b-verse to that of the a-verse; cf. the reverse error at 1233.

475–76 *A plate . . .*: The rationale of judgement, as described in Exod. 28:13–30. With Caiphas's clothing, cf. the description of Iaudas, 'bishop' of Jerusalem, at WA 1652–67; further detail in the howdah can be paralleled in the later description at WA 1686–95.

477–80 *Dauid . . . Iosue . . . Iudas*: The three Jewish worthies (Judas is the Maccabee, not the Iscariot); see PTA 422–61, MA 3300–23 and 3412–21. The error *Ioseph* appears archetypal, and some mss. have scribally emended, correctly in this case. But note BF 362–63 'et tenoit en sa main le livre Moÿses et lisoit les estoires de Joseph et de Pharaon', in fact utilized by the poet in the following quatrain.

477 *lered men of þe lawe*: i.e., 'men learned in the (Mosaic) law,' a fine distinction perhaps ironically querying such learning.

   loude coupe: Perhaps a line to be taken, as 199, as scanning with an adverb in *-e*, *loud-e*. The alternative, the expanded plural *coupe*[*n*], seems to us much less likely.

478 *tolde*: Conceivably an anachronistic Christianization, referring to singing certain numbers of Psalms, as in the Breviary or Primer.

481 *a rolle*: Presumably suggests, in a detail the author adds to BF (as again in 595), knowledge of a Torah scroll, its contents (cf. *Moyses lawe* 484), and the usual way such holy scriptures (a replacement for the actual 'testimony' of Exod. 40:18) were transported. *faiples* 485 may represent a direct response to the specific human 'author' of Caiphas's Jewish—and thus lawless (cf. 499)—law.

482 *how þe folke ran*, **484** *myche of Moyses lawe*: Cf. Exod. 14–15 and 20:1 et seq., respectively.

486 *after*: 'along'; cf. DT 4717.

487 *beme-worde*: A and U are clearly *durior*, and readings like theirs the source of all other mss. evidence. LE appear most removed from the archetype, perhaps from texts with a secondary reading like *and blasons*. The reading we print forms a compound noun, 'the vanguard of trumpets'; *worde* is the common ME reflex of OE *ord*.

488 *somme*: The majority reading *sonne* misinterprets minims. The noun occurs frequently to describe armies or multitudes; see WA 2745, 4196, and 5635; DT 8201 and 8286; WW 192; as well as lines 422 and 615 here.

vneþ: The word, attested only by L, looks like another example of the scribe's fussyness, but we allow copy-text to stand.

492 *a londe*: Our interpretation of L's ambiguous form, a reading more explicit in P *in land*. The break, so early in the speech, seems to us unduly immediate and intrusive.

496 *fayntly*: 'feignedly' (see the parallel adj. in 517), the *durior* reading; cf. also PPA 2.130.

501, 507 The a-verse recurs at DT 1763.

502 *clayme . . . kyng*: Parallels *querels . . . burnes* 501.

504 *paas*: In its connection with Latin *passus*, which can also mean 'biblical passage', the sense C here glosses, the word perhaps places the poem, with its passus, as a gospel continuation. But the term is well established in the sense 'division of an alliterative poem'; cf. WP 161, DT 633, WA 2845, and various rubrics in PP.

505 *mynne*: The rule of copy-text might well obtain here, although we ultimately find *mynne*, in southern mss. and supported by PA and by the echo in line 509, preferable to LC *mynde/mynge*.

507–8 The prepositional phrases of line 508a depend on 507 *querel*, and *þis rebel* is pl. 'these rebels'. L's construction in 507b, in part an effort to avoid

/hw/-/kw/ cross-alliteration (cf. 11 and 626), makes 508b analogously
dependent on 507b: 'he wishes nothing other than to have his legal rights'.
However, in choosing the alliterating reading of the other manuscripts, we
interpret 508b as following directly on 507a ('I surrender his quarrel with
these rebels, except to have [Rome's] legal rights'), with 507b—'whichever
of the two (viz., to demand or not demand tribute) he wishes'—completely
parenthetical. We also drop the *ne* which appears in LA only. In the first of
these copies, it is clearly secondary smoothing, dependent on substituting
for oper for *wheper*; Thornton's use, with *wheper*, seems to mistake the
construction—'whether he wishes it—or not'. This quatrain is distinguishable from the one immediately following by concentrating on Nero's
perquisites as separable from an abstract sense of Roman and Christian
'right'. D eyeskips on midline *Rome* in 508 and 510.

509 Translate: 'but recall in our minds today a greater thing'. UC *mode* is
probably *durior*; the remaining mss. have anticipated the following *myn-*
verb.

510 *realte*: 'Royal status or prerogative' (MED *realte*, sense 1). Were one to
read L *regnance* as 'regnancy', it would be metrical and might be *durior*. But
no such word is elsewhere recorded in ME or OF. A stronger case might be
made for A *Rygalite*, which could represent the synonymous MED *regalite*
(cf. PTA 598) or *regalie*; but Thornton most likely strives to write a clearly
metrical form.

511 *maistre*: We interpret L's *-er* suspension in such a way to accord with
other mss. readings. In the b-verse, we follow P, although L may be
anterior; the other mss. have clearly substituted, most in ways inspired by
the next line.

513 *of*: L's omission of the word probably results from reading the line in
isolation. Although it requires the harder sense, *wynne* 'slay', this choice
destroys both the grammatical connection with line 514 and the b-verse
metre.

518 *wap*: The UDE variant may be connected with OED *weefe*[2], with only
one citation, *Richard Coeur de Lion* 5291.

520 *sternes of stour*: Answering BF 374 'lor fortereces'.

522 We construe the a-verse as a vocative, a decision which commits us to
accepting A *pyn*.

525 *neʒe*: L may consider this a form of the verb 'neigh', but PA *nye* clarifies
the sense (and cf. 532): '(the signal for the Romans) to approach (their)
horses'. Kölbing and Day suggest reading *toneye* 'approach'.

526 *stuffed*: The L b-verse, with *stif*, is not metrical (see Duggan 1986a:94–
97), and A *stuffede* is the most provocative of the readings, confirmed for
sense by UDEC *wedes*. L *stif* and P *stith* seem to have been generated by the

opening of the next line, and the UDEC readings appear a secondary effort to put the line into metrical form. But *steil-wedes vnder* would be equally metrical. With 526–28, cf. WA 900–4.

529 *cormous*: Cf. MA 1809; P *with* is metrically necessary.

530 *tonelande*: MED lists the usage as a hapax legomenon. We interpret the form as a frequentative of OED *tone* v. 'to sound musically', perhaps directly from BF 388 'tonnant'. All other mss. readings are explicable either as homeographs or outright substitutions.

531 *schrikande*: Although A *schakande* might equally support L *schillande*, we find UDC *durior*. Since line 532 apparently describes powerlessness in a situation of threatened pain, we take *As* at the line-head to refer to the Jews, and read the b-verse with a change of subject.

532 We follow Turville-Petre's brilliant gloss of the b-verse: 'when child-birth approaches'. The line translates BF 388 'que l'en ni oist pas dame d'eu tonnant'.

534 (cf. 1126) *As fure out of flynt-ston*: Cf. BF 390 'se ferirent entre eus si fierement', indicating that force of impact is at issue; and see Whiting F 189–90.

535 *dymeden alle*: 'All things grew dark'. Cf. WA 905.

536 *probolande*: P confirms the reading Kölbing and Day originally suggested on the basis of DT 7619 and 12496; they note further examples at Cln 504, 879. Translate: 'as it does when thunderstorms jostle in the heaven'—the line may parallel 534a, rather than depend upon 535 *dymedyn*; cf. BF 390–91 'le ferirent . . . conme se ce fust foudre qui descendist du ciel.'

538 Cf. DT 1199. The b-verse, which allows substitution of variously alliterating adjectives, is part of an elaborate formulaic system; cf. DT 1211, 1222, 1273, 1730 (see *Siege* 1292), 2688, 3633, 4695, 4776, 5912, etc.

539–40 Translate: 'And always the false (Jew) was swooning beneath into death, incapable of further response' (*to swelt* answers 532 *in swem*). Cf. DT 1200, 5753.

541 Cf. WA 3640.

542 *Foriustes þe iolieste*: Cf. AA 502, MA 2088 and 2134, Cln 1216.

544 *ornen*: Preferable to the competing *lafte* (cf. DT 8255), printed by Turville-Petre, which everywhere—except in A—is linked with the noun *bronde* (substituted under the influence of 543 and 547), not *bent*. Cf. with the scribal versions 599b and 607b.

545 *side*: Probably 'flank of the army, portion of the troop', rather than 'flank of his adversary'. Cf. 802 n.

547 *as a bore lokeþ*: Cf. 785 'wroþ as a wode bore'; and see the wealth of uses cited at Whiting B 387–92, to which one might add the description at DPR 1117/26–32.

548 *how*: Although conceivably an example of *e/o* confusion for past tense *hew*, the form probably reflects L's western reflex of OE ēo. Similarly unsightly examples, nonetheless retained as copy-text, occur at lines 65 *ful* ('fell') and 638 *blowen*. Similarly western are sporadic *u*-spellings for OE ȳ, e.g. 552, 657, 900 *fure*; 890 *hure*; 1031, 1144 *fuste*; and back-spellings of *v*- as *f*-, e.g. 453 *fanward*.

549–50 *of . . . Of* are coordinated: 'as beams out of the golden gear and the good stones like beams out of the sun'.

551 *schymerynge*: Supported by BF 393 'li feus et les estenceles des hiaumes et des armeüres resplendissoient'. The verse is a stock; cf. WA 903.

552 *vpon fure*: Translate: 'The field behaved like the sky—as if it were on fire'.

556 *gremed*: We follow the grammatical form of LP. However, the precise adjective, on the basis of P *grimly* and DE *wiþ grame*, would appear to be the pp. of OE *gremian*; ample uses occur elsewhere in the corpus, in Cln, Pat, DT, and AA. Reduction of minims or approximative spellings have produced the easier LUC *greue/grene*; A has a further substitution.

557 The line parallels 558: 'Their spears passed into splinters hastily'. UDEC have a line with four rhyming syllables, but may import the stock of WA 790, DT 1195, 5783, 6406, 7248, 9666–67.

559–60 Translate: 'They shook what was ground to a sharp edge out of sheaths and pounded the metal through merciless hearts'. *mallen* appears in similar contexts at DT 9520, MA 2950 and 3841.

561 The b-verse recurs at DT 1198.

562 Like the preceding, this line is comprised of two parallel statements. L's verb forms represent past plurals, 'they sheared apart'; the verb of the b-verse is 'shatter' (as again at 1121) and its object *burnee* a group singular.

564 *goutes . . . as goteres þey runne*: Uniquely cited by Whiting G 495, but cf. WA 3359, 4923; in the first case, as here, blood runs like streams from wounds.

565 *setteþ hym vp*: Probably either MED sense 2d 'put himself in a prominent position' (he has earlier [437–40] been described as commanding a third troop held in reserve) or 5b 'made an attack'. The stressed *so* refers to events of the preceding lines. The line, as does 976 also, shows that the authorial form of this word is not *swa*, since elsewhere (321, 540, 1149, 1176) /sw/ always rhymes away from /s/.

568–72 P skips on proximate uses of the word *castels*.

569 *Atles*: The sense 'attack' also occurs at DT 6399, 7424. The approved method of elephant-slaughter—to run beneath the beast and stab it to the heart from beneath—comes from BF 398–402 but has biblical warrant; cf. 1 Macc. 6:43–47.

571–72 Translate: 'So that a hundred people clearing away what was left on the field would have enough work burying them'. Alternatively, line 572b could be construed as an adjectival clause modifying 571a. The A reading *bere* for *burie* is quite attractive, especially since Thornton alone appears to understand the preceding line. *Rispen* appears in MED as a unique usage, and *ridders* 'rubbish-removers' is unrecorded.

575 *flasches*: For the general sense, accompanied with a use of this noun, see WA 2174–75 (and, more distantly, KnT 1660 and WA 2049).

577–81 *þe burnes*: The subject of the verbs *wexen* 580 and *diȝeden* 581, with intervening materials modifiers of various sorts. The 'quatrain' has five lines, and the immediately succeeding group of lines only three.

580 The a-verse, on the basis of BF 403–5, should parallel 578a; cf. 'qui estoient tuit avuglé et estordi de la charge des hiaumes et des armeüres et de la noise et de la fumee'. And the destructive weight of the armour inspires the poet's verb *forstoppette*.

    starke-: The L reading *storte-* is certainly defensible, cf. MED *startblind* adj. However, the parallel citations (Trevisa's *Polychronicon* 6:235, the Vernon 'Miracles of the Virgin') come from Southwest Midland texts, composed in dialects resembling the scribal dialect of L. Thus, we suspect that this form represents the scribe's (substantive) dialect substitution, and follow the more northerly texts.

581 *And vnder*: Kölbing and Day supports UDEC *An hundred of*; this reading would restore a regular four-line quatrain. But UDEC seem to us likely to anticipate the similar numeration in lines 587 and 600, and may well seek to provide a second strong a-verse stave—overlooking the double alliteration of *d*rome*d*ary. For a b-verse with similar metrical structure, a trisyllabic past pl. providing a necessary extra syllable, cf. 597.

583 We simply allow this line to stand as a Langlandian verse with mute stave alliteration on *at*; see 165 n. Although we find the secondary alliteration in the b-verse suspicious, it corresponds to BF 415 'la mestre porte' and to the similar translation of that phrase at 651 (= BF 444).

586 *ma*: Both Kölbing-Day and Turville-Petre gloss *made* 'appointed'. But we suspect that P *ma* in fact represents the archetype, misinterpreted as a form of *maken* (rather than of *mo*, although recall 340) and expanded by the other manuscripts. Cf. BF 417–18 'lui douziesme des mestres de la loi'. Duggan (1988:134) notes that the trisyllabic *Moyses* required by the metre also occurs at *Cursor Mundi* 6482; cf. also Mum 1235b 'sith Noeis dayes' or lines 29 and 704.

590 *ilka*: Such a disyllabic form—PEC *iche/eche a* would be equally appropriate—is confirmed by the metre.

591 *to þe berfray*: L is contaminated from line 589.

594 Cf. DT 3170.

599 *in þe felde lefte*: A parenthetical clause parallel to the remainder of the distich: 'He alone felled a hundred of that troop and left them in the field'.

600 *in her helmes*: We retain the L reading, although not especially difficult, on copy-text principles. The other mss. simply vary on the previous line. Perhaps the original read *of helmede*, an unusual absolute participial adjective.

601–2 *fallen so picke As hail*: For this proverb, inspired by BF 408–9 'ausi espessement conme pluie' with alliterative dissimilation, see Whiting H 13–14.

602 *hepe ouer oper*: As BF 408 'l'un sus l'autre' indicates, the common alliterative use of the noun *hepe* as 'troop' (e.g. DT 991). Cf. the battle descriptions at DT 6743 and 7239 'Hurlet hom on hepis' 'knocked them down into heaps'.

603–6 P skips on line-opening *So*.

603 *blody byrunne*: An absolutely formulaic b-verse; cf. DT 1328, 7033, 7299, 9052, etc.; MA 3946, 3971 (and more distantly, 1863, 2144); PTA 62.

604–5 The b-verse of 604 is an parenthetical restatement of 603 *þe bent*. The sense runs across the quatrain boundary: 'the field was so strewn that no horse might . . .'. With the sense, cf. MA 2151–52.

607 *So myche was þe multitude*: For examples of this formulaic a-verse, cf. WA 1050 and 1372; DT 5992, 7543, 9559.

608 *mart*: P *morte* 'dead' is perhaps *durior* and may in fact be the sense of L (although cf. WA 1391 'martirde' in the same context). L could also reproduce the *marred* of other copies, a word widely used in this context in DT, e.g. 1855, 2940, 5700, 6128, 6525. Translate the b-verse: 'It would have been a wonder otherwise'.

609 UDEC might suggest an archetypal reading like 'yet fared the Romans as frik/frekliche as whan they first comen'; cf. 858.

610 *Vnriuen*: As earlier at 411, L *Ronnen* conceals a more difficult verb; and cf. the nearly universal error *roos* for *roof* 59. We follow A *Vnriven* 'unpierced, (hence) unwounded'; the usage parallels 609 *reste* 'undamaged'. Accommodating the substitution *ronnen* requires secondary syntactic variation, conversion of the prefix *vn-/on-* to *ouer*.

611 L is perhaps scribal, as are UDE. Turville-Petre prints an a-verse based on P(612a) +UDEC(611), together with the b-verse of P(612a). But this line looks corrupt, and *breke on* has no parallels in MED (the sense 'start to speak' is not only irrelevant but unrecorded after Katherine Group). Thus, we find the situation one where it is appropriate to invoke the rule of copy-text. Perhaps the archetypal scribe skipped from 609 *come* to 612 *complyn*, with some subsequent efforts at corrections; scribes may have noted these only in part and attempted to fill out the quatrain (note the wealth of extra lines after 612).

612 The b-verse is probably metrically acceptable, an example of the frame prep. + adj. + sb., as line 1150 (Duggan 1988:134 sees it as an anomaly): either [*þe*] *complyn* or UC *complynes* would be certainly metrical.

613 More hyperbolic than BF 425–27, which describes 53,000 dead.

614 *fallen*: This LP(E) reading seems relatively automatic with *fey*; although the *fownden* of the other copies may be preferable, we find this a situation in which to retain copy-text. (BF 425–26 includes no parallel materials.) L's flaccid b-verse appears derived from a form like D's *freke stopid*.

618–19 Cf. the identical line at DT 6018 (with *barres*, not *boltes*), 10739, 11148; 10463–64 closely parallel *Siege* 618–19 (and 10462 has an a-verse like 621, with alliterating b-verse of the same syntactic frame as 617b).

619 *brayden . . . brouden*: Of course, forms of the same word, but here differentiated in sense, 'tugged/pulled . . . twisted'.

620 *pinne*: Translate: 'they pitched it to the ground using the pin (in the works)'; cf. MED sense 4, especially the citation from *Arthur and Merlin* 7055. Turville-Petre, who does not distinguish *pyne* and *pynne* spellings, reads *with pyne* 'with difficulty'.

622 *vnfounded*: MED *founden* v.1, sense 5, cites abundant parallel *-ou*-spellings for OE fandian 'try, test'.

624 Cf. WA 1453.

626 *whappen*: LDE apparently anticipate a series of *quar*-words. L *Quarten* is a hapax legomenon; MED identifies DE with *quatten* (= OF catir, quattir 'to hurl'). But the anterior reading probably involves a /hw/-/kw/ cross-rhyme (cf. lines 11 and 507 above), and we follow P *Whappes* (partly confirmed in A *warppis*; and cf. DT 4743, MA 2103, more distantly WA 2353). We further emend the universally attested, but senseless, *quarters* to *quartes* 'crossbows' (see MED *quart* n., OF quartot, Kölbing and Day's emended form): BF 431–32 reads 'et d'arbalestes ator et de quarriaus'.

626–28 The U omission affects three lines which should stand at the head of a new page: the scribe apparently turned the leaf he was copying and looked ahead to the next paraph in his exemplar.

627 *fote*: 'foot of the wall'.

628 *diche*: We retain L's dialect form, following the rule of copy-text. But U *dike* (cf. A *dikes* and the P scribalism *derke*) is preferable, for its consonance with *dukes*.

631 *ȝede*: 'passed forth'.

632 *wem*: The sense is confirmed by PAUC *wounde(s)*, the form by DE *harme* (although the opening of the word has been attracted to *hadde*). As we print it, this off-verse has implicit 'was there'. But AEC, which lack *þat*, may construe the verse as parallel to line 631b, with 632a fully parenthetical.

635 With the a-verse, cf. DT 10743 (and see the distant parallel at 888 below).

    to: The LP placement of this word appears prosaic, unlike the majority *many wyes to*. But we follow our copy-text.

637 *Rathe*: Although likely an innovation by the very clever and formally conscious D scribe, the reading alliterates and is closer to authorial behaviour than the synonyms of the other copies.

638 *to ryse*: The sense is apparently causative, 'blow to make men rise'. L *aryse* seems simply an error; MED *arisen*, sense 1b, cites this line as a unique and queried usage.

639 *acry*: Presumably representing the prep. phr. *on cry*: 'commanded by a cry what was begun at once, viz.'. BF 441 reads 'fist crier'.

640 *bonke*: L has support from BF 442–43: 'et que l'en asemblast contre les quatre portes de Jherusalem' implies that the action occurs at the ramparts, not in the field, as PA *bent* suggests.

641–42 Translate: 'None should resist stripping the dead or getting girdles'. In 641b, we provide the full inflection *sparen metri causa*. Duggan (1986a:96) rejects line 642b as unmetrical, but his later considerations (1987:34–36) would seem to take such b-verse structures as licit. In any event, the UDEC verse he prefers in his earlier discussion is scribal, a secondary effort at smoothing. (The same scribes suppress another alliterating stave in 643.) With the line, cf. DT 1366, 1373.

646 With the formulaic a-verse, cf. DT 6731, MA 1797, and (especially with the reprise at 1006) WA 1447.

647 *saut*: *a saut/assault* readings simply echo the verb at the head of the line.

648 *Folke*: The subject of *Assembleden* 647. The b-verse might modify either this verb or *saut* 674b; BF 442, which lacks overt mention of the assault, would support the first interpretation.

649 *þat þey taken hadde*: Reproduces BF 443–44 'que il avoient pris', i.e. the towers from the Jews' fallen warbeasts. Thus, the quatrain distinguishes acts of appropriation from new efforts at siegecraft.

652 *Greided*: Kölbing and Day take L *Groded* to be a form of ON greiða assimilated to OE ȝe-rādian. But the spelling probably represents an effort at reproducing the pp. of that ON verb, as in PUD; cf. the ON pa. p. greiddr (and the forms 'Gret' at DT 1659, 'graid' at DT 1664). BF 444 reads 'fist drecieer'.

654 The entire line modifies 653 *wyde*: 'wide enough for five hundred to attack at once'.

655 *þe grecys*: Steps used to climb the garret, rather than ladders to scale the walls.

657 ff. Both the mss. omissions are eye-skips and independent: U responds to the identical b-verses of lines 656 and 663; E apparently skips to similar subject matter, bowmen (with the aid of the paraphs which mark the heads of quatrains).

657 *out*: Confirmed by BF 446 'd'ilec'.

658 *vnarwely*: We follow Kölbing-Day and Turville-Petre in emending to this A reading 'swiftly', confirmed for sense by D and perhaps C. So far as we can determine, the word is a hapax legomenon, but, equally, we can find no example of either the ME adjective, adverb, or verb which does not directly reflect common senses of OE earh 'timid, fearful, slack (hence slow)'. With the line, cf. WA 1513.

663 The construction is *many bold . . . to assayle*; conceivably the original read the clearer *burne bold*. D has fused the similar b-verses of lines 662 and 664, with loss of intervening material.

665 *at a bir*: 'under the force of/against an onslaught'.

667 *bonked*: Modifies *diches* 666. Variation between *aboue* and *aboute* recurs (cf. 577, 756): here we simply follow copy-text, since context might have generated either of the competing readings, e.g. 'under / high above', 'halves about'.

668 *Riȝt*: *Wonder*, scribal hyperalliteration, has been suggested to most scribes by line 666 (note D's exchange of readings).

670 Cf. DT 4739, more distantly WA 1514.

671 The a-verse is formulaic; cf. line 840, DT 5707, WA 3173 (more distantly 1523).

674–77 This piece of detail is derived from BF 452 'la poiz boulie et le plon ardant et le soufre' but ultimately goes back to Josephus's description of the siege of Jotapata (see 789–96 n). His use of heated oil/tar to defend the town is allegedly the first example of this technique in the history of warfare.

675 *brennande*: We adopt the pres. p. on the theory that *leed and brynston* are the compound subject of *schoten*, here a verb of motion 'poured', as in GGK 2314. In the b-verse, we emend to create a metrical line; we might equally have read trisyllabic *barel[e]s*, as we do *kirnel[e]s* 686.

676 *schynande*: UD may point to a *durior* reading; cf. MED *shelfen* (its sense from ON *skelfa* 'to make tremble with fear').

schyre water: Parallel uses, nearly all describing the ocean (DT 270, 1901, 12168; MA 3600), suggest that the water foams to a shiny whiteness. With the image of a waterfall, which the poet here evokes, cf. GGK 2082–83.

679 An unmetrical b-verse, according to Duggan (1988:128), who prefers AUEC, which include *þe* before or after the pp. But we assume that the line is analogous to others with historically inflected plural adjectives, e.g. 217b 'by tenfull-e wayes' or 707b 'with persched[e] sides.' Moreover, all those mss. which have *þe* lack the *durior* reading *clustred* and read *clatered* instead. This use of *clatered* appears unparalleled; for the more normal sense 'fall with a loud noise', cf. Cln 912, GGK 1722, and line 573. For the scattered uses of *clusteren* as an architectural term (the more normal sense refers to gems closely set), see DT 1634, more distantly DT 5476, Cln 951.

680 *der daies worke*: Phrasal *daies worke* and the compound *dai-worke* are essentially equivalent, and we retain our copy-text, in spite of the weight of attestation. The same phrase, in a different sense (a day's costly battle), occurs at MA 4305.

682 The a-verse modifies *wro3t*, the b-verse *pale*.

683 L lacks a line in the quatrain; translate the verse we print here: 'No one might encircle it unless he had wings (lit. feather-clothes)'. *vmfonge* 'encircle' implies movement from the outside (i.e. the Romans cannot be flanked or besieged themselves), as opposed to the following line, which describes movement from inside the palisade.

vmfonge is not recorded in MED. But the form would be a direct reflex of OE *ymbfōn* 'encompass, surround, envelop' and would correspond to quite regular derivations from compounds with OE ymb(e)-, e.g. *um(b)fold* at lines 223 and 1131, WA 4717, DT 8496. *feþerhame* appears at WA 380, 2835, 3822 to describe wings. Possibly, the locution was suggested by BF 498–500, which describes the Jews relying on carrier pigeons in their search for reinforcements and supplies; however, this description occurs only in y copies of BF.

685 *þe diches*: BF 455–56 has plural 'les fossez'; in the following verse, the supply of pronouns (*hit* LPC, *þam* AU) is perhaps scribal.

687 *stewe*: See MED *steue* n.2, sense 1d 'vapour', once from Thornton's medical book; in contrast, *steem* 'vapour' is not especially widely attested. Turville-Petre glosses *of the stewe* 'out of the moat', but the following verse indicates that medieval theories of infection through vapours are at issue here.

688 *cope*: This verb, 'to infect', is an MED hapax legomenon; the related noun (OE coðu), amid its few uses, occurs at WA 2940. But the spelling 'corit' at DT 9686, in a similar context of 'germ-warfare', is probably an error (cf. UD here) for past tense 'coþit'.

689 *cors*: L correctly sees that this noun is plural; most of line 690 elaborates upon the word *cors*, the object of *Stoppen* 'they stop'. Consequently, the verb of the L b-verse is a disyllabic present or past plural. The other scribes apparently read the noun as singular, construe *come* as past singular, and then must intrude an additional syllable to construct a metrical b-verse.

690 *strande*: 'stream'; the word is recorded primarily in northern texts, and later is distinctly Scots; cf. WA 5280, 4202, 5507; Sus 123.

696 *with*: As BF 460–61 'Kaÿfas et les mestres' implies, this is the *with* of accompaniment, dependent on 695 *he*.

698 *ech freke*: An unmarked dative with body-part (cf. 826); *were* is subjunctive 'should be' and its subject *felles*. Translate: 'that each man's skin should be completely flayed off'.

699–700 *Firste . . . And sup*: Probably coordinated with one another, rather than in temporal relation to lines 697–98. *to be* 699 is grammatically antecedent to the string of pp.s which end with *kagged* 704.

700 Cf. DT 12885, 13033.

703 *claures*: According to the etymology provided s.v. MED *clivres*, a blend of OE *clifras* with ME *clawe*.

704 *kagged*: The etymology is unclear (? ON *kǫgurr* 'a fringed quilt', in the sense of something that swaddles); this word 'to tie or bind' does not occur outside the alliterative canon (Cln 1254, Pearl 512, DT 3703, WA 1644).

Foure: Modifies 703a: as BF 470 indicates, there are two of each species; one might cf. the six beasts (subsequently elaborated as three and three) at WW 79–80.

706 *renten*: We retain copy-text, since variation with PA *ryuen* does not seem resolvable. BF 471 'esgratinoient' 'scratch' probably supports L, and the PA archetypal scribe may have anticipated *persched* at the end of the next line.

708 *syed*: We take D to be *durior* here. Although it occurs frequently in Laȝamon, there are only three late fourteenth-century examples of *sien*: *Firumbras* 589, *Otuel* 1393, Chaucer's *Troilus* 5.182. For the summer day, see Whiting S 880.

709 *ledes*: We do not believe PUD engage in scribal hyperalliteration here; the locution is at least partly ironic.

710 *topsailes*: For metricality, we follow Duggan's suggestion that the adverb has the suffix *-es*, as in DT 1219, cited by Turville-Petre. Cf. also the metrical adverbial forms in *-es* at line 30 (*inmyddis*), DT 6638, 7249, 7434 (all *hedstoupis*), and 7485 (*hedlynges*).

712 *þat*: In strictly logical grammar, the antecedent is 710 *a tre*, but the poet also relies on the more distant locution *heye galwes . . . alle folke to byholden* 700–1. The spectacle echoes the crucifixion in which the Jewish elders participated.

 dryuen: See MED *driven* v., sense 10a ('bear, suffer'). Although the disposition of the variants might suggest an anterior *dri(ȝ)en* (cf. 124 above), P *drow* may simply respond to archetypal *drouen* '? drove' '? drew'; see 574.

715 *hem by*: LP *here* shows the attraction both of the subsequent noun *heere* and 714 *here*.

718–24 We perform extensive, although minimalist, surgery throughout this passage, in the belief that originally the construction followed the extensive subordination and parallelism of BF 484–86: 'Puis fist alumer . . . et fist geter . . . Et ilec fist ardoir . . . et puis fist la poudre venter et espandre'. From *bade* until the end of 724 is all Vespasian's speech (including in 723 one bit of directed speech within speech). To convey this, we change a series of scribal efforts to depict simple action with past tense verbs into the series of imperatives which follow on the command here. See further 723 n.

719 *alle*: This line and 725 have apparently exchanged their concluding adjectives. Given the weight of attestation, this transposition, stimulated by the attraction of 726 *Al*, seems more likely to have occurred in L than in the remaining copies (although note D's further exchanges).

720 *browne askes*: With this formulaic b-verse, cf. DT 2646 and 7150, PPC 3.126, more distantly GGK 2.

723 *adoun*: The majority reading *a duke* seems to us secondary, an intrusion of a personal speaker provided by scribes who do not understand that this is a quoted statement. The L grammatical frame for 723 would seem to indicate that L's archetype retained direct speech at this point, but we must provide one final conversion of past *bade* to imperative *bidde* in line 724 to close out Vespasian's direct address.

724 *bible*: An attested form for this verb 'to drink'; cf. Chaucer's 'Reeve's Tale' 4162 vars. and *Chester Plays* 138/153.

726 The majority omission, presumably archetypal, reflects simple eyeskip on the openings *to*brused and *to*ken; the P omission of the following line is a separate error. And another independent omission will occur shortly: E returned to copy a paraph too far along after copying line 729.

727 *In tokne of*: BF 489–93 provides an elaborate 'tokening', an allegorization of the various beasts used in these torments.

729–33 One of the major passages in which *The Siege* and DT converge for several lines; here cf. DT 7348–53. Line 730, in addition to appearing as DT 7350, also occurs at DT 7809 and 9932. And line 729 is DT 6016 (and its b-verse occurs at WA 561), as well as 7348, just as line 733 recurs at DT 6037, as well as 7353 (there converted to rhyme in /t/).

731 *rysten*: Kölbing and Day plausibly identify the word as a reflex of ON *hrista* 'to shake', with a number of Icelandic uses referring to beards and horses' manes. MED, less convincingly, follows L *rusken*, which it associates with the ON verb 'to rush'.

732 A verb of motion is implicit in both half-lines.

736 *chek-wecche*: An MED hapax, with the apparent sense 'watch against checks, i.e. assaults' (cf. the uses of the noun *chek* at Cln 1238, MA 1986, WA 3098).

738 Cf. DT 10096.

742 *lyften*: In the absence of a recorded verb *liftnen*, we take L *lyfteneþ* to be an inadvertently doubled plural inflection. Perhaps L's archetype, like DC's, had *vp*, which the scribe assimilated to the verb; cf. the similar absorption of *on* 595.

743 *with*: 'To the accompaniment of'; 744 further elaborates this halfline.

745 *busked*: This verb specifically means 'put on one's clothes', as *bounys* does not. All texts but L reduce *busked* toward a simple verb of motion, probably under the influence of line 743.

746 *fronte . . . fourche*: Given the subsequent description of Vespasian drawing his byrnie over cloth, the clothing should run from his head or shoulders to his hips. We print those variants which allow such a reading. Most mss., within the exigencies of rhyme, simply have him dress in the proverbial head-to-foot manner.

749 *grate*: Cf. MED *grate* n.3 'seat for a lance in a breastplate' (the only other uses at *Libeaus* 1645, Mirk's *Festial* 133/28).

753 *alofte*: I.e., 'above' his girdled loins (described in the preceding line).

754 *polisched*: L *purged*, although perfectly sensible, probably is the result of assimilation to preceding *pur*. A skips on *gold* at midline from 754 to 756.

758 *hanleþ*: Kölbing and Day conjecture *hauleþ ouer*, i.e. pulls the gloves over the sleeves [sic] of his byrnie. But *han(d)leþ* is well attested with clothing and weaponry; see CIT 376; GGK 289, 570, 2505; WW 413. Moreover, in construing *glowes* 757 as the subject of *hauleþ*, Kölbing and Day create a further grammatical problem: one would expect a more explicit notation of the change of subject at line 758b. We assume that 756–57 describe Vespasian stowing his gauntlets in a way resembling the modern practice of putting gloves beneath an epaulet.

760 *viser and avental*: A conventional a-verse; cf. MA 910 and 2572; AA 408 splits the nouns between halflines.

762 *Rybaunde*: We do not find the variation with *Rayled* resolvable and follow copy-text.

763 *into þe pure corners*: Most scribes strive to remove the apparent descriptive paradox of roundness (the top of Vespasian's helmet) and linearity (the *corners*, the pointed peaks of his coronet).

764 *so*: Another example (cf. 565 n) in a line where the word would alliterate on /s/, not /sw/. But L (and UD) may simply here share a dialect substitution for the form of PA's archetype, *als(e)*. Translate *so* 'similarly', i.e. the sapphires are just as proudly set as the pearls are.

765 *stif*: Cf. the variants at lines 526–27.

766 *liȝt as a lyoun* (cf. 1001 *liouns lote*): With the usage here, cf. WA 5310 ('liȝt lions latis') and DT 5810 'Launsit as a lyoun' (more distantly, but with the same sense of violent activity AA 574). With the b-verse, cf. Day's fragment (1939, pp. 63–64) line 5; and with 1001, line 40 of the fragment. In contrast, lions' *lote(s)* are wrathful and cruel; cf. MA 118–19 and 3831; WA 612 and 3294. For 'light as a lion', see Whiting L 316; for more general uses, like 1001, L 335–36, L 344, L 348, L 350.

767 *sewen*: Arguably pt. of *see* (as most scribes construed it), but more probably the verb *sue* 'follow'.

769 *barres*: We find the variation incapable of resolution and follow our copy-text. With the line, cf. the nearly identical DT 5677.

770 *þat þe bras*: Rather than brass rings, as L assumes, this appears another example of a brazen gate (cf. 310). The proximate source of such an imposing portal is probably Poly 166–69 (and cf. Jos 6.6, fol. 299ᵛ; 5.201–6, 3:261–63), but as line 310 suggests, such architectural features may have recognized as uniquely Palestinian; cf. the Egerton *Mandeville's Travels* (Hakluyt Soc., 2 ser. 101:23): 'From [Gaza] til a hill without bare Samson the forte the gates of the city, the which were made of brass'.

772 Translate: 'Acknowledge him as your king, before you receive more (destruction)'. Cf. e.g. GGK 643 (to catch a wound) or Chaucer's *Troilus* 5.602 (to catch one's bane).

773 UDEC probably omit the line because the archetypal scribe knew he should return to copy following a line which opened with an imperative, but returned to the second such example, rather than the first.

776 The a-verse elaborates 775 *it*, the b-verse 775 *neuer*.

779 *defenden*: Kölbing and Day suggest following AUD *fenden of*, but that construction would then jostle with *aȝens*. We see the verse as loosely modifying 777a: 'the palisade, which forty men can defend against five hundred'.

780 *etnes*: The word may simply mean 'monster', as at WA 4872, but one might compare the abusive descriptions of Arthur's Roman enemies in MA, e.g. the Genovese giant called a warlock at 958 and 1140.

781 *menske*: 'Humane action' probably is the *durior* reading; LD *manschyp* translates the word dialectically but loses much of the semantic force: *manship* usually means 'dignity, worthiness, respect', with strong connotations of manly valour.

782 With the a-verse, cf. DT 7861.

783–84 Translate: 'No Jew speaks, but all watch for their chance (MED *pointe* n.1, sense 5c) to stone any Roman who wanders (from the barrier)'.

783–88 P, which opens line 789 with *þan*, has skipped on that initial word.

785 *wode*: In spite of attestation, we find the variation incapable of resolution and follow copy-text.

788 *owene*: 'acknowledge' (MED *ouen*, sense 1d; cf. DT 8956).

789 *gynful*: We believe this adjective 'tricky' Josephus's usual cognomen (cf. line 813 and the use with John at 1137); *gentyl* is a pallid substitution, only eventually relevant to the character (see 1325).

789–836 Poly 69–70 correctly identifies these events as part of the siege of Jotopata in Galilee (not Jerusalem), which occurred May–July 67 C.E. See Kölbing-Day, pp. xxiii–iv. Josephus was the Jewish commander at Jotapata, and there, after the defeat which he had, he claims, foreseen as inevitable, he defected to the Romans. The poet cleverly fuses this siege, in which water supply was a serious problem for the defenders, with the detail of the interdicted Jerusalem aqueduct (cf. lines 685–88).

792 *and . . . hengen* is correlated with *Made wedes*: the a-verse in this line is a parenthetical modifier of *wedes*. Translate: 'He had woollen cloths plunged into water as if they'd been washed and had them hung from the wall'.

795 *hade wasschyng so ryue*: L is confirmed by Poly 73–74: 'que sic illis abundabat ad vestimentorum lauacrum'.

796 *fayle*: P *tharue* 'have need of' may well be an acceptable *durior* reading, especially since the verb usually appears in an impersonal construction with an infinitive. But cf. P agreeing with UDE in a similar variant for *faylen* four lines later; the word may represent anticipatory substitution.

797 *wel ynow knewe*: L's b-verse is probably a mute stave Langlandian line. The other mss. have imported their reading from line 800a, as D's partial retention of the L reading shows.

801 *note anewe*: After protracted hesitation, we finally reject L, which has misdivided and probably misunderstood the line. *note / anewe*, implied by P, and likely archetypal, appears to us the original reading. Most scribes have, like L, reduced this to adjective + noun phrase and transposed.

802 *by halues*: This line appears pleonastic in its repetition of synonymous *side* and *halues*. *halues* might represent a scribal substitution, in this case already in O', for a reading like *ram(mes)*, which would correspond with Poly 74–75: 'Inde Uespasianus *ictu arietis* murum conturbat'. But in fact, the assault here involves, not battering equipment, but stone-throwers; note especially line 807, which presupposes only an artillery attack, not the ram both Josephus and Higden describe. See further our discussion of Jos at pp. xlvii–iii. Perhaps the best one can do is to construe the line in the spirit of 1185–86, 1191: in such a reading *by halues* might mean 'with separated troops'—cf., rather distantly, DT 13303.

806–7 Another example of the poet's inventive grammatical intricacy. Here the structure is chiastic, with 806a *side* modified by 807b and 806b *sakkes* by 807a.

808 *dyt*: L provides the less familiar word (cf. 252 n) and is arguably the source of other synonymous readings. With the a-verse, Kölbing and Day compare DT 808.

809 *runne to*: Probably 'attacked', answering Poly 77 'e contra' (cf. MED *rennen*, sense 1d(d), virtually always with personal object).

810 *pat*: Modifies *Sipes*, not *sackes*.

812 *flatten*: The uses ('fall flat') here and in line 65 (and perhaps also 1077) are, according to MED, unparallelled elsewhere.

817–18 The U and PA omissions are independent but perhaps similar in aetiology. U skipped from one midline similar to the next (*bote > fote*), and the PA archetype may similarly have returned to copy at mid-818, considered it a line already copied, and passed to the next.

818 *frytted*: Probably represents MED *freten* v.3 'tie or wrap with a thong'.

819 *many sadde hundred*: A b-verse stock; cf. WA 2739, 4011.

821 *brayden*: Here not a verb of motion (as L *bowyn* assumes) but parallel in sense to *bekered* 'threw projectiles'; cf. GGK 2377.

822 *felonsly*: The word is a synonym of *felly* 'fiercely'; scribal substitution has probably been inspired by the usual association of the root with criminality. But cf. *felon* 'adversary' at DT 8063.

823 *Iouken*: Kölbing and Day emend L's *Iolken* to *Iokken* and associate the word with 'choke'; their line thus has /tʃ/-/dʒ/ cross-alliteration (as, for example, GGK 86). But we prefer to link the form with MED *jouken* (which occurs earlier at line 304), here in a sense attested elsewhere only at Malory 238/5: 'jowked downe with her hedys many jantyll knyghtes'. Malory derived this locution from a line not in the extant text of MA but originally preceding line 2875 of Thornton's copy (2875–77 continue /dʒ/ alliteration.) Translate: 'to strike, thus bring to rest', and cf. 'chokkes' at MA 2955, apparently in the same sense. P has lost the subsequent line 824, since the scribe looked for a line ending in a word in *þ-n* and found the second of these, rather than the first.

826 *A burne*: Another ethical dative with body-part; cf. 698 n.

828 *a*: Corresponds to Poly 81–82 'ultra tercium stadium', i.e. more than three.

829 *bounden with barn*: Cf. the similar a-verse of WA 396.

    bely: Confirmed by Poly 83: 'de alui secreto'; *body* has intruded from 831. Cf. the universal bowdlerization of 'þe waast and þe wambe' at AA 578, discussed Hanna, 'A la Recherche du temps bien perdu: The Text of *The Awntyrs off Arthure*', TEXT 4 (1988), 189–205 (193).

830 *of a stayre*: Kölbing and Day read *of a staf-slyng*, following *Titus and Vespasian* 2946, a respectable reading (and perhaps dependent on the coalescence of two separate clauses in Josephus's account); but PAC ('ladder, step in one of the siege towers Josephus describes') is here *durior*. The original reading has, as Kölbing and Day suggest, conceivably been lost, and the poet may have used a word rhyming in /st/ and referring to some kind of siege equipment.

835–36 *Frosletes . . . And many toret*: The compound subject of *tilte*; *þrylled* is a pp. (and echoed in the PA variant *tirlede* 836). With the a-verse of 836, cf. DT 1551.

840 *archelers*: This PAC reading is surely *durior*, and as Duggan notes, necessary for metre. We can find no parallels to add to Kölbing and Day's note, which cites Du Cange for ML *archelharia* 'arbalista vel balista, machina jaculatoria', with two dispersed uses from French sources. The word does not occur in the British Academy *Dictionary of Latin from British Sources*.

842 Virtually the same line occurs at DT 4741.

844 *toles*: We follow P with some tentativeness: this noun 'weapons' may be a scribal guess or may be a representation of the noun *toiles* 'slings' which occurs at MA 3616 (*Toloures* 'slingmen' in 3618). The *Towneley Plays* citation Kölbing and Day adduce is not in fact parallel.

845 *steweþ*: Kölbing and Day identify the verb with the form 'stewede', which they gloss 'restrained', in MA 1489. But that usage seems more likely to mean 'struck down'. We thus would connect the verb with *stowen* 'dispose, place (advantageously)'; cf. Cln 360.

846 *forbeten and bled*: The phrase may deliberately vary on *forbeten and forbled* to imply 'seriously beaten, and they also bled'.

848 *Al: wonder* is simply scribal secondary alliteration, as earlier at 616 (E only) and 668. Such intensifications appeal to the scribes since alliteration on the stem is authorial, e.g. 462, 681, 790, 815.

852 Translate: '(stop them also) with chrism and prayers, prescribed as a medicinal charm'; cf. MED *ordeinen*, sense 7e.

854 *nempned*: P(U)DC *mened* 'lamented' is attractive, but the word could simply result from misconstruing minims. Further, *mened* appears to be secondary variation attached to another scribal error in every ms. in which it occurs. And this verb must also control lines 855–56, which *nempned* does very well ('they mentioned no woe, but dancing'); in contrast, *mened* seems senseless in this respect.

857–62 UDE skip between two uses of *tyme* at line ends, and C only contains the lines through its consultation of a text like A. Line 857 contains the first example of our transcription of L *dou'* 'done' as *don* (cf. 908, 988, etc.).

857 Cf. the frequent repetitions of this line in DT, e.g. 1079, 4814, 5647, 6061, 7133; and more distantly, WA 1628. See further Turville-Petre 1977:86.

859 *forþ with*: Kölbing and Day misconstrue the construction: the adverb + prep. cannot be coalesced into a compound. *kyng* cannot be the subject of the plural verb *Comen*: *with þe kyng* probably modifies *conseil*, and the subject of *Comen* is 860 *knyȝthod*.

862 The line recurs at DT 9862.

863 *ȝernest*: The variation—a comparable set of readings which we handle analogously occurs at 934—is problematic. We take L *on ernest* to be a homeograph and A *in haste* and PC *fyrste* to be synonymous substitutions; with L, cf. D *in iryn* for *ȝerne* at 821. On this basis, we hypothesize an authorial superlative adjective *ȝernest* 'most swiftly, i.e. first' (in 934 'most eagerly'): the word here balances *after* at the line-end. A similar scribal form, in this case confirmed as erroneous by failure of alliteration, occurs at

Mum 1438: 'And yelde hit vp in erniste and yeue hit hym foreuer'. In contrast to the Mum line, most uses of *ȝerne* in alliterative poetry do not rhyme, and the word is especially prevalent in the fourth stress position (cf. 793, 821, 1331 and numerous uses in WA and MA; but contrast GGK 498, 1478, 1526).

864 *of þat werre*: Modifies *wille*.

866 *on hande*: Probably only intensive in force; translate the b-verse 'will befall us here'.

868 *Of*: The preposition connects the a-verse with *tale* 867.

870 *lese*: L *lesne* probably reproduces a weak adj. pl. from OE lēasan; A, accepted by Kölbing and Day, has the same word in a less dialectically tinged form, although Thornton tries to avoid the absolute adj. 'faithless ones'.

871 The a-verse also occurs at DT 2128.

875 *hone*: 'dawdle, be idle', virtually limited to Yorkshire texts in the later Middle Ages. *houer and/ne hone* appears as a doublet in both the York and Towneley cycles.

878 *our strif*: I.e., 'the strife between us and them' (OE *uncer*), not some internecine Roman problem. *whyle* here probably means 'until' (cf. AC), with *marden* a subjunctive.

879 *honte*: 'Attack, chase,' as at MA 4258, RR 3.228, PPB 2.221. The word provides an ironic counterpoint, not just to the events of 889 ff., but to *hoke* at the end of the line (its sense 'depart' also occurs at DT 4621).

880 The sense follows 879b: 'to leave town without hurting *us*'.

881–82 The maximic distich occurs twice in DT, at 5170–71 and 9377–78; for the sentiment, cf. WA 1291.

884 *Apaied*: AUDEC respond to a grammatical problem, since lines 883–84 seem to turn on themselves, *Alle* referring to *þe peple*. But these mss. are surely scribal, and it is unclear whether the lines can be improved. Perhaps translate (evasively): 'All of them, pleased, assented to this opinion which pertained to the siege, just as the prince and the people wished'.

886 DE have skipped from one mid-line to the next. The nouns of the a-verse contextualize the b-verse: men who hold household office in Vespasian's (very fourteenth-century) retinue.

887 *chersly*: L has the harder reading, MED *cherishli(che)* 'affectionately', with only five citations; all the other readings are homeographs. With the line cf. DT 1292 (which reads 'chefely', not 'chersly').

891 *þe reuer*: 'The river-bank', conventionally a hawking locale; cf. MED *rivere*, sense 2, and the uses at Chaucer's 'Thopas' 737, WW 96–100, PTA 208 and 217, *Orfeo* 308.

893 The line requires an implicit verb of motion ('each man will pass', following 891 *Ride*).

897 Nero died 9 June 68 C.E., an event followed, as the poem tells, by civil war, the infamous 'year of four emperors'.

900 *þe senatours*: As Kölbing and Day note, they are unmentioned at Poly 11–12 but available to the poet through commonplace accounts of Nero's reign, e.g. Boethius, *Consolation* 2 m6 (cf. Chaucer, 'Monk's Tale' 2480–81, a direct translation from the Latin). *Senek* is lauded at Mum 305 and 1212, in the company of Sidrac and Solomon, as a model of sage truthful counsel.

901 The line occurs, with only minor variation, at DT 12424; *myd-* for *mylde* recurs at 1081.

903–6 In this description of Nero's death, the poet follows the details of LA ch. 89 (p. 377): 'Romani vero ejus vesaniam ulterius non ferentes, in eum impetum fecerunt et usque extra civitatem persecuti sunt'. The use of 'impetum fecerunt' implies that 903 *resen* represents OE ræsan, not OE rīsan.

906 With the a-verse, cf. DT 5073.

909–10 WA 132 joins materials like the b-verse of 909 and a-verse of 910 into a single /p/ line.

910 *priue*: L's *pore* shows the same difficulty with *r*-suspensions evident in 167 (and cf. the *poke/prikke* variation in 914).
   folwed: We retain as copy-text, although L may still be hearing the /f/ rhyme of the preceding line.

911–13 The A omission follows the PA archetype which apparently transposed so as to place *tronchoun* at midline in 913.

911 The a-verse occurs repeatedly in DT to describe actions involving spear-shafts; cf. 9434, 9540, 9550, 9603, 11096, 11104.

913–14, 919–20 Cf. LA ch. 89 (p. 377): 'fustem dentium morsibus exacuit et se per medium palo transfixit et tali morte vitam finivit'.

913 *with his teeþ he toggeþ*: 'gnaws', literally 'attacks with his teeth' (cf. OED *tug* v., sense 4).

914 *prikkes*: 'spike's'. L *poke* is probably the result of a misunderstood *ri*-suspension: *poke* sb. is a bag (see 1307 and n.), and the parallel verb has no recorded sense relevant to LA's *palus* 'stake' (it usually means either 'nudge' or 'impel').

917–18 *þe tale . . . coppe*: 'No low fellow will be able to boast while he's drinking'.

919 *stykeþ*: Confirmed by LA 'transfixit'.

920 *colke*: Properly the centre of an onion or an apple; the use for the human heart occurs elsewhere only at Laud Troy Book 5717.

923 The b-verse is largely parenthetical: 'it will always be remembered'.

925 At the very least, L has a defective b-verse: *chossen* does not alliterate in this /g/ line. Although the variation seems overly profuse to have been generated by simply the infinitive *gan*, PUDE testify to a three-stress a-verse and to some form of this common verb. (AC have avoided whatever difficulty appeared in the PA(C) archetype by generating a verb out of the adjective *togedres*.) Our solution represents something of a stopgap; the authorial text may not be here recoverable.

928 *lede*: PAU are correct, while other mss. echo the preceding line.

930 *fale*: A legitimate form, from OE feala. WA 2055 has identical stave-words.

931 *more*: Poly 22 'regnauit vij. mensibus' confirms this reading, as opposed to AUC 'no more', even though this alternative seems rhetorically more pointed. Perhaps the author worked from a copy of Poly or Jos where *vij.* was reproduced as *iv*.

933 *Whan*: L has imported *and* from the opening of the preceding line.

934 *ȝernest*: See 863 n.

936 *and hymself quelled*: As Poly 31 says, '[ne] propter eum bellum ciuile surgeret'.

937–48 The full account of Poly 32–40 runs: 'Vitellius post Othonem regnauit quasi mensibus vij., qui cum seuicia notabilis esset, tante tamen ingluuiei fertur indulsisse, vt cum de die sepe quater, sepe quinquies cibaret, in cena tamen quadam duo millia piscium et vij. millia auium apposita traduntur. Hic cum Vespasianum regnare metuerit, Sabinum fratrem eius occidit; deinde cum in quandam cellam timide se conclusisset, a ducibus Vespasiani inde protractus, per urbem nudus palam est ductus, capite erecto, supposito ad mentum gladio, stercore a cunctis impetitus, in Tiberim est proiectus'. There seem to us massive problems, in some measure beyond our abilities to solve, about the reproduction of this material here. Simply in terms of the English text, the quatrain structure seems to us to waver, and connections between a number of distiches appear very likely the result of scribal smoothings to preserve some semblance of a narrative.

We are particularly struck by the almost universally attested 945b–46. This description seems to us to indicate that something like Higden's material on Vitellius as glutton once stood in the poem; only such material actually explains the precision with which the author imagines this assassination. See further 945 n, and cf. 950 *his luper dedes*, a reference far from adequately demonstrated in the surviving text.

We think only a series of distiches from several (the number is impossible to determine) quatrains remain of a more extensive account. Thus, for example, materials about Vitellius's dining habits might well have followed 938. The line-ending *rauȝte* there could be the remains of homeoteleuthon, since it could correspond to Poly 35 'traduntur' (describing the offering of mountains of food to Vitellius). Alternatively, *croune* might be construed as central to the loss: it could conceivably have led to a skip to a later line answering Poly 35–36 'Hic cum Vespasianum regnare metuerit'.

940–41 We leave the first of these lines as the conclusion to a fragmentary sentence-opening. Repetition of materials in these lines seems to us a *prima facie* sign of some omission.

943 *pat as*: All openings to this line are probably scribal smoothings to construct a narrative sequence following losses, and are simply beyond our repair. On the basis of the Latin, we believe the b-verse is object of the verb *drowe* 944b: '[someone] dragged along the new emperor naked [through] all the city'; cf. Poly 38 'protractus, per urbem'. Were the text more continuous, one might feel justified in putting a preposition before *alle*. We delete 944 *hym* as a smoothing construction analogous to the AEC variants at the head of 943.

945 *gorel*: With some trepidation, we emend *gome*, the only point in our labours where we rely upon an unsupported E reading. We recognize that the form may be dittographic attraction to *gored*, but we simultaneously do not believe that it can have been stimulated by 946 *boweled*, since that word did not occur in the common archetype behind UDE. Given our previous lucubrations about the loss in extant manuscripts of materials concerning Vitellius's gluttony (see 937–48 n above), we find the word precise in its sense, infrequent enough in Middle English (only three MED citations) to believe it not an E innovation, quite unlike E's manifest efforts to recast the text, and possibly supported by its assonance with the neighboring verb. We assume *gome* to be a substitution.

946 The a-verse modifies 945 *gored*: 'They butchered the glutton like a beast so that. . .'. Cf. the similar deer-breaking metaphor at 991–92.

947 *ȝermande*: We follow Kölbing and Day in this conjecture; cf. WA 4872, where the verb appears with the verb A here substitutes, *ȝarande* 'crying out'. PE have apparently read this participle as if *ȝarn* < OE iernan and adjusted to appropriately downward motions.

952 *agayn tournen*: '(will) return'; cf. WP 1837 and 4182; 917 and 1087 here, in the latter of which the phrase translates Poly 132 'Redi'.

956 *of . . . was*: L has clarified the ambiguous *of*, 'belonging to?' 'out of?', by reordering the line. Most mss. which retain archetypal word-order accomplish the same end by supplying *oute*.

957–64 et seq. In visualizing the scene, the poet again relies on sources other than Poly. Here cf. LA ch. 67 (p. 301): 'Interea legati Romanorum veniunt, Vespasianum in imperium sublimatum asserunt eumque Romam deducunt. . . . Reliquit autem Vespasianus Titum filium suum in obsidione Jerusalem.' And cf. our discussion of possible Josephan influence, p. xlix.

958 *rapande*: We simply retain L as copy-text. Its form is at least partially confirmed by UD, and we do not believe that we can rationally choose between L and the alternative *durior* reading, P *raykande*.

961 *kny3thod*: Cf. the comparable sense of election at PPB Pro.112; 962b parallels *kny3thod*, another possible analogy to Langland's account (cf. Pro.113, 143–45).

963 *for . . . lord*: The majority word-order is prosaic and may reflect scribal objections to the metrical subordination of the noun. This line and the next assert three different political functions of the ruler—military commander, feudal superior, and opulent head of state. To these Vespasian seeks to add in the council scene an appropriate sense of 'worship' (984), fidelity to his religious oath.

965–66 P skips on proximate repetitions of *lettres*.

969 *Y best wolde*: 'I should wish the best'. The subjunctive apparently anticipates 976 ff.: in possibly breaking his vow, Vespasian would shame not simply himself, but his dependent retinue. But perhaps *wolde* represents simple past for perfect *haue wolde* 'have always wished'. The grammatical difficulty apparently motivates the various scribal substitutions for *wolde*, in PC an overt borrowing from line 971.

970 Translate: 'My son is my greatest intimate, and many others (as if) my closest relations'.

972 D returns to copy after the next line headed by *Sire Sabyn*.

973 *bro3t of blys*: Although perhaps we should follow copy-text, the grammatical neatness of V seems to us compelling. WA 1612 has 'bodword of blis' in the a-verse (and cf. WA 48), but WA 1581 splits the construction across the caesura, as does the V reading we print.

978–79 The majority transposition of these lines, accepted by Kölbing and Day, does not seem to us well-taken. Mss. which do transpose see a crescendo of action, but they retain the L grammatical frame of the sentence, with *Tille* at the head of 978.

978 The line also occurs at PTA 398, 575. Vespasian's vow includes, not only the prophecy which he invokes at 982, but also such a personal reaffirmation as 787–88.

980 *honshed on*: MED follows Kölbing and Day in taking this verb as a unique *houshen* 'humiliated them'. But the form probably represents MED *honischen* (cf. 'destroy', WA 3131 and 3919, perhaps Cln 596; 'spurn, revile, drive away' at PPA 11.48). *on* is unparalleled in the other citations, but it appears in ms. J of PPA and in eleven mss. at PPB 10.62, all of which have various substitutions for the verb. *hem* is ambiguous: either the human inhabitants or—as our punctuation indicates—the physical defences of the town.

981 *Betyn and brosten*: The strength of attestation suggests L has transposed the verbs of the a-verse.

982 Answering line 356; see our note there.

985 *semelich*: Trisyllabic, with either medial *-e-* (cf. Duggan 1988:143) or the *-e* of the vocative.

986 *wyes þe with*: 'Warriors who accompany you'.

987 *bylafte*: 'Committed (to you), having confidence (in you)'; cf. MED *bileven* v.2, sense 4. But the verse is potentially parallel to 986a, and *bylafte* an example of *bileven* v.1, sense 3 ('to remain, stay in a place').

989 *who*: This AV reading creates a metrical b-verse: an equally defensible, although unrecorded, alternative would be line-ending *oþer*.

990 *Schal*: Depending on whether one believes the word to bear stress and alliteration, the /s/ rhyme would confirm authorial *sall*; cf. 383 n.

991–92 The comparison, valorizing, not simply physical savagery, but psychological viciousness, seems stated in reverse (conceivably an archetypal error); translate: 'The man who only holds the foot at its extremity (991b modifies *foot* 992) is just as fierce as the one who flays off the skin'. It is certainly a proverb (Whiting F 112), perhaps a specifically Yorkshire one: 'For swilk a common worde men has / Als gode es he yat haldes als flaas' (*Speculum vitae* 6471–2). For the sense, a deer-breaking metaphor, cf. 879, 946, 1132, and 1308. See further Hanna 1992, pp. 107–9; and cf. the different discussion of counsel as a form of agency at Mum 743–50.

993–94 *Bytake Tytus . . . and to*: Note the variable idiomatic use after this verb 'commit to'.

995 *holde vp myn honde*: 'Pledge myself' (MED *honde* n., sense 1c(a)).
lenge: We follow copy-text; AV *lende* is equally adequate.

998 *eure*: Confirmed by A *tym*, a secondary response to homeographic *houre*, and C *kynde*, an approximating gloss.

999 *þe*: L *þy* is attracted by the neighbouring uses of the pronoun.

1003 *he hym*: In this line and the next, *he* is Titus, *hym* Vespasian (who is also *þe freke* 1013).

1004 *burnes*: In spite of the slender attestation, one must read plural here. In LP, the reference is to Sabin alone. Translate the b-verse: 'as if Titus wished him bliss/to bless him'.

1008 *tohewen be*: Attestation overrrules L's prosaic order, possibly a finicky effort to avoid the erroneous reading nearly all mss. provide.

1010 *Burnes*: We suppress LP *Alle*: these mss. write the line into a class statement (only real nobles get to kiss the book). We believe both *Burnes* and *barouns* refer to the same group, the entire company.

boden to þe honde: 'stretched their hands forth to (the book)'. But *boden* is necessarily polyvocal, since this verb also logically controls *To be leel* 1011: 'promised to be loyal'. But this line might be construed as totally parenthetical, and *To be leel* the direct complement of *swere* 1009.

1012 *þe trewe kyng*: I.e., continuing the argument of delegation or agency which has characterized the council scene, he is his father's proper deputy.

1013 *fayn as þe foul of day*: Cf. Whiting F 561 and F 566.

1014 *carful*: UDC *komeliche* is an attempt to unwrite what appears the deliberated paradox of *fayn/carful*. But cf. 199, 1022 *wepande* and the re-enactment of the paradox in Titus's joyous illness.

1015 Translate: 'You control, in order to preserve them, my bliss and honor'.

1018 *vnder God-riche*: L probably rejects what he believes *riche* adj. 'powerful'. But the UE substitution indicates a more careful reading of the archetype, as *God-riche* 'God's kingdom, heaven'.

1019 *stondande*: Although we think L's pp. *stonden* potentially defensible— it would depend upon 1017 *nold . . . wer* and would parallel 1017 *vntake*— the other mss. seem to us to have clearer grammar. L may have, as occasionally, had difficulty with a pres. p. in *-ande*.

1020 *tilt*: The PA error *tirled* has occurred earlier at 836. Note the nearly identical DT 7184.

1022 With the a-verse, cf. MA 3888.

1024 *herte*: L's sg. 'resolution' is harder than the palpably physical sense of the other mss.

1025 *þe wale stremys*: Cf. the similar b-verses of WA 75, DT 4901, and WW 460. Although conventionally glossed 'swift streams' (*wale* usually means 'choice'), it is at least possible that the line hides the compound 'whale-streams' and corresponds to such an OE reference to the sea as the compound *hron-rād* 'whale-road.'

1027–33 The episode of Titus's illness comes from LA; cf. ch. 67 (p. 301): 'Titus autem, ut in eadem hystoria apocrypha legitur, audiens patrem suum in imperium sublimatum, tanto gaudio et exsultatione repletur quod nervorum contractione ex frigiditate corripitur et altero crure debilitatus paralysi torquetur'. And see further 1039–42 n, 1043–45 n, 1047 n, 1048 n, 1049–54 n, 1057–66 n. Cf. DPR 358/21–24, 27–29: 'Palsye is an hurtinge of a partye of mannes body wiþ wiþdrawinge or wiþ priuacioun of meuynge or of felynge oþir of boþe, and comen somtyme of coolde constreynynge, somtyme of humours stoppinge. . . . [I]f þe senewis of felinge and of meuynge ben istoppid atte fulle or ikorue, þe membre lesiþ felinge and mevinge'. Sickness itself, as DPR 342/6–8 points out, is 'aʒens kynde' (cf. 1033).

1032 *was*: See 1149, 1151, and 1310 for similar examples of *wax/was* variation; and cf. L's variant *face* for *fax* at 364.

lyþy as a leke: Whiting L 181 provides no real parallels, but perhaps cf. PPB 5.81–82.

1033 *Becroked*: L points toward the harder reading; the other copies have emended to respect the quatrain boundary. We read as parallel to line-ending *woxen*; both are pp.'s dependent on *han* 1032.

1034 *so*: 'In such a state', but the brevity of the a-verse produces the expansive PD clarifications.

1036 *condit*: L *condis* is plural.

1038 With the b-verse, cf. WA 30.

1039–42 Cf. LA ch. 67 (p. 301): 'Joseph autem audiens Titum paralysi laborare, causam morbi et tempus morbi diligentissime inquirit'.

1040 *þe gome forto hele*: This UDE b-verse seems to us more attractive than the vapidity of the other texts. But neither version is exactly difficult, and it is hard to see why there is extensive variation here.

1041 *cause*: Although *case* and *cause* overlap in form in ME, the source's 'causam et tempus [the subject of line 1042] inquirit' suggests the poet intended the latter.

1043–45 Cf. LA ch. 67 (p. 301): 'dixit itaque Tito, "si curari desideras, omnes qui in meo comitatu venerit salvos facias". Cui Titus, "quicunque in tuo comitatu venerit, securus habeatur et salvus"'.

1047 Cf. LA ch. 67 (p. 301): '[Josephus] quaerere coepit, an aliquis esset, qui principis inimicus obnoxius teneretur. Et erat ibi servus adeo Tito molestus, ut sine vehementi conturbatione nullatenus in eum posset respicere, nec etiam nomen ejus audire'.

1048 In LA, Josephus arranges a dinner, with the slave at his table directly opposite Titus. In the absence of English mss. evidence, we believe it overadventurous to emend *beddes* to *bordes*, although we recognize the possibility of a virtually automatic archetypal substitution.

1049-54 Cf. LA ch. 67 (p. 301): 'Quem Titus aspiciens molestia conturbatus infremuit et qui prius gaudio infrigidatus fuerat, accensione furoris incaluit nervosque distendens curatus fuit'. The cure takes one standard form of medieval medical practice, of supplying a humour contrary to that causing the disease.

1051 *to brede abrode*: L, as usual, has substituted *spred* (see 292 n), but all mss. include the alliterating infinitive somewhere in the line. The competing variant *with þe hete* represents scribal over-specification, stimulated by the *hote* and *hetterly* of the preceding line.

1052 *resorte*: We allow L to stand as copy-text, since the *to* of all other mss. is implicit in the parallelism *to brede and resorte*.

1056 *Of*: Coordinated with *of* in the prec. line: 'thanks God for his grace and the physician for everything except bringing'.

1057-66 Cf. LA ch. 67 (p. 301): 'Post hoc Titus et servum in sui gratiam et Josephum in sui amicitiam recepit'.

1057 *Iosophus*: The AVC archetype intrudes *sir* because its scribe misses the stress shift in *Io:seph'us* which allows the word to rhyme on /s/, as it probably also does in 1039.

1062 *hym*: Several mss. have difficulties deciding where the caesura should fall; having put three staves into the a-verse, they generated an extra alliterating *gode* here.

1069 *Now*: L has exchanged line-openings with line 1067.

1071 *fourty*: The emendation seems simply commonsensical. Note at BF 501, the P reading 'par xl. iorz', as most MSS., but C's 'trois jorz' could correspond to the poet's source version.

1072 *on to byte*: Perhaps Poly 98-99 'cessantibus emptione et venditione' confirms PD; but the mss. probably anticipate, since the topic recurs, as if previously undiscussed, at 1141, after 'Titus pacem offert'.

1073 *browet*: This word may well be L's scribal doublet for *broþe*, but the competing readings have been imported from the b-verse.

1075 *schone*: Another detail potentially derived from LA ch. 67 (p. 302): 'Tanta enim ibi fames erat, quod calceamenta sua et corrigias comedebant'; Poly 99-100, although including a far longer list, most of it suppressed by the poet, has only 'coria scutorum.' But see also our discussion of Jos, p. xlix above.

1078 *Ded as a dore-nayl*: Cf. Whiting D 352.

1079 *as wolues*: The comparison (the starving Jews ate uncooked food) is inspired by Josephus (see p. xlix)—and exceeds even Vespasian's worst threat in line 786. See the rich array of comparisons gathered as Whiting W 439–41, W 452, W 456, W 465, W 467; and cf. WA 4713–16, where the wolf appears as a figure of dietary rapacity, which will even eat earth; and DT 6424–28, where cannibalism is at issue.

1080 Translate: 'The vigorous gained through war on the weak his completely full belly'.

1084 *is alofte*: We retain L as copy-text; its reading and majority *is on hande* equally reflect Poly 130 'circum*stant*'.

1089 *rych*: The alliterating synonym 'reek, smoke, fumes', which we insert, in spite of unanimous attestation of *smel*. Poly 134–35: 'nidor incense carnis sediciosos allexit' could support either reading.

1093 *in a wode hunger*: Translates the earlier description, Poly 129: 'que fame tabescens'. Here, rather than narrative, the verse may form part of Miriam's speech.

1095 *forþ* (LP): The two mss. here (and E in 1096) may anticipate line 1097, which has then been dissimilated in LP. MED *fecchen* v., sense 3 'to bring before another's view', does include the phrasal *fecchen forþ* 'produce food (from a kitchen)'; cf. Cln 1429, but see the differing uses at WW 281 and 193 above, identical with PTA 549. LP probably seek additional alliteration.

1096 *hire*: plural, i.e. even the ravenous Jews (in Jos's account criminal brigands; see 1137–40 n and cf. Poly 135 'sediciosos') are shocked by the act.

1098 *dwelle*: UDE *duren* is potentially *durior* and may point toward an original reading *driȝen*.

1100 *fine*: L's reading ('end, death') is certainly the *durior*, in fact almost too good, a reading.

1102 *destruyed*: 'Wasted, dissipated'. Those who cannot profit from food and thus are wasting it, as defined in lines 1103–4, should get none. L essentially presents the excluded category as those physically debilitated, whereas UDEC make it a matter of class ('those of no great place').

1105 *to*[1,2]: Coordinate with 1102 *To* and dependent on 1101 *demeden*; most scribes have attempted to respect the putative quatrain boundary.

1106 *þat þe gomes þenke*: 'which the men intend'.

1109–13 Given the subsequent narrative, the Jews here attempt to undermine the enclosing wall which the Romans have built. The passage allows Titus to participate in a scene of personal danger analogous to that faced by Vespasian at 815–18 (cf. Jos 6.2, fol. 296[v] [5.59, 3:219]: 'Titus autem in sua tantum fortitudine sitam esse prospiciens spem salutis'). In Josephus's account, this ambush occurs at an early point in setting the siege, *c.* May 70 C.E.

1113 *after*: We retain L as copy-text, especially given the partial support of AVDE. But Poly 85 'die quadam' more directly supports UC *on*, also partially supported in AVDE.

1114 *sixty*: Poly 86 has 'sexcentis' six hundred, from Jos 6.2, fol. 296ᵛ (5.52, 3:217).

1115 The a-verse is adjectival and modifies *Tytus* 1113, who wanders without the mass of his troops. In contrast, the b-verse is enjambed into the following line and modifies *brake*.

1116 *brigt hedis*: This synecdoche means just what the UDEC specification *helmes* says, 'head-coverings, helmets, i.e. warriors'.

1118 The a-verse modifies *men* 1117.

1121 *schedred*: Perhaps, given majority *shyuerde*, one should hypothesize the rare *schyndred* (cf. GGK 424, 1594; AA 501, 503). The battle at this point may represent the poet's own invention: in the sources, Titus simply manages to dash to safety. But see our discussion of Josephus, p. l.

1122 With the a-verse, cf. DT 6780 and, with *sheldes*, 1195, 9667.

1124 This line and 1196 have been exchanged, either in PAVCEx or in LUDE. The mechanism which stimulated the exchange is fairly apparent: both lines stand at the ends of quatrains, thus inferentially before paraphs, and both begin 'And many + synonym for 'man.'" Moreover, seventy-two lines, which might be roughly a page-opening in a ms. copy (cf. the formats of VU and some pages of L; D is slightly less compressed), separate the two readings.

In such a reconstruction, an archetypal scribe may have turned a page in his exemplar, forgotten that he had done so, and copied the last line on the recto now open before him (a seventy-two-line jump). But then, looking for a paraph following a 'Many a man'-line, he returned to copy in the correct place, at 1125. But, whatever the concatenation of accidents involved in displacement, the surviving mss. indicate some measure of dishonesty as well. When, in our reconstruction, the scribe arrived at 1196, he recognized the line as already copied, rechecked his text, and inserted the overlooked line 1124 in place of 1196. He may have felt the lines similar enough to be fully interchangeable and simply copied on without any indication of his activity; in any event, if he left any signal to transpose these lines into their original positions, it was ignored by those using his copy.

In that mixture of fidelity and error which typifies the entire textual tradition, we believe that the archetypal scribe *gamma*, parent of PAVCEx, transposed the lines but uniquely retained the correct verb in 1196b (see the note there). Line 1196 occurs in a passage derived from Josephus and discussed in our Introduction (pp. l–li); in this martial context, wounds of the sort 1196 describes, brainings or bruisings, 'crushings', would be particularly apt. Correspondingly, *souȝte to þe grounde* would describe the cavalry engagement (cf. 1128) the poet here imagines. Thus, we collate here the readings of AVC 1196; these are the only *gamma*-derived mss. extant at that point in the text.

1125 *hacchen*: We retain L, following Kölbing and Day, as a form of the verb 'hack', with an easy substitution—stimulated by line 1127—elsewhere. But either A (confirmed by CEx) or V (perhaps confirmed by P) is correct in the b-verse: the possibilities seem to us so finely balanced (although *hatel* is otherwise essentially limited to the *Gawain*-poet) that we simply choose that word most proximate to copy-text.

1127 *Of*: 'Off'.

1128 *þe stompe*: 'The decapitated trunk'.

1131 *vmbefeldes*: The *-e-* of *vmbe-* is otiose; see Duggan 1986: 573–74 nn17–18 on alternation of forms from OE ymb- and ymbe- for metrical purposes and cf. line 11.

1131–32 The lines may be flagrantly enjambed, following the underlying structure *vmbefeldes hem As bestes* 'rounds them up like beasts'.

1132 *haþ . . . holpen*: We retain L's perfect tense as copy-text; other scribes may have generated present forms in order to provide consistent tenses.

1133 *tentis*: *tente* sg. reflects scribal literalism: the individual should have only one.

1134 *and men*: An alliterating adjective may have dropped in O'. But the only variant at all suggestive, P *masons* (for *mynours*, not *men*), has been suggested by the collocations at 1111 and 1281.

1136 The *Whan*-clause depends on *After* 1135.

1137–40 *Ion . . . symond of his assent*: Cf. Poly 97–98: 'sed ex parte Iudeorum Simone et Iohanne contradicentibus, tanta in urbe crudelitas et fames inualuit. . .'. These figures, John of Gischala and Simon son of Gioras, are the great villains of Josephus's account. Originally leaders of brigand bands, they become the most powerful forces within Jerusalem (cf. 1160 'þat þe cyte ladde'); but they use their power despotically, both to war upon one another and to plunder the progressively weaker inhabitants.

1138 *An oþer*: 'And a second who agreed, Simon . . .', which requires a plural verb, necessary for metricality, in the b-verse. The other copies have difficulties with *An* 'And' in this context; see p. lxxxvii.

1147 *face chaungen*: 'They change expression', in ME with strong connotations of substantial emotional change as well. Given the plural verb, *face* represents the contracted *fa(ce)s*.

1148 *þat*: Modifies *wymmen* 1147.

1149 *swounen*: The UC pres. p. looks attractive: 'they fall down, swooning, they swelled up'. AE *Some* is *facilior*, an effort to make the half-lines grammatically parallel. As usual, the cluster /sw/ here alliterates apart from /s/. For 'swell as a swine', see Whiting S 956, S 958.

1150 *lanterne*: Duggan (1988:132) explains the word as a metrical form in this context. A lantern-horn forms the quasi-opaque yet extremely thin pane which simultaneously protects the light and allows it to illuminate. A similar and equally unparalleled usage (cf. Whiting L 76–77) occurs at PPB 6.177.

1156 *propfred hem pes*: Titus offered peace at 1135, rejected by John and Simon. We take LDE *hadde* as generated by the second use at line's end and emend to simple past.

1157 In Josephus's account, he has long since defected and acts here as a willing Roman agent from outside the walls.

1157–58 *to enforme*: L's mislineation is probably associated with the scribe's distraction on arriving at a page boundary. Other examples of mislineation occur at A 84, PUDEC 344, E 746, L 775, P 909.

1169 *vp abrode*: One should probably interpret the spelling as equivalent to *vpon brode* 'into clear sight'.

1172b Translate: 'than of the men themselves'.

1173 *tille two ʒeres ende*: Historically, the siege was relatively brief (see 319–20 n); as Kölbing and Day see, the poet here follows LA ch. 67 (p. 301): 'Biennio igitur a Tito Ierusalem obsessa'. A similar chronology is implied in line 955.

1175 The ms. (and archetypal) version, which we allow to stand, is a Piers line with vowel-h crossrhyme, rhyming on *El-*, *hun-*, and *in*.

1178 *warwolues*: We finally reject *warlawes* 'wizards' as the more predictable reading: Jews could well be construed as heathen sorcerers or simply included within the generally abusive sense 'monsters' (cf. MA 3771; WA 3923, 4554); see 780 n. Moreover, *wolf* is supported by line 1079, and Kölbing and Day point out that the noun 'werewolf' is otherwise uncited in OED until Walter Scott.

1179 *profre*, **1180** *taken*: Like the verb forms of the following quatrain, infinitives, parallel to 1178 *To wynne*.

1184 *and*: The variation with *in* (which could be construed with *stondiþ*, as well as *styf*) is irresolvable; we follow our copy-text.

1191–93 U skips on either line-ending *scholde* or line-opening *ech(e)*.

1192 *brenyed*: LDE *brayned* probably anticipates the similarly scribal usage in 1196.

1194 *lyf:* AV *lede* is potentially harder, but might equally represent dissimilation from the preceding pres. p. In this dubious situation, we follow copy-text.

1195 *quasschyng:* This L reading has but a single parallel (from a glossary) and is probably *durior*. The archetypal scribe behind the other mss. apparently read initial *qu* as *cr*, and UDEC *catching* is a second generation rationalization of that reading. Esp. with the scribal form of A, cf. DT 4752.

1196 Cf. 1124 n. Josephus at this point provides the poet's source (see p. li); he describes actions of both miners and rams, resisted by rounds of missiles and stones. We adopt AVEx *brosed* 'crushed' here: it roughly corresponds to Jos's '[Romani] lapidibus frangerentur'. LUDE have been attracted to proximate examples of the stem *brayn*, the erroneous *brayned* 1192 and *brayn* 1203. But the reading may represent an instance when we should follow copy-text; cf. the attack with stones at 833.

1199 *peron:* I.e. on the wall, not the ladder.

1200 *for ston:* 'In spite of the stones the Jews threw at him'.
　steel-ware: The compound, attested only in U, is the prior reading and refers to projectiles launched by the Jews. LA convert *-ware* into *-gere*, which produces the senseless secondary variant VDE *-weede:* this would refer to Sabin's armor, not the missiles thrown at him.

1204 *into þe diche:* Did the poet mistake Poly 152 *confossus* 'pierced' with a form of *fossus* 'ditch'?

1210 *sowe:* 'siege engine', as also at MA 3033; see MED *soue* n.2, sense 3.

1211 *hit:* We assume that *þat* refers to *A sowe* in the preceding line, not the more proximate *Tytus*—implicit in the verb *dryueþ.* This confusion has influenced the scribes' rendition of the subsequent pronoun.

1215 *þis was þe Paske euene:* Cf. Poly 52–53: 'sed secundum Martinum et alios capta fuit in diebus Pasche' and lines 319–20 above. This detail is not Josephan; he, as Poly 49–53 indicates, is the source of the tradition that the destruction of both the First and Second Temples occurred on the same day, 9/10 Av, in late summer (*c.* 30 August 70 C.E.).

1216 *And þe:* We refrain from inserting the *to* of all mss. but L: it may be a scribal clarification of an otherwise unmarked indirect object. The plural termination of *raughten* indicates that the Jews remain the subject.

1219 *agenes:* The rhyme in this line is ambiguous, either on /g/ or /j/, although *gate* 'a (clear) road' (ON *gata*) is the root sense. We simply emend the odd /j/ stave to accommodate it to those in graphemic /g/, while also adjusting to a trisyllabic form, required by the metre and implied in the spellings of most mss.

1221 *al þe ȝeres tyme*: AVC are confirmed by Poly 163–64: 'Nam per annum ferme ante urbis euersionem'. But the signs described in line 1222 in fact, according to the sources, extended over a much longer period—the full forty years of divine forbearance mentioned at 19–24. We also follow A(V)C *ȝete*, although their preceding *ȝitt* is its scribal echo.

1224 *hold*: Confirmed in a general way by Poly 164–65 'in aere'. Translate: 'without any support save whatever came out of heaven'.

1229 *heye*: Neither Poly 174 'patria voce' nor Jos 'uoce maxima' (7.12, fol. 314ᵛ; 6.308, 3:467, to describe the last outcry in 1234–36 here) can resolve the variation with AVC *lowde*.

1231–32 *wo wo wo*: Cf. Jer. 13:27, as filtered through Apoc. 8:13.

1233 This line, attested only in AVC, corresponds to Poly 179 'vsque ad ultimum euersionis diem', as the extra line after 1236 in other mss. does not. We find the latter vacuous, unmetrical, and partially contradicting the sense of line 1236; on these bases, we take it as a scribal supply after noting a quatrain reduced to three lines. Line 1233 probably dropped out of L and UDEC's archetypes because of the repetition of *toun* at midline in two consecutive verses. Note, as typically after line 620, C's reliance on two archetypes: the scribe derived 1233 from that archetype related to AV but also, for completeness's sake, copied in the line after 1236 from his UDE source.

1234 *ȝit*: To improve the metrically defective b-verse, we transfer this word from the line head: given dislocation in several mss. at this point, that seems a modest measure. The reverse error, a word from the line-head transferred to the head of the b-verse, occurs in 474. The reading is confirmed by Josephus, if not Poly; see p. li. But the next line comes directly from Poly 181 'ictu fundibule obiit' and has no Josephan parallel.

1237 *þe vilayns*: The line lacks adequate alliteration, except in a dialect like Langland's with *þ/v* crossrhyme. We assume that *þey* is the remnant of *þe* + noun rhyming in /v/; we simply provide one obvious possibility, *þe vilayns*. In contrast to the overwhelming preponderance of lines with *devisen* rhyming /d/ in alliterating position in *Gawain*-poet and WA, the poet here rhymes the word on /v/ at 489, 760, and 960, and indeed, as Kölbing and Day (p. xxviii) noted, the prefix *de-* never rhymes in the poem (cf. *inter alia*, 1240 *deˈfeteˈ* and 1296 *diˈstroiˈed*).

1238–40 The omissions here, which leave L the only evidence for most of the quatrain, are independent examples of eyeskip: if A's *Than* 1241 reflects the AVC archetype, that skip went from the head of 1237 to that of 1241; the UDEC archetype dropped three lines owing to the similarity of the line endings 1237 *helde* and 1240 *hadde*.

1238 *witen*: As normally in OE and ME, the verb takes a double object; cf. among many examples, PPB 1.31. Translate: 'Blamed their woe on the wrong they had performed'.

1239 *þe byschup seint Iame*: James the Less, identified as 'fratrem Domini' at Gal. 1:19 (cf. Matt. 13:55), appears as the head of the Jerusalem community, thus inferentially its 'bishop', on several occasions in Acts (e.g. ch. 15 and 21:18). Josephus provides the single historical account of his death by stoning *c.* 62 C.E. at *Antiquities* 20.200 (Loeb 9:495–97). Poly 4.6 (4:346) describes his election as bishop of Jerusalem and says he held that see for thirty years; accounts of the martyrdom occur in Poly 4.9 (4:386, 408) and 4.2 (4:280).

1240 The b-verse clarifies *hit*.

1241 There is a mid-line shift of subjects: 'Their gates went up, and they all surrender themselves without . . .'. The line generally resembles WA 2273.

1242 *chertes*: AC *serkes*, which can mean 'undergarments', is attractive. The line at last fulfills Vespasian's threat, delivered by the unfortunate messengers at lines 350–52 and parodied by the Jews' treatment of those messengers at 361.

1243 *none*: UDE *morne*, although an interesting reading (cf. the formula of WA 2168 and 3979), does not alliterate. The variant is a scribal recasting, predicated on reading the a-verse in isolation, under the attraction of the adjective *merke*.

1244 *ay*: After some hesitation (contrast the AVC archetypal scribe's supply of *Ay* in 1108), we insert VUE *ay*, which balances *neuer* in the preceding line.

1245 *takeþ*: As printed, the line confirms a disyllabic form, not *tas*, but note the UEC variation (E requires a monosyllable and substitutes the past tense).

1246 *styken*: We print the present tense—L offers the vocalism of the pt. or pp. 'stuck'—essentially Kölbing and Day's emendation. This means the same as E's gloss *abyde*: because of the stench, no one could stand still in the street.

1248 *and defete*: Virtually all mss. replicate the sense of the b-verse in the earlier *for defaute*: U, with support from D, appears to us anterior and an improvement of the sense.

1250 *fleschy*: We simply retain copy-text: just as L may be influenced by 1249 *lene bones*, other scribes may be attracted by *fayre*.

1251 *balies as barels*: See Whiting B 53, B 55.

   or þat tyme: Although any judgement of the variants (echo? dissimilation?) must contend with *byfore* 1250, this reading appears potentially another example of L's fastidiousness. One might well prefer UD(C) *aforn/ byfor*.

1252 *No gretter þan a grehounde*: Although the sense is pellucid, a reference to the dog's strait waist, there seem to be no parallel uses. MA 1075 has the different simile 'grenned as a grewhounde'.

1253–72 Cf. the destruction of the First Temple, as narrated at Cln 1269– 90 and the appearance of the temple vessels at 1439 ff.

1256 *flikreþ*: *fliketh* is the *durior* reading, although its initial consonant may show influence of *ferde* 1255 and *-fure* here. But neither AUDE *strikes* nor L *stikeþ* is particularly compelling in itself, or in light of the range of variants. But there is no verb *flikken*, and we emend to *flikreþ* 'plays' (of light). MED *flikeren* has only the sense 'flutter' (usually of wings), and OED first cites the modern sense from King Lear.

1258 The b-verse modifies *dyemauntes* 1257. In the a-verse, we interpret the apparent adv. 'marvellously' as if adj. + sb. *lye* 'fire'. We would translate this half-line and 1259: 'The jewelled doors made a marvellous flame so that they shone as a lamp, always shining forth light'. With the sense of 1259–60, cf. DT 8746–48.

1260 *derst*: Representing OE þorfte, not OE dorste; the two verbs routinely share forms in ME.

1264 *brenne hit into grounde*: This conclusion, traditional in the apocryphal literature (see BF 569–70, Poly 50), contrasts with Josephus's account. In what is usually taken as a self-serving presentation of his patron, Josephus describes Titus's protracted efforts to save the temple, including a fullscale debate with his council at 7.9, fol. 312^v (6.236–42, 3:443–45). However, in the course of the assault, the temple was burned, largely, according to Josephus, by accident. During the conflagration, Titus was able to get but a single glimpse of the interior; see 7.10, fol. 313^r (6.260, 3:451). However, after the sack, he received some of the temple implements from surrender- ing priests (7.15, fol. 316^r; 6.387–91, 3:487–89); these he displayed at his triumph in Rome (7.24, fol. 320^r; 7.148–52, 3:549), and depictions of them appear on the Arch of Titus.

1267 *pulsched*: In contrast to Duggan (1988:127), who suggests *pul[i]sched* for b-verse metricality (cf. DT 11942), we take *vessel* to be an uninflected plural, a syntactic frame in which /x/x would be historically equivalent to the metrical form /xx/x.

1268 Cf. DT 3169.

1269 *fele*: L is *durior*. The *ful(l)* of the other mss. has been derived from *fele*, with secondary supply of various adjs.; these scribes, having failed to see that *metals* might be trisyllabic (and thus metrical), attempt to fill out a line they believe too short.

1275 *and iemewes*: Probably identical with the form *gemows* 'clasp(s)' (cf. MED *gemeue* 'a pair of hinges') of MA 2893. The *and* we derive from AUDEC coordinates the word with earlier *iewels*.

1276 *per*: AUE still provide unmetrical b-verses but indicate that some scribes perceived problems with this over short example. We insert the otiose *per* from L 1274, attracted to a sequence of *þ*-words in that context.

1279 *Clene*: Modifies *selke* ('pure'); cf. our note to 477.

1281 Cf. DT 4774. This demolition occurred *c.* 26 September 70 C.E.

1283 *hurled*: The UD reading is durior; cf. MED *hurlen* v., sense 3 ('to drag forcibly'). DT 12007 combines the materials of 1285a and 1283b into a single /w/ verse.

1286 *Tille*: The *alle* which follows in most mss. has been generated by ample neighboring examples (1284a, 1285b, the b-verse here, 1288b), just as has another in 1287a. The b-verse probably should be coordinated with 1285a; translate: 'For a full week, they worked to destroy the wall and looked through the whole city, until it was searched'.

1287–88 The central clause of the sentence is *Maden wast alle þe toun*. Line 1287b probably modifies *tour* 1288.

1293 *-tilt*: Although the AV variants may imply original *-tiȝt* 'pulled down with ropes'.

1295 *þey . . . seiden*: The b-verse requires a plural verb for metricality, and we insert the a-verse variants which allow such a reading.

1300–2 The mislineation of D reflects the scribe's memory that the next line to copy contained *Pilat apere*, but then his misremembering—looking back to his exemplar as if he had already copied that line and taking up the next one. But in that process, the scribe found the second relevant example and not the first—a fact which he quickly recognized (but declined to signal to the reader).

1301–8 The conclusion of the text returns momentarily to the legendary accounts (although cf. 1328 n, 1329–36 n for the poet's equal reliance on 'the historical tradition' for some details of Pilate's death). In both VS verse 18 and BF (see *Middle English Prose* 86/13–87/25), Pilate is still in Jerusalem at the end of the siege and surrenders to Vespasian. The episode narrated here, however, occurs either under the questioning of Tiberius's messenger Velosianus or, in the Harley 595 version of VS, after Velosianus has brought Pilate to Rome (VS verse 23): 'Ait illi Tiberius, "Quid inuenisti in Christo propter quem interfecisti?" Pilatus dixit, "Gens sua et pontifices terre tradiderunt eum mihi"' (fol. 7ᵛ).

1302 *he*: AVEC *Titus* is simply an effort at overspecifying the change of subject.

1302-4 The central clause is *he frayned þe freke Of þe heþyng and þe woundis*. Line 1303 is an adverbial modifier, dependent on 1304 *hadde*.

1304a This extra line, unique to L, is closely modelled on the preceding and following. By intruding it, the scribe compensates for the later line 1312 absent from his exemplar.

1305 *matere*: The widespread variant *maner* was simply generated by scribal anticipation of following *How* (with reenforcement in some copies from scribal *How* 1303).

1307 *poke*: Judas, alone of the disciples, carried a bag (see John 12:6 and 13:29 and the prohibitions of Luke 9:3 and 10:4), as was ceaselessly pointed out in the thirteenth-century arguments about Franciscan poverty.

1307-20 For this infamous detail of the legendary account, cf. VS verse 17 (Harley 595, fols. 6ᵛ–7ʳ): 'Dixit autem Vaspasianus, "Quid faciemus de istis qui remanserunt?" Titus dixit, "Vendiderunt dominum nostrum Ihesum Christum xxxᵗᵃ. argenteis, et nos demus xxxᵗᵃ. Iudeos pro vno argenteo". Et ita fecerunt'. (For the comparable account of BF, see *Middle English Prose* 88/26–30.) Historically, this cheap sale had somewhat less to do with ironic fulfilment of the gospels than with economic realities; cf. Jos 7.15, fol. 316ʳ (6.384, 3:487): 'Sola enim relicta plebe, aliud uulgus cum coniugibus ac liberis, paruo quenque pretio uenundabant. Cum multi autem distraherentur, et emptores pauci essent, quanquam uoce praeconis edixerat'.

1309 *acate*: L's reading *cate* 'sale, bargain', a variant of the stem in *escheat*, is cited by MED as a unique usage. But, given the appearance of *a-* in all other relevant variants (VUE), the form is very likely L's misunderstanding of *þe a cate*, a form the scribe construed as having a double article.

1312 *fourmed*: The line does not alliterate. In the absence of any evidence for an adjective in /f/ early in the line, we follow Kölbing and Day's perception that VC *worth* is the remains of an alliterating verb. We supply *formen* 'to create, give rise to.'

Perhaps a better line would see the initial conjunction (in L's usual form, *þey*) as the remnants of original *þof of*; cf. 7 n. In this interpretation, the second word would have been lost in all mss. through haplography, to the great muddling of the construction; and the archetypal text would have read *had be fourmed* (VC *ben worth* a fairly proximate homeograph). We would translate this reconstruction: 'Although a hundred florins had been created from each farthing'.

1315 This line should grammatically follow on 1313 *marchaundise make*. Both the lack of connection to that antecedent and the local grammar suggest that some connective at the line-head—*for* or *with*?—has probably been lost. The failure of sense may depend upon the intrusive 1314b, a clause modifying *make* 1313. But alternatively, there may be a larger disjunction, with perhaps as much as four lines of text (a distich from each of two quatrains) lost.

1316 *prophete*: Of course, Jesus, as in line 103; UDE may object to the word on the grounds that Jesus is more than just a prophet, God incarnate.

1318 Translate: 'So that all who . . . might have purchases'.

1320 The a-verse, in varying combinations, is formulaic; cf. WA 3134, 3770.

1321–24 BF 579–85, which follows the brief description of the sale of the Jews, adds a comparable statement indicating that this represents the beginning of the Diaspora. Although the siege certainly destroyed traditional biblical Judaism, centred in the observance of Temple sacrifices, historically there was no such clear break. Substantial overseas Jewish communities already existed (in Mesopotamia and Egypt, for example); and, in Palestine itself, the Sanhedrin continued to operate—just as Jewish revolts intermittently continued, until the suppression of the Bar Koḥba rebellion in the 130s.

1324 The a-verse apparently elaborates upon *her lawe* 1323.

1325 *aiorned*: We assume that L *aiorneyd* has assimilated the legalism *adjournen* 'summon, order to appear' to the commoner travel-narrative verb 'to journey.' Poly 183–84 'Titus Romam rediens adduxit secum Iosephum Iudeum' does not offer support for either reading. A's *ajoinen*, although not contemptible, seems to us overly specific: its sense, 'to charge or assign someone a duty' (cf. DT 2197, 2328, 4947), ignores *to* and makes a nameless agent responsible for Josephus's literary efforts. Finally, Josephus loses his Jewish perfidiousness, ceases to be *gynful* (see 789 n) and becomes *gentile*, here probably not just 'noble' but also, as at Pat 62, 'gentile'.

1326 *þer of þis mater*: 'Where, of this matter'. The allusion, following Poly 184–88, is not simply to *De bello Iudaico*, the poet's source, but to the longer *De antiquitatibus* as well.

    made fayr: We assume this b-verse metrical with an historically plural adjective *fayr-e*. But one might equally emend to *ma[k]ed*.

1327 *was*: The original very likely lacked the word, as do VUC; the poet counted on the parallelism 'Josephus was adjourned and Pilate put'. The varying placements of *was* reflect different scribal supplies.

1328 *Vienne*: Confirmed by Poly 2 'Viennam Gallie'; see further 1329–36 n. Poly 1 dates the imprisonment 'tercio imperii anno Gai[i]' (i.e. Caligula); this dating, presumably accurate, places Pilate's imprisonment in the late 30s.

    he poled: Although a more extensive (and, we believe, scribal) inversion is involved, we follow UDEC in placing *he* in the b-verse, where it is necessary for metricality.

1329–36 L provides six lines absent from all other copies but with clear parallels in Poly. However, quatrain structure then fails in this copy, and one must assume that the ms. has lost an additional distich as well. (Note also the UDC colophon, two alliterative lines, a scribal effort at restoring this disruption.) Such a lost couplet would probably correspond to Poly 5–6 'Qui cum moli ingenti alligatus in Tiberim proicetur'. The reference to the Italian river, rather than the Rhone which flows past Vienne, may be responsible for the variant reading *Viterbe* 1328; this error would then be of considerable antiquity in the scribal tradition, from copyings which preceded the O' loss of 1335–36.

1330 *pere*: As the next line shows, Poly 4 *pomum* 'apple' has been emended for the sake of the metre. As Kölbing and Day note (EETS 188:xxvi), this suicide in fact has been assimilated to the story of Pilate from a well-known episode in the life of Herod; see Poly 4.2 (4:286–88), or Jos 1.21, fol. 250^v (1.662, 2:315).

1333 *schef*: As usual, only L cross-rhymes /s/ and /ʃ/. Moreover, the form itself is suspect: *schef* should represent the pa. of OE *scufan*; *schof*, the pa. of the relevant OE *scafan*. Probably one should read *slit(te)* or *snoþ* (only the pres. p. of this verb recorded after Ormm). But there seem also deeper problems: *with þe same* sounds unduly legalistic; one may need an alliterating term for 'knife.' Reconstruction thus would involve a considerable supply of hypothetical readings, e.g. 'And with þe s[charp]e [þe schalk] / sch[o]f hymself to þe herte.'

1334 *kaytif as his kynde*: Probably an allusion to the life in Poly 4.4 (4:316–24); cf. especially the account of Pilate's ancestry (4:318): 'Rex quidam nomine Tirus ex Pila filia cujusdam molendinarii Athus nomine genuit filium, qui ex nomine matris et avi composito vocabulo dicebatur Pilatus'.

1337–40 Cf. BF 587–88: 'Lors se desseja et fist trousser son hernois'. But the echo of 'trousser' in 1338 has at least partial alliterative parallels; cf. DT 1733, MA 3592.

APPENDIX A
THE VINDICTA SALVATORIS

We here attempt to create a consensus text which represents the form of VS current in later medieval England, with some attention to readings of any source that appear relevant to the *Siege*. As Kölbing and Day were aware (p. xvii), the text available to the *Siege* poet and other English readers differed significantly from Tischendorf's *textus receptus*. This state of affairs goes back to at least the eleventh century. The Old English translation of VS shows a transitional form—some readings shared with our text against Tischendorf's, others shared with Tischendorf's text against ours. These readings depend, as Cross has shown, upon a single manuscript, now St Omer, Bibliothèque municipale 202, probably brought to Exeter by Leofric.[1]

We follow, for the most part, majority readings. Many of those relegated to our collations show the persistence of older texts like that Tischendorf printed. Our most flagrant emendations occur in a few places where we wrench the text into line, on the basis of minority evidence, with what the *Siege* poet translated. Our collations generally record only shared variation; a few exceptional examples draw attention to readings like those Tischendorf printed. In these collations, we ignore minor transpositions, words intruded to clarify the sense (especially pronouns and finite verbs), and substitutions of connectives like *enim* and *autem*.

As did Kölbing and Day (pp. 83–85), we use as our base-text British Library, MS Harley 595 (s. xiv[1]), fols. 3^r–9^r, to which we assign the sigil H. This we correct into a form comparable to that available to the *Siege* poet on the basis of the following MSS.:

A   British Library, MS Royal 9 A.xiv (s. xiii[2]), fols. 292rb–94rb
C   Cambridge, St John's College, MS C.12 (s. xiii ex.), fol. 127^{ra-vb}
E   British Library, MS Royal 8 E.xvii (s. xiv in.), fols. 123rb–25rb
Em Cambridge, Emmanuel College, MS 27 (s. xiii[2]), fols. 164ra–65va

---

[1] We are grateful to the late Jimmy Cross for sharing news of his discovery with us in advance of his projected book-length study of the MS.

G   Cambridge, St John's College, MS G.16 (s. xiv in.), fols. 116ra–18va

L   Lambeth Palace Library, MS 527 (s. xiv in.), fols. 63^r–67^v

O   Cambridge, *olim* University Library, MS Oo.vii.16 (s. xiii ex.), fols. 32rb–33vb (now bound as MS Dd.iii.16, fols. 66–67)

S   Bodleian Library, MS Selden supra 74 (s. xiv^1), fols. 28va–31ra

None of these copies appears in Ker. In addition, we cite, as appropriate, readings from versions more closely resembling, especially in verses 6–7, that printed by Tischendorf (B and P provide the same version):

B   Bodleian Library, MS Bodley 90 (s. xiii ex.), fols. 88^v–90^v

Hm San Marino, Huntington Library, MS HM 1342 (s. xv med.), fols. 16^r–23^v (probably continental)

P   Cambridge, Peterhouse, MS 242 (II) (s. xiii), fols. 21va–23ra

We would also note a severely compressed version, apparently derived from Eusebius, at British Library, MS Additional 38787, fols. 215^r–16^r.

on fol. 3^r | 1 In diebus imperii Tiberii Cesaris, tetrarcha [Herodes], sub
SJ 1–6 Poncio [Pilato] Iude traditus fuit Dominus zelatus a Tiberio. In
SJ 25–32 diebus illis erat quidam Titus subregulus Tiberii in regno Aquitannico in ciuitate que dicitur Burdegala. Erat enim insanus in sua nare
dextera, quia cancro dilaceratam habebat in tantum ut faciem teneret 5
vsque ad oculos.

SJ 45–48   2 Exiuit homo quidam de Iudea nomine Nathan filius Nahim; erat
enim Ysmaelita, negocians de terra in terram, de mari in mare,
SJ 49–52 de terminis in terminos orbis terrarum. Missus est enim a[d]
Tiberi[um] imperatore[m] ad portandum ei magnam pecuniam ad 10

1 tetrarcha Herodes] t. Herodes (-de Em) procurante CEm (cf. *Siege* 5–6), tetrarcha AGHLS, *om.* EO, sub tetrarcha Hm sub] *om.* CEmS   2 Pilato] *om.* HL (*perhaps read* Pilato proposito?) Iude] Iudeam CEm, *om.* OHm zelatus] zelotes (-us Em) CEm 3 Titus] *add* nomine AG Tiberii in] *om.* EO   4 insanus] infirmus CEmSHm, non sanus G   5 dextera] *om.* CEmS quia] quam A, *om.* GB cancro] cancrum CEmBHmP dilaceratam] delimatam C, delinitum Em   7 de] a CEm, ex GO Nahim] Naum CEmS, Nahum GL (sim. 21)   8 Ysmaelita] ysmaelitus A, hismaelites (-is Em) CEmS, ismaeliticus EGO, isreliticus BP, hysmahclica Hm negocians . . . terram] pergens de regno in regnum BP (cf. pergens Hm; cf. *Siege* 47–48, which may fuse two distinct sets of readings)   9 de . . . terrarum] *om.* EO est] erat CEm, *om.* S   9–10 ad . . . imperatorem] AHm (cf. *Siege* 50), ad imperatorem CEm, a Tiberio imperatore EGHLO, a imperatore S

vrbem Rome. Erat enim Tiberius insanus wlneratus quasi nouem
annis + a lepra.

|3 Voluit autem Nathan pergere ad Romam cum nauigio per f. 3ᵛ
Tyberym flumen. In[suf]flauit ventus qu[i] dicitur Auster et impulit ⁵ⁿ 53–76
nauigium illius et deduxit eum ad septentrionalem plagam per mare.
At ille recuperantes ubi Garrona fluuium ingreditur mare exierunt ad
ciuitatem que dicitur Burdegala. Et vidit Titus nauigium et cognouit
eum quod transmarinis partibus uenisset. Mirati sunt omnes ⁵ⁿ 77–80
dicentes, 'Numquam talia vidimus'.

4 Iussit Titus uenire ad + se et interrogauit eum dicens, 'Quisnam ⁵ⁿ 81–88
es?' Et dixit ei, 'Ego sum Nathan filius Nahim de gente Grecorum
missus ad vrbem Romanam iubente Pilato ad portandum Tyberio
imperatori pactum tributi eius de Iudea. Et irruit ventus validus in
mare et deduxit me in loc[um] ist[um] et nescio vbi sum'.

5 A[i]t illi Tytus: 'Si potuisses inuenire + aliqua[m] re[m] aut ⁵ⁿ 89–92,
pigmentorum aut herbarum qu[e] potuisset wlnus delere vlcus quod ⁹⁸–¹⁰⁰
in + facie mea habeo, statim ego te restituam sine dubio ante
Tyberium'.

6 Et iurauit illi dicens, 'Vivit dominus, non possum inuenire ⁵ⁿ 93–96
[talia] que mihi denuncias. Sed si in hiis temporibus ante fuisses in
Iudea, inuenire ibi posses verum prophetam nomine Iesum Cristum, ⁵ⁿ 100–10
qui erat missus a Deo et natus ex virgine + vt saluaret genus
humanum | a peccatis eorum, qui faciebat et prodigia coram f. 4ʳ
populo terre. Primum fecit de aqua vinum, deinde leprosos ⁵ⁿ 125–30

11 insanus] infirmus EmSHm   12 annis] ramis CEOS, plagis Em a] wlneratus a
HL, *om.* wlneratus¹ AG   13 ad] *om.* CEEmGOSHm   14 Insufflauit] Inflauit H,
Sufflauit P   qui]que HOS   15 per mare] *om.* CEmS   16 ille] illi AS, ille et socii
sui EO fluuium] fluuius AG, flumen EO   18 eum] *om.* AEEmGOS   quod] quod ex C,
quod a EEmS, quod de G partibus] *om.* CEmS (*corr. later* Em)   Mirati] Et admirati A, Et
mirati CEmS, a`d´miratus Hm Mirati . . . vidimus] *om.* EO   20 Titus] *adds* ducem
illum A, *add* ducem CEmS, *add* illum EGO (EO *prec.* Titus), *adds* eum Hm   se]seipsum
HL   -nam] *om.* EO, iam G   21 Grecorum] hismaelica G   22 missus] *add* fui
AEEmGOSP, *add* sum CHm   Romanam] Rome CEmGS   Tyberio imperatori] Tiberio
CG, *om.* OP   24 locum istum] loco isto EmHLS (*corr. later* Em)   25 Ait]At EHO,
corr. to Et Em   potuisses] posses EOHm   aliquam rem] de aliqua re AHL, aliqua re O
26 herbarum] herbam CEmHm   que] qui HL, quod S, vnde BP, quibus Hm   potuisset]
posset EO, posses BP   wlnus] *add* meum CEmGL   delere] sanare EOHm   vlcus] meum
AS, *om.* CEEmGOBHm   27 in facie mea] *om.* EO facie mea] faciem meam CHL, facie
GHm   restituam] restituerem CEmGSBPHm sine dubio] *om.* CEmGS   29 dicens]
om. CEmS   30 talia] *om.* HLO in] tamen AG (cf. BP), *om.* Em ante] antea EOS, *om.*
CEm   31 ibi] *om.* CEmGSB   posses] potuisses EO, *om.* (*reading* inuenisses) GBHmP
verum] unum AEO, *om.* CEmS, electam Hm (cf. P)   32 ex] de CG   virgine] *add*
Maria CH   33 et] signa et AEGL, *om.* EmS   34 terre] in terra eorum CEmS, *om.*
EO   deinde] inde ACEmGL, postea S

mundauit, cecos illuminauit, [paraliticos] curauit [et] demoniacos 35
[effugauit], mortuos suscitauit, [surdus auditum reddidit, mutos
loqui fecit,] mulierem de fluxu sanguinis liberauit que per xij.
SJ 133–36 annos a medicis curari non potuit. De v^{que}. panibus et duobus
piscibus saciavit quinque milia hominum [et remanserunt de frag-
mentis duodecim scophini pleni]; super vndas maris siccis ambulauit 40
SJ 131–32 pedibus, et talia multa miribilia fecit quorum non est numerus.

SJ 161–64   7 Quod cum vidissent Iudei, inuidia accensi accusantes senioribus
et principibus sacerdotum, tradiderunt principibus propter inuideam
et duxerunt eum + ad mortem et crucifixerunt eum et occiderunt et,
deponentes de lingno, posuerunt in sepulcro. Hunc deus suscitauit 45
die tercia a mortuis sicut ipse ante predixerat; et manifestauit se
discipulis suis in ipsa carne in qua passus est et quadraginta dies cum
illis conuersatus est et, videntibus illis, receptus est in celum et iussit
fideles suos ut baptizarentur in nomine Patris et Filii et Spiritus
Sancti, Amen. Et pollicitus illis se fore cum illis usque ad con- 50
SJ 137–40 summacionem seculi. Et lxx^{a}ij^{os}. discipulos predicare mandauit
resurreccionem suam (et eis qui ab ante dormierant in sanctitate
qui cum ipso resurrexerunt), quia lxx^{ita}. et due lingue erant per
f. 4^{v} mundum +. [Et erat] quedam femina | nomine Veronica in terra
nostra que fluxum saguinis paciebatur per xij^{cim}. annos, nisi per 55
SJ 165–72 ipsum curari non potuit. Et postea pro amore suo wltum suum
figurauit in pallio suo, qui ibi omnes aduenientes infirmos hodierna
die adorantes et osculantes, mox illos tota suauitate optata sanat a
labe.

SJ 173–76   8 Et hec audiens Titus admirans dixit, 'Ve, ve tibi + Tyberi, qui 60
wlneratus lepra circumdatus scandalo, qui tales duces misisti in

35–6 paraliticos . . . effugauit] BHmP (cf. *Siege* 127), demoniacos curauit AGHLS, *om.*
CEEmO   36–7 surdus . . . fecit] BP (cf. *Siege* 129–30), *om.* ACEGHLOSHm
38 a medicis] *om.* CEEmO   39–40 et . . . pleni] BHm (cf. *Siege* 135–36), *om.* rest
40 maris] *om.* EO   41 talia] alia CEmS, *om.* EO   miribilia] miracula CG   fecit] *om.*
AEmGLS, faciebat C   42 accusantes] add eum ACEEmOS   senioribus] add populi
EO   43 principibus²] eum CEEmOS   propter] per EO   44 duxerunt] dedux- AO
eum] *om.* AG, eum vsque HL   46 ante] antea EO, *om.* CEmS   se] se coram CEmS
47 suis] *om.* EmS   dies] diebus CEEmGOS   48 conuersatus est] fuit EO   50–
1 Et . . . Et] *om.* EO   51 mandauit] precepit EO, misit G   52 ab] *om.* ACEmGS
in] *om.* EO   53 qui] et qui CEm   resurrexerunt] surrex- EEmOS, -erant C   quia] et
CEm (*corr. to* secundum quod Em)   54 mundum] add vel terram HL   Et erat
quedam] Quedam uero HL   55 nisi] que nisi A, nisi (*corr. to* que nisi) Em, et nisi GS
56 postea] *om.* CEmGS   pro] post AG   57 pallio] populo C, panno G   qui] et
CEEmOS   infirmos] infirmi COS, infirmitates Em   58 osculantes] deosc- AG
58–9 illos . . . labe] ditat sanitate optata AG, accipiunt sanitates (-em S) optatas (adop- Em,
-em S) CEmS, sanitatem optimam suscipiunt EO   60 dixit] ait CEmOS   Tyberi]
Tyberio HL, *om.* P   61 lepra] es a lepra CEmLS

terram tuam, qui occiderunt filium Dei, liberatorem animarum
nostrarum. Verumptamen si fuissent ante faciem meam, ego eos
occidissem in ore gladii, et aliquos in ligno suspendissem, qui
5 occiderunt quem oculi mei videre non fuerunt digni'.

9 Factum est autem cum hec dixisset Titus—cecidit cancrus de   sj 177–80
facie eius et restituta est caro eius sicut antea, quando pulcrior fuerat,
et factus est sanus. Et clamans Titus dixit, 'Iudex meus et rex meus,   sj 181–88
ego nunquam te uidi, sed quia credidi, sanus factus sum. Iube me
10 super aquas in terra natiuitatis tue venire ut faciam tibi de inimicis
tuis ui[ndict]am et disperdam eos in terra ut non remaneat ex eis
[mingens] ad parietem'.

10 Et cum hoc dixisset, ait ad Nathan, 'Quod signum dedit   sj 189–94
fidelibus suis credentibus in se?' Ipse dixit, 'Hoc iussit | baptiza-   f. 5ʳ
15 rentur in aqua'. Ait Titus, 'Ego credo in eum qui sanum me fecit. Et
tu baptiza me sicut ipse precepit et mandauit'. Et iussit Nathan ut
[eum] + baptizaret in nomine sancte Trinitatis. Et cum hoc factum
fuisset, misit nuncios in Ytaliam ad Vaspasianum fratrem suum, et   sj 195–98
iussit eum venire ad se cum armigeris suis paratis quasi ad bellum.

62 filium] in terra filium EO   64 in ore . . . suspendissem] *om.* AGBP (in ore gladii
om. E)   66 cancrus] cancer CEmS, lepra EO   de] a EOB   67 fuerat] esset C, erat
EEmO, fuit S   68 dixit] ait EO, *om.* G   et] deus et EOBP   70 terra] terram
ACEEmG   venire] peruenire ACEEmGOS, ambulare BHmP   71 uindictam] Em;
vindicem BP (cf. mortem tuam vindicare Hm, cf. *Siege* 188), uictoriam ACEGHLOS
disperdam] dispergam CEm   in] cum EmGOS   72 mingens] AEmGS, quiquam C,
vnus solus EO, vna gens HL, quisquam Hm   ad parietem] *om.* EO   74 Ipse . . . iussit]
Ait nathan CEm, *om.* S   74–5 baptizarentur] -zentur GS   75 sanum] saluum CGS
76 precepit et mandauit] mandauit AG, precepit EO   77 eum baptizaret] baptizaretur
HL (eum *om.* OS)   sancte Trinitatis] *persons named* EOS   hoc] *om.* CEO
78 nuncios] *add* suos ACEmSP   79 venire] ut veniret EO

APPENDIX B
HIGDEN'S POLYCHRONICON

As did Kölbing and Day (pp. 86–89), we provide a text of those portions of Ranulf Higden's *Polychronicon* used by the *Siege* poet. We base our text upon

Hu San Marino, Huntington Library, MS HM 132 (s. xiv med.), fols. 125^r, 127^v, 128^v, 129^r–31^v.

This manuscript, from St Werburgh's, Chester (OSB), contains Higden's holograph corrections; see V. H. Galbraith, 'An Autograph Manuscript of Ranulph Higden's *Polychronicon*', *Huntington Library Quarterly*, 23 (1959–60), 1–18; cf. Ker, p. 50. We cite the very few significant variants in these passages from the two surviving MSS. with medieval provenances most proximate to the locale in which *The Siege* was composed:

H British Library, MS Harley 3600 (s. xv), fols. 119^v–24^r (from Whalley, Lancs. [OCist]; see Ker, p. 197)
L Bodleian Library, MS Laud Misc. 619 (s. xiv/xv), fols. 80^r–84^r (from Fountains, North Yorks. [OCist]; see Ker, p. 89)

Only L's reading at line 99 seems potentially useful for identifying any of the MSS. with the poet's source copy; H is excluded, not only by date but by the error in line 39.

Poly 4.7, fol. 125^r [= Rolls Series 4, 364–66]:

SJ 1327–34   Sed et tercio imperii anno Gaius Pilatum Iudee presidem, in multis accusatum, apud Viennam Gallie exilio relegauit in opprobrium generis sui, quia inde oriundus erat. . . . Missus ergo in carcerem die quadam cultro ad purgandum pomum accomodato propria manu se interemit. Qui cum moli ingenti alligatus in Tiberim 5 proicetur, spiritus maligni maligno applaudantes, inundaciones pestes, tonitrua circa locum commouebant.

Poly 4.9, fol. 127^v [= Rolls Series 4, 394, 398, 412–14]:

SJ 900   Hic etiam, ut similitudinem Troie ardentis conspiceret, plurimam Rome partem per septem dies et noctes incendi fecit, et tunc tragico boatu *Iliadem* decantabat.   10

Nero multos nobiles interfecit, e quibus fuerunt Liuia uxor   sj 898–902
Octaviani, Agrippina mater propria, soror patris sui et uxor [with
an extensive Seneca discussion following].

| Nero una et eadem die Petrum cruce, Paulum gladio, occumbere   f. 128ᵛ
5 fecit. Vespasianum ducem ad subigendum Iudeos, auariciam Flori   sj 898–99
presidis non ferentes, Iudeam mittit. Qui cum audiret Galbam in
Hispania imperatorem creatum, animo concidit. Inde ob mala   sj 903–08,
reipuplice machinata, hostis a senatu pronunciatus, ad quartum ab   923
urbe miliarium fugiens, in suburbano libertini sui semetipsum
20 occidit, anno etatis sue 32°., in quo omnis familia Augusti Cesaris
consumpta est.

Poly 4.10, fols. 129ʳ–31ᵛ [= Rolls Series 4, 418–54, with minor
omissions]:

Galba Servius post Neronem regnauit vij. mensibus, ab Hispanis   sj 925–26,
et Gallis electus anno etatis sue 73., antique nobilitatis senator, cuius   931
vita priuata insignis erat, et sepe consul, sepe proconsul, sepe dux
25 grauium bellorum fuerat. Pisonem nobilem iuuenem in filium et
heredem adoptauit; ambo tamen insidiis Othonis in medio foro   sj 926–32
occubuerunt. Otho Lucius regnauit tribus mensibus, qui cum   sj 933–36
[Vitellium] creatum imperatorem in Gallia per Germanicas legiones
audisset, bella ciuilia molitus est; in quorum tribus primis victor
30 existens, in quarto cum videret suos succumbere, ait se tanti non esse
ut propter eum bellum ciuile surgeret, sicque sese interfecit. Vitellius   sj 949–50
post Othonem regnauit quasi mensibus vij., qui cum seuicia notabilis
esset, tante tamen ingluuiei fertur indulsisse, vt cum de die sepe   cf. sj 945
quater, sepe quinquies cibaret, in cena tamen quadam duo millia
35 piscium et vij. millia auium apposita traduntur. Hic cum Vespasianus   sj 939–48
regnare metuerit, Sabinum fratrem eius occidit; deinde cum in
quandam cellam timide se conclusisset, a ducibus Vespasiani inde
protractus, per urbem nudus palam est ductus, capite erecto,
supposito ad mentum gladio, stercore a cunctis impetitus, in Tiberim
40 est proiectus. Vespasianus regnauit quasi annis viij., qui pecunie
auidus, sed non iniuste auferens, offensarum immemor, conuicia a
causidicis seu philosophie sibi dicta leniter tulit. Hic 'aliquando' ad
Iudeam missus 'a Nerone ad Iudeos compescendos', audita morte
Neronis, dimisit ibidem filium suum Titum, et Romam rediit; tricies

15 ducem] *om.* L subigendum] subiugandum H   16 Qui] Orosius Qui L
20 32°.] 37 H   28 Vitellium] *om.* HuHL   39 gladio] *om.* L   in ... proiectus] *om.*
H (cf. *Siege* 948)

et bis cum hoste in Germania et alibi valide conflixit. *Policratica, libro* 45
3, capitulo 14. . . .

f. 129ᵛ | *Ranulphus.* Hic deficiunt x. anni secundum communes chronicas
inter passionem Domini et tempora Vespasiani, prout supra dicitur
in prologo. *Iosephus, libro septimo.* Iherosolima capitur a Tito,
templum succenditur et solo coequatur, eo videlicet mense et die 50
quo prius incensum fuerat a Caldeis, viijᵃ. die mensis Septembris,
anno a prima construccione sua sub Aggeo dcᵒxxxix.; [sed secundum
sj 1175–76 Martinum et alios capta fuit in diebus Pasche]. *Egesippus.* In hoc
sj 1317–24 excidio vndecies centena milia Iudeorum gladio et fame perierunt,
centum millia captiuorum sunt vendita semper xxx. pro vno denario. 55
sj 313–20 Nongenta milia sunt dispersa. *Ieronimus.* Iccirco tanta multitudo
Ierosolimis tunc erat, quia in diebus Azimorum ex omni Iudea ad
templum confluxerant. *Iosephus.* Non est mirandum de tanta multi-
tudine Iudeorum mortua, capta, aut occisa; nam Nerone aliquando
inquirente de numero Iudaice plebis apud Ierosolimam existentem, 60
sj 49,   quam omnino vilipendebat, rescripsit Cestius preses, quemadmodum
85–86   didicerat a pontificibus, reperta fuisse in die festo Ierosolimis + vicies
centena et septinginta milia, absque pollutis et uiciatis personis,
quibus hostiam offerre non licuit. Hunc autem numerum collegerunt
pontifices per numerum hostiarum, que fuerunt ducenta quinqua- 65
ginta `sex´ milia et quingenta. Nam ad unamquamque ostiam
offerandam decem persone concurrebant. *Egesippus, libro tercio.* In
isto conflictu pericia Romanis erat cum virtute, Iudeis furor cum
sj 789–800 temeritate. Nam Vespasianus primitus, cum siccitas erat, ad urbem
Iotapaten accedens, omnes aqueductus obstruxit; sed Iosephus 70
interius commentum inuenit, quo vestes aquis infusas muris urbis
suspenderet, unde paulatim vaporantibus aquis, externi crederent
aquas illis non deesse ad potum, que sic illis abundabat ad
sj 801–12 vestimentorum lauacrum. Inde Uespasianus ictu arietis murum
conturbat, sed Iosephus saccos paleis repletos ictibus opponens, 75
plagam delusam emollit, nam solida melius per molliora deluduntur;
sed e contra Romani falces contis ligantes funes saccorum succider-
sj 813–32 unt. Iosephus tamen ardenti oleo superiecto omnia machinamenta
exussit; quibus reperandis instans Vespasianus in talo grauiter
vulneratur; quo viso, tanta vis telorum ex parte Titi proruit vt 80
vnius de sociis Iosephi occipicium lapide percussum ultra tercium

47–49 *Ranulphus* . . . prologo] *om.* H   49 a Tito] *om.* L   52–3 sed . . . Pasche]
HL, *marginal addition* Hu   58 *Iosephus*] *adds* libro 7 L   62 vicies] HL, in die festo
vicies Hu   75 repletos] plenos L

stadium excuteretur; fetus etiam cuiusdam mulieris gravide vltra
dimidium stadii de alui secreto propelleretur. . . .

   | *Egesippus, libro quinto.* Vespasiano tandem ad imperium vocato,   f. 130ʳ
85 Titus filius eius ad obsidionem Ierosolime dimissus, dum die quadam   SJ 1113–32
circa vrbem visendam cum sexcentis equitibus deloricatis obambu-
laret, concluditur a tergo a Iudeis exeuntibus; sed animum suum
audacia exacuens, penetrato cuneo ad suos redit. Verum quia acerba
odia metus plerumque comprimit, dissidentes in vrbe ad tempus
90 confederantur. Sed et pluribus Iudeorum pacem a Tito petentibus,   SJ 1105–08
Titum dolum formidans dixit suis, 'Sicut inferiorum est vti insidiis,
sic forciorum est cauere insidias, ne virtuti illudat dolus'. Quassato
ergo cum ariete muro primo, consulit Titus prouide pungnare, ne, si
desit consilium, fortitudo temeraria videatur. In ipsa quoque victoria
95 magis ˋcauendumˊ est, nam | superiorem cum inferiore pariter   f. 130ᵛ
perire victi triumphus est. Quassato tamen muro secundo, Titus   SJ 1133–40
pacem offert; sed ex parte Iudeorum Simone et Iohanne contradicentibus, tanta in urbe crudelitas et fames inualuit, ut cessantibus   SJ 1069–76
emptione et vendicione ac ciborum coctura, coria scutorum man-   cf. SJ 1141
100 derent et purgamenta olerum parietum adherentia, nauseancium
vomitus, vetera boum stercora, exuvie serpentum, equorum
cadauera, ad cibum querebantur; facilior apud aduersarios quam
apud suos pietas; patibulo ponebantur in muris ne quis fugeret; foris
captiuitas, intus fames, utrobique formido. Cingit Titus vrbem nouo
105 muro, qui xl. stadiis vrbem girabat. Girus autem castrorum denis
stadiis numerabatur, ne vllus quidem euaderet custodias ponens.   SJ 1151–56
Inualescente tandem fame, sepultor plerumque sepeliendum preuenit
ad sepulcrum, cum tanto moriencium fetore vt urbis solo ad   cf. SJ 1246
sepulturam non sufficiente, cadauera extra muros ad milia proice-
110 rentur. Quo viso ingemuit Titus, et se veniam optulisse sepius
protestatur. Multi tamen ad Romanos confugerunt, quibus cum   cf.
daretur cibus, aut nulla erat vis edendi aut digerendi. Quidam   SJ 1161–72
autem ex transfugis, dum aluum purgarent, bunones aureos egesse-
runt, quos ante fugam absorbuerant, ne insidiatores aliquid palam
115 reperirent. Comperit id quidam Assirius, et ab vno in omnes opinio
manauit; eripiuntur igitur transfuge Iudei, quamuis contra iussum
Titi, inciduntur ventris secreta, aurum requiritur. Monet Titus   SJ 1157–60
Iosephum vt Iudeos scripturis, exemplis, promissionibus, lacrimis

---

   86 visendam] videndam H   95 cauendum] *int. corr. with expunction* Hu, timendum
HuHL   99 emptione] in vrbe emptione L (cf. *Siege* 1141)   116 eripiuntur]
diripuntur H, diripirentur L

ad dedicionem si possit inflectat, sed nil profuit. *Iosephus, libro* [6]°.
Quin etiam Iohannes et Symon cum complicibus ita omnia obstrux-   120
erunt vt ne quidem Iudeis exitus neque Romanis aditus pateret.
Domus iugiter scrutabantur si quid reperiri posset, negantes truci-
cf.   dabantur. Denique uxores viris, parentes filiis, cibum ex ore
SJ 1079–80   rapiebant; si ostium domus clauderetur, statim aliquis comedere
estimabatur, vnde et domus rumpebatur; inferiores spoliabantur;   125
diciores pro suis pecuniis accusati quasi aut fugere aut urbem
prodere vellent, necabantur. *Egesippus, libro quinto, et Iosephus*
SJ 1081–   *septimo.* Tunc contingit illud factum tam horrendum quam famosum
1100   Marie alienigene, que fame tabescens paruulum quem genuerat
alloquitur in hunc modum, 'Fili mi, seua omnia te circumstant,   130
bellum, fames, incendia, latrones; redde uel semel matri quod ab ea
sumpsisti. Redi in id secretum a quo existi. Feci quandoque quod
pietatis erat, faciamus modo quod fames persuadet'. Hec dicens
filium igne torruit; partem comedit, partem reseruauit; sed nidor
incense carnis sediciosos allexit, quos obiurgans mulier sic affatur,   135
f. 131ʳ   'Silete; | non fui auara, partem uobis seruando', et ad portionem
reseruatam sic loquitur, 'Gratus es mihi, fili mi, vite mee dilatator,
percussorum repressor; qui venerunt necaturi iam facti sunt conuiue.
Gustate ergo quod matrem nouistis gustasse, aut certe totum
reliquum incorporabo. Ne pudeat uos mulierem imitari quam sic   140
epulari fecistis'. Repleuit ilico urbem tanti sceleris nefas, et Titum in
tantum commouit ut manus eleuans sic effaretur, 'Ad bellum
hominum venimus; sed, ut video, contra beluas dimicamus. Quin
etiam fere rapaces a propria spetie abstinent, etiam in summa
necessitate suos fetus fouent; sed isti proprios deuorant. Ipsos ergo   145
SJ 1197–   deleamus, quorum feda sunt omnia'. *Iosephus, libro 7.* Erat inter
1208   Romanos Sabinus quidam genere Sirus, manu et animo promptus,
perpetua laude dignus; hic quidem, niger colore, exilis habitudine,
sed anima heroica in macro corpore virtute enituit. Hic primus cum
xj. sociis murum ascendit, Iudeos fugavit, sed lapide tandem pressus,   150
sagittas et lapides paruipendens, etiam genibus innixus et scuto
protectus multos sauciauit, donec iaculis vndique confossus interiret.
Egesippus. Admotis tandem arietibus ad templum, sed parum
SJ 1237–40   proficientibus, ualuas templi auro tectas incendunt. *Ranulphus.*
Refert hic Iosephus quod propter occisionem Iacobi Iusti excidium   155
urbis et gentis dispersio prouenerit; sed verius propter occisionem

119 6] HL, *om.* Hu   122 posset] posset cibi L   128 quam] tam L
130 circumstant] circumdant L   134 nidor] odor L   142 ef-] a- H

Cristi, secundum illud euangelii, 'Non relinquent in te lapidem super
lapidem, eo quod non cognoueris tempus visitationis tue'. Quia sj 19–24
tamen Dominus non uult mortem peccatoris, sed magis ut con-
160 uertatur, et ut ipsi Iudei de preoccupacione calumpniam aut
excusacionem non haberent, per xl. annos eos expectauit per
apostolorum predicacionem, ad conuertendum sollicitauit, per
signa stupenda eos terrere curauit. Nam per annum ferme ante sj 1221–28
urbis euersionem visa est gladii ignei similitudo supra templum in
165 aere pendere. In ipsa quoque Paschali celebritate vitula in medio
templi immolanda agnum peperit. Orientalis quoque porta templi
solido ere plurimum grauis, viginti vix hominum labore claudi solita,
per plures noctes, fractis repagulis ferreis, sponte aperiebatur vix
iterum claudenda. Visi sunt etiam in nubibus acies armate et currus sj 1225–26
170 volitare per aera. In festo Pentecostes sacerdotes de nocte templum
ingredientes audierunt voces huiuscemodi, 'Transeamus hinc; migre-
mus ex hiis sedibus'. Iesus quoque Ananie filius, vir ruricola, sj 1229–36
quadriennio ante vrbis excidium in ipsis Scenophegie sacrificiis
templum ascendens cepit clamare patria voce, 'Vox ab Oriente, vox
175 ab Occidente, vox a quatuor ventis; Ve! ve! ve! Ierosolimis et
templo'. Hec die et nocte clamabat, | ita ut nec verberibus afflictus f. 131ᵛ
nec precibus rogatus desisteret; quin etiam coram Albino preside
Romano ductus, et dire tractatus proprias iniurias semper negligeret,
patrie excidium proclamaret, vsque ad ultimum euersionis diem, quo
180 murum ascendens predicta repetiit, et dum adiungeret, 'Ve etiam et
mihi', ictu fundibule obiit. *Ranulphus.* Refert Marianus, libro primo,
quod templo succenso, solum templi in odium Iudeorum exaratum
sit. *Ieronimus in prologo super Iosephum.* Post urbem euersam Titus sj 1325–26
Romam rediens adduxit secum Iosephum Iudeum, qui statim septem
185 Iudaice captiuitatis libros Grece conscripsit, quos Titus bibliothece
puplice tradidit; ob cuius ingenii gloriam Iosephus ipse post mortem
suam statuam Rome promeruit. Scripsit etiam iste Iosephus ab
exordio mundi usque ad tempora Domiciani xx. *Antiquitatum* libros.

163 Nam] Egesippus et Iosephus libro 7 Nam L   182 Iudeorum] *adds* vomeribus H

APPENDIX C: EVIDENCE OF MANUSCRIPT AFFILIATIONS

Observed agreement in variation in lines 1–166, 249–82, 370–620:

UDEC 5 emperie; 9 *puȝt was doun; 12 he . . . blode; 13 stoked; 14 blyndfelled; 14 hym; 17 þraste; 18 a[1]; 18 and; 19 hasted; 23 fewere ȝyrys; 24 princes . . . hem; 32 hit . . . togedres; 33 of flesche; 36 þe . . . after; 37–44; 37 sorer+þan; 38 in; 38 laser at; 41 helpe; 42 to; 46 souȝt oft; 50 þe athel; 50 an . . . from; 52 withtake; 52 wolde; 53 Nathan; 53 on his; 54 grounde; 54 myd; 56 on[1]; 58 Cloudes . . . lofte; 64 an hepe; 65 flatte . . . ful; 66 wedour and þe wynde; 66 hem lyked; 68 Toward; 68 kayrande on; 69 ragged tourres; 72 as . . . drenche; 73–74 om.; 77 by þat; 77 were; 78 and; 80 vnpersched; 82 yferked; 83 y am come; 84 sondisman; 84 þe; 85 seriant; 87–88 om.; 89 calleþ; 90 and . . . þou; 90 cure or craft; 93 sayde; 94 kyng; 96 eche; 101 wole y; 103 þrow . . . dedes; 118 inwardly endeles; 118 bygan; 120 þe; 122 careynes; 124 driede; 127 hem; 129 keuered; 130 boþ; 130 dombe-deue; 132 *þe halue; 135 ferre; 138 what; 138 were; 139 hem; 140 atwynne; 142 and; 142 were hoten; 144 þe outwal; 144 of; 146 was hoten; 149 is myche yloued; 150 Tadde and tomas; 153 man; 164 þrow; 165 þat[1]; 165 þat[2]; 165 nempned; 254 hit; 255 wyten; 256 was lazar-liche; 256 lyȝtter; 257 departyng; 259 kerchef; 259 fram hem alle; 259 eyr; 260 þat; 260 pople; 264 hit; 264 and for; 266 tolde hadde; 268 emperour; 270 Iewes; 270 myȝt best on; 270 take; 277 Crouned . . . boþe; 278 geuen; 278 of; 278 *grem; 283 leften; 285 on; 286 Takled and atired; 286 talterande; 289 aflot; 291 streyngþe; 383 atlest; 385 wellande; 391 folke; 396 kene bladdys; 401 brennand; 402 þeraboute; 405 wolde; 406 no[1]; 406 bot; 406 ȝelde; 415 knowe; 416 so . . . schonen; 418 and; 418 with . . . ybetyn; 421 byfor; 423 ward; 433 þe . . . toke; 433 vpon ferst; 434 soudiours; 435 as . . . midward; 435 were; 435 lenge; 437 and . . . þridde; 439 þat . . . was; 439 and; 440 in; 440 here; 448 þe place; 452 *hurdiȝsed; 459 bak; 460 Echon; 463 Many; 468 pileres; 478 tolde; 479 oþer; 481 kyppid; 486 burne kene; 487 for; 488 þrow; 490 þat was; 495 forto venge; 496 þe; 522; 523 þe; 525 þanon; 526 stampen; 526 stuffed . . . vndere; 527 a-; 529 with loude; 529 cry; 533 *dymeden; 536 *þrobolande; 537 launces; 538 crosschen; 538 doun; 541 to; 544 *bent; 545 *Souȝt; 548 hetterly doun; 554 *here; 554 heldiþ; 556 in samen; 557 Spakly; 557 *ȝeden; 560 mallen; 560 *vnmylt; 565 hit so ȝede; 566 Rideþ; 566 folweþ; 569 Atles; 570 Girdiþ; 573 Castels clateren; 573 doun; 578 as alle; 581 and vnder; 581 sone; 583 an anlepy; 583 at; 595 he; 597 herte; 600 one; 601 Iewes; 602 heuen; 605 doun stap; 606 burne, beste; 606 beste; 609 as[2] . . . rome; 610 Vnriuen; 615 of þe somme; 620 picchen (203)

UDC 18 vmbecasten; 18 with; 23 *and; 24 to; 30 he; 33 Also; 36 waspasian; 39 Out of; 39 was; 39 gon; 41 couþ; 42 grym; 48 boþe; 51 Caled; 60 out of; 65 Nathan; 68 yþes; 92 schal; 98 is most; 101 Nay; 101 non; 105 a . . . vnmarred; 106 As¹; 114 þe . . . sone; 127 Pyned; 131 Dide; 143 encresche; 147 was; 152 was; 157 whan; 157 hadde; 157 was; 157 passed; 158 for; 160 and; 160 knewen; 163 doylful; 165 þat; 258 ay ȝelden; 258 alle þo; 259 aireþ; 262 *gayly; 264 teldeþ; 272 þrow; 275 and; 280 and; 292 Brayde; 380 of oure; 385 waspasian; 392 fynde; 393 was; 397 were; 398 Of; 398 wlonkfulle; 398 worde; 398 þer . . . fondyn; 400 swerd; 403 þer; 403 werred; 404 bot ay; 404 *on; 404 þat; 406 entrete; 409–16; 410 al . . . seluere; 417 were; 419 ful of; 421 lenge; 423 sette; 423 scaped; 426 Strogelyng; 429 waspasian; 436 waspasian; 444 blesse . . . lorde; 449 fyf; 459 hadde; 462 lyste; 468 *as; 470 þat . . . bare; 472 with¹; 478 tolde; 479 kyng; 486 *after; 500 fram; 502 saue; 504 who . . . paas; 507 wheþer; 508 þis; 511 mayn; 511 and oþer; 518 *wel; 523 louten; 530 toneland; 531 ȝeuen; 531 schrikande; 536 in; 556 As; 562 gild schroud; 562 schedered burnee; 563 *woxen; 564 and goutes; 564 gold; 564 as . . . runne; 571 forþ; 571 rydders; 572 bent; 574 Dromedaries; 575 flasches; 591 and; 603 bent; 603 ouerbrad; 609 as¹; 609 rest; 610 and; 614 fey fallen; 619 brouden (116)

PA 2 seysed; 11 *bywente; 16 heraboute; 17 þraste; 19 harme; 32 *clocched; 34 nose; 36 waspene; 50 *athel; 56 and; 58 clateren; 58 on lofte; 61 harde; 70 atwynne; 71 of þe sschip; 71 ay; 71 heuen; 73 wende?; 74 yn; 84 þe; 87 londe; 87 lene; 92 schal; 92 þe redly; 94 kyng; 97 Telle; 100 chauntements . . . charmes; 122 *careynes; 135 ferre; 138 what; 139 hem; 148 bone; 148 neuer breke nolde; 162 hette in herte; 165 and; 165 þat; 165 nempned; 249 here; 250 botnyng; 254 blessed; 262 agysen; 264 hit teldeþ; 276 ferþer; 276 to; 278 and . . . stroyed; 279 hadde; 279 hestes; 289 aflot; 369–79 om.; 389 streyȝt; 391 in; 392 botnyng to fynde; 398 wlonkfulle; 402 he; 404 þat; 417 were; 418 sendel; 418 y-; 423 scaped; 432 þis; 435 were; 441 at; 443 ful; 462 wite; 463 Many; 463 was adradde; 464 fond fey; 470–72 om.; 475 was; 483 in . . . drouned; 490 ouerbrad; 501 alle; 505 mynne; 515 pendauntes; 519 tristen; 524 any; 542 Foriustes; 550 gilden; 563 woxen; 576 dascheden; 602 heuen; 602 hepe; 617 to; 620 and (84)

DE 1 tyberyus; 5 vndere; 5 his; 37 neuer; 53 toke; 57 skeweþ; 58 cleue; 61 on; 69 ragged; 76 byr; 77 bernes; 80 many; 83 nowe; 86 om.; 96 softyng and; 102 lif hadde; 116 mene; 118–20; 123 helpe; 140 ay; 149 was; 161 þe paske; 250 my; 250 y bidde; 256 er; 260 symple; 260 myȝt; 279 here; 289 floynes; 384 han þey certifiet; 396 *kene; 402 þeraboute; 405 se; 421 he; 430 and; 433 fanward; 437 fele; 449 twenti; 461 Chares; 461 chosen; 463 was; 466 was; 472 bournde; 474 a; 479 oþer; 483 drouned; 486 burne kene; 498 þe²; 517 þe; 518 wap; 534 ferde; 537 þrow; 545 souȝt . . . side; 551 For; 555 Cam; 556 gremed griffouns; 560 *mallen; 574 camelis; 574 brosten; 578 doust; 589 on;

602 hepe; 607 molde; 611 May; 611 bigly; 611 stonde; 612 om.; 612 there (68)

UC 36 was; 65 ferd; 76 was; 80 many; 83 swiþe; 86 Iewen; 92 þe . . . rewarde; 95 softyng and; 102 londe; 106 of; 112 ben; 122 kynde; 131 in mynde haue; 140 hy; 146 his; 149 was; 253 þe²; 257 his . . . awey; 260 my3t; 260 hit; 264 þe; 275 his; 277 Crouned . . . boþe; 282 Schewyng; 288 hem strengþe; 384 han þey certifiet; 388 be; 395 þe; 396 feet; 400 hadde; 406 trewes; 412 with; 413 was; 424 Sixe; 424 in sercle; 431 Iuggen; 437 fele; 441 lafte; 444 beden; 452 Ay an; 453 þo; 459 busked; 466 was; 467 atired; 467 was; 472 bournde; 509 more þing; 509 myneþ; 522 venge; 525 blonkes; 530 loude; 537 þrow; 545 anoþer; 550 gilden; 556 gremed griffouns; 573 camelis; 599 in; 603 bente; 604 aboute alle; 612 his . . . gan; 612 complyn; 614 a freke (62)

AUDEC 17 þraste; 20 þe; 24 princes; 31 þe¹; 31 þe²; 38 liter; 42 growyng; 59 on; 69 Rapis; 69 vnradly; 69 ragged tourres; 77 atte; 91 þe; 100 Oþer; 100 chauntementes; 104 one; 109 *taknyng; 111 Eche; 127 myd; 135 3itt; 159 3it; 166 hire; 249 lordlynges; 256 was; 257 departyng of stryf; 259 hangyþ; 262 Garde; 271 alle; 277 mychel crist; 281 robbyng; 283 lau3te; 382 ferre; 393 alofte; 432 hym; 442 hors; 442 harnays; 443 blowen; 485 to þe; 488 vneþ; 489 dyuyseþ; 496 hym fayntly; 521 today; 525 blonkes; 527 Stiþe; 533 lepyn; 544 ornen; 546 on þe; 561 hewen; 561 hurtlen; 566 Rideþ; 570 Girdiþ; 595 rolles; 596 myd; 602 froward; 608 mart; 619 brigges (56)

PAUDEC 22 lyte; 31 lyþ; 47 fele; 59 myddel; 82 fraynes; 89 calleþ; 97 better; 99 drenches; 106 as²; 107 saue; 108 30; 126 logge; 126 enys; 128 rered; 130 myd; 132 clerk with countours; 156 on; 254 þrye; 263 hym; 283 leften; 285 yschot; 286 yþes; 291 Galees; 383 be satled; 387 in; 391 *feld; 393 drawen; 432 bigly; 443 on; 446 in; 466 myd; 474 myd; 481 of; 484 mynned; 485 to; 492 Seiþ; 493 noþer; 496 hym fayntly; 519 on¹; 519 on²; 543 he; 559 was; 566 myd; 573 clateren; 582 standeþ; 587 hien; 591 þe²; 607 so . . . multitude; 618 barren; 619 brigges; 620 to (51)

UD 34 nose; 42 gayne; 57 wanned; 115 is þe; 117 euen; 137 sorte; 146 felawys; 156 balwe; 158 þey; 159 were; 161 princes; 164 þe; 252 dyn; 253 visage; 262 agysen; 263 visage; 266 withtane; 278 stroyed; 281 rotlyng; 285 yschot; 292 on; 383 þat; 406 toun; 410 with . . . bordored; 412 wap; 412 wynges; 444 blesse . . . lorde; 459 and; 468 on; 474 was; 507 he wilneþ; 539 Fou3t; 547 þe; 571 forþ; 591 bew-; 606 burne; 616 wonnen (37)

EC 37 þolid; 79 berne; 94 kuþþe; 98 þat²; 133 is; 135 freke; 146 felawys; 155 Suþ; 252 doil; 262 Garde; 262 agysen; 263 visage; 381 our; 391 þe²; 415 burnes; 437 þryuande; 454 and; 455 þer; 483 rede water; 494 burne; 495 þat; 495 come; 499 lat; 500 bou3t; 537 burnes; 541 tourneþ; 576 dale; 583 an anlepy; 602 ouer; 606 burne; 610 renk; 617 ledes (32)

PUDEC 4 in; 14 and; 23 fewere ȝyrys; 34 waspen; 42 no; 50 þe²; 53 toward; 54 yþes; 59 myd; 65 and ful; 108 at; 132 Nis; 257 þan; 270 who; 276 sone dere; 287 faste; 387 in; 391 fauted; 426 in; 433 vpon ferst; 450 of; 485 þis; 519 on no; 535 alle; 536 and; 550 and; 592 þer¹; 613 of (28)

UEC 21 on; 33 a; 56 þe; 65 *flatte; 66 lete; 69 vnradly; 69 vmbe; 91 grete; 112 eldres; 131 Dide; 280 byfor; 432 bigly; 444 now; 453 drowen dromedaries; 454 hosed; 455 Eche; 455 beste; 455 were; 465 *y-armed; 529 with cormous; 532 in swem; 537 beren; 551 of²; 557 þey; 576 dasscheden; 592 stadded; 601 fallen (27)

UE 52 þey; 112 tellen; 132 no; 133 is; 138 chosen; 145 Iacob; 155 he; 252 and dit; 255 alle; 386 layde; 428 bake; 450 on; 473 fyne; 476 perle; 476 pured; 497 hethyng; 524 fende; 535 dymedyn; 559 Schoken; 569 on; 585 tourneþ; 601 in . . . fallen; 603 blody byrunne; 609 were þe romayns; 617 louken (25)

DC 21 ay; 23 as; 55 ouer; 99 graces; 126 leched; 150 ben; 267 commaundiþ; 374 sende; 412 to; 423 noȝt; 442 kepe; 452 hurdised; 473 fyne; 502 one; 511 and; 512 eche; 520 one; 530 trumpes; 535 dymedyn; 559 Schoken; 569 on; 574 swyþe; 614 and (23)

AUDC 51 Caled; 67 schot; 81 hym; 82 he; 93 nyckes; 111 bot; 135 ferre; 157 henen; 165 arst was; 403 lord; 412 sprongyn; 423 to; 430 by; 435 myd-; 525 blowen; 532 hire þe water; 543 Suþ; 562 burnee; 567 came; 599 ferde; 600 *in here helmes; 614 fallen (22)

DEC 54 grekys; 64 hurled; 72 ȝo; 104 and; 125 ene; 132 couþe; 166 veronica; 256 lyȝtter; 275 body; 418 sendel; 427 arwe; 430 weren; 449 defensable; 459 bak; 477 lered; 478 and; 483 were; 518 quelle; 521 today; 532 welter schal; 552 vpon; 581 that (22)

AE 35 hyued; 39 was; 45 Now; 70 tobresteþ; 111 bot; 127 þe palsy; 147 caled; 252 loude; 386 walle; 448 to; 450 bak; 453 doun; 486 batayled; 492 my; 555 ferde; 556 As; 567 kenely; 570 þe; 610 eche (19)

UDE 34 waspen; 37 þis; 66 wedour; 80 vnpersched . . . hadde; 90 vpon; 152 byfor; 156 to-; 256 lyȝtter; 258 grace; 278 stroyed; 383 atlest; 383 sterne; 445 assembled; 475 piȝt; 490 ouerbrad; 518 *wap; 611; 612a (18)

AD 21 on; 47 fele; 49 Sensteus; 63 on; 69 vmbe; 273 wyes; 395 þe; 434 sixtene; 483 ferde; 490 to; 504 paas; 529 with cormous; 530 tabouris; 537 beren; 568 here bake; 572 a; 588 of; 600 honde (18)

AC 61 se; 77 atte; 285 þat; 287 wounden; 404 lokande; 419 gled-fure; 458 ferlich; 503 ne; 505 note; 524 Today; 544 on; 547 þe; 587 An; 611 om. (14)

PUDC 17 þrange; 51 hym; 51 to; 62 naue; 92 and¹; 115 þridde; 132 aluendel; 157 passed; 423 walles; 441 atte; 448 to; 540 om.; 563 baches (13)

AUC 13 Suþ; 55 setteþ; 78 þe; 381 þe; 464 were; 469 white; 498 and; 545 þroȝ; 549 of; 554 to; 555 Cam; 556 gremed griffouns; 620 pinne (13)

PD 13 men; 55 setteþ; 102 lede; 136 of²; 253 availed; 260 hit; 415 burnes; 426 wede; 444 now; 542 Foriustes; 574 ful; 577 aboute; 594 Chaire (13)

PE 18 slowen; 101 Nay; 104 schene; 151 and; 165 arst was; 258 þay ȝelden; 263 þe²; 269 Assembled; 283 leften; 409–12 om.; 430 forþ; 499 neuer; 567 came (13)

PC 35 ȝouþe; 135 þat; 148 his; 156 to-; 419 gled-fure; 481 þe; 488 summe; 493 nys; 508 bot; 527 þin; 543 harde; 565 setteþ; 593 and¹ (13)

PAUDC 55 setteþ; 115 myd; 156 myddel; 399 þis; 400 riches; 403 vpon; 421 formes; 484 mynned; 497 þe¹+and; 564 fram; 600 myd; 616 wunnen (12)

AU 1 þe; 35 hem; 77 banke; 89 into; 141 sorte; 143 þat; 155 Suþ; 421 he; 473 chekes; 514 hard; 607 þe² (11)

In addition, fifty-six different variational groups are recorded ten times or less in the sample. Given their dispersed attestation, we assume that all these are random, in many cases comprised of a group noted above as of frequent occurrence in agreement with an additional manuscript, inferentially from independent coincidence.

LPA 10×; LP, PU 8× each; LA, LUDEC 7×; LE, AUD, PUC, ADE, ADEC, AUEC 6×; PAE 5×; PAU, PDE, PDEC, PAEC, LAUDEC 4×; AEC, PUD, PAD, PDC, PUE, PADC, PUDE, PAUC, PADE 3×; LD, PAC, ADC, AUE, LPC, LAE, PAUD, PUEC, LUEC, LPAE, LAUDC, LPUDEC 2×; LC, LU, PEC, LUD, LUC, LEC, LPE, LUE, AUDE, PAUE, LPAC, LAUE, LDEC, LPUD, LPDE, LPAUC, LPAUD, LPUDE, LPAUDC 1×.

Observed agreement in variation in lines 621–965:

AC 628 dewe; 631 Comen; 633 passen; 634 as-tyt; 636 þe: 642 Geten; 645 kesten; 648 Folke; 648 ferlich; 651 bygonnen; 652 Greided; 660 cacchen; 660 burnes; 662 brosten; 676 Schoten; 683 myght; 688 To; 688 folke; 689 condit; 691 stockes; 692 enclosed; 697 Domesmen; 698 þat; 711 knyt; 727 and trey; 732 walle; 738 litel; 741 whan; 743 burnes; 745 of; 748 browded; 753 belteþ; 778 so; 783 was; 790 whan; 791 Made; 792 hengen; 794 Rich; 794 rises; 795 wenden; 799 abasched be; 806 and; 810 *selly; 827 forþ; 834 wymmen; 842 Dryuen; 842 depe; 844 was; 845 urnes; 847 Tyen; 850 leches; 851 waschen; 859 Comen; 860 knyȝthod; 862 þat . . . tyme; 870 lese; 878 whyle; 885 To . . . called; 891 reuer; 901 Murdred; 905 porayle; 919 hymself; 919 staf; 925 togedres gan; 925 geten; 927 longe; 933 þat; 937 raysen; 943 þat; 943 as; 946 into his breche; 951 septre; 952 for; 955 yn; 956 neuer; 958 rapande; 959 with; 960 louten; 965 þis (79)

UDE 632 wanted; 636 here; 637 schye; 653 hy3te; 655 hi3te; 676 doun; 679 kernels; 688 *þat . . . scholde; 692 þat weren; 699 to be; 714 hundred; 715 Somme; 722 alle; 725 coursed; 738 his; 745 of; 755 he; 758 hanleþ harnays; 763 prudely; 763 perles; 763 into . . . corners; 766 li3t; 789 clerk; 798 þerat; 801 þan; 801 noþyng; 806 on . . . chaf; 813 alle; 822 fou3t, felly; 822 ri3t; 823 *þro3; 837 þat tyme; 841 sponnen; 842 3euen; 845 *steweþ; 855 daunsyng; 857–62 om.; 863 Prayeþ; 863 3ernest; 864 þat²; 866 on hande; 867 þey . . . alle; 880 weme or wounde; 880 or . . . elles; 888 wacche; 888 waled men; 893 to þe solas þat; 894 on; 895 trifflyn; 897 Nero haþ; 899 apostlen; 899 seint; 899 bothe; 900 fured; 903 þe; 909 frendles alone; 913 þat; 915 spekeþ; 918 karl; 918 by þe coppe; 923 mettyn; 925 togedres gan; 934 Othis . . . ernest; 936 sathanas þe soule; 938 hym; 946 As . . . beste; 946 into; 947 3eldeþ; 949 hadde; 951 schold; 955 yn (71)

UDEC 621 wynnen; 625 kernels; 634 vnarmen; 634 resten; 636 be lafte; 637 Rathe; 639 comsed; 641 sparen . . . none; 642 and gere; 642 goode; 643 byes; 655 hyen; 675 leed and brynston; 683 fethyr-; 685 *dommyn; 686 kirneles; 690 Stoppen; 694 anon; 695 by; 701 *alle; 702 *hydeles; 705 Twey; 705 at his armes; 706 þat; 715 hem by þe; 726 om.; 735 chyuentayns out; 740 tourneþ+and; 755 on; 757 were; 758 askeþ; 760 deuysed; 762 vmbe+rounde; 770 bet; 773 om.; 780 scholde; 782 metles marre; 788 spaklokere; 788 owene; 795 here wedes; 798 lordlynges; 798 byddis; 801 *to; 812 doun; 839 on; 841 with; 844 layke . . . toles; 850 loken; 852 in; 854 þey . . . were; 854 no; 856 þe¹; 865 *toures heye; 878 *marden; 893 *lykeþ; 907 assented hem boþe; 910 folwed; 917 þe; 917 rise; 920 and; 930 Othis; 934 entriþ; 941 vpon; 948 þey; 950 þus; 953 *cite; 953 and . . . sege; 962 þro3; 964 (69)

UD 648 þycke; 676 schynande; 677 wariande; 684 my3t; 685 dommyn; 688 coþe; 688 þat . . . scholde; 689 to; 692 enclosed; 710 weren; 710 topsailes; 718 betyn; 728 þrow; 732 on; 733 abrode bette; 739 waltreþ; 740 Ofte; 753 belteþ; 756 bri3t; 756 at þe; 759 haspeþ he; 775 wynne . . . neuer; 781 were hit; 790 fayled; 796 þat; 796 þe; 801 was; 806 and; 806 side; 814 brente; 819 assembled hym to; 819 hundred; 820 oþer; 828 hit . . . feld; 834 walte; 855 daunsyng . . . deil; 866 torfere; 876 *loþe; 883 þe¹; 883 sawe; 884 Apaied; 887 falle; 890 racches; 892 fele . . . beste; 893 lyked; 895 Torneien; 896 oure lord; 909 frendles alone; 914 was; 915 þat; 920 þe colke; 921 and; 923 mynde; 934 was; 938 was; 939 sake; 949 þis; 956 was; 958 rapande (59)

PA 621 wynnen; 635 wacche; 640 bonke; 656 bir; 659 tachen; 666 holwe; 666 diches; 668 helpe; 674 picche; 678 wer; 685 dommyn; 706 renten; 717 *whan; 718 bole-; 728 whan; 732 wacche; 733 betyn; 740 for; 745 busked; 746 fourche; 763 perles; 764 *so; 765 stif; 765 *strikeþ; 769 boweþ; 776 þro3; 776 daies; 790 wondere; 795 hadde . . . ryue; 818 om.; 822 felonsly; 836 tilte; 840 manye; 841 sponnen; 842 adoun; 844 myd; 848 þat;

848 ful; 858 sembled; 867 tourned; 877 ferke; 889 hart; 890 racches; 910 folwed; 923 mynde; 928 *out . . . hym; 929 togedres; 950 þus; 953 of² (49)

EC 630 kene; 632 noȝt; 632 wye; 645 byholde; 650 ȝarken; 656 borow; 678 benden; 685 dommyn; 694 Commaundeþ; 718 betyn; 724 bible; 741 scheden; 745 bounys; 745 of; 746 fourche; 755 hongiþ; 770 brond; 781 were hit; 783 warpiþ; 806 myd; 813 bot; 829 barne; 830 burwe; 831 barne; 838 fende; 841 out; 843 out; 845 stynteþ; 851 stoppen; 853 segge; 863 wye; 868 and; 881 þe; 884 as; 884 wolde; 891 Ride; 897 noye; 904 vnquemed; 916 were; 919 stykeþ; 930 fey; 936 and; 943 þat; 948 kayȝt; 959 bodeworde; 963 chef lorde (46)

UDC 674 playande; 677 waspasian; 677 wariande; 681 þat; 685 corses; 694 consail; 700 hep; 703 *Corres; 711 corres; 718 bole-; 718 corses; 731 and; 731 rysten; 736 *chekwecche; 744 on¹; 750 colour; 752 layþ; 752 on; 752 ynow; 753 alofte; 762 vmbe+rounde; 765 bente; 778 on; 787 or; 788 efte; 797 waspasian; 803 Merken; 812 dasschande; 814 brente; 815 waspasian; 817 þe¹; 824 manye; 833 deþ; 869 Titus . . . to; 894 presen; 902 Combred; 920 þe colke; 922 waspasian; 927 þroȝ; 954 werreþ; 965 vnlappeþ (41)

DE 624 of gret; 626 whappen; 626 with; 627 þat; 628 dale; 632 wem; 633 here; 633 on; 634 as-tit; 641 spoyle; 644 *hewen; 647 saut; 651 rere; 679 kesten; 683 vmfonge; 686 hit; 687 stynk+stewe; 690 ȝede; 699 a; 699 bent; 719 kesten; 740 for; 745 bounys; 761 of; 767 echon; 777 hit who; 810 selly; 814 brennande; 830 of; 830 stayre; 831 fram; 848 werk; 873 walle; 886b–87a om.; 921 þis; 925 togedres gan; 950 þe (37)

DC 636 be lafte; 638 to; 649 þey taken; 655 hyen; 657 of; 658 vnarwely; 660 þrow kernels; 661 wel; 665 bycchet; 671 arblastes; 696 with; 700 on an; 704 to; 713 walles; 713 at; 732 abrode; 736 to; 742 lyften; 747 Suþ; 747 ouer; 749 of; 770 rynges; 771 ȝe; 802 Assaylen; 823 Iouken; 826 þe; 835 *ferst; 837 myd; 840 arblastes; 891 Ride; 900 alle; 921 bytydde; 933 to (33)

AUDEC 623 Tyeþ; 629 withdrowen; 635 vmbe; 635 to; 642 and gere; 643 bryȝt; 647 at; 685 Suþ; 687 of; 703 claures; 716 daschen; 721 Suþ; 723 for; 772 knoweþ; 774 May ȝe; 793 dryed; 801 *note anewe; 805 was Iosophus; 812 into; 820 þe; 821 barres; 821 bekered; 822 foyned; 842 ȝeuen; 847 Tyen; 852 orisoun; 852 charme; 884 Apaied; 945 Suþ; 947 ȝeldeþ (30)

UE 625 alofte; 636 wolle; 638 burnes+to; 655 hyen; 674 picche; 685 Suþ; 692 þat weren; 706 rede peces; 746 cloþes; 747 om.; 775 wede; 792 hengen; 795 hadde . . . ryue; 802 Assaylen; 813 here; 815 *waspasian; 823 Iouken; 831 brayde; 842 ȝeuen; 848 þat; 850 torche-liȝt; 878 marden; 884 þe¹,²; 897 now; 935 monþes bot þre; 950a (26)

UC 622 and; 656 bygonnen; 670 Schoten; 678 were; 689 þe²; 699 blonkes; 719 kesten; 724 of þat; 727 of; 731 fallen; 732 to²; 735 chiden; 740 for tene; 745 busked; 766 out of; 771 caytifes forþ; 781 menske; 787 wordes schewe;

817 *boot; 826 balwe; 845 þe; 850 loken; 866 on hande; 887 chersly; 914 piked; 941 broþer (26)

PAUDEC 630 þe¹; 647 saut; 686 myd; 689 comen+toun; 690 Stoppen; 699 todrawe; 717 adoun; 723 -doun; 797 *wel ynow; 811 rent; 812 into; 845 steweþ; 847 myd; 849 hadden; 891 rere; 909 flowe; 919 myd; 930 falleþ; 930 3af; 936 3elde; 963 worþe (21)

PC 630 walles; 696 þey lau3te; 698 were; 702 þe; 732 ny3t; 737 cacchen; 761 vpon lofte; 762 Rybaunde; 857 derk; 863 3ernest; 877 mowe þey; 893 hymself; 899 apostlen; 912 glowande; 912 grounde; 918 Of; 944 drowe; 949 þis; 958 Comen (19)

PAC 623 Tyeþ; 626 with; 659 Taysen; 688 coþe; 699 a; 741 attwynne; 778 þat; 778 þe²; 780 in; 799 abasched be; 801 noþyng; 863 Prayeþ; 883 þe¹; 911 of; 915 abideþ þat burne; 929 Amydde; 932 and; 952 tournen (18)

DEC 674 3eten; 690 a; 690 strande; 704 þeyes; 709 lered; 769 bide; 783 waytes; 783 poyntes; 812 flatten; 818 of þe frytted; 818 in; 854 no; 863 Prayeþ; 865 and; 876 ay; 876 li3t; 879 scholde (17)

PUDEC 635 walles; 677 wendeþ; 683 -hames; 702 vpon; 740 Ofte; 757 þat; 767 sayþ; 781 3it; 789 a . . . Iosophus; 789 þe; 848 Al; 867 graunten; 890 þis; 892 þe; 894 presen; 956 of (16)

AUDC 646 weyes . . . þey; 667 aboute; 730 Merked; 750 he casteþ; 751 oþere; 753 belteþ; 785 wode; 787 þis; 793 dryeden; 798 þerat; 803 manglouns; 836 temple; 853 Suþ; 892 fele; 965 þis (15)

AE 706 þe; 727 of; 742 vpon; 767 sewen; 777 pi3t haue; 785 a; 798 loude; 806 walle; 811 Ra3ten; 813 gynful; 878 wolde; 887 may; 898 pyned; 904 quyk (14)

PU 623 tourres; 698 felles; 704 þeyes; 713 at; 725 ended; 752 lacchetes; 799 No; 804 þey; 812 dasschande; 812 flatten; 816 hard; 835 om.; 869 hem; 870 lese (14)

AUD 650 3arken; 673 werien; 678 benden; 696 þe; 756 aboue; 762 vmbe; 769 barres; 779 defenden; 828 or; 837 saut; 863 princes; 892 Se; 932 þo (13)

AD 632 wye; 635 wyes; 713 þe²; 728 deþ; 737 hem; 748 þicke; 753 swerd; 783 warpiþ; 786 dey; 791 wete for-; 856 nakerer; 903 seyen (12)

AUC 679 kesten; 697 swyþe; 708 tyme; 722 blowen; 771 forþ; 777 who; 809 runne; 827 gretter; 854 was; 873 in; 886 men; 931 more (12)

PUDC 639 comaundeþ; 677 walles; 704 kagged; 744 blowyng; 749 of . . . and; 756 myd; 765 ouer; 767 sewen; 834 stones; 854 *nempned; 891 þe; 903 rosen (12)

PD 679 and; 681 a; 743 busken; 781 byseche; 793 dropeden; 793 dryeden; 823 engynes; 874 and; 877 here; 891 and; 908 was; 928 þat (12)

AEC 625 kepten; 632 ne non þat; 654 in; 681 han; 685 Suþ; 686 Crammen; 703 Corres; 723 crieþ; 806 side; 806 myd (10)

PUDE 633 passen; 669 benden; 685 diche; 698 quyk; 800 fayleþ; 813 engynes; 888 of; 918 how; 940 of blode; 955 wynter (10)

PE 714 *here; 721 walle; 729 þe skyes; 734 carpen; 757 þe; 767 sayþ to oþer; 888 of; 892 om.; 914 prikkes; 932 þo (10)

PAUC 632 *wem; 638 blowen; 653 wroӡt; 708 syed; 729 dymmed; 745 busked; 887 chargeþ; 905 his; 950 loste (9)

UEC 629 hem; 637 Rathe; 706 renten; 717 lete; 738 passus div.; 798 lawӡþe; 841 and; 856 nakerer; 908 *þey . . . ӡolden (9)

PUD 649 þey; 794 hem; 804 of; 806 myd; 863 wye; 890 hure; 951 þat; 955 þis (8)

AU 666 with; 686 hit; 742 leuerockes; 783 poyntes; 785 wendeþ; 807 stones; 824 þrewen; 921 after (8)

PAUDC 668 Riӡt; 711 kene; 744 on[1]; 750 casteþ; 803 myd; 808 dyt; 852 and; 896 þey ledde (8)

Smaller groups include: LP, PADC 7×; PAD, ADEC, AUEC 6×; LA, LE, LC, PAU, PUC, ADC, AUDE 5×; PDC, PDEC, PADEC 4×; PAE, ADE, PDE, AUE, PUE, PAUE, LDEC 3×; LD, LUD, PEC, LUE, PAUD, PAEC, PADE, PUEC, LAEC, LUDE 2×; LU, LAD, LPA, LAC, LDC, LPE, LDE, LPAC, LAUC, PAUEC, LAUEC, LPAEC, LPAUD, LPUDE, LPADEC, LAUDEC 1×.

Observed agreement in variation after line 966:

UDE 969 wolde; 980 honshed on hem; 981 betyn and brosten; 982 neuer; 982 ston . . . stede; 984 may; 998 In honour; 998 as . . . schapiþ; 1006 Made weys; 027 for; 029 fayndom; 032 leke; 036 keuere; 041 and; 049 saw; 050 hote yre; 051 to brede; 052 resorte; 053 alle þe fetoures; 054 ryseþ; 056 was; 057 haþ þe holpyn; 062 graunted; 063 with . . . Ioye; 066 he kepiþ; 068 bylompyn; 070 is byfalle; 071 þey no fode; 073 browet, broþe; 078 Ded; 078 hundred; 080 alle; 083 rewful; 085 batail; 087 þerfore; 093 worþi; 097 dwelle; 100 lengþen our; 103 elde; 104 myӡt noӡt stonde; 108 and; 114 sixty speres; 115 outwith; 129 þe[2]; 131 Fel; 135 After; 136 stoken; 138 Anoþer; 138 of; 151 þe . . . myche; 152 were ded; 157 þo; 157 he; 158 Forto saue; 158 and; 159 þe sawe; 161 Myche . . . prechyng; 180 to; 182 Tyen euen; 188 of; 200 for ston; 209 þe; 210 A sowe; 214 þe dukes; 220 soure; 226 sundrede; 228 and; 231 on; 234 O; 237 and[1]; 238–40 om.; 242 in here bare; 243 none; 243 þe; 243 neuer ne cesed; 250 byfore; 253 Tytus; 253 for þat; 261 on; 267 pulsched vessel; 281 han+souӡte; 282 pykeyse and ponsone; 289 Nas; 297 hym; 298 Alle; 304 þat; 310 wexe; 313 bot . . . make; 316 forto; 316 þe prophete; 323 scholde (91)

EC 967 burne; 978 taken; 979 ȝet; 980 holde; 985 onone; 995 lenge; 1002 anon; 010 burnes; 011 leel; 016 treuþ; 018 glowande; 019 alofte; 021 *þus; 021 laccheþ; 022 wende; 023 Praieþ; 026 maked; 034 segge; 041 was comen; 043 complet; 044 burne; 046 ferkiþ; 046 ful blyue; 049 segge; 061 segge; 063 rauȝte; 064 byes; 082 brad; 084 Sayþ; 090 fele; 094 barn; 100 fyne; 103 wymmen; 105 touche; 120 tourneþ; 123 brunyes . . . yren; 123 blody; 124 segge; 133 toward; 147 falwed; 147 face; 164 bytauȝt; 176 Swalten; 187 freke; 191 assaute; 194 eche; 194 lyf; 205 wepyþ; 213 lyȝten; 229 wye; 236 dynt; 245 Titus; 249 lene; 257 ful of; 261 warien; 262 euer; 263 commaundyþ; 266 gaddes; 268 bryȝt; 276 freke; 280 wye; 299 as hy; 301 apered; 302 þe freke; 304 þe²; 307 postel; 309 þe kyng; 313 schal; 320 þrongen; 327 for; 328 þoled (71)

AV 972 fele; 976 myȝt; 978 haue; 980 suþ; 985 seiþ; 995 lenge; 1009 on²; 015 to; 019 alofte; 032 lost; 043 complet; 046 ferkiþ; 049 eyen; 052 here; 060 be; 066 with; 066 he kepiþ; 084 Sayþ; 086 withyn; 097 þey went; 104 myȝt noȝt stonde; 132 bretnes; 133 hym sone; 139 Sayn; 151 was; 154 Into; 154 diche; 154 falle; 155 vouched; 168 lest; 168 fongen, schold; 187 XV; 187 ilk a; 188 maner; 188 engyne; 194 lyf; 200 or for; 204 diche; 206 lede; 206 lost; 212 diche; 221 Or; 226 Ouer . . . were; 229 on . . . cried; 230 þe; 242 and; 243 Fram; 243 merke; 256 glowande; 258 made; 259 a lampe; 264 Doun; 264 into grounde; 268 oþer; 273 same; 275 Iemewes; 276 Floreynes; 284 for; 284 of þe; 286 serched . . . al; 323 lawe; 325 aiorned; 328 vienne (64)

UD 979 *ȝet, ȝolden; 991–92 om.; 998 to; 1004 þe; 021 he; 030 was; 038 couþe¹; 039 þe self; 045 was; 052 synwes; 056 yn on; 060 and; 062 to; 062 hym; 066 he kepiþ; 067 on; 071 for; 071 byfor; 083 rigge, rib; 090 þat; 104 mardyn; 108 is; 131 vmbefeldes; 142 bite; 147 wymmen; 147 here; 149 *swallen; 153 wenten; 155 vouched; 157 to preche; 164 graunteþ hem; 164 grace; 180 taken; 181 alle for; 190 at; 206 loue; 209 same; 211 alle; 212 lyȝten; 215 þis . . . euen; 220 ben satled; 221 byfore; 232 toun; 237 deuysed; 241 bot; 246 no man; 246 stoken; 249 ladies; 251 or; 255 ferde; 263 Out; 264 Doun; 272 doun; 280 wale; 283 hem; 285 woke; 286 was; 287 Maden . . . wappe; 302 with; 303 of; 306 whan he deþ, 309 made; 316 þe prophete; 320 in¹; 323 leued (65)

UDEC 985; 987 *and . . . owen; 988 elles; 996 here; 015 to kepe; 018 riche; 048 yn; 052 here; 058 and . . . bote; 066 *with; 069 were; 073 beste vpon lyue; 077 fellen; 079 þycke; 080 on; 082 gledis; 084 our; 087 þat; 092 *hadde; 092 layned; 103 of; 104 in; 106 for gile; 112 *Grobben; 114 segges; 116 hedis; 135 After; 139 Sayn; 154 þe ded doun; 155 þe; 160 *þat oþer segge; 164 graunteþ; 174 hit by; 175 Iewes; 187 XV; 195 quasschyng; 200 or for; 201 Syx; 225 vpon; 225 ost-; 228 lombe; 230 om.; 236 þrow; 236a haplich was; 250 were fleschy; 253 tarieþ; 253 wendiþ; 259 þat ay; 270 In copper;

270 and in; 271 pure gold; 297 suþ Tytus; 304 and; 313 schal; 328 he . . . deþ; 338 Trossen, trompen; 339 han . . . forþred (57)

DE 966 Ouerlokeþ; 970 next; 998 eure schapiþ; 1017 toures heye; 019 þe; 025 wale; 027 so mychel; 037 aboute; 046 ful; 049 sodeynly; 053 byfore; 072 fisch, flesch; 086 neȝ; 086 our; 100 lengþen our; 116 broke; 127 hed; 131 Fel; 146 a . . . gyuen; 157 to enforme; 160 þat oþer segge; 162 Tyen; 162 bysecheþ; 174 þey; 176 by[1,2]; 181 as-tyt; 187 fightyng men; 189 -ȝate; 192 belfrayes; 193 dyn and dyt; 200 ston; 203 brast; 203 boþ; 218 on; 219 a; 222 þynges; 230 A; 246 þe stret; 260 rise; 268 bassynes of brend; 269 fele; 282 pykeyse and ponsone; 289 þe; 289 alofte; 290 Mulle; 292 blake; 317 ost a; 320 in[2]; 328 At (50)

AVC 982 neuer; 1004 with . . . burnes; 014 kysseþ; 029 fayndom; 057 Iosophus; 063 with; 073 browet; 076 þat; 085 aboute; 108 *and; 119 hem; 119 wal; 121 yþrelled; 125 an; 127 attonys; 131 Fel; 136 stoken; 140 reioyced; 148 Feynte and; 150 Som; 155 to; 157 þo; 168 lest; 178 eche; 185 on; 189 Tytus; 191 setteþ; 193 was noȝt bot; 193 dyn and dyt; 193 deye; 199 wynneþ; 204 into; 212 þat; 229 heye; 232 þe Iewen; 237–40 om.; 241 and; 243 ne; 246 stoken; 261 tyme; 289 Nas; 297 sett hym; 297 on; 298 Alle; 323 in (45)

UE 967 riseþ; 972 fele; 977 heyȝt; 980 kepyn; 998 be; 1018 vnder god; 048 þe; 051 bygan; 075 scheldes and schone; 090 þe sauere; 091 scholde þe berde; 099 ȝit; 107 hym; 108 afere; 125 hetter; 140 reioyced; 146 haue gyuen; 148 Feynte; 158 hem-; 161 ȝatis; 174 hadde; 218 þe[1]; 226 tymes; 228 at; 229 cried . . . heye; 232 þe Iewen; 234 word; 236a how . . . neuere; 25 rayled; 265 in þe place; 277 riche; 277 and; 309 corsed; 323 leued; 325 clerk; 327 was (36)

AVUDEC 966 ech a; 995 here; 996 herte; 1008 to hewen þe; 010 þe honde; 034 wepyþ; 057 sayþ; 059 aȝen; 093 seiþ; 097 sayn; 111 myne; 113 after; 113 vmbe; 131 folke; 139 Sayn; 180 Armen; 182 Tyen; 198 leyþ; 200 or for; 213 þe; 214 han so dere; 216 and; 236 a; 245 his; 246 on; 252 on; 261 werke; 272 ledyn; 274 tresours; 289 Nas; 293 and; 295 sow; 297 Tytus suþ; 299 callen; 329–34 om. (35)

VC 988 may; 991 fers; 1004 forto; 007 boþere; 013 freke; 029 þe[1]; 039 *þe self; 052 resorte; 056 yn on; 059 þy; 082 brad; 108 fairest; 119 hadde; 122 schalke; 140 reioyced; 155 trewe; 155 vouched; 169b–70a; 184 many; 184 and; 190 where; 196 burne; 200 for ston; 228 and . . . ewe-; 229 wondere; 241 bot; 243 ne; 248 defaute; 259 lemaunde; 288 in[1,2]; 312 eche a; 312 be worth; 322 after; 327 was (34)

AC 978 Tille; 980 on; 982 in þat stede; 982 *oþere; 992 þat[2]; 998 schapiþ; 1021 he; 055 þe; 059 þerfor; 076 chewe; 083 Rostyþ; 087 þerfore; 107 hape; 118 Iambers; 127 Of; 129 þe[2]; 134 þe; 135 profreþ; 189 -ȝate; 190 at; 199

þoʒ; 204 and; 204 into; 236 þrow; 242 chertes; 248 enfamyned; 255 and; 270 cast; 277 princes; 279 selke; 289 alofte; 310 fenged (32)

UDC 990 werke; 993 forto; 1000 soudiours; 000 by; 008 to-; 014 kysseþ; 014 carful; 020 alle; 027 þe; 049 eyen; 055 þonkeþ; 065 forsakeþ; 069 Now; 105 lord; 112 þe; 139 leuer, lengen; 167 Ful; 174 souʒt; 181 *for; 183 neʒen; 190 Merkeþ; 220 soure; 221 Or; 242 brunee and; 297 Tytus suþ; 305 *melys; 340ab (27)

UC 974 as þis; 975 sey; 990 þe; 1017 nold; 017 vntake; 019 þe; 037 seggys; 077 grounde; 098 and; 113 after; 146 Nold; 149 Swounen; 149 wexen; 160 þat oþer segge; 169 vp; 200 and; 207 y trowe; 216 out; 245 his; 246 ded; 251 burges; 273 vpon; 289 þe; 290 om.; 300 prouost was; 305 melys (26)

AE 967 bordes; 1008 to-; 020 -tourned and; 035 þey; 080 his; 091 Doun; 132 helpes; 140 out; 148 so; 178 To . . . hit; 178 of; 202 on hym; 204 felle; 229 wal; 278 bies; 283 ston; 285 wal; 290 fallen; 299 Criours; 324 þus; 326 þer (21)

PA 967 burne; 968 þis; 995 hem; 997 þe; 1008 hennes; 015 weldeþ; 020 tilt; 032 here; 062 hym; 068 hem; 086 neʒ; 112 on; 121 sone; 122 Many; 130 issed; 139 lengen (16)

VUDEC 1001 lote; 011 þat[1]; 050 *riseþ; 054 in; 079 wakned; 084 Sayþ; 084 on; 112 on; 146 goode; 179 Neuer; 187 fightyng; 199 happned; 235 worþly; 250 fleschy; 309 Now (15)

AUDEC 976 y myʒt; 1056 þat; 069 in; 069 tore; 083 *Rostyþ; 092 þis; 097 sore; 105 After; 118 Iambers; 183 nakerers; 194 layeþ on; 269 fele; 295 Suþ; 303 whan (14)

VE 967 doun; 974 þis; 1024 han; 076 was . . . chewe; 081 meschef; 091 dey; 104 here; 128 leueþ; 131 vmbefeldes; 134 Makeþ; 226 sundrede; 252 No; 269 masly; 310 þe (14)

VU 1036 condit; 060 serued; 089 roos; 093 þat; 107 hape; 116 vp; 119 and; 124 þat; 130 eʒte; 195 kernel; 211 þer; 219 agenes; 249 lafte; 298 as (14)

DC 966 Ouerlokeþ; 968 Calleþ; 981 brosten; 1008 here; 012 Sire; 091 þei daschen; 164 gaylers; 234 wye; 244 ay; 256 on; 319 ay; 326 þer (12)

DEC 976 and; 052 self; 073 vpon lyue; 105 graunteþ noʒt; 118 Iambers; 148 so faire were; 189 at; 219 agenes; 224 holde; 224 one; 228 -lombe; 324 commaundyþ (12)

AU 1031 fustes; 065 þe[1]; 101 þat deil was; 119 Iambers; 197 laste; 222 *selcouþe; 257 were; 276 wanted; 297 a; 297 sete; 300 beden apere (11)

AUDE 1119 hadde; 137 Ion; 158 *ʒelde; 166 was . . . strengþe; 176 sweng; 180 no; 183 þe; 252 medil; 256 flikreþ; 337 vp; 338 here (11)

AD 1088 a; 169 vp; 173 two; 180 Ne; 181 Armen; 196 burne; 197 saute; 260 whan clerkes scholde; 310 þe; 326 mater; 327 was (11)

AVUDC 977 *heylich; 1005 wol; 007 heste; 013 þe[1]; 036 delyueryn; 083 rigge, rib; 095 feccheþ; 160 þe; 171 Goren; 234 sayþ (10)

AVEC 1002 To . . . anon; 031 and[1]; 076 *chewe; 109 wal; 125 hacchen; 148 fallen; 173 Ay; 215 preien; 283 hurled; 302 he (10)

PAVUDEC 995 myd; 1024 byhot; 033 be; 040 graunteþ; 043 haue; 051 *abrode; 052 resorte; 111 mynours, masouns; 112 Grobben; 125 hacchen (10)

In addition, there is an extremely large number of agreements infrequently attested (at least in part the product of simple probability, given the presence of nine manuscripts rather than eight):

PV, PAV, VUD, VUDC 8×; LC, AVE, AUC, ADE, UEC, PAVC 7×; VD, VDC, VDE, AVD, VEC, LUDE, VUDE 6×; LA, PD, AEC, AUEC, AVDE, ADEC 5×; LP, PAC, AUD, AVU, PUDE, AVUD, PAUD, AVUC, AVDC, AVUEC, PAVUC, AVDEC 4×; LE, PE, LD, PU, VUE, VUC, AUE, AUDC, VDEC, LDEC, PAVEC, PVUDEC, LAVUDEC 3×; PC, LU, PUD, PAE, PAU, PUC, LAV, LDE, LUDC, LUEC, LUDEC, AVUDE, PAVUDC 2×; PVC, ADC, PUE, PEC, LEC, LDC, LAC, PAEC, PAVE, PAUE, PVUC, PDEC, AVUE, LAVC, LAVU, LUDE, PUDEC, LPAUD, LAVUC, PVDEC, LPVDC, PAVDE, PVDEC, LPAVC, LADEC, PAUDEC, PAVDEC, LAVUDC, LVUDEC 1×.

GLOSSARY

This glossary is intended to provide our interpretation of the forms found in the edited text. We generally attempt to provide complete references for every word which occurs in the poem. For the few exceptions, some names and function words of frequent occurrence whose senses closely confirm to modern usage, we give the first five uses. Readings we discuss in our textual notes have "(n.)" after the line reference; this is the only indication we give here that a reading we print may lack manuscript support.

We adopt the following principles of alphabetization. ȝ (yogh) appears immediately following g, and þ (thorn) follows t. We have separated the interchangeable spellings u/v. Vocalic v appears with u and consonantal u with v. When y is merely a spelling variation for i, it is alphabetized with i; when it performs a consonantal function, it follows w. Words with modern English *j* are usually spelled i or I in the mss.: we present these forms separately in the modern alphabetic order.

a *indef. art.* a, an, one 9, 13, 14, 17, 18, etc.; **an** 64, 172, 301, 336, 440, etc.; see also **on** *card. num.*

a *card. num.* a single one 518, 614, 1185, 1287; see also **on** *card. num.*

a *interj.* ah, alas 173 (2×), 181.

a see **at** *prep.*, **on** *prep.*

abasched *pp. as adj.* downcast 799.

abide *v.* risk battle, withstand 312 (n.); **habiden** suffer, endure 820; *pr. 3 sg.* abideþ stands his ground, stands at bay 915.

ablode *pred. adj.* bloody, bloodstained 563.

aboute *adv.* round about, here and there 254, 318, 410, 535, 563, 575, 628, 1037; over (an extent of) 292; on all sides 338, 413, 604, 730, 739, 1286.

aboute *prep.* around, about 268, 424, 664, 682, 1085; postposited at 325, 489, 491, 764, 836, 889, 1117.

aboue *adv.* overhead, above 577, 667; higher up 756.

abrod(e) *adv.* wide, apart, widely 409, 722; over a large area, far and wide 733; throughout, freely 1051; *vp* ~ into clear sight 1169 (n.); see also **brode.**

ac *conj.* but 217.

acate *n.* purchase 1309.

acounte *v.* reckon, regard 1240.

acry *adv., prep. phrase* (on cry), crying, with a cry 639 (n.).

adoun *adv.* down, downward 717, 723, 842.

adradde *pp.* afraid, frightened 463.

afere *adv.* from a distance, afar 1108.

affray *v.* alarm, terrify 672.

aflot *adv.* at anchor 289.

afowe *pr. 1 sg.* make a vow, swear 203.

after *adv.* after, next 147, 366; after, afterwards, 160, 863, 921, 1105, 1135, 1322; behind, following 255, 284 (with implicit 'went'), 323.

after *prep.* after 388, 858, 1113, 1244; postposited at 587, 598; on account of 36, 261; along 486; ~ *þe sonne* after daybreak 388.

agenes see **aȝen** *prep.*

agysen *v.* deck out, ornament 262 (n.).

aȝen *adv.* again, back, back again, in return 346, 374, 917, 1087; **agayn** 952.

aȝen(s) *prep.* about the time of, toward 161; against, opposing 428; over against, opposite 650; in opposition to 779; as protection against 807; contrary to 1033, 1227; **agenes** 1219; at 161; in return for 1059.

ay *adv.* always, ever, constantly 21, 71, 140, 232, 306, 404, 452, 539, 876, 1173, 1259, 1319; again and again 1244.

ayere *n.* air 1225.

aireþ *pr.3 sg.* proceeds, goes 259 (n.).

aiorned *pp.* summoned, ordered 1325 (n.).

al(le) *pron.* all, everything, everyone 12 (n.), 64, 73 (n.), 76, 111, etc.

al(le) *adj.* (may denote total number; totality, entirety, perfection) all 19, 26, 86, 88, 112, etc.; often post-posited, as in 1172; ~ *þei,* ~ *þey, þey . . . ~, hem* ~ them all, all of them 162, 259.

al(le) *adv.* completely, utterly, totally 172, 240, 254, 290, 325, etc.

alas *interj.* alas 1098.

alofte *adv.* on top, high above 335, 625; up high 393, 527; upright, erect 582; upright 1019, 1184, 1289; on top, above 753; in the air, in the ascendent 1084; up, on high 1198; *striden* ~ mounted 527.

alone *adv.* unaided, single-handed 909, 1201.

aloude *adv.* loudly, in a loud voice 523, 916.

also *adv.* also, moreover 4, 33, 395.

als-tite see **tit**.

aluendel *n.* half, the half part 132.

am see **be**.

amydde *prep.* in the middle of, amidst 929.

amys *adv.* wrongfully 1310.

among(e) *prep.* among, amid 674, 890.

an see **on**.

an(d) *conj.* and 4, 8, 10, 14, 18, etc.; if 976; **an** and 452 (2nd use), 471, 936, 1138.

anewe *adv.* afresh, once again 801.

angren *v.* afflict, injure 705.

any *pron.* anyone 784.

any *adj.* any 99, 690; any at all, any whatever 90, 524, 880, 1140, 1166, 1208.

anlepy *adj.* single, just one 583.

anoynted *pp.* smeared, daubed 702; **ynoyntid** anointed, consecrated 303.

anon *adv.* at once, immediately, shortly, soon 57, 62, 525, 533, 597, 617, 694, 809, 903, 968, 985, 1002, 1014.

anoþer *pron.* another, a second 925; another (person) 989; the other (side), the opposite (side) 1186.

anoþer *adj.* another, a second 141, 545, 951; the second, the other 274.

apaied *pp.* as *adj.* satisfied, contented 884.

apere *v.* present oneself, appear 1300; *pr. 3 sg.* **apered** 1301.

apys *n. pl.* apes 705.

aposteles *n. pl.* apostles 142; *poss. pl.* **apostlen** 899; see also **postel**.

appul *n.* sphere, orb, ball, globe; *gilde* ~ golden orb, symbol of imperial authority 330.

aproched *pt. 3 sg.* went, came near to, approached 247.

arblastes *n. pl.* cross-bows 671, 840.

archelers *n. pl.* catapults, stone-throwers 840 (n.).

armen *pr. 3 pl.* arm, equip for battle 1181; *pp.* as *adj.* **armed** equipped for battle, armed 395, 451, 1225; **y-armed** 465, 487; *with arwes* ~ depicted as armed with arrows 395.

armes *n. pl.* arms (of a person) 705; see also **armys**.

armyng *n.* equipping for battle, arming 427.

armys *n. pl.* armorial bearings, coat of arms 334, 750; **armes** weapons; *man of* ~ warrior 438, 460.

armure *n.* weapons and armour collectively, arms 611.

arst *adv.* first 165.

arwe *adj.* slow, sluggish, lazy 427.

arwes *n. pl.* arrows 395, 658, 671, 840.

as *conj.* as 5, 23, 66, 75, 112, etc.; as if 58, 72, 552, 1126, 1193; to introduce a conjuration 202; just as 263, 884; as though 534; when 957; that 73 (n.); *as . . . as* 106, 119, 180, 609, 943, 991–992 (and *as for (as) . . . as* 637, 766); see also **þer as**.

as *prep.* like 12, 14, 365, 390, 419, etc.

askes *n. pl.* ashes 720.

askeþ *pr. 3 sg.* demands, requires 206, 506; requests 758, 1043; *pt. 3 sg.* **asked** required 293; *pt. 3 pl.* **asked** 216.

aspyed *pp.* discovered, detected 1169.

assaute *n.* armed attack, assault 1191; see also **saute**.

assayle(n) *v.* attack 567, 656, 663, 802, 1177; *pt. 3 pl.* **assayled** assaulted 627.

assembled *pr. 3 sg.* assembled, convened, came together 269; *pr. 3 pl.* gathered 819; *pr. 3 pl.* **assembleden** 647; *pp.* **assembled** gathered together 388, 445; see also **sembled**.

assent *n.* consent, sanction 962, 1000, 1138; *of his* ~ in agreement with him, of his party 1138.

assenteden *pr. 3 pl.* consented, agreed 214, 883; *pr. 3 pl. refl.* **assented hem** agreed 907.

assyned *pp.* as *adj.* assigned, appointed 434.

assised *pp.* set, arranged, put in place 401.

as-tyt see **tit**.

at *prep.* at, in 38, 70, 87, 126 (2×), etc.; through 108; by, with 76, 125, 321; of 283, 1021; on 505, 824; against, to withstand 665; for 889; **atte** at the 75, 77,

229, 441, 669, 991, 1196; at 392; ~ *þe bak(e)* behind them 294, 306; ~ *ere* through the ear, through speech 108.

athel *adj.* noble 50.

atired *p.pl.* fitted out, equipped 286, 446; **atyred** ornamented 467.

atlest *pr. 2 sg.* intend, plan 383; *pr. 3 sg.* **atles** attacks, takes aim at 569 (n.); *p.pl.* **atled** sought, planned, arranged 370.

atte see **at**.

attyr *n.* poison 658.

attonys *adv.* at once, immediately 342; simultaneously, immediately 626; together 1127.

atwynne *adv.* in two, asunder, apart 70; **attwynne** 741.

atwynne *pp.* separated 140.

aughte see **owene**.

auntred *pr. 3 sg. refl.* dared, put (himself) at risk 151.

availed *pr. 3 sg.* lowered 253.

avental *n.* the lower front piece of a helmet 760.

away *adv.* away 255; aside 585; on one's way 1022, 1339; **awey** away 423.

awide *adv.* all around, in every direction 861.

bachelere *n.* a knight, ranking just below the hereditary nobleman 494.

baches *n. pl.* streams 563.

bade see **bidde**.

bayne *imper. sg.* prepare, make ready, grant 185 (n.).

bak(e) *n.* back 363, 568; *at þe* ~ behind them 294, 306; *on* ~ on their backs 428, 450, 459.

bal *n.* sphere, ball 401; rounded missile or shot 832.

bale *n.* evil, harm 187; tribulation (of this world), torment 500, 596, 814, 1058, 1145.

balies see **bely**.

balwe *n.* as *adj.* evil, destructive 156, 826; ~ *tre* death-bringing tree, gallows 156.

band *n.* bond 590.

baners *n. pl.* banner-bearers, standard-bearers 444.

baneres *n. pl.* banners 487, 490.

banke see **bonke**.

baptemed *pp.* baptized 192.

bare *adj.* bare, despoiled 306; nude 640,

1242; *in her* ~ *chertes* scantily clad, wearing only their shirts 1242.

bare see **bere**.

barel *n.* barrel 675; *pl.* **barels** 1251.

bargayned *pp.* sold, bartered 1308, 1321.

bargaynes *n. pl.* business transactions, buying and selling 1315.

barge *n.* a sailing vessel of moderate size 79.

barn *n.* infant, (unborn) child 829, 831, 1082, 1094, 1096.

baronage *n.* the body of nobles or retainers of a ruler, the nobility 196.

baroun *n.* baron, great lord 494; *pl.* **barouns** 77, 233, 491, 1010.

barre *n.* bar of a court-room 1301; *pl.* **barres** barrier, barricade outside the gate of a walled city 769, 821.

barren *pr. 3 pl.* bar, bolt 618.

barst see **brestyþ**.

bassynes *n. pl.* basins, dishes 1268.

bastiles *n. pl.* fortified encampments (for an army besieging a walled city), towers 682.

batail *n.* battle, combat, armed conflict 381, 459, 1099; army 664, 1085.

batayled *pt. 3 sg. refl.* drew up in battle formation 432; *pt. 3 pl.* 486.

battes *n. pl.* chunks (of bread) 136 (n.).

be *n.* bee 14; *pl.* **bees** 34, 36.

becroked *pp.* as *adj.* made crooked, mis-shapen 1033.

bedde *n.* bed 743, 745; *poss.sg.* **beddes** of his bed 1048.

beden *pr. 3 pl.* present, announce themselves 444; see also **bidde**.

bekered *pt. 3 pl.* engaged in combat, threw projectiles 821.

beldes see **bilde**.

belfray *n.* moveable tower used in siege operations 390, 392, 413; **berfray** 591; *pl.* **belfrayes** 1192.

bely *n.* belly, abdomen 829; *pl.* **balies** 1251.

belles *n. pl.* bells 410.

belteþ *pr. 3 sg.* attaches (a sword) to or with a belt, buckles on 753.

bemes *n. pl.* trumpets 525, 638, 743; **bemys** 443.

beme-word *n.* vanguard of trumpets 487 (n.).

bemys *n.* beams, rays (of the sun) 420, 549.

be(n) v. be 204, 298, 300, 303, 349, etc.; *pr.*
1 sg. am (as auxiliary of the perfect)
have 83; *pr. 3 sg.* is is 86, 95, 98, 111,
113, etc.; (as auxiliary of the perfect) has
1025, 1028, 1068, 1070; his is 773; *pr. 1
pl.* beþ are 369; ben are 380, 521, 986;
pr. 2 pl. ben are 969; *pr. 3 pl.* beþ (*with
sg. subj.*) is 800; ben are 112, 117, 150,
517, 871, etc.; (as auxiliary of the perfect) have 952; *imper.sg.* be 192, 799,
1060; was *pt. 1/3 sg.* was 3, 8, 9, 36,
37, etc.; (as auxiliary of the past perfect)
had 1141; became 221; *pt. 3 sg. without
subject* there was, it was 37, 182, 244,
251, 281, etc.; *pt. 3 pl.* was were 213,
463, 559, 1032; were(n) were 77, 80,
118, 138, 140, etc.; *pp.* be(n) been 175,
837, 838, 1058; *pr. 1 sg. subj.* were 72
(2nd use); *pr. 2 sg. subj.* be be, are 15;
were 94; *pr. 3 sg. subj.* be be, are 204,
865, 1309; were were, should be, would
be, may be 87 (2×), 204, 404, 464, etc.;
pr. 2 pl. subj. were were 780; *pt. 1 sg.
subj.* were 83; *pt.2 sg. subj.* 94; *pt. 3 sg.
subj.* were were, was 7, 404; *pt. 3 pl. subj.*
wer 698; *negative forms: pr. 3 sg.* nis,
nys (there) is not 132, 493; (as auxiliary
of the perfect) has not 495; *pt. 3 sg.* nas
(there) was not 41, 1289.

benden *pt. 3 pl.* drew back the string of (a
bow), bent 669; prepared a siege engine
for shooting or casting 678; *pp.* bent
824.

bent(e) *n.* open field 312, 486, 544, 549,
572, 603, 699, 744, 765.

bere *v.* carry, bear 368; *pr.* (*pt.?*) *3 pl.*
beren bear 537; *pt. 3 sg.* bar bore (up),
gave birth to 1082, 1096; *pt. 3 pl.* 470; *pp.*
born carried, borne 76, 832, 967; born
104, 202; *beren prow* stab, pierce 537;
born doun taken down 967.

berde see burde.

berdis *n. pl.* beards 364.

berelepes *n. pl.* large baskets 136.

berfray see belfray.

berly *n.* as *adj.* barley 134.

berne see burne.

besauntes *n. pl.* gold coins (first struck in
Byzantium), a bezant used as an ornament 643, 1064, 1142, 1278.

best(e) see goode, wel.

beste *n.* (fabulous) creature, monster 401,
415; beast, animal 455, 593, 606, 1073,

1308; *poss.* beast's 946; *pl.* bestes 427,
449, 487, 568, 691, 726, 1132.

bete *v.* beat, raze, level 1264; *pt. 3 pl.*
beten 661; *pp.* beten beaten, flogged
10; betyn beaten, levelled 981, 1292;
pr. 3 sg. betiþ strikes 543; *pt. 3 sg.* bet
on struck 546, 770; *pp.* as *adj.* ybetyn
embroidered 418; betyn inlaid 472;
~ *doun* razed, destroyed 661.

betyn *imper. pl.* kindle, light 718; *pt. 3 pl.*
betyn 733.

bet(t)er see goode, wel.

betyng *n.* beating, flogging 498.

beþ see be(n).

bew-clerkes *n. pl.* excellent clerics, good
scholars 591.

by *n.* byre, cowshed 104 (n.).

by *conj.* when, by the time that 356.

by *prep.* by 51, 77, 140 (2×), 191, etc.
(postposited 478); at 918; in accord with
984, 1000; through, by means of 989,
1176 (2×); ~ *somme* in sum 422; ~ *þat*
after that, then, when, by that time 285,
443, 663, 681, 729, etc.; be þat 464;
~ *þanne* thereby, thereupon 823, 1141.

by(e) *v.* buy 1142, 1315; *pr. 3 pl. subj.* byen
pay for 514; *pt. 3 sg.* bouȝt saved, freed
(from damnation) 500; *pp.* bouȝt bought
1308, 1321, bouȝte 1214; ~ *hard* pay
dearly for 514; dere bouȝte hard-won,
dearly paid for 1214.

bible *v.* drink (heartily) 724.

bycchyd *pp.* as *adj.* vile, accursed, difficult
589; bycchet 665.

bidde *pr. 1 sg.* pray for 250; command,
demand, require, order 349; *imper.* 724;
pr. 3 sg. byddis 798; *pt. sg.* bade 233,
718; *pt. 3 pl.* beden 1300.

biddyng *n.* bidding, command 369.

biden *v.* await 432; bide make a stop, halt
769.

byen see by(e).

bies, byes *n. pl.* bracelets, torques 643,
1064, 1278.

byfelle *pt. 3 sg.* came about, happened,
occurred 237; *pp.* byfalle 1070.

byfor, before *adv.* earlier 280; previously,
beforehand 1053, 1071, 1250.

byfor *prep.* before, in front of 152, 377,
421.

big *adj.* big, mighty, great 455, 665, 778.

byggid *pp.* built, established 665.

bygynne *v.* begin 647, 801; *pr. 3 sg.*

begynneþ 869; *pt. 3 sg.* **bygan** 118, 225, 1051; *pt. 3 pl.* **bygonn** 361; **bygonnen** 651, 656; **bygonne** 1111.

bigly *adv.* stoutly, strongly 413; vigorously 432; firmly 618.

byhold(e) *v.* behold, gaze upon, stare at 232, 338, 645, 666, 875, 1247; **byholden** 701, 1247; *pr. 3 sg.* **byholdeþ** 553, 861, 965; *pr.3 pl.* **byholden** 794; *imper. pl.* **byholdeþ** 497.

byhot *pp.* promised 1024.

byhouyþ *pr. 3 sg. impers.* it is obligatory; *sey þe* ~ you must say 975.

biker *n.* a nest of wild bees 34.

bylafte *pp.* committed (to you), having confidence (in you) 987 (n.).

bilde *n.* building 1264; *pl.* **beldes** 661.

byleue *n.* faith, religion 206, 517.

byleue *pr.1.sg.* believe 201.

bylompyn *pp.* happened, befallen 1068.

byndyng *n.* fettering (of a prisoner) 498.

bynyþe *adv.* lower down 709.

byr, bir *n.* following wind, favourable wind 76, 294; onslaught 656, 665.

byrunne *pp.* as *adj.* drenched; *blody* ~ drenched in blood 603, 1123.

bischup, byschup *n.* bishop 589, 596, 1239; *poss. sg.* **bischop** 724; *pl.* **bischopes** 349.

byseche *v.* beg or pray for 781; *pr. 3 pl.* **byseche** beg, beseech 1162; *pt. 3 sg.* **bysouȝt** 1244.

bystrode *pt. 3 sg.* mounted, rode 1208.

bytake *imper. sg.* entrust (to), commit (to) 993.

bytauȝt *pt. 3 sg.* committed (them to) 1164.

byte, bite *v.* eat 1072, 1142; *pr. 3 sg.* **byteþ** gnaws, bites 913; *pt. 3 sg.* **boot** pierced 817.

biterly *adv.* sorely, bitterly 225; **biterlych** sharply, sternly, harshly 915.

bytide *pt. 3 sg.* befell, happened, came to pass 33; **bytydde** 921; *pt. 3 pl.* **bytidde** 238.

bytrayede *pt. 3 sg.* betrayed 354.

bitter *adj.* grievous, severe 250.

bytwene *prep.* between 534 (postposited).

bladde *n.* cutting edge, blade, sword 546; *pl.* **bladdys** 396.

blake *adj.* black, dark 1292.

bleche *n.* ink, black pigment or dye 366 (n.).

blecken *pr. 3 pl.* stain, dye, blacken 366.

bled *pp.* covered with blood 846 (n.).

blesse *v.* bless 1004; *pr. 3 sg. subj.* 444; *pt. 3 sg.* **blessed** 254.

blessed *adj.* honoured, gracious 185; consecrated, holy 192.

blew, blewe, blewen see **blowe.**

blyndfelled *pp.* as *adj.* blindfolded 14 (n.).

blys *n.* joy, happiness 973; **blysse** 1029.

blyue *adv.* immediately, quickly 218; eagerly, willingly, gladly 759, 1046.

blod, blode *n.* blood 12, 500, 544, 575, 590, 940, 1051; lineage 969; mood 1096; *broþer of* ~ (blood) brother 940.

blody *adv.* bloody; ~ *byrunne* drenched with blood 603, 1123.

blonke *n.* horse, steed 275; *pl.* **blonkes** 525, 699.

blowe *v.* blow, sound (a signal) 732; *pr. 3 pl.* **blowen** 443, 525, 638; *imper.* **blowen** 722; *pt. 3 sg.* **blewe** 61; *pr.p.* **blowyng** 744.

bobbed *pt. 3 sg.* buffeted, struck in jest 16.

bocklyd *pp.* as *adj.* buckled 756.

boden *pt. 3 pl.* bade; *boden to* stretched forth toward 1010 (n.).

bodeword(e) *n.* message 959, 973.

body *n.* body 10, 156, 228, 254, 275, 366, 498, 831; *pl.* **bodies** 604, 640, 1085, 1152; **bodyes** 1315.

boffetis *n.* blows with the hand, cuffs 14.

boke *n.* book 1009; *pl.* **bokes** 595, 1326.

bold(e) *adj.* brave, noble, impudent 233, 275, 381, 455, 491, 663, 906, 956, 1192.

bole-fur *n.* blazing fire, especially for burning human corpses 718.

bolned *pt. 3 sg.* swelled up, surged 61.

boltes *n. pl.* bolts, bars 618.

bonden see **bounden.**

bon(e) *n.* bone 720, 817; *pl.* **bones** 1094, 1249.

bone *n.* commandment 148; petition, request 185.

bonke *n.* coast 294; hill, ridge 640; artificial earthwork, embankment 669, 778, 824; **banke** shore 77; *pl.* **bonkes** 890.

bonked *pp.* as *adj.* provided with an embankment 667.

boot see **byte.**

borden *adj.* wooden 363.

bordes *n. pl.* tables; ~ *born were doun* tables were taken down and removed 967.

bordored *pp.* bordered 410.

bore *n.* boar 547, 785.

bor(o)w see **burwe**.

born see **bere** *v.*

bost *n.* boast 301, 799.

bot *n.* boat 79.

bot *adv.* only, but 111, 112, 379, 800, 935.

bot *prep.* except, but 307, 425, 801, 1074, 1193, 1249.

bot *conj.* but 21, 94, 101, 116, 160, etc.; except, unless 183, 204 (n.), 406, 508, 514, 605, 1104; than 276; ~ *3if* unless 668.

bote *n.*¹ boot 817.

bote *n.*² deliverance, defence 1058.

boteles *adj.* incurable, irremediable 1145.

botnyng *n.* cure 250; help 392.

boþ(e) *correlative conj.* both 130, 159, 312, 511, 744, 899, 907, 1288; postposited 48.

boþ(e) *adj.* both 667, 907, 1203, 1231; (as *pron.* both 236, 277); **our boþere** *g.pl.* of both of us 1007.

bou3t(e) see **by(e)**.

boun *adj.* ready, prepared 349, 409, 664; *busken* ~ get ready, prepare 187, 678.

bounden *pt. 3 pl.* tied, bound 363, 589; *pp.* 373, 381, 829; *pp.* as *adj.* **bonden** 10; ~ *with barn* pregnant 829.

bounys *pr. 3 sg.* gets ready; ~ *of bedde* gets out of bed 745.

bourd *n.* joke, trick 1169.

bournde *pp.* as *adj.* polished, burnished 472.

boweled *pp.* as *adj.* disembowelled 946.

boweþ *pr. 3 sg.* goes 769.

bowmen *n. pl.* archers 669.

brad *pt. 3 s.* roasted 1082; *pp.* **brad** 1094.

brad, brayd see **brede**.

brayd(e) *n.* moment; *at o* ~, *atte* ~ instantly, forthwith 70, 1099, 1196.

brayde, brayden, braydyn see **breydeþ**.

brayn *n.* brains 544, 826, 1203.

brayned *pp.* brained, killed by the brain being crushed 833.

brake see **breke**.

bras(s) *n.* brass, gates made of brass 310, 770.

brast see **brestyþ**.

breche *n.* underwear 946.

bred *n.* bread, food 1073, 1145.

bred see **breydeþ**.

bredde *pt. 3 sg.* bred 34.

brede *v.* spread out, extend 1051; *pp.* **brad** 409.

breydeþ *pr. 3 sg.* brandishes 547; *pr. 3 pl.* **brayden** tug, pull 619; *pt. 3 sg.* **brayde** dashed, flew 831; *pt. 3. pl.* **braydyn** hastened, rushed 821 (n.), 831; *pp.* as *adj.* **brayd** scattered 292; **brouden** twisted, woven, interlinked 619 (n.); **browded** 748.

breke *v.* break 148; *pt. 3 s.* **brake vp** sprung into action, issued abruptly 1116; *pp.* **broken** 136.

brenyed *pp.* mail-clad, wearing a coat of mail 1192.

brenne(n) *v.* burn 718, 1264; *imper.pl.* **brennen** 720; *pr.p.* as *adj.* **brennand, brennande** 401, 472, 675, 814; **brennyng** 1223; *pt. 3 sg.* **brente** 814; *pt. 3 pl.* 306; **brenten** 661; **brent** 1292; *pp.* as *adj.* **brent** 726; **brend** burnished 1268.

breste *n.* breast 475.

brestyþ *pr. 3 sg.* bursts, breaks 1086; *pt. 3 sg.* **barst** 59; **brast** 1203; *pt. 3.pl.* **brosten** 20, 310, 537, 573, 662; *pp.* 610, 981.

brestplate *n.* breastplate 748.

bretages see **britage**.

bretful *adj.* brimful, crammed 390.

bretnes see **brytten**.

bridul *n.* rein, bridle 785.

brigges *n. pl.* drawbridges 619.

bri3t, bry3t *adj.* pure, virtuous 202; brilliant, splendid 338, 959, 1242; bright, shining 410, 756, 846, 1116, 1123, 1268; shining, gleaming 543, 593, 606, 753, 1223; lustrous, sparkling 643; bright, blazing 733.

bri3tned *pt. 3 sg.* shone, glittered 549.

bri3tnesse *n.* radiance 415.

brynge *v.* bring, fetch, send 354, 1044; *pr. 3 sg.* **bryngeþ** 1048; *pt. 3 sg.* **bro3t** 263, 928; *pt. 3 pl.* **bro3t** 196, 235; **bro3ten** 591, 649; **bro3te** 596; *pp.* **bro3t** 933, 973, 1009, 1056, 1169, 1321; **ybro3t** 301.

brynye *n.* coat of mail, corselet 748; **burnee** 562; **brunee** 1242; *pl.* **brynnyis** 281; **bruneys** 959; **brunyes** 1123.

brynston *n.* brimstone, burning sulphur 675.

britage *n. pl.* defensive structure on the back of an elephant, defensive barricade or parapet 593; *pl.* **bretages** 577; **britages** 662, 981.

britaged *pp.* provided with a parapet or barricade 338; **ibrytaged** 413.

brytten *v.* slay 906; *pr. 3 sg.* **bretnes**

butchers, dismembers, destroys 1132; *pp.*
britned 408; brytned 940; brutned
1239.

broches *n. pl.* brooches (jewelry) 643,
1064, 1278.

brod(e) *adj.* broad, wide, large 61, 70, 292,
450, 604, 662, 664, 755, 1009; ~ *se* open
sea 61, 292.

brode *n.* breadth; *on* ~ on every side 638;
see also abrod(e).

bro3t, bro3te, bro3ten see brynge.

broken see breke.

brond(e) *n.* sword, blade 543, 547, 770.

brosed *pp.* crushed, beaten 833, 1196.

brosten see brestyþ.

broþ(e) *n.* broth, soup 724, 1073.

broþer *n.* brother 152, 940, 941, 994, 1004,
1132.

brouden see breydeþ.

broun *adj.* shining, polished, bright 546;
browne brown, dark 720.

browded see breydeþ.

browet *n.* soup, stew 1073.

brunee, bruneys, brunyes see brynye.

brutned see brytten.

burde *n.* maiden, woman 104; berde 1091.

burges *n. pl.* citizens 1251.

burie *v.* bury 572, 1152.

burne *n.* man, soldier, esp. a knight 225,
275, 486, 494, 606, 663, 799, 915, 956,
967, 1044, 1048, 1196; unmarked dative
with body part 826; berne 16, 79; *pl.*
burnes 373, 415, 501, 537, 577, 638,
660, 743, 833, 845, 969, 1004, 1010;
bernes 77.

burnee see brynye.

burnesched *pp.* as *adj.* polished, burnished
753.

burwe *n.* town, citadel, fortified place 373,
408, 443, 450, 568, 663, 682, 722, 824,
832, 906, 956, 1044, 1152, 1223, 1239;
poss. sg. the town's, of the town 744;
borwe 310, 312, 490, 1085; borow 656;
burowe 778.

buschment *n.* ambush, body of men lying
in ambush 1116; ~ *brake vp* troops
attacked from ambush 1116.

busy *adj.* busy, occupied 572.

buske *v. reflex.* prepare, get ready 187; *pr.
3 pl.* busken hasten 373, 743; *pt. 3 sg.*
busked set forth, hastened 459; dressed,
arrayed 745; *pp.* busked made ready,

prepared 678; ~ *out of bedde* get up
743; ~ *me boun* get myself ready 187.

cacchen *v.* get, take 737; *pr. 2 pl.* cacche
receive, get 772; *pr. 3 pl.* cacchen seize,
pick up 528; receive, meet 660; *pt. 3 pl.*
cau3ten took, captured 588; kay3t took
948; *pp.* cacched driven 728; cau3t
overcome, afflicted 1030.

caytifes *n. pl.* wretches, poor persons 123;
scoundrels, wicked persons 771; chaytyfes 143; see also kaytif.

calf *n.* calf 1227.

calleþ *pr. 3 sg.* calls 89, 968; *pr. 3 pl.*
callen 1299; *pt. 3 sg.* called 261; *pp.*
caled called, named 36, 51, 147; ycalled
6; called summoned 213, 885; calde
named 938.

calued *pt. 3 sg.* calved, gave birth 1227.

cam(e) see come *v.*

cameles *n. pl.* camels 457, 573.

cancred *pp.* as *adj.* ulcerated, diseased 129.

candel *n.* candle 1260.

canker *n.* tumour 32, 178.

canste *pr. 2 sg.* know of 90; *pt. 3 sg.*
couþ(e) understood 81, 805; knew of
93; could, was/were able, knew how
41, 132, 1036, 1038 (2nd use), 1151,
1274; *pt. 3 pl.* couþ(e) 477, 1038 (1st
use).

care *n.* distress, hardship, misfortune 40,
1240.

careynes see karayn.

carful *adj.* anxious 1014.

carpyn *v.* speak 361; *pr. 3 pl.* carpen 734;
pt. 3 sg. carped 200.

carte *n.* cart; *pl.* cartes 1006; ~ *fulle* cart
load 1279.

caste *n.* throwing of darts or stones 625,
630.

castel *n.* castle (battlemented structures
containing armed men carried on an
elephant's back) 466, 584, 588; *pl.* castels 428, 450, 567, 573.

ycasteled *pp.* provided with fortified
towers 290.

casteþ *pr. 3 sg.* throws, casts 750; *pt. 3 sg.*
kest 1332; *pt. 3 pl.* kesten 645; kast
948; caste planned, plotted, determined,
devized 163; casten 1109; kesten
hurled missiles with a siege engine 679;
imper. pl. kesten cast, throw 719; *pp.*
cast cast (in metal) 1270.

cattes *n. pl.* cats 703.

cauȝt(en) see **cacchen**.

cause *n.* reason, cause, purpose 344, 348, 495, 1041.

certayn *adj.* certain, specific 85.

certifiet *pp.* directed, instructed 384.

cesed *pt. 3 sg.* ceased 1243; *pp.* ended 1141.

chaf *n.* chaff, straw 806.

chaynes see **cheyne**.

chaire, chayre *n.* chair, throne 471, 473, 594.

chaytyfes see **caytifes**.

chambre *n.* room, apartment 736.

charbokel *n.* as *adj.* carbuncle (precious stone of a red or fiery color, e.g., ruby or garnet) 594; *n. pl.* **charboklis** 329; **charbokles** 473.

chares *n. pl.* chariots 461.

charge *v.* command, impose a duty on 347.

charge *pr. 1 sg.* order, command, request 100; *pr. 3 sg.* **chargeþ** 887; *pt. 3 pl.* **charged** 368; appointed, assigned 736; *pp.* **charged** loaded 461.

charme *n.* medicinal charm, magic spell; *in ~* in the form of an incantation 852; *pl.* **charmes** 100.

chaunce *n.* event, esp. one that is unforeseen or beyond human control; *for ~ þat may falle* no matter what happens 887.

chaundelers *n. pl.* candlesticks 471, 594.

chaunge *v.* change, alter 1024; *pr. 3 sg.* **chaungeþ** 1096; *pr. 3 pl.* **chaungen** 1147.

chauntements *n. pl.* enchantments, acts of magic or witchcraft 100.

chef *adj.* highest in rank or authority, chief 341, 963.

cheffare *n.* goods in trade, merchandize 1318 (n.).

cheyne *n.* chain 766; *pl.* **chaynes** 619.

cheke *n.* cheek, jaw 31, 91; *pl.* **chekes** sides 473.

chek-wecche *n.* officer who watches against assaults 736.

chepe *v.* buy, bid for 1318 (n.).

chepis *n. pl.* bargains, purchases 1318 (n.).

chersly *adv.* affectionately, tenderly 887.

chertes see **scherte**.

ches *pt. 3 sg.* chose 143; *pt. 3 pl.* **chosen** took 341; *~ . . . out* selected 735; **chossyn** 158; *pp.* **chosen** 138, 963; *pp.* as *adj.* choice, excellent 471; *pp.* as *n.*

chosen or choice men 461; *~ her wey* picked, took their way 341.

chese *n.* cheese 368 (n.); *pl.* **cheses** 384.

cheuentayn *n.* ruler, chieftain, commander 341; **chyuentayn** 368, 963; *pl.* **cheuentayns** 329; **chyuentayns** 735; *chef ~* commander in chief 341.

chewe *v.* eat, consume 1076.

chiden *pr.* (*pt.?*) *3 pl.* argue 735.

child *n.* child 108.

chyuentayn see **cheuentayn**.

choppyn *pr. 3 pl.* mount (a piece of metal) 329 (n.).

chosen, chossyn see **ches**.

churche *n.* church 143.

cite, cyte *n.* a walled town or city, populace, inhabitants of a city 315, 319, 325, 339, 343, 357, 405, 420, 424, 445, 488, 615, 647, 684, 712, 802, 837, 868, 900, 907, 953, 962, 1035, 1037, 1065, 1141, 1158, 1160, 1174, 1222, 1226, 1273, 1286; (one) city 46; (through) the city 944; *pl.* **citees** 139; **cytees** 299.

citezeins *n. pl.* freemen of a city 78.

clayme *n.* claim 502.

clansed *pt. 3 sg.* became clear or bright 245; *refl. ~ hitself* grew bright 245.

clarioun *n.* as *adj.* trumpet 529.

clateren *pr. 3 pl.* crash, clatter 58, 573.

claures *n. pl.* claws 703 (n.).

clef *n.* cliff 106.

clene *adj.* clean, pure, unsullied, uninjured 95, 106, 122, 631, 761, 860, 1270, 1279.

clene *adv.* entirely, completely 698, 831.

clenly *adv.* entirely, completely 178.

clere *adj.* bright 245.

clerk, clerke *n.* learned man, scholar, administrator, priest, ecclesiastic 132, 584, 711, 789, 1325; *pl.* **clerkes** 318, 714, 719, 725, 1260.

cleue *v.* split apart 58; *pp.* **cloue** cracked, split 826.

clymyþ *pr. 3 sg.* climbs 1198.

cloched *pt. 3 sg.* stuck together, formed a lump 32.

closed *pp.* enclosed, encased 457, 761, 778.

cloþ(e) *n.* cloth 171, 228, 240, 242, 248, 474; *pl.* **cloþes** clothes 746; cloths 1279; **cloþys** 328.

cloudes *n. pl.* clouds 58.

cloue see **cleue**.

clustred *pp.* as *adj.* gathered in a bunch, thickly placed 679.

cogges *n. pl.* ships 290.

cold *adj.* cold 538.

colde *n.* disease produced by excessive 'coldness' (one of the four 'qualities'), such as gout or paralysis 1030.

colke *n.* core, centre or bottom of the heart 920 (n.).

colour *n.* heraldic colour 750; *pl.* **coloures** armorial bearings 335.

comaundeþ see **commaundiþ**.

combred *pp.* harassed, harmed 902.

come *n.* coming 348, 495.

come(n) *v.* come 267, 360, 428, 588; *pt. 2.sg.* **cam** came 1088; *pt. 3 sg.* **cam**, **came** came 123, 465, 555, 567, 1322; **come** 212, 630, 1066; *pt. 3 pl.* **come**, **comen** came 160, 218, 375, 445, 450, 457, 485, 609, 631, 646, 689, 859, 958; **comyn** 339, 1054; *imper.pl.* **comeþ** come 771; *pp.* **come, comen** 83, 493, 1041; **comyn** 275; *of his body* ~ fathered by him 275; ~ *in* returned to, regained 1054.

comyng *n.* coming 344.

comlich *adj.* noble 768; **comelich** 954, 961, 1216.

commaundiþ, commaundyþ *pr. 3 sg.* commands, demands 267, 1263, 1324; **comaundeþ** 639; **commaundeþ** 694; **commaundys** 1293.

complet *pp.* finished, completed 1043.

complyn *n.* as *adj.* compline (the last of the seven daily services or 'hours') 612.

comsed *pp.* begun, undertaken 639.

comunes *n. pl.* common people 318.

conceyued *pt. 3 sg.* conceived 108.

condit *n.* conduit, water channel 689; safe-conduct 1036, 1043, 1066.

confort *n.* remedy 248.

consail, consayl *n.* meeting, conference, council 213, 267, 694, body of advisers 734, 968; **conseil, conseyl** 89; a devious or secret plan 354; advice, scheme 728, 859, 983, 1177; *kyþe* ~ give advice, advize 983.

constables *n. pl.* high military officers 885.

contreys *n. pl.* countries, regions 47; **contrees** 318.

coppe *n.* drinking vessel, goblet, cup 918; *by þe* ~ in drinking 918.

copper *n.* copper 1270.

corde *n.* rope, cord, string 367.

cormous *n.* as *adj.* hornpipe (early form of bagpipe) 529.

corners *n. pl.* angles, points 763.

corres *n. pl.* mongrels, stray dogs 703, 711.

corrours *n. pl.* messengers, couriers 195.

cors *n.* body, corpse 224, 948; *pl.* **corses** 685, 718, 1246.

cors see **cours**.

corsed *pp.* accursed, damned 1309; as *adj.* 688; **coursed** 725.

corsedlich *adv.* damnably 1334.

corteys *adj.* gracious, merciful 181.

coste *n.* coast, district 195; *pl.* **costes** 68.

cote *n.* cloak, garment decorated with armorial bearings to wear over armour 750.

coþe *v.* to infect with disease 688.

coueyte *v.* desire strongly 344.

couered see **keuered**.

countours *n. pl.* counters, disks used for computing 132.

cours *n.* course 195; *pl.* **cors** 689; ~ *nomen* started on their way 195.

coursed see **corsed**.

couþ, couþe see **canste**.

couenaunt *n.* promise, pledge 999.

couered *pp.* as *adj.* covered 474; **keuered** 466.

craft(e) *n.* power 90, 190.

craftly *adv.* skilfully 1270; **craftily** 466.

crayers *n. pl.* small vessels 290.

crammen *pr. 3 pl.* stuff 686.

cramp *n.* cramp, disease characterized by contortion or spasms 1030.

crepel *n.* (implicitly possessive) cripple's 1033.

cry *n.* shout, cry, noise, outcry 18, 529, 1195; see also **acry**.

crye *v.* proclaim; *imper.* **crieþ** shout, cry 723; *pt. 3 sg.* **cried** called, cried 248, 1229; *pr. 3 pl.* **criande** calling, crying 200; ~ *a market* announce the holding of a market 1317.

criours *n. pl.* officers in a court of law who summon witnesses or the accused 1299.

cristalle *n.* crystal 106.

Cristen *adj. n.* Christian 194, 428, 839, 902.

croys *n.* cross 18, 272.

croysen *pr. 3 pl.* cross, make the sign of the cross 528.

croked *pp. adj.* as *n. pl.* lame, misshapen 129.

crosschen *pr. 3 pl.* smashed, shattered 538.

croune *n.* crown 17, 303, 761, 931, 938, 997.

crouned *pp.* as *adj.* crowned 277.

cud *adj.* courteous 215 (n.); see also **kyþe**.

cur(e) *n.* cure, remedy 90, 198, 1043.

cured *pp.* restored to health, cured 272.

cuþe *n.* country 40; **kuþþe** 94.

day *n.* day 128, 463, 637, 729, 741, 857, 957, 1013, 1078; dawn 430; **day, dawe** 188, 1303; *poss. sg.* **daies** 680; *pl.* **daies** 776, **dayes** 1071; *by* ~ at daylight 430; *on a* ~ one day 957; *to do of dawe* (lit. to put out of days) to deprive of life, put to death 188, 1303; *daies worke* something built in a day 680; *daies in your lyue* during your life 776.

dale *n.* valley, dell 576, 628.

dartes *n. pl.* javelins or spears 842.

daschen *pr. 3 pl.* threw (themselves) down, knocked down 716; **daschen** strike, knock 1091; *pt. 3 pl.* **daschenden** rushed, dashed 576; *pr.p.* **dasschande** 812.

daunsyng *n.* dancing 855.

dawe see **day**.

ded(e) *adj.* dead 128, 204, 604, 640, 685, 717, 1078, 1152, 1204, 1207, 1212, 1246; as *n.* dead men, corpses; bodies 645 (2×), 1154.

ded(e) *n.* action, deed 155, 163, 183, 908, 988, 1059, 1306; *pl.* **dedes** 103, 950; **dedis** 153.

deden see **do(n)**.

deep see **depe** *n.*

defaute *n.* lack (of food) 1077.

defence *n.* defence, act of defending oneself 622, 672, 871.

defende(n) *v.* defend 316, 779.

defensable *adj.* ready and able to fight 449.

defete *pp.* disfigured, changed in appearance, overcome by hunger 1248.

defye *v.* digest 1166.

dey *v.* die 695, 776, 786, 1091; **deye** 1099, 1193; *pt. 3 sg.* **deyed** 6, 94, 920, 932; **deyd** 1236; **deied** 1334; *pt. 3 pl.* **diȝeden** 581.

deyes *n.* dais 697; *on* ~ presiding over the court, (sitting) in judgement 697.

deil *n.* grief, sorrow 645, 716, 1101; mourning, lamenting 855; **doil** 252;

was ~ *to byholde* was distressing to see 645.

dele *v.* deal, treat 1108.

delyueryn *pr. 3 pl.* bestow, grant 1036.

demen *v.* judge, believe 988; *pt. 3 sg.* **dempte** decreed 138; *pt. 3 pl.* **demeden** agreed, decided 271, 1101; passed judgement 697; *pp.* **demed** 989, 1337.

departe *v.* separate 234.

departyng *n.* departure, end 257.

depe *adj.* deep 842; *as n.* **depe,** deep deep water, sea 56, 72, 285; bottom 1154.

dere *adj.* dear, excellent 130, 479, 680; dear, beloved 184, 226, 276; noble 479.

dere *adv.* dearly, at a high cost 204 (n.), 300, 1214.

dered *pt. 3 pl.* harmed, damaged 808.

dereworþ *adj.* precious 300.

derk *n.* darkness, night 857.

derkned *pt. 3 sg.* grew dark 1284.

derst *pt. 3 sg.* there needed 1260.

dest see **do(n)**.

destruyed *pt. 3 pl.* wasted, dissipated 1102; *pp.* **distroied** destroyed 1296.

deþ(e) *n.* death 128, 163, 183, 188, 204, 226, 300, 323, 370, 574, 660, 695, 728, 833, 898, 901, 1102, 1196, 1214, 1303, 1306, 1328.

deue *adj.* as *n. pl.* deaf people 130.

deuel *n.* devil 786; *pl.* **deueles** 188; *þe* ~ *haue þat recche* may the devil have (it), whoever may care 786.

deuelich *adv.* horribly, terribly, awfully 453.

deuysed see **dyuyseþ**.

dewe *n.* dew, moisture 628.

diademe *n.* diadem, crown 932.

diche *n.* ditch, trench, moat 629, 812, 1154, 1204, 1212, 1284; *pl.* **diches** 666, 685.

dide see **do(n)**.

dyemauntes *n. pl.* diamonds 1257.

diȝeden see **dey**.

diȝt *pp.* arrayed, set 521; gone 430; *weren* ~ *forþ* had gone out 430.

dymedyn *pt. 3 pl.* grew dark, grew dim 535; **dymmed** 729.

dyn *n.* noise, din, clamour 252, 578, 1129, 1193.

dyner *n.* dinner, the dinner table 957.

dynnyng *n.* noise, blaring 855.

dynt(e) *n.* blow of a weapon or combat

missile, stroke 1202, 1204, 1212, 1236;
pl. **dyntes** 803.

disciples *n. pl.* disciples 138.

distroied see **destruyed**.

dit, dyt *n.* clamour, outcry, noise 252, 808,
1193.

dyuyseþ *pr. 3 sg.* inspects, looks upon,
observes 489; *pt. 3 pl. refl.* **deuysed**
considered 1237; **deuysed** *pp.* designed,
contrived 760.

dyzs *n. pl.* dice 808; *nozt a* ~ not a bit, not
at all 808.

dogges *n. pl.* dogs 786.

doil see **deil**.

doylful *adj.* terrible, piteous 163, 226.

dom(e) *n.* sentence, judgement, fate 271,
370, 695, 908, 989; law 1101; *demeden a*
~ passed a law (made a judgement) 989,
1101; *demeden by* ~ judged 271; *by* ~
judicially 695.

dombe *adj.* as *n. pl.* dumb, deaf-mutes
130.

domesmen *n. pl.* judges, magistrates 697.

dommyn *pr. 3 pl.* dam, fill up, choke 685.

do(n) *v.* do 138, 908; put 188; **done** 216;
pr. 2 sg. **dest** 1000; *pr. 3 sg.* **doþ** does
314; acts 989; *pr. 1 pl.* **don** do 988; *pt. 3
sg.* **dide** performed 131; *pt. 3 pl.* put 323;
deden delivered 342; *pp.* **don** completed, concluded, over 183, 729, 857,
1236, 1303, 1306, 1337; *diden to þe deþe*
put to death 323; *do of dawe* (lit. put out
of days) deprive of life 188, 1303.

dongen *pt. 3 pl.* knocked 680.

donked *pp.* made wet, moistened 628.

dore *n.* door 1091; *pl.* **dores** 1257.

dore-nayl *n.* door-nail 1078.

doþ see **do(n)**.

douȝti, douȝty *adj.* brave, worthy 479,
994; *superl.* **douȝtiest** 1207; as *n. pl.* 463.

doun *adv.* down, below, downward, on or
to the ground 9, 72, 171, 326, 453, 538,
540, 548, 573, 578, 605, 661, 676, 708,
716, 773, 793, 812, 836, 874, 947, 967,
981, 1077, 1091, 1148, 1154, 1264, 1272,
1292.

doust *n.* dust, ashes, powder 535, 578, 723,
1284.

dragoun *n.* dragon (used as a battle standard) 284, 393; *pl.* **dragouns** 331.

drawen *v.* pull, draw, drag, carry 717; *pt. 3
sg.* **drowe** dragged 944; *pt. 3 pl.* **drowen**
went 430, 453, 574; drew, folded 1337;

refl. betook themselves 323; **drow** drew,
went 1186; *pp.* **drawyn** hoisted 393.

dreden *pr. 1 pl.* fear 370.

drenche *v.* sink, go under 72.

drenches *n. pl.* tonics, medicinal potions
99.

dressed *pp.* put in order, built, lifted up
393; as *adj.* **ydressed** prepared 282.

dryeden *pt. 3 pl.* dried 793.

driede *pt. 3 sg.* suffered, endured 124.

Driȝten *n.* the Lord (God or Christ) 521.

drynke *n.* drink 723.

drynke *v.* drink 1074.

dryueþ *pr. 3 sg.* aims a blow 1210; drives,
impels, travels 56, 62; *pr. 3 pl.* **dryuen**
hurl, shoot 842; *pt. 3 sg.* **drof** drifted,
was blown 535; *pt. 3 pl.* **driuen** suffered,
endured 712; *pp.* **dryuen** studded, set
1257.

dromedaries *n. pl.* camels 453, 574, 581.

dromound a large sea-going ship 56.

dropeden *pt. 3 pl.* dripped, trickled 793.

droppe *n.* drop 776.

drouned *pp.* drowned 483.

drowe, drownen see **drawen**.

duk(e) *n.* duke, leader 932, 994, 1129,
1186; warrior 1207; *poss. sg.* **dukes**
1214; *pl.* **dukes** 220, 271, 436, 629, 957.

dwelle *v.* tarry, remain 1098, 1323; *pt. 3 sg.*
dwelde dwelt 313.

ech(e) *adj.* each, every 96, 111, 135, 195,
305, etc.; **eche a** 610, 802, 966, 1312; see
also **ilka**.

echon *pron.* each one, every single one 460,
767, 780.

efte *adv.* in return, in reply 788.

egle *n.* eagle 330.

eȝte *card.num.* as *adj.* eight 1130.

eyen *n. pl.* eyes 1001, 1049.

eyȝt *ord.num.* as *adj.* eighth 149.

eyr *n.* air 244, 259.

elde *n.* (old) age 1103.

eldres *n. pl.* old authorities 112.

eleuen *card.num.* as *adj.* eleven 1175.

elleueþ *ord.num.* eleventh 151.

ellis, ellys *adv.* besides, otherwise 352,
608, 962; **elles** 880, 988.

emperie *n.* imperial rule 5.

emperour *n.* emperor 1, 50, 173, 233, 268,
904, 924, 934, 943, 964, 998, 1026;
empererour 216.

enclosed *pp. adj.* confined, imprisoned 692.

encresche *v.* increase, make larger or stronger 143.

ende *n.* end 71, 168, 177, 301, 515, 914, 991 (n.), 1173; *to þe last* ~ all the way through 966; *the scharpe* ~ spear point 1122.

ended *pt. 3 sg.* died 725, 924; **endid** came to an end 464.

endeles *adj.* eternal 117, 118.

ene *adv.* first of all 125 (n.).

enemy *n.* enemy 1056.

enfamyned *pp.* starved 1248.

enforme *v.* instruct 1157.

engyne *n.* siegecraft, a mechanical device to assault or throw stones at walls or towers 1188, 1209; *pl.* **engynes** 324, 678, 813, 823, 1191.

enys *adv.* once 126; *at* ~ at the same time, simultaneously 126.

entriþ *pr. 3 sg.* takes possession 934; *imper.sg.* **entre** enter 1088; *pp.* **entred** entered 1026.

enuenymyd *pp.* as *adj.* poisoned 658.

er *adv.* formerly, previously 256; *super.* **erst** first 924.

er *conj.* before 339, 588; see also **or**.

eraunde *n.* errand, mission 50; **erand** 216.

ere *n.* ear 108 (n.); *at* ~ through the ear, through speech 108.

erye *v.* plough (up) 1294.

erles *n. pl.* earls, nobles 268.

erst see **er**.

erþe *n.* world, ground, soil 9, 118, 121, 175, 538, 579, 1292; *vpon* ~ on earth, anywhere, at all 90, 170, 244, 1146.

est *n.* east 1230.

etyþ *pr. 3 sg.* eats 1088; *pt. 3 pl.* **eten** 1075, 1168.

etnes *n. pl.* monsters, giants 780 (n.).

eued *pt. 3 sg.* gave birth to (a lamb or kid) 1228.

eure *n.* destiny, fate, fortune 998 (n.).

euen(e) *adv.* exactly 150, 1215; equally, alike 117, 456; directly, straight, 1026, 1182.

euer(e) *adv.* ever, at any time 79, 88, 1208, 1262; always, forever 120, 297.

euerech(e) *adj.* every 502, 650, 711, 720; **euereche a** 690, 853, 1171.

ewe-lombe *n.* female lamb 1228.

face *n.* face 30, 179; *pl.* expressions 1147.

fader(e) *n.* father, God the father 33, 113, 119, 198 (an unmarked dative); *poss.sg.* father's 1029.

fayle *v.* (*usually impers.*) lack, be lacking 796; *pr. 3 sg.* **fayle** they lack 800; is scarce, is lacking 881; *pt. 3 sg.* **fayled** they lacked 790; *pt. 3 pl. fayleden herte* lacked courage, lost heart 597.

fayn *adj.* glad, happy 1013; *comp.* **fayner of** more eager for, more desirous of 1172.

fayndom *n.* joy 1029.

faynt see **feynt(e)**.

fayntly *adv.* feignedly, treacherously 496.

faire, fayre *adj.* excellent 198; light-coloured 364; considerable, sizable 555; beautiful, attractive 1148, 1250; courteous, eloquent 1302, 1326; *superl.* **fairest** 1108.

fayre *adv.* splendidly 745.

fayþ *n.* faith 207; loyalty 972.

faiþles *adj.* infidel, perfidious 485, 496, 513; **feyþles** 597.

fale see **fele**.

falle *v.* happen 887; *pr. 3 sg.* **fallyþ** belongs, pertains 510; **falleþ** falls 1204; *pr.* (*pt.?*) *3 pl.* **fallen** 242, 377, 601, 731, 1148, 1154; *pt. 3 sg.* **ful** fell 65; **fel** 1131; *pt. 3 pl.* **felle** 946; **fellen** 1077, 1117; *pp.* **fallen** 614, 1028, 1042, 1290.

falleþ see **fele v.**

fals *adj.* un-Christian 517; treacherous 599, 601, 1131; as *n.* 539, 555.

falsede *n.* treachery, falsehood 1108.

falwed *pt. 3 pl.* turned pale, blanched 1147.

fanes *n. pl.* banners, pennants 291.

fanward *n.* vanguard 433, 553.

farcostes *n. pl.* boats 289.

faste *adv.* quickly, instantly 234, 458, 1147; firmly 287; vigorously, hard 539, 1112.

fastyng *part. adj.* fasting 1090.

faucoun *n.* falcon 314; *pl.* **faucouns** 892.

fauchoun *n.* falchion, broad sword, dagger 399; **fauchyn** 396.

faute *n.* blemish, flaw 179.

fauted *pt. 3 sg. impers.* was lacking 391.

fax *n.* hair 364.

feble *adj.* weak, feeble 882.

fecche *v.* bring back 215; obtain 774; *pr. 3 sg.* **feccheþ** fetches, brings (forth) 1095.

fedde *pt. 3 sg.* fed 134; **fedyng** *pr.p.* feeding 1330.

feet *n.* deed 1038.

feet see fot(e).

feffyt *pt. 3 sg.* presented 1330.

fey mortally wounded, dying, dead 464, 614, 774, 930.

feynt(e) *adj.* timid, cowardly 517; **faynt** 1166; weak, feeble 881.

feynte *pr. 3 pl.* grow weak 1148.

feyþles see faiþles.

fel *n.* skin 992; *pl.* **felles** 698.

fel see falleþ.

felawys *n. pl.* companions, disciples 146.

feld(e) *n.* field, battle ground 371, 388, 391, 458, 464, 485, 539, 599, 601, 614, 828; *pl.* **feldes** 416.

felde see falleþ.

felden *pt. 3 pl.* felt, smelled 1090; **felleden** 243.

fele *adj.*¹ many 47, 309, 902, 972, 1090, 1269; as *n.* 207; **fale** 930.

fele *adj.*² fierce, bold 871 (n.).

fele *v.* fell, strike down 892; *pr. 3 sg.* **falleþ** attacks, fells 930; *pt. 3 sg.* **felde** felled 599 (1st use) (n.).

felle(n) see falle.

felleden see felden.

felles see fel *n.*

felonsly *adv.* fiercely 822 (n.).

fende *n.* fiend, devil, Satan 524, 838.

fenged see fongen.

fer *adv. adj.* far 82; **ferre** *comp.* further, more 135, 371, 382, 877; *adj comp.* **ferre** far, farther, opposite 991.

ferce see fers.

ferde *n.*¹ fear 65.

ferde *n.*² army, troop 483, 555, 599.

ferde *pt. 3 sg.* appeared, looked, was 1255; *impers.* it behaved, it was 534, 552; *pt. 3 pl.* behaved 1079.

ferke *v.* go 877; *pr. 3 sg.refl.* **ferkiþ** go out or away 1046; *pp.* **yferked** driven 82.

ferly *n.* wonder, marvel 33, 133, 198; miracle 237.

ferlich *adj.* wondrous 458; *adv.* extremely, exceedingly 648.

ferre see fer.

fers *adj.* fierce, proud 838, 991; **ferce** 871.

ferst *n.* roof-tree, roof, ceiling 835 (n.).

ferst see firste.

ferþe *ord.num.* as *pron.* fourth 145.

ferþer *adv.* more distant, further away 276.

ferþyng *n.* farthing, one-quarter penny 1312.

ferþing-worþ *n.* a farthing's worth, a miniscule amount 1143.

fete see fot(e).

fetoures *n. pl.* features or parts of the body 1053.

fettes *pr. 3 sg.* fetches, brings 1046; *pt. 3 pl.* **fetten** 193.

feþer-hames *n. pl.* wings 683.

feþres *n. pl.* feathers 731.

fewe *adj.* few 1114, 1311; *comp.* **fewer** 23.

fif, fyf *card.num.* as *adj.* five 133, 134, 449, 1117; **fyue** 654, 779.

fifþe *ord.num.* as *pron.* fifth 146.

XV *card. num.* fifteen 1187.

fiȝt *n.* fighting, battle, conflict 464, 513, 517.

fiȝt(en) *v.* fight, battle 654; **fiȝt** 862; *pt. 3 pl.* **fouȝt** 539, 822; **fiȝtyng** *pr.p.* as *adj.* 1117; **fyghtyng** 1187.

fynde *v.* find, discover, obtain 371, 392, 1038; *pr. 1 sg.* **fynde** read, calculate 23; *pt. 3 pl.* **fondyn** 398; **founden** 1274; *pp.* **fond** found 464.

fyne *n.* end, death 1100.

fyne *adj.* fine, excellent, precious, costly 473, 746; pure 1276.

fyngres *n. pl.* fingers 1031.

firmament *n.* firmament, sky 552, 701.

first *ord.num.* first 113; *as adj.* **furst** 862.

firste *adv.* (at) first 699; **ferst** 433.

fisch *n.* fish 1072; *pl.* **fisches** 134.

fyue see fif, fyf.

flambande *pr.p.* as *adj.* flaming, ablaze 657.

flasches *n. pl.* standing pools, swamps, puddles 575.

flatte *pt. 3 sg.* fell flat, dropped down 65; *pt. 3 pl.* **flatten** 812 (n.).

flatte *adj.* flat 1077 (perhaps the prec.).

flauour *n.* odor, fragrance 243.

flawe *pt. 3 sg.* flowed, was wafted 243.

fle(e) *v.* fly 409, 892; *pt.3 sg.* **flow(e)** flew 828, 1126; *pt. 3 pl.* **flowen** 657.

fleyn *pp.* flayed; *quyk ~* skinned alive 698; see also **of-fleis**.

flesch(e) *n.* flesh 179, 706; meat 1072; *fader of flesche* earthly father, ancestor 33.

fleschy *adj.* plump 1250.

fleþe *pr. 3 sg.* flees, retreats 524; *pt. 3 sg.*

flowe fled 909; *pt. 3 pl.* **flowen** 314, 615; ~ *any fote* retreats any distance at all 524.

flikreþ *pr. 3 sg.* flickers 1256.

flynt-ston *n.* a hard stone, flint-stone 534; *pl.* **flynt-stonys** 1126.

flode *n.* current, sea 82; **floode** 483.

floynes *n. pl.* small ships 289.

flor *n.* ground, foundation 835.

floreyns, floryns *n. pl.* florins, foreign gold coins 1143, 1168, 1172, 1276, 1312.

flow, flowe, flowen see **fle(e), fleþe.**

flowen *pt. 3 pl.* flayed, shaved 364.

fode *n.* food 774, 877, 881, 1071, 1143, 1166, 1248; **foode** 1081.

foyned *pt. 3 pl.* thrust, lunged 822.

folis *n.poss.* steed's, horse's 818.

folke *n.* people, persons 133, 207, 391, 399, 447, 482, 485, 496, 513, 597, 622, 627, 641, 648, 672, 688, 701, 838, 1090, 1103, 1131.

folowe *v.* follow, succeed 984; *pr. 3 sg.* **folweþ** 494, 566; *pt. 3 pl.* **folwed** 910.

folowed *pt. 3 pl.* baptized 207 (n.); **foulled** 193.

foman *n.* enemy, foe 1060; *pl.* **fomen** 1168.

fomed *pt. 3 sg.* gushed, spurted 575.

fond, fondyn see **fynde.**

fongen *v.* seize 1168; *pt.3 sg.* **fenged** received 1310.

font *n.* font-stone 193 (n.).

foode see **fode.**

foot see **fot(e).**

for *conj.* for, because 38, 81, 266, 407, 517, etc.; so 193.

for *prep.* in spite of 19, 1200 (2×); for, because of 38, 65, 81, 155, 162, etc.; for the sake of 724; as 103, 189, 264, 963; instead of 96, 158; on behalf of 194, 868; in exchange for 322; against 810.

forbesyn *n.* example 399.

forbeten *pp.* severely beaten or wounded 846.

foreuere *adv.* forever, permanently 923, 1296, 1327.

forgyue *v.* pardon, absolve 1163.

foriuggyd *pp.* as *adj.* condemned 302.

foriustes *pr.3 sg.* jousts destructively, unhorses, defeats in combat 542.

forlong *n.* furlong 828.

formes *pr. 3 sg.* deploys, arranges 421; *pp.*

fourmed created, given rise to 113, 1312 (n.).

forsakeþ *pr. 3 sg.* refuses, rejects 1065; *pt. 3 sg.* **forsoke** 1159; *pt. 3 pl.* **forsoken** 1138.

forschorne *pt. 3 pl.* cut to pieces 562 (n.).

forstoppette *pp.* as *adj.* completely shut off, smothered 580.

forto *conj.* to (usually to mark the infinitive and to adjust b-verse syllable count to achieve metricality) 187, 348, 409, 495, 555, etc.

forþ(e) *adv.* forward 1097, 1301; out 193, 430, 444, 571, 771, 827, 859, 1299; away 631, 1046, 1097; *weren diȝt* ~ had set/ gone out 430; *beden* ~ called out 444.

forþmyd *prep.* among, before 237.

forþred see **furþer.**

forwarde *n.* agreement, contract 280.

fot(e) *n.* foot, base (of a wall) 447, 524, 627 (n.), 731, 818; **foot** 992; *pl.* **feet** 396, 701, 1031, 1053, 1128; **fete** 223; *vpon* ~ on foot, walking 447; *any* ~ the smallest distance 524; *fallen to* ~ fall to the ground 731.

fouȝt see **fiȝt(en).**

foul(e) *n.* bird 314, 1013; *pl.* **foules** 731, 891.

foulled see **folowed.**

founden see **fynde.**

foure *card. num.* four 292, 329, 396, 397, 416, 421, 447, 470, 648, 704, 923, 931, 1230.

fourche *n.* fork of the body, crotch 746.

fourmed see **formes.**

xl. *card. num.* forty 23.

fourty *card. num.* as *pron.* forty (men) 779.

fourty *card.num.* as *adj.* forty 440, 1071.

fraynes *pr.3 sg.* asks 82; ~ *of* enquires about 1302 (n.).

fram *prep.* from 46, 50, 85, 116, 174, etc.; of 831; **from** 1092.

frasche *adj.* fresh, untired 622; **fresch** 287; *comp.* **frescher** 862.

freke *n.* man, warrior, person 135, 223, 614, 683, 698 (dative of person with body part), 909, 991, 1013, 1029, 1038, 1072, 1187, 1276, 1302; *pl.* **frekes** 1172.

frende *n.* friend, comrade 1060; *pl.* **frendes** ? relatives 972.

frendles *adj.* without friends 909.

frendschup *n.* friendship 1060.

fresch see **frasche.**

freschly *adv.* anew, afresh, suddenly 627.

frytted *pp.* as *adj.* tied or wrapped with a thong 818 (n.).

fro *prep.* from 128, 575, 629, 652, 773, 787, 794 (postposited), 835.

frosletes *n. pl.* strongholds, towers 835.

frounte *n.* foremost line 654; **fronte** forehead, head 746.

froward *prep.* (away) from 67, 602, 973.

frut *n.* fruit 1330.

ful, fulle *adj.* full, filled, in compounds with nouns indicating capacity 334, 419, 461, 675, 762, 1167, 1257, 1279.

ful(l) *adv.* very, quite, most, completely 95, 218, 298, 306, 309, etc.

ful see **falle**.

fulfille *v.* fulfil, comply with 280.

fulle *n.* fill 135.

fure *n.* fire 534, 552, 657, 1126; *pl.* **fures** 733; *vpon (a)* ~ on fire 552; *of* ~ with fire 657.

fured *pt. 3 sg.* set on fire 900.

furst see **first**.

furþer *v.* promote, advance 986; *pp.* **forþred** 1339.

fuste *n.* fist, hand 1144; *pl.* **fustes** 1031; *to pay in þe* ~ to pay in hand 1144.

gaddes *n. pl.* bars, ingots 1266.

gay *adj.* gleaming, bright 330.

gaylers *n. pl.* jailers 1164.

gayly *adv.* splendidly, richly 262.

gayne *v.* heal 42.

galees *n. pl.* galleys 291.

galwes *n.* gallows, ?cross for crucifixion 700.

gan *pt. 3 sg. as auxil. with infin.* did (indicating continuance, rather than commencement of action) 612; *pt. 3 pl.* 925 (with implicit verb of motion).

gapande *pr.pl.* gaping, (of the mouth) wide open 394.

garde *pt. 3 sg.* caused (to be) 262, 347.

garrite *n.* seige tower 651.

gate *n.* (clear) road 1219 (n.).

gate see **gete(n)**.

gawged *pt. 3 sg.* reached (above), projected 414 (n.).

gentile *adj.* noble, pagan 1325.

gere *n.* gear, armor, tackle 550, 593, 642, 751; weapons 669; goods 1268.

gete(n) *v.* get, take, capture 642, 1180; *pr.*

3 pl. **geten** 925; *pt. 3 sg.* **gate** 26; *pp.* **geten** 1219; see also **ʒete** *pp.*

geuen see **ʒeuen**.

gilden *adj.* golden, gilded, decorated with gold 550; **gilde** 330; **gild** 562.

gile *n.* guile, deceitfulness 1106.

gynful *adj.* ingenious, tricky 789, 813; **ienfulle** 1137.

gyng *n.* company, body of retainers 284.

girdel *n.* belt (for carrying a purse or sword) 751; *pl.* **girdeles** 642.

girdiþ *pr. 3 sg.* beats, thrusts 570; *pr. 3 pl.* **girden** strike, attack 556.

gyue(n) see **ʒeuen**.

glad *adj.* pleased, delighted 1045.

glad *adv.* joyfully, cheerfully 199.

glade *v. refl.* comfort, cheer up 39.

gled-fure *n.* fire of burning coals 419, 1256.

gledis *n. pl.* live coals 1082.

glitered *pt. 3 sg.* sparkled, glittered, shone 419.

glowande *pr.p.* as *adj.* glowing, shining 912, 1018, 1256.

glowes *n. pl.* (armour) gloves or gauntlets 757.

gnawen *pp.* gnawed 1094.

go *v.* go 347, 1040, 1062; *pr. 3 sg.* **gooþ** goes 1023; *pt. 3 sg.* **ʒede** went, passed 241, 578, 690, 853, 947, 1065, 1185, 1303; happened, transpired 565; *pt. 3 pl.* **ʒede** went 357; passed forth 631; **ʒeden** 1241; passed into, changed into 557; *pp.* **gon** gone 39, 933, 952; *to þe swerd/deþ ʒede* was slaughtered, died 321, 1299.

gobet *n.* morsel 1146.

God *n.* God 111 (2×), 199, 201, 258, 519, 1023, 1055, 1112, 1155, 1163, 1324; *poss.* **goddis** God's 184.

God-riche *n.* God's kingdom, heaven 1018.

goions *n. pl.* pegs or blocks of metal, pivots 470 (n.).

gold *adj.* gold 564, 746.

gold(e) *n.* gold 88, 262, 284, 330, 331, 394, 401, 419, 470, 472, 475, 564, 642, 644, 746, 749, 751, 754, 756, 757, 761, 912, 1018, 1064, 1167, 1171, 1256, 1266, 1268, 1271, 1276, 1278; *of* ~ made of gold 330, 394, 470, 475, 644, etc.; *clene* ~ pure gold 761; *brennande* ~, *brend* ~, *bournde* ~ gold refined by fire, burnished gold 401, 472, 1268.

golden *adj.* made of gold, golden 291.

gold-hewen *adj.* gilded, ornamented with (beaten) gold 759; see also **hewen** *pp.*

gollet *n.* throat, gullet 394.

gome *n.* man 88, 169, 926, 1040, 1045, 1167, 1171, 1180; *pl.* **gomes** 347, 1106.

gommes *n. pl.* gums or resins used medicinally 99.

gon see **go**.

good(e) *n.* goods, possessions 88; wealth 1146.

goode *adj.* good 1055, 1059; effective 99; precious, valuable 550, 642; *comp.* **beter** 1099; *super.* as *n.* **beste** 541, 892, 969; *goode dede* kindnesses, benefactions 1059.

gooþ see **go**.

goren *pr. 3 pl.* disembowel, butcher 1171; *pt. 3 sg.* **gored** 945.

gorel *n.* glutton, fat man 945.

goste *n.* spirit, ghost; *þe Holy* ~ the Holy Spirit 107, 115, 120.

goteres *n. pl.* gutters, ditches, water channels 564.

gottes see **guttes**.

goutes *n. pl.* streams (of water) 564.

grace *n.*[1] grace, kindness, mercy 278, 519, 1023, 1055, 1059, 1062, 1164, 1180; thanks 258.

grace *n.*[2] plant or herb of healing power 42; *pl.* **graces** 99.

gray *adj.* bright, shining, gleaming 624, 749, 757.

grayn *n.* class, subdivision 111.

grate *n.* lance-rest 749.

graunte *v.* grant 1045, 1110; *pr. 3 sg.* **gr, granteþ** assents 1003; **graunteþ** consents 1040; promises 1106; grants 1164; *pr. 3 pl.* **graunten** grant 867; *imper. sg.* **graunte** grant 1059; *pt. 3 sg.* **graunted** 1062.

grecys *n. pl.* stairs 655.

grehounde *n.* greyhound 1252.

greided *pp.* built, constructed 652 (n.).

grem *n.* anger, injury, trouble 278 (n.), 926.

gremed *pp.* as *adj.* enraged 556.

gret *n.* grit, sandstone 624.

grete *adj.* great, large 91, 291, 328, 331, 583, 622, 624, 652, 1266; noble 258; splendid, magnificent 284, 751, 1254; much, a lot of 808, 1156, 1183; as *n.*

nobles 858, 925, 952; *comp.* **gretter** larger, bigger 827, 1252; *superl. as n.* **grettist** 651.

grete *adv.* greatly 199 (n.).

griffouns *n. pl.* griffins 556.

grym *adj.* severe 42; tempestuous 54; fierce 331.

grym *adv.* severely, sorely 169.

grype *v.* encircle 1252; seize, snatch 1266.

grobben *pr. 3 pl.* dig 1112.

gronnand *pr.p.* murmuring, complaining 199.

grounde *n.* ground, earth, floor 222, 470, 554, 652, 716, 1077, 1112, 1124, 1264; earth, world 169, 912; land, domain 54 (n.); shut, down level with the ground 620; *þe Grekys* ~ the Mediterranean 54; *to* ~ to the ground, to the earth, down 680, 1283; *hewyn to* ~ strike to the ground, kill 311; *on* ~ in the world 169, 912; *to* ~ *broȝt* slain 933.

grounded *pp.* as *adj.* established, grounded 519.

grounden *pp. as adj.* ground, sharpened 570; **ygrounde** 559.

growyng *pr.p.* growing 42; *pp.* **growyn** born, produced 114.

gult *n.* crime 1163.

guttes *n. pl.* guts, entrails 570, 945; **gottes** 1167.

ȝaf see **ȝeuen**.

ȝarken *pr. 3 pl.* set, place, erect 650.

ȝate *n.* gate 583, 650; *pl.* **ȝates** 310, 351, 421, 447, 617, 648, 979, 1173, 1221, 1241; **ȝatis** 490, 1161.

ȝe *pron. nom. 2 sg.* you (formal) 344; *pl.* 771, 772, 774 (2×), 775 (2×), etc.; *acc.dat.pl.* **ȝou** 304, 774, 1095, 1231; **ȝour** *poss. adj.* 299, 303, 343, 344, 372, etc.; *emphatic reflex.* **ȝourselfen** yourselves 1217.

ȝede(n) see **go**.

ȝelde *v.* yield, surrender, give up 351, 406, 1158; *pr. 3 sg.* **ȝeldeþ** 936, 947; *pres. (pt.?) 3 pl.* **ȝelden** give 258; yield 1241; *imper.sg.* **ȝeld** give back 1087; *pp.* **ȝolden** repaid 204; paid for 300; given, rendered 908; surrendered 979.

ȝemyd *pt.3.sg.* cared for, had charge of 64.

ȝerdes *n. pl.* rods (signs of office) 351.

ȝere(s) see **ȝyrys**.

ȝermande *pr.p.* screaming 947.

3erne *adv.* quickly 793; eagerly 821, 1331; 3ernest *super.* first 863 (n.); most eagerly 934 (n.).

3ete *v.* heed 369.

3et(e) *pp.* granted, given 979, 1221; see also gete(n), vn3et.

3eten *pr. 3 pl.* pour 674.

3euen *pr. 3 pl.* grant, give 531, 842; *pt.1 sg.* 3af gave 1087; *pt. 3 sg.* gave 22, 219, 930; *pr. 3 sg. subj.* 3yue give 896; gyue 1112; *pp.* geuen given 278; gyuen 1146.

3if *conj.* if 15, 21, 784, 786, 984, 1007; *bot* ~ unless 668.

3yrys *n. pl.* years 23; *poss. sg.* 3eres of a year 1221; *poss. pl.* 3eres of . . . years 1173.

3it *adv.* yet, still, up to now 135, 159, 263, 339, 609, 781, 1095, 1099, 1234.

3yue see 3euen.

3o *pron.* she 72, 105, 108, 166, 222, 228, 1082, 1096; *acc., dat.* hir her, to her 109, 168, 532; *poss.adj.* hir her 166, 168, 1082.

3olden see 3elde.

3ong *adj.* young 1129, 1186.

3ou, 3our, 3ourselfen see 3e.

3oupe *n.* youth 35.

habiden see abide.

hacchen *pr.3 pl.* hack 1125.

hacchys *n. pl.* ship's decks, hatches; *vnder* ~ below decks 65.

hadde(n) see haue.

hail *n.* hail, hailstones 602.

half *n.* side 702; *pl.* halues 667; halves (of an army) 802 (n.).

half *adj.* half; half wynter six months 955.

hamberkes *n. pl.* hauberks, coats of mail or plate armour 446, 644, 849.

han see haue.

hande *n.* hand 351, 448, 773, 866, 949, 1067; honde 600, 995, 1010, 1213; *pl.* hondis 13, 251, 363; handes 1178; *on* ~ at hand, immediately 773, 866, 1067.

hande-darte *n.* javelin 816.

handwhyle *n.* moment 172.

hangyþ see hengen.

hanleþ *pr. 3 sg.* handles, holds 758.

hap *n.* luck, fortune, fate 1007.

hape pr. 3 sg. subj. befall 1107.

hapneþ *pr. 3 sg.* has the good fortune 172; *pt. 3 sg. subj. impers.* happned should befall 1199.

hard *n.* hard part 816.

hard(e) *adj.* hard 579, 1125, 1283; harsh, violent 497, 1304; intense 1068.

hard(e) *adv.* violently 61; with hardship, bitterly 514; fiercely 543; vigorously, quickly 657, 841; firmly 1030.

hardy *adj.* valiant 655.

harme *n.* pain, injury 19, 875; *pl.* harmes 442; harmys 499.

harme *v.* injure, damage 671.

harmeles *adj.* uninjured, unharmed 636.

harnays *n.* armor and trappings for a war-beast 442, 454, 514, 758.

hart *n.* male of the red deer 889.

haspeþ *pr. 3 sg.* fastens, buckles 759.

haste *n.* haste, speed; *vpon* ~, *in* ~ speedily, in a hurry 269, 386.

hasted *pt. 3 sg.* hastened, hurried 19.

hated *pt. 3 sg.* hated 927, 1047, hatide 7.

haþ see haue.

hatte *pt. 3 sg.* was called, was named 166; *pp.* hoten called, named 142, 146; see also hey3t.

haue *v.* have, possess 508, 951, 1318; *pr.1 sg.* haue 131, 996; *pr. 3 sg.* haþ 96, 166; *pr. 1 pl.* haue 516; *pr. 3 sg. subj.* haue 524, 786; *pt. 3 sg.* hadde 19, 30, 35, 102, 135, 178, etc.; *pt.3 pl.* hadde(n) 120, 279, 294, 795, 847, etc. (~ *of* took off 849); as *auxil. v.* haue 1146; *pr.1 sg.* 183, 777, 977, 978, 1005, etc.; *pr. 3 sg.* haþ 343, 778, 897, 955, 1027, etc.; *pr. 3 sg. subj.* haue 1043; *pr. 1 pl.* haue 370; han 1219; *pr. 3 pl.* han 384, 407, 681, 908, 963, etc.; *pt. 3 sg.* had(de) 80, 82, 109, 157, 266, etc.; *pt. 3.* hadde 400, 649, 696, 1037, 1119; negative forms: *pt.3.sg.* nadde 175; *pt. 3 sg. subj.* nad 838.

hangyþ see hengen.

hauen(e) *n.* harbor 76, 196.

he *pron. 3 sg. nom.* he 8, 19 (2×), 30, 35, etc.; *acc. dat.* hym (to, for) him 14, 22, 24, 29, 49, etc.; *poss. adj.* his 5, 10, 11, 17, 20, etc. (of, on him 908); *emphatic reflex.* hymself 893, 919, 936, 990, 1298, 1330, 1333; hym 39, 151, 1297; hym-sulf 2, 155, 276.

hed *n.* head 17, 35, 247, 715, 1127; *pl.* hedis warriors 1116 (n.).

hede *imper.sg.* protect, look after 522.

heer *n.* hair 715.

hey(e) *n.* high, height; *an/on* ~ on high, aloft, above 55, 232, 452, 547.

hey(e) *adj.* great, divine 120, 522; high, tall 666, 700, 865, 981, 1017, 1192; **hy3e** 417.

hey(e) *adv.* high 650, 667; loudly 1229.

heyly *adv.* solemnly, devoutly, earnestly, sincerely 203; **heylych** 977.

hey3t *pt. 3 sg.* promised 977; see also **hatte.**

held, helde see **hold(e).**

heldiþ *pr. 3 sg.* falls, collapses 554.

hele *n.*[1] heel 816.

hele *n.*[2] health 127; healing 203.

hele *v.* become healed, recover 172; cure, heal 1040; *pp.* **heled** 178.

yheled *pp.* as *adj.* covered 454.

helm *n.*[1] helm, tiller 64.

helm(e) *n.*[2] helmet 759, 762, 1127; *pl.* **helmes** 426, 440, 551, 600, 644, 849; warriors 613, 1189; **helmys** 528.

helmed *pp.* as *adj.* helmeted 587.

helpe *n.* cooperation 107; support 1224.

helpe *v.* cure 41; save 123; *pr. 3 sg.* **helpys** helps 782; *pr. 3 pl. subj.* **helpe** assist 668; *pp.* **holpen** helped, saved 1132; **holpyn** helped 1057.

hem see **þei, þey.**

hemmyd *pp.* bordered 757.

hemself see **þei, þey.**

hengen *v.* hang 792; *pr. 3 sg.* **hangyþ** hangs, floats 259; **hengeþ** 399; **hongiþ** 755; **hengyþ** depends upon 1016; *pt. 3 sg.* **henged** hung, was suspended 1223.

hennes *adv.* hence, from this place 157 (n.), 1008, 1314.

hente *v.* receive or parry a blow, receive 548; *pt. 3 pl. reflex.* **hent** seized, took hold of 715.

hep(e) *n.* heap 64; troop 602 (n.), 700; *hurled on an* ~ crashed down in confused masses 64; *on an* ~ as a group, together 700; ~ *ouer oþer* one troop over another 602.

here *n.* army 311, 440, 554, 636, 996.

here *v.* hear, listen to, understand 133, 344, 825, 859; **hure** 890, 1101; *pt. 3 sg.* **herde** heard 1129.

her(e) *adv.* here 150, 493, 977, 995, 1008, 1058, 1315; here (is) 249; ~ *ben* these are 150.

heraboute *adv.* near here, here 16.

heried *pp.* harrowed 157.

heritage *n.* hereditary succession 5.

hert(e) *n.* heart 162, 279, 500, 597, 919,

1050, 1086, 1333; life 996; resolution 1024; *pl.* **hertes** 560, 882.

heste *n.* promise, vow 1007; *pl.* **hestes** 279.

hette *pt. 3 pl.* grew hot or heated 162.

hetter *adj.* savage, violent 1125.

hetterly *adv.* violently 548, 1050.

heþen *adj.* heathen 311, 613, 636; **heþyn** 554; as *n.* (*pl.*) 561, 955.

heþes *n. pl.* heaths, moors 889.

heþyng *n.* contempt, scorn 497, 1304, 1314.

heuen *n.* heaven 71, 115, 512, 602, 1224.

Heuen-kyng *n.* King of Heaven, God, Christ 522, 1213.

heueþ *pr. 3 sg.* raises, lifts 1213.

hewen *pr. 3 pl.* hack, hew, chop, cut 561, 1127; *pt. 3 sg.* how hacked 548; *pt.3 pl.* **hewyn** 311; *pp.* **hewen** hewed, hacked 1283.

hewen *pp.* ornamented, inlaid 640; see also **gold-hewen.**

hy see **þei, þey.**

hyde *n.* skin; *of flesche and of* ~ of any kind 179.

hydeles *adj.* without skin; as *n. pl.* flayed ones, skinned ones 702.

hien, hyen *pr. 3 pl.* hasten 587; rush 655.

hy3e see **hey(e)** *adj.*

hy3te *n.* height 653; *vpon* ~ on high 655.

hym, hymself see **he.**

hir see **3o.**

his see **be, he.**

hit *pron. neut. nom., acc. dat.* 22, 25, 32, 61, 163, etc.; it 775; *reflex.* **hitself** 245.

hitteþ (on) *pr. 3 sg.* hits, strikes 1202; *pt. 3 pl.* **hytte** 807; *pp.* **hytte** 829.

hyued *pt. 3 sg.* made a nest, lived as in a hive 35.

hoke *v.* depart, proceed 879 (n.).

hold *n.*[1] stronghold, castle 980.

hold *n.*[2] support, assistance 1224.

hold(e) *v.* hold 267; keep, preserve 1007, 1024; *pr.1 sg.* **holde** raise 995; *pr. 3 sg.* **holdeþ** 992; *pr. 3 pl.* **holden** regard as 264; *pt. 3 pl.* **held** held 232; **helde** considered, regarded as 1237; *pp.* **holden** 955; ~ *up my honde* pledge myself 995 (n.).

hole *adj.* whole, entire 664.

holy *adj.* holy 162; *þe Holy* ~ the Holy Spirit 107, 115, 120.

holy *adv.* entirely, wholly, completely 311.

holpen, holpyn see **helpe.**
holwe *adj.* hollowed out, deep 666.
hom *adv.* home, homeward 1340.
hond(e), hondis see **hande.**
hone *v.* hesitate, dawdle, be idle 875 (n.).
honget *pp.* hanged 700.
hongiþ see **hengen.**
hony *n.* honey 702.
honour n. honour 998.
honshed (on) *pp.* destroyed 980 (n.).
honte *v.* attack, chase 879 (n.); **hunten at** hunt 889.
hors *n.* horse 442, 446, 514, 758 (the first two uses perhaps *pl.*); *on* ~ on horseback, mounted 446; ~ *ne harneys* horse(s) nor its (their) equipment 442.
hosebondes *n. poss. sg.* husband's 107.
hosed *pp.* as *adj.* supplied with armour for the lower leg 454 (n.).
hote *adj.* hot 674; severe, keen 882, 1068, 1086; intense 1050.
hoten see **hatte.**
houe *n.* hood 365 (n.).
how *adv.* how 82, 360, 482, 554, 918, etc.
how see **hewen.**
hulte *n.* hilt 754.
hundred *card. num.* hundred 336, 440, 446, 452, 454, 571, 587, 600, 613, 654, 714, 779, 819, 1078, 1117, 1130, 1143, 1175, 1211, 1312.
hunger *n.* hunger 879, 882, 1068, 1086, 1093, 1176.
hunten see **honte.**
hurdised *pp.* provided with a defensive framework 452.
hurdizs *n. pl.* wooden frames used for defense in a siege 579.
hure see **her(e)** *v.*
hurled *pt. 3 pl.* rushed violently, charged 64 (n.); dragged, threw 1283 (n.); ~ *on an hepe* rushed or fallen in a heap 64.
hurt *n.* malady, disease 203; *pl.* **hurtes** wounds, injuries 850.
hurtlen *pr. 3 pl.* rush, dash, charge 561; *pt. 3 pl.* **hurtled** 579.

I, Y *pron.nom.* 23, 83, 87, 92, 100, etc.; *acc., dat.* me (to, for) me 87, 97, 185, 189, 203, etc.; *refl.* **myself** 970, 976; **myselue** 1235; me 187; *poss.adj.* my 91, 185, 203, 224, 250, etc., **myn** 995, 1094.
y-armed etc.: for past participles with

prefixed **i-, y-,** see the simple verb form, here **armen.**
ybroȝt see **brynge.**
ygrounde see **grounden** *pp.*
ilka *adj.* each, every 128, 590, 1167, 1187.
in, yn *prep.* in 1, 2, 4, 12, 29, etc.; upon 24; of 331; into 791, 818, 1042, 1054; upon 24; within 906.
yn(ne) *adv.* in, inward, inside 287, 780, 955, 1294; within 455, 1048, 1056.
inmyddis *prep.* amidst 1317; in the middle of 30.
ynoyntid see **anoynted.**
ynow(e) *adj.* enough, plenty of, many 124, 208, 673, 752, 1188.
ynow *adv.* extremely, enough 797.
into *prep.* into 89, 241, 623, 720, 812, etc.; to 195, 948, 1026, 1089, 1264, 1292; until, so far as 260, 763.
inwardly *adv.* in the inner being, in the spirit 118.
yre *n.* fit of anger 1050.
yren *n.* iron 618; armour 846, 1123.
is see **be.**
issed *pt. 3 sg.* issued, made a sortie 1130.
yþes *n. pl.* waves 54, 68, 286.
yþrelled see **þrylled.**
ywroȝt see **wirche, wyrche.**

iambers *n. pl.* armor for the legs 1118.
iemewes *n. pl.* clasps, hinges 1275.
ienfulle see **gynful.**
iepouns *n. pl.* tunics (worn over or under armor) 1118.
iewels *n. pl.* treasures, jewelry 1063, 1275.
iewes *n.* judicial sentence 270; **iewyse** 353; ~ . . . *take upon* sentence, punish 270; ~ . . . *to take* be sentenced, be punished, suffer a penalty 353.
ioye *n.* joy, pleasure 896, 1027, 1112; *with* . . . *made* ~ received . . . joyfully, welcomed 1063.
ioyned *pt. 3 pl.* met, came ashore 296 (n.).
ioynyng *n.* hostile encounter 542.
ioyntes *n. pl.* joints 1031.
ioly *adj.* beautiful, fine 1232, 1275; *superl.* as *n.* **iolieste** most vigourous 542.
iouke *v.* sleep, rest, dwell 304; *pr. 3 pl.* **iouken** 823 (n.); ~ *proȝ* strike and thus bring to rest 823.
iuge *n.* judge 86.
iugge(n) *v.* try in a court of law, condemn (to death) 176, 1298; decide, determine

270; bring judgement (on the last day)
431.

iuggement *n.* (my) verdict 353.

iustice *n.* a high official (such as a Roman
governor) who exercizes judicial power)
4; judge 1298; **iustise** 86.

kagged *pp.* as *adj.* bound, tied 704.

kay3t see **cacchen**.

kayrande *pr.p.* riding, travelling 68.

kaytif *adj.* wretched, accursed 1334; see
also **caytifes**.

karayn *n.* dead body, corpse 686; **careynes** *poss. sg.* of flesh, fleshly 122; *take
~es kynde* assume a mortal body 122.

karl *n.* low fellow, churl 918.

kast see **caste**þ.

kaue *n.* tunnel, pit 1115.

keyes *n. pl.* keys 979, 1216; *3olden* þe ~
surrendered control (of the city) 979.

kempe *n.* warrior, man 1332.

kende *pp.* lit 1260.

kene *adj.* fierce, sharp 396, 486, 660, 810;
deadly 630; savage 711.

kenely *adv.* bravely, boldly, vigorously
567; **kenly** 625.

kepe *v.* keep, hold 279; protect, preserve
from harm 442, 612, 1015; protect,
defend 621, 688, 888, 937; take (by
force), capture 993; *pr. 3 sg.* **kepi**þ
desires 1066; *pr.3 pl.* **kepyn** defend
980; *pt. 3 pl.* **kepten** worshiped 242
(n.); defended 625, 839; *pp.* **kept** kept,
honoured, preserved 999.

kepyng *n.* care, responsibility 224.

kerchef *n.* kerchief, headcloth, veil 211,
215, 218, 224, 245, 259.

kernel *n.* embrasure in battlements 1195;
pl. **kernels** battlements 625, 660, 679;
kirneles 686.

kerneld *pp.* provided with battlements
335.

kest(en) see **caste**þ.

keuere *v.* return or bring back to health,
cure 1036; *pt. 3 sg.* **keuered** 129, 211.

keuered *pp.* as *adj.* covered 466; **couered**
474.

kylle *v.* strike, assault, kill 784; *pt. 3 pl.*
kilden (**on**) struck, assaulted 839; see
also **quelle**.

kynd(e) *n.* form, shape 122; people, race
303, 1220; creation, the natural order of
things, Nature 1033, 1227; nature 1052,

1054; lineage, family 1334; *careynes* ~
the flesh, human nature 122; *a3en(s)* ~
against nature, abnormally, monstrously
1227.

king, kyng *n.* king 6, 40, 89, 94, 108, 173,
178, 181, 194, 303, 377, 479, 493, 502,
631, 639, 717, 734, 768, 772, 859, 885,
906, 918, 920, 954, 961, 983, 1041, 1045,
1047, 1054, 1061, 1216 (an unmarked
dative), 1309; lord, regent 1012, 1036;
pl. **kynges** 277, 737.

kyngdomes *n. pl.* kingdoms 47.

kyppid *pt. 3 sg.* seized, took 481.

kirke *n.* church, temple 240.

kirneles see **kernel**.

kysseþ *pr. 3 sg.* kiss 1014; *pr. 3 pl.* **kyssen**
1010.

kyst *n.* chest, ark 481.

kyþ**e** *imper.* show, reveal 983; **ky**þ**e**þ *pr. 3
sg.* utters, declares 968; *pp.* **cud** illus-
trious, courteous 215.

knaue *n.* male offspring, son 108.

kne-dep *adj.* knee-deep, up to the knees
576.

knees *n. pl.* knees 242, 377.

kneleþ *pr. 3 sg.* kneels 171.

knew, knewe, knewen see **know(e)**.

knyf *n.* knife 1332.

kny3t *n.* knight 437, 480, 493, 938, 983;
poss. **kny3tes** knight's 367; *pl.* **kny3tes**
77, 192, 215, 218, 242, 267, 346, 361,
377, 528, 538, 612, 737, 768, 874, 1014.

kny3thod *n.* nobility, body of knights 860,
961.

knyt(te) *pt. 3 pl.* tied 367, 711, 809; *pp.*
knyt 704.

know(e) *v.* perceive, recognize, know 335,
415, 488; *imper pl.* **knowe**þ acknowledge
772; *pt. 3 sg.* **knewe** 47; perceived 797;
pt. 3 pl. **knew(en)** knew 160; recognized,
acknowledged 190.

kuþ**þe** see **cu**þ**e** *n.*

lacchetes *n. pl.* loops (as fastening) 752.

laccheþ *pr. 3 sg.* takes 1021; *pr. 3 pl.*
lacchen take up 533; *pt. 3 pl.* **lau3te**
took 283; *pp.* **lau3te** taken, captured 404,
696.

ladde(n) see **lede** *v.*

ladder *n.* ladder 1198.

ladies *n. pl.* women 1076, 1249.

lafte, laften see **leue**þ.

lay see **lygge**.

layde, laye, layeþ see **layþ.**

layk *n.* fight, contest, encounter, game 876.

layke *v.* engage in a contest or sport, play 844; fight 870.

layned *pp.* kept secret, concealed 1092.

layþ *pr. 3 sg.* lays, places 752; **leyþ** 1198; **layeþ** 1194; *pt. 3 sg.* **layde** 386; *pp.* **leyd** buried 175; ~ *on* strikes at, rains blows on 1194; *layde wecche to* kept watch on 386.

lampe *n.* lamp 1259.

langour *n.* distress, misery 75, **langur** 1100.

lanterne hornes *n.* the horn panes of a lantern 1150 (n.).

lasar-liche *n.* sickly corpse 256 (n.); see also **laser.**

laschyng *pr.p.* as *adj.* flashing, burning strongly 308.

laser *n.* leper, diseased person 38; *pl.* **lasares** 126; see also **lasar-liche.**

last(e) *n.* last or final thing; *atte/at þe* ~ finally, in the end 75, 229, 726, 928.

last(e) *adj.* last 153, 966; *to þe* ~ *ende* see **ende.**

laste *v.* last, endure, survive 516; **lasteþ** *pr.3 sg.* continues 422; endures 996; *pt. 3 sg.* **last(e)** lasted 425, 546; continued 1176, 1197.

laste *adv.* last, the last time 16.

lat see **lete.**

lauȝ *v.* laugh 499; *pt. 3 sg.* **lawȝþe** 798.

lauȝte see **laccheþ.**

launces *n. pl.* spears, javelins 533, 537.

lawe *n.* law 206, 340, 477, 709, 1323; *þe* ~ the Law (as opposed to the Gospel) 320; *Moyses* ~ Mosaic law, Jewish law 484, 586.

lawles *adj.* lawless 499.

leche *n.* physician, surgeon 41, 844, 1035, 1055; *pl.* **leches** 850.

leched *pt. 3 sg.* cured, healed 126.

lede *n.* man, warrior 102, 246, 928, 1206; nation, people 974; *pl.* **ledes** followers, army 523, 1170; men 617, 696, 709, 987, 1021; **ledis** 499.

lede *v.* lead, rule, command 768, 1011; *pr. 3 pl.* **ledyn** brought, took 1272; *pt. 3 sg.* **ladde** ruled 439, 1137, 1160; *pt. 3 pl.* **ladden** brought 568; **ledde** lived 896.

leed *n.* lead 675.

leel *adj.* loyal, faithful 1011.

leeue see **leue.**

lef *n.* page, leaf 965.

lefte *adj.* left 294.

left(e) see **leueþ.**

leften see **lyfte.**

leyd, leyþ see **layþ.**

leke *n.* leek 1032.

lemaunde *pres. p.* shining, glowing 1259.

lendis *n. pl.* loins, hips 752.

lene *adj.* lean, thin 1150, 1249.

lene *pr. 3 sg. subj.* grant 87.

lenge(n) *v.* remain 421, 435, 977, 995, 1110, 1139.

lengþen *v.* prolong, lengthen 1100.

lent *pp.* remained 358.

lepyn *pr. 3 pl.* spring 533; **lepen** 617; ~ *to* rush forward 617.

lered *pp.* as *adj.* learned, educated 477, 709.

lese *adj.* as *n. pl.* faithless ones 870 (n.).

lest *conj.* lest, that . . . not 1168.

lestenyþ *imper.pl.* listen to 492.

lete *pt. 3.sg.* allow, let 66; caused to 717; *imp.pl.* **lat** let 499, 513.

lette *pr. 3 sg.* impede, hinder 1218.

lettered *adj.* literate, educated 696.

lettres *n. pl.* letters, documents 960, 964, 965, 974; **leteres** 85.

leue *n.* leave; **leeue** permission 1170; *lacchep* ~ asks for and obtains permission to go 283, 1021.

leued see **leueþ**[1] and **leueþ**[2].

leuer *comp.adj.* better, preferable 844; *ben* ~ *to* prefer to be (with dat.) 87, 1139.

leuerockes *n. pl.* larks 742.

leueþ *pr. 3 sg.*[1] believes (in) 171; *pt. 3 sg.* **leued** 1323; *pt. 3 pl.* **leued** 190, 902.

leueþ *intr. pr. 3 sg.*[2] remains 1128; *pt. 3 sg.* **lafte** remained 607; *pt. 3 pl.* **leued** 135; **lafte** left behind, 441, 572; **lefte** 294; *trans. pt. 3 sg.* **left(e)** left (behind) 168, 599 (n.), 932; **lafte** 189; *pt. 3 pl.* **laften** 306; *pp.* **left** 582, **lafte** 636, 1249.

lyande see **lygge.**

lycam *n.* body 175.

lye *n.* fire, flame 308; light, brilliance 1238.

lif, lyf *n.* life 102, 516, 896, 928, 950; **lyue** 41, 79, 582, 776, 1073; condition, mode of living 1098, 1139; person 1194; *poss. sg.* **lyues** life's 168; *vpon lyue* living, alive 41, 79, 582, 1073; ~ *hadde* was alive 102; *out of* ~ *broȝt* killed 928.

liflode *n.* food 1076.

lifte *pr. 3 sg.* raises, lifts 1001; *pr. 3 pl.*

lyften 742; *pt. 3 pl.* leften erected, set up 283; *pp.* lifte raised 403.

lygge *v.* lie 873; *pr. 3 sg.* lyþ 31, 738; liþe 512; *pt. 3 sg.* lay 38; *pr.p.* lyande 332.

liȝt, lyȝt *n.* light 246, 1259.

liȝt *adj.* brave, valiant, fierce, swift, active 766; *comp.* lyȝtter more free of pain 256.

liȝt *pr. 3 sg.* falls 876; *pt. 3 pl.* lyȝten 1212.

lyk *n.* form, shape 332 (n.).

lykeþ *pr. 3 sg.impers.* it pleases 893, 1280; *pt. 3 sg.* lyked(e) 66, 1062; as hem lyked as they pleased, as they liked 66.

lyknesse *n.* likeness, image 249.

lyme *n.* limb 516.

lympis *pr. 3 sg. impers.* befalls, occurs; *vs ~ þe worse* it turns out worse for us 870.

lyne *n.* line (of writing) 966.

lyoun *n.* lion 766; *poss. sg.* liouns lion's 1001; *pl.* lyouns 332.

lyppe *n.* lip, edge (of an ulcer) 31.

lyste *pt. 3 sg.* desired, chose 462; *pt. subj.* should desire to 1266.

lyte *n.* little; *maken bot ~ of* care little about, hold of small account 379.

lyte *adv.* little 22.

litel *n.* little 709.

litel *adj.* little 875.

litel *adv.* briefly, little 738.

liter *n.* litter, bed 38.

lyþ, liþe see lygge.

lyþy *adj.* weak, feeble 1032.

lyue *v.* live 1100; *pres. p.* lyuande 1194.

lyuered *pp.* as *adj.* clotted, coagulated 31.

lyues see lif, lyf.

lo *interj.* lo 249.

lofte *n.* sky, high place 742; (*vp*)*on ~ on* high, high above, above 58, 403, 465, 535, 761.

logge *n.* hut, rude shelter 126; tent 738.

loke *v.* look, gaze 246, 1150, 1250; *pr. 3 sg.* lokeþ 547, 1022; *pr. 3 pl.* loken examine 850; *pr.p.* lokande 404; *~ on* look at, gaze upon 246, 1150, 1250; *~ as* look like 547.

londe *n.* land, country, kingdom 4, 87, 102, 296, 297, 308, 317, 358, 404, 492, 512, 1321, 1323.

longe *adj.* long 987.

longe *adv.* for a long time 227, 896, 927; long 1098, 1174.

longed *pt. 3 sg.* were part of, pertained 883; *pt. 3 pl.* 391.

lord(e) *n.* nobleman, lord 283, 403, 927,

960, 963, 965, 974, 985, 1011, 1105, 1170; Lord (God) 75, 87, 185, 444, 896, 1340; *pl.* lordes noblemen, lords 41, 258, 358.

lordlynges *n. pl.* noblemen, young lords (term used by a superior to those of lower rank) 249, 492, 798.

lordschip *n.* sovereignty, government 512.

lore *n.* doctrine, religious teachings 206.

loste *pt.3 sg.* lost 950; *pp.* lost 1032, 1206.

lote *n.* expression, gesture, look 1001.

loþe *n.* injury, harm, hardship, misfortune, evil 876.

loude *adj.* loud 252, 529, 743.

loude *adv.* in a loud voice, loudly 200, 248, 411, 443, 477, 530, 798.

louken *pr. 3 pl.* lock, fasten 617.

loused *pp.* unleashed, let loose 766.

louten *pr. 3 pl.* bow to, kneel to 523, 960.

loue *n.* love 168.

loue *v.* love 1206; *pt.3 pl.* loued 277.

yloued *pp.* praised 149.

loues *n. pl.* loaves 134.

low *adv.* low, deep 175.

lowere *adj. comp.* lower 1316.

lumpe *n.* lump 31.

luþer *adj.* wicked, treacherous 153, 950; grievous 1076.

ma see mo.

made(n) see make.

mahound *n.* idol 239.

may *n.* maiden 98.

may *pr. 2 sg.* may 297; *pr. 3 sg.* 516; is able to 873; may 887, 984, 988, 999, 1180; moun 298; *pr. 2 pl.* may 774; *pr. 3 pl.* mowe 825, 877; *pt. 1 sg. subj.* myȝt 976; *pt. 3 sg.* myȝt could, might 227, 246, 260, 405, 488, etc.; *pr. 3 pl.* myȝt 232, 270, 415, 588, 692, etc.

mayde *n.* maiden, virgin 105, 122, 202.

maieste *n.* (tenure of) majesty, kingship 935.

mayle *n.* chain mail, armour 454.

mayn *n.* strength, vigour 511.

mayntened *pp.* kept control of, retained 931.

maister, mayster *n.* master 226; chief 374; *pl.* maistres masters 340; maystres 586.

maistre *n.* mastery, lordship 511.

make *v.* make 319, 374, 1313, 1315; cause (to be) 640; *pr. 3 sg.* makeþ causes 1134;

pr. 3 pl. make(n) 799; regard, think of 379; *pt. 2 sg.* made made 999; *pt. 3 sg.* made caused 791, 808, 1063, 1309, 1317; composed 1326; *pt. 3 pl.* made(n) 194, 280, 359, 622, 646, etc.; *pp.* made created 116; appointed 176; sent 340; made, created, constructed 934, 1006, 1258, 1269; maked 1026; *made ioye with* received joyfully, welcomed 1063.

malady *n.* sore 30.

mallen *pt. 3 pl.* hammered, pounded 560.

mametes *n. pl.* idols, representations of pagan gods 239.

man *n.*[1] man 149, 153, 158, 438, 488, 935, 988, 1047, 1151, 1184, 1244 (2×), 1246, 1305; *pl.* men 128, 142, 268, 387, 451, 455, 460, 477, 491, 527, 587, 655, 871, 886, 888, 1092, 1117, 1134, 1142, 1187, 1192, 1225, 1275; *gen. pl.* mannes 13.

man *n.*[2] crime, sin 105, 170 (n.).

manace *n.* threatening 379.

maner *n.* kinds (of), manner (of) 288, 387, 1188.

manglouns *n. pl.* mangonels, machines used for hurling stones 803.

many(e) *adj.* many (a) 47, 80, 289, 295, 310, 316, 321, 451, 463, 476, 486, 635, 660, 663, 675, 682, 819, 824, 836, 840, 843, 874, 970, 1034, 1078, 1122, 1124, 1184, 1188, 1196, 1279; mony(e) 435, 680; as *n. pl.* many 608.

mannes see man.[1]

mansed *pp.* as *adj.* damned, accursed 158.

marble *n.* marble 624.

marchals *n. pl.* military commanders, generals 886.

marchaundise *n.* business transactions, deals, bargains 1313.

marchaunt(e) *n.* merchant 48, 1310.

marden, mardyn see marre.

marener *n.* mariner, navigator 44.

market *n.* market-place, forum 929; market 1317; *a ~ to crye* announce the holding of a market 1317.

marre *v.* perish 782; marden *pt. 3 pl.* ruined, destroyed 804; mardyn 1104; *pt. 3 pl. subj.* marden dissipated 878 (n.); *pp.* mart wounded, overcome; or ? morte dead 608 (n.).

masers *n. pl.* mace-bearers 886.

masly *adv.* massively, strongly, sturdily 1269.

masouns *n. pl.* masons, workers in stone 1111, 1281; *gen. pl.* masons' 804.

mater(e) *n.* material, subject matter, narrative 1305, 1326.

me see I, Y.

medecyn *n.* medical treatment 98.

medil see myddel.

mekly *adv.* humbly, courteously 342.

melys *pr. 3 sg.* speaks 1305.

men see man.

mene *adj.* intervening; *~ whyle* meantime 1175.

mene *adv.* conjointly 116.

mened *pt. 3 sg.* lamented, regretted 183.

menske *n.* humane action 781.

mercy *n.* clemency, mercy 781, 1244.

mereuail *n.* wonder, marvel 608.

mergeri *n.* pearl 1258; *~ perle* pearl 1281.

merke *adj.* dark 1243.

merked *pt. 3 pl.* darkened, grew dark 730.

merken *v.* aim (blows) at 803; *pr. 3 sg.* merkeþ assigns, directs 1190; *pp.* merked created 116; assigned, designated 435.

merueylous *adj.* wonderful 1258.

meschef *n.* misfortune, suffering, disaster 170, 1070; lack, deprivation 1081, 1092; myschef misfortune 921.

meselry *n.* sickness, leprosy, skin disease 170.

message *n.* message; *deden here ~* delivered their message 342; *~ to make* to carry a message 374.

messageres *n. pl.* messengers, couriers 214; messengeres 340.

metalles see metel.

mete *n.* food, sustenance 136, 1070, 1092, 1165.

mete *v.* meet, confront, encounter 555; *pr. 3 pl.* metyn clash together 63; *pt. 3 pl.* metten did battle 929; chanced upon, came across 1165.

metel *n.* metal 560; *pl.* metalles 1269.

meteles *adj.* without food, deprived of food 782.

mettyn *pp.* as *adj.* measured, exact 923.

my, myn see I, Y.

michel, myche(l) *adj.* much, great 48 (postposited), 75, 298, 607, 616, 814, 844, 866, 897, 926, 1027, 1151; many 439, 898, 1161; as *n.* myche much, a great deal 484, 804, 805.

mychel *adv.* much, greatly 149, 277.

myd *prep.* amid, among 54.

myd *prep.* with 59, 115, 127, 130, 230, etc.; with, by (means of) 474, 726, 837; filled with 806.

mydday *n.* mid-day, noon 346.

myddel *n.* middle, midst 59; middle 156; medil waist 1252.

myd-ward *n.* the middle section 435.

my3t *n.* power 117, 511, 782.

my3t see may.

myld(e) *adj.* gentle, well-born 901, 1081.

myle *n. pl.* miles 292, 416, 923.

mynde *n.* memory 1313; *in* ~ *haue* remember 131.

mynden *v.* remember 923.

myne *n.* tunnel, mine 1134.

myne *v.* tunnel 1111, 1190; *pp.* myned undermined 1119.

mynne *v.* remember 505; *imper.* myneþ 509; *pt. 3 sg.* mynned recorded, related 484.

mynours *n. pl.* mining engineers, men who undermine fortifications, tunnel into a town, etc. 1111, 1134, 1188, 1190, 1281.

mynt *n.* intention (to strike) 379 (n.).

myracles *n. pl.* miracles 131.

myschef see meschef.

myself, myselue see I, Y.

mo *adj.* more (in number) 131; ma 586 (n.); as *n.* others 1326.

mode *n.* spirit, mind 509.

moder-naked *adj.* as naked as from the womb 350.

mody *adj.* proud, valiant 1047.

modir *n.* mother 901.

molde *n.* earth, ground 607; soil, earth 1281.

money *n.* money 1310.

mony(e) see many(e).

montayns *n. pl.* mountains 730.

monþe *n. pl.* months 921; monþes 931, 935, 949.

morayne see moryne.

mor(e) *adj.* additional, further, more 362, 540, 1120, 1234; greater, more 509, 781; as *n.* more, further, additional 772, 828, 911, 921, 931, 953; *super.* most greatest, best 98.

mor(e) *adv.* any more, any longer 304; more, further 705, 1066, 1179; *super.* moste chiefly 279; most 1047; *no* ~ no further, no longer 735.

mores *n. pl.* moors 730.

moryne *n.* pestilence, widespread death 1070; morayne 1151.

morowe *n.* morning, morrow, the next day 387.

morter *n.* mortar, plaster 1290.

most see mor(e) *adj.*

moste see mor(e) *adv.*

moun, mowe see may.

mouþe *n.* mouth 342, 395; *by* ~ aloud 342.

mude-walle *n.* mud-wall 1290.

mulle *n.* dust, dirt 1290.

multitude *n.* large number 607.

murdred *pt. 3 sg.* killed; ~ *to deþe* killed 901.

nad(de) see haue.

nay *n.* utterance of the word 'no', denial 93; *nyckes with* ~ see nyckes.

nay *interj.* no 101, 1217.

nayled *pt. 3 sg.* nailed, transfixed 817.

naked *adj.* naked, bare; ~ *as an nedul* stark naked 943.

nakened *pt. 3 pl.* stripped; ~ *as a nedel* stripped bare 365.

nakerers *n. pl.* players on nakers or kettle drums 1183; *gen. pl.* nakerer of naker-players 856 (n.).

name *n.* name 51, 191; *pl.* names 144.

nas see be.

naue *n.* ship 62.

ne *adv.* not (forming emphatic negatives) 503, 1243.

ne *conj.* nor 42, 116, 170 (2×), 183, 184, etc.

nebbe *n.* face 180.

necke *n.* neck 756.

nedel *n.* needle 365; nedul 943.

nediþ *pr. 3 sg.* is necessary 505.

ne3 *adv.* almost, nearly 1086.

ne3e *v.* draw near, approach 525; *pr. 3 sg.* ne3eþ 532; *pl.* ne3en 1183; *pt. 3 sg.* ne3et 29.

nehyng *n.* neighing 425.

nempne *imper. sg.* name, call on 191; *pt.1 sg.* nempned spoke of, mentioned 165; *pp.* nempned mentioned 854 (n.).

neþer *adj.* lower 365.

neþer see noþer.

neuer(e) *adv.* never 37, 105, 113, 148, 180, etc.

newe *adj.* unblemished 180; new, recently appointed 943, 959.

newen *v.* renew 186.

next *adj. comp.* nearest 970.

nyckes *pr. 3 sg.* denies 93; ~ . . . *with nay* answers 'no', 93.

ny3t *n.* night 425, 634, 1243; *poss. sg.* ny3tes night's 265.

ny3t-tyme *n.* night-time 856.

ny3t-wacche *n.* patrol kept during the night 732.

nis, nys see be(n).

no *adj.* no 23, 41, 42, 132, 167, etc; non 265, 908.

no *adv.* no 276, 371, 382.

noble *adj.* noble 26, 480; splendid, magnificent 315, 644; valiant, bold 871; renowned 939, 1039.

no3t *pron.* nothing, naught 160, 307, 425, 1106, 1142, 1193, 1249; no one 423.

no3t *adv.* not, not at all 19, 142, 370, 505, 610, 614, 632, 636, 808, 1104, 1240, 1253.

noye *n.* suffering 29, 51; affliction 186; wrath 265; misfortune, suffering 897; *hadde* ~ was angry 265.

noyse, noyce *n.* noise, sound 856, 1183.

nold(e) see wole.

nome *pt. 3 sg.* took 53; *pt. 3 pl.* nomen 195; ~ *on his way* made his way, went 53; *cours* ~*n* made their way, journeyed 195.

non see no.

non(e) *pron.* none 93, 101; no one 322, 582, 632, 641, 783, 1323.

nonbre *n.* number 458, 462.

none *n.* the ninth canonical hour, noon, midday 1243.

nones *n. for the* ~ for the occasion, expressly 434, 760.

norþ *n.* the North 62.

nose *n.* nose 34.

noseþrylles *n. pl.* nostrils 1203.

note *n.* occasion 505; task, work 801; practice, work 804; *at þis* ~ on this occasion 505.

noþer *conj.* neither 519, 1072, 1291; nor 493; neþer 116; noþer . . . ne neither . . . nor 519, 1072.

noþyng *pron.* nothing 801.

now *adv.* now 45, 101, 185, 299, 301, 444, 877, 897, 953, 973, 1025, 1069, 1177, 1207, 1217, 1281, 1296, 1309, 1340.

o see on *card. num.* as *adj.*

odour *n.* aroma, fragrance 244.

of *adv.* off 364, 698, 849, 1127.

of *prep.* of 6, 15, 25, 34, 39, etc.; since 35, 987; in 517, 1112; with 390, 657, 1167; of, from among 143, 303; out of, from 49, 104, 125, 141, 188, etc.; concerning, regarding, about 78, 153, 160, 211, 360 (2×), etc.; of, from 83, 106, 114, 122, 125, etc.; for 155, 203, 252, 344, 714, etc.; off 364; (made) of 11, 284, 310, 326, 327, etc.; following a numeral 133.

of-fleis *pr. 3 sg.* flay off 992; see also fleyn.

offryng *pr.p.* as *adj.* pertaining to giving religious offerings; ~ *tyme* the time designated for religious sacrifices 1228.

oft *adv.* often, repeatedly 7, 46; ofte 151, 740.

o3t *pron.* anything 391; ou3te 411.

oyle *n.* oil 814, 852.

olde *adj.* old 1075.

olyfaunt(e) *n.* elephant 451, 465, 583; *pl.* olyfauntes 427, 449, 569.

on *adv.* onward 56 (2nd use), 69, 633; upon 1150, 1231; upon the case of 694.

on *prep.* on 8, 13, 17, 18, 20, etc.; upon 595, 1022, 1131, 1220, 1250; at 1067, 1329; with 12; from 595; in 156, 171, 443, 637, 1246, etc.; into 557; against 1209; about, concerning 740, 1038; to 62, 200, 423, 1056, 1185; in 31, 59, 171, 829; onto 558; one in 104 (n.); an on 50, 55, 452, 547; in 12, 59, 351; a 492.

on *card. num.* as *adj.* a certain 25, 45, 926, 1081; one 71; o one, a single 70, 110, 111 (2×), 117, 125, 137, 632, 776, 1099, 1234; a 518, 614; *card. num.* as *pron.* on(e) one 112, 273, 773; see also a *card. num.*

one *adv.* alone, only 252, 336, 502, 520, 600, 1224.

open *adv.* open; *wide open* lying at full length 834.

or *conj.*[1] before 24, 118, 177, 227, 350, etc.; see also er.

or *conj.*[2] or 79, 90, 99, 100, 217, etc.; oþer . . . or or . . . or 99, 100; see also oþer.

ordeyned *pp.* as *adj.* prescribed 852.

orible *adj.* terrifying, monstrous, huge 569.

orisoun *n.* prayer 852.

ornen see renne.

ost *n.* host, army 1115, 1130; crowd 1317; oste 733.

ost-wyse *adv.* in the manner of an army 1225.

oþer *pron.* (the) other, the next, another 46, 72, 767, 982, 1194, 1313; *pl.* others 349, 432, 602, 629, 678, 693, 905, 970 (n.), 1020, 1291; other things 511.

oþer *adj.* other, second 427, 479, 627, 751, 908, 955, 972, 1138, 1160, 1268.

oþer *conj.* or 79, 88, 820, 1224; oþer . . . or or . . . or 99, 100.

ouer *prep.* over, across, on, above 46, 54, 55, 73, 86, etc. (postposited in 308).

ouer(e) *adv.* over 355, 1153; *alle* . . . ~ over all, everywhere 1271.

ouerbrad *pp.* covered over, overspread 490, 603.

ouerlokeþ *pr. 3 sg.* scans, peruses 966.

ouertilt *pp.* destroyed 1293.

ouertourned *pp.* as *adj.* demolished 1020.

ouerwalte *pt. 3 sg.* overthrew, threw down 1211.

ouȝte see oȝt.

our(e), ous see we.

out *adj.* extant, in existence, at all 96 (n.).

out *adv.* out 457, 465, 570, 590, 626, 657, 735, 831, 841, 910, 1088, 1126, 1203, 1216, 1263.

out of *prep.* from, out of 39, 60, 83, 373, 450, etc.

outwale *n.* outcasts 144.

outwith *prep.* outside, away from 1115.

owen *adj.* own 987, 1054, 1082, 1094; owne 522.

owene *pr. 1 sg. subj.* acknowledge 788; owen *pr. 3 pl.* owe 972; *pt. 3 sg.* owede possessed, owned 221; aughte 88.

paas *n.* passage, chapter 504 (n.).

pay *v.* pay 322, 1144, 1319.

paynted see peynted.

palace *n.* palace 231; palice 241; paleys 905.

pale *n.* palisade, paling intended as a fortification 681, 777.

paled *pp.* hung with cloth 333.

pallen *adj.* made of fine cloth, of pall 326, 747; ~ *webbes* rich cloths 326.

palsy *n.* palsy, paralysis 127.

pane *n.* rich fur or fabric 1277.

panne *n.* brain-pan, skull 827.

pardoun *n.* an indulgence 219.

paren *v.* peel 1331.

partyis *n. pl.* divisions, quarters, parts 397.

passe *v.* pass, leave 684, 956, 1316; cross 777; *pr.1 sg.* 356, 1008; go 1314; *pr. 3 sg. subj.* 372, 382; passyþ proceeds, processes 116 (n.); *pr. 3.pl.* passen 633; *pt. 3 sg.* passed 219; went on his way 231; proceeded 240; escaped 322; *pp.* escaped 80; left 157.

passioun *n.* narrative of (Christ's) suffering 504.

passyþ see passe.

paueloun *n.* tent, especially a large one used for military encampments 333, 468; *pl.* pauelouns 326, 633, 894; *piȝten* ~*s* pitched tents 326.

pauyes *n. pl.* large shields, designed to protect the whole body 448.

pauyment *n.* street 1247.

peces, pecis see pese.

peynted *pp.* portrayed 167; decorated 1271; paynted 333.

peys *n.* full statutory weight 1267; see also pese.

pelour *n.* fur 1277.

pelours see pyler.

pendauntes *n. poss. sg.* pendant's, of a pendant ornament 515.

peny *n.* penny, an English silver coin 1319; *pl.* penyes money, cash, the pieces of silver Judas received 322 (n.), 1307, 1311.

penseles *n. pl.* small pennons, used to identify a lord and his men-at-arms 417.

peple *n. pl.* people, crowd, persons 439, 503, 674, 863, 884, 898, 910, 1157, 1161, 1247; pople 234, 260.

per(e) *n.* pear 1330, 1331.

peryles *n. pl.* dangers 80.

perische *v.* perish, suffer physical destruction or decay 1262.

perschid *pp.* pierced 611; persched 1282; *pp.* as *adj.* 707.

peritotes *n. pl.* chrysolites, peridots, green gem stones 1255.

perle *n.* pearl 476; *pl.* perles 763, 1255, 1258.

persone *n.* person 121; *pl.* persones 110.

pes *n.* peace 1135, 1156; pees 1179, 1215.

pesan *n.* a piece of metal or mail attached to the helmet and extending over the neck and upper breast 515.

pese *n.* piece 827; *pl.* peces bits, bits of flesh 239, 706; pecis pieces of plate

1267; ~s of peys coins of great value 1267.

pyble n. pebble, stone used as a missile in warfare 827.

picche n. pitch, tar 674.

picchen pr. 3 pl. hurl, cast 620; pt. 3 pl. piȝten pitched, placed, fixed, set (down) 326; pp. piȝt 397, 468, 475, 777; pyȝt set up 9; attached, fastened 417; set, adorned 763.

piked adj. pointed, sharpened 914.

pykeyse n. pl. pickaxes 1282.

pyler n. pillar, post 9; pl. pileres pillars, columns 468; pelours 1269.

pyne n. torture, torment 24.

pyne(n) v. torture, torment 503; endure, languish 1327; pt. 3 sg. pyned 898; pp. pyned 8, 707; crucified 164; pp. as n. those afflicted 127.

pinne n. pin 620 (n.).

pypyng n. piping (of musical instruments), sound of music 257.

pipis, pypys n. pl. pipes, flutes 529, 855, 1182; see also cormous.

pite, pyte n. pity 503, 1135, 1156, 1247; mercy 1179.

place n. place 110, 493, 1255, 1262, 1265, 1271; an open area (for battle) 448, 1294; in o ~ of equal rank 110.

play n. joy, pleasure, merriment 257.

playande pr.p. as adj. boiling 674.

playn adj. flat 9.

plain adv. plainly, distinctly 167.

plate n. breastplate of a Jewish high priest 475; plate armour, a cuirass 515; pl. platis works of silver or gold, such as chalices or platters 1267.

platte pt. 3 sg. fell flat 222.

plente n. plenty, abundance 1265.

plowes n. pl. ploughs; in ~ to putte to begin to plow up 1294.

plunge v. plunge, immerse, dip 791.

poynt n. jot, the least bit, detail 167, 611; spot 914; pl. poyntes points 397; chances, opportunities 783 (n.).

poke n. bag, pouch 1307.

polisched pp. as adj. polished, burnished 754; pulsched 475, 1267.

pomel n. round ornament on the top of a tower 417; pommel, knob on the hilt of a sword 754.

ponsone n. pointed tool, punch 1282.

pope n. pope 205, 219, 222, 234, 236, 241, 253, 898.

pople see peple.

pore adj. poor 142.

poreil n. poor people 317; porayle 905.

port n. the port 296.

portecolis n. pl. portcullis 620.

postel n. apostle 1307; see also apostel.

posterne n. side gate, secret entrance 910; attrib. side 1161.

postes n. pl. posts, pillars 652.

powder n. dust, ashes 722; pouder 1284.

praieþ, prayeþ pr. 3 sg. requests, entreats 863, 1023, 1331; pr. 3 pl. preien pray (for), plead for 1215; pt. 3 sg. praied 1157.

preche v. preach 139, 152; proclaim 1157; pt. 3 sg. preched preached 205; pt. 3 pl. urged, exhorted 320.

prechyng n. preaching, proclamation 1161.

precious, precyous adj. precious, valuable, rare 1262, 1265, 1311; preciose 476.

preysed pp. as adj. commendable, admirable 103.

prelates n. pl. priests 161, 317.

prente n. image, imprint 241.

pres n. crowd, throng, company 220, 231.

presen pr. 3 pl. press forward, push forward, hasten 894; pt. 3 pl. presed 24; preset pushed 448; pressed crowded together 905; presed in attacked, assailed 24.

presented pt. 3 sg. introduced 236.

prestes n. pl. priests 320.

preueþ pr. 3 sg. proves 504; pp. preued acknowledged 103; as adj. experienced, manifest 110.

prikkes n. poss. sg. spike's 914.

prime, pryme n. the first canonical hour, usually 9 A.M. 372, 382, 707.

prince n. prince, ruler 3, 176, 247, 372, 439, 747, 884, 899, 1311; pl. princes 24, 152, 161, 220, 317, 436, 633, 863, 894, 1144, 1277.

pris n. value, worth, price 15, 1316, 1319; of ~ excellent, noble 15; in money, apiece 1316.

pris adj. noble, splendid 611.

prisoun n. prison 1327.

priue adj. secret, concealed 910.

processioun n. religious procession 220.

profer *n.* offer 1138.

profre *v.* offer 1179; *pr. 3 sg.* **profreþ** 1135; *reflex.* **proffriþ** 1301; *pr. 3 pl.* **profren** 1144; *pt. 3 sg.* **propfred** 1156; ~*iþ hym forþ* ventures forth, comes out 1301.

prophecie *imper. sg.* prophesy 15.

prophete *n.* prophet 15, 103, 1316.

prouynce the province (i.e., Syria) 439.

prouost *n.* provost, representative of king or emperor, chief magistrate 3, 164, 176, 1300.

prudely *adv.* proudly, splendidly, magnificently 763.

prute *adj.* proud 142.

psalmys *n. pl.* psalms 478.

pulled *pt. 3 pl.* pulled, tore 715.

pulsched see **polisched**.

pure *adj.* pure 754, 1271; very 763; *into þe* ~ *corners* even into the corners 763.

pured *adj. pp.* cut and polished 476.

purely *adv.* completely, openly 167.

putte *v.* put; *pr. 3 sg.* **putteþ** 747; *pr. 3 pl.* **put** delayed, postponed 382; *pt. 3 sg.* **put(te)** brought 127; raised 247; *pp.* **put** placed, affixed 8, 1327; *in plowes to* ~ to begin to plow up 1294.

quaynte *adj.* elaborate, strange, marvellous 335.

quarels *n. pl.* bolts for a crossbow, arbalest, or siege engine 657; **querels** 626.

quasschyng *pr.p.* as *n.* clashing, striking together 1195.

quartes *n. pl.* crossbows, seige engines 626 (n.).

quelle *v.* slay, kill 518, 904, 1085; *pt. 3 sg.* **quelled** 898, 936; **quelde** 918; *pp.* **quelled** killed 898, 1308; see also **kylle**.

querel *n.* legal suit, complaint, accusation 507; *pl.* **querels** 501.

quyk *adj.* living, alive 501, 698.

quyk *adv.* quickly, at once, immediately 904.

quyrboyle *n.* hardened (boiled) leather 11.

quyte-clayme *pr. 1 sg.* abandon a dispute, reliquish the right to redress of a wrong 501; **quit-cleyme** 507.

quod *pt. 3 sg.* said, exclaimed 97, 101, 173, 189, 191, 1217, 1309.

racches *n. pl.* hunting dogs 890.

racke *n.* drifting clouds, storm 59.

radde see **redeþ**.

radly *adv.* quickly, swiftly 69.

ragged *adj.* jagged, rugged, rough 69 (n.).

raȝte *pt. 3 sg.* dealt (a blow) 14; **rauȝte** gave 1063; *pt. 3 pl.* **raȝten** reached, caught 811; **raȝten** gave 1216; **rauȝte** granted, gave 938; **rauȝten** 960; ~ *to* reached for 811; ~ *out* held out with their hand, handed over 1212.

rayn *n.* rain 12, 536.

rayled *pp.* as *adj.* adorned, decorated 1254.

raisen, raysen *pr. 3 pl.* erect, set up 327; raise, promote, exalt 937.

ran *pt. 3 sg.* touched, struck 409 (n.).

ran see **renne**.

rapis *pr. 3 sg.* goes swiftly, hurries, rushes 69; *pr.p.* **rapande** hurrying, hastening 958.

rappis *n. pl.* bowels, intestines 571.

rathe *adv.* quickly, soon; ~ *as* as soon as 637.

rauȝte, rauȝten see **raȝte**.

rawe *adj.* raw, abraded 706.

realte *n.* royal status 510.

rebel *n. pl.* rebels 508 (n.).

rebies *n. pl.* rubies 1254.

recche *pr. 3 sg. subj.* cares 786.

receyue *v.* accept 997; *pt. 3 sg.* **receyued** 230; ~ *þe croune* be crowned 997.

red(e) *adj.*[1] red 12, 308, 482, 637, 706; *þe* ~ *day* the dawn 637.

rede *adj.*[2] violent 59 (n.).

rede *n.* counsel; ~ *take* to get advice, follow advice 407.

redeþ *pr. 3 sg.* reads 504; *pr. 3. pl.* **redeþ** explain, state 964; *pt. 3 sg.* **radde** read 482; *pt. 3 pl.* **redde** 595; *pr. 3 sg. subj.* **rede** may guide 1340; **redde on** read aloud 595.

redeþ see **ride**.

redy *adj.* ready 411.

redly *adv.* immediately, without delay 92.

reioyced *pt. 3 sg. subj.* should rejoice in 1140.

rekene *v.* count, reckon, estimate 132.

relyk *n.* relic 264.

renayed *pr.p.* as *adj.* apostate; traitorous, disloyal 173.

renk(e) *n.* warrior, knight; man 610, 843 (unmarked dative with **leuer**), 937, 1140; *pl.* **renkes** 958.

renne *v.* run 890; *pr. 3 pl.* **runne** 564, 809; *pr.p.* **rennande** flowing 230 (but see n.);

pt. 3 sg. **ran** ran, flowed 12, 482; *pr. 3 pl.* **ornen** 544; *runne to* run forward, attack 809.

renten *pt. 3 pl.* tore apart, tore limb from limb 706; tore, pulled 1272; ~ *asonder* tore apart 811.

rere *v.* erect 651; **rere vp** arouse, disturb, flush out 891; *pt. 3 sg.* **rered** raised 128.

rereward *n.* rear, rear-guard 566.

resen *pt. 3. pl.* attacked, charged 903 (n.).

resorte *v.* return 1052.

resoun n. justice, legal right 508, 510.

rest see **resten**.

reste *n.* rest, sleep 265, 737.

resten *pr. 3 pl.* rest, sleep 634; *pp.* as *adj.* rest undamaged 609.

resting *n.* setting 843.

reuer *n.* riverbank 891.

reuerence *n.* reverence, honor 230.

rewarde *v.* reward 92.

rewful *adj.* pitiable, piteous 1083.

rewþe *n.* misery, mischief, cruelty 903.

rib *n.* rib; *rigge and* ~ completely 1083.

rybaunde *pp.* trimmed, bordered 762.

rich *n.* smoke 307; steam 794, 1089.

riche *adj.* noble, high-born, powerful 3, 173, 964; rich, precious 327, 419, 474, 595, 643, 749, 762, 1275, 1277; splendid, magnificent 307, 906, 1297.

riche *adv.* richly, splendidly, lavishly 467.

rydders *n. pl.* ridders, rubbish removers 571.

ride *v.* ride 891, 997; *pr. 3 sg.* **rideþ** 566, 584; **redeþ** 1113; *pr. 3 pl.* **riden** 1340; *pr. 3 pl. subj.* ~ *on* ride to attack 407.

rigge *n.* back; ~ *and rib* completely 1083.

riȝt *adv.* very, extremely 668, 822; just, exactly 676; right, straight 1089.

ryng *n.* ring, link in chain mail 610; *pl.* **ryngys** rings 1064; **rynges** 1278.

ryngen *v.* ring, resound 411; *pr. 3 sg.* **rynges** 770.

rise *v.* result 405; arise, be spread abroad 917; get up 1260; **ryse** arouse, waken, get up 638; *pr.3 sg.* **riseþ** rises, stands up 967; stirs 1050; **rises** 794; **ryseþ** 1054; *pt. 3 sg.* **rose** 637; **roos** 1089.

rispen, *pr. 3 pl.* break, burst 571.

rysten *pr. 3 pl.* (of birds) shake their wings 731 (n.).

ryue *adj.* abundant, plentiful 795.

robbyng *n.* polishing 281.

roddes *n. pl.* rods, sticks, poles 809.

rode *n.* cross; *put on þe* ~ crucified 8.

rolle *n.* scroll, torah, roll of Jewish scripture 481; *pl.* **rolles** 595.

rome *n.* room, building 264 (n.).

roof *n.* vault, ceiling 1254.

roof *pt. 3 sg.* broke, sundered 59 (n.); see also **vnriuen**.

roos see **rise**.

ropis *n. pl.* ropes, cords 327, 811, 1320.

roryng *n.* wailing, lamentation 307.

rose see **rise**.

rost *n.* roast, roast meat 1089.

rostyþ *pr. 3 sg.* roasts 1083.

rotlyng *n.* disturbance 281.

rounde *adj.* round 762.

route *n.* troop, army 566.

rowe *adj.* rough, rugged, wild 890.

runne see **renne**.

sacrifice *n.* sacrifice 319.

sad *adj.* heavy, hard 545; **sadde** in a compact group 819.

sadly *adv.* resolutely, directly 325, 357.

saghtlyng *n.* reconciliation, agreement 405.

saȝtles *pr. 3 sg.* is reconciled, makes peace 1061.

say *v.* say 100; **sey** 384, 953, 975; **seyn** 868; *pr. 3 sg.* **saiþ, sayþ** 767, 1057, 1084, 1093, 1234; **seiþ** 492, 985; *pr. 3 pl.* **sayen** 343; **sayn** 961, 1098, 1139; *imper. pl.* **sayþ** 349, 369; *pt. 3 sg.* **saide** 90, 200, 223; **sayde** 93, 983; **sayd** 1231; **seide** 83, 181, 212; *pt. 3 pl.* **sayde** 15, 523; **seiden** 1295; *pp.* **seid** 1003.

say see **se** *v.*

sail, sayl *n.* sail 55, 70.

sake n. sake, consideration 304, 939, 944.

sakkes *n. pl.* sacks, bags 806; **sackes** 810.

sakles *adj.* innocent 7.

sale *n.* selling, trade 1141.

salt *n.* salt 55, 1295; ~ *water* sea 55.

salue *n.* ointment, salve, remedy 96.

same *adj.* same 1209, 1233, 1273; *pron.* 383, 1333.

samen *adv.* together; *in* ~ together 556.

samned *pp.* gathered 319 (n.).

saphyres *n. pl.* sapphires 764.

satled *pp.* befall; *be* ~ *on* befall, be turned against, press heavily on 383, 1220.

saue *v.* save 1158; **sauy** 976; *pp.* **saued** 1061; kept 1095.

saue *prep.* except 107, 502, 583, 615, 1039, 1224.

saue þat *conj.* except 1056.

sauere *n.* smell, aroma 1090; *felden þe ~* smelled the odor 1090.

sauy see saue.

saut(e) *n.* assault, siege 647, 837, 1124, 1197; see also assaute.

saw see se.

sawe *n.* opinion, speech 883; request 1159; *pl.* sawes doctrines, teachings 139.

sawters *n. pl.* psalters 478.

scaped *pt. 3 sg. subj.* escape 423; skaped *pt. 3 sg.* escaped, survived 614.

schadew *n.* shadow, darkness 741.

schafts *n. pl.* shafts, lances 1121.

schal *pr.1 sg.* shall 92, 187, 355, 1313; *pr. 2 sg.* schalt 997; *pr. 3 sg.* schal 97, 300, 303, 356, 371, etc.; *pr. 1 pl.* schul 875; must 1098; *pr. 2 pl.* schul 787; *pt. 3 sg.* schold(e) was to, was meant to, should 288, 387, 402, 641, 695, etc.; *pt. 1 pl.* scholde 879; *pt. 2 pl.* scholde 776, 780; *pt. 3 pl.* schold(e) appeared 73 (n.); were appointed to 688; should 360, 572, 1168, 1190, 1193, 1260.

schalke *n.* man, warrior 1122.

schame *n.* shame; *vpon ~ wyse* shamefully, in an ignominious way 376.

schapiþ *pr. 3 sg.* ordains, determines 998.

scharpe *adj.* as *n. pl.* ? violent (men), ? weapons 282 (n.).

scharpe *adj.* sharp, keen 559, 703, 1122.

scharply *adv.* violently 670; eagerly 1075.

scheden *pr. 3. pl.* divide, separate from each other 741.

schedered *pt. 3 sg.* shattered 562; *pp.* schedred 1121 (n.).

schef *pt. 3 sg.* thrust 1333.

scheld *n.* shield 755, 1009; pl. scheldes 282, 551, 558, 606, 1075, 1121.

schende *pp.* reproached, disgraced 376.

schene *adj.* beautiful, fair 104; splendid 670.

scher *pt. 3 sg.* ran swiftly, swerved 67 (n.).

scherte *n.* shift, undershirt 352; *pl.* chertes 1242; *in her bar ~es* wearing only their shifts 1242.

scheþes *n. pl.* sheaths, scabbards 559.

schewe *v.* show 198, 440; reveal 394; speak, utter 787; proclaim 864; *pt. 3 sg.* schewed displayed 246; spoke 345; told 1002; to schewe ? displayed 440.

schewyng *pr.p.* as *n.* displaying, muster 282.

schidwod *n.* split wood, splinters 558.

schye see skyes.

schymeryng *n.* gleaming, shining 551.

schynande see schonen.

schynyng *n.* brightness, brilliance 551.

schip *n.* ship 67; sschip 71; *pl.* schippis 285.

schir, schyr *adj.* bright, clear 676, 741.

schoken *pt. 3 pl.* drew 559.

schold, scholde see schal.

scholdir *n.* shoulder 755; schoulder 1088; *pl.* scholdres 558.

schone *n. pl.* shoes 1075.

schonen *pt. 3 pl.* shone, were bright 416, 1259; *pr.p.* schynande sparkling, glistening 676; *pr.p.* as *adj.* polished, shiny 755.

schore *n.* slope; *vpon ~* aslant 67 (n.).

schorne *pp.* shorn, shaved 376.

schoten *pr. 3 pl.* shoot 670, 676; *pt. 3 sg.* schot sped 67; *pp.* yschot launched 285.

schoulder see scholdir.

schout *n.* noise, shout 531.

schred *pp.* rigged 285.

schrikande *pr.p.* as *adj.* screeching 531.

schrynken *pr. 3 pl.* flinch, draw back in fear 531.

schroud *n.* armor 562.

schul see schal.

scourgis *n. pl.* whips, scourges 10.

se *n.* sea 46, 60, 61, 292, 295.

se *v.* see, look at 260, 405, 488, 712; be seen 420; watch 892; *pt. 1 sg.* sey saw 184; *pt. 3 sg.* say 585; saw 1049; *pt. 3 pl.* sey saw 1034; seyen 903; *pp.* sen seen 825; sein 990; seyn 1222, 1226.

secunde *ord. num.* as *n.* second 114; as *adj.* 121.

sede *n.* stock, kind 114.

sege *n.* siege 325, 339, 422, 1174, 1338; besieging army 868, 883, 953, 1114.

segge *n.* man 684, 853, 893, 939, 949, 951, 971, 1034, 1042, 1049, 1057, 1061, 1065, 1124, 1160, 1322; *pl.* segges 767, 825, 942, 1114; seggys 1037.

segyþ *pr. 3 sg.* besieges, lays siege to 1067.

sey, seye, seyen see say and se *v.*

seid, seide, seiden see say.

seignour *n.* lord 84.

sein, seyn see say and se *v.*

seint *n.* Saint 222, 236, 899, 1239.

seysed *pt. 3 sg.* was in legal possession 2; *pp.* **seised** taken, captured 837.

seiþ see **say.**

seke(n) *v.* seek 371, 951; *pt. 3 sg.* **souȝt** journeyed, went 46, 197; went 545; *pt. 3 pl.* **souȝte** 295; fell 1124; **souȝten** 1035; **souȝt** attacked 1174; *pp.* **souȝt** searched 1037, 1273, 1286; explored, probed 1281; *souȝte to þe grounde* fallen dead 1124.

seken *v.* sigh 297 (n.).

selcouþ *adj.* miraculous, marvelous 1222; as *n.* a marvel 78; *pl.***selcouþes** 825.

self *adj.* very, same 119, 1039; own, proper 1052; *þe ~ Fadere* the Father himself 119; *here ~ kynde* their own nature 1052.

selke *n.* silk 418, 1279.

selly *adv.* extremely, marvellously 810.

seluere *n.* silver 262, 410, 418, 468, 469, 1270.

sembled *pt. 3 pl.* assembled 858.

semelich(e) *adj.* good, appropriate, honorable 985; as *n. pl.* good men 141.

sen see **se** *v.*

senatours *n. pl.* senators 269, 900, 907; *poss. pl.* of the senators 962.

sende *v.* send, dispatch 92, 214, 1023; *pr. 3 sg.* **sendeþ** 210, 346; *pr. 3 pl.* **sende** 384; *imper. sg.* **sende** 203; *pt. 3 sg.* **sende** 139; sent 49, 174, 942; *pt. 3 pl.* **sente** 1035; *pp.* sent 84, 121, 343.

sendel *n.* costly fabric 418.

septre *n.* sceptre 949, 951.

serchen *v.* inquire about, ascertain 343; *pp.* **serched** searched through 1286.

sercle *n.* circle 424.

sergis *n. pl.* large wax candles, usually for religious services 472.

seriant *n.* servant, officer (in a lord's retinue) 85.

serue *v.* serve 521; *pt. 3 pl.* **serued** 838.

serued *pp.* deserved 1060.

sete *n.* seat 1297.

seten, sette, setteþ see **sitte.**

setteþ *pr. 3 sg.* raises, hoists 55; sets up 1191, 1209; *pt. 3 sg.* **sett** struck 60; set, posted 423; placed 806, 1297 (*reflex.*); *pt. 3 pl.* **setten** (vpon) attacked 305; *pp.* **sett** 315; **sette** 339; seated 474; set, mounted 764; *pr. 3 sg. refl.* **setteþ** (vp) makes an attack 565 (n.); *sette sege* laid siege 325.

seuen *card.num.* as *adj.* seven 615, 714, 949.

seuenty *card.num.* as *n.* seventy 137.

seueþ *ord.num.* as *n.* seventh 147, 1202.

sewen *pr. 3 pl.* follow 767; *pt. 3 pl.* **suwed** 137, 141.

sib *n.* kin, relation, kinsman 276, 970.

side, syde *n.* part, direction 60; part, region, area 305, 1322; side (of the body) 545; side, party (in a battle) 613; side 721, 802, 806, 1048, 1084, 1185, 1191, 1209; (of an animal) 818; (of meat) 1095; *pl.* **sydes** sides 764; **sides** (of the body) 11, 707; *out of þe souþ ~* from the south 60.

syed *pt. 3 sg.* descended, set 708.

sygne *n.* banner, device 283.

siȝt, syȝt *n.* sight, spectacle 78, 184.

sike *adj.* as *n. pl.* sick 211.

siker(e) *adj.* faithful, reliable 346; strong, doughty 438.

syknes(se) *n.* sickness 37, 1028, 1042.

silk *n.* silk 327.

sille *v.* sell 1311; *pt. 3 sg.* **solde** 154, 1307; *pt. 3 pl.* 1316.

symple *adj.* lowly, common 260.

synful *adj.* sinful, unrepentant 174.

synge *v.* sing, chant 477; *pr.p.* **syngyng** singing 1339.

synne *n.* sin 7, 1262.

synwys *n. pl.* sinews, nerves 1028; **synwes** 1052.

sire *n.* lord, master 37, 83; (as title prefixed to name) Lord, Sir 2, 438, 565, 939, 944, 971, 975, 983, 985, 1003, 1012, 1185, 1197, 1201.

sitte *v.* sit, meet in session (on) 694; *pr. 3 sg.* **sitteþ** 91; *pr. 3 pl. reflex.* **seten** seat themselves 478; *pp.* **sette** seated 957.

syþ *conj.* since, because 1206.

siþes *n. pl.* scythes, curved blades 810.

six(e) *card.num.* as *adj.* six 424, 921; as *n.* **syx** 1201.

sixte *ord.num.* as *n.* sixth 147.

sixtene *card.num.* as *adj.* sixteen 434, 437.

sixti, sixty *card.num.* as *adj.* sixty 422, 1114.

skaped see **scaped.**

skeweþ *pres. 3 sg.* makes cloudy, grows dark 57.

skyes *n. pl.* heavens, sky 536, 729; **schye** *sg.* 637.

slepiþ *pr. 3 sg.* sleeps 738.

slynge *n.* sling 1236.

slowe *pt. 3 sg.* killed 155; **slow** slew 1201;

pt. 2 pl. **slowen** 771; *pt. 3 pl.* 18, 272,
496, 1170, 1299; **slow** 714; *on crois* ~*n*
crucified 272.

so *adv.* thus, so, in this way 123, 372, 565,
603, 707, etc.; so (intensifying) 80, 245,
375, 607, 608, etc.; to such a degree 416;
likewise, in a similar manner 764; so . . .
that 795, 1027, 1030, 1050; just as 32;
who so 504.

so *conj.* therefore, so 123, 612, 707, 999,
1285, 1308, etc.; so . . . that, so . . . as
so . . . that 63–64, 601–2.

sodeynly *adv.* suddenly 1042, 1049; **soudeynly** 1028.

soferayn *n.* sovereign 990.

softe *v.* soothe, relieve 91.

softynge *n.* remedy, alleviation 96.

solas *n.* entertainment, recreation 893.

solde see **sille**.

som *pron.* some, a portion 1095; *pl.*
som(me) . . . **som(me)** some . . .
others 715–16, 1149–50.

somere *n. attrib.* summer 708.

somme *n.* sum, number 422; company,
host 488, 615; *by* ~ in all 422.

sonder *adv. in* ~ apart, asunder 811.

sondisman *n.* messenger, emissary 84;
sondesman 197; *pl.* **sondismen** 346,
357.

sone *n.* son, God the Son 45, 114, 119 (2nd
use), 121, 184, 212, 276, 970, 993, 1084.

sone *adv.* at once, immediately, quickly 60,
89, 119 (1st use), 160, 210, 214, 269, 388,
445, 581, 639, 819, 849, 858, 1003, 1121,
1131, 1133.

sonne *n.* sun 388, 549, 684, 708, 843, 858;
poss. sun's 420.

soper *n.* supper 853; *attrib.* 260.

sore *n.* wound, sore 91, 96; *pl.* **sores**
afflictions, wounds 42.

sore *adv.* severely, painfully 815; cruelly,
grievously 848, 1097.

sorer *comp. adj.* more painful 37.

sory *adj.* accursed, wicked 1220.

sorow(e) *n.* remorse, contrition 155;
misery 186; misfortune, tribulation 299,
924, 1084, 1140; sorrow 635, 714; agony,
torture 712.

sorte *n.* group, class, category 137, 141.

soþe *n.* truth 210, 380.

soudeynly see **sodeynly**.

soudiours *n. pl.* soldiers 434, 1000; **soudeours** 295.

souȝt, souȝte, souȝten see **seke(n)**.

soule *n.* soul 524, 724, 936, 947.

sour *adv.* bitterly, harshly, severely 1220.

souþ *adj.* south 60.

sow *v.* sow 1295.

sowe *n.* mobile siege engine used to shelter
besiegers while they advance towards
and mine the walls of a town or castle
1210.

space *n.* time 22.

spakly *adv.* quickly, immediately 557;
comp. **spakloker** more prudently, more
wisely 788.

sparen *v.* spare, refuse, decline 641.

speche *n.* speech 381, 492, 788, 968.

spedde *pt. 3 sg. impers.* prospered, profited
by 22.

speke *v.* speak 788; *pr. 3 sg.* **spekeþ** 915;
pr. 3 pl. **spekeþ** state, declare 974.

speres *n. pl.* spears 557, 570, 822, 841;
spearmen, warriors 1114, 1130; **grounden speres** sharpened spears 570.

spilide *pt. 3 pl.* destroyed, killed 22; *pp.* as
adj. spilt slain 641.

spoyle *v.* strip (of arms and armour) 641.

sponnen *pt. 3 pl.* thrust 841.

sprynges *pr. 3 sg.* grows, springs 106; *pt. 3
sg.* **sprongyn** blew 412; *pp.* **sprongen**
dawned 857.

spryngoldes *n. pl.* siege catapults 841.

sprongen, sprongyn see **sprynges**.

sprotes *n. pl.* splinters, slivers 557.

sschip see **schip**.

stadded *pt. 3 sg.* stationed, placed 592.

staf *n.* stick, rod 919; *pl.* **stauys** 363.

stage *n. pl.* turrets, parapets 336.

stayned *pp.* stencilled or painted (with a
coat of arms) 334.

stayre *n.* ladder 830 (n.).

stalwourþe *adj.* secure, solidly built 1296.

stampen *pr. 3 pl.* stamp, tread heavily 526.

standard *n.* siege tower 389, 592.

standeþ see **stonde**.

stap *v.* step, take a step 605.

starke-blynde *adj.* utterly blind 580.

stauys see **staf**.

stede *n.*[1] place 227, 336, 526, 982, 1019,
1289, 1296; **stonde in stede** be of use
1104.

stede *n.*[2] horse, steed 605, 765, 1208; *poss.*
steed's 1128; *pl.* **stedis** 425, 526; **stedes**
576, 894; *vnder* ~ *feet* on the ground,
beneath horses' hooves 1128.

steel *n.* steel 749, 757, 1125, 1128; steel armour 1208; **steil** 526; **stele** protective trappings of steel (for a war-beast) 457, 546, 580; *attrib.* ~ *wede* garments of steel, armour 426, 429, 605.

steel-ware *n.* projectiles 1200 (n.).

sternes *n.* fierceness, sternness 520.

stertis *pr. 3 sg.* moves; ~ *on stray* straggles, moves off the right path, comes into range 784.

steuenes *n. pl.* voices; *lyften her* ~ they sing 742.

stewe *n.* vapor 687 (n.).

steweþ *pr. 3 sg.* dispose, place (advantageously) 845 (n.).

stif, styf *adj.* strong, powerful, mighty 13, 765, 1184.

styken *v.* stand still, stay 1246; see also **stoken**.

stykeþ *pr. 3 sg.* stabs 919.

stynk(e) *n.* stink, stench 687, 1246.

stynkande *pr.p.* as *adj.* stinking, putrefying 691.

stynt(e) *v.* stop, cease, end 227, 878; *pr. 3 sg.* **stynteþ of** 845.

stire *v.* trouble, incite 186.

stiropys *n. pl.* stirrups 527.

stiþe *adj.* strong, hardy, valiant 527.

stockes *n. pl.* tree-trunks or branches, logs 691.

stode see **stonde**.

stof *n.* supplies, provisions 288.

stoked *pt. 3 pl.* made fast, set, confined 13.

stoked *pp.* filled 334.

stoken *pp.* imprisoned, trapped 1136; see also **styken**.

stole *n.* stool, seat 13.

stompe *n.* torso, decapitated trunk 1128.

ston *n.* stone, gem 356 (2×), 826, 830, 874, 982, 1019, 1200, 1289; as if *pl.* collective 1283; *pl.* **stones** 476, 550, 594, 624, 642, 691, 762, 807, 834; projectiles 784; **stonys** 1265; see also **flynt-ston**.

stonde *v.* stand 356, 1104; *pr. 3 sg.* **stondiþ** 1184, 1200; **standeþ** 582; *pt. 3 sg.* **stode** stood 227, 1287; was raised 592; *pr. 3 sg. subj.* **stond** 982; *pr.p.* **stondande** 1019, 1289; **stondyng** *p.pl.* as *adj.* upright, erect 336.

stoppe *v.* stop up, block 1134; *pr. 3 pl.* **stoppen** 690; staunch (bleeding) 851.

stor(e) *n.* supplies, provisions 288, 878, 1104.

storyj *n.* story, history 830; *pl.* **storijs** 479; pictorial representations of events 334.

stormes *n. pl.* storms, tempests 74.

stounde *n.* a time, a while; accusative of extent 'for a time' 39, 1205.

stoure *n.* battle 520, 845.

stoure *adj.* resolute, strong, powerful 1184; *in a* ~ *wyse* resolutely, defiantly 389.

stray *n.* the action of wandering 784; *stertis on* ~ see **stertis**.

strande *n.* stream 690.

streem *n.* river, stream 690; *pl.* **stremes** currents, seas 74; **stremys** 1025.

streȝt *adv.* directly, all the way 919.

streyȝt *pt. 3 sg.* raised 389 (n.).

streyngþe see **strengþ(e)**.

strengþ(e) *n.* military might 520; physical strength 881, 1032, 1166; **streyngþe** power 291; force 807.

strengþe *v.* make strong 288.

stret(e) *n.* street 12, 1089, 1246.

strideþ *pr. 3 sg.* mounts 765; *pr. 3 pl.* **striden** 527.

strif, stryf *n.* hardship, trouble 257; waging war, siege 878.

strike *v.* strike, attack 314; strike 874; spread, be carried 687; *pr. 3 sg.* **strikeþ** hastens, darts, goes 765, knocks 827; *pt. 3 sg.* **stroke** sailed, dashed, made his way 74; **strike doun** fell 874.

strogelyng *n.* struggle (into clothes) 426 (n.).

stroyed *pp.* overcome, cured 278.

stroke *n.* blow 807.

stroke see **strike**.

stronge *adj.* strong 681.

stuffed *pp.* as *adj.* padded 526.

stuffyng *n.* padding 426.

stuny *v.* stun 874.

suche *adj.* such 176.

summe see **somme**.

sundrede *adj.* various, different; ~ *tymes* many times, several times 1226.

sunne see **sonne**.

surgyan *n.* surgeon 1039.

suþ *adv.* then, next, after that 13, 155, 197, 254; afterwards, also 338, 367, 543, 685, 700, 721, 747, 853, 945, 980, 1295, 1297, 1322.

suwed see **sewen**.

swallen *pt. 3 pl.* swelled (from hunger) 1149.

swalten *pr. 3 pl.* perish 1176.

swar *n.* answer, word; *without ~ more* without another word 540.

swart *adj.* black, wan, pallid 1149.

swelt *n.* faint, swoon 540.

swem *n.* swoon 532.

sweng *n.* fighting, battling 321, 1176.

swere *n.* neck 367.

swere *v.* swear, take an oath 1009.

swerd *n.* sword 321, 400, 753, 1176, 1223; *ʒede to þe ~* were slaughtered, died 321.

swetter *comp.adj.* sweeter, more fragrant 244.

swykel *adj.* as *n.* one who is deceitful or treacherous 321.

swyn *n.* swine, pigs 1149.

swyþe *adv.* quickly, swiftly 231, 327, 574, 633, 697, 958; **swythe** 56.

swounen *pr. 3 pl.* faint, swoon 1149.

swowande *pr.p.* fainting, swooning 540.

tabernacle *n.* canopied dais, turret, booth 467.

tabourris *n. pl.* small drums, tabors, drums 530.

tachen on *pr. 3 pl.* attack 659.

tail(le) *n.* tail 402; rear 441.

taysen *pr. 3 pl.* aim an arrow 659.

take(n) *v.* take 122, 270, 1263; receive 353, 1180; *pr. 1 sg.* entrust, commit, grant 224; *pr. 3 sg.* **takeþ** takes 1245; *pr. 3 pl.* **taken** take 1171; *pt 3 sg.* **toke** assumed control of 433; carried 911; *pt. 3 pl.* **token** took 81; seized, captured 309, 362; *imper.pl.* **take** seize 1217; *pp.* **tak** captured, taken 865; **take** taken 407, 1177; received 1027; **taken** seized, taken 649, 978, 1005, 1233; *~þ his way* makes his way 1245.

takled *pp.* as *adj.* equipped 286.

taknyng *n.* token, sign 109 (n.).

tale *n.* tale, story 378, 917, 1002, 1155; message 359; talk 362, 1120; tally 456; opportunity to speak, 867.

talkyng *n.* talking, speaking 869.

talterande *pr.p.* as *adj.* tossing, rolling 286.

tarie *v.* linger, dwell 1005; *pr. 3 sg.* **tarieþ** delays 1253; *pt. 3 sg.* **taried on** waited, lingered in expectation 21 (n.).

teldes *n. pl.* buildings, dwellings 309.

teldeþ *pr. 3 pl.* build 264 (n.).

telle *v.* tell 52; relate 101; tell 347, 433, 1069, 1151; recount 1274; *pr. 3 sg.* **telleþ**

tells 830; *pr. 3 pl.* **tellen** 112; *pt. 3 sg.* **tolde** 210, 1305; *pt. 3 pl.* **tolde** chanted, recited 478; **tolden** told 359, 378; *imper. sg.* **telle** 97, 189; *imper. pl.* **telliþ** 372; *pp.* **told** told, said 266, 1155; as *adj.* counted, reckoned 456.

temple *n.* temple 238, 836, 1020, 1227, 1232, 1253, 1288, 1291, 1293.

ten *card.num.* as *n.* 150.

ten *card.num.* as *adj.* 126, 441, 460, 1189.

tene *n.* trouble, affliction 847, 866, 1067, 1069; anger 740.

tenful(le) *adj.* menacing, fearful 217, 238, 414; difficult 872.

tente *n.* tent 337, 693; *pl.* **tentis** 328, 441, 847, 1133, 1337.

teris *n. pl.* tears 230.

teþ *n. pl.* teeth 913.

tide *n.* tide, time 293.

tyde *v. impers.* happen, befall 97; *pr. 3 sg.* (me) **tydiþ** befalls me 1007; (vs) **tides** will befall us 866; *pt. 3 sg.* **tydde** 25; *pp.* **tid** 378.

tydyng *n.* (piece of) news 1027.

tyeþ *pr. 3 pl.* draw, drag 623; **tyen** go, turn 847, 1162, 1182; **tyʒten** *pt. 3 pl.* drew, hoisted 293.

til(le) *prep.* until, till, to 168, 612, 1173, 1243; of, to be referred to 182 (postposited).

til(le) *conj.* until 12, 25, 124, 140, 404, 628, 708, 914, 978, 1005, 1012, 1043, 1286.

tilte *pt. 3 pl.* fell 836; *pp.* as *adj.* **tilt** fallen 1020.

tymbre *n.* wood, material for building 1291; *pl.* **tymbris** timbrels, drums or tamborines 530.

tyme *n.* time, reign, occasion, space of time 1, 29; time 21, 25, 161, 260, 320, 484, 612, 708, 713, 804, 837, 862, 987, 1113, 1221, 1228, 1251, 1261, 1285, 1329; unmarked dative 'at that time' 205, 804, 1233; *pl.* **tymes** 1226.

tyre *n.* clothing 380.

tit, tyt *adv.* soon, quickly 97, 189, 359; **as-tyt** at once, as quickly as possible 634, 1181; **als-tite** 362.

to *card. num.* as *adj.* two 332 (n.).

to *adv.* forward 541, 617, 809.

to *prep.* to, into 24, 29, 46, 49, 50, etc. (postposited 869); to introduce the dative 186; from 276; on 386; to, towards 633,

670, 701, 1120, 1182; into 1180, 1327; with infinitive 'to', 20, 39, 42, 52, 91, etc.

tobresteþ *pr. 3 sg.* breaks apart 70; *pt. 3 sg.* **tobreste** burst apart 156.

tobrused *pp.* as *adj.* mangled 726.

tocleuen *pr. 3 pl.* split asunder 558; *pt. 3 sg.* **toclef** 920.

tocrased *pt. 3 pl.* broke 240.

today *adv.* today 509, 521, 524.

todrawe *pp.* pulled or drawn apart 699.

togedre(s) *adv.* together 32, 110, 561, 579, 734, 925, 929; **togedris** 533.

toggeþ *pr. 3 sg.* tugs, attacks 913; ~ *wiþ his teþ* gnaws 913 (n.).

tohewen *pp.* hewn to pieces 1008.

toke(n) see **take(n)**.

tokne *n.* sign, evidence 189; *in* ~ *of* as a sign of 380, 727.

told(en) see **telle**.

toles *n. pl.* weapons 844 (n.).

tolles *pr. 3 sg.* brings down 541.

tomorow *adv.* tomorrow 350.

tomorowe *n.* tomorrow; ~ *prime* tomorrow at 9 A.M. 372, 382.

tomortled *pt. 3 pl.* crumbled 239.

tonelande *pr.p.* sounding musically 530 (n.).

tonge *n.* language 81; tongue 1274.

tonnes *n. pl.* barrels 623.

topsail *n.* topsail 293; *poss. sg.* as *adv.* **topsailes** headdown, upside down 710.

torche-liȝt *n.* torch-light 850.

tore *adj.* difficult 1069.

toret *n.* turret 316, 460, 836; *pl.* **torettes** 337.

torfere *n.* difficulty 866.

torkeys *adj.* Turkish 328.

tormented *pt. 3 sg.* tortured 1324; *pp.* **tourmented** 710.

torneien *pr. 3 pl.* take part in tournaments 895.

touche *v.* touch (on) 1105; *pt. 3 sg.* **touched** had sexual contact with 105; touched 228, 253; *pp.* **touched** touched, affected 109.

toun *n.* town, fortified place 309, 316, 328, 406, 414, 598, 689, 740, 865, 872, 879, 895, 978, 993, 1005, 1012, 1017, 1067, 1069, 1110, 1113, 1144, 1162, 1177, 1182, 1232, 1233, 1245, 1288; (fate of this) town 1016; *pl.* **tounnes** 298, 307.

toun-ȝate *n.* town-gate 1189.

tour *n.* tower 309, 316, 414, 455, 456, 467,

1288; *pl.* **toures** 649, 659, 662, 679, 865, 1017; **tourres** 623; mountainous waves 69.

toured *pp.* supplied with towers 337; as *adj.* turreted, towered 872, 978.

tourmented see **tormented**.

tourne *v.* convert 21; turn 402; turn, return 780; *pr. 3 sg.* **tourneþ** turns, returns 541, 585, 693, 740, 869, 1002, 1120; *reflex.* 1133; *pt. 3 pl.* **tourned** converted 207; *pt. 3 pl.* **tourned** turned, returned 598, 867; *imper. sg.* **tourne** return 1087; *imper. pl.* **tourneþ** return 917; *pp.* **tourned** turned out, stripped 380; **tournen** returned 952; **tournen agayn** return 917, 952 (n.), 1087.

toward to, toward *prep.* 53, 68, 71, 458, 598, 1133.

towe *adj.* tough 359; *made* (*it*) ~ pressed aggressively 359.

trayled *pt. 3 sg.* trailed 402.

traytours *n. pl.* traitors 917, 1217.

trauail *n.* hardship, labour 274.

tre(e) *n.* tree, wood; cross, gallows 710; roof- or door-tree 1291; *balwe* ~ death-bringing tree, gallows 156; *of* ~ wooden 460, 649, 911.

trey *n.* pain, affliction 727.

trenchour *n.* knife 1332.

tresoun *n.* treason, treachery 727.

tresour *n.* treasure 1016, 1263, 1338; *pl.* **tresours** 1274.

trete *n.* treaty 406.

trete *v.* treat, bargain, negotiate 506, 1105.

treuþ *n.* troth, fidelity 1016.

trewe *n.* truce 506, 1105, 1110; *pl.* **trewes** safe-conduct 216, 217; (with sg. meaning) truce 406.

trewe *adj.* true, legitimate, unquestioned 1, 1012, 1155, 1324.

tribute *n.* tribute 52, 217, 266, 506.

trifflyn *pr. 3 pl.* dally, loiter, spend time idly 895.

triste *pr. 1 sg.* have confidence, trust 971; *pr. 3 sg.* **tristiþ** 886; *pr. 3 pl.* **tristen** 519.

trompen vp *pr. 3 pl.* call by trumpet 1338.

trompis *n. pl.* trumpets 1182.

tronchoun *n.* staff 911, 913.

trossen *pr. 3 pl.* carry off 1338.

trowe *pr. 1 sg.* trust, believe 1207.

twey see **two**.

xij *card. num.* twelve 233, 346, 652;

twelf(e) *card.num.* as *adj.* 471, 586, 725; twelue 136, 141; twelf(e) *card.num.* as *n.* twelve (men) 373.

xxᵗⁱ *card.num.* twenty 215; twenty *card.-num.* as *n.* 456; twenticard.*num.* as *adj.* 449.

two *card.num.* as *n.* 140 (2×); twey 137; two *card.num.* as *adj.* 134, 1173; twey 273, 705, 711.

þay see þei, þey.

þan *conj.* than 37, 88, 131, 782, 844, 862, 1100, 1140, 1172, 1252, 1316; than then 1209.

þan(ne) *adv.* then, next, in addition 181, 195, 213, 225, 233, etc.; *by* ~ thereby, thereupon 823, 1141 (see also by).

þanked see þonkeþ.

þat *dem. adj.* that 3, 40, 71, 72, 86, etc.; *pl.* þo those 258, 271.

þat *dem. pron.* that, what 404, 988; *pl.* þo those (ones) 101.

þat *rel. pron.* that, which, who(m) (with ellipsis of antecedent): that which, what, the one who, he who, whoever, those who 7, 19, 20, 22, 24, etc.

þat *conj.* that, because, so that, when 79, 87, 209, 221, 348, etc.; so that 64 (n.), 135, 167, 232, 260, etc.; *by* ~ then, after that, when 77, 285, 443, 663, 681, etc. (see also by); *whan* ~ when 6, 933; *saue* ~ except that 1056.

þe *def. art.* the 1, 8, 9, 12, 19, etc.

þe see þou.

þeȝ see þoȝ.

þei, þey *pron. 3 pl. nom.* they 15, 21, 52, 58, 158, etc.; þay 232; hy 140, 1299; *acc., dat.* hem them, to them, for them 20, 22, 24, 35, 66 (with impers. vb.), etc.; *emphatic refl.* hem themselves 634, 1181; hemself themselves 528, 714, 1074, 1158; *poss.adj.* here their 42, 144, 238, 278, 279, etc.; hire 1096.

þey see þoȝ.

þeyes *n. pl.* thighs 704.

þenke see þynkeþ.

þer *adv.* where 94, 313, 324, 358, 398, etc.; there 193, 408, 432, 462, 592 (2nd use), etc.; ~ *as adv.* where 94, 584, 881, 882.

þer *adv.* the expletive use, usually preceding the verb 41, 45, 95, 102, 137, etc.

þeraboute *adv.* around it 402.

þeraȝens *adv.* towards them 219.

þerat *adv.* at it 798.

þerby *adv.* whereby, thereby 405; beside it, near by 471.

þerfor(e) *adv.* therefore, on that account 1059, 1087.

þerfro *adv.* therefrom, from it 243, 416.

þeryn(ne) in it, in that place 469, 719.

þermyd *adv.* in addition 192.

þerof *adv.* of which, concerning this, about them 209, 397, 805.

þeron *adv.* on it 1199.

þerouer *adv.* on top of this 750.

þerto *adv.* to that, to it 10.

þervnder *adv.* under it 332.

þy see þou.

þicke *adj.* thick, crowded, dense, heavy, solid 536; þykke 324, 623.

þicke, þycke, þykke *adv.* densely, abundantly, in a crowd 453, 601, 648, 661, 748, 1079, 1257.

þing *n.* thing, matter 509; *pl.* þinges, þynges 238, 431, 1222.

þynkeþ *pr. 3 sg. impers.* thinks 740; þenke *pr. 3 pl.* intend 1106; *pt. 3 sg.* þoȝt, þouȝte it seemed (to him) 78, 596; ~ *on* thinks of 740.

þy(n) see þou.

þis *pron.* this 768, 1215.

þis *dem. adj.* this 37, 144 (1st use), 169, 224, 265, etc.; *pl.* þis these 41, 144 (2nd use), 177, 357, 384, etc.; ~ *worlde* here (as opposed to eternity) 144.

þyself see þou.

þo *adv.* then 453, 932, 1157.

þo see þat.

þoȝ *conj.* although, though, when 322, 774, 775, 776, 780, 799, 1058, 1199; þey though, although 7, 22, 40, 1312; þou 596; þeȝ 854.

þoȝt see þynkeþ.

þoled(e) *pt. 3 sg.* endured 37, 40, 1306, 1328.

þonder *n.* thunder 536.

þonkeþ *pr. 3 sg.* thanks, gives thanks to 1055, 1213; *pt. 3 sg.* þanked 199.

þornen *adj.* of thorns, thorny 17.

þou *pron. 2 sg.* you (thou) 15, 90, 94, 202, 297, etc.; *acc.dat.* þe 16, 92, 97, 100, 182, etc.; *poss. adj.* þy(n) 175, 183, 188, 204, 301, etc.; *emphatic refl.* þyself 383, 1000, etc.

þou see þoȝ.

þouȝte see þynkeþ.

þousand *card.num.* as *adj.* thousand 434, 613, 1175, 1187, 1189.

þousand *card.num.* as *n.* thousand 133, 422, 424, 437, 441, 446, 615.

þrange *adj.* tight, pressing 17.

þraste *pt. 3 pl.* thrust 17.

þre *card.num.* as *n.* 112; þre *card.num.* as *adj.* three 110, 935.

þrewen *pt. 3 pl.* shot 824.

þridde *ord.num.* as *n.* third 115, 437.

þrye, þries *adv.* thrice 191, 254; *at þries* thrice 191.

þrylled *pt. 3 pl.* pierced, penetrated 835; *pp.* yþrelled 1121.

þritty, þrytty *card.num.* as *adj.* thirty 1307, 1320.

þryuande *pr.p.* as *adj.* excellent 437.

þrobolande *pr.p.* jostling 536 (n.).

þro3 *adv.* through 823; see also iouke.

þro3, þrow *prep.* (of motion) through 74 (postposited), 240, 482, 488, 537, etc.; (of means) by, with 103, 354, 728, 962, 1236; (of agent) by 8, 164, 272; because of 927.

þrom *n.* crowd 1320.

þrongen *pp.* crowded together, bound 1320.

þrow see þro3.

þrow-schot *pp.* transfixed 1122.

þus *adv.* thus, in this way, like this 380, 384, 636, 725, 870, 924, 950, 964, 1021, 1100, 1324.

vmbe *adv.* round about 333, 635.

vmbe *prep.* about, around 69, 635, 752, 762, 1113.

vmbecasten *pt. 3 pl.* surrounded 18.

vmbefeldes *pr. 3 sg.* surrounds, rounds up 1131; *pt. 3 sg.* vmbefelde embraced 223.

vmbywente *pt. 3 pl.* encircled 11 (n.).

vmfonge *v.* encircle 683.

vnarmen *pr. 3 pl. reflex.* disarm, take off armour 634.

vnarwely *adv.* swiftly 658.

vnbaptized *pp.* unbaptized, heathen 159.

vnbuxum *adj.* unwilling 369.

vnclene *adj.* dirty, foul 32.

vnclosed *pt. 3 sg.* unwrapped, undid 228.

vncouþ *adj.* unknown, unfamiliar, foreign 68.

vnder(e) *prep.* under, beneath 175, 396, 512, 526, 581, etc. (postposited in 526,

590, 686); below, beneath 65, 315; under the authority of 3, 5, 299.

vnder *adv.* beneath, underneath 539, 666.

vndertoke *pt.3 pl.* undertook, took on 274.

vneþ *adv.* scarcely, hardly 488.

vnfounded *pt. 3 pl.* untried, untested 622 (n.).

vn3et *pp.* unconquered, unyielded 1173; see also geten, 3ete.

vnhende *adj.* rough, violent 1202.

vnknowen *adj.* unrecognized, unfamiliar, unacknowledged 123.

vnlappeþ *pr. 3 sg.* unfolds 965.

vnlele *adj.* disloyal, treacherous 153.

vnmarred *adj.* unblemished 105.

vnmeke *adj.* cruel 30.

vnmete *adj.* immeasurable, huge 803.

vnmy3ty *adj.* powerless 1165.

vnmylt *adj.* harsh, merciless 560 (n.).

vnpersched *adj.* alive, unscathed 80.

vnquemed *pp.* displeased, troubled 904.

vnriuen *pt. 3 pl.* unpierced, unwounded 610; see also roof *pt. 3 sg.*

vntake *pp.* uncaptured, not taken 1017.

vnto *prep.* until, up to 197.

vp(pe) *adv.* up, upwards, at hand 35, 61, 247, 293, 296, etc.

vpon *prep.* on, upon 9, 41, 79, 90, 170, etc.; in 67, 269, 376, 582, 1073, etc.; on top of 645; into 706; ~ *erþe* at all 90; ~ *ferst* at first, first 433; ~ *haste* in haste 269; ~ *hy3te* on high 653; ~ *lyue* alive 41, 79; ~ *lofte* on high 403, 465, 535, 742; ~ *schame wyse* in a shameful manner 376.

vs see we.

vseþ *v.* uses 98.

vsselue see we.

vale *n.* vale 430, 489, 553, 563, 604.

veil *n.* veil 166; vail(e) 235, 253, 263.

veynys *n. pl.* veins 20; vaynes 1051.

vengaunce *n.* vengeance 1237; veniaunce 1328.

venge(n) *v.* avenge 20, 188, 348, 495, 941.

veniaunce see vengaunce.

vernycle *n.* vernicle 261.

vessel *n. coll.* vessels 1267 (n.).

vile *adj.* vile, miserable 1102, 1328.

vyleny *n.* dishonour, wickedness 20.

vilayns *n. pl.* villains, evil ones 1237.

visage *n.* (imprint of the) face 166, 253, 263; *pl.* 366.

viser *n.* visor, moveable front part of the helmet 760.

vitelys *n. pl.* victuals, provisions, food 1102.

voiden *v.* clear away, remove 1102.

voys *n.* voice 1230 (3×).

vouched *pt.sg.* swore, affirmed as true 1155.

wacche *n.* guard, watch 635, 888; **wecche** 386.

way *n.* course, way, road 53, 1218; **wey** 341, 1119, 1245; *pl.* **way(e)s** 217, 1109; **wey(e)s** 646, 1006.

waytes *n. pl.* watchmen 732.

waytes *pr. 3 sg.* awaits, watches 783; **waiteþ** looks searchingly 861; *pl.* **wayten** keep watch 895; look 1261; *imper. pl.* **wayteþ** look 773.

wakned *pt. 3 sg.* was stirred up 1079.

wal(le) *n.* wall 386, 721, 732, 787, 792, 873, 1109, 1119, 1153, 1190, 1198, 1201, 1210, 1218, 1229, 1234, 1285, 1287; *attrib.* 806; *pl.* **walles** 355, 423, 616, 621, 630, 635, 646, 654, 664, 670, 673, 677, 687, 713, 744, 773, 832, 839, 888, 1006, 1022, 1183, 1282.

wale *n. attrib.* whale 1025; ~ *stremes* whale's streams, sea 1025 (but perhaps merely the *adj.* 'choice, noble').

wale *pt. 3 sg.* chose 1280; **waled** *pp.* as *adj.* chosen 888.

walte(n) *v.* overturn, turn upside down 73; hurl 355; *pt. 3 pl.* **walten** threw (themselves) 713; threw 1153; *pp.* **walte** thrown down 834; *pp.* as *adj.* **walten** turned 710.

waltreþ *pr. 3 sg.* tosses 739.

walwyþ *pr. 3 sg.* rolls around 739; *pp.* as *adj.* **walwed** tossed about, rolled from side to side 469.

wanned *pr. 3 sg.* dimmed, grew dark 57.

wanteþ *pr. 3 sg.* is lacking 167, 1280; *pt. 3 sg.* **wanted** lacked 632, 1248, 1276.

wap(pe) *n.* blow, gust 412; *at a* ~ at one blow, all at once 518, 1287.

ward *n.* watch 423; guard, defence 1218.

warded *pt. 3 sg.* guarded 1329.

ware *adj.* aware 209, 221, 805; prudent 1107.

waried see **werry**.

warieþ *pr. 3 sg.* curses 1205; *pr. 3 pl.*

warien 1261; *pr.p.* **wariande** cursing 677.

warned *pt. 3 sg.* admonished, instructed 386.

warpiþ *pr. 3 sg.* utters 783; *pt. 3 sg.* **warp** took away 229.

warwolues *gen. pl.* of werewolves 1178.

was see **ben**.

waschen *pr. 3 pl.* wash 851.

waspys *n. pl.* wasps 209, 255; **waspen(e)** *gen.* as *adj.* waspish, wasp-like 34, 36.

wasschyng *n.* washing 795.

wast *n.* destruction; *maden* ~ destroyed 1287.

water *n.* water 55, 57, 63, 125, 192, 287, 482, 676, 692, 790, 796, 800, 1074; birth-water 532 (n.).

waterles *adj.* without water 775.

water-waschen *pp.* as *adj.* washed (with water) 792.

wawes *n. pl.* waves 73.

we *pron. 1 pl. nom.* we 370, 380, 516, 521, 875, etc.; *acc., dat.* **vs** (to, for) us 112, 343, 371, 444, 500, etc.; **ous** 1340; *emphatic refl.* **vsselue** ourselves 876; *poss. adj.* **our(e)** 75, 102, 206, 380, 381, etc.; of us 1007.

webbes *n. pl.* woven cloths, fabrics 326.

wecche see **wacche**.

wede *n.* cloth 221, 229; garment 352; clothes, apparel 426, 429, 605, 959, 1242; *pl.* **wedes** 747; cloths 791, 793, 795.

wede *pr. 2 pl. subj.* go insane, go mad 775.

wedour *n.* weather, storm, wind at sea 63, 66.

wey, weyes see **way**.

weyke *adj.* weak 1103.

wel *adv.* very 248, 661; fully, quite 518, 795; well 797; *comp.* **better** 97; *super.* **best** 270, 969.

weldeþ *pr. 2 pl.* have in one's power or control 1015.

wele *n.* well-being, prosperity, riches 1015, 1280.

wellande *pr.p.* welling, boiling 385.

welter *v.* writhe 532.

wem(e) *n.* injury 632, 880.

wemlese *adj.* without blemish, spotless 201.

wemmyd *pp.* blemished 180.

wende *v.* go, come 233, 271, 355, 585; *pr.1 sg.* **wende** turn 787; *pr. 3 sg.* **wendeþ,**

wendiþ goes, turns 677, 785, 1253; *pt. 3 sg.* wende went 73, 1022; went(e) 1211, 1329; *pt. 3 pl.* went(en) went 736, 1097, 1153, 1339; *imper.* wende 721; *pp.* went gone 922, 1025.

wenen *pr. 3 pl.* expect, imagine, think 518; *pt. 3 pl.* wenden imagined, supposed 795.

wenes *n. pl.* wagons 1006.

went(en) see wende.

wepe *v.* weep 225; *pr. 3 sg.* wepyþ 1034, 1205; *pr.p.* wepande 1022, 1097.

wepyng *n.* weeping 251.

wepne *n.* weapon 545; *coll. pl.* weapons 390, 461, 545, 1195.

were *v.* wear 1277; *pt. 3 sg.* wered wore 1208.

wer(en) see be.

wery *adj.* weary 848.

werien *pr. 3 pl.* defend 673.

werk(e) *n.* action, work 848, 990; worke 182, 680; handiwork, a wrought object 1261; *pl.* werkes deeds, actions 162.

werre *n.* war 398, 542, 800, 805, 864, 1181, 1210.

werry *v.* make war 922; *pr. 3 sg.* werreþ 954; *pt. 3 sg.* werred 403; waried gained through warfare 1080; *pt. 3 sg. subj.* would go to war for 194 (n.); *pt. 3 pl.* werred 860.

west *n.* the west 1230.

wete *n.* wet, water 791.

wexe(d) *pt. 3 sg.* grew, became 245, 1310; *pt. 3 pl.* wexen 580, 1149; woxen 563; *pp.* become 1033.

whan *conj.* when 6, 157, 163, 176, 221, etc.; when 361; whan/when þat 933.

whappen *pr. 3 pl.* cast violently, shoot, throw 626.

what *pron.* what 344; whatever 1280; *pron. rel.* what 138.

what *adj.* what 98, 189, 695, 773, 1070; whatever 1044.

when see whan.

where *rel. adv.* where, wherever 1062, 1152, 1190; see also þer.

wheþer *inter. conj.* which of the two 507; untranslatable 'is it' 99.

why *inter. adv.* why 175.

which *n.* chest, ark 469.

whiche *inter. adj.* which 16.

why3tly see wy3tly.

whyle *n.* (space of) time 265, 1175; *in þe mene* ~ in the meantime 1171.

while, whyle *conj.* while 3, 102, 422, 425, 516, 546, 996, 1176, 1197; until 29, 878 (n.).

whyppes *n. pl.* whips 11.

white *adj.* white 11, 352, 469.

who *inter. pron. nom.* who 270, 777; *acc., dat.* whom whom 165, 201, 250.

who *rel. pron.* who, whoever 773, 989.

whoso *pron.* whosoever 462, 504, 548, 1145, 1266, 1319.

wicked *adj.* difficult, dangerous 668.

wide *adj.* wide 646, 653.

wide, wyde *adv.* wide(ly) 394; ~ *open* lying at full length 834.

wye *n.* man 208, 352, 632, 796, 864, 1229, 1234, 1280, 1329; *poss. sg.* wyes man's 635; *pl.* wyes men 273, 345, 375, 429, 861, 916, 986, 1211.

wif, wyf *n.* woman 95, 165, 1081, 1093; wife 901.

wyght, *adj. as n.pl.* vigorous ones, 1080.

wy3tly *adv.* vigorously, actively 1199; why3tly 621.

wilde *adj.* wild 73.

wile, wyle *n.* guileful behavior, strategem 790, 797; *pl.* wyles 668, 673, 800.

wille, wylle *n.* wish, desire, will 343, 864, 1219; pleasure, will 978, 1339; desire, purpose 1125.

willeþ see wole.

wilneþ *pr. 3 sg.* wishes, desires 507; *pt. 3 sg.* wylned 1045.

wymmen see womman.

wynd(e) *n.* wind 59, 63, 66, 412; *attrib.* wynde 721; *pl.* wyndes 74; wyndis 1230.

wyndiþ *pr. 3 sg.* turns 739; *pt. 3 pl.* wounden hoisted 287.

wyn(e) *n.* wine 125, 287, 851, 1074.

wynges *n. pl.* wings 409, 412.

wynne *v.* conquer, win, gain 408, 513, 665, 668, 872, 1178; procure, attain, get 692, 775, 877; *pr. 3 sg.* wynneþ wins his way 1199; *pr. 3 pl.* wynnen 621; *pt. 3 pl.* wonnen gained, attained 310, 616; *pp.* wonnen won, 400, 1233; wonne come 177.

wynter *n.* winter, year 955; *pl.* years 23.

wirche, wyrche *v.* make, create, cause 187, 875; do, act, work 1159, worche 66, 984; worchyn create, 1109; *pr. 3 pl.*

worchen 1000; *pt. 1 sg.* **wroȝt** did, performed 182; acted, did 976; *pt. 3 sg.* caused 814; performed 124, 208; made 125; caused 1163; did 727; **wroȝte** did 1238; **wrouȝten** worked 1285; *pp.* **wroȝt(e)** done, made 298; made, worked 331, 653; made 681; performed 790; caused 897; made 1119, **ywroȝt** made, worked 466; *pp.* as *adj.* **wroȝt** made 1210; ~ *to* brought to (a state) 24, 51; ~ *vp* built up, raised 653.

wyse *n.* manner, way 376, 389, 589, 1178, 1273; *on eche* ~ completely 1178.

wise *adj.* wise 1107.

wite *v.* know, know of 462; *pt. 3 sg.* **wist** knew, learned of 1136; **wyste** 1041.

wyten *pr. 3 pl.*[1] depart 255.

wyten *pr. 3 pl.*[2] blame on 1238.

wiþ *prep.* with 1114; with 10, 18, 56, 75, 85, etc. (postposited 986); by (means of) 13, 625, 699; to the accompaniment of 743.

withdrowen *pt. 3 pl. reflex.* withdrew 629.

withyn *prep.* within 305, 616 (both postposited).

withyn(ne) *adv.* within, inside 452, 1086, 1136.

without(en) *prep.* without 107, 179, 217, 362, 447, etc.

withtake *v.* withhold, keep back 52; *pp.* **withtane** withheld 266.

witt *n.* wisdom 984.

wlonk *adj.* proud 298.

wlonkfulle *adj.* proud 398.

wo *n.* misery, distress, trouble, crying, woe, grief, pain, sorrow 124, 251, 255, 298, 616, 713, 773, 820, 854, 880, 1079, 1097, 1107, 1136, 1199, 1205, 1231 (3×), 1235 (2×), 1238.

wode *adj. adv.* furious, mad 385, 1093; wild 785.

woke *n.* week; *alle þe* ~ *tyme* the space of an entire week 1285.

woke *adj.* as *n.* weak (ones) 1080.

wolcon *n.* sky 57.

wol(e) desire, wish, be willing, intend (and as aux. indicating futurity) *pr. 1 sg.* will 101, 984, 1005; **wolle** 953; *pr. 1 pl.* **wol** 889; *pr. 2 pl.* **wol** 786; *pr. 3 pl.* **wol** 1315; **willeþ** 381; **wolle** 636; *pt. 2 sg.* **wolde** wished, desired 1058; *pt. 3 sg.* 5, 75, 1058; *pt. 3 pl.* 52, 884, 1240, 1318; *pt. 1 sg. subj.* would wish 969 (n.); *pt. 3 sg.*

subj. would, might wish to 72, 314, 322, 344, 405, etc.; *pt. 1 pl. subj.* 878; *pt. 3 pl. subj.* 21, 58, 312; **wolden** 820; negative forms: **nold(e)** *pt. 3 sg.* would not, did not want 148, 1110, 1146; *pt. 1 sg. subj.* would not wish 1017.

wolle *n.* wool 791, 851.

wolues *n. pl.* wolves 1079.

wombe-fille *n.* bellyfull, satiety 1080.

womman *n.* woman 95, 221, 229, 532, 829; *pl.* **wymmen** women 834, 1103, 1147.

wonder *adj.* marvellous 462, 790.

wonder *adv.* marvellously, extremely 359, 666, 681, 1229.

wondres *n. pl.* marvels, miraculous deeds 124, 208.

wonderliche *adv.* marvellously, extremely 653, 815.

wone *n.* (dwelling)place 796, 873, 1235.

wonne(n) see **wynne.**

wope *n.* weeping, tears 1074.

worche(n), worchyn see **wyrche.**

word *n.* word 125 (n.), 345, 783, 1234; *pl.* **wordes,** 130, 177, 787, 916, 1014, 1083, 1295; **wordis** 1302.

worde see **world(e).**

worke see **werk(e).**

world(e) *n.* world 144, 518; **worde** 398 (n.).

world-riches *n. pl.* kingdoms of this world, the world 400.

worlich(e) *adj.* honorable 95, 165.

worschup *n.* honor 986, 1015; **worschip** 984.

worse *adv. comp.* worse 870.

worst *adj. super.* worst 873.

worþe *v.* be, become 963; *imper.* **worþ** fall (upon) 1231; *pr. 2 pl. subj.* **worþe** might become 774.

worþi, worþy *adj.* worthy, distinguished 182, 1093; worshipful, noble 201.

worþly *adj.* noble 1235.

wounde *n.* wound 820, 880; *pl.* **woundes** 497, 842, 851, 930; **woundis** 250, 1304.

wounded *pp.* wounded 169, 815, 848, 854.

wounden see **wyndiþ.**

woxen see **wexe(d).**

wrake *n.* destruction 585.

wrecche *n.* wretch, miserable creature 174, 873; *pl.* **wrecchys** 302.

wrecken *v.* avenge 820.

wriȝtes *n. pl.* workmen, carpenters 681.

wryngyng *n.* wringing 251.
wro3t(en) see wyrche.
wronge *n.* wrong, injustice 1238.
wroþ(e) *adj.* angry 375, 385, 785.

xij see twelue.
xl see four-.
xv see fif-.
xxᵗⁱ see twenti.

PROPER NAMES

Andreu the apostle Andrew 151.
Barnabe the apostle Barnabas 159.
Bertholomewe the apostle Bartholomew 148.
Bethleem Bethlehem 104, 202, 301.
Burdewes *poss.* of Bordeaux 76, 196.
Cayphas Caiaphas 354, 360, 474, 481, 584; cayphas 694, 719, 725; *poss.* Cayphases Caiaphas's 704.
Cesar Caesar, the Roman emperor 174; sesar 2, 7; *poss.* cesaris Caesar's 297.
Crist Christ, Jesus 6, 94, 157, 160, 171, etc.; messiah 190; *poss.* Cristes Christ's 228.
Dauid king David 479.
Domycian Domitian, Vespasian's nephew, later emperor 1129, 1186; Domyssian, 994.
Gabba the emperor Galba 926, 933.
Galace Galatia in Asia Minor 39.
Galile Galilee 6.
Gascoyne Gascony, southern France 26.
Gyan Guienne, southern France 26.
Grecys the Greeks 45; *gen. pl.* grekys the Greeks' 54.
Helle Hell 157.
Herode Herod 5 (n.).
Iacob the apostle James the Less 145; see also Iame.
Iaf Jappa 296 (n.).
Iame the apostle James the Less, first bishop of Jerusalem 1239 (n.).
Iames the apostle James the Greater 145.
Ierico Jericho 302.
Ierusalem Jerusalem 302, 313, 324, 1232.
Iewe Jew 304, 480, 789; *pl.* Iewes 50, 86, 154, 313, 324, etc.; Iewys 270; *poss. pl.* Iewen of the Jews, Jewish 4, 1232.
Ihesu Jesus 154, 353, 431; *poss.* Ihesus Jesus's 304.
Ion¹ the apostle John 145.
Ion² the Jewish rebel John of Gischala 1137 (n.), 1159.
Iosophat Jehosophat, the valley of Last Judgement 431 (n.).

Iosophus Josephus 313, 789, 805, 813, 1039, etc.
Iosue Joshua 480.
Iudas¹ Judas Iscariot 154.
Iudas² Judah Maccabee 480.
Iudees *gen.* Judaea's, of Judaea 4, 296.
Lucyus see Othis Lucyus.
Marie Mary, a Jewish matron 1081.
Mathu the apostle Matthew 149.
Mathie the apostle Matthias (named to replace Judas) 158.
Moyses *poss.* Moses's 484, 586.
Nathan Nathan 45, 101, 191, 212, 266; Nathan 53, 65, 93; *poss.* Nathannys Nathan's 62.
Neymes *poss.* Nahum's (Nathan's father) 45, 212.
Nero the emperor Nero 51, 53, 84, 186, 212, etc.; *poss.* neroes Nero's 29.
Othis Lucyus the emperor Otho Lucius 927, 930, 934.
Paske Pesaḥ, the Passover 1215; ~ *tyme* the Passover season 161, 320.
Peter the apostle and first pope Peter 145, 205, 222, 236; Petre 899; *poss.* Petres Peter's 152.
Pharao Pharaoh 483.
Phelip the apostle Philip 146.
Pilat Pontius Pilate 164, 176, 1300, 1301, 1327; Pylat 3, 8.
Poule the apostle Paul 159, 899.
Romayns Romans 407, 609, 794, 809, 903, etc.; Romaynes 264.
Rome Rome 2, 25, 38, 49, 67, etc.
Sabyn¹ Sir Sabinus of Syria 438, 565, 971, 975, 985, etc.
Sabyns² *poss.* Sabinus's, of Sabinus (Vespasian's brother) 939, 944.
Sathanas *dat.* to Satan 936.
Senek Seneca the younger 900.
Sensteus Cestius, governor of Palestine 49; sensteus 85.
Sesar see Cesar.
Symond¹ the apostle Simon 147.

Symond[2] the Jewish rebel Simon son of Gioras 1138 (n.) 1160.

Syone Zion, the mountain of the temple 299; Syon 315.

Surrie the Roman province Syria (including both Judaea and Galilee) 305, 438, 942, 971, 975; Surrye 1185, 1197; Surye 49; Surre 83; Suree 297.

Tadde the apostle Thaddeus 150.

Tiberyus *poss.* of Tiberius the Roman emperor, Tiberius's 1.

Tybre the river Tiber 948.

Tytus Titus 25, 541, 598, 993, 1049, etc.; Titus 81, 97, 189, 274, 433, etc.

Tomas the apostle Thomas 150.

Trinyte *n.* Trinity 109, 191.

Vaspasian see Waspasian.

Veronyk Veronica 166, 235, 261, 263.

Vienne Vienne in the Rhone valley 1328.

Vitel the emperor Vitellius 938, 941.

Waspasian Vespasian, 36, 209, 273, 345, 375, etc.; Vaspasian 235, 261, 489, 553, 941.

W